Machine Learning Algorithms for Problem Solving in Computational Applications:

Intelligent Techniques

Siddhivinayak Kulkarni
University of Ballarat, Australia

Information Science
REFERENCE

Managing Director:	Lindsay Johnston
Senior Editorial Director:	Heather A. Probst
Book Production Manager:	Sean Woznicki
Development Manager:	Joel Gamon
Development Editor:	Myla Harty
Assistant Acquisitions Editor:	Kayla Wolfe
Typesetter:	Deanna Jo Zombro
Cover Design:	Nick Newcomer, Lisandro Gonzalez

Published in the United States of America by
Information Science Reference (an imprint of IGI Global)
701 E. Chocolate Avenue
Hershey PA 17033
Tel: 717-533-8845
Fax: 717-533-8661
E-mail: cust@igi-global.com
Web site: http://www.igi-global.com

Library of Congress Cataloging-in-Publication Data

Machine learning algorithms for problem solving in computational applications
: intelligent techniques / Siddhivinayak Kulkarni, editor.
    p. cm.
  Includes bibliographical references and index.
  Summary: "This book addresses the complex realm of machine learning and its
applications for solving various real-world problems in a variety of
disciplines, such as manufacturing, business, information retrieval, and
security"-- Provided by publisher.
  ISBN 978-1-4666-1833-6 (hardcover) -- ISBN 978-1-4666-1834-3 (ebook) -- ISBN
978-1-4666-1835-0 (print & perpetual access) 1. Machine learning. I.
Kulkarni, Siddhivinayak, 1970-
  Q325.5.M3215 2012
  003'.3--dc23
                              2012003492

British Cataloguing in Publication Data
A Cataloguing in Publication record for this book is available from the British Library.

All work contributed to this book is new, previously-unpublished material. The views expressed in this book are those of the authors, but not necessarily of the publisher.

Table of Contents

Section 1
Machine Learning Applications

Section 2
Computational Intelligence Techniques and Applications

Section 3
Miscellaneous Techniques in Machine Learning

Detailed Table of Contents

Section 1
Machine Learning Applications

Chapter 1

    Siddhivinayak Kulkarni, University of Ballarat, Australia

Developments in the technology and the Internet have led to increase in number of digital images and videos. Thousands of images are added to WWW every day. Content based Image Retrieval (CBIR) system typically consists of a query example image, given by the user as an input, from which low-level image features are extracted. These low level image features are used to find images in the database which are most similar to the query image and ranked according their similarity. This chapter evaluates various CBIR techniques based on fuzzy logic and neural networks and proposes a novel fuzzy approach to classify the colour images based on their content, to pose a query in terms of natural language and fuse the queries based on neural networks for fast and efficient retrieval. A number of experiments was conducted for classification and retrieval of images on sets of images, and promising results were obtained.

Chapter 2

    Hong Lee, Central Queensland University, Australia
    Brijesh Verma, Central Queensland University, Australia
    Michael Li, Central Queensland University, Australia
    Ashfaqur Rahman, Central Queensland University, Australia

Handwriting recognition is a process of recognizing handwritten text on a paper in the case of offline handwriting recognition and on a tablet in the case of online handwriting recognition and converting it into an editable text. In this chapter, the authors focus on offline handwriting recognition, which means that recognition system accepts a scanned handwritten page as an input and outputs an editable recognized text. Handwriting recognition has been an active research area for more than four decades, but some of the major problems still remained unsolved. Many techniques including the machine learning techniques have been used to improve the accuracy. This chapter focuses on describing the problems of handwriting recognition and presents the solutions using machine learning techniques for solving major problems in handwriting recognition. The chapter also reviews and presents the state of the art techniques with results and future research for improving handwriting recognition.

Unsupervised learning is a class of problems in machine learning which seeks to determine how the data are organized. Unsupervised learning encompasses many other techniques that seek to summarize and explain key features of the data. One form of unsupervised learning is blind source separation (BSS). BSS is a class of computational data analysis techniques for revealing hidden factors that underlie sets of measurements or signals. BSS assumes a statistical model whereby the observed multivariate data, typically given as a large database of samples, are assumed to be linear or nonlinear mixtures of some unknown latent variables. The mixing coefficients are also unknown. Sometimes more prior information about the sources is available or is induced into the model, such as the form of their probability densities, their spectral contents, et cetera. Then the term blind is often replaced by semiblind. This chapter reports the semi BSS machine learning applications on audio and bio signal processing.

The applications of machine learning algorithms to the analysis of data sets of DNA sequences are very important. The present chapter is devoted to the experimental investigation of applications of several machine learning algorithms for the analysis of a JLA data set consisting of DNA sequences derived from non-coding segments in the junction of the large single copy region and inverted repeat A of the chloroplast genome in Eucalyptus collected by Australian biologists. Data sets of this sort represent a new situation, where sophisticated alignment scores have to be used as a measure of similarity. The alignment scores do not satisfy properties of the Minkowski metric, and new machine learning approaches have to be investigated. The authors' experiments show that machine learning algorithms based on local alignment scores achieve very good agreement with known biological classes for this data set. A new machine learning algorithm based on graph partitioning performed best for clustering of the JLA data set. Our novel k-committees algorithm produced most accurate results for classification. Two new examples of synthetic data sets demonstrate that the k-committees algorithm can outperform both the Nearest Neighbour and k-medoids algorithms simultaneously.

Cancer is one of the most complex diseases, and one of the most effective treatments, radiation therapy, is also a complicated process. Informatics is becoming a critical tool for clinicians and scientists for improvements to the treatment and a better understanding of the disease. Computational techniques such as machine learning have been increasingly used in radiation therapy. As complex as cancer is, this book chapter shows that machine learning technique has the ability to provide physicians information for better diagnostic, to obtain tumor location for more accurate treatment delivery, and to predict radiotherapy response so that personalized treatment can be developed.

Chapter 6

Many applications of machine learning in law aim to support lawyers or litigants by predicting court outcomes, retrieving past cases from document repositories, or assembling arguments for use in advancing assertions. Law is a unique application field for machine learning, because for many decades, jurisprudence scholars have provided theoretical insights about the nature of legal reasoning. Concepts including open texture and discretion directly impact on the application of machine learning in law. This chapter discusses how these and other concepts influence the selection of cases for learning, the way in which outliers are dealt with, and how cases with contradictory outcomes can be interpreted. These points are made with reference to a number of machine learning applications in fields of law including family law, refugee law, and eligibility for legal aid.

Chapter 7

Recognizing objects based on their appearance (visual recognition) is one of the most significant abilities of many living creatures. In this study, recent advances in the area of automated object recognition are reviewed, where the authors specifically looked into several learning frameworks to discuss how they can be utilized in solving object recognition paradigms. This includes reinforcement learning, a biologically-inspired machine learning technique to solve sequential decision problems and transductive learning, and, a framework where the learner observes query data and potentially exploits its structure for classification. The authors also discuss local and global appearance models for object recognition, as well as, how similarities between objects can be learnt and evaluated.

Chapter 8

This chapter describes a novel multistage method for linguistic clustering of large collections of texts available on the Internet as a precursor to linguistic analysis of these texts. This method addresses the practicalities of applying clustering operations to a very large set of text documents by using a combination of unsupervised clustering and supervised classification. The method relies on creating a multitude of independent clusterings of a randomized sample selected from the International Corpus of Learner English. Several consensus functions and sophisticated algorithms are applied in two substages to combine these independent clusterings into one final consensus clustering, which is then used to train fast classifiers in order to enable them to perform the profiling of very large collections of text and web data. This approach makes it possible to apply advanced highly accurate and sophisticated clustering techniques by combining them with fast supervised classification algorithms. For the effectiveness of this multistage method, it is crucial to determine how well the supervised classification algorithms are going to perform at the final stage, when they are used to process large data sets available on the Internet. This performance may also serve as an indication of the quality of the combined consensus clustering obtained in the preceding stages. Experimental results in the chapter compare the performance of several classification algorithms incorporated in this multistage scheme and demonstrate that several of these classification algorithms achieve very high precision and recall and can be used in practical implementations of our method.

Chapter 9

Keyword suggestion is an automatic machine learning method to suggest relevant keywords to users in order to help users better specify their information needs. In this chapter, the author adopts two semantic analysis models to build a keyword suggestion system. The suggested keywords returned from the system not only with a certain semantic relationship, but also with a similarity measure. The benefit of the author's method is to overcome the problems of synonymy and polysemy over the information retrieval field by using a vector space model. This chapter shows that using multiple semantic analysis techniques to generate relevant keywords can give significant performance gains.

Section 2
Computational Intelligence Techniques and Applications

Chapter 10

Content-based image retrieval is a difficult area of research in multimedia systems. The research has proven extremely difficult because of the inherent problems in proper automated analysis and feature extraction of the image to facilitate proper classification of various objects. An image may contain more than one object, and to segment the image in line with object features to extract meaningful objects and then classify it in high-level like table, chair, car, and so on has become a challenge to the researchers in the field. The latter part of the problem, the gap between low-level features like colour, shape, texture, spatial relationships, and high-level definitions of the images is called the semantic gap. Until this problem is solved in an effective way, the efficient processing and retrieval of information from images will be difficult to achieve. In this chapter, authors explore the possibilities of how emergence phenomena and fuzzy logic can help solve these problems of image segmentation and semantic gap.

Chapter 11

Engineered floodplain filtration (EFF) system is an eco-friendly low-cost water treatment process wherein water contaminants can be removed, by adsorption and-or degraded by microorganisms, as the infiltrating water moves from the wastewater treatment plants to the rivers. An artificial neural network (ANN) based approach was used in this study to approximate and interpret the complex input/output relationships, essentially to understand the breakthrough times in EFF. The input parameters to the ANN model were inlet concentration of a pharmaceutical, ibuprofen (ppm) and flow rate (md– 1), and the output parameters were six concentration-time pairs (C, t). These C, t pairs were the times in the breakthrough profile, when 1%, 5%, 25%, 50%, 75%, and 95% of the pollutant was present at the outlet of the system. The most dependable condition for the network was selected by a trial and error approach and by estimating the determination coefficient (R2) value (>0.99) achieved during prediction of the testing set. The proposed ANN model for EFF operation could be used as a potential alternative for knowledge-based models through proper training and testing of variables.

Chapter 12

D. Jude Hemanth, Karunya University, India
J. Anitha, Karunya University, India

Medical image classification is one of the widely used methodologies in the biomedical field for abnormality detection in the anatomy of the human body. Image classification belongs to the broad category of pattern recognition in which different abnormal images are grouped into different categories based on the nature of the pathologies. Nowadays, these techniques are automated and high accuracy combined with low convergence rate has become the desired features of automated techniques. Artificial Intelligence (AI) techniques are the highly preferred automated techniques because of their superior performance measures. In this chapter, the application of AI techniques for pattern recognition is explored in the context of abnormal Magnetic Resonance (MR) brain image classification. This chapter illustrates the theory behind the AI techniques and their effectiveness for practical application in medical image classification. Few experimental results are also provided to aid the conclusions. Algorithmic approach of the AI techniques such as neural networks, fuzzy theory, and genetic algorithm are also dealt in this chapter.

Chapter 13

Satvir Singh, Shaheed Bhagat Singh College of Engineering & Technology, India
J. S. Saini, Deenbandhu Chhotu Ram University of Science & Technology, India
Arun Khosla, Dr. B. R. Ambedkar National Institute of Technology, India

In most of fuzzy logic system (FLS) designs, human reasoning is encoded into programs to make decisions and/or control systems. Designing an optimal FLS is equivalent to an optimization problem, in which efforts are made to locate a point in fitness search-space where the performance is better than that of other locations. Number of parameters to be tuned in designing an FLS is quite large. Also, fitness search space is highly non-linear, deceptive, non-differentiable, and multi-modal in nature. Noisy data, from which to construct the FLS, may make the design problem even more difficult. This chapter presents a framework to design Type-1 (T1) and Interval Type-2 (IT2) FLSs using Particle Swarm Optimization (PSO). This framework includes the use of Nature Inspired (NI) Toolbox discussed in the previous chapter.

Chapter 14

B. Verma, Central Queensland University, Australia

This chapter presents the state of the art in classifier ensembles and their comparative performance analysis. The main aim and focus of this chapter is to present and compare recently developed neural network based classifier ensembles. The three types of neural classifier ensembles are considered and discussed. The first type is a classifier ensemble that uses a neural network for all its base classifiers. The second type is a classifier ensemble that uses a neural network as one of the classifiers among many of its base classifiers. The third and final type is a classifier ensemble that uses a neural network as a fusion classifier. The chapter reviews recent neural network based ensemble classifiers and compares their performances with other machine learning based classifier ensembles such as bagging, boosting, and rotation forest. The comparison is conducted on selected benchmark datasets from UCI machine learning repository.

Chapter 15

Jagannathan Krishnan, Universti Teknologi MARA, Malaysia
Eldon Raj Rene, University of La Coruña, Spain
Artem Lenskiy, University of Ulsan, South Korea
Tyagarajan Swaminathan, Indian Institute of Technology Madras, India

Volatile organic compounds (VOCs) belong to a new class of air pollutant that causes significant effect on human health and environment. Photocatalytic oxidation is an innovative, highly efficient, and promising option to decontaminate air polluted with VOCs, at faster elimination rates. This study pertains to the application of artificial neural networks to model the removal dynamics of an annular type photoreactor for gas – phase VOC removal. Relevant literatures pertaining to the experimental work has been reported in this chapter. The different steps involved in developing a suitable neural model have been outlined by considering the influence of internal network parameters on the model architecture. Anew, the neural network modeling results were also subjected to sensitivity analysis in order to identify the most influential parameter affecting the VOC removal process in the photoreactor.

Section 3
Miscellaneous Techniques in Machine Learning

Chapter 16

Tomoharu Nakashima, Osaka Prefecture University, Japan
Gerald Schaefer, Loughborough University, UK

This chapter presents an overview of pattern classification. In particular, the authors focus on the mathematical background of pattern classification rather than discussing the practical analysis of various pattern classification methods, and present the derivation of classification rules from a mathematical aspect. First, they define the pattern space without the loss of generality. Then, the categorisation of pattern classification is presented according to the design of classification systems. The mathematical formulation of each category of pattern classification is also given. Theoretical discussion using mathematical formulations is presented for distance-based pattern classification and statistical pattern classification. For statistical pattern classification, the standard assumption is made where patterns from each class follow normal distributions with different means and variances.

Chapter 17

Satvir Singh, Shaheed Bhagat Singh College of Engineering & Technology, India
Arun Khosla, Dr. B. R. Ambedkar National Institute of Technology, India
J. S. Saini, Deenbandhu Chhotu Ram University of Science & Technology, India

Nature-Inspired (NI) Toolbox is a Particle Swarm Optimization (PSO) based toolbox which is developed in the MATLAB environment. It has been released under General Public License and hosted at Source-Forge.net (http://sourceforge.net/projects/nitool/). The purpose of this toolbox is to facilitate the users/designers in design and optimization of their systems. This chapter discusses the fundamental concepts of PSO algorithms in the initial sections, followed by discussions and illustrations of benchmark optimization functions. Various modules of the Graphical User Interface (GUI) of NI Toolbox are explained with necessary figures and snapshots. In the ending sections, simulations results present comparative performance of various PSO models with concluding remarks.

Chapter 18

Bernadetta Kwintiana Ane, Institute of Computer-aided Product Development Systems, Universitaet Stuttgart, Germany

Dieter Roller, Institute of Computer-aided Product Development Systems, Universitaet Stuttgart, Germany

To date, cancer of uterine cervix is still a leading cause of cancer-related deaths in women in the world. Papanicolau smear test is a well-known screening method of detecting abnormalities of the cervix cells. Due to scarce number of skilled and experienced cytologists, the screening procedure becomes time consuming and highly prone to human errors that leads to inaccurate and inconsistent diagnosis. This condition increases the risk of patients who get HPV infection not be detected and become HPV carriers. Coping with this problem, an adaptive intelligent system is developed to enable automatic recognition of cancerous cells from. Here pattern recognition is done based on three morphological cell characteristics, i.e. size, shape, and color features, and measured as numerical values in terms of N/C ratio, nucleus perimeter, nucleus radius, cell deformity, texture heterogeneity, wavelet approximation coefficients, and gray-level intensity. Through a supervised learning of multilayer perceptron network, the system is able to percept abnormality in the cervix cells, and to assign them into a predicted group membership, i.e. normal or cancerous cells. Based on thorough observation upon the selected features and attributes, it can be recognized that the cancerous cells follow certain patterns and highly distinguishable from the normal cells.

Chapter 19

Constanta-Nicoleta Bodea, Academy of Economic Studies, Romania

Adina Lipai, Academy of Economic Studies, Romania

Maria-Iuliana Dascalu, Academy of Economic Studies, Romania

The chapter presents a meta-search tool developed in order to deliver search results structured according to the specific interests of users. Meta-search means that for a specific query, several search mechanisms could be simultaneously applied. Using the clustering process, thematically homogenous groups are built up from the initial list provided by the standard search mechanisms. The results are more user oriented, as a result of the ontological approach of the clustering process. After the initial search made on multiple search engines, the results are pre-processed and transformed into vectors of words. These vectors are mapped into vectors of concepts, by calling an educational ontology and using the WordNet lexical database. The vectors of concepts are refined through concept space graphs and projection mechanisms, before applying the clustering procedure. Implementation details and early experimentation results are also provided.

Márcio Porto Basgalupp, Federal University of Sao Paulo (UNIFESP), Brazil
Rodrigo Coelho Barros, University of Sao Paulo (ICMC-USP), Brazil
André C. P. L. F. de Carvalho, University of Sao Paulo (ICMC-USP), Brazil
Alex A. Freitas, University of Kent, UK

Decision tree induction algorithms are used in a variety of domains for knowledge discovery and pattern recognition. They have the advantage of producing a comprehensible classification model and satisfactory accuracy levels in several application domains. Most well-known decision tree induction algorithms perform a greedy top-down strategy for node partitioning that may lead to sub-optimal solutions that overfit the training data. Some alternatives for the greedy strategy are the use of ensemble of classifiers or, more recently, the employment of the evolutionary algorithms (EA) paradigm to evolve decision trees by performing a global search in the space of candidate trees. Both strategies have their own disadvantages, like the lack of comprehensible solutions (in the case of ensembles) or the high computation cost of EAs. Hence, the authors present a new algorithm that seeks to avoid being trapped in local-optima by doing a beam search during the decision tree growth. In addition, the strategy keeps the comprehensibility of the traditional methods and is much less time-consuming than evolutionary algorithms.

Liang-Bin Lai, National Taiwan University, Taiwan, ROC
Shu-Yu Lin, National Taiwan University, Taiwan, ROC
Ray-I Chang, National Taiwan University, Taiwan, ROC
Jen-Shiang Kouh, National Taiwan University, Taiwan, ROC

Understanding the ability of learning in both humans and non-humans is an important research crossing the boundaries between several scientific disciplines from computer science to brain science and psychology. In this chapter, the authors first introduce a query based learning concept (learning with query) in which all the minds' beliefs and actions will be revised by observing the outcomes of past mutual interactions (selective-attention and self-regulation) over time. That is, moving into an active learning and aggressive querying method will be able to focus on effectiveness to achieve learning goals and desired outcomes. Secondly, the authors show that the proposed method has better effectiveness for several learning algorithms, such as decision tree, particle swarm optimization, and self-organizing maps. Finally, a query based learning method is proposed to solve network security problems as a sample filter at intrusion detection. Experimental results show that the proposed method can not only increase the accuracy detection rate for suspicious activity and recognize rare attack types but also significantly improve the efficiency of intrusion detection. Therefore, it is good to design and to implement an effective learning algorithm for information security.

Preface

Machine Learning stream evolved from the broad area of Artificial Intelligence, which adopts the intelligent capacity of humans. The main aim of machine learning is to use previous data or experience for solving a particular problem and to make machine "learn" in an intelligent way. The components of machine learning are used for last few years to solve real world problems. It includes the development of new learning algorithms and its applications in various disciplines. Machine Learning deals with the design and development of new algorithms based on various types of data and has wide range of applications in today's world.

This book mainly focuses on improvement in machine learning algorithms and its use for real world applications. The book addresses state-of-the art solutions for many real-world problems in business, science and the engineering disciplines. Some of the applications include: image processing/retrieval, security, computer vision, handwritten characters recognition, bioinformatics, health, law, text analysis.

The book is intended for academics, researchers, scientists and professionals who are engaged in research and development in the area of machine learning. It provides the development of new algorithms and their implementations as well as recent advances in the field.

The book includes 21 chapters that are broadly organized into three sections. Section 1, titled Machine Learning Applications, contains nine book chapters and details new algorithms for solving real world problems in the field of image retrieval, computer vision, handwritten character recognition, medicine, bioinformatics, text analysis, and legal databases. These chapters cover detail information about methodology, experiments, and analysis of their results. Section 2, titled Computational Intelligence Techniques and Applications, contains six chapters and deals with novel algorithms and hybrid techniques in machine learning. Computational intelligent techniques such as artificial neural networks and fuzzy logic are proposed for image segmentation, biomedical image processing, floodplain filtration system, noisy data systems, classifier ensembles, and photocatalytic reactor. Section 3, titled Miscellaneous Techniques in Machine Learning, contains six chapters and details in the area of pattern recognition, nature-inspired toolbox to design and optimize systems, intelligent systems for recognition of cancerous cervical cells, ontology-based clustering of the web search results, decision tree induction algorithm, and network security.

Section 1: Machine Learning Applications

Chapter 1 is titled *Machine Learning Approach for Content Based Image Retrieval.* In this chapter, Kulkarni investigates the problem of efficient and fast searching of images based on their low level features. Colour is prominent feature for most of the images. This chapter reviews various image retrieval techniques based on computational intelligence such as fuzzy logic and neural networks and proposes these techniques for posing a natural language query, classification, and fusion of multiple queries. Proposed technique was developed for a single query and later extended for multiple queries. It works effectively for searching specific images on large image database. Number of experiments was conducted, and promising results were obtained. Machine learning approach for content based image retrieval would be used for retrieving images in health, security, arts and many other areas.

Chapter 2 is titled *Machine Learning Techniques in Handwriting Recognition: Problems and Solutions*. In this chapter, Lee, Verma, Li, and Rahman focus on offline handwritten character recognition. Handwritten character recognition is an active research area for more than four decades, but some of the major problems are still unsolved. The proposed system gets a scanned handwritten page as input and provides an output in the form of editable recognized text. Problems and solutions for handwritten recognition techniques using machine learning have been identified in the chapter. The state of the art techniques and useful applications of handwriting recognition have been reviewed and presented. The binary segmentation with neural validation processes were discussed for improvement of the segmentation accuracy with expectation of better word recognition rate. In addition, very advanced architectural models, such as multiple experts systems and ensemble systems, have been discussed to achieve better performance and accuracy.

Chapter 3 is titled *Semi Blind Source Separation for Application in Machine Learning*. In this chapter, Naik and Kumar discuss semi Blind Source Separation (BSS) machine learning applications on audio and bio signal processing. BSS is one form of unsupervised learning and is a class of computational data analysis techniques for revealing hidden factors that underlie sets of measurements or signals. BSS assumes a statistical model whereby the observed multivariate data, typically given as a large database of samples, are assumed to be linear or nonlinear mixtures of some unknown latent variables. This chapter also establishes the applicability of BSS for biomedical applications and identifies the shortcomings related to order and magnitude ambiguity.

Chapter 4 is titled *Machine Learning Algorithms for Analysis of DNA Data Sets*. In this chapter, Yearwood, Bagirov, and Kelarev investigate that the applications of machine learning algorithms to analysis of data sets of DNA sequences are very important. This chapter discusses applications of several machine learning algorithms for the analysis of a JLA data set consisting of DNA sequences derived from noncoding segments in the junction of the large single copy region and inverted repeat A of the chloroplast genome in Eucalyptus. Machine learning algorithms based on local alignment scores achieve very good agreement with known biological classes for this data set. A new machine learning algorithm based on graph partitioning performed best for clustering of the JLA data set. Authors also claims that a new machine learning algorithm based on graph partitioning performed best for clustering of the JLA data set.

Chapter 5 is titled *Machine Learning Applications in Radiation Therapy*. In this chapter, Zhang, Meyer, Shi and D'Souza propose machine learning technique for health informatics. Cancer is one of major cause of death, and most patients go through radiation therapy during their treatment. Authors discuss the proposed use of computational techniques such as machine learning in radiation therapy for better diagnostic for obtaining tumor location for more accurate treatment. In addition, the chapter also reveals the review of recent advancement of machine learning applications in radiation therapy.

Chapter 6 is titled *Insights from Jurisprudence for Machine Learning in Law*. In this chapter, Stranieri and Zeleznikow focus on use of machine learning for legal database. The chapter provides basic information about approach of machine learning based on previous court cases and their outcomes. In addition, the chapter provides detailed literature for overview of machine learning techniques in law, jurisprudence concepts, and related case studies. It also introduces the novel concept of machine learning in family law-split up. Limitations of knowledge discovery are extracted and proposed solutions based on various parameters are detailed in this chapter.

Chapter 7 is titled *Machine Learning Applications in Computer Vision*. In this chapter, Harandi, Taheri, and Lovell review recent advances in the area of automated object recognition mainly considering various learning frameworks for solving object recognition problems. Intelligent techniques such as reinforcement learning and machine learning are discussed, as well as their use for solving sequential decision problems. In addition, this chapter discusses local and global appearance models for object recognition and how similarities between objects can be learnt and evaluated.

Chapter 8 is titled *Applications of Machine Learning for Linguistic Analysis of Texts*. In this chapter, Torney, Yearwood, Vamplew, and Kelarev describe a novel multistage method for linguistic clustering of large collection of text available on the Internet. This method addresses the practicalities of applying clustering operations to a very large set of text documents by using a combination of unsupervised clustering and supervised classification. The method relies on creating a multitude of independent clustering of a randomized sample selected from the International Corpus of Learner English. Experimental results compare the performance of several classification algorithms incorporated in the multistage scheme and demonstrate that several of these classification algorithms achieve very high precision and recall and can be used in practical applications.

Chapter 9 is titled *An Automatic Machine Learning Method for the Study of Keyword Suggestion*. In this chapter, Chen describes two semantic analysis models to build a keyword suggestion system. The suggested keywords returned from the system have certain semantic relationship with similarity measure. The proposed system overcomes the problem of synonymy and polysemy over the information retrieval field by using vector space model. In addition, the benefit of semantic graph is to find the terms easily with semantic relationships by using a graph search. This system solves the problem of finding any two objects with a semantic relationship and calculating the similarity degree between these two objects.

Section 2: Computational Intelligence Techniques and Applications

Chapter 10 is titled *Emergence Phenomenon and Fuzzy Logic in Meaningful Image Segmentation and Retrieval*. In this chapter, Deb and Kulkarni discuss the problem of extracting meaningful image segmentation using emergence phenomenon. The chapter provides useful information about basics of emergence index, definitions, and its performance on various real world images. Extracting meaningful objects from images is a challenging task in content based image retrieval and helps to overcome the problem of semantic gap. Computational Intelligence techniques such as artificial neural networks and fuzzy logic are proposed for identifying the problem of image classification and similarity measure. Artificial neural networks have been proposed to classify images based on their structure, features, and objects. Fuzzy logic has been used to calculate the similarity between segmented objects and shapes and their colours.

Chapter 11 is titled *Predicting Adsorption Behavior In Engineered Floodplain Filtration System Using Backpropagation Neural Networks*. In this chapter, Rene, Behera, and Park propose artificial neural networks to approximate and interpret the complex input/output relationships, essentially to understand the breakthrough times in EFF (EFF). Authors claim that engineered floodplain filtration system is an eco-friendly low-cost water treatment process wherein water contaminants can be removed, by adsorption and-or degraded by microorganisms, as the infiltrating water moves from the wastewater treatment plants to the rivers. The chapter discusses various related areas such as wastewater treatment processes, flood plain filtration for wastewater treatment, and mechanism and usefulness of flood plain filtration. The chapter is detailed with various experiments and their analysis.

Chapter 12 is titled *Computational Intelligence Techniques for Pattern Recognition in Biomedical Image Processing Applications.* In this chapter, Hemanth and Anitha first describe medical image classification and challenges in abnormality detection in the anatomy of the human body. The application of AI techniques for pattern recognition is explored in the context of abnormal Magnetic Resonance (MR) brain image classification. This chapter also illustrates the theory behind the AI techniques and their effectiveness for practical application in medical image classification. Algorithmic approach of neural networks, fuzzy theory, and genetic algorithm are also discussed in this chapter.

Chapter 13 is titled *A PSO-Based Framework for Designing Fuzzy Systems from Noisy Data Set.* In this chapter, Singh, Siani, and Khosla present a framework to design fuzzy logic systems using Particle Swarm Optimization (PSO). The chapter describes basics of fuzzy sets and systems along with lower and upper membership functions and fuzzy operators. PSO based framework is described using Nature-Inspired Toolbox in detailed steps and its application for designing fuzzy logic systems from noisy data.

Chapter 14 is titled *Neural Network Based Classifier Ensembles: A Comparative Analysis.* In this chapter, Verma presents the state of the art in classifier ensembles and their comparative performance analysis. Three types of neural classifier ensembles are considered and discussed. The first type is a classifier ensemble that uses a neural network for all its base classifiers. The second type is a classifier ensemble that uses a neural network as one of the classifiers among many of its base classifiers. The third and final type is a classifier ensemble that uses a neural network as a fusion classifier. The chapter reviews recent neural network based ensemble classifiers and compares their performances with other machine learning based classifier ensembles such as bagging, boosting, and rotation forest.

Chapter 15 is titled *Development of an Intelligent Neural Model to Predict and Analyze the VOC Removal Pattern in a Photocatalytic Reactor.* In this chapter, Krishnan, Rene, Lenskiy, and Swaminathan present an application of artificial neural networks to model the removal dynamics of an annular type photoreactor for gas. Volatile Organic Compounds (VOCs) belong to a new class of air pollutant that causes significant effect on human health and environment. Photocatalytic oxidation is an innovative, highly efficient, and promising option to decontaminate air polluted with VOCs, at faster elimination rates. The various steps involved in developing a suitable neural model have been outlined by considering the influence of internal network parameters on the model architecture.

Section 3: Miscellaneous Techniques in Machine Learning

Chapter 16 is titled *An Introduction to Pattern Classification.* In this chapter, Nakashima and Schaefer present an overview of pattern classification. The chapter discusses on the mathematical background of pattern classification rather than practical analysis of various pattern classification methods, and presents the derivation of classification rules from a mathematical aspect. Pre-processing and normalisation is often necessary in order to reduce the number of features and use only salient features that are important for classification. In distance-based pattern classification systems, a simple metric such as Euclidean distance between a training pattern and an unseen pattern is used to classify the unseen pattern. On the other hand, probabilistic assumption for patterns and classes are used in statistical pattern classification systems. This chapter also discusses statistical pattern classification from the view point of minimising classification costs. The property of classification boundaries were also explained for both distance-based and statistical pattern classification.

Chapter 17 is titled *Nature-Inspired Toolbox to Design and Optimize Systems.* In this chapter, Singh, Saini and Khosla discuss the fundamental concepts of Particle Swarm Optimization algorithms in the initial sections, followed by discussions and illustrations of benchmark optimization functions. Various modules of the Graphical User Interface (GUI) of Nature-Inspired Toolbox are explained with necessary figures and snapshots. In addition, the chapter also describes simulations results and comparative performance of various Particle Swarm Optimization models.

Chapter 18 is titled *Adaptive Intelligent Systems for Recognition of Cancerous Cervical Cells Based on 2D Cervical Cytological Digital Images.* In this chapter, Kwintiana and Roller claim that cancer of uterine cervix is still a leading cause of cancer-related deaths in women in the world. Due to scarce number of skilled and experienced cytologists, the screening procedure becomes time consuming and highly prone to human errors that leads to inaccurate and inconsistent diagnosis. This chapter provides detailed information about related studies and machine learning techniques, backpropagation learning algorithm. Experiments are conducted on various sets of images, and their detailed analysis is provided.

Chapter 19 is titled *Ontology-based Clustering of the Web Meta-Search Results.* In this chapter, Bodea, Lipai, and Dascalu present a meta-search tool developed in order to deliver search results structured according to the specific interests of users. Meta-search means that for a specific query, several search mechanisms could be simultaneously applied. Using the clustering process, thematically homogenous groups are built up from the initial list provided by the standard search mechanisms. The results are more user oriented, as a result of the ontological approach of the clustering process. After the initial search made on multiple search engines, the results are pre-processed and transformed into vectors of words. These vectors are mapped into vectors of concepts, by calling an educational ontology and using the WordNet lexical database. The vectors of concepts are refined through concept space graphs and projection mechanisms, before applying the clustering procedure. Implementation details and early experimentation results are also provided.

Chapter 20 is titled *A Beam Search Based Decision Tree Induction Algorithm.* In this chapter, Basgalupp, Barros, Carvalho, and Freitas claim that decision tree induction algorithms are highly used in a variety of domains for knowledge discovery and pattern recognition. They have the advantage of producing a comprehensible classification model and satisfactory accuracy levels in several application domains. This chapter presents a new algorithm that seeks to avoid being trapped in local-optima by doing a beam search during the decision tree growth. In addition, proposed strategy keeps the comprehensibility of the traditional methods and is much less time-consuming than evolutionary algorithms.

Chapter 21 is titled *Learning with Querying and its Application in Network Security.* In this chapter, Lai, Lin, Chang, and Kouh present a framework of query based learning concepts for different models of supervised and unsupervised learning. The chapter introduces a query based learning concept in which all the minds' beliefs and actions are revised by observing the outcomes of past mutual interactions over time. Experiments show that the proposed method increases the accuracy detection rate for suspicious activity and significantly improve the efficiency of intrusion detection.

Siddhivinayak Kulkarni
University of Ballarat, Australia

Acknowledgment

First I would like to thank academic editor of IGI Global for inviting me to organize and edit this book.

My sincere thanks goes to 49 contributing authors, from 13 countries who made great contributions to this book by submitting quality chapters and reviewing them. I appreciate their support and cooperation.

I would like to thank the Centre for Informatics and Applied Optimization at the University of Ballarat, for its support.

I wish to extend my special thanks to all IGI Global publishing staff for their valuable communication and suggestions during the development of this book.

Last, but not least, I am very thankful to my wife Pradnya, daughter Tejal, son Tanmay, and my parents Arvind and Anuradha for their patience, support, and understanding during last two years.

Siddhivinayak Kulkarni
University of Ballarat, Australia

Section 1
Machine Learning Applications

Chapter 1
Machine Learning Approach for Content Based Image Retrieval

Siddhivinayak Kulkarni
University of Ballarat, Australia

ABSTRACT

Developments in technology and the Internet have led to an increase in number of digital images and videos. Thousands of images are added to WWW every day. Content based Image Retrieval (CBIR) system typically consists of a query example image, given by the user as an input, from which low-level image features are extracted. These low level image features are used to find images in the database which are most similar to the query image and ranked according their similarity. This chapter evaluates various CBIR techniques based on fuzzy logic and neural networks and proposes a novel fuzzy approach to classify the colour images based on their content, to pose a query in terms of natural language and fuse the queries based on neural networks for fast and efficient retrieval. A number of experiments were conducted for classification, and retrieval of images on sets of images and promising results were obtained.

INTRODUCTION

The concept of content-based image retrieval (CBIR) is a very interesting in computer science field that involves retrieving specific images from small to large size image databases based solely on the feature content of the images. The size of the digital image collection is increasing very rapidly due to the advancement in technological devices. These images are stored digitally and transmitted over the Internet at a very high speed.

To retrieve the images based on their content effectively and efficiently is essential for further processing of the images. But how to retrieve the images based on their content? There are few image retrieval systems developed commercially as well as academically. Most of the CBIR systems use example image (query image) for retrieving the images from the database.

One of the most common techniques for adding the images into a database is to store images together with some descriptive text or keywords assigned by human operators. These text or key-

DOI: 10.4018/978-1-4666-1833-6.ch001

words are developed based on most prominent feature of an image. For example, for the image of sunset, the most prominent object will be sun or red/orange colour the top of the image. Image retrievals are performed by matching the query texts with the stored descriptive keywords. The images are ranked based on these keywords for similarity. There are several problems with the keyword based matching as this approach is exclusively text based and no visual properties of underlying data are employed. First of all this is very time consuming process, as text descriptions of image contents have to be assigned and keyed in by human operators, also due to enormous volumes of image data, it is also very subjective and incomplete. Human may find different objects or colours or textures in the same image. Retrieval will fail if the user forms the query based on a different set of keywords, or the query refers to the image contents that were not initially described. An ideal system should allow both a keyword and a concept search, in conjunction with a content-based search. The system receives images that are similar to the users' query and ranks them on the basis of similarity. Many strategies and algorithms have been proposed for similarity based retrieval from the high dimensional index structure. However, there has been little work on query processing based on natural language and fusion of multiple queries. The main task of the image retrieval system to retrieve images based on user's query. This query may be in the form of keywords, natural language and/or example image. In most of the CBIR systems, the different features such as colour, texture, shape objects are extracted and used for posing a query in the form of example image. The features of the query image and all other images in the database are compared and the distance between them is calculated using similarity measures.

Most of the current CBIR systems such as QBIC (Flickner et al., 1995), Virage (Gupta, 1996), Photobook (Pentland et al., 1996) and Netra (Ma and Manjunath, 1999) use a weighted linear method to combine similarity measurements of different feature classes. QBIC (Flickner et al., 1995) executes the queries by calculating the similarity between the pre-extracted features of the images in a database. QBIC allows queries based on example images, user-constructed sketches or/and selected colour and texture patterns. The percentage of a specific colour in an image is adjusted by moving sliders. To perform a query in Photobook (Pentland et al., 1996), the user selects some images from the grid of still images displayed and/or enters annotation filter. The images obtained with the query are refined to make another search. VisualSEEK (Chang and Smith, 1996) determines the similarity by measuring image regions using both colour parameters and spatial relationships. To pose a query, the user sketches a number of positions and dimensions them on the grid and selects a colour for each region. Also, the user can indicate boundaries for location and size and spatial relationships between regions. Netra (Ma and Manjunath, 1999) depends upon image segmentation to carry out region based searches that allow the user to select example regions and lay emphasis on image attributes to focus the search. The user can select any one image as query image from 2500 images, clustered into 25 classes and 100 images for each class. The images are segmented into various homogenous regions and the user can select any one of the region for possible matching based on colour, texture, spatial location and shape. The main motivation for the development of this system is that region-based search improves the quality of the image retrieval. Therefore the system incorporates an automated region identification algorithm. Region-based querying is also used in Blobworld (Carson et al., 1998) where global histograms are shown to perform comparatively poorly on images containing distinctive objects. The user first selects a category, which already limits the search space. In an initial image, the user selects a region (blob), and indicates the importance of the blob. Next, the user indicates the importance of each blob based on fuzzy terms such as 'not', 'somewhat', 'very'. Multiple regions are used for querying. In Chabot (Ogle, V., and Stonebraker, M., 1995), the user is presented with a list of search criteria such as keywords, colours, photographer etc. The colour criterion offers the options in terms of specific content of the each colour. The concept in an image is demonstrated by a descriptive keyword and specific colour related to the keyword.

Fuzzy logic offers a good solution for posing a query in terms of natural language based on the various features of an image. Fuzzy logic has been extensively used at various stages of image retrieval such as region groupings within the images as a feature extraction technique, for measuring the similarity between the target image and the images in the database. Fuzzy logic is proposed for the computation of fuzzy colour histogram as well as posing the queries in CBIR. This chapter reviews the prominent CBIR systems along with fuzzy logic based techniques and proposes a technique based on fuzzy logic and neural networks for retrieving the images using natural language query for colour and texture features. The rest of the book chapter is organised as follows: Section 2 reviews CBIR techniques based on computational intelligence techniques such as fuzzy logic and neural networks, Section 3 proposes feature extraction algorithm and fuzzy mapping of images, Section 4 describes neural based fusion of classes, Section 5 details experimental results in brief and chapter is concluded in Section 6 with Conclusion.

BRIEF REVIEW OF CONTENT BASED IMAGE RETRIEVAL TECHNIQUES

Fuzzy logic based technique has been applied for solving the problems in CBIR. Fuzzy logic is used for measuring the similarity between the two images as fuzzy hamming distance, region groupings, colour histogram as feature extraction techniques, and posing the queries etc.

Fuzzy colour histogram is proposed by considering the colour similarity of each pixel's colour associated to all the histogram bins through fuzzy-set membership function (Han and Ma, 2002). Stricker and Dimai's method (Sticker and Dimai, 1997) segments each image into five partially overlapping fuzzy regions and extracts first two colour moments of each region both weighted by membership functions of the region to form a feature vector for the image. A colour space for CBIR is presented which provides both the ability to measure similarity using fuzzy logic and psychologically based set theoretic similarity measurement. These properties are shown to be equal or superior to the conventional colour space (Seaborn and Hepplewhite, 1999). Fuzzy logic based colour histogram and their corresponding fuzzy distances are proposed for the retrieval of colour images for image database (Vertan and Boujemaa, 2000). Fuzzy logic is applied to the traditional colour histogram for solving the problem of inaccuracy in typical colour feature. The similarity is defined through a balanced combination between global and regional similarity measures incorporating all the features. A secondary clustering technique is developed to improve the retrieval efficiency that also saves the query processing time significantly without compromising the retrieval precision (Zhang and Zhang, 2002). C. Vertan et al. propose fuzzy colour histogram that classifies fuzzy techniques as crude fuzzy, fuzzy paradigm based, fuzzy aggregational and fuzzy inferential (Vertan and Boujemaa, 2000).

The Fuzzy Hamming Distance (FHD) is an extension of Hamming Distance for real valued vectors. Because the feature space of each image is a real-valued, the fuzzy Hamming Distance can be successfully used as image similarity measure. FHD is applied for colour histograms of the two images. The authors claim that FHD not only considers the number of different colours but also the magnitude of this difference (Ionescu and Ralescu,

2004)(Ionescu and Ralescu, 2005). In (Yang, 2001) supports concept-based image retrieval as well as the inexact match with a fuzzy triple matching performed when evaluating queries.

In (Chen and Wang, 2002) an image is represented by a set of segmented regions each of which is characterised by a fuzzy feature reflecting colour, texture and shape properties. The resemblance between two images is then defined as the overall similarity between two families of fuzzy features and quantified by unified feature matching. Non-Boolean fuzzy and similarity predicates are used to rank tuples according to fuzzy based algebra (Ciaccia, et al., 2001). Soft queries in image retrieval systems present the use of soft computing and user defined classifications in multimedia database systems for content based queries (Shahabi, and Chen, 2000). A CBIR system which automatically clusters images using features of those images which are fuzzy in nature. Image is described on a fuzzy rule based compact composite descriptor which includes global image features combining brightness and texture characteristics (Chatzichristo□s and Boutalis., 2010).

The resultant clusters must be described by linguistic variables which are more meaningful to humans than traditional approaches, also fuzzy features result in better clustering than traditional approach. Fuzzy image labelling method that assigns multiple semantic labels together with confidence measures to each region in an image (Paterno et al., 2004). E. Walker describes several aspects of Internet information retrieval where fuzzy logic can be applied (Walker, 2002). In Berkeley Digital Library Project (Carson and Ogle, 1996), the user can select the colours along with their amount in the picture. The coloured regions can be categorized in various sizes such as 'any', 'small', 'medium' and 'large.' In (Aboulmagd, H., Gayar, N., and Onsi, H., 2009), image is represented by a fuzzy attributed relational graph that describes each object in the image with its attributes and spatial relation and graph

matching technique is used that resembles with human thinking.

The query in CBIR system may be based on single feature (colour, texture etc.) or complex, dealing with combination of features (such as colour and texture or texture and shape etc.) It is easy to retrieve images based on single query compared to multiple or complex queries. Many efficient algorithms have been proposed for range of queries and its variants and are implemented in some CBIR systems (Beckmann et al., 1990). Fagin (Fagin, 1996) and Chaudhari and Gravano (Chaudhari and Gravano, 1996) have addressed the problem of solving complex queries. Both approaches have used fuzzy logic to arrive at the sorted list to evaluate and answer the complex queries. Byrne and Klein (Byrne and Klein, 2003) proposed combination of a traditional information retrieval technique with named entity recognition, CBIR and relational database tools. Combining these techniques with CBIR, that look at the physical characteristics of images in terms of colour and shape was less successful. Durai et. Al., (Durai, Duraisamy, and Sahasranaman, 2010) developed the fuzzy relaxation pattern matching technique using rotational invariance has been developed in the framework of fuzzy set and possibility theory. Paper presented by Yu and Dunham (Yu S., and Dunham M., 2011) proposed fuzzy logic based method to automatically generate the description of spatial relationship among objects and graph based fuzzy linguistic metadata schema for topology and relationship for a set of objects. Linguistics query terms were used for a single colour and a content type such as mostly red, few green for retrieving images based on single content and colour (Kulkarni et al., 1999) and experiments were performed for classification of texture features of the images (Verma and Kulkarni, 2004).

Computational intelligence based techniques such as neural networks have also been applied by some researchers to develop a prototype for CBIR. Neural networks have also been proposed for feature extraction (Oja et al., 1997), similarity measurement (Muneesawang and Guan, 2002), relevance feedback technique (Lee and Yoo, 2001a, Lee and Yoo, 2001b) etc. Various developed algorithms such as error back propagation, self organizing map, radial basis function etc. have been successfully applied to solve the various problems in image retrieval as well as to bridge the semantic gap used for processing high level query posed by a user and low level features extracted by the system (Tsai et al., 2003b). Images are compared through a weighted dissimilarity function which can be replaced as a "network of dissimilarities." The weights are updated via an error back-propagation algorithm using the user's annotations of the successive set of the result images (Fournier et al. 2001). It allows an iterative refinement of the search through a simple interactive process. Not much work has been done in the area of fuzzy logic based linguistic queries for image retrieval. Fuzzy logic has impressive power to represent the queries in terms of natural content of the image. The next section describes the proposed technique for colour feature extraction and fuzzy mapping of images.

FEATURE EXTRACTION AND FUZZY MAPPING

Colour feature extraction forms the basis of colour image retrieval. The distribution of colour is a useful feature for image representation. Colour distribution, which is best represented as a histogram of intensity values, is more appropriate as a global property which does not require knowledge of how an image is composed of different objects. So this technique works extremely well to extract global colour components from the images. A colour histogram technique is used for extracting the colours from the images. The colour of any pixel may be represented in terms of the components of red, green and blue values. These histograms are invariant under translation and rotation about

the view axis and change only under the change of angle of view, change in scale and occlusion. Therefore, the colour histogram is a suitable quantitative representation of image content.

Let F_S denote the set of features used to represent colour content, F_S = {colour}. The feature representation set of colours is rep (colour) = {red, green, blue, white, black, yellow, orange, pink, purple}.

An image histogram refers to the probability mass function of the image intensities. This is extended for colour images to capture the joint probabilities of the intensities of the three-colour channels. More formally, the colour histogram is defined by

$$h_{rgb} = N \cdot prob\left\{R = r,\ G = g,\ B = b\right\}$$

where R, G, B represent the three-colour channels and N is the number of pixels in an image. These RGB values are converted into Hue (0, 360), Saturation (0, 1) and Value (0, 1).

Maximum and minimum values for RGB were calculated. Saturation (S) is the ratio of the difference between maximum and minimum values to the maximum value (12). After getting these terms, HSV were calculated.

NEURAL BASED FUSION OF CLASSES

It is very important to learn the meaning of the classes for fusion of queries. A neural network based technique is the best solution to learn those classes. Different neural network algorithms can be categorized by, for example, the learning method and architecture of the network. The supervised learning neural network is efficient to learn the colours and content types. Concept of neural network ensemble has been used to implement the fusion of classes. Neural Network Ensembles

Algorithm RGB_to_HSV (r, g, b:real; var h, s, v:real)

```
{Given: r, g, b, each in (0, 1).
Desired: h in (0,360), s and v in (0, 1) expect if s=0, then h=UNDEFINED
begin
Red -> val(RED) > val(GREEN) + val(BLUE)
GREEN -> val(GREEN) > val(BLUE) && val(Green) > val(RED)
BLUE -> val(BLUE) > 0.5 (val(RED) + val(GREEN))
WHITE -> val(RED) > 200 && val(BLUE) > 200 && val(GREEN)> 200
BLACK -> val(RED) < 30 && val(GREEN) < 30 && val(BLUE) <30
YELLOW -> h > 42 && h < 62 && s> 0.6 && v > 0.95
ORANGE -> h > 2 && h < 40 && s >.7 && v >.93
PINK-> h > 320 && s <.5
PURPLE -> (h > 320 && h < 330) && (s >.50) && (v >.60 && v <.8)
end
Colour {Red, Green, Blue, White, Black, Yellow, Orange, Pink, Purple}
Content {Very low, Low, Medium, High, Very high}
Fuzzy terms for colour contents for each image:
verylow ->(0.05, 0.1)
low -> (0.11, 0.35)
medium -> (0.36, 0.65)
high -> (0.66, 0.80)
veryhigh-> (0.81, 1)
```

(NNE) divide the data into smaller areas and becomes easier to learn the meaning of each class. NNE is robust compared to single neural network for processing large amount of data and therefore produces better final decision. Separate neural networks were formed for each of the content type ranging from very low to very high.

Fuzzy class for colour contents for each image is described in the last section. As each of the neural networks is learned on classes and not on the database, it avoids retraining of the neural networks. The query is consisted of a colour and type of content in natural language terms. There are total 55 classes (11 colours and 5 content types). In this approach, the user has the opportunity to select the colour and the content type in natural language terms rather than having to use technical terms. The user also has the advantage of retrieving images without having an example/query image.

NN indicates the Neural Network designed for a specific content. For low content, low=0.11 with increment of 0.01 till reaches max value which is 0.35 in this case. Similarly neural network was designed for each content class. This process helps to build training pairs for each class. It is an efficient way to classify images based on their content and search images for a specific query and content.

EXPERIMENTAL RESULTS

Image Dataset Preparation and Feature Extraction

Image Dataset was prepared from various sets of images and consists of five thousand images. These images are taken from various categories

Figure 1. Neural based fusion

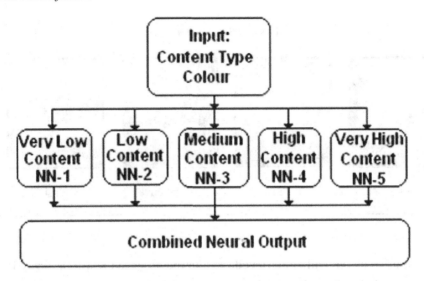

such as images of babies, beaches, birds, boats, cars, dogs, fireworks, flowers, landmarks, nature, planes, planets, sunsets, waterfalls and weddings. Number of experiments was conducted by various queries and some of the results are mentioned in this section. Features were extracted from all images and stored in feature image database in appropriate classes.

Image Retrieval for Single Query

In the image retrieval section, the images retrieved are based on the query submitted by the user. As an example, the query was submitted in terms of fuzzy logic as high content of blue colour. Images will be searched only in a single class, avoids all other classes for searching and therefore minimizes the time in searching of images. The results for first top ranked two images are shown in Figure 2. Percentage of colour content is shown along with ranked images. Similarly, number of experiments was conducted for different sets of queries such as low content for red colour, medium content for green colour and so on.

Fusion of Queries Using Neural Networks

The natural language query is used to match with the image in the image set and the relevant images will be classified into the query class. First experiments were conducted on single colour and query type and later results were fused using combination of neural networks based on con-

Figure 2. Results for single query: Blue + very high

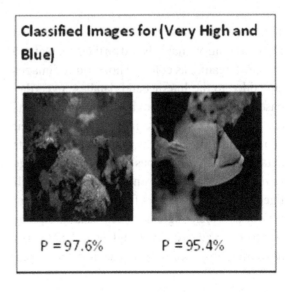

Figure 3. Image retrieval results using multiple queries

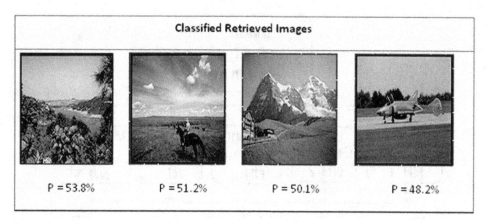

tent type. The classified image will be retrieved and shown in descending order long with their percentage for the relevant colour. For example, if user provides Medium + Blue and Medium+ Green, the names of the images are listed with the percentages which have a medium content of Blue and Green colours.

The images are retrieved with their percentage. Each percentage is used for indexing. Sorting algorithm is used and the percentages are sorted in descending order. The classified images are then displayed in descending order.

CONCLUSION

This chapter evaluates the problem of efficient and fast searching of images based on their content and low level feature as colour. Thousands of images are added to the Internet and database everyday based on their applications in health, security, arts etc. It is vital to retrieve images based on their content in an effective way. This chapter presents detailed review of various content based image retrieval systems based on computational intelligence technique such as fuzzy logic and neural networks. Fuzzy logic has been used at various stages in image retrieval and neural networks have been proposed for classficiation of images.

In the proposed research, fuzzy logic is used for identifying the meaning of the queries in terms of natural language such as low content and high content of a specific colour in an image. Based on content and colour, images are classified to the specific class. Neural network is used to fuse the results obtained from various queries. This proposed approach works well for efficient searching for large image database. Proposed technique was developed for single query and later extended for multiple queries. Experiments were conducted for combination of queries and promising results were obtained.

REFERENCES

Aboulmagd, H., Gayar, N., & Onsi, H. (2009). A new approach in content-based image retrieval using fuzzy logic. *Journal of Telecommunication Systems*, *40*(1-2), 55–66. doi:10.1007/s11235-008-9142-9

Beckmann, N., Kriegel, H.-K., Schneider, R., & Seeger, B. (1990). The R*-tree: An efficient and robust access method for points and rectangles. *Proceedings of the ACM SIG-MOD International Conference on Management of Data*, (pp. 322-331).

Byrne, K., & Klein, E. (2003). Image retrieval using natural language and content-based techniques. *Proceedings of the 4ᵗʰ Dutch-Belgian Information Retrieval Workshop*, (pp. 57-62).

Carson, C., Belongie, S., Greenspan, H., & Malik, J. (1998). Blobworld: Image segmentation using expectation-maximization and its application to image querying. *Journal of Pattern Analysis and Machine Intelligence*, *24*(8), 1026–1038. doi:10.1109/TPAMI.2002.1023800

Carson, C., & Ogle, V. (1996). Storage and retrieval of feature data for a very large online image collections. *Bulletin of the IEEE Computer Society Technical Committee on Data Engineering*, *19*(4), 19–27.

Chatzichristo□s, S., & Boutalis, Y. (2010). Content based radiology image retrieval using a fuzzy rule based scalable composite descriptor. *Journal of Multimedia Tools and Applications*, *46*(2-3), 493-519.

Chaudhari, S., & Gravano, L. (1996). Optimizing queries over multimedia repositories. *Bulletin of the IEEE Computer Society Technical Committee on Data Engineering*, (pp. 45-52).

Chen, Y., & Wang, J. (2002). A region based fuzzy feature matching approach to content based image retrieval. *IEEE Transactions on Pattern Analysis and Machine Intelligence*, *24*(9), 1252–1267. doi:10.1109/TPAMI.2002.1033216

Ciaccia, P., Montesi, D., Penzo, W., & Trombetta, A. (2001). Fuzzy query languages for multimedia data. In Syed, M. R. (Ed.), *Design and management of multimedia information systems: Opportunities and challenges*. Hershey, PA: Idea Group Publishing. doi:10.4018/978-1-930708-00-6.ch010

Durai, R., Duraisamy, V., & Sahasranaman, K. (2011). Content based image retrieval using fuzzy relaxation and rotational invariance for medical databases. *Proceedings of International Conference on Process Automation, Control and Computing*, (pp. 1-3).

Fagin, R. (1996). Combining fuzzy information from multiple systems. *Proceedings of Fifteenth ACM Symposium on Principles of Database Systems*, (pp. 216-226).

Flickner, M., Sawhney, H., Niblack, W., Ashley, J., Huang, Q., & Dom, B. (1995). Query by image and video content: The QBIC system. *IEEE Computer*, *28*(9), 23–32. doi:10.1109/2.410146

Fournier, J., Cord, M., & Philipp-Foliguet, S. (2001). Back-propagation algorithm for relevance feedback in image retrieval. *Proceedings of International Conference on Image Processing*, (Vol. 1, pp. 686-689).

Gupta, A. (1996). *Visual information retrieval: A Virage perspective*. Technical Report, Revision 4. San Diego, CA: Virage Inc. Retrieved from http://www.virage.com/wpaper

Han, J., & Ma, K. (2002). Fuzzy colour histogram and its use in colour image retrieval. *IEEE Transactions on Image Processing*, *11*(8), 944–952. doi:10.1109/TIP.2002.801585

Ionescu, M., & Ralescu, A. (2005). Image clustering for a fuzzy hamming distance based CBIR systems. *Proceedings of the Sixteen Midwest Artificial Intelligence and Cognitive Science Conference, MAICS-2005*, (pp. 102-108).

Ionescu, M., & Ralescu, R. (2004). Fuzzy hamming distance in a content based image retrieval systems. *Proceedings of FUZZ-IEEE 2004*, Budapest.

Kulkarni, S., & Verma, B. (2002). An intelligent hybrid approach for content based image retrieval. *International Journal of Computational Intelligence and Applications, 2*(2), 173–184. doi:10.1142/S1469026802000567

Kulkarni, S., Verma, B., Sharma, P., & Selvaraj, H. (1999). Content based image retrieval using a neuro-fuzzy technique. *Proceedings of IEEE International Joint Conference on Neural Networks,* (pp. 846-850). Washington, USA.

Lee, H., & Yoo, S. (2001). Applying neural network to combining the heterogeneous features in content-based image retrieval. *Proceedings of SPIE Applications of Artificial Neural Networks in Image Processing, 4305*(13), 81–89.

Lee, H., & Yoo, S. (2001). A neural network based image retrieval using nonlinear combination of heterogeneous features. *International Journal of Computational Intelligence and Applications, 1*(2), 137–149. doi:10.1142/S1469026801000123

Ma, W., & Manjunath, B. (1999). NETRA: A toolbox for navigating large image databases. *Journal of ACM Multimedia Systems, 7*(3), 184–198. doi:10.1007/s005300050121

Muneesawang, P., & Guan, L. (2002). Automatic machine interactions for CBIR using self organized tree map architecture. *IEEE Transactions on Neural Networks, 13*(4), 821–834. doi:10.1109/TNN.2002.1021883

Ogle, V., & Stonebraker, M. (1195). Chabot: Retrieval from a relational database of images. *IEEE Computer, 28*(9), 40-48.

Oja, E., Laaksonen, J., Koskela, M., & Brandt, S. (1997). Self organising maps for content based image database retrieval. In Oja, E., & Kaski, S. (Eds.), *Kohonen Maps* (pp. 349–362). Amsterdam.

Paterno, M., Lim, F., & Leow, W. (2004). Fuzzy semantic labelling for image retrieval. *International Conference on Multimedia and Expo,* (Vol. 2, pp. 767-770).

Pentland, A., Picard, R., & Sclaroff, S. (1996). Content-based manipulation of image databases. *International Journal of Computer Vision, 3,* 233–254. doi:10.1007/BF00123143

Seaborn, M., & Hepplewhite, L. (1999). Fuzzy colour category map for content based image retrieval. *Tenth British Machine Vision Conference,* (pp. 103-112).

Shahabi, C., & Chen, Y. (2000). Soft query in image retrieval systems. *Proceedings of the SPIE Internet Imaging (EI14), Electronic Imaging, Science and Technology,* San Jose, California, (pp. 57-68).

Smith, J., & Chang, S. (1996). Querying by colour regions using the VisualSEEK content-based visual query system. In Maybury, M. T. (Ed.), *Intelligent multimedia information retrieval* (pp. 23–41). AAAI Press.

Sticker, M., & Dimai, A. (1997). Spectral covariance and fuzzy regions for image indexing. *Machine Vision and Applications, 10,* 66–73. doi:10.1007/s001380050060

Tsai, C., McGarry, K., & Tait, J. (2003). Using neuro-fuzzy technique based on a two stage mapping model for concept-based image database indexing. *Proceedings of the Fifth International Symposium on Multimedia Software Engineering,* Taiwan, (pp. 10-12).

Vertan, C., & Boujemaa, N. (2000). Embedding fuzzy logic for image retrieval. *19th International Conference of the North American Fuzzy Information Processing Society,* (pp. 85-89).

Walker, E. (2002). Image retrieval on the Internet - How can fuzzy help? *Proceedings of the Annual Conference of the North American Fuzzy Information Processing Society, NAFIPS '00*, (pp. 526-528).

Yang, J. (2001). An image retrieval model based on fuzzy triples. *Journal on Fuzzy Sets and Systems*, *121*(3), 459–470. doi:10.1016/S0165-0114(00)00056-7

Yu, S., & Dunham, M. (2011). A graph-based fuzzy linguistic metadata schema for describing spatial relationships. *Proceedings of International Symposium on Visual Information Communication*, Article no. 14.

Zhang, R., & Zhang, Z. (2002). A clustering based approach to efficient image retrieval. *14th IEEE Conference on Tools with Artificial Intelligence*, (pp. 339-346).

KEY TERMS AND DEFINITIONS

Classifier Ensembles: A combination of multiple classifiers by training them and fusing their decisions to produce the final decision.

Colour Image Retrieval: Retrieving the digital images based on colour feature of an image.

Content-based Image Retrieval: Searching of the digital images from database or from Internet based on the contents (or features) of an image.

Fusion of Queries: Two or more queries are combined together to achieve better results.

Fuzzy Query: (1) Analysis of queries posed by the user in terms of natural language and converting them into numerical values. (2) Flexible queries or queries in terms of natural language. These queries are expressed to reduce the semantic gap between the user and computer. The search results obtained with fuzzy query are usually more robust.

Neural Networks: A neural network is an interconnected group of artificial or biological neurons, generally used for learning and classification of input data.

Chapter 2
Machine Learning Techniques in Handwriting Recognition:
Problems and Solutions

Hong Lee
Central Queensland University, Australia

Brijesh Verma
Central Queensland University, Australia

Michael Li
Central Queensland University, Australia

Ashfaqur Rahman
Central Queensland University, Australia

ABSTRACT

Handwriting recognition is a process of recognizing handwritten text on a paper in the case of offline handwriting recognition and on a tablet in the case of online handwriting recognition and converting it into an editable text. In this chapter, the authors focus on offline handwriting recognition, which means that recognition system accepts a scanned handwritten page as an input and outputs an editable recognized text. Handwriting recognition has been an active research area for more than four decades, but some of the major problems still remained unsolved. Many techniques, including the machine learning techniques, have been used to improve the accuracy. This chapter focuses on describing the problems of handwriting recognition and presents the solutions using machine learning techniques for solving major problems in handwriting recognition. The chapter also reviews and presents the state of the art techniques with results and future research for improving handwriting recognition.

DOI: 10.4018/978-1-4666-1833-6.ch002

INTRODUCTION

Personal Digital Assistants (PDA), Electronic Pen (E-Pen), Electronic-Mail (Email), mobile phones, computers, and so forth are the examples of the representatives in modern communication methodologies. In the last few decades, communication sectors have been changed dramatically from classical manual methods to electronic automations in the ways of delivering or storing the information. The automatic conversion of recognizing handwritten texts is not exceptional. For the last few decades, attempts to digitize machine-printed, known as Optical Character Conversion (OCR), have been very successful. In fact, OCR applications are commercially available off the shelves nowadays, and the performance and accuracy in conversion are very close to perfection. Along with the success in OCR, the research efforts have been made to convert human-printed, 'handwritten' texts to digital format. Handwriting is a methodology to aid and expand finite biological human memory by making artificial graphical marks on a surface, which represent symbols in each language. The purpose of handwriting is to communicate with others through the common understanding of symbols in languages, known as characters and letters. Until the dawn of a paper-free society, the primitive communication method, handwriting, will persist, and will play important and convenient role as a means of recording information. So long as the primitive communication method is used, the corresponding handwriting recognition technology will thrive to simulate machine reading of human manuscripts.

Depending on the input methods of handwritten data into recognition systems, handwriting recognition techniques diverge into two flavors, on-line or dynamic and off-line or static respectively. In the dynamic or on-line type method, a special pen is commonly used on an electronic liquid crystal display surface with a sensor to digitize the pen's motion trails. The motion trails, writings, are stored in order of two dimensional coordinates in timely manner. However, in off-line or static systems, a paper with handwritten data is scanned and digitized through an optical scanner, and only two-dimensional information is stored. The information of stroke order and time is not available in off-line system (Plamondon & Srihari, 2000; Vinciarelli, 2002). However, there are common challenges to be addressed in both methods. They are the variations of human handwriting, such as position, size, slant or slope, different models and connectivity.

The remainder of this chapter describes the ideal applications of handwriting recognition systems, the problems of handwriting recognition, the state of the art handwriting recognition systems and solutions using machine learning techniques.

Handwriting Recognition Applications

Handwriting recognition is a series of processes to interpret clusters of graphical marks on a surface into meaningful symbolic representations of a related language. For an instance of English language, the symbolic representations would be alphabet characters and letters. The importance and need of handwriting recognition has been arising in many real world applications such as postal address recognition, bank cheques processing, hand-filled forms processing, conversion of field notes and historical manuscripts. One of the major applications of the handwriting recognition is automation in processing bank checks for handwritten legal amount (Xu, Lam, & C Suen, 2003). Handwriting recognition systems also contribute very much into automation for processing of postal codes (Alginahi, 2009) and postal addresses (Akiyama, 2004). A highly effective application of handwriting recognition is to process handwritten form data (Cheriet, 1995). A vast amount of handwritten historical manuscripts can be easily converted into electronic representation for sharing and searching (Wuthrich, 2009).

Problems with Handwriting Recognition

In this section, the steps involved in handwriting recognition are described to categorize the problem domains. The major steps for handwriting recognition incorporate pre-processing, segmentation and recognition. First, the problems of the handwriting recognition are described through the sample examples of handwritten images.

How it Works: Offline Handwriting Recognition

The stereotype of involving steps in off-line handwriting recognition systems consists of pre-processing, segmentation and recognition. However, some of the stages are merged or omitted, depending on the methods of recognition. In general, the pre-processing and normalization algorithms are independent of the recognition approach of the system, but segmentation is tightly coupled with recognition algorithms (Lorigo & Govindaraju, 2006). The general off-line handwriting recognition system is shown in Figure 1.

Pre-Processing

A series of document analysis tasks are required prior to recognizing letters from scanned documents. Some common processes are thresholding, noise removal, slant and slope correction as normalization, and thinning. The main objective of the pre-processing is to produce an image containing the word to be recognized without any other disturbing elements.

Noise Reduction

It is common that there are introduction of the noises such as salt and pepper while digitization of a handwritten image through scanning processes. In addition, certain handwritten images like bank checks includes organization textured backgrounds, grids or underlines. Especially in handwritten text recognition, it's not quite unusual that the neighboring text lines are interfering with each other. These kinds of factors, as known as noises, raise serious complications for successive processes like segmentation and recognition. In (Agrawal & Doermann, 2009), the approach in-

Figure 1. General steps in handwriting recognition systems

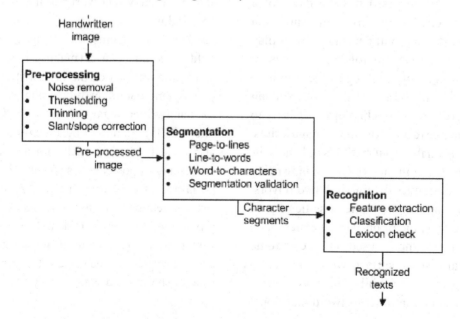

troduced a clutter detection and removal algorithm for complex document images. The distance transform based approach is independent of clutter's position, size, shape and connectivity with text. In (Eglin, Bres & Rivero, 2007), a biologically inspired, global and segmentation free methodology was proposed for manuscript noise reduction and classification.

Binarization

The core objective of thresholding is to extract the foreground pixels from the background. Digitized text images from scanning processes are normally stored in a grey-scaled format, which starts from 0 (representing white pixels) to 255 (black pixels). Depending on the researching methodologies, it is required or preferred to convert a grey-scaled image into a binary image of 1 and 0. However, it is arguable that the recognition process should be done based on the features directly extracted from grey-level format, which preserves the originality of the image. On the other hand, many researchers prefer a binary image because of ease in image processing. There are two main streams of thresholding algorithms. In (Dawoud & Kamel, 2004), global adaptive approach was proposed to obtain a single threshold for the entire image. Meanwhile, locally adaptive techniques measure the threshold of each pixel in an image referencing to the information from the neighborhood (Trier & Taxt, 1995).

Normalization

It is well known that all the natural handwritten materials from different writers lack uniformities such as character sizes, writing angles of characters and lines. Therefore, the core idea of normalization is to reduce the variances from the different writing styles. Slant and slop correction or character resize could be one of the sub-tasks of the normalization. An ideal model of handwriting is a word written horizontally with ascenders and descenders aligned along the vertical direction. Slope is the angle between the horizontal direction and the direction of the implicit line on which the word is aligned, and slant is the angle between the vertical direction and the direction of the strokes supposed to be vertical (Vinciarelli, 2002). The normalized images are invariant with respect to the sources of slant and slope. On the contrast, the normalized standard form might destroy the writing style information, which might be helpful to recognition process. Size normalization could be added to this stage, to adjust the character size to a certain standard (Arica & Yarman-Vural, 2001).

Thinning

As known as skeletonization, thinning process is to normalize the variances of stroke width from the different writing mediums and it could be referred as a meaningful process for retaining information about a character pattern such as geometric and topological properties. At the same time, the positive outcomes from this process are that it reduces the noises mentioned above, and compresses the images. Whereas, it imposes a number of unexpected serious problems, such as relatively large processing time, distortion in resulting skeletons, and appearance of false skeleton components and disappearance of others. As the result of the significant research, there have been appearing successful algorithms. In (Lam, Lee & Suen, 1992), sequential approach is proposed by examining the contour points of an image in a predetermined order. In (Zhang & Suen, 1984), parallel thinning algorithms mark and delete a pixel based on the information from the previous iteration. Finally, non-iterative thinning algorithms are proposed to decide a centre line by run-length encoding or line following (Baruch, 1988). The examples of original input images (A) and preprocessed images (B) are shown in Figure 2.

Figure 2. Examples of handwritten input images before (A) and after (B) pre-processing

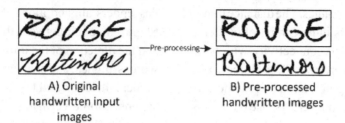

A) Original
handwritten input
images

B) Pre-processed
handwritten images

Segmentation

In handwriting recognition systems, the entry point of recognition is acquiring the handwritten images by scanners. Generally, the unit of acquisition of the handwritten image is a page. The acquired page needs to be chunked down into smaller units, which are lines. The process of chunking a page into lines is called line segmentation. Furthermore, each line is dissected into words, which is called word segmentation. Finally, each word is cut down into individual characters. The final process

is called character segmentation. The examples of line segmentation, word segmentation and character segmentation are shown in Figure 3. However, one of the most difficult segmentation is character segmentation. As shown in Figure 4, characters in a word are touching or connected very often. Therefore, it is very hard to find a precise letter boundary within connected components. In handwriting recognition context, segmentation normally refers to characters segmentation. From now on, segmentation refers to character segmentation if not explicitly annotated.

Figure 3. Examples of line segmentation (A → B), word segmentation (B → C) and character segmentation (C → D)

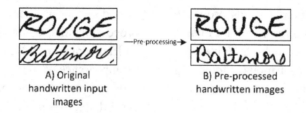

A) Original
handwritten input
images

B) Pre-processed
handwritten images

Figure 4. Example words projecting problems in handwriting recognition systems: A) underlined, B) noisy, C) stamped and D) connected to a word from the line below. Moreover, characters in the words are connected.

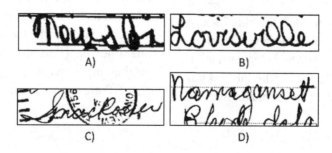

A)

B)

C)

D)

Segmentation is an operation that seeks to decompose an image of a sequence of characters into sub-images of individual symbols (Wshah, 2009). It is clearly stated that segmentation is one of the most important stages because the separation of words, lines, or characters directly affects the recognition rate of the script (Natarajan, 2009). As the result of this stage, paragraphs, sentences, words, or letters are isolated through the document analysis. As shown in Figure 5, characters in words can be separated easily by white spaces vertically like A). In handwriting recognition, words are written more like B) rather than A). Characters in B) are connected, and the segmentation points are very hard to locate. Moreover, the last segmentation point from B) indicates the further problem, which the segmentation points are not necessarily linear. That's why the perfect character segmentation in handwriting recognition is virtually impossible. That's the ill effect to the overall handwriting recognition performance.

A survey on character segmentation techniques from the existing literature, presents four categories of segmentation paradigms. They are dissection techniques, recognition-based segmentation, over-segmentation, and holistic approaches. The distinction of the holistic strategy from the others is that it avoids segmentation process. Rather, it attempts to recognize the whole image as classification token. It is expressively defined the implicit segmentation as an easier method to achieve (Vinciarelli, 2002). By introducing over-segmentation methods, the number of spurious cuts, needs not to be limited. Finally, the hybrid way of mixed strategies between implicit and explicit have been proposed to yield better results.

Holistic Approach

Segmentation module in handwriting recognition plays a crucial role for successful performance. However, it is very difficult to find precise character boundaries without knowledge about characters. So, to avoid the error prone process, segmentation-free approach has been proposed as one of the segmentation strategies. The approach from (Benouareth, Ennaji & Sellami, 2008) used holistic method for Arabic word recognition. To build a feature vector sequence, two segmentation schemes are incorporated to divide a word into frames. The first one is uniform segmentation, which vertically divides a word into equal sized frames. The second one is non-uniform segmentation. This time the size of frames varies. After word segmentation into frames, statistical and structural features are extracted by capturing ascenders, descenders, dots, concavity, and stroke direction. Another approach from (Vinciarelli, 2005) used similar technique for information retrieval of writer dependent documents. Prior to

Figure 5. Examples of characters segmentation: A) The segmentation of the word 'AFB' is relatively easy because each character is separated. B) The segmentation of the word 'Orange' is very hard because characters are connected; therefore white space does not separate characters. Also, the segmentation points are more likely non-linear.

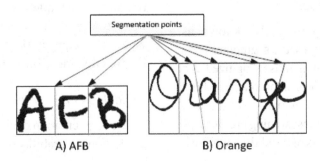

the information retrieval, word recognition of the handwritten document proceeds first. Using fixed size of sliding window, density feature is extracted for HMM to perform recognition by calculating the likelihood of a word against lexicon.

However, the main pitfalls of segmentation-free approaches heavily depend on the size of lexicon, and they are only suitable for recognition domains with limited or small size lexicons. Because lexicon size greatly affects the recognition performance, reduction of unlikely lexicon words would increase the chances to find correct matching lexicon words during the recognition process. A lexicon reduction scheme is proposed in (Mozaffari, Faez, Margner & El-Abed, 2008) for static Farsi handwriting recognition by analyzing dots within characters.

Segmentation by Dissection

Referred as dissection techniques in the literature, the explicit segmentation is the process of cutting up the image into meaningful components without using specific class of shape information. Available methods take advantages of general features such as white space and pitch, vertical projection analysis, connected component analysis, landmarks, and evaluation of linguistic context. In the literature (Vinciarelli, 2002), it is described that the explicit segmentation is a difficult and error prone process and a letter cannot be segmented before having been recognized and cannot be recognized before having been segmented. Until now, no methods were developed which are able to segment handwritten words exactly into letters.

Segmentation by Recognition

Segmentation by recognition also known as recognition-based strategies, the segmentation is based on whether a component is recognized as a legal character or not. The essential concept behind is to use a sliding window, which scans through images from left to right for searching pre-defined components. As the results of the sliding window,

the decision of the segmentation points considers the recognition confidence as well as semantic and syntactic fitness of the overall result. In (Zimmermann, Chappelier & Bunke, 2006), combined dynamic programming and neural networks were employed as classifiers with the sliding window methods. In (Nopsuwanchai, Biem & Clocksin, 2006), the researcher proposes the Hidden Markov Model (HMM) as the classifiers.

Hybrid Techniques

The hybrid strategies tend to be a combination of the first two traditional segmentation methods. Dissection is employed to over-segment the word or connected component into a sufficient number of components, as to encompass all segmentation boundaries present. In the next step, classification is used to determine the optimum segmentations from a set of possible segmentation hypotheses. The hybrid techniques yield better results compared to the traditional methods. However, error detection and correction mechanisms should be embedded into the systems to improve accuracy, as well as the wise use of context and classifier confidence, which implies the adoption of the Artificial Neural Networks (ANNs) (Blumenstein & Verma, 2001). ANN has abilities to generalize, adapt, and learn implicit concepts, which are particularly well suited to address the problems caused by high variability between handwriting samples. Especially, the trained ANN is capable of identifying similarities and patterns among different handwriting samples (R. Ghosh & M. Ghosh, 2005; Marinai, Gori & Soda, 2005). Moreover, ANN has been a predominant method among researchers to implement the error detection, and correction module in segmentation stage along with over-segmentation strategies (Bortolozzi, Britto, Oliveira & Morita, 2005).

Difficulties in Segmentation

As the segmentation constraints, the main factors are the non-separability of characters, the diversity of character patterns, ambiguity and illegibility of characters, and the overlapping nature of many characters in a word (Elnagar & Alhajj, 2003). Because of such factors, the most existing segmentation algorithms confront major problems, such as inaccurate character cuttings, missing segmentation points, and over-segmentation of a same character. Research surveys prove that the segmentation is one of the most difficult and error prone process. It directly contributes to the poor cursive handwriting recognition performance, and the research in the area is largely open to improve the existing recognition systems. The limited capabilities in segmentation process encourage the adaptation of error detection, and correction mechanisms embedment into systems. Alternatively, holistic approach is presented to avoid the segmentation process, but it is only effective with a small lexicon (Espana-Boquera, 2010).

Recognition

During the recognition process, generally the shape features are extracted from the segmented images, and the appropriate class is assigned to the observed character. As fast methods for implementing classifiers, Artificial Neural Networks have been presented in the literature. Besides, algorithms based on nearest-neighbor methods are indicated to produce the higher accuracy, but to be slower (Liu, Nakashima, Sako & Fujisawa, 2003). Finally, word recognition algorithms typically attempt to produce a ranking by associating the word image to choices in a lexicon. As the examples of algorithms, analytic and holistic approaches are presented. However, combining the results of both methods are suggested to achieve a higher level of performance. Hidden Markov Models (HMMs) are a good learning algorithm to cope with the characteristics that are difficult to describe intuitively. Approaches from (Benouareth, Ennaji & Sellami, 2008; Espana-Boquera, 2010; Günter & Bunke, 2004; Saleem, Cao, Subramanian, Kamali, Prasad & Natarajan,

2009) show the competitiveness of the HMM as the recognizer. As a new generation learning system based on recent advances in statistical learning theory, Support Vector Machines (SVM) deliver the state-of-the art performance in real-world applications such as text categorization, hand-written character recognition, image classification and bio-sequence analysis. The SVM recognizers are well established and described in (S. Basu, Das, Sarkar, Kundu, Nasipuri and D. Basu, 2010; Camastra, 2007; Justino, Bortolozzi & Sabourin, 2005; Khemchandani & Chandra, 2007). In artificial neural networks, each simple rule is presented as a neuron to handle simple tasks. Depending on the problems or rules, networks of the neurons are interconnected to process the inputs through the final layer. During the processing, each element adds contribution to be considered in the decision stage. The contribution criterion is trained by the training data during the training process. The effectiveness of the neural networks as the recognizers is proven through the countless literature (Al-Omari & Al-Jarrah, 2004; Desai, 2010; Marinai, Gori & Soda, 2005; Montazer, Saremi & Khatibi, 2010; Shrivastava & Singh, 2010).

State of the Art Handwriting Recognition Systems

The performance of handwriting recognition applications has been reported by measuring the recognition rate either in individual character or whole word recognition. In the former, correct individual character matching against a given fixed alphabet are counted as a successful recognition. On the other hand, the latter focuses on searching for the most likely word from a set of recognized individual characters against a fixed given lexicon. Statistically, recognition rates for on-line method are much higher than the one for off-line (Lorigo & Govindaraju, 2006; Plötz & Fink, 2009; Vinciarelli, 2002). On-line handwriting recognizers are normally shipped with Personal Digital Assistance

(PDA), or Tablet PCs, and their performances are fairly acceptable for processing handwritten letters and symbols. In contrast, off-line systems are reluctantly bundled with scanner and printers. However, the performances are less than the industrial standard for ordinary uses. So, it is put in use in only constrained domains such as postal addresses and courtesy amounts on bank checks.

As shown in Table 1, various approaches are proposed to improve the word recognition accuracy. Overlapping sliding windows with features of percentiles of pixel intensity, values, angle, correlation and energy were proposed in Arabic word recognition with HMM and n-gram based classifiers (Saleem, Cao, Subramanian, Kamali, Prasad & Natarajan, 2009). Sliding window technique is used in word recognition with an ensemble classifier on IAM database (Günter & Bunke, 2005). Over-segmentation and direction feature extraction approach was adapted to recognize Arabic words with a neural classifier on local database (Hamad & Zitar, 2010). Mean gray value and center of gravity of the pixels are suggested for English word recognition with recurrent neural classifier on IAM database (Graves, Liwicki, Fernandez, Bertolami, Bunke &Schmidhuber, 2009). Over-segmentation and contour transition histogram of each segment in the horizontal and vertical directions were proposed

to recognize the English words with HMM and neural classifiers on SRTP database (Koerich, Sabourin & Suen, 2005).

In Table 2, various strategies are proposed to improve the character classification accuracy. Directional distance distribution feature extraction approach was suggested to improve the handwritten numeral character classification. The classifier was calibrated into modular neural networks and the experiment was conducted on NIST benchmark database (Oh & Suen, 2002). The feature of division points of sub images are proposed for English character classification with RBF-SVM on CEDAR pre-segmented characters (Vamvakas, Gatos & Perantonis, 2010). Several feature extraction techniques, using different approaches, are extracted and evaluated by an ensemble classifier of neural networks. The experiment was conducted on C-Cube benchmark database (Cruz, Cavalcanti & Ren, 2009).

As shown in Table 3, various digit recognition approaches were suggested. In (S. Basu, Das, Sarkar, Kundu, Nasipuri and D. Basu, 2010), the handwritten images are rastered in four directions; row-wise, column-wise and major diagonals. The longest run lengths are used to digit recognition with RBF-SVM classifier on MNIST database. The feature extraction of foreground pixel counts in four directions in 3x3 pixel frame was experi-

Table 1. Word recognition accuracy in the state-of-the-art handwriting recognition systems in the literature: Each technique is enlisted with the feature extraction method, segmentation incorporation, recognizer, experiment database, language and accuracy.

Techniques	Feature	Segmentation	Language	Recognizer	Database	Accuracy
(Saleem, Cao, Subramanian, Kamali, Prasad & Natarajan, 2009)	Overlapping slide window	N/A	Arabic	HMM + n-gram	Local	70%
(Günter & Bunke, 2005)	Sliding window	Holistic	English	Ensemble	IAM	75.6%
(Hamad & Zitar, 2010)	Direction feature	Hybrid	Arabic	Neural networks	Local	82.98%
(Graves, Liwicki, Fernandez, Bertolami, Bunke &Schmidhuber, 2009)	Geographical features	N/A	English	Recurrent neural networks	IAM	74.1%
(Koerich, Sabourin & Suen, 2005)	Contour transition histogram	Hybrid	English	HMM + neural networks	SRTP	72.39%

Table 2. Character classification accuracy in the state-of-the-art handwriting recognition systems in the literature: Each technique is enlisted with the feature extraction method, recognizer, experiment database, language and accuracy.

Techniques	Feature	Language	Recognizer	Database	Accuracy
(Oh & Suen, 2002)	Directional distance distribution	English	Modular neural networks	NIST	91.99%
(Vamvakas, Gatos & Perantonis, 2010)	Division points of sub images	English	RBF SVM	CEDAR	85.11%
(Cruz, Cavalcanti & Ren, 2009)	Structural characteristics, Modified edge map, image projections, multi zoning, concavities, gradient directional, medial gradient, Camastra 34D	English	Ensemble of neural networks	C-Cube	89.34%

Table 3. Digit recognition accuracy in the state-of-the-art handwriting recognition systems in the literature: Each technique is enlisted with the feature extraction method, recognizer, experiment database, language, and accuracy.

Techniques	Feature	Language	Recognizer	Database	Accuracy
(S. Basu, Das, Sarkar, Kundu, Nasipuri and D. Basu, 2010)	Longest run feature	Latin, Bangla, Devanagari, Urdu	RBF SVM	MNIST	96.10%
(Desai, 2010)	Foreground pixels counts in four directions of 3 x 3 pixel frame	Gujarati	MLP	Local	81.66%
(Montazer, Saremi & Khatibi, 2010)	Feature points: terminal, branch, cross points	Farsi digit	Neuro-Fussy	Local	98%
(Ko, Cavalin, Sabourin & Britto, 2009)	Circular mean direction and variances	English digit	HMM	NIST	98.88%

mented for Gujarati character classification with MLP classifier. Region growing based segmentation approach was suggested for extracting English character with a MLP classifier (Desai, 2010). Terminal, branch and cross feature points are adapted to improve the character classification with neuro-fuzzy classifier for Farsi numerals (Montazer, Saremi & Khatibi, 2010). A circular mean direction and variance feature extraction approach was introduced to improve character classification with HMM classifier on NIST database (Ko, Cavalin, Sabourin & Britto, 2009).

Many researchers have been tackling the offline handwriting segmentation problems in various approaches as shown in Table 4. Segmentation approach on pixel density threshold was articulated to extract characters for Gurumukhi language (Kumar & Singh, 2010). Region growing based segmentation algorithm is suggested for Arabic language on local database (Saeed & Albakoor, 2009). A junction point based oversegmentation algorithm and stroke component based primitive merging algorithm were suggested to segment English uppercases with fuzzified decision rule algorithm (Jayarathna & Bandara, 2006). Over-segmentation algorithm based on vertical histogram minima of main body and segment checking validation method are incorporated to segment English and Greek words (Kavallieratou, Stamatatos, Fakotakis & Kokkinakis, 2000).

Table 4. Character segmentation accuracy in the state-of-the-art handwriting recognition systems in the literature: Each technique is enlisted with the feature extraction method, segmentation, recognizer, experiment database, language, and word recognition.

Techniques	Feature	Segmentation	Language	Recognizer	Database	Accuracy
(Kumar & Singh, 2010)	N/A	Dissection	Gurumukhi	N/A	Local	91.01%
(Saeed & Albakoor, 2009)	N/A	Dissection	Arabic	MLP	Local	80%
(Jayarathna & Bandara, 2006)	Fuzzy features	Hybrid	English up-percases	Decision rules	Local	100%
(Kavallieratou, Stamatatos, Fakotakis & Kokkinakis, 2000)	Segmentation position	Hybrid	Greek	Decision rules	Local	82.4%

Solutions Using Machine Learning Techniques

Machine learning algorithms can be used at two stages of handwriting recognition problem – segmentation validation and character recognition. A classifier can produce a binary output to indicate the validity of a segmentation point. Similarly a classifier can predict a character from the segments produced in the previous stage. The literature (Verma, Gader & Chen, 2001; Zhang, Bui & Suen, 2007) indicates the use of individual as well as ensemble of classifiers for this purpose. Commonly used individual classifiers are Artificial Neural Networks (ANN), Support Vector Machine (SVM), k Nearest Neighbor (k–NN), and Decision Tree (DT). With ensemble of classifiers multiple base classifiers provide decisions that are combined to produce the final classification verdict. The use of ensemble classifier for handwriting recognition deserves attention in two areas: (i) ensemble classifier architecture and (ii) decision fusion methods.

Multiple feature sets can be used for the purpose of classification. Let there be N feature sets $Fset_1,..., Fset_N$. The ensemble classifier can be produced in three different ways (Figure 6). The first possibility is presented in Figure 6(a) where each base classifier trained on a separate feature set. The decisions produced by the base classifiers are fused to obtain the final decision. The second

alternative is presented in Figure 6(b) where an ensemble of classifiers is trained on each feature set and the decisions produced by the ensemble classifiers are combined for class prediction. The last possibility (Figure 6(c)) is to construct a feature set by combining all feature sets i.e. $[Fset_1 ... Fset_N]$ and train an ensemble classifier on the combined feature set. Note that the base classifiers can be of the same or different types although the former is common in the literature (Cruz, Cavalcanti & Ren, 2009).

The output of the base classifiers can be discrete decisions or continuous valued confidence measures. The commonly used fusion methods (Polikar, 2006) for combining discrete decisions are majority voting, weighted majority voting, behavior knowledge space, and Borda count. The commonly used fusion methods for combining continuous outputs are algebraic combiners (Kittler, Hatef, Duin & Matas, 1998) including mean rule, weighted average, trimmed mean, min/max/median rule, product rule, and generalized mean. The continuous valued confidence measures are also combined using a fusion classifier (Cruz, Cavalcanti & Ren, 2009).

One of the good examples of ensemble classifier systems in handwriting recognition is found in (Verma, Gader & Chen, 2001). In the approach, ranks and confidence values are fused to produce final results from three neural experts. The word recognition results were 91%, which was the high-

Figure 6. Different ensemble classifier architectures used in handwriting recognition

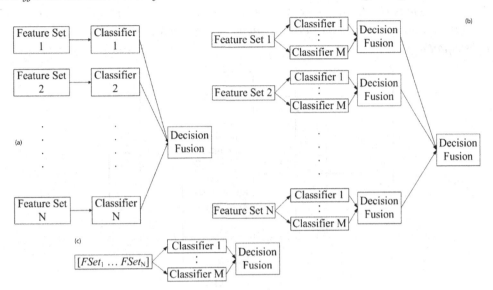

est among the published results for handwritten words. In (Zhang, Bui & Suen, 2007), a cascade ensemble classifier system for the recognition of handwritten digits was proposed. The system aimed at attaining a very high recognition rate and a very high reliability at the same time, in other words, achieving an excellent recognition performance of handwritten digits. The trade-offs among recognition, error, and rejection rates of the new recognition system were analyzed. Experiments conducted on the MNIST handwritten numeral database were shown with encouraging results: a high reliability of 99.96% with minimal rejection, or a 99.59% correct recognition rate without rejection in the last cascade layer.

Neural Dictionary Matching Strategy

The final stage of the handwriting recognition system is to find the best matching word from the provided lexicon words. In the stage, neural networks can be trained on lexical words and find the best matching lexical word for a given string of recognized characters. To compose a feature vector from an input character string, ASCII values for English alphabets are used. To extract a feature

vector from a character string, an ASCII value of each character was divided by the highest value from 52 class characters. However, one of the challenging problems was to set the number of input feature space since the numbers of characters in words are different. Also, the number of characters in input character strings was observed to be larger than the corresponding lexical words since some segments are partial characters. To overcome this challenge, the size of the feature space was set to the doubled number of characters from the longest lexicon word. When the number of the characters in a character string is less than the number of the feature space, the unused feature space was padded with zeros. The architectural overview of neural dictionary is shown in Figure 7.

Some Recent Ideas for Improvement

During the discussion of the general handwriting recognition system, the segmentation step was singled out as one of the most difficult part in the systems. In the recognition step, the successful rates are very dependant to the outcomes of the segmentation process. Therefore, various attempts have been made to increase the segmentation ac-

Figure 7. Architectural overview of neural dictionary, A) n characters in the input string, B) r feature space; When r > n, remainder feature spaces (from n+1 to r) are padded with zeros, C) neural dictionary takes r input feature elements and outputs s numbers of confidence values, D) the number of the lexical words equal to j

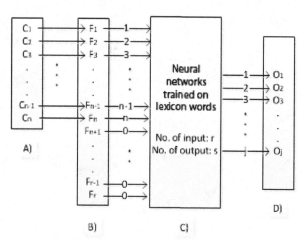

curacy with expectation of the better recognition rate. In (Lee & Verma, 2009), binary segmentation with neural validation algorithm is proposed to produce better segmentation hypotheses for word recognition. Over-segmentation and validation is a well anticipated segmentation strategy in cursive off-line handwriting recognition. Over-segmentation is a means of locating all possible character boundaries, and the excessive segmentation points called over-segmentation points. Validation is a process to check and validate the segmentation points whether or not they are correct character boundaries by commonly employing an intelligent classifier trained with knowledge of characters. The existing algorithms use ordered validation which means that the incorrect segmentation

points might account for the validity of the next segmentation point. The ordered validation creates problems such as chain-failure. The binary segmentation with neural validation targeted to reduce the chain-failure. The approach contains modules of over-segmentation and validation but the main distinctive feature of the approach was an un-ordered segmentation strategy. The proposed algorithm was evaluated on CEDAR benchmark database. The results of the experiments were 4.33% of segmentation errors in average, and 84.54% of word recognition rate. In Figure 8, the sample segmentation results are shown from the binary segmentation with neural validation algorithm (Lee & Verma, 2009).

Figure 8. Example words of segmentation results from (Lee & Verma, 2009)

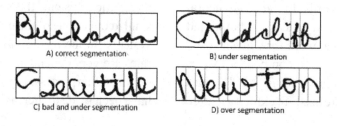

CONCLUSION

This chapter has discussed the major processes involved in handwriting recognition and use of machine learning techniques to improve the overall word recognition accuracy. The state of the art techniques and useful applications of handwriting recognition have been reviewed and presented. Despite the rising interests in the applications, the maturity of the handwriting recognition systems is below the standards of real world applications. During the discussion of the general handwriting recognition systems, the segmentation process was singled out as one of the main problems. To increase the segmentation and recognition performances, various machine learning techniques were presented and discussed. Especially, multiple experts systems and ensemble systems have been discussed which are very promising architectural models to achieve better performance in handwriting recognition. The binary segmentation with neural validation processes were discussed for improvement of the segmentation accuracy with expectation of better word recognition rate.

REFERENCES

Agrawal, M., & Doermann, D. (2009). Clutter noise removal in binary document images. *International Conference on Document Analysis and Recognition,* (pp. 556-560).

Akiyama, T. (2004). Handwritten address interpretation system allowing for non-use of postal codes and omission of address elements. *International Workshop on Frontiers in Handwriting Recognition,* (pp. 527-532).

Al-Omari, F., & Al-Jarrah, O. (2004). Handwritten Indian numerals recognition system using probabilistic neural networks. *Advanced Engineering Informatics, 18*(1), 9–16. doi:10.1016/j. aei.2004.02.001

Alginahi, Y. (2009). A proposed hybrid OCR system for Arabic and Indian numerical postal codes. *International Conference on Computer Technology and Development,* (Vol. 2, pp. 400-404).

Arica, N., & Yarman-Vural, F. (2001). An overview of character recognition focused on off-line handwriting. *IEEE Transactions on Systems, Man and Cybernetics. Part C, Applications and Reviews, 31*(2), 216–233. doi:10.1109/5326.941845

Baruch, O. (1988). Line thinning by line following. *Pattern Recognition Letters, 8*(4), 271–276. doi:10.1016/0167-8655(88)90034-7

Basu, S., Das, N., Sarkar, R., Kundu, M., Nasipuri, M., & Basu, D. (2010). A novel framework for automatic sorting of postal documents with multi-script address blocks. *Pattern Recognition, 43*(10), 3507–3521. doi:10.1016/j.patcog.2010.05.018

Benouareth, A., Ennaji, A., & Sellami, M. (2008). Semi-continuous HMMs with explicit state duration for unconstrained Arabic word modeling and recognition. *Pattern Recognition Letters, 29*(12), 1742–1752. doi:10.1016/j.patrec.2008.05.008

Blumenstein, M., & Verma, B. (2001). Analysis of segmentation performance on the CEDAR benchmark database. *Sixth International Conference on Document Analysis and Recognition* (pp. 1142-1146).

Bortolozzi, F., Britto, A., Oliveira, L. S., & Morita, M. (2005). Recent advances in handwriting recognition. *Proceedings of the International Workshop on Document Analysis* (pp. 1-30).

Camastra, F. (2007). A SVM-based cursive character recognizer. *Pattern Recognition, 40*(12), 3721–3727. doi:10.1016/j.patcog.2007.03.014

Cheriet, M. (1995). A formal model for document processing of business forms. *International Conference on Document Analysis and Recognition,* (Vol. 1, p. 210).

Cruz, R., Cavalcanti, G., & Ren, T. (2009). An ensemble classifier for offline cursive character recognition using multiple feature extraction techniques. *IEEE International Joint Conference on Neural Networks* (pp. 744-751).

Dawoud, A., & Kamel, M. S. (2004). Iterative multimodel subimage binarization for handwritten character segmentation. *IEEE Transactions on Image Processing, 13*(9), 1223–1230. doi:10.1109/TIP.2004.833101

Desai, A. (2010). Gujarati handwritten numeral optical character reorganization through neural network. *Pattern Recognition, 43*(7), 2582–2589. doi:10.1016/j.patcog.2010.01.008

Eglin, V., Bres, S., & Rivero, C. (2007). Hermite and Gabor transforms for noise reduction and handwriting classification in ancient manuscripts. *International Journal on Document Analysis and Recognition, 9*(2-4), 101–122. doi:10.1007/s10032-007-0039-z

Elnagar, A., & Alhajj, R. (2003). Segmentation of connected handwritten numeral strings. *Pattern Recognition, 36*(3), 625–634. doi:10.1016/S0031-3203(02)00097-3

Espana-Boquera, S. (2010). Improving offline handwritten text recognition with hybrid HMM/ANN models. *IEEE Transactions on Pattern Analysis and Machine Intelligence, 99.*

Ghosh, R., & Ghosh, M. (2005). An intelligent offline handwriting recognition system using evolutionary neural learning algorithm and rule. *Journal of Research and Practice in Information Technology, 37*(1), 73–87.

Graves, A., Liwicki, M., Fernandez, S., Bertolami, R., Bunke, H., & Schmidhuber, J. (2009). A novel connectionist system for unconstrained handwriting recognition. *IEEE Transactions on Pattern Analysis and Machine Intelligence, 31*(5), 855-868. Retrieved from 10.1109/TPAMI.2008.137

Günter, S., & Bunke, H. (2004). HMM-based handwritten word recognition: On the optimization of the number of states, training iterations and Gaussian components. *Pattern Recognition, 37*(10), 2069–2079. doi:10.1016/j.patcog.2004.04.006

Günter, S., & Bunke, H. (2005). Off-line cursive handwriting recognition using multiple classifier systems--On the influence of vocabulary, ensemble, and training set size. *Optics and Lasers in Engineering, 43*(3-5), 437–454. doi:10.1016/j.optlaseng.2004.01.004

Hamad, H., & Zitar, R. (2010). Development of an efficient neural-based segmentation technique for Arabic handwriting recognition. *Pattern Recognition, 43*(8), 2773–2798. doi:10.1016/j.patcog.2010.03.005

Jayarathna, U., & Bandara, G. (2006). New segmentation algorithm for offline handwritten connected character segmentation. *First International Conference on Industrial and Information Systems,* (pp. 540-546).

Justino, E., Bortolozzi, F., & Sabourin, R. (2005). A comparison of SVM and HMM classifiers in the off-line signature verification. *Pattern Recognition Letters, 26*(9), 1377–1385. doi:10.1016/j.patrec.2004.11.015

Kavallieratou, E., Stamatatos, E., Fakotakis, N., & Kokkinakis, G. (2000). Handwritten character segmentation using transformation-based learning. *15th International Conference on Pattern Recognition,* (Vol. 2, pp. 634-637).

Khemchandani, R., & Chandra, S. (2007). Twin support vector machines for pattern classification. *IEEE Transactions on Pattern Analysis and Machine Intelligence, 29*(5), 905–910. doi:10.1109/TPAMI.2007.1068

Kittler, J., Hatef, M., Duin, R. P. W., & Matas, J. (1998). On combining classifiers. *IEEE Transactions on Pattern Analysis and Machine Intelligence, 20*(3), 226–239. doi:10.1109/34.667881

Ko, A., Cavalin, P., Sabourin, R., & Britto, A. (2009). Leave-one-out-training and leave-one-out-testing hidden Markov models for a handwritten numeral recognizer: The implications of a single classifier and multiple classifications. *IEEE Transactions on Pattern Analysis and Machine Intelligence, 31*(12), 2168–2178. doi:10.1109/TPAMI.2008.254

Koerich, A. L., Sabourin, R., & Suen, C. Y. (2005). Recognition and verification of unconstrained handwritten words. *IEEE Transactions on Pattern Analysis and Machine Intelligence, 27*(10), 1509–1522. doi:10.1109/TPAMI.2005.207

Kumar, R., & Singh, A. (2010). Detection and segmentation of lines and words in Gurmukhi handwritten text. *Advance Computing, IEEE International Conference on (pp. 353-356).*

Lam, L., Lee, S., & Suen, C. Y. (1992). Thinning methodologies-a comprehensive survey. *IEEE Transactions on Pattern Analysis and Machine Intelligence, 14*(9), 869–885. doi:10.1109/34.161346

Lee, H., & Verma, B. (2009). Binary segmentation with neural validation for cursive handwriting recognition. *IEEE International Joint Conference on Neural Networks, IJCNN 2009* (pp. 1730-1735).

Liu, C., Nakashima, K., Sako, H., & Fujisawa, H. (2003). Handwritten digit recognition: Benchmarking of state-of-the-art techniques. *Pattern Recognition, 36*(10), 2271–2285. doi:10.1016/S0031-3203(03)00085-2

Lorigo, L. M., & Govindaraju, V. (2006). Offline Arabic handwriting recognition: A survey. *IEEE Transactions on Pattern Analysis and Machine Intelligence, 28*(5), 712–724. doi:10.1109/TPAMI.2006.102

Marinai, S., Gori, M., & Soda, G. (2005). Artificial neural networks for document analysis and recognition. *IEEE Transactions on Pattern Analysis and Machine Intelligence, 27*(1), 23–35. doi:10.1109/TPAMI.2005.4

Montazer, G. A., Saremi, H. Q., & Khatibi, V. (2010). A neuro-fuzzy inference engine for Farsi numeral characters recognition. *Expert Systems with Applications, 37*(9), 6327–6337. doi:10.1016/j.eswa.2010.02.088

Mozaffari, S., Faez, K., Margner, V., & El-Abed, H. (2008). Lexicon reduction using dots for offline Farsi/Arabic handwritten word recognition. *Pattern Recognition Letters, 29*(6), 724–734. doi:10.1016/j.patrec.2007.11.009

Natarajan, P. (2009). Stochastic segment modeling for offline handwriting recognition. *International Conference on Document Analysis and Recognition,* (pp. 971-975).

Nopsuwanchai, R., Biem, A., & Clocksin, W. F. (2006). Maximization of mutual information for offline Thai handwriting recognition. *IEEE Transactions on Pattern Analysis and Machine Intelligence, 28*(8), 1347–1351. doi:10.1109/TPAMI.2006.167

Oh, I., & Suen, C. (2002). A class-modular feedforward neural network for handwriting recognition. *Pattern Recognition, 35*(1), 229–244. doi:10.1016/S0031-3203(00)00181-3

Plamondon, R., & Srihari, S. N. (2000). Online and off-line handwriting recognition: A comprehensive survey. *IEEE Transactions on Pattern Analysis and Machine Intelligence, 22*(1), 63–84. doi:10.1109/34.824821

Plötz, T., & Fink, G. A. (2009). Markov models for offline handwriting recognition: A survey. *International Journal Document Analysis and Recognition, 12*(4), 269–298. doi:10.1007/s10032-009-0098-4

Polikar, R. (2006). Ensemble based systems in decision making. *IEEE Circuits and Systems Magazine, 6*(3), 21–45. doi:10.1109/MCAS.2006.1688199

Saeed, K., & Albakoor, M. (2009). Region growing based segmentation algorithm for typewritten and handwritten text recognition. *Applied Soft Computing, 9*(2), 608–617. doi:10.1016/j.asoc.2008.08.006

Saleem, S., Cao, H., Subramanian, K., Kamali, M., Prasad, R., & Natarajan, P. (2009). Improvements in BBN's HMM-based offline Arabic handwriting recognition system. *International Conference on Document Analysis and Recognition,* (pp. 773-777).

Shrivastava, S., & Singh, M. P. (2010). Performance evaluation of feed-forward neural network with soft computing techniques for hand written English alphabets. *Applied Soft Computing, 11*(1), 1156–1182. doi:10.1016/j.asoc.2010.02.015

Trier, I. D., & Taxt, T. (1995). Evaluation of binarization methods for document images. *IEEE Transactions on Pattern Analysis and Machine Intelligence, 17*(3), 312–315. doi:10.1109/34.368197

Vamvakas, G., Gatos, B., & Perantonis, S. J. (2010). Handwritten character recognition through two-stage foreground sub-sampling. *Pattern Recognition, 43*(8), 2807–2816. doi:10.1016/j.patcog.2010.02.018

Verma, B., Gader, P., & Chen, W. (2001). Fusion of multiple handwritten word recognition techniques. *Pattern Recognition Letters, 22*(9), 991–998. doi:10.1016/S0167-8655(01)00046-0

Vinciarelli, A. (2002). A survey on off-line cursive word recognition. *Pattern Recognition, 35*(7), 1433–1446. doi:10.1016/S0031-3203(01)00129-7

Vinciarelli, A. (2005). Application of information retrieval techniques to single writer documents. *Pattern Recognition Letters, 26*(14), 2262–2271. doi:10.1016/j.patrec.2005.03.036

Wshah, S. (2009). Segmentation of Arabic handwriting based on both contour and skeleton segmentation. *International Conference on Document Analysis and Recognition,* (pp. 793-797).

Wuthrich, M. (2009). Language model integration for the recognition of handwritten medieval documents. *International Conference on Document Analysis and Recognition,* (pp. 211-215).

Xu, Q., Lam, L., & Suen, C. (2003). Automatic segmentation and recognition system for handwritten dates on Canadian bank cheques. *Seventh International Conference on Document Analysis and Recognition* (Vol. 2, pp. 704-708).

Zhang, P., Bui, T. D., & Suen, C. (2007). A novel cascade ensemble classifier system with a high recognition performance on handwritten digits. *Pattern Recognition, 40*(12), 3415–3429. doi:10.1016/j.patcog.2007.03.022

Zhang, T. Y., & Suen, C. Y. (1984). A fast parallel algorithm for thinning digital patterns. *Communications of the ACM, 27*(3), 236–239. doi:10.1145/357994.358023

Zimmermann, M., Chappelier, J., & Bunke, H. (2006). Offline grammar-based recognition of handwritten sentences. *IEEE Transactions on Pattern Analysis and Machine Intelligence, 28*(5), 818–821. doi:10.1109/TPAMI.2006.103

KEY TERMS AND DEFINITIONS

Binarization: The core objective of thresholding is to extract the foreground pixels from the background.

Character segmentation: an operation that seeks to decompose an image of a sequence of characters into sub-images of individual symbol.

Noise Reduction: It is common that there are introduction of the noises such as salt and pepper while digitization of a handwritten image through scanning processes. Noise reduction is procedures to remove unwanted information as much as possible.

Normalization: It is well known that all the natural handwritten materials from different writers lack uniformities such as character sizes, writing angles of characters and lines. Therefore, the core idea of normalization is to reduce the variances from the different writing styles.

Offline handwriting recognition: the ability of a computer to receive and interpret intelligible handwritten input from sources such as paper documents.

Recognition: During the recognition process, generally the shape features are extracted from the segmented images, and the appropriate class is assigned to the observed character.

Thinning: to normalize the variances of stroke width from the different writing mediums and it could be referred as a meaningful process for retaining information about a character pattern such as geometric and topological properties.

Chapter 3
Semi Blind Source Separation for Application in Machine Learning

Ganesh Naik
RMIT University, Australia

Dinesh Kumar
RMIT University, Australia

ABSTRACT

Unsupervised learning is a class of problems in machine learning which seeks to determine how the data are organized. Unsupervised learning encompasses many other techniques that seek to summarize and explain key features of the data. One form of unsupervised learning is blind source separation (BSS). BSS is a class of computational data analysis techniques for revealing hidden factors that underlie sets of measurements or signals. BSS assumes a statistical model whereby the observed multivariate data, typically given as a large database of samples, are assumed to be linear or nonlinear mixtures of some unknown latent variables. The mixing coefficients are also unknown. Sometimes more prior information about the sources is available or is induced into the model, such as the form of their probability densities, their spectral contents, etc. Then the term blind is often replaced by semiblind. This chapter reports the semi BSS machine learning applications on audio and bio signal processing.

INTRODUCTION

Blind source separation (BSS), is the separation of a set of signals from a set of mixed signals, without the help of information (or with very little information) about the source signals or the mixing. BSS relies on the hypothesis that the source signals do

not correlate with each other. For instance, the signals may be mutually statistically independent or decorrelated. BSS thus separates a set of signals into a set of other signals, such that the steadiness of each resulting signal is maximized, and the regularity between the signals is minimized (i.e. statistical independence is maximized). BSS is an unsupervised learning which is closely related to relate to the problem of density estimation in

DOI: 10.4018/978-1-4666-1833-6.ch003

statistics. However unsupervised learning also encompasses many other techniques that seek to summarize and explain key features of the data. The basic method of unsupervised learning is clustering technique. Another method is blind source separation based on Independent Component Analysis (ICA) (Bell & Sejnowski, 1995; Hyvärinen, Karhunen, & Oja, 2001; Lee, 1998).

BSS can be seen as an extension to the classical methods of Principal Component Analysis and Factor Analysis. BSS is a much richer class of techniques, however, capable of finding the sources when the classical methods, implicitly or explicitly based on Gaussian models, fail completely. In many cases, the measurements are given as a set of parallel signals or time series. Typical examples are mixtures of simultaneous sounds or human voices that have been picked up by several microphones, muscle activities measurements from multiple Electromyography (EMG) sensors, several radio signals arriving at a portable phone, or multiple parallel time series obtained from some industrial process. Perhaps the best known single methodology in BSS is ICA, in which the latent variables are non-Gaussian and mutually independent. However, criteria other than independence can be used for finding the sources. One such simple criterion is the non-negativity of the sources. Sometimes more prior information about the sources is available or is induced into the model, such as the form of their probability densities, their spectral contents, etc. Then the term "blind" is often replaced by "semiblind."

In BSS, we assume that a set of observations is generated via an instantaneous linear mixing of underlying source signals, following the standard model: x = As. There, x is a vector with the observations, s are the underlying source signals, and A expresses the mixing process. In order to solve the BSS problem, a set of general assumptions needs to be made, either on the sources or on the mixing. ICA, one of the most widely used tools to estimate the BSS solutions, assumes the sources to be statistically independent. An addi-

tional assumption is the non-Gaussian distribution of those sources. Algorithms performing ICA can be based on concepts such as negentropy, maximum likelihood, or mutual information. There is a considerable amount of algorithms capable of performing ICA (Bell & Sejnowski, 1995; Bofill, 2000; P. Bofill & Zibulevsky, 2001; J. Cardoso & Souloumiac, 1996; J. F. Cardoso, 1997; Hyvärinen, 1999; Lewicki & Sejnowski, 2000; Zibulevsky & Pearlmutter, 2001).

In this research we propose following semi blind BSS machine learning methods for audio and bio signal applications:

- Hand gesture recognition using BSS of EMG
- Evaluate the use of ICA for the separation of bioelectric signals when the number of active sources may not be known and
- Determining the number of sources in given set of audio recordings using BSS

The authors have explored the various machine learning applications of BSS and in audio and biomedical signal processing. The robustness of the BSS machine learning techniques has been tested using different classification tools including twin support vector machine and neural networks.

SEMIBLIND ICA FOR SOURCE SEPARATION AND IDENTIFICATION

Source separation and identification can be used in a variety of signal processing applications, ranging from speech processing to medical image analysis. The separation of a superposition of multiple signals is accomplished by taking into account the structure of the mixing process and by making assumptions about the sources. When the information about the mixing process and sources is limited, the problem is called "blind." Independent Component Analysis (ICA) is a technique suitable for blind source separation - to separate signals from different sources from the mixture. ICA is a method for finding underlying factors or components from multidimensional (multivariate) statistical data or signals (Hyvarinen, Cristescu, & Oja, 1999; Hyvärinen, et al., 2001; Hyvärinen & Oja, 1997a, 1997b; Hyvärinen & Oja, 2000).

ICA builds a generative model for the measured multivariate data, in which the data are assumed to be linear or nonlinear mixtures of some unknown hidden variables (sources); the mixing system is also unknown. In order to overcome the underdetermination of the algorithm, it is assumed that the hidden sources have the properties of non-Gaussianity and statistical independence. These sources are named Independent Components (ICs). ICA algorithms have been considered to be information theory based unsupervised learning rules. Given a set of multidimensional observations, which are assumed to be linear mixtures of unknown independent sources through an unknown mixing source, an ICA algorithm performs a search of the unmixing matrix by which observations can be linearly translated to form independent output components. When regarding ICA, the basic framework for most researchers has been to assume that the mixing is instantaneous and linear, as in Infomax. ICA is often described as an extension to Principal Component Analysis (PCA) that uncorrelates the signals for higher order moments and produces a non-orthogonal basis. More complex models assume for example, noisy mixtures (Hansen, 2000; Mackay, 1996), nontrivial source distributions (Kab'an, 2000; Sorenson, 2002), convolutive mixtures (Lee, 1998), time dependency, underdetermined sources (Bofill, 2000; P. Bofill & Zibulevsky, 2001; Lewicki & Sejnowski, 2000; Zibulevsky & Pearlmutter, 2001), mixture and classification of independent component (Kolenda, 2000; Lee, Lewicki, & Sejnowski, 1999; Lee, Lewicki, Girolami, & Sejnowski, 1999). A general introduction and overview can be found in (Lee, 1998).

CHALLENGES OF SOURCE SEPARATION IN BIO SIGNAL PROCESSING

In biomedical data processing, the aim is to extract clinically, biochemically or pharmaceutically relevant information (e.g metabolite concentrations in the brain) in terms of parameters out of low quality measurements in order to enable an improved medical diagnosis (Rajapakse, Cichocki, & Sanchez, 2002). Typically, biomedical data are affected by large measurement errors, largely due to the non-invasive nature of the measurement process or the severe constraints to keep the input signal as low as possible for safety and bio-ethical reasons. Accurate and automated quantification of this information requires an ingenious combination of the following four issues:

- An adequate pre-treatment of the data,
- The design of an appropriate model and model validation,
- A fast and numerically robust model parameter quantification method and
- An extensive evaluation and performance study, using in-vivo and patient data, up to the embedding of the advanced tools into user friendly user interfaces to be used by clinicians

A great challenge in biomedical engineering is to non-invasively asses the physiological changes occurring in different internal organs of the human body. These variations can be modeled and measured often as biomedical source signals that indicate the function or malfunction of various physiological systems. To extract the relevant information for diagnosis and therapy, expert knowledge in medicine and engineering is also required.

Biomedical source signals are usually weak, geostationary signals and distorted by noise and interference. Moreover, they are usually mutually superimposed. Besides classical signal analysis tools (such as adaptive supervised filtering, parametric or non parametric spectral estimation, time frequency analysis, and higher order statistics), Intelligent Blind Signal Processing (IBSP) techniques can be used for pre-processing, noise and artifact reduction, enhancement, detection and estimation of biomedical signals by taking into account their spatio-temporal correlation and mutual statistical dependence.

- Exemplary ICA applications in biomedical problems include the following:
- Fetal Electrocardiogram extraction, i.e removing/filtering maternal electrocardiogram signals and noise from fetal electrocardiogram signals (Rajapakse, et al., 2002).
- Enhancement of low level Electrocardiogram components (Rajapakse, et al., 2002).
- Separation of transplanted heart signals from residual original heart signals (He, Clifford, & Tarassenko, 2006)
- Separation of low level myoelectric muscle activities to identify various gestures (Calinon & Billard, 2005; Kato, Chen, & Xu, 2006; Naik, Kumar, & Palaniswami, 2008; Naik, Kumar, Singh, & Palaniswami, 2006; Naik, Kumar, & Weghorn, 2007; Naik, Kumar, Weghorn, & Palaniswami, 2007).

One successful and promising application domain of blind signal processing includes those biomedical signals acquired using multi-electrode devices: Electrocardiography (ECG) (Rajapakse, et al., 2002; Scherg & Von Cramon, 1985), Electroencephalography (EEG) (Rajapakse, et al., 2002; Ricardo Vigário, Jousmáki, Hämäläinen, Hari, & Oja, 1998; R. Vigário, Särelä, Jousmäki, Hämäläinen, & Oja, 2000), Magnetoencephalography (MEG) (Hämäläinen, Hari, Ilmoniemi, Knuutila, & Lounasmaa, 1993; Mosher, Lewis, & Leahy, 1992; Parra, Kalitzin, & Lopes, 2004;

Tang & Pearlmutter, 2003; Ricardo Vigário, et al., 1998) and sEMG. sEMG is an indicator of muscle activity and related to body movement and posture. It has major applications in biosignal processing.

Challenges of Source Separation in Audio Signal Processing

One of the most practical uses for BSS is in the audio world. It has been used for noise removal without the need of filters or Fourier transforms, which leads to simpler processing methods. There are various problems associated with noise removal in this way, but these can most likely be attributed to the relative infancy of the BSS field and such limitations will be reduced as research increases in this field (Bell & Sejnowski, 1995; Hyvärinen, et al., 2001).

Audio source separation is the problem of automated separation of audio sources present in a room, using a set of differently placed microphones, capturing the auditory scene. The whole problem resembles the task a human listener can solve in a cocktail party situation, where using two sensors (ears), the brain can focus on a specific source of interest, suppressing all other sources present (also known as cocktail party problem) (Hyvärinen, 1999; Lee, 1998).

Blind separation of audio signals is, however, much more difficult than one might expect. This is because the basic ICA model is a very crude approximation of the real mixing process. Some of the major problems in audio source separation are highlighted here:

1. The mixing is not instantaneous. Audio signals propagate rather slowly, and thus they arrive in the microphones at different times. Moreover, there are echoes, especially if the recording is made in a room. Thus the problem is more adequately modeled by a convolutive version of the ICA model (Hyvärinen, 1999; Lee, 1998).

2. Typically, the recordings are captured with two microphones only. However, the number of source signals is probably much larger than 2 in most cases, since the noise sources may not form just one well-defined source. Thus we have the problem of overcomplete bases.
3. The nonstationarity of the mixing is another important problem. The mixing matrix may change rather quickly, due to changes in the constellation of the speaker and the microphones. For example, one of these may be moving with respect to the other, or the speaker may simply turn his head. This implies that the mixing matrix must be re-estimated quickly in a limited time frame, which also means a limited number of data (Hyvärinen, 1999; Lee, 1998).
4. Another major problem is undercomplete audio source separation where there exist more microphones than the number of sources. Hence there is need for removal of redundant information, which can improve the quality of audio separation.

Due to these complications, it may be that the prior information, independence and non-Gaussianity of the source signals, are not enough. To estimate the ICA model with a large number of parameters, and a rapidly changing mixing matrix, generally requires more information on the signals and the matrix First, one needs to combine the assumption of non-Gaussianity with the different time structure assumptions (Matsuoka, Ohya, & Kawamoto, 1995; P. Pajunen, 1998). Second, one may need to use some information on the mixing. For example, sparse priors could be used (Karthikesh, 2000). Speech signals have auto-correlations and non-stationarities, so this information could be used for third problem (Ikeda & Murata, 1999; Lee, 1998). Removing redundant recorded data is always a challenging task in ICA source separation. In the recent past there have been some work done to tackle this

problem (Joho, Mathis, & Lambert, 2000; Joho & Rahbar, 2003; Liu & Randall, 2005; Nishikawa, Abe, Saruwatari, & Shikano, 2004; J. Stone, 2004; J. V. Stone, 2002), but still there exist two major issues:

*   identification of dependency and independency measure and
*   removal of redundant data to improve the signal to noise ratio

Hence there is a need for proper source separation method to improve the quality of source estimation in undercomplete ICA.

SEMIBLIND ICA FOR BIO SIGNAL APPLICATIONS

Hand Gesture Recognition Using Semi Blind ICA and Neural Network

Gesture identification has various human computer interface (HCI) applications related to controlling machines, computers, for rehabilitation, disabled and defence. There are number of methods to identify the gestures and actions. The traditional techniques rely on movement or position sensed by accelerometers, capacitive techniques (Rekimoto, 2001) or proximity sensors worn on different parts of the body. These techniques require the users to noticeably move their limbs. On the contrary, electromyographic (EMG) signals can convey information about isometric muscular activity: activity related to very subtle or no movement at all. EMG is a biosignal related to muscle contraction. Studies on the use of EMG for gesture recognition have been reported, but none of them takes explicit advantage of its subtlety, the fact that commands can be issued without the generation of observable movements. Any hand or finger movement is a result of a complex combination of many flexors and extensors present in the forearm. Since all these muscles present in the forearm are close to each other, myo-electric activity observed from any muscle site comprises the activity from the neighbouring muscles as well, referred to as cross-talk. When the muscle activity is small (subtle), the signal strength is small and the impact of cross talk and noise is very high. This is further exaggerated when considering different subjects since the size of the muscles, presence of subcutaneous fat layer and also the training level varies for each person. Extraction of the useful information from such kind of surface EMG becomes more difficult for low level of contraction mainly due to the low signal–to–noise ratio. At low level of contraction, EMG activity is hardly discernible from the background activity. Therefore to correctly classify the gestures more precisely, EMG needs to be decomposed to identify activities of individual muscles. There is little or no prior information of the muscle activity, and the signals have temporal and spectral overlap, making the problem ideal for BSS or ICA for the separation of muscle activities.

Methodology

Experiments were conducted to evaluate the performance of the proposed ICA based technique. sEMG was recorded while the participant maintained isometric finger flexions. The recordings were statistically tested to evaluate the reliability of separation and then tested using a back-propagation neural network. Overall methodology approach is shown in Figure 1.

Surface EMG Recording

Experiments were conducted after obtaining approval from RMIT University human experiments ethics committee. Five subjects, ages ranging from 21 to 32 years (four males and one female) volunteered for the experiments. sEMG was recorded using a Delysis eight channel sEMG acquisition system (Boston, MA, USA). Each channel has a pair of electrodes mounted together with a fixed inter-electrode distance of 10mm and a gain of 1000. Four electrode channels were placed over four different muscles. A reference electrode was placed at Epicondylus Medialis.

Before placing the electrodes, the subject's skin was prepared by lightly abrading with skin exfoliate to remove dead skin. This was done to reduce the skin impedance to less than 60 kOhm. Skin was also cleaned with 70% v/v alcohol swab to remove any oil or dust on the skin surface. The experiments were repeated on two different days. The forearm was resting on the table with elbow at an angle of approximately 90 degree and in a comfortable position. Five isometric wrist and finger flexions were performed and each was repeated for a total of 24 times for each action over the two sessions (Table 1). The signal was sampled at 1024 samples/second. The actions were selected because these required four multiple muscles to be contracting at the same time and

Figure 1. Flowchart of the system

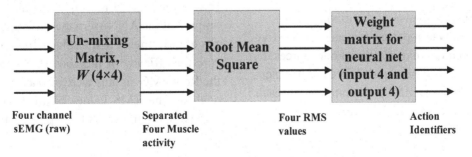

Four channel sEMG (raw)   Separated Four Muscle activity   Four RMS values   Action Identifiers

Table 1. List of four wrist and finger flexion actions

Gestures
Wrist flexion
Index and middle finger flexion
Little and ring finger flexion
Finger and wrist flexion together

thus could test the ability of the system and this ensured that the estimated unmixing matrix was square. Markers were used to obtain the isometric contraction signals during recording. A suitable resting time was given between each experiment. There was no external load.

Surface EMG Feature Extraction

The aim of these experiments was to test the use of BSS along with known properties of the muscles for separation of sEMG signals for the purpose of identifying isometric (subtle) finger movements. The analysis was performed using Hyvearinen's fixed point algorithm (FastICA) by keeping the mixing matrix constant at each instance.

The wideband EMG signal was broken into 12 narrow band signals each of length approximately 2500 samples. The mixing matrix A was computed for the first set of data only and kept constant throughout the experiment. The independent sources of motor unit action potentials that mix to make the EMG recordings were estimated using the following equation.

$$\hat{s} = Wx = WAs \qquad (1)$$

where, W is the inverse of the mixing matrix A. This process was repeated for each of the five Finger movements experiments. Four sources *sa, sb, sc* and *sd,* were computed in each instance. Root Mean Squares (RMS) was computed for each separated sources using the following.

$$S_{rms} = \sqrt{\frac{1}{N} \sum_{i=1}^{n} s_i^2} \qquad (2)$$

where s is the source and N is the number of samples. This results in one number representing the muscle activity for each channel for each finger movements. RMS value of muscle activity of each source represents the muscle activity of that muscle and is indicative of the force of contraction generated by each muscle.

Classification of Finger Movement Data

This chapter presents the use of Back Propagation (BPN) type Artificial Neural Network. The size of the hidden layer and other parameters of the network were chosen iteratively after experimentation with the back-propagation algorithm. There is an inherent trade off to be made. More hidden units results in more time required for each iteration of training; fewer hidden units results in faster update rate. These experiments used sigmoid as the threshold function and gradient descent and adaptive learning with momentum as training algorithm. A learning rate of 0.05 and the default momentum rate were found to be suitable for stable learning of the network. The training stopped when the network converged and the network error is less than the target error. The weights and biases of the network were saved and used for testing the network. The data was divided into subsets of training data, validation, and test subsets. One fourth of the data was used for the validation set, one-fourth for the test set, and one half for the training set. The four RMS EMG values were the inputs to the ANN. The outputs of the ANN were the different isometric finger movements RMS values. In order to measure the efficacy of the above BSS techniques, the Raw EMG signals were also analyzed. In the analysis, the RMS values of all the four channels were computed. A back propagation neural

Table 2. Over all experimental results (average) for hand gesture identification

Methods	Wrist flexion	Index and Middle Finger flexion		Little and ring finger flexion	Finger and wrist flexion together.
Method 1	60%	60%	60%	60%	60%
Method 2	65%	65%	65%	65%	65%
Method 3	97%	97%	97%	97%	97%

network was then trained and tested with these RMS values taken as feature vector.

The results of the experiments demonstrated the performance of the semi blind ICA algorithm on sEMG in classifying the four different subtle finger movements using back propagation ANN learning algorithm. The results of testing the back propagation ANN to correctly classify the test data based on the weight matrix generated using the training data for semi blind ICA algorithm is tabulated in Table 2.

Method 1: Experimental results for Hand Gesture Identification using Raw sEMG (without using ICA)

Method 2: Experimental results for Hand Gesture Identification using muscle activity separated from sEMG using traditional (matrix repeated) ICA

Method 3: Experimental results for Hand Gesture Identification using muscle activity separated from sEMG (using fixed matrix) ICA

SEMIBLIND ICA FOR AUDIO SIGNAL APPLICATIONS

BSS consists of two major issues; source number estimation and source separation. For conceptual and computational simplicity, most ICA algorithms assume that the number of sources is equal to the number of recordings and this result in the mixing matrix to be a square matrix. This simplifies estimation of the mixing matrix A and un-mixing matrix W, because square matrix can be inverted. However, this equality assumption is in general not accurate for number of applications. If the number of sources exceeds the number of sensors (recordings) then the situation is referred to as 'over-complete' while when the number of sources is less than the number of recordings, it is referred to as 'under-complete'.

Researchers have studied the over-complete situation extensively. In over-complete situation, application of standard ICA can result in incorrect separation and this has been demonstrated by (Lewicki & Sejnowski, 2000). (P. Bofill & Zibulevsky, 2001) have attempted to identify the number of sources in a mixture for over-complete situation. While under-complete situation has not been studied extensively, it is often encountered for applications where the numbers of sensors exceed the number of sources such as in sensor networks for environmental or defense monitoring, or when the sources are not independent (Amari, 1999; Joho, et al., 2000; Joho & Rahbar, 2003).

The mixture of unknown sources is referred to as under-complete when the numbers of recordings M, are more than the number of sources N. Since standard ICA techniques assume number of sources as same as number of recordings, dimensional reduction is generally required to estimate the sources for under-complete ICA. Often the number of independent sources in the mixture is unknown. If ICA is applied on the assumption of the matrix being square, this results in estimating more number of independent sources than exist and can result in poor quality of separation. For successful implementation of ICA when the number of recordings may be greater than the number of independent sources, the number of independent sources needs to be determined ahead of source separation. This research proposes a new measure to identify the number of independent sources in an under-complete ICA situation. It demonstrates that after determining the numbers of independent sources, and by randomly removing the extra recordings, it is possible to separate the sources with high quality of separation using standard ICA techniques such as FastICA algorithm. Such a technique is more efficient than any other under-complete ICA technique.

Global matrix G is the product of the mixing matrix A and un-mixing matrix W. If the number of recordings, M is equal to the number of independent sources, N, and the separation is accurate, then G is a unity matrix (or very close to). Based on the independence criterion, the value of the determinant of G would be unity after normalization (Meyer, 2000).

Methodology

Two sets of experiments were conducted. The first experiment was to establish the relationship between the normalized value of the Det G and the number of independent sources N in M recordings. The second experiment was conducted to test the hypothesis that once the number of independent sources, N is known, ICA can be used to separate any N recordings to get good estimate of the original signals. The second experiment was in two steps. The first step was to estimate the number of independent sources K (and compare with N) from M recordings based on the value of

the determinant of G as established in the first experiment. The next step was to randomly select N number of recordings from the total M number of recordings and using ICA on the N recordings. Quality of separation was measured using Signal to Interference Ratio (SIR). The experiments were repeated 10 times.

In simulated conditions, the G can be calculated using the known mixing matrix, A and the estimated un-mixing matrix, W. In real experiments, A is not known, and G is estimated by multiplying estimated unmixing matrix from one time window, W_p, with the inverse of the estimated unmixing matrix of the other time window, W_q. If the separated signals are independent, each of the unmixing matrices should be the inverse of the mixing matrix but for the ambiguity due to the order and arbitrary scaling (Cichocki & Amari, 2002; Hyvärinen, et al., 2001). In this situation, the global matrix (the product of these) should be sparse with typically one dominant cell in each row and column while the other cells should be close to zero (Meyer, 2000).

Experiment 1

Experiments were conducted using four independent audio recordings and synthetically mixed according to Table 3. The values of the mixing equations parameters ($a_{i,j}$) were in the range 0.4 to 0.9. Using FastICA, the unmixing matrices, W_p and W_{p+1} were estimated for two subsequent segments.

Table 3. Criterion of mixing sources to generate the four recordings

Criterion	Sources	Recordings
Four Independent Sources (Independent)	Four independent audio files s_1, s_2, s_3 and s_4.	$x_i = a_{i,1}s_1 + a_{i,2}s_2 + a_{i,3}s_3 + a_{i,4}s_4$, for i= 1 to 4
Three Independent and one Dependent Source (Dependent)	Three independent audio files s_1, s_2 and s_3.	$x_i = a_{i,1}s_1 + a_{i,2}s_2 + a_{i,3}s_3 + a_{i,4}s_1$, for i= 1 to 4
Two Independent and two Dependent Sources (Double dependent)	Two independent audio files s_1 and s_2.	$x_i = a_{i,1}s_1 + a_{i,2}s_2 + a_{i,3}s_2 + a_{i,4}s_1$, for i= 1 to 4
All Dependent Sources- High level dependency.	Only one independent source s_1.	$x_i = a_{i,1}s_1 + a_{i,2}s_1 + a_{i,3}s_1 + a_{i,4}s_1$, for i= 1 to 4

$$G = W_p \times \left(W_{p+1}\right)^{-1} \qquad (3)$$

The determinant of the G matrix was computed and normalized using Frobenius Norm of determinant of G (FN_det G) which is based on the square root of the sum of squares.

Experiment 2

Based on the results of experiment 1 (Table 4), the determinant value of the estimated G was used as the indicator of the numbers of independent sources K from the total M recordings. K out of M number of recordings were randomly selected. Source separation was conducted using fastICA on these K recordings. The quality of separation was estimated using signal to interference ratio

(SIR) (Cichocki & Amari, 2002). For comparison purposes, the source separation was conducted on all M recordings and the FN along with the SIR was computed.

Results-Experiment 1

Examples of the global matrix along with the values of the determinants have been provided below for each of the 4 categories in Table 4. The values of the normalized determinants (FN_det G) have been tabulated for all the four categories in Table 4. From the global matrix, it is observed that when there are four independent sources there is only one dominant value in each row and column. When there are less than four independent sources, there are multiple dominant values in each row and column indicating that the output

Table 4. Example of global matrices, G and Det_FrobeniusNorm for the four criterion

Criterion	Global Matrix G	FN_det G
Independent	$\begin{bmatrix} -\mathbf{1.7555} & -0.1522 & -0.0608 & -0.0665 \\ -0.0806 & 0.1189 & -0.0201 & \mathbf{1.2224} \\ -0.0760 & \mathbf{0.9003} & 0.0124 & 0.0538 \\ -0.1653 & -0.0046 & \mathbf{0.8451} & -0.0054 \end{bmatrix}$	-0.6628
Single Dependency	$\begin{bmatrix} \mathbf{1.0000} & \mathbf{0.6988} & 0.2026 & \mathbf{0.3688} \\ 0.0215 & \mathbf{0.8923} & \mathbf{0.6681} & \mathbf{1.0000} \\ \mathbf{1.0000} & \mathbf{0.8296} & 0.1738 & \mathbf{0.5944} \\ 0.3293 & 0.0001 & \mathbf{1.0000} & \mathbf{0.5071} \end{bmatrix}$	-0.05456
Double Degree Dependency	$\begin{bmatrix} \mathbf{0.9955} & \mathbf{-1.2131} & -0.5903 & \mathbf{0.9328} \\ \mathbf{0.4400} & 0.2165 & \mathbf{0.6893} & -0.3979 \\ -\mathbf{1.1664} & \mathbf{0.9400} & \mathbf{2.0976} & \mathbf{-2.0100} \\ -0.2226 & \mathbf{-0.8282} & -0.1252 & 0.1048 \end{bmatrix}$	-0.0242
Very High Dependency	$\begin{bmatrix} 0.2328 & 0.2467 & \mathbf{0.9154} & \mathbf{1.0000} \\ 0.0425 & 0.0595 & \mathbf{0.9666} & \mathbf{1.0000} \\ 0.1199 & 0.0972 & \mathbf{1.0000} & \mathbf{0.9980} \\ 0.0939 & 0.0597 & \mathbf{1.0000} & \mathbf{0.6754} \end{bmatrix}$	0.000809

would not be a good estimate of the sources. It is also observed from Table 4 that as the dependency increases between sources, the value of FN_Det *G* decreases. This is further confirmed from Table 4 and 5 from where it is observed that values of FN_Det *G* when all four sources are independent is greater than 0.4. When there are three out of the four are independent sources, the value ranges between 0.1 and 0.04. When there are two independent sources and 4 mixtures, the value of FN_det *G* ranges between 0.01 and 0.005. When there is only one source and 4 mixtures, FN_det *G* is below 0.001.

Results- Experiment 2

The average and standard deviation of the second experiment have been tabulated in Table 6. This table gives the SIR of the separated signals when ICA is performed on all the *M* recordings and for *K* recordings. It is observed that the average SIR value for *M* recordings is 11 dB and average FN_det *G* is 0.0077 (SD 0.0007). Based on these values of FN_det *G*, and comparing with Table 5, it is observed that in each of the experiments the value indicates that there are two independent sources (*K* = 2) in the mixture which from prior knowledge is correct.

The results also indicate that when *N* numbers of recordings were considered, the SIR of the separated signals increase to 19 dB, and the FN_det *G* to 0.485 (SD 0.022). Value of FN_det *G* is now comparable when all the sources are independent (Table 5).

Observations

The summary of the observations is listed below:

- From Table 4 and 5, it is observed that the value of the normalized determinant (FN_det *G*) of the global matrix (from ICA) is high when the sources in the mixture are independent while this value decreases with the increase in dependency between the sources. The results indicate that when there are 4 recordings with 4 independent sources, the average FN_det *G* value is 0.558 ±0.24, reduces to 0.057 ±0.02 with 3 independent sources, to 0.077 ±0.007 with 2 independent sources, and to 0.007 ±7 E -5 with only 1 independent source.
- Comparing Table 5 and 6, it is observed that FN_det *G* is a good indicator of the number of independent sources in a mixture.
- From Table 6, it is observed that random selection of recordings to match with the number of independent sources prior to applying ICA improves the quality of separation of the output signals as measured using Signal Interference Ratio (SIR) from 11 to 19 dB (average).

DISCUSSIONS AND CONCLUSION

This research first establishes the applicability of BSS for biomedical (Electromyography) applica-

Table 5. Average and standard deviation of FrobeniusNorm _det of G for the four criterions

Criterion	Average FN_det *G*
Independent	0.558 ± 0.24
Single Dependency	0.057 ± 0.02
Double Degree Dependency	0.0077 ± 0.0007
Very High Dependency	0.0007 ± 7E-05

Table 6. Mean and standard deviation of FN_det G and mean SIR (in dB) for experiment 2

Experiment	Determinant Norm of G Mean and SD	SIR of Output (Mean)
FastICA on M recordings	0.0077 ±0.0007	11 dB
FastICA on N recordings	0.485 ± 0.022	19 dB

tions and also identifies the shortcomings related to order and magnitude ambiguity. It has then developed, a mitigation strategy for these issues by using a single unmixing matrix and neural network weight matrix corresponding to the specific user. The research reports experimental verification of the technique and also the investigation of the impact of inter-subject and inter-experimental variations. The results demonstrate that while using surface EMG without separation gives only 60% accuracy, and surface EMG separated using traditional BSS gives an accuracy of 65%, this approach gives an accuracy of 99% for the same experimental data. Besides the marked improvement in accuracy, the other advantages of such a system are that it is suitable for real time operations and is easy to train by a lay user.

The second part of this research conducted to evaluate the use of ICA for the separation of bioelectric signals when the number of active sources may not be known. The work proposes the use of value of the determinant of the Global matrix generated using sparse sub band ICA for identifying the number of active sources. The results indicate that the technique is successful in identifying the number of active muscles for complex hand gestures. The results support the applications such as human computer interface. This research has also developed a method of determining the number of independent sources in a given mixture and has also demonstrated that using this information, it is possible to separate the signals in an undercomplete situation and reduce the redundancy in the data using standard ICA methods.

This research has proposed and verified the use of determinant values of the global matrix generated by ICA to identify the number of independent sources in a given mixture. Given a set of recordings of mixture of unknown sources, using this method, it is possible to identify the number of independent sources in the mixtures. This chapter has also proposed and verified that after the number of independent sources have

been identified to be K, ICA be performed on a random selection of K recordings. There is a marked improvement of the separation compared to when all the recordings were used for estimating the independent sources. This technique is simple two step approach. It is efficient and not based on any assumptions regarding the number of sources in the mixture. The technique does not require any prior information of the sources or even the independence between the sources. However in the present form, this is based on the assumption that the mixing matrix is linear and stationary.

FUTURE RESEARCH DIRECTIONS

An important line of future research is application of the proposed techniques to real-world problems. For example, the change detection approach based on variational Bayesian learning could be applied to real process monitoring tasks. The faster semi blind ICA algorithms could be useful for analysis of other types of spatio-temporal datasets. This is a start of a new set of signal quality enhancement techniques using semi blind ICA method, and there are number of opportunities to extend this work. One important task required to be undertaken is to determine the limitations of this technique in regards to the signal statistical properties. It is also important to develop a streamlined approach to make this technique suitable for real-time filtering of the signal recordings. It is also important to determine the impact of change in the distance between speaker, noise sources and the microphone because it would violate the need for stationarity for simple FastICA. In the future, we would like to more carefully explore the combination ICA and non negative matrix factorisation (NMF) to denoise non-stationary noise, and we plan to explore multi-scale temporal regularization to capture even longer-term patterns.

REFERENCES

Amari, S.-I. (1999). Natural gradient learning for over- and under-complete bases in ICA. *Neural Computation, 11*(9), 1875–1883. doi:10.1162/089976699300015990

Bell, A. J., & Sejnowski, T. J. (1995). An information-maximization approach to blind separation and blind deconvolution. *Neural Computation, 7*(6), 1129–1159. doi:10.1162/neco.1995.7.6.1129

Bofill, P. (2000). *Blind separation of more sources than mixtures using sparsity of their short-time Fourier transform.* Helsinki, Finland.

Bofill, P., & Zibulevsky, M. (2001). Underdetermined blind source separation using sparse representations. *Signal Processing, 81*(11), 2353–2362. doi:10.1016/S0165-1684(01)00120-7

Calinon, S., & Billard, A. (2005). *Recognition and reproduction of gestures using a probabilistic framework combining PCA, ICA and HMM.* Paper presented at the ICML '05: 22nd International Conference on Machine Learning.

Cardoso, J., & Souloumiac, A. (1996). Jacobi angles for simultaneous diagonalization. *SIAM Journal on Matrix Analysis and Applications, 17*(1), 161–164. doi:10.1137/S0895479893259546

Cardoso, J. F. (1997). Infomax and maximum likelihood for blind source separation. *IEEE Signal Processing Letters, 4*(4), 112–114. doi:10.1109/97.566704

Cichocki, A., & Amari, S.-I. (2002). *Adaptive blind signal and image processing: Learning algorithms and applications.* John Wiley & Sons, Inc. doi:10.1002/0470845899

Hämäläinen, M., Hari, R., Ilmoniemi, R., & Knuutila, J., & Lounasma. (1993). Magnetoencephalography, theory, instrumentation, and applications to noninvasive studies of the working human brain. *Reviews of Modern Physics, 65*(2), 413–497. doi:10.1103/RevModPhys.65.413

Hansen, L. K. (2000). Blind separation of noicy image mixtures. In Girolami, M. (Ed.), *Advances in independent components analysis* (pp. 159–179). Springer-Verlag. doi:10.1007/978-1-4471-0443-8_9

He, T., Clifford, G., & Tarassenko, L. (2006). Application of independent component analysis in removing artefacts from the electrocardiogram. *Neural Computing & Applications, 15*(2), 105–116. doi:10.1007/s00521-005-0013-y

Hyvärinen, A. (1999). Fast and robust fixed-point algorithms for independent component analysis. *IEEE Transactions on Neural Networks, 10*(3), 626–634. doi:10.1109/72.761722

Hyvarinen, A., Cristescu, R., & Oja, E. (1999). *A fast algorithm for estimating overcomplete ICA bases for image windows.* Paper presented at the International Joint Conference on Neural Networks, IJCNN '99.

Hyvärinen, A., Karhunen, J., & Oja, E. (2001). *Independent component analysis.* Wiley-Interscience. doi:10.1002/0471221317

Hyvärinen, A., & Oja, E. (1997). A fast fixed-point algorithm for independent component analysis. *Neural Computation, 9*(7), 1483–1492. doi:10.1162/neco.1997.9.7.1483

Hyvärinen, A., & Oja, E. (2000). Independent component analysis: algorithms and applications. *Neural Networks, 13*(4-5), 411–430. doi:10.1016/S0893-6080(00)00026-5

Ikeda, S., & Murata, N. (1999). A method of ICA in time-frequency domain. *Proceedings of the International Workshop on Independent Component Analysis.*

Joho, M., Mathis, H., & Lambert, R. (2000). Overdetermined blind source separation: Using more sensors than source signals in a noisy mixture.

Joho, M., & Rahbar, K. (2003). *Joint diagonalization of correlation matrices by using Newton methods with application to blind signal separation.*

Kab´an. (2000). *Clustering of text documents by skewness maximization.*

Karthikesh, R. (2000). *Sparse priors on the mixing matrix in independent component analysis.* Paper presented at the Workshop on Independent Component Analysis and Blind Signal Separation (ICA2000).

Kato, M., Chen, Y.-W., & Xu, G. (2006). *Articulated hand tracking by PCA-ICA approach.* Paper presented at the FGR '06: The 7th International Conference on Automatic Face and Gesture Recognition.

Kolenda, T. (2000). Independent components in text. In Girolami, M. (Ed.), *Advances in independent components analysis* (pp. 229–250). Springer-Verlag. doi:10.1007/978-1-4471-0443-8_13

Lee, T.-W. (1998). *Independent component analysis: Theory and applications.* Kluwer Academic Publishers.

Lee, T.-W., Lewicki, M., & Sejnowski, T. (1999). *Unsupervised classification with non-Gaussian mixture models using ICA.* Paper presented at the 1998 Conference on Advances in Neural Information Processing Systems II.

Lee, T.-W., Lewicki, M. S., Girolami, M., & Sejnowski, T. J. (1999). Blind source separation of more sources than mixtures using overcomplete representations. *IEEE Signal Processing Letters*, 6(4), 87–90. doi:10.1109/97.752062

Lewicki, M. S., & Sejnowski, T. J. (2000). Learning overcomplete representations. *Neural Computation*, 12(2), 337–365. doi:10.1162/089976600300015826

Liu, X., & Randall, R. B. (2005). *Redundant data elimination in independent component analysis.* Paper presented at the Eighth International Symposium on Signal Processing and Its Applications, 2005.

Mackay, D. J. C. (1996). *Maximum likelihood and covariant algorithms for independent component analysis.*

Matsuoka, K., Ohya, M., & Kawamoto, M. (1995). A neural net for blind separation of nonstationary signals. *Neural Networks*, 8(3), 411–419. doi:10.1016/0893-6080(94)00083-X

Meyer, C. D. (2000). *Matrix analysis and applied linear algebra.* Cambridge, UK: Cambridge Press. doi:10.1137/1.9780898719512

Mosher, J. C., Lewis, P. S., & Leahy, R. M. (1992). Multiple dipole modeling and localization from spatio-temporal MEG data. *IEEE Transactions on Bio-Medical Engineering*, 39(6), 541–557. doi:10.1109/10.141192

Naik, G., Kumar, D., & Palaniswami, M. (2008). *Multi run ICA and surface EMG based signal processing system for recognising hand gestures.* Paper presented at the 8th IEEE International Conference on Computer and Information Technology, CIT 2008.

Naik, G., Kumar, D., Singh, V., & Palaniswami, M. (2006). *Hand gestures for HCI using ICA of EMG.* Paper presented at the VisHCI '06: The HCSNet Workshop on Use of Vision in human-Computer Interaction.

Naik, G., Kumar, D., & Weghorn, H. (2007). *Performance comparison of ICA algorithms for isometric hand gesture identification using surface EMG.* Paper presented at the 2007 3rd International Conference on Intelligent Sensors, Sensor Networks and Information, Melbourne, Australia.

Naik, G., Kumar, D., Weghorn, H., & Palaniswami, M. (2007). *Subtle hand gesture identification for HCI using temporal decorrelation source separation BSS of surface EMG*. Paper presented at the 9th Biennial Conference of the Australian Pattern Recognition Society on Digital Image Computing Techniques and Applications (DICTA 2007), Glenelg, Australia.

Nishikawa, T., Abe, H., Saruwatari, H., & Shikano, K. (2004). *Overdetermined blind separation for convolutive mixtures of speech based on multistage ICA using subarray processing*. Paper presented at the IEEE International Conference on Acoustics, Speech, and Signal Processing, 2004 (ICASSP '04).

Pajunen, P. (1998). Source separation using algorithmic information theory. *Neurocomputing, 22*, 35–48. doi:10.1016/S0925-2312(98)00048-4

Parra, J., & Kalitzin, S., & Lopes. (2004). Magnetoencephalography: An investigational tool or a routine clinical technique? *Epilepsy & Behavior, 5*(3), 277–285. doi:10.1016/j.yebeh.2004.02.003

Rajapakse, J. C., Cichocki, A., & Sanchez. (2002). *Independent component analysis and beyond in brain imaging: EEG, MEG, fMRI, and PET*. Paper presented at the 9th International Conference on Neural Information Processing, ICONIP '02.

Rekimoto, J. (2001). GestureWrist and GesturePad: Unobtrusive wearable interaction devices. *Proceedings Fifth International Symposium on Wearable Computers*, (pp. 21-27).

Scherg, M., & Von Cramon, D. (1985). Two bilateral sources of the late AEP as identified by a spatio-temporal dipole model. *Electroencephalography and Clinical Neurophysiology, 62*(1), 32–44. doi:10.1016/0168-5597(85)90033-4

Sorenson, P. A., Winther, O., & Hansen, L. K. (2002). Mean field approaches to independent component analysis. *Neural Computation, 14*, 889–918. doi:10.1162/089976602317319009

Stone, J. (2004). *Independent component analysis: A tutorial introduction*. The MIT Press.

Stone, J. V. (2002). Independent component analysis: an introduction. *Trends in Cognitive Sciences, 6*(2), 59–64. doi:10.1016/S1364-6613(00)01813-1

Tang, A., & Pearlmutter, B. (2003). *Independent components of magnetoencephalography: Localization* (pp. 129-162).

Vigário, R., Jousmáki, V., Hämäläinen, M., Hari, R., & Oja, E. (1998). *Independent component analysis for identification of artifacts in magnetoencephalographic recordings*. Paper presented at the NIPS '97: The 1997 Conference on Advances in Neural Information Processing Systems, Denver, Colorado, United States.

Vigário, R., Särelä, J., Jousmäki, V., Hämäläinen, M., & Oja, E. (2000). Independent component approach to the analysis of EEG and MEG recordings. *IEEE Transactions on Bio-Medical Engineering, 47*(5), 589–593. doi:10.1109/10.841330

Zibulevsky, M., & Pearlmutter, B. (2001). Blind source separation by sparse decomposition in a signal dictionary. *Neural Computation, 13*(4), 863–882. doi:10.1162/089976601300014385

ADDITIONAL READING

Adali, T. (2009). Independent component analysis and signal separation. *Proceedings 8th International Conference, ICA 2009*, Paraty, Brazil, March 15 - 18. Berlin, Germany: Springer.

Baker, J. J., Scheme, E., Englehart, K., Hutchinson, D. T., & Greger, B. (2010). Continuous detection and decoding of dexterous finger flexions with implantable myoelectric sensors. *IEEE Transactions on Neural Systems and Rehabilitation Engineering, 18*(4), 424–432. doi:10.1109/TNSRE.2010.2047590

Comon, P. (2010). *Handbook of blind source separation: Independent component analysis and blind deconvolution* (1st ed.). Boston, MA: Elsevier.

De Lucia, M., Michel, C. M., & Murray, M. M. (2010). Comparing ICA-based and single-trial topographic ERP analyses. *Brain Topography*, *23*(2), 119–127. doi:10.1007/s10548-010-0145-y

Deco, G., & Obradovic, D. (1996). *An information-theoretic approach to neural computing*. New York, NY: Springer.

Girolami, M. (1999). *Self-organising neural networks: Independent component analysis and blind source separation*. London, UK: Springer.

Girolami, M. (2000). *Advances in independent component analysis*. London, UK: Springer.

James, C. J., Abasolo, D., & Gupta, D. (2007). Space-time ICA versus ensemble ICA for ictal EEG analysis with component differentiation via Lempel-Ziv complexity. *Conference Proceedings;... Annual International Conference of the IEEE Engineering in Medicine and Biology Society. IEEE Engineering in Medicine and Biology Society. Conference, 2007*, 5473–5476. doi:10.1109/IEMBS.2007.4353584

Kelly, R. E., Wang, Z., Alexopoulos, G. S., Gunning, F. M., Murphy, C. F., & Morimoto, S. S. (2010). Hybrid ICA-seed-based methods for fMRI functional connectivity assessment: A feasibility study. *International Journal of Biomedical Imaging*, 2010.

Kurisu, N., Tsujiuchi, N., & Koizumi, T. (2009). *Prosthetic hand control using motion discrimination from EMG signals* (pp. 6922–6925). IEEE Engineering in Medicine and Biology Society.

Kurzynski, M., & Wolczowski, A. (2009). Control of dexterous bio-prosthetic hand via sequential recognition of EMG signals using fuzzy relations. *Studies in Health Technology and Informatics*, *150*, 799–803.

Margadan-Mendez, M., Juslin, A., Nesterov, S. V., Kalliokoski, K., Knuuti, J., & Ruotsalainen, U. (2010). ICA based automatic segmentation of dynamic H(2)(15)O cardiac PET images. *IEEE Transactions on Information Technology in Biomedicine*, *14*(3), 795–802. doi:10.1109/TITB.2007.910744

Meilink, A., Hemmen, B., Seelen, H. A., & Kwakkel, G. (2008). Impact of EMG-triggered neuromuscular stimulation of the wrist and finger extensors of the paretic hand after stroke: A systematic review of the literature. *Clinical Rehabilitation*, *22*(4), 291–305. doi:10.1177/0269215507083368

Min, B.-W., Yoon, H.-S., Soh, J., Yang, Y.-M., & Ejima, T. (2002). *Hand gesture recognition using hidden Markov models*. Paper presented at the Systems, Man, and Cybernetics, IEEE International Conference on Computational Cybernetics and Simulation.

Moeller, F., Levan, P., & Gotman, J. (2010). Independent component analysis (ICA) of generalized spike wave discharges in fMRI: Comparison with general linear model-based EEG-fMRI. *Human Brain Mapping*, *32*(2), 209–217. doi:10.1002/hbm.21010

Naik, G. R., & Kumar, D. K. (2010). Identification of hand and finger movements using multi run ICA of surface electromyogram. *Journal of Medical Systems*, *36*(2), 841–851. doi:10.1007/s10916-010-9548-2

Puntonet, C. G., & Lang, E. W. (2006). *Blind source separation and independent component analysis: Selected papers from the ICA 2004 Meeting*. Elsevier.

Roberts, S., & Everson, R. (2001). *Independent component analysis: Principles and practice*. Cambridge, UK: Cambridge University Press.

Ryali, S., Glover, G. H., Chang, C., & Menon, V. (2009). Development, validation, and comparison of ICA-based gradient artifact reduction algorithms for simultaneous EEG-spiral in/out and echo-planar fMRI recordings. *NeuroImage, 48*(2), 348–361. doi:10.1016/j.neuroimage.2009.06.072

Selvan, S. E., Mustatea, A., Xavier, C. C., & Sequeira, J. (2009). Accurate estimation of ICA weight matrix by implicit constraint imposition using lie group. *IEEE Transactions on Neural Networks, 20*(10), 1565–1580. doi:10.1109/TNN.2009.2027017

Starck, T., Remes, J., Nikkinen, J., Tervonen, O., & Kiviniemi, V. (2010). Correction of low-frequency physiological noise from the resting state BOLD fMRI--Effect on ICA default mode analysis at 1.5 T. *Journal of Neuroscience Methods, 186*(2), 179–185. doi:10.1016/j.jneumeth.2009.11.015

Stone, J. V. (2004). *Independent component analysis: A tutorial introduction.* Cambridge, MA: MIT Press.

Subasi, A., & Kiymik, M. K. (2010). Muscle fatigue detection in EMG using time-frequency methods, ICA and neural networks. *Journal of Medical Systems, 34*(4), 777–785. doi:10.1007/s10916-009-9292-7

Theis, F. J., & Meyer-Bäse, A. (2010). *Biomedical signal analysis: Contemporary methods and applications.* Cambridge, MA: MIT Press.

Zhang, H., Zuo, X. N., Ma, S. Y., Zang, Y. F., Milham, M. P., & Zhu, C. Z. (2010). Subject order-independent group ICA (SOI-GICA) for functional MRI data analysis. *NeuroImage, 51*(4), 1414–1424. doi:10.1016/j.neuroimage.2010.03.039

Chapter 4
Machine Learning Algorithms for Analysis of DNA Data Sets

John Yearwood
University of Ballarat, Australia

Adil Bagirov
University of Ballarat, Australia

Andrei Kelarev
University of Ballarat, Australia

ABSTRACT

The applications of machine learning algorithms to the analysis of data sets of DNA sequences are very important. The present chapter is devoted to the experimental investigation of applications of several machine learning algorithms for the analysis of a JLA data set consisting of DNA sequences derived from non-coding segments in the junction of the large single copy region and inverted repeat A of the chloroplast genome in Eucalyptus collected by Australian biologists. Data sets of this sort represent a new situation, where sophisticated alignment scores have to be used as a measure of similarity. The alignment scores do not satisfy properties of the Minkowski metric, and new machine learning approaches have to be investigated. The authors' experiments show that machine learning algorithms based on local alignment scores achieve very good agreement with known biological classes for this data set. A new machine learning algorithm based on graph partitioning performed best for clustering of the JLA data set. Our novel k-committees algorithm produced most accurate results for classification. Two new examples of synthetic data sets demonstrate that the authors' k-committees algorithm can outperform both the Nearest Neighbour and k-medoids algorithms simultaneously.

DOI: 10.4018/978-1-4666-1833-6.ch004

INTRODUCTION

Machine learning algorithms have useful applications in broad areas and are very important. Many valuable results on machine learning techniques have been obtained in the literature recently. To illustrate the broad character of associated applications let us just refer to a few articles by Bagirov & Yearwood (2006), Bagirov, Rubinov & Yearwood (2002), Haidar, Kulkarni & Pan (2008), Pan, Haidar & Kulkarni (2009), Verma & Kulkarni (2007), Witten & Frank (2005), Yearwood et al. (2009), Yearwood & Mammadov (2010).

On the other hand, the data sets of nucleotide and protein sequences have been rapidly growing, see Baldi & Brunak (2001) and Gusfield (1997). Enormous amounts of DNA, RNA and protein data are continuously being generated. This is why it is especially important to devise efficient machine learning algorithms in order to automate the analysis of nucleotide sequences.

Nucleotide and protein sequences stored in databases are very long. They cannot be accurately represented using short tuples of values of numerical or nominal feature attributes, and cannot be regarded as points in a finite dimensional space. In order to achieve agreement between classifications produced by machine learning algorithms and biological classifications, sophisticated local alignment scores have to be used as a measure of similarity between DNA sequences. These scores do not satisfy axioms of Minkowski metrics, which include as special cases the Euclidean distance, Manhattan distance, and max distance.

To verify the effectiveness of new machine learning methods for automated classification and clustering of DNA sequences, the researchers have to rely on classes and groupings of known data sets that have already been considered in the biological literature. A comparison of the results produced by new machine learning algorithms with known groupings is essential for automating further classifications and clusterings and the development of new advanced machine learning programs that may lead to discoveries of biological significance.

The present paper is devoted to experimental analysis of several algorithms for clustering and classification of a JLA data set derived from the non-coding segments in the junction of the large single copy region and inverted repeat A of the chloroplast genome in Eucalyptus collected by Australian biologists. We compare the effectiveness of several algorithms in their ability to achieve agreement with known biologically significant classes already obtained for this data set by Freeman, Jackson & Steane (2001).

Our experimental analysis shows that all algorithms based on local alignment scores achieve better results than straightforward alternatives using simple statistical measures. The experiments compare the results of k-medoids, Nearest Neighbour, k-committees algorithms, and a machine learning algorithm based on graph partitioning in their ability to achieve agreement with the results published in the biological literature before. All of these algorithms rely on local alignments. For unsupervised clustering of the JLA data set, the machine learning algorithm based on graph partitioning performed best. For supervised classification, the k-committees algorithm produced the most accurate results. Finally, we present two examples of synthetic data sets, where our novel k-committees algorithm outperforms both the classical Nearest Neighbour algorithm and the k-medoids algorithm.

The results demonstrate that machine learning algorithms based on local alignments achieve good agreement with classifications published in the biological literature. They can be used to obtain biologically significant machine learning results.

PRELIMINARIES AND BACKGROUND INFORMATION

We use standard machine learning terminology and notions and refer the reader to the monographs by Kaufman & Rousseeuw (1990), Witten & Frank (2005), Yearwood & Mammadov (2010) for prerequisites on machine learning techniques, and to Baldi & Brunak (2001), Gusfield (1997) for background information on nucleotide sequences.

Chloroplast and Nucleotide Sequences

Chloroplast genome represents valuable opportunity for the development of machine learning techniques applicable to the analysis of DNA information, since its structure is well understood and is simpler than that of nucleus DNA. We are hoping that the methods, which can first be tested in this setting, will then become available for applications to the analysis of various other collections of DNA sequence data. It is also likely that such methods will be applicable to the analysis of protein molecules, which can be regarded as sequences over a 20-letter alphabet encoded with the genetic code, as explained, for example, by Gusfield (1997).

Chloroplasts are small specialized subunits within cells found in plants and other eukaryotic organisms that conduct photosynthesis. They have their own specific functions and are enclosed within individual membranes. Chloroplasts typically occur in green plants. They are the site of photosynthesis and perform a number of further synthetic processes.

Chloroplasts have their own circular DNA, which codes for proteins involved in electron transport in photosynthesis. Their DNA shows substantial similarity to bacterial genomes. The chloroplasts are inherited along the female line, which is known as maternal inheritance. This is why the whole chloroplast DNA sequence is useful for studying the evolutionary history of plants. In particular, it is more closely linked to the geographic location. Such information is also very valuable for investigating the genetics behind common diseases. Besides, genetic modifications to the chloroplast DNA do not transfer to other unmodified plants, pose significantly lower environmental risks and have attracted a lot of research with a view to agricultural applications.

Chloroplast DNA is organized into large clusters of coding regions containing transcribed genes. Large structural changes in chloroplast DNA, such as segmental, deletion, insertion and mutation in gene order, are relatively rare and evolutionarily useful in making phylogenetic inferences. The chloroplast DNA of most plants contains two special segments called the inverted repeats A and the inverted repeats B. These segments are commonly separated by two single copy sequences called the large single copy region and the small single copy region, as explained, for example, by Palmer (1985) and Sugiura (1989). The JLA segment is a non-coding sequence in the junction of the large single copy region and inverted repeat A of the chloroplast genome. These sequences contain highly repetitive elements and are comparatively highly variable. They have been actively investigated, for example, by Raubeson & Jansen (2005).

Our experiments used a data set with sequences of a JLA region in the chloroplast DNA of several species from all different subgenera and sections of Eucalyptus collected by Australian biologists. For a detailed description of the data set the reader is referred to Freeman, Jackson & Steane (2001).

The Watson-Crick complementarity allows us to encode every nucleotide molecule as a string over a 4-letter alphabet: A, C, G, T in the case of DNA, and A, C, G, U in the case of RNA, respectively. Likewise, protein sequences can be encoded as strings over a 20-letter alphabet.

In order to achieve biological significance in measuring the similarity or distance between sequences we use local alignment scores, see Baldi & Brunak (2001) and Gusfield (1997). These scores do satisfy axioms of Minkowski metrics, which include as special cases the Euclidean distance, Manhattan distance, and max distance. It is impossible to calculate new DNA sequences from given ones. One cannot compute the arithmetical average, or mean, of several sequences. These circumstances make it impossible to utilize previous implementations of the machine learning algorithms. We had to develop novel algorithms and adjust familiar ones.

In order to achieve strong agreement between clusterings produced by machine learning algorithms and biological classes, we use local alignment scores, which have not been applied in this context before.

Sequence Alignment Scores for Machine Learning Algorithms

Local alignments and their scores are very well known tools of the computational biology. Every alignment algorithm produces an alignment score, which measures the similarity of the nucleotide or amino acid sequences. This score is then used to evaluate optimal local similarity between the sequences. These scores do not satisfy the axioms of Minkowski metrics, which include as special cases the standard Euclidean distance used in previous implementations, Manhattan distance, and max distance.

The alignment scores in our algorithms provide a measure of similarity that is significant biologically. To illustrate let us suppose that we have a long DNA sequence L, and an identical copy S of a segment within the sequence L. Obviously, every correct biological clustering should place both L and S in the same cluster. This may however be difficult to determine using other metrics. Indeed, L and S may have seriously different values of statistical parameters. Therefore traditional statistical approaches, mapping L and S into an n-dimensional space and using standard Euclidean norm there, may not notice their similarity at all. In contrast, sequence alignment will immediately show that there is a perfect match between S and a segment in the sequence L.

All our algorithms rely on the use of local alignment scores as a measure of the similarity of

the nucleotide sequences. Our experiments used a data set with sequences of a JLA region in the chloroplast DNA of several species from all different subgenera and sections of Eucalyptus. We have used the groupings in the data set identified by several Australian biologists. For a detailed description of the data set we refer to Freeman, Jackson & Steane (2001).

We used the BLOSUM matrices, or blocks of amino acid substitution matrices, which are substitution matrices based on local alignments common in all implementations of the alignment algorithms, since they "encourage local alignment algorithms to produce alignments highlighting biologically important similarities" as explained by Gusfield (1997). Alignment scores have properties that are seriously different from those of the Euclidean norms and their simple modifications discussed, for example, in Section 6.4 of the book by Witten & Frank (2005). Hence our algorithms had to be designed differently and have been encoded with the Bioinformatics Toolbox of Matlab. We used the *swalign(Seq1,Seq2)* function of the Bioinformatics Toolbox, which returns the optimal local alignment score. Higher alignment scores correspond to lower distances between closely associated sequences. Every alignment score between each pair of the given sequences is found once during a pre-processing stage.

CLASSIFICATIONS OF A MACHINE LEARNING ALGORITHM BASED ON GRAPH PARTITIONING WITH ALIGNMENT SCORES

At first glance it might appear impossible to use graph partitioning program METIS for classification tasks, since it specializes in finding optimal unsupervised clusterings only, see Karypis & Kumar (1999). However, we have managed to overcome this problem by constructing a special weighted graph in such a way that every optimal solution to the clustering problem in this graph automatically solves a classification problem.

In order to apply the METIS unsupervised partitioning program, described by Karypis & Kumar (1999), to a supervised classification of the JLA data set, we use the training set to construct an appropriate weighted graph for clustering, where artificial weights of edges are chosen so that every optimal clustering of the graph automatically clusters all vertices of the training set correctly. Every DNA sequence in the JLA data set is represented by a vertex of the graph. There is an undirected edge connecting each pair of vertices, so that the graph is complete. Initially, we labeled each undirected edge with the alignment score of the DNA sequences corresponding to the vertices incident to the edge. After that, we found the sum S of all alignment scores, i.e., the sum of all initial labels of all edges. Then we replaced the labels on all edges incident to the pairs of the vertices in the training set, where the class membership of DNA sequences was known in advance. If two vertices of the training set belong to the same class, then we associate the weight S to the undirected

edge connecting them. If they belong to two different classes, then we remove their edge from the graph, or equivalently, associate zero weight with that edge.

The choice of very large value S for all edges connecting the vertices in the same class of the training set ensures that METIS keeps these edges intact when it finds an optimal cut with minimal weight of the cuts producing the partition. In this way every optimal partition of the new graph found by METIS is guaranteed to represent a clustering of the original data set which respects correct groupings of the training set. We used the standard tenfold cross validation, explained by Witten & Frank (2005), Section 5.3.

The experimental results on classifications are presented in Table 1. We have also included the average accuracies of three traditional classification algorithms using simple statistics as features. For small values of d, we used the numbers of occurrences of all short sequences of letters of length d, also called d-graphs, in every given sequence. This approach produced much worse

Table 1. Average accuracies of classifications obtained by machine learning algorithms

Machine learning algorithms		Local alignment scores		
		BLOSUM30	BLOSUM60	BLOSUM90
k-medoids		58.43	59.35	58.93
NN		63.28	64.43	63.69
k-committees	r=2	62.28	63.49	62.83
	r=3	66.38	67.14	66.64
	r=4	70.09	71.28	70.51
	r=5	72.04	73.49	72.92
Machine learning algorithm based on graph partitioning		63.33	64.35	63.63
		Simple statistics: d-graphs		
		d=2	d=3	d=4
J4.5		20.53	21.58	21.83
Neural networks		20.84	21.65	21.96
SVM		20.12	20.73	21.02

results, and has been included just to illustrate the advantages of using local alignments.

CLASSIFICATIONS OF THE K-MEDOIDS MACHINE LEARNING ALGORITHM WITH ALIGNMENT SCORES

The k-means algorithm and the Nearest Neighbour algorithm are very well known. Complete explanations of these methods are given, for example, in Chapter 4 of the book by Witten & Frank (2005). Both of them can be used for classification and clustering. Traditional k-means algorithm finds the mean of the points in each class as a centroid. Every new point is then assigned to the class of its nearest centroid. The complexity of the k-means algorithm is $O(k)$.

In this chapter we consider a modification of the k-means algorithm known as the k-medoids algorithm, see for example, Kaufman & Rousseeuw (1990). It chooses each centroid among the elements of the given data set. For DNA sequences it is impossible to find the "mean" of several sequences and the standard k-means algorithm cannot be used. Besides, the squares of distances used in the k-means algorithm do not make sense either, since the squares of the alignment scores do not have any geometrical meaning. For the alignment scores, there does not exist a simple arithmetical calculation computing a DNA sequence that is the "midpoint" or "mean" of the given DNA sequences in order to use it as a new centroid.

Our algorithm operates on the set of given sequences only and does not create any new sequences as means of the given ones. As a centroid of the class C our algorithm uses a sequence x in the data set, which the sum of all distances to all other sequences of C. In other respects, the algorithm proceeds as the k-medoids algorithm.

The average success rates of this method for classifying new sequences in comparison with

the classes obtained and published by Freeman, Jackson & Steane (2001) are represented in Table 1. We used the percentage of correctly classified instances as a measure of accuracy. The JLA regions are highly variable, and so the results obtained demonstrate very good agreement of new machine learning classifications with the already known biological classes.

The complexity of the k-medoids algorithm is $O(k)$.

CLASSIFICATIONS OF THE K-COMMITTEES MACHINE LEARNING ALGORITHM WITH ALIGNMENT SCORES

This subsection is devoted to the k-committees algorithm developed by Yearwood, Bagirov & Kelarev (2009). Instead of one centroid, we select a small number of representatives in each class. These representatives form a *committee* of the class. Let us denote the number of the representatives chosen in each class by r. When the training is complete, during the classification stage every new sequence is then assigned to the class of its nearest committee member. If every class has the same number r of committee members to indicate this number explicitly, then we call our method the *k-committees of r representatives* algorithm.

The set of representatives in a class will be called a *committee* of the class. As a committee of r representatives of the class C our algorithm uses the points the set X of r points from C such that the largest distance from any point y in C to the set X achieves a minimum. Intuitively speaking, this means that the k-committees algorithm approximates every class by a union of `spheres', i.e., sets of points with given members of the committee as their centroids. When the committees have been prepared, the algorithm assigns every new sequence to the class of its nearest committee member. The complexity of the k-committees algorithm is $O(kr)$.

CLASSIFICATIONS OF THE NEAREST NEIGHBOUR MACHINE LEARNING ALGORITHM WITH ALIGNMENT SCORES

The standard implementations of the Nearest Neighbour classifier could not be applied directly to the JLA data set of nuclear ribosomal DNA, because they handle data represented as points in an n-dimensional Euclidean space. Thus we had to encode a new version of the Nearest Neighbour algorithm based on optimal local alignments of the given sequences.

The situation in this case is much simpler compared to the case of the k-means or k-medoids algorithm, and all modifications for the case of the Nearest Neighbour classifier are straightforward. We have found the average success rates of this method comparing classes produced by our algorithm for various alignment scores with the classes obtained by Freeman, Jackson & Steane (2001). The results on the accuracy of this algorithm are presented in Table 1.

The Nearest Neighbour algorithm compares each new sequence with all previous sequences, and assigns it to the class of the nearest known sequence using the alignment scores. The complexity of this algorithm is O(n), where n is the number of all sequences in the data set. Since n>k, applying the Nearest Neighbour algorithm to classify new sequences is slower.

CLUSTERINGS OF A MACHINE LEARNING ALGORITHM BASED ON GRAPH PARTITIONS WITH ALIGNMENT SCORES

We used local alignment scores to define a complete weighted graph representing the JLA data set and applied graph partitioning package METIS

of Karypis & Kumar (1999) with multilevel algorithms for partitioning of weighted graphs and hypergraphs. To apply the METIS program for the clustering of JLA data set, a special weighted graph has to be introduced. Every DNA sequence is represented by a vertex or node of the graph. There is an undirected edge connecting each pair of vertices, so that the graph is complete. It is important to associate correct weights to the edges of the graph so that the weights reflect the biological similarity of DNA sequences and METIS produces a biologically significant clustering.

In our case, the METIS program is applied to a complete weighted undirected graph with weights associated to edges only. Given a graph of this sort, METIS produces a partition, which minimizes the total weight of the cut. This ensures that the vertices in each cluster are connected by edges with high weights. We label every edge of the graph with the alignment score of the DNA sequences corresponding to the vertices incident to the edge. Higher alignment scores correspond to more closely related sequences. Since "shorter" edges have higher weights, their vertices are more likely to end up in the same cluster.

Experimental results on performance of the machine learning algorithms are included in Table 2, which uses average cluster purity as a standard measure of effectiveness of clustering algorithms. It is defined as the average ratio of a dominating class in each cluster to the cluster size, see Kaufman & Rousseeuw (1990).

For comparison, we have also included the average cluster purities of the Nearest Neighbour and k-means algorithms using simple statistics as features. We used simple counts of the numbers of occurrences of all d-graphs in the sequence for small values of d. This approach produces substantially worse results, and has been included just to illustrate the advantages of using local alignment scores.

Table 2. Average cluster purities of the clusterings obtained by machine learning algorithms

		Local alignment scores		
		BLOSUM30	**BLOSUM60**	**BLOSUM90**
k-medoids		50.12	52.48	51.51
NN		53.32	55.16	54.63
k-committees	r=2	51.49	52.20	52.72
	r=3	55.33	56.07	55.64
	r=4	59.47	60.10	59.80
	r=5	61.18	62.04	60.06
Machine learning algorithm based on graph partitioning		65.41	67.11	66.86
		Simple statistics: d-graphs		
		d=2	d=3	d=4
NN		21.78	22.23	22.75
k-means		22.02	23.21	23.75

CLUSTERINGS OF THE K-MEDOIDS MACHINE LEARNING ALGORITHM WITH ALIGNMENT SCORES

The k-medoids algorithm is a natural modification of the k-means clusterer, described by Kaufman & Rousseeuw (1990). It operates on the set of given sequences only and does not create any new sequences as means of the given ones. This is essential for the JLA data set, because there is no way of calculating new DNA sequences from the given ones.

Every alignment score between each pair of the given sequences is found once during a pre-processing stage of the algorithm, and then these scores are looked up in a table during the search for centroids. The average rates of agreement between clusters obtained using this method and biologically significant clusters obtained and published by Freeman, Jackson & Steane (2001) are presented in Table 2.

CLUSTERINGS OF THE K-COMMITTEES MACHINE LEARNING ALGORITHM WITH ALIGNMENT SCORES

This section is devoted to a novel k-committees clustering algorithm introduced and considered by Yearwood, Bagirov & Kelarev (2009) recently. Instead of considering a single centroid for each cluster, the k-committees algorithm selects a certain (very small) number of representatives for each of the k clusters to be determined. These representatives form a *committee* for the cluster. They are selected among the elements of the given finite data set – the algorithm does not compute any new points, since such computations would be impossible in the case of DNA data.

The algorithm makes a random selection of the initial centroids. Every new sequence is then assigned to the cluster of its nearest committee member. When the initial clusters have been determined, in order to begin an iteration process, the algorithm finds new committees representing the clusters. A new committee for the cluster C is then found as a set of r points $x_1,...,x_r$ in C minimizing the sum $\Sigma_{y \text{ in } C}(\min_{i=1,...,r}\|x_i-y\|)$. In other words, a new committee of the cluster C is found as a set X of r points from C such that the maximum distance of a point y in the cluster C to the set X achieves a minimum. The process then continues recursively. Every sequence assigned to the new cluster of its nearest committee member. The iterations continue until the committees stabilize or converge.

If every cluster has the same number r of committee members and it is desirable to indicate this number explicitly, then we call our method the k-committees of r representatives algorithm, or the (k,r)-*committees* algorithm.

It is well known that the k-means algorithms achieves high accuracy in situations where every cluster can be represented by one centroid. If approximations like this are not accurate, then higher success rates can be achieved by using several representatives. Intuitively speaking, this version of our k-committees algorithm approximates every cluster by a union of 'spheres'.

CLUSTERINGS OF THE NEAREST NEIGHBOUR MACHINE LEARNING ALGORITHM WITH ALIGNMENT SCORES

The section deals with an analogue of the Nearest Neighbour clustering algorithm applied to the JLA data set. The standard implementations of the Nearest Neighbour clusterer handle data represented as points in an n-dimensional Euclidean space. Usually these points correspond to the weights of features. These implementations could not be directly applied to the JLA data set, and we had to encode a modified version of the Nearest Neighbour algorithm based on optimal local alignments of the given sequences.

The Nearest Neighbour clustering algorithm chooses a random set of k sequences as representative of clusters. Then it compares new sequences with all previous sequences, finds a nearest neighbor, and assigns every sequence to the cluster of

its nearest neighbor. This process continues until all points are assigned to the clusters.

The situation in this case is more straightforward in comparison with the case of the k-means algorithm, and all modifications are easy to implement. We have found the average success rates of this method comparing clusters produced by our algorithm for various alignment scores with the clusters obtained by the Australian biologists Freeman, Jackson & Steane (2001). The results on performance of this algorithm are illustrated in Table 2, which contains average cluster purities of the clusterings obtained by these algorithms.

EXAMPLES OF SYNTHETIC DATA SETS

We have generated special new synthetic data sets, where the k-medoids algorithm turns out at least as accurate as the Nearest Neighbour, and the k-committees method happens to be the most accurate one. The ideas behind these examples are illustrated in Figures 1 and 2. Created with the PyX package in Python.

The data set in Figure 1 has two clusters. The points in the clusters are represented by small circles arranged on a large unit circle. Both the

Figure 1. Example where k-committees clusterer outperforms k-means and NN

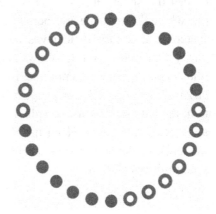

Figure 2. Example where k-committees classifier is better than k-means and NN

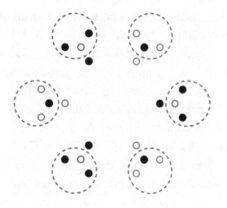

Nearest Neighbour and the k-medoids clusterer divide the large circle into two arcs approximately equal to half-circles. Hence their average cluster purity is equal to 50%. In the k-committees algorithm, if the initial randomly chosen representatives in the selected seeding pair of each cluster are adjacent to their second representative of the same pair, then the algorithm also divides the large circle into two approximately equal arcs and achieves 50% average cluster purity. The probabilities of events can be approximated by the lengths of arcs, which can be found using definite integrals. It follows that the initial representatives of each cluster are adjacent with probability approaching 1/3 for a large number of points in the set. On the other hand, if the points in each pair are separated by the points in the pair of the other cluster, then the k-committees algorithm divides the sphere into 4 approximately equal arcs, where the opposite arcs belong to the same cluster. In this case it achieves average cluster purity approaching 3/4. It follows that the average cluster purity of the k-committees is equal to $(1/3)(1/2)+(2/3)(3/4) = 2/3$. For a large number of points in the data set of our example, the approximate success rates are 50% for the Nearest Neighbour and k-medoids clusterers, and 66.67% for the k-committees clusterer.

The second example is in Figure 2. There are two classes in the data set of this diagram. They are represented by small circles and small disks (or large dots), respectively. Training set is inside large dashed circles. The success rates are 0% for the Nearest Neighbour, 50% for the k-medoids, and 65% for the k-committees algorithm with r=3.

CONCLUSION

The JLA regions are highly variable and our experimental results demonstrate that algorithms based on local alignment scores achieve sufficiently high accuracies in the agreement of their results with known biologically significant classes. The machine learning algorithm based on graph partitioning performs best for clustering, and the k-committees algorithm is the most accurate for classification of the JLA data set. The results show that the algorithms based on local alignments achieve good agreement with classifications published in the biological literature and can be used in practice. Two new synthetic data sets demonstrating that our novel k-committees algorithm can outperform both the k-medoids and Nearest Neighbour algorithms simultaneously. An interesting future direction is to investigate the performance of these algorithms for observations from large online databases of DNA sequences discussed, for example, by Baldi & Brunak (2001).

ACKNOWLEDGMENT

The first author was supported by Queen Elizabeth II Fellowship and Discovery grant DP0211866. The first and second authors were supported by Linkage grant LP0990908 from Australian Research Council. The second author was supported by Discovery grant DP0666061 from Australian Research Council. The third author was supported by Discovery grant DP0449469 from the Australian Research Council.

REFERENCES

Aha, D., & Kibler, D. (1991). Instance-based learning algorithms. *Machine Learning, 6,* 37–66. doi:10.1007/BF00153759

Bagirov, A. M., Rubinov, A. M., & Yearwood, J. (2002). A global optimization approach to classification. *Optimization and Engineering, 3,* 129–155. doi:10.1023/A:1020911318981

Bagirov, A. M., & Yearwood, J. L. (2006). A new nonsmooth optimization algorithm for minimum sum-of-squares clustering problems. *European Journal of Operational Research, 170,* 578–596. doi:10.1016/j.ejor.2004.06.014

Baldi, P., & Brunak, S. (2001). *Bioinformatics: The machine learning approach.* Cambridge, MA: MIT Press.

Bouckaert, R. R., Frank, E., Hall, M., Kirkby, R., Reutemann, P., Seewald, A., & Scuse, D. (2010). *WEKA manual for version 3-7-1.* Retrieved November 15, 2010, from http://www.cs.waikato.ac.nz/ml/weka/

Duda, R. O., Hart, P. E., & Stork, D. G. (2001). *Pattern classification* (2nd ed.). Wiley-Interscience.

Fan, R.-E., Chen, P.-H., & Lin, C.-J. (2005). Working set selection using second order information for training SVM. *Journal of Machine Learning Research, 6,* 1889–1918.

Fisher, D. (1987). Knowledge acquisition via incremental conceptual clustering. *Machine Learning, 2*(2), 139–172. doi:10.1007/BF00114265

Freeman, J. S., Jackson, H. D., Steane, D. A., McKinnon, G. E., Dutkowski, G. W., Potts, B. M., & Vaillancourt, R. E. (2001). Chloroplast DNA phylogeography of Eucalyptus globules. *Australian Journal of Botany, 49,* 585–596. doi:10.1071/BT00094

Gusfield, D. (1997). *Algorithms on strings, trees, and sequences. Computer Science and Computational Biology.* Cambridge, MA: Cambridge University Press. doi:10.1017/CBO9780511574931

Haidar, I., Kulkarni, S., & Pan, H. (2008). Forecasting model for crude oil prices based on artificial neural networks. In *Proceedings of ISSNIP 2008, Fourth International Conference Intelligent Sensors, Sensor Networks & Information Processing,* December 15-18, 2008, Sydney, (pp. 103-108).

Hall, M., Frank, E., Holmes, G., Pfahringer, B., Reutemann, P., & Witten, I. H. (2009). The WEKA data mining software: An update. *SIGKDD Explorations, 11*(1), 10–18. doi:10.1145/1656274.1656278

Hsu, C.-W., Chang, C.-C., & Lin, C.-J. (2003). *A practical guide to support vector classification.* Dept. Computer Science, National Taiwan University. Retrieved April 15, 2010, from http://www.csie.ntu.edu.tw/~cjlin

Jain, A. K., & Dubes, R. C. (1988). *Algorithms for clustering data.* London, UK: Prentice Hall.

Jain, A. K., Murty, M. N., & Flynn, P. J. (1999). Data clustering: A review. *ACM Computing Surveys, 31*(3), 264–323. doi:10.1145/331499.331504

Karypis, G., & Kumar, V. (1999). A fast and high quality multilevel scheme for partitioning irregular graphs. *SIAM Journal on Scientific Computing, 20*(1), 359–392. doi:10.1137/S1064827595287997

Kaufman, L., & Rousseeuw, P. J. (1990). *Finding groups in data: An introduction to cluster analysis.* New York, NY: John Wiley & Sons.

Keerthi, S. S., Shevade, S. K., Bhattacharyya, C., & Murthy, K. R. K. (2001). Improvements to Platt's SMO algorithm for SVM classifier design. *Neural Computation, 13*(3), 637–649. doi:10.1162/089976601300014493

Kelarev, A., Kang, B., & Steane, D. (2006). Clustering algorithms for ITS sequence data with alignment metrics. *Advances in Artificial Intelligence, 19th Australian Joint Conference on Artificial Intelligence, AI06, Lecture Notes Artificial Intelligence, 4304,* (pp. 1027-1031).

Palmer, J. D. (1985). Comparative organization of chloroplast genomes. *Annual Review of Genetics, 19,* 325–354. doi:10.1146/annurev.ge.19.120185.001545

Pan, H., Haidar, I., & Kulkarni, S. (2009). Daily prediction of short-term trends of crude oil prices using neural networks exploiting multimarket dynamics. *Frontiers of Computer Science in China, 3*(2), 177–191. doi:10.1007/s11704-009-0025-3

Raubeson, L. A., & Jansen, R. K. (2005). Chloroplast genomes of plants. In Wallingford, H. R. J. (Ed.), *Plant diversity and evolution: Genotypic and phenotypic variation in higher plants* (pp. 45–68). doi:10.1079/9780851999043.0045

Sugiura, M. (1989). The chloroplast chromosomes in land plants. *Annual Review of Cell Biology, 5,* 51–70. doi:10.1146/annurev.cb.05.110189.000411

Verma, B., & Kulkarni, S. (2007). Neural networks for content-based image retrieval. In Zhang, Y. (Ed.), *Semantic based visual information retrieval* (pp. 252–272).

WEKA. (n.d.). *Waikato environment for knowledge analysis.* Retrieved October 30, 2010, from http://www.cs.waikato.ac.nz/ml/weka

Witten, I. H., & Frank, E. (2005). *Data mining: Practical machine learning tools and techniques.* Amsterdam, The Netherlands: Elsevier/Morgan Kaufman.

Yearwood, J., Webb, D., Ma, L., Vamplew, P., Ofoghi, B., & Kelarev, A. (2009). Applying clustering and ensemble clustering approaches to phishing profiling. *Proceedings of the 8th Australasian Data Mining Conference: AusDM 2009 Data Mining and Analytics 2009,* 1-4 December 2009, Melbourne, Australia, (pp. 25-34).

Yearwood, J. L., Bagirov, A. M., & Kelarev, A. V. (2009). Optimization methods and the k-committees algorithm for clustering of sequence data. *Journal of Applied & Computational Mathematics, 1,* 92–101.

Yearwood, J. L., & Mammadov, M. (2010). *Classification technologies: Optimization approaches to short text categorization.* Hershey, PA: Idea Group Inc.

KEY TERMS AND DEFINITIONS

Alignment Scores: Scores used in the optimization of alignments of DNA sequences.

BLOSUM: Blocks of amino acid substitution matrix, is a matrix based on local alignments.

Centroid: The mean of all observations in a cluster.

Classification: The process of identifying the known classes to which new observations belong.

Clustering: The assignment of observations from a data set into subsets called clusters.

DNA Sequence: A sequence of letters representing a real DNA molecule or strand.

k-Committees Algorithm: A generalization of the k-means algorithm.

k-Means Algorithm: An iterative clustering algorithm specifying each cluster by the mean of its observations.

Machine Learning Algorithms: Algorithms designed to develop correct procedures based on empirical data.

Chapter 5
Machine Learning Applications in Radiation Therapy

Hao H. Zhang
University of Maryland School of Medicine, USA

Robert R. Meyer
University of Wisconsin-Madison, USA

Leyuan Shi
University of Wisconsin-Madison, USA

Warren D. D'Souza
University of Maryland School of Medicine, USA

ABSTRACT

Cancer is one of the most complex diseases and one of the most effective treatments, radiation therapy, is also a complicated process. Informatics is becoming a critical tool for clinicians and scientists for improvements to the treatment and a better understanding of the disease. Computational techniques such as Machine Learning have been increasingly used in radiation therapy. As complex as cancer is, this book chapter shows that a machine learning technique has the ability to provide physicians information for better diagnostic, to obtain tumor location for more accurate treatment delivery, and to predict radiotherapy response so that personalized treatment can be developed.

INTRODUCTION

Cancer is a leading cause of death worldwide and can affect people at all ages. There are over one million cases of cancer diagnosed each year just in the United States, and many times that number in other countries. About 60% of US cancer patients are treated with radiation therapy, and increas-ingly complex radiation delivery procedures are being developed in order to improve treatment outcomes. A key goal of radiation therapy is to determine appropriate values for a large set of delivery parameters in order to ensure that as large a fraction as possible of the radiation that enters the patient is delivered to the tumor as opposed to depositing it in adjacent non-cancerous organs that can be damaged by radiation (the latter are termed organs-at-risk (OARs)). As complex as

DOI: 10.4018/978-1-4666-1833-6.ch005

cancer is, radiation therapy is also a complicated process. Informatics is becoming a critical tool for clinicians and scientists for improvements to the treatment and a better understanding of the disease. Computational techniques such as Machine Learning (ML) have been increasingly used in radiation therapy to help accurately localize the tumors in images, precisely target the radiation to the tumors, analyze treatment outcomes, and improve treatment quality and patient safety.

Machine learning tools are commonly used to extract implicit, previously unknown, and potentially useful information from data. This information, which is expressed in a comprehensible form, can be used for a variety of purposes. The idea is to build programs or models that sift through raw data automatically, seeking regularities or patterns. Strong patterns, if found, will likely generalize to yield accurate predictions on future data. Machine learning algorithms need to be robust enough to cope with imperfect data and to extract regularities that are inexact but useful. In order to achieve this, machine learning algorithms typically involve solving rigorous mathematical optimization (linear or non-linear) programs to obtain the coefficients for describing regression models or to derive rules, trees and networks for classification.

Recently, machine learning has gained great popularity in many aspects of cancer research, including tumor localization, prediction of radiotherapy response and image processing and pattern recognition. Regression methods are essential to any cancer data analysis which attempts to describe the relationship between a response variable (outcome) and any number of predictor variables (input features). Regression analysis helps us understand how the typical value of the outcome changes when any one of the predictor variables is varied, while the other predictor variables are held fixed. Most commonly used methods include linear regression and ordinary least squares regression, in which the regression function is defined in terms of a finite number of unknown coefficients that are estimated from the data.

Frequently in medical image analysis, situations involving discrete variables arise. In this circumstance, machine learning still plays an essential role, because objects such as lesions, cancer foci and organs in medical images cannot be modeled accurately by simple equations. Thus, it is natural that tasks in medical image analysis require essentially "learning from examples". Logistic regression analysis extends the techniques of multiple regression analysis to research situations in which the outcome variable is categorical, that is, taking on two or more possible values. In cancer research, the goal of logistic regression analysis is to find the best fitting and most parsimonious, yet biologically reasonable model to describe the relationship between an outcome and a set of predictor or explanatory variables. But logistic regression requires many data points to ensure the stability of the model and has a disadvantage with respect to interpretability of the model in the face of multicollinearity.

One of the most popular uses of machine learning in medical image analysis is the classification of objects such as lesions into certain categories (e.g. abnormal or normal, lesions or non-lesions). This class of machine learning uses features (e.g. diameter, contrast, and circularity) extracted from segmented objects as information for classifying objects. Most commonly used techniques include artificial neural networks, support vector machines and decision trees. These methods involve solving an optimization problem in which the objective function has a measure of the errors in the model (e.g.: squared error) and may include a term that measures the complexity of the model (e.g.: norm of the weights of input features). An example of one such technique is the use of a sequential minimal optimization algorithm for "training" a support vector regression model, which employs a quadratic data fitting problem whose objective function is comprised of a weighted combination of two terms: the first term is a quadratic error measure and the second is a model complexity term defined by a norm of the weights selected for the input features. Training a support vector machine (SVM) is accomplished by the solution of a large constrained quadratic programming optimization problem in order to determine the optimal weights of those linear terms in the model.

The rest of the chapter is organized as follows: First, the authors' previous work is used as detailed examples of applying machine learning methods to radiation therapy. Then some related work by other researchers is reviewed. Section 2 shows ML applications in predicting radiation induced complications: xerostomia (dry mouth) in head and neck cancer and rectal bleeding in whole pelvis/prostate cancer. The minimum knowledge required for ML models to achieve adequate accuracy for predictions is addressed in Section 2 as well. Section 3 shows utilization of ML method in localizing thorax tumor motion in radiation therapy. Section 4 provides a summary of recent advances of ML applications in three major areas: medical image processing and diagnostics, real-time tumor localization and radiotherapy response prediction.

MODELING CLINICAL COMPLICATIONS USING MACHINE LEARNING TOOLS IN A MULTI-PLAN INTENSITY-MODULATED RADIATION THERAPY (IMRT) FRAMEWORK

Radiation treatment planning requires consideration of competing objectives: maximizing the radiation delivered to the planning target volume (PTV) and minimizing the amount of radiation delivered to all other tissues. The tradeoff between the above factors leads to consideration of multi-criteria objective techniques (Gopal & Starkschall 2002, Rosen et al. 2005, Zhang et al. 2006, Yu 1997, Xing et al. 1999, Romeijn et al. 2004, Craft & Bortfeld 2008). Despite the literature, a limitation of the current planning approach is that

the relationship between the achieved plan dose-volume (DV) or dose levels and the DV or dose constraint settings is not known *apriori*. Further, the current planning approach does not allow for inferential determination of the ideal DV constraint settings that will yield desired outcomes (achieved DV levels or plan-related complication levels).

We have previously described a multi-plan framework which provides for the generation of many plans that differ in their DV constraint settings (Meyer et al. 2007). The rationale for this work is: (1) DV constraints are implicitly handled by optimization algorithms in commercial planning systems as inequalities through the introduction of penalty variables. These penalty variables account for differences between the actual plan DV values and the DV constraint settings. As a result, the achieved DV levels for an organ-at-risk (OAR) are frequently not equal to the DV constraint settings even in the case that the constraints for that OAR are satisfied. (2) Altering the DV constraint settings for a given OAR has an effect on the actual DV values corresponding to all involved OARs in the clinical case even if the DV constraint settings on the other OARs are unchanged. (3) Without a suitable knowledge base of plans for a given patient it is generally impossible to determine the DV constraint setting ranges for each OAR that will yield the desired output DV values (and thus prevent OAR complications). It would be ideal if the computation of a limited number of plans combined with suitable modeling tools enabled the construction of a *plan surface* representing achieved DV levels for a given OAR as a function of DV constraint settings corresponding to *all* involved OARs. Taking into consideration (1)-(3) we seek to predict OAR complications on the basis of the DV constraint settings (without explicit plan computation for those settings), thereby guiding the selection of OAR constraint settings for all involved OARs.

The purpose of this section is to describe an approach to guide the selection of DV constraint settings by predicting plan-related OAR complications (and achieved DV levels as an intermediate step) as a function of DV constraint settings directly without explicit plan computation (Zhang et al. 2009a & 2009b). We hypothesize that such a prediction is possible using machine learning algorithms. We selected two frequently encountered OAR complications: xerostomia (dry mouth) in head and neck IMRT and rectal bleeding in prostate IMRT.

Dose-Volume Thresholds: Relationship to OAR Complications

Previous research has described the relationships (derived retrospectively) between plan DV levels and OAR complications. These data served as the *"ground truth"* for the actual calculation of OAR complications against which our prediction of OAR complications is compared. A large ML knowledge base was generated for one head and neck case (125 plans were generated by varying the DV constraints on the left parotid, right parotid and spinal cord) and one prostate case (256 plans were generated by varying the DV constraints on the rectum, bladder and small bowel).

Saliva Flow Rate

Retrospective studies have shown that specific volumes of the parotid glands (66%, 45% and 24%) receiving specific doses (15 Gy, 30 Gy and 45 Gy) (Gy is the symbol for Gray, which is unit of absorbed radiation dose of ionizing radiation.) correlated with post-treatment saliva flow rate (Eisbruch et al. 1999, Eisbruch et al. 2001, Chao et al. 2001). Chao et al. (2001) presented an equivalent uniform dose (EUD)-based model to calculate post-treatment saliva flow rate, which we use as the *ground truth* for each of the 125 plans. The saliva flow rate (mL/min) is normalized to that before treatment. The model is

$$F = [\exp(-A \cdot EUD_R - B \cdot EUD_R^2) + \exp(-A \cdot EUD_L - B \cdot EUD_L^2)] / 2$$

$$(1)$$

where A and B are fitted parameters (0.0315 and 0.000168 respectively), F is the expected resulting fractional saliva output, and EUD is the equivalent uniform dose to the left (L) and right (R) parotids as defined in Equation (2).

$$EUD = \left(\frac{1}{N} \sum_{i=1}^{N} D_i^a \right)^{1/a}$$

$$(2)$$

where, N is the total number of voxels corresponding to a given structure, D_i is the dose to the ith voxel, and $a = 1$, is a structure-specific parameter that describes the dose-volume effect.

Rectal Bleeding

Retrospective studies have shown a correlation between rectal bleeding and 25-70% of the rectal volume receiving 60-75 Gy (Boersma *et al.* 1998, Jackson 2001, Jackson *et al.* 2001, Yorke 2003, Fiorino *et al.* 2003, Cozzarini *et al.* 2003) (25-30% for 70 Gy, the most often cited DV level). Therefore, we used a threshold of 25%/70 Gy to determine a binary classification for the plans in the prostate case. The volume of 25% also corresponds to one of the rectum DV constraint settings in this work.

Modeling the Radiation Treatment Plan Surface

Our goal is to predict OAR complications (referred to as *labels*) during the treatment planning process as a function of the DV constraint settings (referred to as *features*) corresponding to all involved OARs. In some cases, in order to accurately predict treatment related complications, an intermediate step of modeling achieved plan DV levels (referred to as *plan properties*) corresponding to one OAR as a function of DV constraint settings (*features*) for the full set of OARs is employed (Equation 3):

$$plan\ properties_{OARi} =$$
$$f(features_{OAR1}, features_{OAR2}, ..., features_{OARn})$$
$$(3)$$

where *i* corresponds to the OAR whose plan properties are being modeled and *n* corresponds to the number of involved OARs. Details of modeling *plan properties* as a function of *features* were described previously in Meyer et al. (2007). This intermediate modeling step was utilized in the head and neck case. *Plan properties* (specifically dose to 24%, 45% and 66% of the parotids) were modeled as a function of the input constraint settings (*features*) using quadratic functions and employing linear programming data fitting tools as described in Meyer et al. (2007).

Machine Learning Algorithms

We use ML algorithms to predict treatment related complications for an OAR as a function of DV constraint settings (*features*) corresponding to all involved OARs and *modeled* achieved dose and dose-volume levels (*plan properties*) corresponding to the OAR in question if necessary as the input of Equation 4.

The goal of ML in this research is to build and validate the numerical prediction or decision models (described in Equation 4) from the knowledge base. The knowledge base is the collection of plans arising from our multi-plan framework coupled with properties of those plans.

The details of the modeling process are summarized in Figure 1. The outputs of the ML models (*labels*) are the plan-related OAR complications. In our work, *features* alone served as the input parameters in the ML model used to predict *labels* (as in the prostate case) if acceptable prediction accuracy was achieved (solid path). Otherwise, these inputs were supplemented by modeled *plan properties* (achieved DV levels), i.e., dashed path. In summary, 11 inputs (5 *features*, and 3 predicted *plan properties* for each parotid) were used to predict saliva flow rate in the head and neck case and 5 inputs (5 *features*) were used to predict Grade 2 rectal bleeding complication in the prostate case using ML. These inputs to the ML algorithms are summarized in Table 1.

Both the construction and the validation of the models were accomplished through the repeated use of a two-fold cross-validation process. In this process, the knowledge base (set of all computed IMRT plans for a case) is first randomly partitioned into *training* and *testing* subsets, each consisting of an equal number of samples (plans). A model is constructed using only the subset of the data in the *training* subset (50% of the total number of plans), and the quality of the model is evaluated by applying it to the data in the *testing* subset (data not included in the *training* subset) and assessing the accuracy of the results produced on that subset. This process was repeated 50 times and the average errors along with 95% confidence intervals are reported.

Two machine learning algorithms were explored: support vector machines (SVM) and decisions trees. While both approaches were tested for each of the two cases, it was determined that SVMs yielded superior results in predicting sa-

Equation 4.

$$complications_{OARi} = g(features_{OAR1}, ..., features_{OARn}, plan\ properties_{OARi}) = g(features, f(features))$$

Figure 1. Summary of modeling process involving ML prediction of OAR complications using features and predicted plan properties (if necessary)

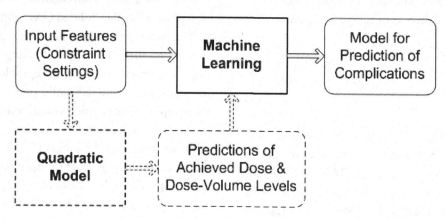

Table 1. Input variables used in modeling the achieved dose volume and dose levels in the head and neck case and the OAR complications in the head and neck and whole pelvis case

	Input Variables (dose settings at following volume levels)				
Head and Neck	33% Left Parotid	66% Left Parotid	33% Right Parotid	66% Right Parotid	Max Cord
Pelvis/ Prostate	25% Bladder	50% Bladder	25% Rectum	50% Rectum	30% Bowel

liva flow-rate and decision trees yielded superior results in predicting rectal bleeding.

Sequential Minimal Optimization for SVM

The method that we used to predict the saliva flow rate from *features* and the *modeled plan properties* was the construction of a linear model (Equation 4) via a sequential minimal optimization (SMO) algorithm (Platt 1999, Shevade et al. 2000) for "training" a support vector regression model, which is essentially a quadratic data fitting error minimization problem whose objective function is comprised of a weighted combination of two terms: the first term is a quadratic error measure and the second is a model complexity term defined by a norm of the weights selected for the input features. The SMO algorithm employs a linear model of the form $k + l\,u$ where u denotes the vector of input variables and k and l denote the fitting parameters

(k a scalar, l a vector) to be generated by SMO. Training a SVM is accomplished by the solution of a large constrained quadratic programming optimization problem in order to determine the optimal weights of those linear terms. In support vector regression, an accuracy threshold ε is set so that model prediction errors that are below this threshold yield a penalty of 0 in the objective function. In order to model these error thresholds functions, appropriate inequality constraints are used in the weight optimization problem:

minimize

$$\frac{1}{2}ll + c(dd + ee)$$

subject to

$$-d^i - \varepsilon \le p^i - k - l \cdot u^i \le \varepsilon + e^i$$
$$\text{for } i = 1,...,K \quad d \ge 0, e \ge 0$$

where, c is a weighting factor for the sum of errors terms $dd+ee$ and ll is a model complexity measure. d and e are variables measuring violation of the threshold.

Decision Trees for Binary Classification

The binary classification method in predicting Grade 2 rectal bleeding is an optimized decision tree, whose generation process via supervised learning is outlined below (1-5). Referencing Figure 2, note that the non-leaf nodes (that is, the nodes that have successor nodes below them, shown as ellipses in Figure 2) represent univariate inequality tests that are followed by further tests at lower nodes until the final tests leading to the leaf nodes (shown as rectangles in Figure 2) yield classification decisions (Quinlan 1993, Witten & Frand 2005).

A general approach to the construction of decision trees starts with the selection of a branching test at the root node at the top of the tree and can be summarized as following:

1. Choose an attribute-value pair that leads to the best partition of the training instances with respect to the output attribute.
2. Create a separate branch for each range of value of the chosen attribute.
3. Divide the instances into subgroups corresponding to the attribute value range of the chosen node.
4. For each subgroup, terminate the attribute partitioning process if:
    a) All members of a subgroup have the same value for the output attribute.
    b) No further distinguishing attributes can be determined. Label the branch with the output value seen by the majority of remaining instances.
5. Else, for each subgroup created in 3 for which the attribute partitioning process is not terminated in 4 at a leaf, repeat the above branching process.

This stage of the algorithm is based on the training data, and generally produces a large and complex decision tree that correctly classifies all of the training instances. In the second stage of the tree generation process, this decision tree is then pruned by considering the test data and removing parts of the tree that have a relatively high error rate or provide little gain in statistical accuracy.

Figure 2. Optimized decision tree algorithm schematic

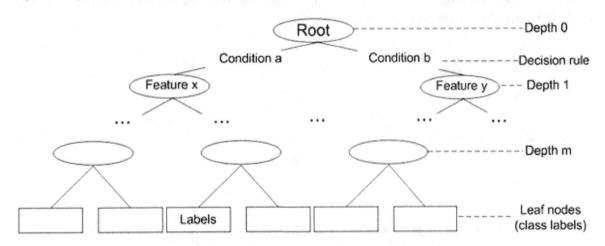

ML Modeling Results

Modeling IMRT Treatment Plan Properties

We used Equation 3 to determine the achieved *plan properties* as a function of *features* in the head and neck case. Figures 3 shows the results of modeling *plan properties* for the left and right parotids, respectively, i.e., the comparison between the predicted *plan properties* and the actual *plan properties*. The indices of the 125 treatment plans are reordered in each subfigure, so that the displayed achieved doses are in increasing order. This reordering is done to show the distribution of the actual delivered doses and to better allow comparisons of delivered doses (red points) with the corresponding doses as predicted by Equation 3 (blue points). As we can see, the relative prediction errors varied from 0 to 6%.

Prediction of Saliva Flow Rate

The results for predicted saliva flow rate using the SMO algorithm are shown in Figure 4. The x-axis was the actual flow rate (normalized to the pre-treatment saliva flow rate) for each of the 125 plans in the knowledge base (plans were sorted according to increasing saliva flow-rate).

The actual saliva flow rate was obtained using Equation 1. The y-axis was the mean predicted saliva flow-rate obtained from the 2-fold cross-validation process. From Figure 4, it can be seen that the normalized saliva flow rate ranged from 20-30% for the case considered. The further a point is from the diagonal (which represents equality of actual and predicted values), the larger the prediction error is. The mean absolute error (averaged over 50 simulations in cross-validation) for saliva flow-rate prediction compared with the ground truth obtained from the EUD-exponential model in Equation 1 was 0.42% with a 95% confidence interval [0.41%, 0.43%].

Classification of Rectal Bleeding

Figure 5 shows a representative decision tree resulting from 2-fold cross-validation method applied to the 256 prostate treatment plans. Each decision node of the tree represents one dose-volume histogram (DVH) constraint, which is an input to the planning system. For example, *25Bldr* is the DVH constraint setting for 25% of the bladder volume. The numbers on the branches show the dose level partitions. Each leaf node represents a classification result, and the number in parenthesis is the number of instances that were classified correctly/incorrectly. Each leaf

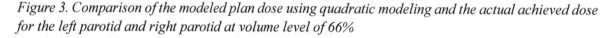

Figure 3. Comparison of the modeled plan dose using quadratic modeling and the actual achieved dose for the left parotid and right parotid at volume level of 66%

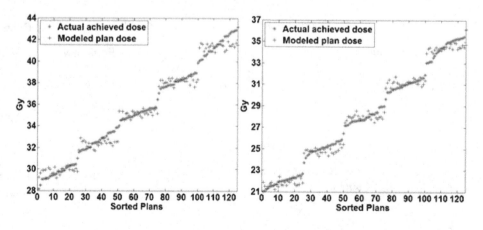

Figure 4. Comparison of the mean (obtained from the 2-fold cross-validation process) predicted saliva flow rate (normalized to the pre-treatment saliva flow rate) using Equation 4 to the actual saliva flow rate (calculated using Equation 1)

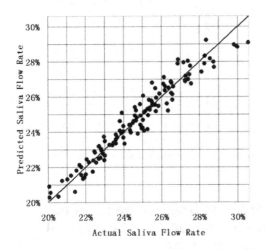

OAR Complications as a Function of DV Constraints

Figure 6 shows an example of the results for the prediction of normalized saliva flow rate as a function of the DV constraints using the approach described in this work. The contours in each plot correspond to the percentage saliva flow rate normalized to the pre-treatment saliva flow rate as a function of DV constraint settings for two of the OARs and a fixed constraint setting for the third OAR. It can be observed that the plot for saliva flow rate as a function of the DV constraint settings on one parotid gland (left or right) and the maximum dose constraint to the spinal cord for a fixed DV constraint setting for the other parotid gland is near linear or near quadratic

Figure 7 shows an example of the results for the prediction of Grade 2 rectal complications. The shaded region in the plot corresponds to the complication region for a range of DV constraint settings for two OARs and a fixed constraint setting for the third OAR. We attribute the unshaded region (lack of rectal bleeding) in Figure 7 corresponding to increasing the bladder and bowel

node corresponds to the set of inequalities on the path from the top-most node to that leaf. Using 2-fold cross validation 50 times, we achieved an average classification accuracy of 97.04% with a 95% confidence interval of [96.67%, 97.41%] for Grade 2 rectal bleeding.

Figure 5. Decision tree for Grade 2 rectal complication classification - An example

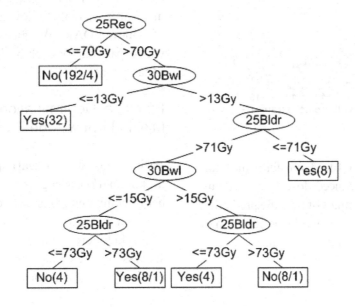

Figure 6. Prediction of saliva flow rate (expressed as a percentage of the pre-treatment saliva flow rate) as a function of the dose constraint settings for the three OARs: (a) fixed cord constraint, ranges for left parotid (LP) and right parotid (RP), (b) fixed RP constraint, ranges for cord and LP and (c) fixed LP constraint, ranges for cord and RP

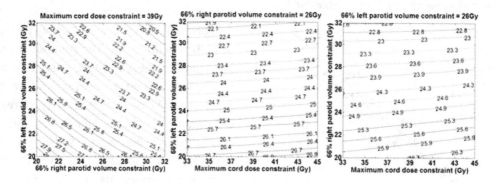

Figure 7. Prediction of Grade 2 rectal complications as a function of the dose constraint settings when fixing rectum constraint and ranging for bladder and bowel

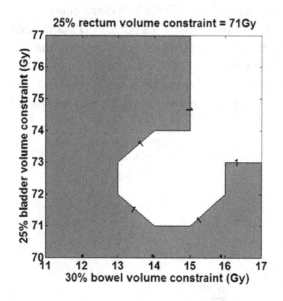

Minimum Knowledge Base for Predicting OAR DV Levels and Complications

Computerized planning for IMRT is a complex process involving a large amount of input data and vast numbers of delivery variables whose calculation for a given patient may pose significant computational challenges. Generation of the full knowledge base (described above) automatically without planner intervention takes approximately 20-24 hours. We also investigated if a much smaller knowledge base is adequate for the development of models that allow accurate predictions of achieved OAR DV values and complications with 5 patients for each of the two disease sites (Zhang et al. 2010).

Empirical Determination of the Minimal Knowledge Base

settings to an associated dose transfer to the bladder and bowel and reduced dose to the rectum. These results are examples of how the prediction of OAR complications can guide the selection of DV constraint settings for all OARs.

We introduce an empirical approach to determine the minimal knowledge base size (minimum number of computed plans) needed to build accurate representations of the IMRT plan surface (as shown in Figure 6 and 7). Our approach involved successively reducing the size of the assumed explicitly computed knowledge base, referred to as the training data, to build the machine learning model and then evaluating the model on the remaining data (testing data). The training data is used to build the model (to obtain functions (see equations 3 and 4)), and then the model is applied to the testing data to determine model accuracy. The size of the training data thus corresponds to the assumed computed knowledge base required to obtain the model. Knowledge bases of various sizes (comprising subsets of the full knowledge base) were used to determine the sizes needed to obtain accurate plan surface models and accurate complication predictions. The testing data consisted of the full knowledge base less the number of plans in the training data set. We used knowledge bases corresponding to 15, 30, 62, and 125 plans in the training data for the head and neck cases and 16, 32, 64, 128, 256 plans for the whole pelvis/prostate cases.

To obtain accurate statistical measures of our method, for each training data size and each patient, fifty instances of random samples were tested and the results corresponding to the average, quartiles and confidence intervals over the testing data sets were determined. For example, when using 15 plans in the training data, a single sample consisted of 15 plans randomly selected from the total 125 plans to build the model. The model was tested on the rest of the 110 plans. This process was repeated 50 times (each time 15 different plans were randomly selected) to obtain the average result. Relative prediction error for continuous values (achieved DV levels and saliva flow rate) and correct prediction percentage for categorical values (grade 2 rectal bleeding complication) were analyzed over 10 patients (5 patients for each disease site). If full knowledge base was used as training data (e.g. 125 plans for head and neck patients or 256 plans for prostate patients), the average of the modeling errors (only based on training data sets) of the 5 patients were reported.

Prediction Results of Parotid and Rectum DV Levels

Figure 8 shows the distribution of errors in predicting DV levels (D66 and D25) of left and right parotid and rectum respectively. The line in the middle of each box is the median of the mean errors of the predictions, and the lower and upper edges of boxes represent 25% and 75% quartiles over the 50 runs in five cases. The whiskers are extreme ranges of the predictions (as explained below). The points outside the whiskers are outliers. The extreme ranges were decided as follow: points are shown as outliers if they are larger than $2q_3$-q_1 or smaller than $2q_1$-q_3, where q_1 and q_3 correspond to the 25th and 75th percentiles, respectively. The notches within the boxes are 95% confidence intervals on the median. The errors increase when the knowledge base sizes decrease, but remain acceptably small over a wide range of knowledge bases. For each head and neck patient, when using different knowledge base sizes, the errors ranged from less than 1% to slightly more than 3% in predicting DV levels of parotids. From patient to patient, the variation was less than 2%. Note that the ranges of errors also increase when the knowledge base sizes decrease. This means the model stability decreases for smaller knowledge bases. Overall, 30 plans were sufficient to predict achieved DV levels of parotid with less than 3% relative error. For the pelvis/prostate patients, the prediction results for rectum DV levels (D25) were very stable compared to predicting DV levels of parotids in the head and neck cases. The errors for rectum levels ranged from less than 1% to a little more than 1%. This range is tighter than predicting DV levels of the parotids, which means higher accuracy was achieved for the rectum than the parotid. 32 plans were sufficient to predict achieved DV levels of rectum with less than 2% relative error.

Figure 8. Distribution of relative errors in predicting D66 for the left parotid and right parotid in the head and neck cases and D25 in the prostate cases as a function of knowledge base size

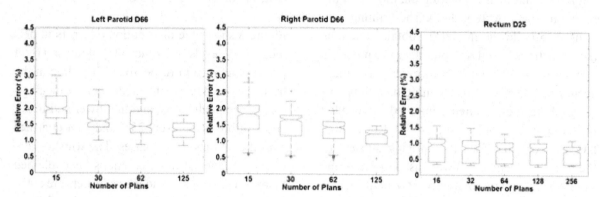

Prediction Results of Saliva Flow Rate and Rectal Bleeding

Figure 9 shows the distribution of errors when predicting saliva flow rate and rectal bleeding. The performance of our approach is very stable when predicting saliva flow rate (error always less than 2%). The variation from patient to patient was also less than 2%. It is seen that when the knowledge base size decreases, there are more prediction outliers (more outlier occurrences in the model validation process). Our results suggest that 30 plans were sufficient to predict saliva flow rate with less than 2% relative error. In predict-

ing rectal bleeding complications (formulated as a binary classification), the correct prediction percentage ranged from 80% to 98%. When the knowledge base decreases, not only does the accuracy decrease, but low-accuracy outliers (less than 70% correct prediction percentage) appear as well. Overall, rectal bleeding complications can be predicted with greater than 90% accuracy using 64 plans.

The goal of this research was to investigate the feasibility of predicting OAR complications (*labels*) as a function of input *features* or DV constraint settings during the IMRT treatment planning process. Conventional IMRT treatment

Figure 9. Distribution of relative errors in predicting saliva flow rate and correct prediction percentage in predicting rectal bleeding as a function of knowledge base size

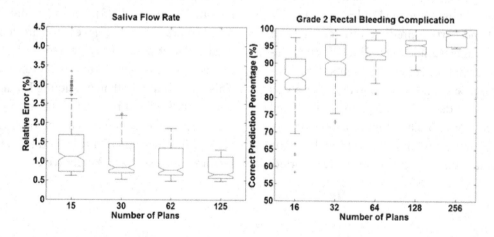

planning is usually an iterative process after plan generation. Planners evaluate the plan and modify the plan if the plan quality is not adequate. Our results show that the ability to predict OAR complications as a function of DV constraint settings could guide the selection of such *features* (corresponding to all involved OARs in the case). Using the methods described here, plan-related OAR complications can be predicted as a function of DV constraint settings. ML tools can be used to guide planners to select DV constraint settings corresponding to all involved OARs in a knowledge-driven manner.

MACHINE LEARNING FOR INTRA-FRACTION TUMOR MOTION MODELLING WITH RESPIRATORY SURROGATES

Advances in radiation therapy for cancer have made it possible to deliver conformal doses to the tumor while sparing normal healthy tissues. However, one of the difficulties radiation oncologists face is targeting moving tumors, such as those in the thorax, which can change position during normal respiration. Tumor motion can be determined by directly monitoring tumor position using continuous x-ray imaging or electromagnetic transponders placed in the tumor that emit a signal. These approaches require potentially unnecessary radiation to the patient or acquisition of expensive technology. Alternatively, one can image the patient intermittently to determine tumor location and external markers placed on the patient's torso. The external surrogates can then be used to determine an inferential model that would determine the tumor position as a function of external surrogates. These external surrogates can be monitored continuously in order to determine the real-time position of the tumor. In order to do that, it is necessary to know whether the relationship between internal tissue motion and external tissue motion is constant during a single treatment

fraction. In this section, we evaluate a machine learning algorithm for inferring intra-fraction tumor motion from external markers using a database obtained via the Cyberknife Synchrony™ system (D'Souza et al. 2009).

Cyberknife System Data

The Cyberknife Synchrony™ system intermittently localizes fiducials implanted in or near the tumor using fluoroscopy and models tumor positions from continuously tracked optical marker positions. We analyzed a database of Cyberknife system files comprising 128 treatment fractions from 62 lung cancer patients, 10 treatment fractions from 5 liver cancer patients, and 48 treatment fractions from 23 pancreas cancer patients. The Cyberknife files for each fraction included both the 3D positions of three optical markers affixed to the abdomen and/or chest and the 3D positions of the centroid of a set of three fiducial markers implanted in or near the tumor (determined through fluoroscopic imaging). Each fraction contained 40-112 (mean=62) stereoscopic radiographs acquired over a mean treatment fraction of 64 minutes. In next subsection, we show how we used these Cyberknife system data to create and test a machine learning model of tumor motion from external markers.

Machine Learning for the Prediction of Tumor Positions

The goal of machine learning is to provide a framework for building and validating numerical prediction or decision models from a knowledge base. In this tumor position prediction context, the knowledge base is the collection of positions from different external markers coupled with properties of those markers (actual position of the tumor). The model that is constructed below for numerical prediction (real coordinates) employs multivariate quadratic functions (whose input variables (features) in the machine learning context, are coordinates of external markers). The outputs of the model (labels in machine learning) are the properties that are of interest - in this case, true position of tumor represented by fiducial markers. Both the construction and the validation of the models are accomplished in conjunction with the repeated use of the cross-validation process. The quality of the model is evaluated by applying it to the data in the testing subset and assessing the accuracy of the results produced on that subset. The method that we used to predict the continuous value of positions is SMO for training a support vector regression model as described in previous section.

We also used same empirical approach to reduce the knowledge base size (i.e., number of fluoroscopic image acquisitions) based on machine learning approaches. The size of the training data corresponds to the knowledge base, the number of fluoroscopic image acquisitions required to obtain the model. We used 50%, 25%, 12.5%, 6% of the full knowledge base as training data and the rest of knowledge base as testing data. For each fractional value 20 random samples of the corresponding size were used as training sets. Mean absolute prediction errors were reported. (Note that the number of data points in each fraction of each patient was different. Future work will investigate same number of data points in the training data set, which means always using the same number of fluoroscopic image acquisitions to build the model.)

Results of Tumor Positions Modeling

We tested our method on three motion directions of tumors (superior-inferior (SI), medial-lateral (ML) and anterior-posterior (AP)) of the three types of cancer: lung, liver and pancreas. Each motion direction was modeled separately. The mean absolute error in millimeter (mm) was reported. The detailed results are shown in Table 2. From Table 2, we can see that the predicted errors using machine learning increased monotonically when using fewer data points in the training set. We can achieve less than 2mm to 3mm error with 5 to 15 training data points for all three tumor sites. Based on real-time application experience, we believe that using 12.5% of the full knowledge base (8 data points on average) can provide enough prediction accuracy, which corresponding to 8 fluoroscopic image acquisitions.

Figure 10 shows the details of prediction errors when using about 8 data points as training set in machine learning algorithm. We can see that tumor motions on the medial-lateral directions can be predict with the highest accuracy. Prediction accuracy on anterior-posterior directions is the second highest and on superior-inferior direction is the lowest. From Figure 10, there is no clear evidence showing which of the three tumor sites could be modeled more accurately.

We further investigated the results by looking at the distributions of the prediction errors. Figure 11 shows the boxplot of these errors. The lines in the middle of each box in the figure were the median of the errors of the predictions and the

Table 2. Tumor motion prediction error summary (in mm)

	Lung			Liver			Pancreas		
	SI	**ML**	**AP**	**SI**	**ML**	**AP**	**SI**	**ML**	**AP**
50%	0.8	0.7	0.8	0.9	0.5	0.6	0.9	0.8	0.8
25%	0.9	0.8	0.9	1.1	0.6	0.6	1.0	0.9	0.9
12.5%	1.2	0.9	1.1	1.5	0.8	0.9	1.3	1.1	1.1
6%	2.1	1.7	2.0	3.0	1.4	1.6	2.2	1.8	1.8

Figure 10. Prediction summary using 12.5% of full knowledge base as training set for lung, liver, and pancreas cases

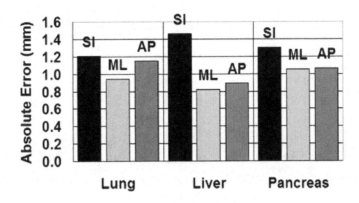

lower and upper edge of boxes represented 25% and 75% quantiles. The whiskers were estimated extreme ranges of the predictions (not considering outliers). The points outside the whiskers were outliers. The notches within the boxes were 95% confidence intervals on the median. From Figure 11 we see that the stability of machine learning algorithm varied when applied to different tumor sites: there were more outliers for the lung cases than liver and pancreas cases and the outliers ranged from more than 2mm to 1cm.

Because more prediction outliers occurred for lung patients, we plotted the error distributions for different tumor locations within the lung patients (Figure 12). The patients were differentiated to six categories: left upper lobe, left lower

lobe, right upper lobe, right middle lung, right lower lobe and other locations. From Figure 12, we noticed that for the left and right lower lobe the outliers were under 8mm, for the right upper lobe the outliers were under 5mm and right middle lung the outliers were under 3mm. For other locations, the outliers spread to 1cm. Most outliers occurred for the left upper lobe and other locations. This provided information about which tumor location in the lung had a better chance to be modelled accurately.

Our aim for this initial research was to investigate machine learning as a method for creating models of instantaneous tumor positions based on a limited number of fluoroscopic image acquisitions. By minimizing image acquisitions, we

Figure 11. Prediction error distributions with 12.5% of full knowledge base as training set

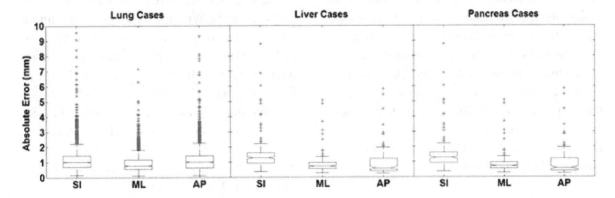

Figure 12. Error distributions of lung tumor position prediction within different locations

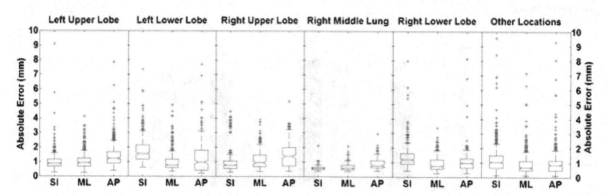

decrease the in-room time for the patient and improve the efficiency of treatment delivery. We were able to achieve accurate intra-fraction motion modelling using 8 (mean error less than 2mm) samples corresponding to individual image acquisitions. Thus, our results indicate that machine learning algorithm shows potential for use in intra-fraction motion modelling in real-time systems. Future work will focus on investigating the consequences of prospectively (rather than randomly) selecting the training data points.

REVIEW OF RECENT ADVANCEMENT OF ML APPLICATIONS IN RADIATION THERAPY

In recent years, there have been special sessions dedicated to applications in radiation therapy at international machine learning conferences. Even in national medical conference (2010 American Association of Physicists in Medicine annual meeting), there has been one special session dedicate to machine learning in radiation therapy. It is therefore appropriate to survey advancements in this area. The purpose of this section is to provide a summary of the research results in the radiotherapy community presented in these conferences and published in medical journals.

Machine Learning for Medical Image Processing

Machine learning plays an essential role in medical image analysis, because objects such as lesions and organs in medical images cannot be modeled accurately by simple equations; thus, tasks in medical image analysis require essentially "learning from examples". One of the most popular uses of machine learning in medical image analysis is the classification of objects such as lesions into certain categories (e.g., abnormal or normal, lesions or non-lesions). This class of machine leaning uses features (e.g., diameter, contrast, and circularity) extracted from segmented objects as information for classifying the objects. Machine learning techniques in this class include linear discriminant analysis, a k-nearest neighbor classifier, an artificial neural network, and a support vector machine.

Early uses of ML were by Wolberg et al. (1994 & 1995) of the Wisconsin group. They built an interactive computer system via ML to evaluate and diagnose breast cancer based on cytologic features derived directly from a digital scan of fine-needle aspirate (FNA) slides. FNA accuracy is traditionally limited by, among other factors, the subjective interpretation of the aspirate. The authors increased breast FNA accuracy by coupling digital image analysis methods with ML techniques. The ML approach captured nuclear features that were prognostically more accurate than estimates based on tumor size and lymph node status. The method was tested on consecutive series of 569 patients. A 166-patient subset provided the data for the prognostic study. An additional 75 consecutive, new patients provided samples to test the diagnostic system. The projected prospective accuracy of the diagnostic system was estimated to be 97% by 10-fold cross-validation, and the actual accuracy on 75 new samples was 100%. The projected prospective accuracy of the prognostic system was estimated to be 86% by leave-one-out testing.

Based on the evidence suggesting that ML can help improve the diagnostic performance of radiologists in their image interpretations, many investigators have continued the research in developing schemes for detection/diagnosis of lesions in medical images, such as detection of lung nodules in chest radiographs (Suzuki et al. 2005a & 2005b), and thoracic CT (Arimura et al. 2004), detection of microcalcifications or masses in mammography, breast MRI, and detection of polyps in CT colonography (Suzuki et al. 2006 & 2008).

For example, a supervised lesion segmentation method based on a massive-training artificial neural network (MTANN) filter in a computer aided diagnostic scheme for detection of lung nodules in CT was developed by Suzuki et al. (2003). Tested on 69 instances of lung cancer patient data, the MTANN filter yielded a sensitivity of 96% (66/69), with 1.2 false positives per CT slice. Overall, the MTANN-based segmentation method was effective in segmenting lesions in medical images with improved sensitivity and specificity.

In mammography, ML classifiers were proposed for breast cancer diagnosis (Ramos-Pollán et al. 2011). The method was evaluated to classify feature vectors extracted from segmented regions (pathological lesion or normal tissue) on craniocaudal (CC) and/or mediolateral oblique (MLO) mammography image views, providing BI-RADS diagnosis (BI-RADS stands for breast imaging

reporting and data system, which is a scheme for putting the findings of mammograms into a small number of well-defined categories). Appropriate combinations of image processing and normalization techniques were applied to reduce image artifacts and increase mammogram details. 286 cases extracted from an image repository, where specialized radiologists segmented regions on CC and/or MLO images (biopsies provided the golden standard), were evaluated. Around 20,000 ML configurations were tested with different parameter combinations, obtaining classifiers achieving an area under the ROC curve of 0.996 when combining features vectors extracted from CC and MLO views of the same case.

Machine Learning in Real-Time Tumor Localization

In recent years, the substantial risks of surgical resection of tumors in the lungs, liver, and pancreas, and the fact that a large percentage of patients are not surgical candidates because their disease is too far advanced or their health is poor, have motivated the investigation of stereotactic body radiation therapy. Stereotactic body radiation therapy involves delivery of a high dose of radiation that conforms precisely to the tumor volume in just a few fractions with the objective of tumor ablation.

However, a significant challenge of radiation therapy with advanced technologies is the great need of delivering very precise treatments to moving targets during respiration. Therefore, methods to track tumors during normal respiration need to be developed. The extent of respiratory motion for tumors in various organs is observed with technologies such as fluoroscopy, surrogate markers (spirometry, fiducials), 4D-CT and dynamic MRI. Then a tumor motion compensation method can be employed. A number of real-time technologies are being developed to account for respiratory motion. These systems require real-time radiation target position information for both respiratory gating and tracking. Classification schemes based on machine learning techniques such as artificial neural networks (Lin et al. 2009b) and SVM (Cui et al. 2008) were used to separate the fluoroscopic images into beam on or off classes. ML regression models have also been proposed to localize tumor position in real-time as we have shown in previous section.

A traditional technique to account for tumor motion is to expand treatment target with margins. The undesirable outcome of these margins is higher doses to the surrounding normal tissue and the increased risk of toxicity. ML methods, such as neural networks, have been used for real-time spatial and temporal tracking of radiotherapy treatment targets during free breathing (Murthy et al. 2002, Sharp et al. 2004, Isaakson et al. 2005, Murphy & Dieterich 2006). These techniques will allow the reduction and possible elimination of dose-limiting motion margins in external-beam radiation delivery plans. Murphy has shown that, despite the widely varying characteristics of 27 test examples of breathing, neural network based ML technique was able to make temporal predictions 300 ms into the future with high accuracy (Murthy 2008), which enabled its use in radiotherapy for motion tracking.

Ruan & Keall (2010) extended ML methods from a single dimension to multi-dimensional processing. However, the amount of data required for such extensions grows exponentially with the dimensionality of the problem. They investigated a multi-dimensional prediction scheme based on kernel density estimation in an augmented covariate-response space. Principal component analysis (PCA) was utilized to construct a proper low-dimensional feature space, where kernel density estimation is feasible with the limited training data. The dimension reduction idea proposed in their work was closely related to feature extraction used in ML, particularly SVMs. To test the performance of their method, 159 lung target motion traces were obtained with a Synchrony respiratory tracking system. Prediction performance of the low-dimensional feature learning-based multi-dimensional prediction method was compared against an independent prediction method where prediction was conducted along each physical coordinate independently. The proposed method showed uniformly better performance, and reduced the case-wise 3D root mean squared prediction error by about 30-40%.

While tracking implanted fiducial markers showed sufficient accuracy, this procedure may not be widely accepted due to the risk of pneumothorax. Cui et al. (2008) proposed a gating method that includes formulating the problem as a classification problem and generating the gating signals from fluoroscopic images without implanted fiducial markers via template matching methods (Cui et al. 2007). The classification problem (gating the beam to be ON or OFF) was solved by SVM. The ground truth was the reference gating signal, which was manually determined by a radiation oncologist. The proposed technique was tested on 5 sequences of fluoroscopic images from 5 lung cancer patients and compared to template matching method alone. SVM was slightly more accurate on average (1-3%) than using template matching method by itself with respect to delivering the target dose. SVM is thus a potentially precise and efficient algorithm for generating gating signals for radiotherapy.

In order to compensate for the shortcomings of template matching methods, which may fail when the tumor boundary is unclear in fluoroscopic images, Lin et al. (2009a) proposed a framework of markerless gating and tracking based on machine learning algorithms. A similar two-class classification tracking problem was solved by PCA and Artificial Neural Network (ANN). The tracking problem was formulated as a regression task, which employs the correlation between the tumor position and nearby surrogate anatomic features in the image. Proposed methods were tested on 10 fluoroscopic image sequences of 9 patients. For gating, the target coverage (the precision) ranges from 90% to 99%, with mean of

96.5%. For tracking, the mean localization error is about 2.1 pixels and the maximum error at 95% confidence level is about 4.6 pixels (pixel size is about 0.5 mm). Following the same framework, different combinations of dimensionality reduction techniques (PCA and four nonlinear manifold learning methods) and two machine learning classification methods (ANN and SVM) were evaluated later (Lin et al. 2009b). PCA combined with either ANN or SVM achieved a better performance than the other nonlinear manifold learning methods. Overall, ANN combined with PCA is a better candidate than other combinations for real-time gated radiotherapy. Generalized linear discriminant analysis (GLDA) was recently applied to the same problem (Li et al. 2009). The fundamental difference relative to conventional dimensionality reduction techniques is that GLDA explicitly takes into account the label information available in the training set and therefore is efficient for discrimination among classes. It was demonstrated that GLDA outperformed PCA in terms of classification accuracy and target coverage at a lower nominal duty cycle.

Machine Learning for Predicting Radiotherapy Response

Radiation-induced outcomes are determined by complex interactions between treatment techniques, cancer pathology, and patient-related physiological and biological factors. A common obstacle to building maximally predictive treatment outcome models for clinical practice in radiation oncology is the failure to capture this complexity of heterogeneous variable interactions and the ability to adapt outcome models across different institutions. Methods based on ML can identify data patterns, variable interactions, and higher order relationships among prognostic variables. In addition, they have the ability to generalize to unseen data (El Naqa 2010). In this section, we briefly summarize the work to utilizing ML for predicting radiotherapy response.

As in the case of our example of using constraints to build treatment plan surface to predict organ complications, Buettner et al. (2009) propose to predict radiation-induced rectal bleeding and loose stools using Bayesian logistic regression with high-order interactions. Binary features (constraint satisfied or failed) were used as predictive variables in multivariate logistic regression to build the probabilistic model. The 10-fold cross-validation of the model for loose stools resulted in an average area under the ROC curve (AUC) of 0.72 with a standard deviation of 0.11. For rectal bleeding an AUC of 0.64 ± 0.08 was achieved. From the results of these models, they were able to derive a new type of geometrical dosimetric constraint which showed more predictive power than traditional constraints. Similarly, Bayesian logistic regression together with feature selection was also applied to predict esophagitis and xerostomia (El Naqa et al. 2006).

In addition to applications in tumor motion localization, neural networks and decision trees have also been utilized in predicting radiotherapy response because of their ability to detect nonlinear patterns in the data. In particular, neural networks were used to model post-radiation treatment outcomes for cases of lung injury (Munley et al. 1999, Su et al. 2005) and prostate cancer (Lennernas et al. 2004). However, these studies have mainly focused on using a single class of neural networks, namely feed-forward neural networks with different types of activation functions. A different neural network architecture, referred to as generalized regression neural network, was shown to outperform classical neural networks (El Naqa et al. 2005). The major drawback of using neural network methods was that they are based on greedy heuristic algorithms with no guarantee of global optimality or robustness, in addition to the extensive computational burden associated with them. This drawback led to introduction of SVM methods from medical imaging applications (El Naqa et al. 2002 & 2004) to the area repose modeling (El Naqa et al. 2008).

The Washington University group applied ML techniques for the prediction of radiation pneumonitis in lung cancer patients (Oh et al. 2009). The authors compared several widely used classification algorithms in the machine learning field, including SVM, decision trees, random forest and naïve bayes, to distinguish between different risk groups of pneumonitis. The performance of these classification algorithms was evaluated in conjunction with several feature selection strategies (SVM-recursive feature elimination, correlation based, chi-square and information gain based feature selection) and the impact of the feature selection on performance was further evaluated. In conclusion, kernel based SVMs showed greatly higher Matthew's correlation coefficient (a metric that is widely used as a performance measure) values than not only linear SVM but also other competing classification algorithms after correction for imbalance.

Oh & El Naqa (2009) continued research along this line for lung cancer patients. Instead of SVM, a Bayesian network was applied to not only predict the probability that a given treatment plan for a patient will result in a treatment complication but also for developing better understanding of the clinical decision making process. Feature selection was used to reduce the time and space complexity associated with Bayesian structure learning. The authors demonstrated that Bayesian network was able to identify the relationship between the dose-volume parameters and pneumonitis (distinguishing the control group from the disease group based on the trained Bayesian network).

Das et al. (2008) provided a simple hybrid ML method, in which they fuse the results of four different machine learning models (Boosted Decision Trees, Neural Networks, Support Vector Machines, Self Organizing Maps) to predict the risk of lung pneumonitis in patients undergoing thoracic radiotherapy. Fusion was achieved by simple averaging of the 10-fold cross validated predictions for each patient from all four models. To reduce prediction dependence on the manner

in which the data set was split, 10-fold cross-validation was repeated 100 times for random data splitting. The area under the receiver operating characteristics curve for the fused cross-validated results was 0.79, higher than the individual models and with lower variance.

Lung cancer has been the most frequent tested disease site utilizing ML, especially via neural networks (Chen et al. 2007a) and SVM (Chen et al. 2007b, Dehing-Oberije et al. 2009). However, Bayesian networks were hypothesized to have an advantage with respect to handling missing data. Dekker et al. (2009) provided a comparison between an SVM and Bayesian network model regarding the handling of missing data for predicting survival in lung cancer. A Bayesian network model outperformed the SVM model in the case of missing data. If an important feature was missing that could not be inferred by the Bayesian model, a strong change in AUC was noticed (AUC resulted from Bayesian network was from 0.72 to 0.82 while AUC resulted from SVM was 0.68 to 0.76) when the patients with missing data are removed from the validation set.

To emphasize the advantage of ML in dealing with heterogeneous data from multiple institutions, El Naqa et al. (2009) described a ML methodology that can screen for nonlinear relations among prognostic variables and generalize to unseen data. An independent RTOG dataset from multiple institutions was used for model validation. The database contained different cancer disease sites including complications such as esophagitis, pneumonitis and xerostomia. The distribution of patient groups was analyzed using PCA to uncover potential nonlinear behavior. Results suggested that an SVM kernel method provided superior performance on leave-one-out testing compared to logistic regression and neural networks in cases in which the data exhibited nonlinear behavior on PCA. In prediction of esophagitis and pneumonitis endpoints, 21% and 60% improvements was reported, respectively.

CONCLUSION

Cancer is a leading cause of death worldwide and most patients go through radiation therapy during their treatment. As complex as cancer is, we have shown that machine learning technique has the ability to provide physicians information for better diagnostic, to obtain tumor location for more accurate treatment delivery, and to predict radiotherapy response so that personalized treatment can be developed.

ACKNOWLEDGMENT

The authors would like to thank Dr Ruijiang Li for sharing his presentation at 2010 AAPM annual conference. The research presented in this chapter was supported in part by a grant from the NIH/NCI CA130814 and by grants from the NSF DMI-0355567 and DMI-0400294.

REFERENCES

Arimura, H., Katsuragawa, S., Suzuki, K., Li, F., Shiraishi, J., Sone, S., & Doi, K. (2004). Computerized scheme for automated detection of lung nodules in low-dose computed tomography images for lung cancer screening. *Academic Radiology, 11*, 617–629. doi:10.1016/j.acra.2004.02.009

Boersma, L., van den Brink, M., Bruce, A., Shouman, T., Gras, L., te Velde, A., & Lebesque, J. (1998). Estimation of the incidence of late bladder and rectum complications after high-dose (70-78Gy) conformal radiotherapy for prostate cancer, using dose-volume histograms. *International Journal of Radiation Oncology • Biology • Physics, 41*, 83-92.

Buettner, F., Gulliford, S., Webb, S., & Partridge, M. (2009). Using Bayesian logistic regression with high-order interactions to model radiation-induced toxicities following radiotherapy. *Proceedings of 8th International Conference on Machine Learning and Applications,* (pp. 451-456).

Chao, K., Deasy, J., Markman, J., Haynie, J., Perez, C., Purdy, J., & Low, D. (2001). A prospective study of salivary function sparing in patients with head-and-neck cancers receiving intensity-modulated or three-dimensional radiation therapy: Initial results. *International Journal of Radiation Oncology • Biology • Physics, 49*, 907-916.

Chen, S., Zhou, S., Yin, F., Marks, L., & Das, S. (2007b). Investigation of the support vector machine algorithm to predict lung radiation-induced pneumonitis. *Medical Physics, 34*, 3808–3814. doi:10.1118/1.2776669

Chen, S., Zhou, S., Zhang, J., Yin, F., Marks, L., & Das, S. (2007a). A neural network model to predict lung radiation-induced pneumonitis. *Medical Physics, 34*, 3420–3427. doi:10.1118/1.2759601

Cozzarini, C., Fiorino, C., Ceresoli, G., Cattaneo, G., Bolognesi, A, Calandrino, R., & Villa, E. (2003). Significant correlation between rectal DVH and late bleeding in patients treated after radical prostatectomy with conformal or conventional radiotherapy (66.6-70.2Gy). *International Journal of Radiation Oncology • Biology • Physics, 55*, 688-694.

Craft, D., & Bortfeld, T. (2008). How many plans are needed in an IMRT multi-objective plan database? *Physics in Medicine and Biology, 53*, 2785–2796. doi:10.1088/0031-9155/53/11/002

Cui, Y., Dy, J., Alexander, B., & Jiang, S. (2008). Fluoroscopic gating without implanted fiducial markers for lung cancer radiotherapy based on support vector machines (SVM). *Physics in Medicine and Biology, 53*(315-N), 327.

Cui, Y., Dy, J., Sharp, G., Alexander, B., & Jiang, S. (2007). Robust fluoroscopic respiratory gating for lung cancer radiotherapy without implanted fiducial markers. *Physics in Medicine and Biology, 52,* 741–755. doi:10.1088/0031-9155/52/3/015

D'Souza, W., Malinowski, K., & Zhang, H. (2009). Machine learning for intra-fraction tumor motion modeling with respiratory surrogates. *Proceedings of 8th International Conference on Machine Learning and Applications,* (pp. 463-467).

Das, S., Chen, S., Deasy, J., Zhou, S., Yin, F., & Marks, L. (2008). Decision fusion of machine learning models to predict radiotherapy-induced lung pneumonitis. *Proceedings of 7th International Conference on Machine Learning and Applications,* (pp. 545-550).

Dehing-Oberije, C., Yu, S., De Ruysscher, D., Meerschout, S., Van Beek, K., Lievens, Y., ... Lambin, P. (2009). Development and external validation of prognostic model for 2-year survival of non-small-cell lung cancer patients treated with chemoradiotherapy. *International Journal of Radiation Oncology • Biology • Physics, 74,* 355-362.

Dekker, A., Dehing-Oberije, C., De Ruysscher, D., Lambin, P., Komati, K., & Fung, G. ... Lievens, Y. (2009). Survival prediction in lung cancer treated with radiotherapy - Bayesian networks vs. support vector machines in handling missing data. *Proceedings of 8th International Conference on Machine Learning and Applications,* (pp. 494-497).

Eisbruch, A., Ship, J., Kim, H., & Ten Haken, R. (2001). Partial irradiation of the parotid gland. *Seminars in Radiation Oncology, 11,* 234–239. doi:10.1053/srao.2001.23484

Eisbruch, A., Ten Haken, R., Kim, H., Marsh, L., & Ship, J. (1999). Dose, volume, and function relationships in parotid salivary glands following conformal and intensity-modulated irradiation of head and neck cancer. *International Journal of Radiation Oncology • Biology • Physics, 45,* 577-587.

El Naqa, I. (2010). Machine learning as new tool for predicting radiotherapy response. *Medical Physics, 37,* 3396. doi:10.1118/1.3469271

El Naqa, I., Bradley, J., Blanco, A., Lindsay, P., Vicic, M., Hope, A., & Deasy, J. (2006). Multivariable modeling of radiotherapy outcomes, including dose-volume and clinical factors. *International Journal of Radiation Oncology • Biology • Physics, 64,* 1275-1286.

El Naqa, I., Bradley, J., & Deasy, J. (2005). Machine learning methods for radiobiological outcome modeling. *AAPM Symposium Proceedings, 14,* 150-159.

El Naqa, I., Bradley, J., & Deasy, J. (2008). Nonlinear kernel-based approaches for predicting normal tissue toxicities. *Proceedings of 7th International Conference on Machine Learning and Applications,* (pp. 539-544).

El Naqa, I., Bradley, J., Lindsay, P., Hope, A., & Deasy, J. (2009). Predicting radiotherapy outcomes using statistical learning techniques. *Physics in Medicine and Biology, 54,* S9–S30. doi:10.1088/0031-9155/54/18/S02

El Naqa, I., Yang, Y., Galatsanos, N., Nishikawa, R., & Wernick, M. (2004). A similarity learning approach to content based image retrieval: Application to digital mammography. *IEEE Transactions on Medical Imaging, 23,* 1233–1244. doi:10.1109/TMI.2004.834601

El Naqa, I., Yang, Y., Wernick, M., Galatsanos, N., & Nishikawa, R. (2002). A support vector machine approach for detection of microcalcifications. *IEEE Transactions on Medical Imaging, 21*, 1552–1563. doi:10.1109/TMI.2002.806569

Fiorino, C., Sanguineti, G., Cozzarini, C., Fellin, G., Foppiano, F., Menegotti, L., … Valdagni, R. (2003). Rectal dose-volume constraints in high-dose radiotherapy of localized prostate cancer. *International Journal of Radiation Oncology • Biology • Physics, 57*, 953-962.

Gopal, R., & Starkschall, G. (2002). Plan space: representation of treatment plans in multidimensional space. *International Journal of Radiation Oncology • Biology • Physics, 53*, 1328-1336.

Isaakson, M., Jalden, J., & Murphy, M. (2005). On using an adaptive neural network to predict lung tumor motion during respiration for radiotherapy applications. *Medical Physics, 32*, 3801–3809. doi:10.1118/1.2134958

Jackson, A. (2001). Partial irradiation of the rectum. *Seminars in Radiation Oncology, 11*, 215–223. doi:10.1053/srao.2001.23481

Jackson, A., Skwarchuk, M., Zelefsky, M., Cowen, D., Venkatraman, E., Levegrun, … Ling, C. (2001). Late rectal bleeding after conformal radiotherapy of prostate cancer (II): Volume effects and dose-volume histograms. *International Journal of Radiation Oncology • Biology • Physics, 49*, 695-698.

Lennernas, B., Sandberg, D., Albertsson, P., Silen, A., & Isacsson, U. (2004). The effectiveness of artificial neural networks in evaluating treatment plans for patients requiring external beam radiotherapy. *Oncology Reports, 12*, 1065–1070.

Li, R., Lewis, J., & Jiang, S. (2009). Markerless fluoroscopic gating for lung cancer radiotherapy using generalized linear discriminant analysis. *Proceedings of 8th International Conference on Machine Learning and Applications,* (pp. 468-472).

Lin, T., Cerviño, L., Tang, X., Vasconcelos, N., & Jiang, S. (2009a). Fluoroscopic tumor tracking for image-guided lung cancer radiotherapy. *Physics in Medicine and Biology, 54*, 981–992. doi:10.1088/0031-9155/54/4/011

Lin, T., Li, R., Tang, X., Dy, J., & Jiang, S. (2009b). Markerless gating for lung cancer radiotherapy based on machine learning techniques. *Physics in Medicine and Biology, 54*, 1555–1563. doi:10.1088/0031-9155/54/6/010

Meyer, R., Zhang, H., Goadrich, L., Nazareth, D., Shi, L., & D'Souza, W. (2007). A multi-plan treatment planning framework: A paradigm shift for IMRT. *International Journal of Radiation Oncology • Biology • Physics, 68*, 1178-1189.

Munley, M., Lo, J., Sibley, G., Bentel, G., Anscher, M., & Marks, L. (1999). A neural network to predict symptomatic lung injury. *Physics in Medicine and Biology, 44*, 2241–2249. doi:10.1088/0031-9155/44/9/311

Murphy, M. (2008). Using neural networks to predict breathing motion. *Proceedings of 7th International Conference on Machine Learning and Applications,* (pp. 528-532).

Murphy, M., & Dieterich, S. (2006). Comparative performance of linear and nonlinear neural networks to predict irregular breathing. *Physics in Medicine and Biology, 51*, 5903–5914. doi:10.1088/0031-9155/51/22/012

Murphy, M., Jalden, J., & Isaksson, M. (2002). Adaptive filtering to predict lung tumor breathing motion during image-guided radiation therapy. *Proceedings of 16th International Congress on Computer Assisted Radiology and Surgery,* (pp. 539-544).

Oh, J., Al-Lozi, R., & El Naqa, I. (2009). Application of machine learning techniques for prediction of radiation pneumonitis in lung cancer patients. *Proceedings of 8th International Conference on Machine Learning and Applications,* (pp. 478-483).

Oh, J., & El Naqa, I. (2009). Bayesian network learning for detecting reliable interactions of dose-volume related parameters in radiation pneumonitis. *Proceedings of 8th International Conference on Machine Learning and Applications,* (pp. 484-488).

Platt, J. (1999). Fast training of support vector machines using sequential minimal optimization. *Advances in kernel methods: Support vector learning,* (pp. 185-208).

Quinlan, J. (1993). *C4.5: Programs for machine learning.* Morgan Kaufmann Publishers.

Ramos-Pollán, R., Guevara-López, M., Suárez-Ortega, C., Díaz-Herrero, G., & Franco-Valiente, J., Rubio-Del-Solar, … Ramos, I. (2011). Discovering mammography-based machine learning classifiers for breast cancer diagnosis. *Journal of Medical Systems*; epub ahead of print. doi:10.1007/s10916-011-9693-2

Romeijn, H., Dempsey, J., & Li, J. (2004). A unifying framework for multi-criteria fluence map optimization models. *Physics in Medicine and Biology, 49,* 1991–2013. doi:10.1088/0031-9155/49/10/011

Rosen, I., Liu, H., Childress, N., & Liao, Z. (2005). Interactively exploring optimized treatment plans. *International Journal of Radiation Oncology • Biology • Physics, 61,* 570-582.

Ruan, D., & Keall, P. (2010). Online prediction of respiratory motion: multidimensional processing with low-dimensional feature learning. *Physics in Medicine and Biology, 55,* 3011–3025. doi:10.1088/0031-9155/55/11/002

Sharp, G., Jiang, S., Shimizu, S., & Shirato, H. (2004). Prediction of respiratory tumour motion for real-time image-guided radiotherapy. *Physics in Medicine and Biology, 49,* 425–440. doi:10.1088/0031-9155/49/3/006

Shevade, S., Keerthi, S., Bhattacharyya, C., & Murthy, K. (2000). Improvements to SMO algorithm for SVM regression. *IEEE Transactions on Neural Networks, 11,* 1188–1193. doi:10.1109/72.870050

Su, M., Miften, M., Whiddon, C., Sun, X., Light, K., & Marks, L. (2005). An artificial neural network for predicting the incidence of radiation pneumonitis. *Medical Physics, 32,* 318–325. doi:10.1118/1.1835611

Suzuki, K., Armato, S., Li, F., Sone, S., & Doi, K. (2003). Massive training artificial neural network (MTANN) for reduction of false positives in computerized detection of lung nodules in low-dose CT. *Medical Physics, 30,* 1602–1617. doi:10.1118/1.1580485

Suzuki, K., Li, F., Sone, S., & Doi, K. (2005a). Computer-aided diagnostic scheme for distinction between benign and malignant nodules in thoracic low-dose CT by use of massive training artificial neural network. *IEEE Transactions on Medical Imaging, 24,* 1138–1150. doi:10.1109/TMI.2005.852048

Suzuki, K., Shiraishi, J., Abe, H., MacMahon, H., & Doi, K. (2005b). False-positive reduction in computer-aided diagnostic scheme for detecting nodules in chest radiographs by means of massive training artificial neural network. *Academic Radiology, 12,* 191–201. doi:10.1016/j.acra.2004.11.017

Suzuki, K., Yoshida, H., Nappi, J., Armato, S., & Dachman, A. (2008). Mixture of expert 3D massive-training ANNs for reduction of multiple types of false positives in CAD for detection of polyps in CT colonography. *Medical Physics, 35,* 694–703. doi:10.1118/1.2829870

Suzuki, K., Yoshida, H., Nappi, J., & Dachman, A. (2006). Massive-training artificial neural network (MTANN) for reduction of false positives in computer-aided detection of polyps: Suppression of rectal tubes. *Medical Physics, 33*, 3814–3824. doi:10.1118/1.2349839

Witten, I., & Frand, E. (2005). *Data mining: Practical machine learning tools and techniques* (2nd ed.). San Francisco, CA: Morgan Kaufmann.

Wolberg, W., Street, W., & Mangasarian, O. (1994). Machine learning techniques to diagnose breast cancer from image-processed nuclear features of fine needle aspirates. *Cancer Letters, 77*, 163–171. doi:10.1016/0304-3835(94)90099-X

Wolberg, W., Street, W., & Mangasarian, O. (1995). Image analysis and machine learning applied to breast cancer diagnosis and prognosis. *Analytical and Quantitative Cytology and Histology, 17*, 77–87.

Xing, L., Li, J., Donaldson, S., Le, Q., & Boyer, A. (1999). Optimization of importance factors in inverse planning. *Physics in Medicine and Biology, 44*, 2525–2536. doi:10.1088/0031-9155/44/10/311

Yorke, E. (2003). Biological indices for evaluation and optimization of IMRT. *Intensity-Modulated Radiation Therapy: The State of the Art: AAPM Medical Physics Monograph Number, 29*, 77-114.

Yu, Y. (1997). Multiobjective decision theory for computational optimization in radiation therapy. *Medical Physics, 24*, 1445–1454. doi:10.1118/1.598033

Zhang, H., D'Souza, W., Shi, L., & Meyer, R. (2009a). Modeling plan-related clinical complications using machine learning tools in a multiplan IMRT framework. *International Journal of Radiation Oncology • Biology • Physics, 74*, 1617-1626.

Zhang, H., Meyer, R., Shi, L., & D'Souza, W. (2010). The minimum knowledge base for predicting organ-at-risk dose-volume levels and plan-related complications in IMRT planning. *Physics in Medicine and Biology, 55*, 1935–1947. doi:10.1088/0031-9155/55/7/010

Zhang, H., Shi, L., Meyer, R., & D'Souza, W. (2009b). Machine learning for modeling dose-related organ-at-risk complications after radiation therapy. *Proceedings of 8th International Conference on Machine Learning and Applications*, (pp. 457-462).

Zhang, X., Wang, X., Dong, L., Liu, H., & Mohan, R. (2006). A sensitivity-guided algorithm for automated determination of IMRT objective function parameters. *Medical Physics, 33*, 2935–2944. doi:10.1118/1.2214171

KEY TERMS AND DEFINITIONS

Decision Trees: Used in statistics, data mining and machine learning, as a predictive model which maps observations about an item to conclusions about the item's target value.

Dose-Volume Constraint: Specifies lower or upper bound on amount of dose delivers to portion (partial volume) of an organ.

Neural Networks: Non-linear processing models that carry out a mapping of an input space onto an output space using a set of parameters (synaptic weights). Synaptic weights vary their value according to a certain learning algorithm.

Principal component analysis: Is a mathematical procedure that uses an orthogonal transformation to convert a set of observations of possibly correlated variables into a set of values of uncorrelated variables called principal components.

Radiation Therapy or Radiotherapy: Is the medical use of ionizing radiation, generally as part of cancer treatment to control malignant cells.

Rectal Bleeding: Refers to any blood that passes from anus or bleeding from lower colon or rectum.

Support Vector Machine: A concept in statistics and computer science for a set of related supervised learning methods that analyze data and recognize patterns, used for classification and regression analysis.

Xerostomia: Is the medical term for the subjective complaint of dry mouth due to a lack of saliva.

Chapter 6
Insights from Jurisprudence for Machine Learning in Law

Andrew Stranieri
University of Ballarat, Australia

John Zeleznikow
Victoria University, Australia

ABSTRACT

The central theme of this chapter is that the application of machine learning to data in the legal domain involves considerations that derive from jurisprudential assumptions about the nature of legal reasoning. Jurisprudence provides a unique resource for machine learning in that, for over one hundred years, significant thinkers have advanced concepts including open texture and discretion. These concepts inform and guide applications of machine learning to law.

1 INTRODUCTION

Many applications of machine learning in the legal domain have sought to predict Court outcomes. In these approaches, key elements of past cases are represented in a database for presentation to a machine learning algorithm so that, once patterns are learnt, the algorithm can predict the outcome of other cases. The main algorithms used include case based reasoning exemplified by Ashley (1992), neural networks (Stranieri and Zeleznikow 2005) and rule induction (Bench-Capon et al 1993). Jur-

isprudential assumptions described below inform machine learning by determining the kinds of cases that are suitable, appropriate mechanisms for dealing with contradictory cases and approaches to evaluate the accuracy of predictions. Many of the issues that arise will be discussed in the context of a sample application: the Split Up project reported by Stranieri et al (1999).

In the Split Up project, Stranieri et al (1999) collected data from cases heard in the Family Court of Australia dealing with property distribution following divorce. The objective was to predict the percentage split of assets that a judge in the Family Court of Australia would be likely to award both

DOI: 10.4018/978-1-4666-1833-6.ch006

parties of a failed marriage. Australian Family Law is generally regarded as highly discretionary. The statute presents a 'shopping list' of factors to be taken into account in arriving at a property order. The relative importance of each factor remains unspecified in the legislation and many crucial terms are not precisely defined. For example, the age, state of health and financial resources of the litigants are explicitly mentioned in the statute as relevant factors yet their relative weightings are unspecified. The Act clearly allows the decision-maker a great deal of discretion in interpreting and weighing factors.

The next section of this chapter provides an overview of diverse applications of machine learning in law. Following that, jurisprudence concepts of open texture and stare decisis are described in order to illustrate the role these concepts play in machine learning exercises. Points raised in that section are illustrated in practice in the Split Up system before a discussion on the limitations of machine learning in law.

2 OVERVIEW OF MACHINE LEARNING IN LAW

Philipps (1989) was among the first to demonstrate the application of neural networks in law with a hypothetical example from Roman Law. The will of a hypothetical citizen whose wife was pregnant read thus: "If a son is born to me let him be heir in respect of two thirds of my estate, let my wife be heir in respect of the remaining part; but if a daughter is born to me, let her be heir to the extent of a third; let my wife be heir to the remaining part"

Philipps trained a feed forward neural network with backpropagation of errors to deliver the correct output when exposed to scenarios that involved the birth of a boy and of a girl but not both. He then put forward a case that necessarily defeats these rules; one in which twins, a boy and a girl are born. In this case, the network that had

not been exposed to this scenario during training, produced an outcome that indicated the mother receives two shares, the son receives three and the daughter receives four. Philipps argued this outcome is reasonable in that it represents an equilibrium based on past cases. However, Hunter (1994) pointed out that the notion of equilibrium with past cases is jurisprudentially flawed. There is neither a notion of moral correctness nor any appeal to rationales that reflect higher principles.

Another instance of the application of connectionism for modeling defeasible rules in law can be seen in the work of Thagard (1989). He advanced a theory of explanatory coherence that modelled the way in which competing hypotheses are supported, to a greater or lesser extent, by available evidence. Some nodes in the network represent propositions that represent each hypothesis. Other nodes represent available evidence. Links exist between evidential nodes and hypothesis nodes, which have an associated weight. These weights may be excitary or inhibitory. To determine which hypothesis has more support, the network is activated. Nodes feed activation (or inhibition) to other nodes that feed back to each other until equilibrium is reached. The network is then said to be settled.

FeuRosa (2000) advanced a unique application of machine learning in the State Supreme Court Judge in Brazil. His 'Judges on Wheels' program involves the transportation of a judge, police officer, insurance assessor, mechanical and support staff to the scene of minor motor vehicle accidents. The team collects evidence, the mechanic assess the damage, and the judge makes a decision and drafts a judgement with the help of a program called the Electronic Judge before leaving the scene of the accident. The Electronic Judge software uses a KDD approach that involves neural networks. Although the judge is not obliged to follow the suggestion offered by the Electronic Judge, the software is used in 68% of traffic accidents by judges in the state of Espirito Santo. The system plays an important role in enhancing the consistency of judicial decision-making.

The automatic categorization of text represents another application of machine learning in law. Legal publishers expend considerable resources to determine the most appropriate list of keywords for each published case. Thompson (2001) describes comparative trials with machine learning techniques, that applies clustering and rule induction for automated case indexing. Merkl et al (1999) used self organising maps to automatically group thousands of European Parliament cases into clusters where each contains cases that are similar. Other applications of machine learning include that of Brüninghaus and Ashley (2001) who used machine learning to elicit case factors automatically from case summaries. Machine learning has also been applied to the detection of concept drift in law initially by Rissland and Friedman (1997). They collected data from US Bankruptcy cases over a ten-year period and asked whether significant shifts in judicial decision-making could be automatically discovered. Their aim was to discover a method for detecting a change in the way the concept of 'good faith' was used by Courts. The onset of a leading decision was automatically detected from case data using a metric they devised.

In a different kind of application, Oatley and Ewart (2003) describe the OVER Project that aimed to assist police with the high volume crime, burglary from dwelling houses. A software system they developed enabled the trending of historical data, the testing of 'short term' hunches, and the development of 'medium' and long term' strategies to burglary and crime reduction, based upon victim, offender, location and details of victimisations. Predictions on the likelihood of burglary were calculated by combining all of the varying sources of evidence into a Bayesian belief network.

Dozier et al (2003) used text-mining techniques to create an on-line directory of expert witnesses from jury verdict and settlement documents. The supporting technologies that made the application possible included information extraction from text via regular expression parsing, record linkage through Bayesian based matching and automatic rule-based classification. Their research shows that text-mining techniques can be used to create useful special-purpose directories for individuals involved in legal proceedings. McCue (2007) describes other applications of conventional data mining in law enforcement.

On the fringe of law, Van Dijk et al (2009) applied a genetic algorithm as a data mining search to discover profiles of successful complaints in an Ombudsman database. They identify the importance of involving legal expertise in the mining and claim that difficulties in doing so, account for the relatively low uptake of data mining in law.

Although applications of machine learning to law are wide ranging, concepts from jurisprudence, discussed next, inform the process substantially.

3 JURISPRUDENCE CONCEPTS

The jurisprudence of legal positivism exemplified by Hart (1958) emphasises the role of statutes and underlying principles in determining case outcomes. A judge determines a case outcome by initially making a finding on the facts of a case then applyies rules to the fact scenario. Adherents to the jurisprudential movement known as critical legal studies (CLS) assign judicial discretion a far more prominent role and diminish the importance of legal principles. Kennedy (1986) provides a CLS account of the way in which a fictitious judge creatively exercises discretion in pre-determining a desired outcome. His acronym HIWTCO (how I want to come out) guides the application of interpretive discretion.

The legal realism movement is less concerned with legal doctrine than with observation of the law in process. The common catch cry of the realist is that to understand the law it is necessary to understand what lawyers do and not what they say they do. Llewellyn (1962 p55-57) tabulates common points of departure that distinguish adherents of the school of realism from other jurisprudential schools and includes a theory of rationalisation that, assigns rules and principles a different status than is the case with theorists from positivist schools. For positivist scholars, rules, principles and standards determine a judicial decision. Legal realism scholars believe that rules and principles may be invoked after a decision has been reached in order to ensure that a decision is just, moral and legally correct. Appellate court decisions can be seen in legal realist terms to lay down guidelines that a first instance judge can use to justify a decision. The Critical Legal Studies movement takes an extreme interpretation of this in order to claim that rules are often irrelevant in determining an outcome.

The extent to which a judge is required to follow past cases in determining a case differs in common law, civil law and hybrid legal systems. Common law is the legal tradition that evolved in England from the 11th century onwards. Its principles appear for the most part in reported judgments, usually of the higher courts, in relation to specific fact situations arising in disputes that courts have adjudicated. Common law is the foundation of private law, not only for England, Wales and Ireland, but also in most U.S. states, Canadian provinces and countries that first received that law as colonies of the British Empire.

Civil law has its origin in Roman law, as codified in the Corpus Juris Civilis of Justinian1 and as subsequently developed in Continental Europe and around the world. Civil law eventually divided into two streams: the codified Roman law (as seen in the French Civil Code of 1804 and its progeny and imitators - Continental Europe, Québec and Louisiana being examples); and uncodified Roman law (as seen in Scotland and South Africa). Civil law is highly systematised and structured and relies on declarations of broad, general principles, often ignoring the details.

The way past cases impact on future decisions is central to perspectives on jurisprudence and differences in legal systems. Concepts of open texture and discretion, discussed in the next section impact directly on machine learning.

3.1 Open Texture

Legal reasoning is characteristically indeterminate in that many key concepts are open textured. Open texture was a concept first introduced by Waismann (1951) to assert that many concepts are necessarily indeterminate in that they cannot be precisely defined outside a specific context. Hart (1958) presents a local government ordinance that prohibits vehicles from entering a municipal park and argues that there can be expected to be little disagreement that the statute applies to automobiles. A definition of vehicle is never complete and closed because new cases can always emerge to challenge a definition. Would roller blades, perambulators, or a military tank on parade be considered a vehicle?

Berman and Hafner (1988) indicate, legal reasoning inherent in the prediction of a case is essentially indeterminate because key variables are open textured. The definition of vehicle sufficiently concise to unequivocally classify roller blades one way or another only emerges once the multiple interpretations are tested in Court. At first sight this would seem to invalidate the application of machine learning to the prediction of case outcomes at Court. However, although every possible extension for an open textured concept cannot be completely known in advance, it is plausible to estimate the extent to which the extensions known represent all possible uses. Practitioners seem to estimate the degree to which a field of law is open textured, in order to offer a prediction. Few practitioners would argue that the concept of vehicle that arises in Hart's scenario seems less subject to new uses than the concept of a social group that arises in the determination of refugee status according to the United Nations Convention Relating to the Granting of Refugee Status (1958).

The open textured continuum cannot have definite end-points. No task is completely open textured and no task in law is totally well defined. To say that a task is totally well defined is to say that only one interpretation alone can ever be found. This may occur in systems such as mathematics, where one can prove theorems from axioms by the use of inference rules. But, this is not the case in law, at least according to most jurisprudence theorists with the exception of some extreme positivists. To propose that a legal concept can be tightly defined presumes a preposterous knowledge of future events. At the other extreme, no task is totally open textured. To be so would be to interpret the task and terms in any way whatsoever.

An assessment of the degree to which a field of law is open textured is necessarily subjective. Different analysts may classify the same task in different ways. A determination is not made on the basis of clear metrics that measure criteria derivable in an objective fashion from theory. Rather, the determination of the degree of open texture involves some subjective judgment and thus leads to the conclusion that the machine learning exercise is as much an art as it is a science.

The concept of discretion is related to that of open texture in jurisprudence. Dworkin (1977) presents a systematic account of discretion by proposing two basic types of discretion, which he called strong and weak discretion. Weak discretion describes situations where a decision-maker must interpret standards in his own way whereas strong discretion characterises those decisions where the decision-maker is not bound by any standards and is required to create his or her own standards.

Dworkin (1977) identified two types of weak discretion and a type he characterizes as strong. Strong discretion characterizes that reasoning that involves the liberty, on the part of the reasoner to incorporate standards of his or her own choosing. Dworkin proposes that this is the nature of the position of the judge in a situation where usual standards or rules do not apply. Weak discretion

of type one exists when one's decision is bound by standards that may inherently have variable interpretations, but nevertheless, those rules apply. The second type of weak discretion exists when a decision is made according to applicable rules and standards but the decision maker's decision stands as final, as in an umpire's call.

A family law expert, aware that a judge may interpret concepts such as a) marriage length, b) financial contributions, c) health needs and other factors in many possible ways; or will exercise discretion in weighting the factors; will suggest a likely outcome with some caution. An expert on road traffic law will suggest that a judge will interpret the terms driver, blood alcohol test and legal limit in only one way. Because it is less open textured than family law, the law relating to drink driving appears to be more predictable than family law. Open texture may be an all or nothing affair for theoreticians but, for practitioners, there are degrees of open texture.

Consequently, as assessment of the extent to which a particular prediction task in law is suitable for a machine learning approach is made on the basis of the degree of open texture apparent. Essentially, tasks suited to a machine learning exercise are those that involve a degree of open texture and discretion demonstrated by:

a) many ambiguous or vaguely defined concepts in statutes and past judgements

b) tasks underpinned by statutes that embed a shopping list of factors without being presciptive about how the factors are to be combined

c) a socio-political environment that encourages ambiguity or discretion

Open texture is an important concept in jurisprudence. Stare decisis, discussed next is also important for machine learning exercises.

3.2 Types of Cases Suited to Machine Learning: The Concept of *Stare Decisis*

Stare decisis is a fundamental principle in common law legal systems. The principle dictates that the reasoning, loosely, ratio decidendi, used in new cases must follow the reasoning used by decision-makers in courts at the same or higher level in the hierarchy. The concept of stare decisis informs the application of machine learning to law and is discussed next.

Wassestrom (1961) describes *traditional stare decisis* as the principle that a lower court must follow the decision of a higher court. Another type of stare decisis, called *personal stare decisis*, is used to describe the observation that most judges attempt to be consistent with their previous decisions. This manifests itself in the Family Court, as the tendency an individual judge has to be consistent with the way he or she exercised discretion in past, similar cases. The third type of stare decisis, called *local stare decisis* represents the tendency of a group of judges that make up a current court to follow its own decisions. This type of *stare decisis* is represented in property division in Australian family law, as a desire for Family Court judges to exercise discretion in a manner that is consistent with other judges of the same registry of the Court, at the same time.

Within law, those decisions from appellate courts which form the basis of later decisions and provide guidance to lower courts do provide a fundamental lesson, or normative structure for subsequent reasoning. Pound (1908) considers such cases to be formal, binding and inviolate prescriptions for future decision-making, whilst McCormick (1978) sees them as beacons from which inferior or merely subsequent courts navigate their way through new fact situations. The common name for such cases is landmark cases. However, most decisions in any jurisdiction are not landmark cases. Most decisions are commonplace, and deal with relatively minor matters such as vehicle accidents, small civil actions, petty crime, divorce, and the like. These cases are rarely, if ever, reported upon by court reporting services, nor are they often made the subject of learned comment or analysis. More importantly, each case does not have the same consequences as the landmark cases.

Landmark cases are therefore of a fundamentally different character to commonplace cases. Landmark cases will individually have a profound effect on the subsequent disposition of all cases in that domain, whereas commonplace cases will only have a cumulative effect, and that effect will only be apparent over time. Take, for example, the case of *Mabo v Queensland (No.2)*. Prior to *Mabo* the indigenous people of Australia, the aborigines, had few, if any, proprietary rights to Australian land. Under British colonial rule, their laws were held to be inchoate and Australia itself was held to be terra nullius, 'empty land' at the time of white settlement. Hence, the only property laws applicable were those stemming from the introduction of white rule, laws which were less than generous in their grant of land to Aborigines. In *Mabo*, the High Court held that previous decisions holding that Australia was terra nullius at settlement, and decisions holding that Aborigines had no property laws affecting land, were simply wrong at law. Hence, the High Court said, Aborigines had sovereignty over parts of Australia under certain conditions. Whether one agrees with the High Court's interpretive technique, it is indisputable that this is the landmark case in the area, and has formed the basis of future decisions in the area. Indeed, *Mabo*, like many other leading cases, was the spur for political action and we soon saw the introduction of the Federal Native Title Act. Thus, landmark cases have the dual effect of determining (to some degree) the interpretation of subsequent fact situations as well as influencing the invocation of normative legislative processes.

Landmark cases rarely occur in common practice and are reported and discussed widely. These cases set a precedent that alters the way in which subsequent cases are decided. Further, there are very large numbers of commonplace cases whereas there are comparatively few landmark cases. For example, in the last two decades, the number of landmark cases in the Family Court of Australia is in the order of hundreds while the number of commonplace cases is in the order of multiple tens of thousands.

Consequently, landmark cases are not well suited to machine learning exercises. Rather, commonplace cases can be used to learn that the way traditional, personal and local *stare decisis* has been applied by judges in a particular jurisdiction. The use of commonplace cases is illustrated in the Split Up application, discussed in the next section

3.3 Split up: Machine Learning in Family Law

Written judgments of commonplace cases are very useful source materials because the explanations for decisions detail factors that the judge has used even if the way the factors have been combined or weighted is often left unspecified. However, a written judgment will not necessarily make explicit every factor a judge uses in order to reach a decision. Commonly assumed knowledge is necessarily used by judges in reaching a property decision but is unlikely to be made explicit in a written judgment. A judge may argue that the wife, at seventy years of age, is elderly. This argument will rarely be elaborated on because it is commonly accepted that 70 years of age is classified as elderly.

The style of judgments varies from judge to judge though there are discernible features most have in common. For example, all judgments reiterate the evidence placed before the court and, where evidence is in disagreement, indicate a preference for one set over another. Most judgments also indicate a percentage to each party and detail the property orders to realise that percentage.

For example, Mullane J in the Marriage of Coulter (1989) 13 Fam LR 421 writes:

"The material before us is sufficient to enable a finding that the contributions of the parties under s 79(4) were approximately equal. The property of the parties came to a total of $422,318. The wife should receive 50% of this based on contribution"

It can be seen from this judgment that Mullane J. has compared contributions of the husband against those of the wife to arrive at a relative contribution assessment. The relative contribution of the husband (to the wife), in this case is equal. Domain experts confirm that practitioners also determine a relative contribution in order to predict the Court's outcome. The vast majority of unreported judgments convey a similar assessment of contributions of one spouse relative to the other.

Mullane J, in the same judgment performs the same comparison with respect to future needs:

"Her lack of employment experience in that area, and her other skills provide only a very limited future earning capacity relative to that of the husband."

He continues to reach a final outcome:

"A just and equitable result in my view would be for the wife to receive an additional $150,000 in respect of the 75(2) factors, giving a total of $361,000"

The final outcome is equivalent to 85% of the property. The reasoning is represented diagrammatically in Figure 1

Some written judgments represent the contribution of each party to the marriage as a percentage, the 75(2) factors as a percentage and then combine these two percentages to yield a final percentage which is the basis for a property order. For example, Hannon J. in The Marriage of B ML4336 19951 states:

"Having regard to the relevant contributions of the parties, including substantial financial con-

Figure 1. The relative contributions and relative needs as relevant factors for a percentage split determination

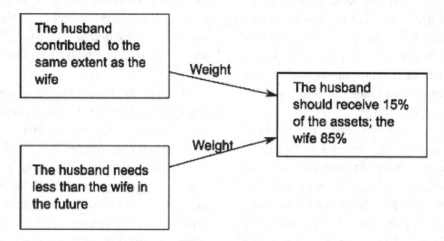

tribution of the husband from the funds received from the sale of his mother's house, I assess their respective contributions as to 60 per cent to the husband and 40 per cent to the wife."

Hannon J then explains arguments relevant for his assessment of 75(2) factors.

"I turn now to a consideration of the section 75(2) factors, which require a consideration of the present and future needs and the means, resources and earning capacity of the parties. Both parties are in good health and that is not a relevant consideration. There is at present a distinction between the income and financial resources of each of the parties..."

After considering a number of relevant factors he concludes:

"The section 75(2) factors favour the wife, and I make an adjustment of 15 per cent under this head. The wife is therefore entitled to 55 per cent of the available assets, and the husband is entitled to 45 per cent. The wife is entitled to receive $67,650 "

A framework of relevant factors can be sketched by perusing past judgments in consulta-

tion with domain experts. Figure 2 below illustrates a tree of relevant factors that are apparent from the excerpts of the two judgments above.

Figure 2 represents a small part of the hierarchy of relevant factors that culminate in the final percentage split outcome. No attempt is made in this representation to model the way in which subordinate factors are weighted to infer superior factors. Thus we can see from Figure 2 that health and financial resources are relevant factors for a future needs assessment.

The assumption made is that once the factor tree is identified the weights of factors can be discovered by applying data from real cases to machine learning algorithms. Attempts to elicit the weightings of factors directly from experts or judges is inappropriate on pragmatic and also on conceptual grounds. It is very difficult for experts to specify how factors are combined specifically enough to reproduce the reasoning process in a computer implementation. Experts know that judges weigh relative needs against relative contributions and indeed, experts are adept at doing this themselves to predict a courtroom outcome, yet articulating exactly how these two factors interact is very difficult.

The complete tree comprises 94 factors and culminates in a percentage split for the husband.

Figure 2. Some relevant factors for the percentage split task

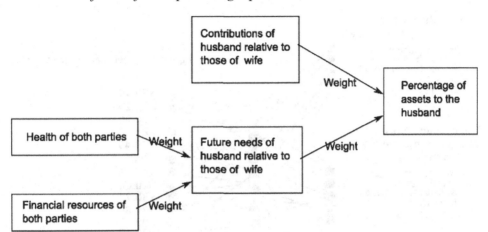

Split Up is a partitioned rule/neural hybrid hybrid because the claim of some arguments are inferred with the use of neural networks whereas the claim of other arguments are inferred with rule sets. The network at the first level of the tree is illustrated in Figure 3. A feed forward network was trained with backpropagation of errors. The 13 output nodes represent outcomes a judge may make regarding the percentage split of assets. The fifteen input nodes represent three variables, the extent to which the husband has contributed to the marriage relative to the wife, the extent to which the husband needs resources in the future and the level of wealth of the marriage.

4 LIMITATIONS OF KNOWLEDGE DISCOVERY FROM DATABASES

Theoretical and pragmatic issues limit the application of machine learning techniques in the legal domain. From a theoretical perspective, Tata (1998) argues that legal reasoning cannot be decomposed or deconstructed to a set of variables inter-linked together in a similar way from one case to another. Rather, legal reasoning is a holistic process where a decision maker selects and processes facts of interest in a way that cannot be pre-specified before a case is encountered.

As a holistic process, any attempt to systematically encode a judgment as a chain of reasoning steps that link facts to conclusions is superficial at best. Any machine learning attempt to glean some unknown knowledge from data from many superficially encoded judgments can lead to the discovery of so-called knowledge that is quite misleading.

Hobson and Slee (1994) studied a handful of cases from the UK theft act and also use neural networks to predict the outcome of theft cases. They used a series of leading cases in British theft law to train a network to predict a courtroom outcome. Results they obtained were less than impressive which they attributed to flaws in the use of neural networks in legal reasoning. This criticism was too harsh. Neural networks have much to offer KDD. However, any application of machine learning to data drawn from the legal domain must be carefully performed. Due attention is required so that key assumptions made at each phase of the learning process are clearly articulated and have some basis in jurisprudence. For example, the cases used in the Hobson and Slee study involved cases known as landmark cases. As described below, we believe that landmark cases are not well suited to a machine learning exercise involving neural networks.

Figure 3. Neural network for percentage split determination

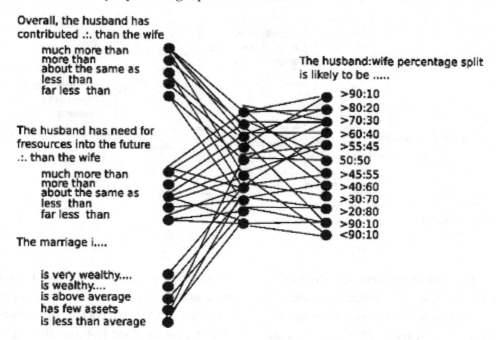

Hunter (1994) raise concerns about the use of neural networks in law based the explication deficiencies of neural networks, the assembly of appropriate data and methods used for network training. Explanation is important in law as it is not acceptable in most jurisdictions for a judge to simply announce an outcome without having offering a justification. The lack of explication facility inherent in the connectionist paradigm weighs heavily against their use in law. However, the reasoning to reach a conclusion and explaining that conclusion can be seen to be two distinct processes. Drawing this distinction enables the design of systems that use neural networks to infer conclusions and another system to explain them. An outcome may be reached by a machine learning algorithms on the basis of the facts inputted. However, rules, principles and the facts of a case, in addition to the decision itself, are necessary in order for a justification to be advanced. In the Split Up system, the explanation is generated from additional information in the structure of the tree, known as an argument tree. Discretion, defined as the ability of individual judges to as-

sign different relative weights to relevant factors, is modelled by the machine learning algorithm in arriving at an outcome without reference to the reasoning steps. Viewed as useful tools for justifying a decision, legal concepts can be applied by an artificial reasoner to justify or explain any decision. A family law expert displays the same capacity. Given the same set of facts an expert is able to justify a property decision of 70% (to the husband) and yet, is also able to create a justification for an output of 50%.

A simple example illustrates that an appropriate explanation may not equate with the line of reasoning. We may engage ourselves with the task of dividing 240 by 16. Using a long division algorithm, we reach the conclusion, 15. If asked to explain that result, we are unlikely to reproduce all or even a subset of the algorithm. Instead we explain the result by claiming that 15 * 16 = 240. In this trivial case, the explanation is quite different from the reasoning steps used to achieve the result, and indeed much simpler.

Zeleznikow and Hunter (1994) state that an explanation is an attempt by a computer system to indicate or clarify its actions, reasoning and recommendations. It is a collection of reasoning steps that connects facts to a legal conclusion about those facts. There are three reasons why explanation is important in legal decision support systems:

1. Users of the system need to satisfy themselves that the program's conclusions are basically correct for their particular use.
2. Knowledge engineers need to satisfy themselves that knowledge is being applied properly.
3. Domain experts need to see a trace of the way in which their knowledge is being applied, in order to judge whether knowledge elicitation is proceeding successfully.

The adoption of a stance that inferencing is a process distinct from the generation of explanation is practically useful in the development of a reasoner for the discretionary domain of family law. It is possible to develop artificial reasoners that operate by invoking neural networks if, another, quite separate process, is invoked to generate an explanation for conclusions reached by neural networks. This notion of how an explanation is generated is in keeping with views on decision-making advocated by proponents of the school of legal realism.

Stranieri et al (2001) make the assumption that an explanation is separate from the steps used to infer a solution and that explanation for discretionary reasoning is further removed from the reasoning steps than is the case in less discretionary domains. This is particularly important when using neural networks or other statistical KDD techniques to model reasoning in discretionary legal domains.

In domains characterised with traditional stare decisis, reasons for a first instance decision often involve principles laid down by appellate Courts. In the absence of traditional stare decisis, explanations cannot derive rigidly from principles because appellate Courts have laid none down in

a specific way. Explanations must necessarily be further removed from the sequence of reasoning steps used to infer an outcome.

Although there is a risk that misleading conclusions can be drawn as a result of a machine learning exercise in law, those risks are offset against potential gains. Currently, the analysis of judicial decisions occurs in a non-transparent manner. Practitioners develop experience in understanding decision-making processes in specific jurisdictions. This experience is transferred informally to colleagues and is rarely subjected to rigorous analysis. Further, even the busiest practitioner can know of only a small number of cases. Legal scholars analyse major decisions and trends in greater detail. However, rarely do they regularly explore thousands of cases. Judges cannot easily allay public concerns that decisions are inconsistent. Furthermore, their decisions are not always readily predictable. KDD can promise to make law more transparent, and predictable.

Zeleznikow (2000) claims that the development of legal decision support systems has led to:

- **Consistency:** by replicating the manner in which decisions are made, decision support systems are encouraging the spreading of consistency in legal decision-making.
- **Transparency:** by demonstrating how legal decisions are made, legal decision support systems are leading to a better community understanding of legal domains. This has the desired benefit of decreasing the level of public criticism of judicial decision-making[1].
- **Efficiency:** One of the major benefits of decision support systems is to make firms more efficient.
- **Enhanced support for dispute resolution:** Users of legal decision support systems are aware of the likely outcome of litigation and thus are encouraged to avoid the costs and emotional stress of legal proceedings. Zeleznikow and Bellucci (2003)

indicate how legal decision support systems can aid in resolving disputes.

Perhaps the greatest obstacle to the widespread use of KDD techniques is the absence of large structured datasets. As society becomes more information-based, data will inevitably be collected in a structured fashion. Currently, legal firms, Courts and related professionals, are rapidly utilising case management systems. Non--profit organisations such as LegalXML (2004).

5 CONCLUSION

Over the past decade, there has been a phenomenal advance in the application of machine learning from database techniques in many fields. Not surprisingly, progress has been less spectacular in the field of law. As we noted in this chapter, this has occurred because of the differences between legal and other data. Legal data is typically unstructured and the amount of data is small.

The over-arching claim we make is that machine learning techniques are particularly adept at discovering patterns of judicial reasoning in discretionary fields of law, provided the data that reflects the reasoning processes is collected. We must draw the distinction between local, personal and traditional stare decisis and clearly articulate any jurisprudential assumptions we make with regard to discretion. When using machine learning in law, we must focus upon commonplace rather than landmark cases.

Although there is a risk that misleading conclusions can be drawn as a result of a KDD exercise, those risks are offset against potential gains. KDD can promise to make law more accessible, affordable, predictable and transparent.

REFERENCES

Ashley, K. D. (1992). Case-based reasoning and its implications for legal expert systems. *Artificial Intelligence and Law, 1*(2), 113–208. doi:10.1007/BF00114920

Bench-Capon, T. J. M. (1993). Neural networks and open texture. In the *Proceedings of the Fourth International Conference on Artificial Intelligence and* Law (pp. 292-297). Amsterdam, The Netherlands: ACM Press.

Berman, D. H., & Hafner, C. D. (1988). Obstacles to the development of logic-based models of legal reasoning. In Walter, C. (Ed.), *Computer power and legal reasoning* (pp. 183–214). New York, NY: Quorum Books.

Brüninghaus, S., & Ashley, K. D. (2001). Improving the representation of legal case texts with information extraction methods. In H. Prakken & R. Loui (Eds.), *Proceedings of the Seventh International Conference on Artificial Intelligence and Law (ICAIL-2001),* St. Louis, MO

Dozier, C., Jackson, P., Guo, X., Chaudhary, M., & Arumainayagam, Y. (2003). Creation of an expert witness database through text mining. *Proceedings 9th International Conference on Artificial Intelligence and Law,* (pp. 177-184). Edinburgh, Scotland: ACM Press.

Dworkin, R. (1977). *Taking rights seriously.* Cambridge, MA: Harvard University Press.

FeuRosa. P. V. (2000). The electronic judge. *Proceedings of AISB'00 – Symposium on Artificial Intelligence & Legal Reasoning,* Birmingham, UK, April, (pp. 33-36).

Hart, H. L. A. (1958). Positivism and the separation of law and morals. *Harvard Law Review, 71*, 593–629. doi:10.2307/1338225

Hobson, J. B., & Slee, D. (1994). Indexing the Theft Act 1968 for case based reasoning and artificial neural networks. *Proceedings of the Fourth National Conference on Law, Computers and Artificial Intelligence.* Exeter.

Hunter, D. (1994). Looking for law in all the wrong places: Legal theory and neural networks. In Prakken, H., Muntjewerff, A. J., Soeteman, A., & Winkels, R. (Eds.), *Legal knowledge based systems: the relation with legal theory.* Lelystad, The Netherlands: Koninklijke Vermende.

Lawler, R. (1964). *Stare decisis* and electronic computers. In Schubert, G. (Ed.), *Judicial behaviour: A reader in theory and research* (pp. 492–505). Chicago, IL: Rand McNally & Company.

LegalXML. (2004). Retrieved March 15, 2004, from http://www.legalxml.org/

Llewellyn, K. (1962). *Jurisprudence.* Chicago, IL: University of Chicago Press.

McCormick, D. N. (1978). *Legal reasoning and legal theory.* Oxford, UK: Clarendon Press.

McCue, C. (2007). *Data mining and predictive analysis intelligence gathering and crime analysis.* Elsevier, Inc.

Merkl, D., Schweighofer, E., & Winiwarter, W. (1999). Exploratory analysis of concept and document spaces with connectionist networks. *Artificial Intelligence and Law, 7*(2-3), 185–209. doi:10.1023/A:1008365524782

Philipps, L. (1989). Are legal decisions based on the application of rules or prototype recognition? Legal science on the way to neural networks. In *the Pre-Proceedings of the Third International Conference on Logica, Informatica, Diritto,* (p. 673). Florence, Italy: IDG.

Phillips, L., & Sartor, G. (1999). From legal theories to neural networks and fuzzy reasoning. *Artificial Intelligence and Law, 7*(2-3), 115–128. doi:10.1023/A:1008371600675

Pound, R. (1908). Mechanical jurisprudence. *Columbia Law Review, 8,* 605. doi:10.2307/1108954

Rissland, E. L., & Friedman, M. T. (1995). Detecting change in legal concepts. *Proceedings of the 5th International Conference on Artificial Intelligence and Law,* Melbourne, Australia, June 30 – July 4, (pp. 127-136). New York, NY: ACM Press.

Stranieri, A., & Zeleznikow, J. (2005). *Knowledge discovery from legal databases.* Berlin, Germany: Springer, Kluwer Law and Philosophy Series.

Stranieri, A., Zeleznikow, J., Gawler, M., & Lewis, B. (1999). A hybrid rule- neural approach for the automation of legal reasoning in the discretionary domain of family law in Australia. *Artificial Intelligence and Law, 7*(2-3), 153–183. doi:10.1023/A:1008325826599

Stranieri, A., Zeleznikow, J., & Yearwood, J. (2001). Argumentation structures that integrate dialectical and monoletical reasoning. *The Knowledge Engineering Review, 16*(4), 331–348. doi:10.1017/S0269888901000248

Tata, C. (1998). The application of judicial intelligence and "rules" to systems supporting discretionary judicial decision-making. *Artificial Intelligence and Law: International Journal, 6*(2-4), 203–230. doi:10.1023/A:1008274209036

Thagard, P. (1989). Explanatory coherence. *The Behavioral and Brain Sciences, 12,* 435–502. doi:10.1017/S0140525X00057046

Thompson, P. (2001). Automatic categorization of case law. *Proceedings of the Eighth International Conference on Artificial Intelligence and Law, ICAIL 2001,* May 21-25, 2001, St. Louis, Missouri, (pp. 70-77). ACM Press. ISBN 1-58113-368-5 van Dijk, J., Choenni, S., & Leeuw, F. (2009). Analyzing a complaint database by means of a genetic-based data mining algorithm. *Proceedings of the 12th International Conference on Artificial Intelligence and Law*, Barcelona, Spain, (pp. 226-227). ACM Press.

Waismann, F. (1951). Verifiability. In Flew, A. (Ed.), *Logic and language*. Cambridge, UK: Blackwell.

Wassestrom, R. (1961). *The judicial decision. Toward a theory of legal justification*. Stanford, CA: Stanford University Press.

Zeleznikow, J. (2000). building judicial decision support systems in discretionary legal domains. *International Review of Law Computers & Technology, 14*(3), 341–356. doi:10.1080/713673368

Zeleznikow, J., & Bellucci, E. (2003). Family_ Winner: Integrating game theory and heuristics to provide negotiation support. In D. Bourcier, (Ed.), *Legal Knowledge and Information Systems. JURIX 2003: The Sixteenth Annual Conference*. (pp. 21-30). Amsterdam, The Netherlands: IOS Press.

Zeleznikow, J., & Hunter, D. (1994). *Building intelligent legal information systems: Knowledge representation and reasoning in law, 13*. Kluwer Computer/Law Series.

ENDNOTE

[1]   Judges of the Family Court of Australia are worried about criticism of the court, which has led to the death of judges, and physical attacks on courtrooms. They believe enhanced community understanding of the decision making process in Australian Family Law will lead to reduced conflict.

Chapter 7
Machine Learning Applications in Computer Vision

Mehrtash Harandi
NICTA, Australia & The University of Queensland, Australia

Javid Taheri
The University of Sydney, Australia

Brian C. Lovell
NICTA, Australia & The University of Queensland, Australia

ABSTRACT

Recognizing objects based on their appearance (visual recognition) is one of the most significant abilities of many living creatures. In this study, recent advances in the area of automated object recognition are reviewed; the authors specifically look into several learning frameworks to discuss how they can be utilized in solving object recognition paradigms. This includes reinforcement learning, a biologically-inspired machine learning technique to solve sequential decision problems and transductive learning, and a framework where the learner observes query data and potentially exploits its structure for classification. The authors also discuss local and global appearance models for object recognition, as well as how similarities between objects can be learnt and evaluated.

INTRODUCTION

The very first question comes into mind when thinking about machine learning and computer vision is: "How can a machine recognize and interpret images/scenes?" Without a doubt, among the various capabilities that humans beings have, recognizing objects based on their appearance (visual recognition) is one of our most significant

abilities. Human beings can recognize familiar objects with little difficulty; whereas, artificial vision systems are far from matching the accuracy, speed and generality of human vision (Ponce, Hebert, Schmid, & Zisserman, 2007). In fact, creating a machine with similar capabilities to human beings is one of the main goals of computer vision research. Upon achieving this ultimate goal, a wide variety of powerful applications would emerge. Face recognition – the task of identifying a person from his/her images – is probably the best

DOI: 10.4018/978-1-4666-1833-6.ch007

known application of computer vision and pattern recognition. In fact, any task that makes use of a scene to identify objects is a potential application; content-based image retrieval, object tracking, robot navigation, automated surveillance, etc are among many that come to mind.

In this chapter, several machine learning approaches devised for recognizing objects will be introduced. Influential works along recent topics in the area of object recognition and machine learning will also be discussed. This chapter is organized as follows. In Section 1, local and global appearance models for object recognition are described. Section 2 is dedicated to Reinforcement learning and the insight it has brought to solve computer vision applications. Section 3 then discusses Transductive learning. Finally Section 4 concludes by discussing how similarities between objects can be evaluated, as well as describing methods to learn similarity among objects.

1 OBJECT DESCRIPTION AND REPRESENTATION IN COMPUTER VISION

Objects can be described by different cues. For example, objects can be described by geometrical primitives like boxes, spheres, cones, and cylinders. Describing and representing objects based on their appearance is a widely studied approach in the literature (Bartlett, Movellan, & Sejnowski, 2002; Belhumeur, Hespanha, & Kriegman, 1997; Dorko & Schmid, 2005; Lowe, 2004; Mikolajczyk, Leibe, & Schiele, 2005; Serre, Wolf, Bileschi, Riesenhuber, & Poggio, 2007; Shechtman & Irani, 2007; Turk & Pentland, 1991; H. Zhang, Gao, Chen, & Zhao, 2006). The general idea of appearance-based object recognition is to extract useful and robust information from only the appearance of the object-of-interest that is usually captured by different two-dimensional views. Appearance-based methods can be sub-divided into two main classes: local and global approaches.

1.1 Global Appearance Models for Object Recognition

Global appearance-based methods for object recognition try to project original input images onto a suitable lower dimensional representation. By choosing different optimization criteria for the projected data different methods can be derived.

1.1.1 Principal Component Analysis (PCA)

PCA was introduced to Computer Vision by Kirby and Sirovich (Sirovich & Kirby, 1987) and is the most well-known projection in this area. It was popularized as the influential Eigenface method of Turk and Pentland in face recognition in 1991 (Turk & Pentland, 1991). In the Eigenface method, images are considered to be high dimensional vectors and a given image x_i of size $h \times w$ is arranged as a vector $\in \mathbb{R}^d$, where $d=hw$. If a set of images $\mathbf{X} = \left\{ \mathbf{x}_1, \mathbf{x}_2, ..., \mathbf{x}_N \right\}, \mathbf{x}_i \in \mathbb{R}^d$ are available for training then the Eigenface method uses PCA projection to derive a lower dimension representation of images in the form of $\mathbf{y}_i = \mathbf{U}_{d \times m}^T \mathbf{x}_i, m \ll d$. Not only has PCA and its extensions been widely used as object descriptors (Gottumukkal & Asari, 2004; K. I. Kim, Jung, & Kim, 2002; C. Liu, 2004; C. Liu & Wechsler, 2000; Moghaddam, 2002; Vidal, Ma, & Sastry, 2005; J. Yang, Frangi, Yang, Zhang, & Jin, 2005; J. Yang, Zhang, Frangi, & Yang, 2004) but it has been also considered as a pre-processing step for other methods like Fisherface (Belhumeur, et al., 1997) or ICA-based approaches (Bartlett, et al., 2002). A numerically robust way to compute PCA projection is based on Singular Value Decomposition (SVD). This algorithm is illustrated in Table 1.

Table 1. PCA based on SVD algorithm

Input: $\mathbf{X} = \left\{ \mathbf{x}_1, \mathbf{x}_2, ..., \mathbf{x}_N \right\}$, *where* $\mathbf{x}_i \in \mathbb{R}^d$.

Compute sample mean vector $\overline{\mathbf{x}} = \dfrac{1}{N} \sum\limits_{i=1}^{N} \mathbf{x}_i$

Compute the centered-samples

$\hat{\mathbf{x}}_i = \mathbf{x}_i - \overline{\mathbf{x}}$

$\hat{\mathbf{X}} = \left\{ \hat{\mathbf{x}}_1, \hat{\mathbf{x}}_2, ..., \hat{\mathbf{x}}_N \right\}$

Apply SVD $\hat{\mathbf{X}} = U \Sigma V$

Compute eigenvalues $\lambda_i = \dfrac{\sigma_i^2}{N-1}$ where σ_i are the singular values of $\hat{\mathbf{X}}$ encoded in Σ.

Output: *PCA projection basis* $U = \left\{ u_1, u_2, ..., u_{N-1} \right\}$ and eigenvalues λ_i.

1.1.2 Linear Discriminant Analysis

As PCA technique finds orthogonal dimensions of maximal variance (or energy), if substantial changes in illumination, pose or expression are presented in the training set, the resulting descriptor then does not necessary encode similarities between faces (Jain & Li, 2005). To alleviate this problem, if class labels are provided in the training set, this additional information can be used for learning. Linear Discriminant Analysis (LDA) is a linear projection that simultaneously (1) maximizes distances among different classes, and (2) reduces distances among samples inside each class. More specifically, for a training set $\left\{ \left(\mathbf{x}_1, y_1\right), \left(\mathbf{x}_2, y_2\right), ..., \left(\mathbf{x}_N, y_N\right) \right\}$, where $y_i \in \left\{ 1, 2, ..., C \right\}$ is the class label for sample x_i, LDA computes a classification function $g(\mathbf{x}) = \mathbf{W}^T \mathbf{x}$ to minimizes within-class scatter (Equation (1)) and maximizes the between-class scatter (Equation (2)).

$$S_w = \frac{1}{N} \sum_{i=1}^{c} \sum_{x \in C_i} (x - m_i)(x - m_i)^T \qquad (1)$$

$$S_b = \frac{1}{N} \sum_{i=1}^{c} N_i (m_i - m)(m_i - m)^T \qquad (2)$$

In Equations (1) and (2), m and m_i are the mean of all samples and the mean of samples in class i, respectively. The solution to LDA problem is given by computing the eigenvectors for $S_w^{-1} S_B$. The rank of $S_w^{-1} S_B$ is at most C-1. As a result, when the number of classes is less than the feature dimension, singularity occurs and the eigen problem cannot be solved. To overcome this problem, several solutions were proposed, e.g, (Belhumeur, et al., 1997; Chen, Liao, Ko, Lin, & Yu, 2000; Huang, Liu, Lu, & Ma, 2002; Yu, 2001; Zhuang & Dai, 2005, 2007).

1.1.3 Independent Component Analysis

Independent Component Analysis (ICA) was introduced in signal processing for blind source separation (Comon, 1994). This problem is often described by the task of identifying a single speaker in a group of speakers –cocktail-party problem – where the goal is to express a set of N

random variables $\mathbf{x}_1, \mathbf{x}_2, ..., \mathbf{x}_N$ as a combination of statistically independent random variables $\mathbf{s}_i$:

$$\mathbf{x}_i = a_{i,1}\mathbf{s}_1 + a_{i,2}\mathbf{s}_2 + ... + a_{i,n}\mathbf{s}_n \qquad (3)$$

The goal of ICA is to estimate the original components $\mathbf{s}_i$ or, equivalently, the coefficients $a_{i,j}$. To compute the ICA projection several objective functions in which independence was also taken into account were developed (Hyvärinen, Karhunen, & Oja, 2001). Bartlett et al. introduced ICA for object recognition (face recognition) by considering face images as a linear mixture of statistically independent basis images (Bartlett, et al., 2002). In past years, extensive study has also been directed toward improving the accuracy of ICA based face recognisers (Dagher & Nachar, 2006; J. Kim, Choi, Yi, & Turk, 2005; Kwak & Pedrycz, 2007; S. Z. Li, Lu, Hou, Peng, & Cheng, 2005; C. Liu & Wechsler, 2003; Vasilescu & Terzopoulos, 2005; J. Yang, et al., 2005; Yuen & Lai, 2002).

1.2 Local Appearance Models for Object Recognition

Local descriptors describe a region/patch –or its identified local neighbourhood– by a region/point detector with certain invariance properties. Here, invariance implies that the descriptors should be robust against various image variations such as translation distortions, scale changes, illumination changes, pose variations and etc. The descriptors performance depends strongly on the power of the detector. Wrong detections of the region's location or shape will drastically change the appearance of the descriptor. Among the considerable research in developing robust local descriptors, SIFT and LBP descriptors are briefly discussed in the following.

1.2.1 SIFT Descriptor

One of the most influential works in object recognition is Scale Invariant Feature Transform (SIFT)

developed by David Lowe (Lowe, 2004). The SIFT algorithm benefits from a combination of detector and descriptor with superior performance as shown in Figure 1. (Mikolajczyk & Schmid, 2005). The detector/descriptor combination uses a scale invariant region detector, called difference of Gaussian (DoG), to extract interest key-points from images. SIFT descriptors are 3D histograms of gradient locations and orientations; locations are quantized into a 4×4 location grid and the gradient angle is quantized into 8 orientations. The resulting descriptor is of dimension 128. The scale invariant property of the descriptor is based on the scale invariant detection behaviour of the DoG key-point detector. Though the descriptor is not affine invariant by itself, it is possible to calculate SIFT on other type of detectors, so that it can inherit affine invariance as well.

1.2.2 Local Binary Patterns

Local Binary Patterns (LBP) are texture descriptors initially proposed by Ojala *et al.* (Ojala, Pietikäinen, & Mäenpää, 2002). LBP is a binary coding of intensity values that have been used in different applications (Ahonen, Hadid, & Pi-

Figure 1. The SIFT descriptor is computed on a 4×4 grid with 8-bin orientation histogram

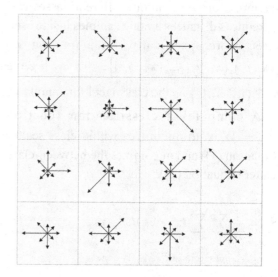

etikainen, 2006; Heikkilä & Pietikäinen, 2006; Heikkilä, Pietikäinen, & Schmid, 2009; Lian & Lu, 2007; Mäenpää & Pietikäinen, 2004; Nanni & Lumini, 2008; X. Wang, Gong, Zhang, Li, & Zhuang, 2006; H. Zhang, et al., 2006; G. Zhao & Pietikäinen, 2007)).

In its simplest form, a 3×3 pixel patch, intensity value of surrounding pixels (p_1 to p_8) are compared against the central pixel $I(p_0)$ (see Figure 2(a)) and a bit is assigned for each pixel according to Equation (4). The LBP value, LBP(p0), is then obtained by weighted summation of all bits (see Figure 2(b)).The LBP values of a region are usually furthermore combined in a LBP histogram to form a distinctive region descriptor.

$$b(p_i) = \begin{cases} 1, & I(p_i) \geq I(p_0) \\ 0, & otherwise \end{cases} \qquad (4)$$

The basic definition of the LBP approach can be extended to include other types of circular neighbourhoods with any number of pixels by bi-linear interpolation of the pixel intensity as well (Ojala, et al., 2002). LBPs are invariant to monotonic gray value transformations. To make them robust against rotation, the neighbouring points can be rotated clockwise as many times as

a maximal number of most significant bits start from zero (Ojala, et al., 2002).

2 REINFORCEMENT LEARNING AND COMPUTER VISION

Reinforcement Learning (RL) is a biologically-inspired machine learning technique to solve sequential decision problems. In RL, through interacting with the environment, an agent receives a reinforcement feedback signal to evaluate relevance of its decisions. From a biological perspective, when this signal becomes positive, the agent experiences pleasure/reward. On the contrary, a negative reinforcement implies a sensation of pain/ punishment. In RL, the agent is neither told what the optimal actions are, nor whether one of its decisions was optimal. Rather, an agent has to solely discover most promising actions by constituting a representative between its states and its environment, as well as by understanding the influence of its decisions on future reinforcements.

RL has received enormous attentions as a potential solution for various computer vision problems (Borji, Ahmadabadi, Araabi, & Hamidi, 2010; M. T. Harandi, Nili Ahmadabadi, & Araabi,

Figure 2. (a) Pixel neighbourhood points and (b) their weights for the simplest version of local binary patterns

P_4	P_3	P_2
P_5	P_0	P_1
P_6	P_7	P_8

8	4	2
16	P_0	1
32	64	128

(a) (b)

2009; S. Jodogne & Piater, 2007; Norouzi, Nili Ahmadabadi, & Nadjar Araabi, 2010; Paletta, Fritz, & Seifert, 2005).

2.1 Optimal Local Basis for Face/Object Recognition

Among different approaches proposed for object recognition and specifically for face recognition, statistical learning methods with the main object of deriving an appropriate basis have been studies the most (Bartlett, et al., 2002; Belhumeur, et al., 1997; He, Yan, Hu, Niyogi, & Zhang, 2005; Turk & Pentland, 1991). Statistical learning theory offers a lower dimensional description of objects that is crucial in learning; mainly because, the number of examples required for achieving a given performance exponentially grows with the dimension of the representation space. On the other hand, low dimensional representations of visual objects have some biological roots as suggested by Edelman and Intrator (Edelman & Intrator, 1997): "perceptual tasks such as similarity judgment tend to be performed on a low-dimensional representation of the sensory data." Principal Component Analysis (PCA) (Turk & Pentland, 1991; J. Yang, et al., 2004), Linear Discriminate Analysis (LDA) (Belhumeur, et al., 1997), Independent Component Analysis (ICA) (Bartlett, et al., 2002; C. Liu & Wechsler, 2003), Locality Preserving Projections (LPP) (Cai, He, Han, & Zhang, 2006; He, et al., 2005), kernel machines (K. I. Kim, et al., 2002; C. Liu, 2004; Lu, Plataniotis, & Venetsanopoulos, 2003; J. Yang, et al., 2005; M. H. Yang, Ahuja, & Kriegman, 2000) and graph embedding (Yan et al., 2007) are successful examples of applying statistical learning theory to face recognition by introducing a single basis for face representation.

Despite great success of traditional statistical approaches, there are some important issues to be addressed: Is a holistic basis sufficient for a complicated task like face recognition or do we have to introduce different basis for different parts of face space (individuals) to achieve best possible recognition? How does a single basis interpret the holistic and feature analysis behaviours of human being (W. Zhao, Chellappa, Phillips, & Rosenfeld, 2003)? Apparently using the same projection for all individuals is in direct contrast to human feature analysis behaviour in face recognition.

Introducing different basis for recognition can be studied under the Ensemble-Learning framework (Cheng, Liu, Lu, & Chen, 2006; Lu, Plataniotis, Venetsanopoulos, & Li, 2006; Su, Shan, Chen, & Gao, 2009; X. Wang & Tang, 2006; J. Zhang, He, & Zhou, 2006). Optimal Local Basis (OLB) is another discipline that utilizes reinforcement learning to generate a set of bases for a face space (see Figure 3) (M. T. Harandi, et al., 2009).

Consider a local approximation to an N dimensional subspace R^N is demanded where only some prototype points, $\{\mathbf{x}_1, \mathbf{x}_2, ..., \mathbf{x}_M\}$, each belonging to one of the available classes, $\{\omega_1, \omega_2, ..., \omega_C\}$ are accessible. In face recognition, the number of samples per class is usually small (Small Sample Size problem SSS). In such cases, it is possible to choose every sample in the training set as a prototype. If the number of samples per class in a specific problem is large, prototypes can be selected by vector quantization techniques (Gersho & Gray, 1991).

For each prototype $\mathbf{x}_i$, the goal of learning is to produce an m dimensional subspace that maximize the prototype discrimination power from its neighbours –provided that the directions of the m dimensional subspace are parallel to the holistic N dimensional space. In other words, a mapping $R^N \xrightarrow{T_i} R^m$ is sought where T_i is a binary diagonal transform matrix. To find the best transform T_i for prototype $\mathbf{x}_i$, firstly the necessary knowledge about the discrimination power of each direction in R^N is acquired utilizing a special version of RL called Q-learning (Sutton & Barto, 1998); then, the most appropriate directions are selected by thresholding the discrimination powers.

Figure 3. Illustrative example of the optimal local basis for recognition. For each sample/subject in a face space, OLB tries to find the most discriminant basis/feature from a set of fixed directions/features. (Adapted from (M. T. Harandi, et al., 2009))

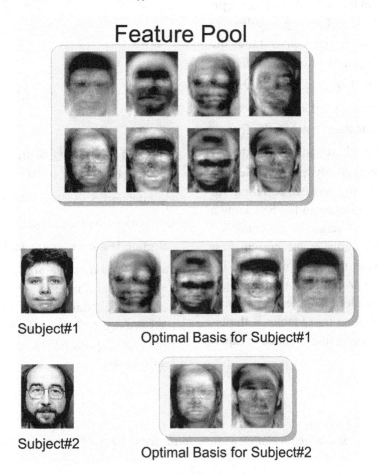

To give a simple view of how the learning method handles the feature selection problem, consider an intelligent agent who wants to figure out which features have the maximum discrimination for a given prototype. In this case, the agent traverses in the environment and picks up a feature from the available features at each step. The environment responds with a reward signal to reflect the discrimination power of the selected features. The agent strives to learn policies to maximize its accrued rewards over time. To employ the RL, the agent's life is modelled with a Markov Decision Process (MDP); i.e., the agent perceives a finite set of distinct states in its environment where it also has a set of finite distinct actions to perform.

At each discrete time step i, the agent senses the current state S_i, chooses action a_i to execute. The environment, in turn, responds the agent with a reward r_i and a new state S_{i+1}.

The environment in OLB algorithm is modelled with a first order MDP. In this model, actions are feature selections in R^N and the environmental states are merely the last selected feature (see Figure 4). States are represented by two Q-tables $\left\{ Q^0, Q^1 \right\}$ of size $\left\{ N, N \times N \right\}$, respectively. Q^0 and Q^1 represent the environment states of a zero and first order MDP respectively. In a zero order MDP, selecting a feature is independent of the previously selected features. In a first order

MDP, selecting a feature only depends on the previously selected features. Q^0 is used for selecting the best feature in the beginning of each episode (every run of the Q-learning is called an episode). The element $Q^0(i_0)$ demonstrates the expected value of received reward by selecting feature i_0. The element $Q^1(i_0, i_1)$ of the Q-table Q^1 demonstrates the expected value of received reward by selecting feature i_1 when the feature i_0 is previously selected. Actions are selected by ε-greedy policy. In ε-greedy policy, selection switches probabilistically between searching for better actions and re-evaluating the best known action. In this case, an action is randomly selected with the probability ε; the current best action is selected with the probability *1−ε*. By letting ε decreases over time, the agent changes its behaviour from exploration to exploitation.

The updating equation for Q-tables is the famous Q-learning updating rule as stated in Equations (5) and (6).

$$Q^0(i_j) =$$
$$Q^0(i_j) + \alpha(r + \gamma \max_l Q^1(i_j, i_l) - Q^0(i_j)) \tag{5}$$

$$Q^1(i_0, i_j) =$$
$$Q^1(i_0, i_j) + \alpha(r + \gamma \max_l Q^1(i_j, i_l) - Q^1(i_0, i_j)) \tag{6}$$

In (5) and (6), r is the received reward of selecting feature i_j; $\alpha \ (0 < \alpha \leq 1)$ is the learning rate; and $\gamma \ (0 \leq \gamma \leq 1)$ is the discount factor. As the Q-values for selecting feature i_l after selecting feature i_j is available through Q^1, this value is used for updating Q^0 in (5).

For generating the reward signal, the *k*-nearest neighbours of the studied prototype in the subspace defined by the selected features are found and Equation (7) is used to determine the reinforcement.

Figure 4. A schematic view of the learning system to derive a basis (Adapted from (M. T. Harandi, et al., 2009))

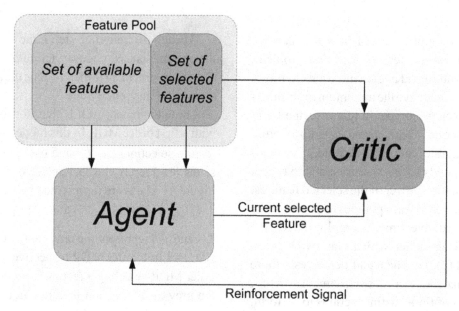

$$r = \sum_{j=1}^{K} \left(f_j(\omega_i) \times R_C(j) + \left(1 - f_j(\omega_i)\right) \times P_{NC}(j) \right) \tag{7}$$

In (7), $f_j(\omega_i)$ is a binary value function representing whether the *j-th* neighbour has the same class label as ω_i or not.

$$f_j(\omega_i) = \begin{cases} 1 & \text{if the } j\text{ - }th \text{ neighbor has the same class label as } \omega_i. \\ 0 & \text{otherwise} \end{cases} \tag{8}$$

$R_C(j)$ and $P_{NC}(j)$ are the learning parameters to express weighting for rewarding or punishing an agent upon its correct and incorrect hits, respectively. The agent receives the maximum reward if the *k* nearest neighbours have the same class labels as ω_i; it is punished for every misclassification with the weight of $P_{NC}(j)$.

The agent keeps track of the selected features in a vector called ***trace_vec*** in order not to select a feature twice in each episode. Also Q^0 is up-dated once at the beginning of each episode when no information about the last selected feature is still available. In the following steps of learning in each episode, the Q^1 gets updated. The learning algorithm can be summarized as shown in Table 2. It is worth mentioning that although the environment model is a first order MDP, since the Q-learning seeks for the policy that brings the maximum reward to the agent in the long run, the agent is able to derive a set of the more discriminant features.

After completing the learning process, prototype features are sorted in descending order of discrimination using the already learned Q-tables. Then, Q^0 is used to extract the most discriminant feature. The remaining features are found using the last selected feature (which is updated in the selection process) and tracing the position of maximum in the Q^1-table where selected features in previous steps are excluded from the selection task. The final step of learning process is to choose a subset of sorted features by simply thresholding the discrimination factors. Figure 5 shows the results of such ordering Eigenface basis for dif-

Table 2. OLB derivation algorithm

Select randomly a prototype $\mathbf{x}_i$ from the training dataset.
Initialize the corresponding Q-tables randomly.
for *iteration=1 to* Number_of_Episods **do**

$$\textbf{trace\_vec} = \left(\overbrace{0, 0, \ldots 0}^{N} \right)$$

repeat

Select a feature a_l by ε Greedy policy.

Update the selected feature vector, $\textbf{trace\_vec}(a_l) = 1$.

Project all the prototype points $\mathbf{x}_j$, $j = 1 \cdots M$ in training dataset into space defined by $\textbf{trace\_vec}$, i.e.

$$\mathbf{p}_j = diag(\mathbf{x}_j \otimes \textbf{trace\_vec}).$$

Find the class labels of the k-nearest neighbors of the projected data from $\mathbf{p}_i$.
Update the corresponding cell of Q-table according to Equations 1 and 2.

until in C_{hits} consequent steps, the agent receives the maximum reward or if all the features are selected.
endfor

Figure 5. The result of ordering the eigenfaces for different subjects after OLB learning

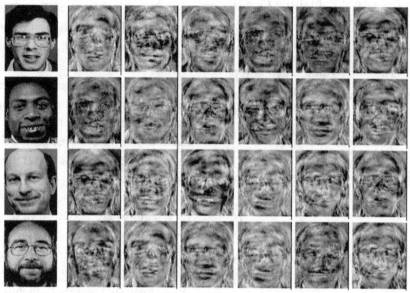

Table 3. Sorting the features in OLB algorithm

Algorithm Ordering the features according to their discrimination power.

$fC = 1$

$$trace\_vec = \left(\overbrace{1,1,\ldots 1}^{N} \right)$$

$a_0 = \arg\max_j(Q^0(a_j))$

$ordered\_features = (a_0)$

$trace\_vec(a_0) = 0$

$cState = \left(a_0 \right)$

while $fC \leq N$ **do**

Select all values described by the last selected action $cState$ *in* Q^1 *i.e.* $Row(Q^1) = (cState, a_j), \quad j = 1\ldots N$. This vector has length N.

$a_{fC} = \arg\max_j(Row(Q^1)) \,|\, trace\_vec(j) = 1$

$ordered\_directions = (ordered\_directions, a_{fC})$

$trace\_vec(a_{fC}) = 0$

$cState = \left(a_{fC} \right)$

$fC = fC + 1$

end while

ferent images in a recognition task. The pseudo code of the ordering algorithm is illustrated in Table 3.

Toward this end, the problem is modelled by a set of prototypes where the learning algorithm finds the best discriminant subspace associated to each one (the number of dimensions varies across prototypes). To assess the similarity of a query datum to all stored prototypes, simple similarity judgment based on ordinary distance measures does not work, because prototypes have different dimensions and features. To make different subspaces comparable, the reward signal is used as the similarity measure. To compute the similarity between a query datum $\mathbf{x}_q$ and prototype $\mathbf{x}_i$, firstly $\mathbf{x}_q$ as well as all prototypes $\mathbf{x}_j$, $j = 1 \ldots M$ are projected into the space defined by $\mathbf{T}_i$ to find the most discriminant subspace associated to prototype $\mathbf{x}_i$, i.e $\mathbf{x}_j \xrightarrow{\mathbf{T}_i} \mathbf{p}_j$ and $\mathbf{x}_q \xrightarrow{\mathbf{T}_i} \mathbf{p}_q$. Then, the label of K-nearest neighbours of $\mathbf{p}_q$ is found and Equation (9) is applied.

$$S(\mathbf{x}_q, \mathbf{x}_i) = \sum_{j=1}^{K} R_C(j) f_j(\omega_i) \qquad (9)$$

In (9), $f_j(\omega_i)$ is a binary value function to demonstrate whether the class label of the *j-th* neighbour of $\mathbf{p}_q$ is ω_i or not (Equation (8)). $R_C(j)$ is the reward values used in (7). Based on (9), the class Ω similarity measure is defined by adding the similarity measures of all prototypes belonging to it, i.e.

$$S_\Omega = \sum_i (S(\mathbf{x}_q, \mathbf{x}_i) \mid \omega_i = \Omega) \qquad (10)$$

To classify a query input in this case, the similarity measure for all classes are computed using (10) and the most similar match is assigned as the output of the classifier. Therefore, the classifica-

tion scheme is a competitive approach which is solved by reinforcement signal in a non-metric space.

The effect of generating local representation using OLB approach will be evaluated for a task of face recognition and a task of object categorization in sequel. The near frontal poses (C05, C07, C09, C27 and C29) of the CMU PIE face database (Sim, Baker, & Bsat, 2003) were used for the face recognition task. CMU PIE database contains more than 40,000 facial images of 68 individuals with variations of poses, illumination and expressions. The recognition accuracies and its standard deviation are compared in Table 4. This table reveals that the recognition accuracy can be significantly improved when local bases are employed. For example the improvement for Eigenface and Orthogonal Laplacianface methods are more than 14% and 5%, respectively.

ETH-80 database (Leibe & Schiele, 2003) was used to assess the efficiency of OLB algorithm for the task of object categorization. The ETH-80 database contains images of the following eight categories: apples, cows, cups, dogs, horses, pears, tomatoes, and cars. An instance of each category is shown in Figure 6. Each category includes the images of ten objects (e.g., ten different dogs as shown Figure 7) pictured at a total of 41 orientations, results in a total of 410 images per category.

Table 4. Recognition accuracies and their associated standard deviations for the studied methods over PIE database

Method	Accuracy
Eigenface (Turk & Pentland, 1991)	23.85, σ=4.0
Fisherface (Belhumeur, et al., 1997)	49.94, σ=7.6
Orthogonal Laplacianface (Cai, et al., 2006)	54.84, σ=8.3
OLB on Eigenface	38.4, σ=7.2
OLB on Fisherface	55.55, σ=7.6
OLB on Laplacianface	60.05, σ=9.7

Figure 6. Example images for each of the eight categories in the ETH-80 database

Figure 7. Sample images for each of the ten different dogs in the ETH-80 database

To obtain the feature space, the silhouette of the object, i.e., the contour that separates the object from the background, are first extracted (Figure 8). Then the centroid of this silhouette is computed and the lengths of lines that connect the centroid with the silhouette points are obtained along with the angles of the lines; see Figure 8. Finally the mean value of all distances lie in a fixed sector (for example a sector between zero degrees to 7.2 degrees) are computed and considered as features. In this experiment, a total of 50 non-overlap sectors (each covers 7.2 degrees) were used; as a result, the dimension of feature space become 50. To reduce the effects of object orientation, the obtained features are regrouped so that the maximum length is always seen as the first element of the feature vector. To test the categorization accuracy, three images from each object were randomly selected for training and the rest were used for testing. The tests were repeated ten times and the average accuracy is re-

Table 5. Comparison of recognition accuracy of the OLB and the holistic approach using the ETH-80 database

Method	Accuracy
Holistic	60.02%, σ=2.3
OLB algorithm	67.00%, σ=1.4

ported. The recognition accuracy of the OLB algorithm over the holistic approach is shown in Table 5. This table also confirms that the OLB approach outperformed the holistic method.

2.2 Reinforcement Learning of Visual Classes

Learning in MDP is conceptually easy for problems with small discrete state and/or action spaces. Solving the learning problem over continuous and very large, discrete state spaces typically demands for using functional approximations. Although functional approximations permit local generalization across similar states, they are not individually adequate for very high-dimensional state spaces spanned by images –curse of dimensionality (S. Jodogne, 2006). Visually similar images may represent states that require distinct actions; and, very dissimilar images may represent the exact same scenes (under different imaging conditions) that require similar actions. To tackle the problem of continuous and large perceptual space Jodogne *et al.* proposed Reinforcement Learning of Visual Classes (RLVC) (Sebastien Jodogne & Piater, 2005; S. Jodogne & Piater, 2007) in which a continuous or very large discrete perceptual space is adaptively and incrementally splits into discrete states (see Figure 9).

Figure 8. Lengths of the lines connecting the centre of each object to its silhouette are extracted from the contours of the ETH-80 objects and used for describing the objects

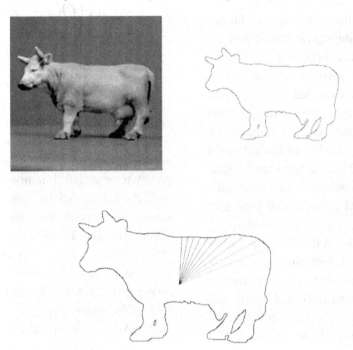

Figure 9. Splitting a discrete perceptual space into discrete states using RLVC (adapted from (S. Jodogne, 2006))

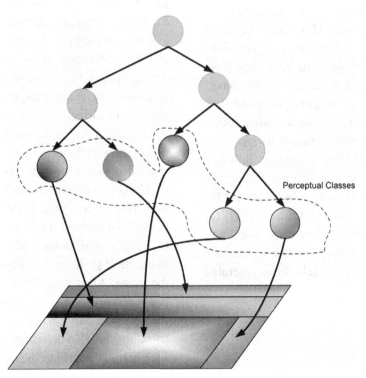

RLVC consists of two learning processes: an RL agent and an image classifier. The RL agent learns discrete state-action mappings in a classical RL manner; the state representation and the determination of the current state are provided by an image classifier that partitions the perceptual spaces into discrete states called visual classes. The two learning processes are interleaved. Initially, the entire perceptual space is mapped to a single visual class; i.e., a variety of distinct world states that requires different actions are lumped together into a single perceptual state for the RL agent. As a result, the RL agent cannot learn a set of actions to earn high rewards. The failure of the RL agent, which can be determined through a measure of residual error, hints the image classifier that the perceptual space must be further decomposed into more distinct visual subclasses. By iterating this procedure, perceptually-aliased visual classes are identified and split such that aliasing in maximally reduced.

To detect when a perceptual-aliasing visual state has happened, RLVC analyses the Bellman residuals error (Sutton & Barto, 1998). More specifically, RLVC assumes if the magnitudes of the Temporal-Difference (TD) errors (Equation (11)) of a given state-action pair (s,a) remained large, perceptual aliasing must have happened. This is inspired by the fact that the world behaves predictably; and therefore, TD errors must vanish over time (Detry, Pugeault, & Piater, 2009). Thus, whenever perceptual aliasing happens, the corresponding visual class s requires different actions and need to be split into two states. The splitting policy is similar to the rule used by CART (Breiman, Friedman, Stone, & Olshen, 1984) for building regression trees. Here also, it seeks to split a state so that the sum of the variances of the TD errors is minimized in each of the generated two new states.

$$\Delta_t = r_{t+1} + \gamma \max_{a'}\left(Q(s_{t+1},a') - Q(s_t,a_t)\right)$$

(11)

An example application of the RLVC over the visual Gridworld is shown in Figure 10; here, the problem is a discrete 2D maze that constituted of walls and cells with only one exit. In each cell, the agent has four possible actions: go up, go right, go down, or go left. If a move results in hitting a wall, the location of the agent will not change. If a move hits the exit, the agent is randomly transferred to another location in the maze. The agent earns a reward whenever it reaches the exit, and a penalty for any other move. This task is closely related to the grid-world problem (Sutton & Barto, 1998). The major difference is that instead of the feedbacks on agent positions, the agent obtains an image from its sensory input, and positions are implicitly encoded as images. In each cell, a different object is stored under a transparent glass, and sensors of each agent return a colour picture of the object underneath (see Figure 10). From each image, visual features like SIFT (Lowe, 2004) are extracted. Figure 11 shows locations of interest detected by SIFT algorithm for some of the images in the maze. In SIFT algorithm, interest-point candidates are detected as local extrema of difference-of-Gaussian (DoG) filters in a Gaussian Scale Space of the input image. Key points showing low contrast or lying on edges are discarded as they are not stable.

Upon perception of a new image, the RLVC will create a new perceptual class. The ultimate goal of an agent here is to encode a mapping between visual states and available actions to direct itself to the exit cell from any other cell in the maze. After completion of RLVC learning phase, as can be seen in Figure 12 and Figure 13, the agent not only classifies the perceptual space correctly, but also determines the best path from each cell in the grid to the exit point.

Figure 10. Visual Gridworld Maze, cells with crosses are walls, and the exit is indicated by a gray background. Empty cells are labelled by a picture (inspired from (S. Jodogne, 2006)).

Figure 11. Location of SIFT feature for some examples from the 2D maze problem. White circles demonstrate the location of interest points detected by the SIFT algorithm.

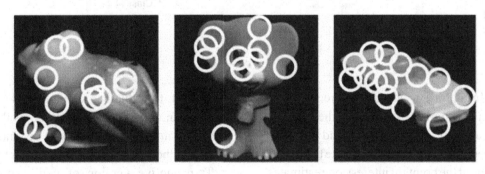

3 TRANSDUCTIVE LEARNING

A large amount of effort in supervised classification has been put toward optimizing the performance of classifiers over all possible future query data. From a practical point of view, it is neither possible nor necessary to classify all possible future samples. This also contradicts the fact that only a particular set of query or working data is usually of real interest. Transductive inference is motivated by such philosophy (Vapnik, 2000). By explicitly including the working set data in problem formulation, a better generalization can be expected on problems with insufficient labelled points. One of the most profound definitions of transductive learning is provided by Vapnik as

Figure 12. Left) the computed optimal policy for this classification algorithm. Right) label of the perceptual class that is assigned to each empty cell by RLVC algorithm (inspired from (S. Jodogne, 2006)).

→	→	↓
✕	G	✕
→	→	↑

1	2	6
✕		5
7	3	4

Figure 13. A typical classifier obtained from RLVC algorithm that tests the presence of the circled local-appearance features (inspired from (S. Jodogne, 2006)).

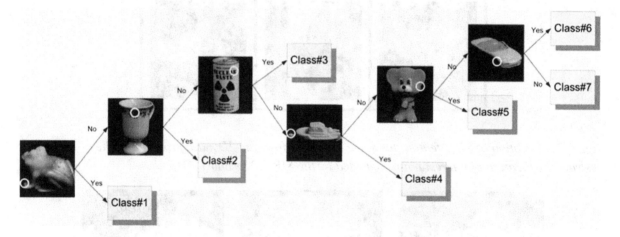

follows: "In contrast to inductive inference where one uses given empirical data to find the approximation of a functional dependency and then uses the obtained approximation to evaluate the values of a function at the points of interest, one estimates the values of a function at the points of interest in one step" (Vapnik, 2000). In other words, in the transductive learning, the learner can observe sample data in the test set and potentially exploit their structures based on their distributions. An interesting analogy to explain this type of leaning: "inductive learning is like an in-class exam, where the questions are not known in advance, and a student needs to prepare for all possible questions;

in contrast, transductive learning is like a take-home exam, where the student knows the exam questions and needs not prepare beyond those" (Zhu, Goldberg, Brachman, & Dietterich, 2009).

Transductive version of many supervised classification schemes such as k-nearest neighbour classifier (Proedrou, Nouretdinov, Vovk, & Gammerman, 2002), support vector machine (Thorsten Joachims, 1999), graph-based learning (T. Joachims, 2003) have been introduced recently. Realization of k-nearest neighbour classifier for transductive learning is based on a strangeness value as follows:

$$\alpha_{iy} = \frac{\sum_{j=1}^{k} D_{ij}^{y}}{\sum_{j=1}^{k} D_{ij}^{-y}} \qquad (12)$$

where D_{ij}^{y} stands for the j-th shortest distance from sorted sequence of distances between example i and samples with the classification label y, and D_{ij}^{-y} is the j-th shortest distance from sorted sequence of distances between example i and samples with different classification from y.

The strangeness measure is the ratio of the sum of the k nearest distances from the same class y divided by the sum of the k nearest distances from all the other classes $-y$. The strangeness of a sample increases either when distances from samples of a class become larger or when its distances from other classes become smaller.

Based on the strangeness value, one defines the p-value function. The p-value implies the strangeness of putative label y for new sample $\mathbf{x}_{new}$ given the set of training samples $\left\{ \left(\mathbf{x}_1, y_1 \right), ..., \left(\mathbf{x}_n, y_n \right) \right\}$. Equation (13) shows how p-value can be computed. As a rule of thumb, the larger the p-value, the less strange is an example $\mathbf{x}_{new}$ with label y compared with the rest of the examples $\left\{ \left(\mathbf{x}_1, y_1 \right), ..., \left(\mathbf{x}_n, y_n \right) \right\}$. In analogy to statistical hypothesis testing, it can also be described as testing the null hypothesis $H0$: "$\mathbf{x}_{new}$ given label y is not strange" against the alternative hypothesis $H1$: "$\mathbf{x}_{new}$ given label y is strange". The pseudo code of transductive kNN classifier (TCM-kNN for simplicity) is shown in Table 6.

$$p(\alpha_{new}) = \frac{\#\left\{ i : \alpha_i \geq \alpha_{new} \right\}}{n+1} \qquad (13)$$

The application of transductive learning in face authentication was first studied by Li *et al.* (F. Li & Wechsler, 2005). The fundamental assumption in open Set recognition is that not all probes have a corresponding match in the gallery; and thus, a rejection option is required. For small sample-sized problems (e.g. face recognition), transductive learning seems very appropriate as it can efficiently deploy its query data to make its decisions. Moreover, as Vapnik mentioned: results of transductive inference are true even when the data points of interest and the training data are not independent and identically distributed (i.i.d). This issue is quite important in small-sample-sized problems where lack of training data always cause doubt whether the model properly expresses the unknown distribution of the trained data.

In open-set authentication using TCM-kNN, the p-values for a new probe sample are exploited as a likelihood measure to determine whether new samples come from a putative subject in the gallery or not. If a p-value is relatively high and significantly outscores the others, new sample can be matched to the corresponding subject class. If the top ranked choices (highest p-values) are very close to each other and outscore others, although the top choice can still be accepted, its recognition is questionable because of its ambiguity as well as its low confidence level. If all p-values are randomly distributed and none of them significantly outscores the others, any recognition choice will be questionable and the new sample should be rejected.

Transductive learning has recently been applied to the problem of matching an image-set to a single image problem (M. B. Harandi, Abbas ; Lovell, Brian C., 2010). Image-set matching, *i.e.* exploiting set information, is a promising and emerging research path in visual object recognition and categorization (Wolf & Shashua, 2003a; Yamaguchi, Fukui, & Maeda, 1998a; Zhou, Krueger, & Chellappa, 2003). Besides having greater accuracy and robustness as compared to approaches utilizing single images, devices for capturing sequence of images are also becoming more affordable every day. While much effort has been dedicated to improving the accuracy of image-set face recognizers, a large family of

Table 6. TCM-kNN algorithm

Input: Training data $\left\{\left(\mathbf{x}_1, y_1\right), ..., \left(\mathbf{x}_n, y_n\right)\right\}$, $\mathbf{x}_i \in \Re^D$, $y_i \in \left\{1, 2, ..., c\right\}$, $\mathbf{x}_{new}$ new unlabeled sample, k the number of nearest neighbors to be used.
Output: The class label of $\mathbf{P}$

%% Compute statistics of training data
for i=1 **to** n **do**

  Compute $D_i^{y_i}$ and $D_i^{-y_i}$
endfor
for i=1 **to** n **do**

Compute strangeness value α_i for $\left(\mathbf{x}_i, y_i\right)$ using *(12)*

endfor
%% Compute distances from new unlabeled sample to training data
for i=1 **to** n **do**

$$dist(i) = d\left(\mathbf{x}_i, \mathbf{x}_{new}\right)$$

endfor
for j=1 **to** c **do**
$idS \leftarrow$ indices of training examples with label j
$idD \leftarrow$ indices of training examples with label different from j

  %% Recalculate statistics using the new sample $\left(\mathbf{x}_{new}, j\right)$

for $t \in idS$ *do*

if $D_{tk}^j > dist(t)$ *then*

Compute strangeness value α_t for $\left(\mathbf{x}_t, y_t\right)$ using *(12)*

  endif
  endfor
for $t \in idD$ *do*

if $D_{tk}^{-j} > dist(t)$ *then*

Compute strangeness value α_t for $\left(\mathbf{x}_t, y_t\right)$ using *(12)*

  endif
  endfor
  %% Compute p-value

$p_i \leftarrow$ p-value for $\left(\mathbf{x}_{new}, i\right)$ *using* (13)(12)

  endfor

---

solutions fail to adapt to scenarios where only one single still image per subject exists in the gallery. Although matching a set against a single image looks very challenging and relatively obscure, it has many practical applications such as advanced surveillance, smart access control, and many more. Transductive Mutual Subspace Method or TMSM utilizes transductive learning to exploit the Mutual Subspace Method (MSM) (Yamaguchi, et al., 1998a) –a well known set to set scheme–in a set to single image matching (M. B. Harandi,

Abbas ; Lovell, Brian C., 2010). In TMSM, for each query image-set, the smallest strangeness values with every putative class label is used to determine the final decision (see Figure 14).

Given a recognition problem of matching an unknown probe image-set $\mathbf{P} = \left\{p_1, p_2, ..., p_M\right\}$ against a gallery set with one sample per class $\left\{\left(g_i, l_i\right) : i = 1, ..., N\right\}$, in TMSM for a putative class label y, k different pairs of sets $\left\{\left(\mathbf{P}_j, \mathbf{P}_j^{'}\right), j = 1, ..., k\right\}$ are generated using $\mathbf{P}$ and

Figure 14. Illustrative example of the proposed transductive scheme. Instead of matching the probe image-set against gallery images, for a putative class, different image-sets using the gallery image and probe images are built. The strangeness of the probe image-set for the putative class is measured using the constructed image-sets and the class with least strangeness is considered as the output of decision. (differently labelled samples) lie outside the smaller circle by some finite margin. (Adapted from (Weinberger & Saul, 2009)).

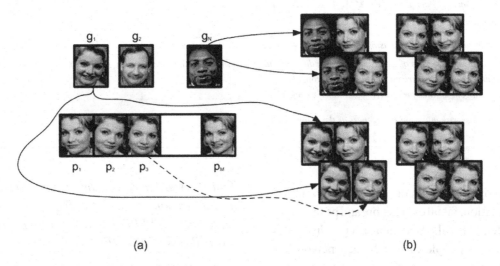

(a)   (b)

g_y as shown in Figure 3. Although the pair generation is purely random, no common vectors are allowed in a pair, *i.e. if* $p_i \in \mathbf{P}_j \Rightarrow p_i \notin \mathbf{P}_j'$. Then, the strangeness of the unknown probe image-set $\mathbf{P}$ with putative label y is defined as:

$$\alpha_y = \frac{\sum_{j=1}^{k} \Omega_E(\neg y, j)}{\sum_{j=1}^{k} \Omega_I(y, j)} \quad (14)$$

$$\Omega_I(y, j) = CC(\mathbf{P}_j \bigcup \{g_y\}, \mathbf{P}_j') \quad (15)$$

$$\Omega_E(\neg y, j) = CC(\bigcup_{M_1}^{k \neq y} g_k, \mathbf{P}) \quad (16)$$

where Ω_I and Ω_E are intra-person and inter-person subspace distances, k denotes the number of pairs, and $\neg y$ represents sample data with class labels different form y.

In (15), $\mathbf{P}_j$ and $\mathbf{P}_j'$ are two subspaces randomly extracted from $\mathbf{P}$. In (16), $\bigcup_{M_1}^{k \neq y} g_k$ is a random subset of gallery images with cardinality M_1 and class labels different from y. The intra-person and inter-person subspace distances are computed utilizing principal angles.

The strangeness value demonstrates the level of confidence in labelling a probe image-set to class y. Large values of strangeness represent either large distances between a probe set with the assumed class or small distance between the probe and other classes; both indicate lower confidence of assumed hypothesis. Small strangeness values, on the contrary, reflect large inter-person and small intra-person distances, respectively; therefore, higher confidence of assumed hypothesis.

To conclude this section, TMSM's efficiency is assesses using two popular and publicity available face databases including Extended Yale B (Lee, Ho, & Kriegman, 2005) and CMU PIE (Sim, et al., 2003). The selected databases address dif-

Table 7. The pseudo code of TMSM method

Input: Gallery set $G = \left\{ (g_i, l_i) \mid g_i \in \mathbb{R}^d, i = 1, ..., N \right\}$ and unknown probe set $\mathbf{P} = \left\{ p_1, p_2, ..., p_M \mid p_i \in \mathbb{R}^d \right\}$
Output: The class label of $\mathbf{P}$

Generate k *random pair from* $\mathbf{P}$, $\left\{ \left(\mathbf{P}_j, \mathbf{P}_j' \right), j = 1, ..., k \right\}$.
  for i=1 to N **do**
Compute the intra-person distances using $\left\{ \left(\mathbf{P}_j, \mathbf{P}_j' \right), j = 1, ..., k \right\}$ *and* g_i *from* (2).
  Generate randomly k subsets of gallery images with different class label than i. Each set contains M_i samples. Compute the inter-person distance using the generated subsets and $\mathbf{P}$ *from* (3).
  Compute strangeness value for putative class label i *using* (1).
  end for
Choose the class with minimum strangeness as the output of classification.

ferent recognition challenges including variation in illumination, facial expression, and pose changing. Extended Yale B database contains 2414 images of 38 people in which each person has almost 64 front-view face pictures with various lighting. From CMU PIE database five near frontal poses (C05, C07, C09, C27, C29) which exhibits different illumination and expressions were used. For each database, the experiments were repeated five times by randomly selecting one image per class for training and grouping the remaining images of each class into sets. The maximum number of images per set was confined to ten. The proposed methods were assessed against well-known benchmarking methods of Eigenface (Turk & Pentland, 1991) and Local Binary Pattern (LBP) (Ahonen, et al., 2006). LBP has shown to provide a set of highly discriminant features for representing faces (Ahonen, et al., 2006; Heusch, Rodriguez, & Marcel, 2006; Shan, Gong, & McOwan, 2005; Tan & Triggs, 2007). For Eigenface and LBP methods, the minimum distance between the query set and gallery images is considered for evaluation. Table 8 provides the average recognition accuracy along with standard deviations for benchmarking methods on the studied databases. For example, this table reveals that the difference between the Transduc-

Table 8. Average recognition rates and standard deviations comparisons for Transductive-MSM, Eigenface, and LBP methods across ten runs on YALE-B and CMU-PIE

	Extended Yale B	**PIE**
PCA	66.52±2.3	33.06±2.4
LBP	74.21±1.7	71.47±2.6
TMSM	94.84±1.0	78.28±2.8

tive method and LBP method is more than 20% on the extended Yale B dataset,

4 DISTANCES IN COMPUTER VISION AND DISTANCE METRIC LEARNING

The performance of many computer vision algorithms greatly depend on the associated distance and/or metric function defined over their input space. For instance, extensively used nearest-neighbour classifiers in computer vision need to be equipped with appropriate metrics to be able to reasonably reflect/discover important relationships among the input data.

A function $f : B \times B \to \mathbb{R}^+$ is called 'a distance function' on a non-empty set B, if for all $x, y, z \in B$:

$$\begin{cases} f(x,y) = 0; & iff \; x = y \\ f(x,y) = f(y,x) \end{cases}$$

The function f is called a 'metric function' if and only if f is a distance function that also satisfies the triangle inequality,

$$f(x,z) \leq f(x,y) + f(y,z)$$

Minkowski's distance,

$$L_r(x,y) = \left(\sum_i \left| x_i - y_i \right|^r \right)^{\frac{1}{r}},$$

is widely used in computer vision and pattern recognition. For example, the L_1 distance has been used for computing similarity among points in subspaces, colour histograms, and gradient histograms.

4.1 Histograms Distances

Histogram $H = \left\{ h_i \right\}$ is a mapping from a set of d-dimensional feature vectors to a distribution of nonnegative reals. It can be considered as a measure of the distribution of mass of the underlying feature space. For instance, in a grey-level image histogram, the set of possible grey values are split into N intervals where h_i is the number of pixels in the image that have a grey value in the interval indexed by i.

Histogram matching plays a vital rule in computer visions. For example, Content-Based Image Retrieval (CBIR) (see Figure 15) systems usually represent image features by multi-dimensional colour histograms or texture features[1] (Gonzalez & Woods, 2006). Beside their simplicity in computation, histograms are conveying interesting properties. For example colour histograms are invariant to translation and rotation of the viewing axis, and change slowly under changes of angle of view, scale, and occlusion.

The similarity measures between histograms can be categorized into two groups: bin-by-bin and cross-bin approaches. In the bin-by-bin approach, two histograms $H = \left\{ h_i \right\}$ and $K = \left\{ k_i \right\}$ are compared through comparison of only h_i 's with k_i 's for all i; In the cross-bin approach, similarity measures is performed to also include non-corresponding bins comparisons of h_i 's with k_j 's for $i \neq j$.

Representative methods in bin-by-bin similarity measure are Minkowski's distance, K-L divergence, and histogram intersection.

Figure 15. Colour histograms are extensively used in CBIR systems. In CBIR, the system searches through a large database and analyses the content of images for possible matches of a query, here for example, a butterfly.

The histogram intersection (Swain & Ballard, 1991), $\sum_i \min(h_i, k_i) \Big/ \sum_i k_i$, is able to handle partial matches when areas of two histograms (sum over all bins) are different. Differences between areas of histograms are the result of matching a model against an image while the number of pixels in the model is different (usually smaller) than the image. $\sum_i \min(h_i, k_i)$ is called the intersection and represent the number of pixels from the model that have corresponding pixels of the same colour in the image. It is shown that when the areas of the two histograms are equal, the histogram intersection is equivalent to the (normalized) L_1 distance.

A major drawback of the bin-by-bin similarity measures are their dependency on the correspondence between same index bins, and neglecting the information across bins. Figure 16 illustrates this problem by showing three one dimensional gray-scale histograms. Comparison between histograms Figure 16b Figure 16c with histogram is shown in Figure 16a. A bin-by-bin similarity measure like L_1 distance incorrectly results in larger distances for Figure 16b. This is in contrast to obvious perceptual dissimilarity of histograms in Figure 16a and Figure 16c.

It is possible to design more meaningful similarity measures if some information about the ground distance between histogram bins (for in-

stance perceptual similarity of bins) is also available. A natural extension of L_2 distance is the quadratic form distance

$d_Q(H, K) = \sqrt{(h - k)^T A (h - k)}$ that can capture the similarity between bins i and j when $i \neq j$. In quadratic form similarity measure, $A = \left[a_{ij} \right]$ is the similarity matrix and a_{ij} denote similarity between bins i and j. Niblack *et al.* proposed to use $a_{ij} = 1 - \dfrac{d_{ij}}{d_{Max}}$ (Niblack et al., 1993) where d_{ij} is the ground distance between bins i and j of the histogram, and $d_{Max} = \max(d_{ij})$. The quadratic form distance does not enforce a one-to-one correspondence between elements in the two histograms; that is an element in the first histogram is simultaneously compared against different bins of the second histogram.

Another way to benefit from ground data in matching histograms is the Earth Mover's Distance (EMD) (Rubner, Tomasi, & Guibas, 2000). Given two distributions, one distribution can be considered as a mass of earth spread in space and the other distribution can be seen as a collection of holes in space. The EMD measures the least amount of work needed to fill the holes with earth. Computing the EMD is based on a solution to the well-known Monge-Kantorovich transportation problem that returns back to 18th century (Rachev,

Figure 16. Example where L_1 distance between the model (a) and query (b) and (c) do not match the perceptual similarity. The L_1 distance between (a) and (b) is larger than L_1 distance between (a) and (c) while (b) is more similar to (a).

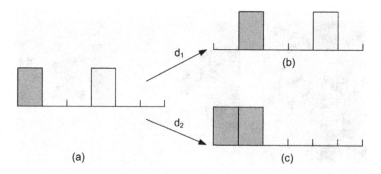

1985). In this problem, it is supposed that several suppliers with individual amount of goods are required to supply consumers with individual limited capacities. For each pair of supplier-consumer, the cost of transporting a single unit of goods is given. The transportation problem is to find the cheapest flow of goods from the suppliers to the consumers that satisfy the consumers' demand. By defining one histogram as the supplier and the other one as the consumer histogram matching can be considered as a transportation problem. The cost for a supplier-consumer pair is equal to the ground distance between an element in the first histogram and an element in the second. Based on this formalism, the solution is then the minimum amount of "work" required for transforming one histogram into the other.

This solution to the EMD can be formalized as a linear programming problem. If the workflow from bin i in the first histogram $H = \{h_i\}$ to bin j in the second histogram $K = \{k_i\}$ is denoted by f_{ij} then the solution is the matrix $F = [f_{ij}]$ that minimizes the overall cost

$$WORK(H, K, F) = \sum_i \sum_j a_{ij} f_{ij} \qquad (17)$$

Subject to the following constraints:

$$f_{ij} \geq 0 \qquad (18)$$

$$\sum_j f_{ij} \leq h_i \qquad (19)$$

$$\sum_i f_{ij} \leq k_j \qquad (20)$$

$$\sum_i \sum_j f_{ij} = \min(h_i, k_j) \qquad (21)$$

In (17) a_{ij} denote similarity between bins i and j, constraint (18) allows moving "supplies" only

from H to K (and not vice versa), constraint (19) limits the amount of supplies can be sent from H to the bin values, constraint (20) limits the bins in K to receive no more supplies than their bin values, and constraint (21) forces to move the maximum amount of supplies possible (the total flow). Based on the solution of the transportation problem, *i.e.* the optimal flow F, the earth mover's distance is defined as the following normalized flow:

$$EMD(H, K) = \frac{\sum_i \sum_j a_{ij} f_{ij}}{\sum_i \sum_j f_{ij}} \qquad (22)$$

The EMD extends the notion of a distance between single elements to that of a distance between sets, or distributions, of elements and allows partial matches in a very natural fashion. This is important in dealing with occlusions and clutter in image retrieval applications. EMD and its extensions have been successfully deployed in several application including similarity measure in object tracking (Monari, Maerker, & Kroschel, 2009; Q. Zhao, Yang, & Tao, 2010), object recognition (Demirci, Shokoufandeh, Keselman, Bretzner, & Dickinson, 2006; Grauman & Darrell, 2005; J. Zhang, Marszałek, Lazebnik, & Schmid, 2007), and image retrieval (Jing, Li, Zhang, & Zhang, 2004; Y. Liu, Wang, Wang, Zha, & Qin, 2010; Rubner, et al., 2000).

4.2 Distance between Sets

Patterns can be broadly represented in three possible ways: point, subspace, and manifolds (R. Wang, Shan, Chen, & Gao, 2008). A subspace by definition is a vector space, i.e.

- if x and y belong to the subspace S; then, $x+y$ also belongs to S.
- if x belongs to the subspace S and r is a real number; then, rx also belongs to S.

As a result, a subspace is a linear model spans by a set of samples. Though a subspace can be considered as a set of samples, common similarity measures for sets like Hausdorff distance and its extensions (Dubuisson & Jain, 1994; C. Zhao, Shi, & Deng, 2005) are not considered the most appropriate ones specially in applications like object recognition from video or image-sets (L. Wang, Wang, & Feng, 2006). Toward solving this problem, more appropriate similarity measures among subspaces has been defined over the past few years. To the best of authors of this chapter, no unified definition for the distance between two subspaces (denoted by $d(\mathbf{S}_1, \mathbf{S}_2)$) has been unanimously agreed; The concept of principal angles, however, is most commonly exploited because of its straight forward computation method and favourable performance (T.-K. Kim, Arandjelovic, & Cipolla, 2007; Wolf & Shashua, 2003b; Yamaguchi, Fukui, & Maeda, 1998b).

If $\mathbf{S}_1 \in \mathbb{R}^{d \times n_1}$ and $\mathbf{S}_2 \in \mathbb{R}^{d \times n_2}$ are two linear subspaces in $\mathbb{R}^d$ with minimum rank $r = \min rank(n_1, n_2)$; then, there are exactly r uniquely defined principal angle between $\mathbf{S}_1$ and $\mathbf{S}_2$ that can be computed as follows:

$$\cos \theta_i = \max_{x_i \in \mathbf{S}_1} \max_{y_j \in \mathbf{S}_2} x_i^T y_j \qquad (23)$$

s.t.

$$x_i^T x_i = y_i^T y_i = 1 \text{ and } x_i^T x_j = y_i^T y_j = 0, i \neq j \qquad (24)$$

where θ_i is the principal angle between the two subspaces and $0 \leq \theta_i \leq \dots \leq \pi/2; i \in \{1, 2, \dots, r\}$. One straight and numerical robust way to compute the principal angles is based on Singular Value Decomposition (SVD). Considering O_1 and O_2 are orthogonal bases for subspaces $\mathbf{S}_1$ and $\mathbf{S}_2$, the cosine of the principal angles are the singular values of $O_1^T O_2 = U \Lambda V^T, \Lambda = diag(\sigma_i)$ *i.e.* $\cos(\theta_i) = \sigma_i$.

Based on principal angles, other similarity measures between subspaces like Binet-Cauchy or Procrustes distances can be defined. The Binet-Cauchy distance (Wolf & Shashua, 2003b) between two subspace $\mathbf{S}_1$ and $\mathbf{S}_2$ is defined by:

$$d_{BC}(\mathbf{S}_1, \mathbf{S}_2) = \sqrt{1 - \prod_i \cos^2(\theta_i)} \qquad (25)$$

The Procrustes distance is the minimum distance between different representations of two subspaces and defined by (Hamm & Lee, 2008):

$$d_{\text{Procrustes}}(\mathbf{S}_1, \mathbf{S}_2) = 2\sqrt{\sum_i \sin^2(\theta_i/2)} \qquad (26)$$

Subspaces are appropriate models for studying the effects of variations on images; e.g., an acceptable and widely used approximation for photometric invariance under restricted conditions of no shadowing, Lambertian reflectance and etc., is a four dimensional linear space (Adini, Moses, & Ullman, 1997). Linear subspaces are, however, not adequate enough when different types of variations (pose, illumination, clutter and etc.) are considered/combined together. Manifolds unlike vector space are curved. In computer vision two types of manifolds namely Grassmann and Stiefel manifolds are often appeared in applications (Turaga, Veeraraghavan, & Chellappa, 2008). It is known that subspaces can be seen as points on Grassmann manifolds. Lui *et al.* adopted arc-length to compare subspaces on a Grassmann manifold (Lui, Beveridge, Draper, & Kirby, 2008). The arc-length distance or geodesic distance between two points (subspaces) $\mathbf{S}_1$ and $\mathbf{S}_2$ is defined by:

$$d(\mathbf{S}_1, \mathbf{S}_2) = \sqrt{\sum_i \theta_i^2} \qquad (27)$$

Comparing two manifolds M_1 and M_2 can be achieved by comparing subspaces (R. Wang, et al., 2008). Considering a dataset $X = \{\mathbf{x}_1, \mathbf{x}_2, ..., \mathbf{x}_n\}, \mathbf{x}_i \in \mathbb{R}^d$ is given where samples are assumed to come from a low-dimensional manifold M. The local modes can be generated by partitioning the data X into a set of disjoint samples C_i. That is,

$$X = \bigcup_i C_i \qquad (28)$$

$$C_i \cap C_j = \varnothing \qquad (29)$$

Different metrics can be used in order to cluster the samples into disjoint sets. Wang *et al.* employed the pair-wise geodesic distance (Tenenbaum, Silva, & Langford, 2000) as a criterion for clustering (R. Wang, et al., 2008), i.e. two samples are considered to be in a subspace if their geodesic distance is smaller than a ratio of their Euclidean distance. Based on the local subspaces for each manifold, the distance between two manifolds M_1 and M_2 can be defined as:

$$d\left(M_1, M_2\right) = \min_{C_i \in M_1} \min_{C_j' \in M_2} d(C_i, C_j') \qquad (30)$$

4.3 Distance Metric Learning

Distance metric learning (DML) aims to construct an appropriate distance metric for the given learning task. One can intuitively expect superior performance in a classification problem if samples of the same class are kept close and samples from different classes are separated far apart. A large family of DML algorithms consider the learning of Mahalanobis distance metric. The Mahalanobis distance between two d-dimensional samples x_i and x_j is defined as:

$$D_{Mah}(\mathbf{x}_i, \mathbf{x}_j) = \left\| \mathbf{x}_i - \mathbf{x}_j \right\|_M^2$$
$$= (\mathbf{x}_i - \mathbf{x}_j)^T \mathbf{M}(\mathbf{x}_i - \mathbf{x}_j) \qquad (31)$$

where $\mathbf{M}$ is a $d \times d$ symmetric positive semi-definite matrix. As a result, a Mahalanobis DML method needs to estimate d^2 parameter.

In this study, only the supervised approaches for DML are further explained. In contrast to typical supervised learning, where training samples are labelled with their class labels, the label information in distance metric learning is usually specified in the form of pair-wise constraints on the data as follows:

(1) Equivalence constraints: The given pairs are semantically-similar and should be close together in the learned metric. The set of equivalence constraints is denoted by $S = \left\{(\mathbf{x}_i, \mathbf{x}_j) \mid y_i = y_j\right\}$.

(2) Inequivalence constraints: The given points are semantically-dissimilar and should not be near in the learned metric. The set of equivalence constraints is denoted by $D = \left\{(\mathbf{x}_i, \mathbf{x}_j) \mid y_i \neq y_j\right\}$.

Based on the definition of set S and D, a criterion for the desired metric is to demand pairs of points in S that have small squared distance between them, *i.e.* $\sum_S \left\| \mathbf{x}_i - \mathbf{x}_j \right\|_M^2$. The trivial solution of this criteria, *i.e.* $\mathbf{M}=\mathbf{0}$ can collapse the dataset into a single point. Xing *et al.* add another constraint to ensure the trivial solution would not happen and formulated the problem of finding the positive semi-definitive $\mathbf{M}$ into the following convex programming Problem (Xing, Ng, Jordan, & Russell, 2002):

$$\min_{\mathbf{M}} \left(\sum_{(\mathbf{x}_i, \mathbf{x}_j) \in S} (\mathbf{x}_i - \mathbf{x}_j)^T \mathbf{M}(\mathbf{x}_i - \mathbf{x}_j) \right) \qquad (32)$$

s.t.

$$\sum_{(\mathbf{x}_i,\mathbf{x}_j)\in D}\left(\mathbf{x}_i - \mathbf{x}_j\right)^T \mathbf{M}\left(\mathbf{x}_i - \mathbf{x}_j\right) \geq 1$$

The choice of the constant '1' in the right hand side of (32) is arbitrary but not important, and changing it to any other positive constant c results only in $\mathbf{M}$ being replaced by $c^2\mathbf{M}$. In addition to general algorithms for distance metric learning like (32), several studies aimed to learn appropriate distance metrics for the KNN or SVM classifiers.

Neighbourhood Component Analysis (NCA) algorithm learns a Mahalanobis distance metric for the KNN classifier by minimizing the expected leave-one-out classification error (Goldberger, Roweis, Hinton, & Salakhutdinov, 2004). Given a point $\mathbf{x}_i$, a 'soft' neighbour of $\mathbf{x}_i$ is defined by p_{ij} as the probability for $\mathbf{x}_j$ to be selected as the neighbour of $\mathbf{x}_i$.

$$p_{ij} = \begin{cases} \dfrac{\exp\left(-\left\|\mathbf{Lx}_i - \mathbf{Lx}_j\right\|^2\right)}{\sum_{k\neq i}\exp\left(-\left\|\mathbf{Lx}_i - \mathbf{Lx}_k\right\|^2\right)} & if\ i \neq j \\ 0 & if\ i = j \end{cases}$$

(33)

In (33) $\mathbf{M}$ is in the form of $\mathbf{M}=\mathbf{L}^T\mathbf{L}$. Under this stochastic selection rule, the probability p_i that point i will be correctly classified is given by:

$$p_i = \sum_{j\in C_i} p_{ij}$$

(34)

where C_i denote the set of points in the same class as i. The objective to maximize is the expected number of points correctly classified, *i.e.* $f(L) = \sum_i \sum_{j\in C_i} p_{ij}$. Differentiating f with respect to the transformation matrix $\mathbf{L}$ yields the gradient learning rule in Equation 35.

In NCA, there is no free parameter k for the number of nearest neighbours. Instead, the scale of $\mathbf{L}$ determines the size of neighbourhoods. The objective function for NCA differs in one important aspect from general algorithm for DML. Although $f(\mathbf{L})$ is continuous and differentiable with respect to its parameters, as the distance metric is not convex, the gradient ascent algorithm proposed by NCA does not guarantee escaping local maxima.

Motivated by learning in support vector machines (SVMs), Weinberger *et al.* proposed a large margin nearest neighbour (LMNN) classification (see Figure 17) (Weinberger & Saul, 2009). In LMNN for each input $\mathbf{x}_i$ k 'target' neighbours are defined (see Figure 3). The target neighbours have the same label as y_i and the goal is to minimize the distance of target neighbours to $\mathbf{x}_i$. If no prior knowledge is available, the target neighbours can simply be identified as the k nearest neighbours, determined by Euclidean distance, that share the same label y_i. If $\eta_{ij} \in \{0,1\}$ indicates whether input $\mathbf{x}_j$ is a target neighbour of $\mathbf{x}_i$ or not, then a cost function similar to SVM cost function for maximizing the margin can be defined as Equation 36.

In Equation (36) the term $[z]_+ = \max(z,0)$ and $y_{il}=1$ if and only if $y_i=y_l$, and $y_{il}=0$ otherwise. The cost function consists of two terms, one which acts to pull target neighbours closer together, and the other to push differently labelled examples

Equation 35.

$$\frac{\partial f}{\partial L} = 2\mathbf{L}\sum_i \left(p_i \sum_k p_{ik}\left(\mathbf{x}_i - \mathbf{x}_k\right)\left(\mathbf{x}_i - \mathbf{x}_k\right)^T - \sum_{j\in C_i} p_{ij}\left(\mathbf{x}_i - \mathbf{x}_j\right)\left(\mathbf{x}_i - \mathbf{x}_j\right)^T \right)$$

Figure 17. Illustration of target neighbours and imposters before training (a) and after training (b) in LMNN. The distance metric is optimized so that: (i) its k=3 target neighbours lie within a smaller radius after training; (ii) imposters (differently labelled samples) lie outside the smaller circle by some finite margin. (Adapted from (Weinberger & Saul, 2009)).

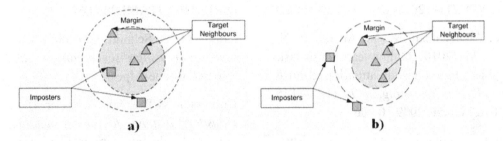

Equation 36.

$$f(L) = \sum_i \sum_j \eta_{ij} \left\| \mathbf{L}(\mathbf{x}_i - \mathbf{x}_j) \right\|^2 + c \sum_i \sum_j \sum_l \eta_{ij}(1 - y_{il}) \left[1 + \left\| \mathbf{L}(\mathbf{x}_i - \mathbf{x}_j) \right\|^2 - \left\| \mathbf{L}(\mathbf{x}_i - \mathbf{x}_l) \right\|^2 \right]_+$$

further apart. The second term in the loss function penalizes small distances between differently labelled examples. For a sample $\mathbf{x}_i$ with label y_i and target neighbour $\mathbf{x}_j$, an impostor (Figure 3) is any example $\mathbf{x}_l$ with label $y_l \neq y_i$ such that

$$\left\| \mathbf{L}(\mathbf{x}_i - \mathbf{x}_l) \right\|^2 \leq 1 + \left\| \mathbf{L}(\mathbf{x}_i - \mathbf{x}_j) \right\|^2 \qquad (37)$$

If the imposters lie in a safe distance away from $\mathbf{x}_i$ then the inequality does not hold. As a result the second term in loss function will become a negative argument and has no effect on the overall loss function. Equation (36) only penalizes large distances between inputs and their target neighbours. It is because accurate kNN classifier does not require all similarly labelled inputs be tightly clustered.

The LMNN framework can be viewed as the logical counterpart to SVMs in which kNN classification replaces linear classification. LMNN hold several useful properties; e.g. unlike SVMs that usually involve combining the results of many binary classifiers to handle multiclass problems, LMNN has no explicit dependence on the number of its classes.

REFERENCES

Adini, Y., Moses, Y., & Ullman, S. (1997). Face recognition: The problem of compensating for changes in illumination direction. *IEEE Transactions in Pattern Analysis in Machine Intelligence, 19*(7), 721-732. doi: http://dx.doi.org/10.1109/34.598229

Ahonen, T., Hadid, A., & Pietikainen, M. (2006). Face description with local binary patterns: Application to face recognition. *IEEE Transactions in Pattern Analysis in Machine Intelligence, 28*(12), 2037-2041. doi: http://dx.doi.org/10.1109/TPAMI.2006.244

Bartlett, M. S., Movellan, J. R., & Sejnowski, T. J. (2002). Face recognition by independent component analysis. *IEEE Transactions on Neural Networks, 13*(6), 1450–1464. doi:10.1109/TNN.2002.804287

Belhumeur, P. N., Hespanha, J. P., & Kriegman, D. J. (1997). Eigenfaces vs. fisherfaces: Recognition using class specific linear projection. *IEEE Transactions on Pattern Analysis and Machine Intelligence, 19*(7), 711–720. doi:10.1109/34.598228

Borji, A., Ahmadabadi, M. N., Araabi, B. N., & Hamidi, M. (2010). Online learning of task-driven object-based visual attention control. *Image and Vision Computing, 28*(7), 1130–1145. doi:10.1016/j.imavis.2009.10.006

Breiman, L., Friedman, J., Stone, C., & Olshen, R. A. (1984). *Classification and regression trees.* Chapman and Hall/CRC.

Cai, D., He, X., Han, J., & Zhang, H. J. (2006). Orthogonal laplacianfaces for face recognition. *IEEE Transactions on Image Processing, 15*(11), 3608–3614. doi:10.1109/TIP.2006.881945

Chen, L. F., Liao, H. Y. M., Ko, M. T., Lin, J. C., & Yu, G. J. (2000). New LDA-based face recognition system which can solve the small sample size problem. *Pattern Recognition, 33*(10), 1713–1726. doi:10.1016/S0031-3203(99)00139-9

Cheng, J., Liu, Q., Lu, H., & Chen, Y. W. (2006). Ensemble learning for independent component analysis. *Pattern Recognition, 39*(1), 81–88. doi:10.1016/j.patcog.2005.06.018

Comon, P. (1994). Independent component analysis, a new concept? *Signal Processing, 36*(3), 287-314. doi: http://dx.doi.org/10.1016/0165-1684(94)90029-9

Dagher, I., & Nachar, R. (2006). Face recognition using IPCA-ICA algorithm. *IEEE Transactions on Pattern Analysis and Machine Intelligence, 28*(6), 996–1000. doi:10.1109/TPAMI.2006.118

Demirci, M. F., Shokoufandeh, A., Keselman, Y., Bretzner, L., & Dickinson, S. (2006). Object recognition as many-to-many feature matching. *International Journal of Computer Vision, 69*(2), 203–222. doi:10.1007/s11263-006-6993-y

Detry, R., Pugeault, N., & Piater, J. H. (2009). A probabilistic framework for 3D visual object representation. *IEEE Transactions on Pattern Analysis and Machine Intelligence, 31*(10), 1790–1803. doi:10.1109/TPAMI.2009.64

Dorko, G., & Schmid, C. (2005). *Object class recognition using discriminative local features.* INRIA - Rhone-Alpes.

Dubuisson, M. P., & Jain, A. K. (1994). *A modified Hausdorff distance for object matching.* Paper presented at the International Conference on Pattern Recognition Jerusalem, Israel.

Edelman, S., & Intrator, N. (1997). Learning as extraction of low-dimensional representations. In Medlin, D. L., Goldstone, R. L., & Philippe, G. S. (Eds.), *Psychology of learning and motivation (Vol. 36*, pp. 353–380). Academic Press.

Gersho, A., & Gray, R. M. (1991). *Vector quantization and signal compression.* Kluwer Academic Publishers.

Goldberger, J., Roweis, S., Hinton, G., & Salakhutdinov, R. (2004). *Neighborhood component analysis.* Paper presented at the Neural Information Processing Systems (NIPS'04).

Gonzalez, R. C., & Woods, R. E. (2006). *Digital image processing* (3rd ed.). Prentice-Hall, Inc.

Gottumukkal, R., & Asari, V. K. (2004). An improved face recognition technique based on modular PCA approach. *Pattern Recognition Letters, 25*(4), 429–436. doi:10.1016/j.patrec.2003.11.005

Grauman, K., & Darrell, T. (2005). *Efficient image matching with distributions of local invariant features.*

Hamm, J., & Lee, D. D. (2008). *Grassmann discriminant analysis: a unifying view on subspace-based learning.* Paper presented at the 25th International Conference on Machine Learning, Helsinki, Finland.

Harandi, M. T., Bigdeli, A., & Lovell, B. C. (2010). *Image-set face recognition based on transductive learning.* Paper presented at the International Conference on Image Processing (ICIP2010), Hong Kong.

Harandi, M. T., Nili Ahmadabadi, M., & Araabi, B. N. (2009). Optimal local basis: A reinforcement learning approach for face recognition. *International Journal of Computer Vision, 81*(2), 191–204. doi:10.1007/s11263-008-0161-5

He, X., Yan, S., Hu, Y., Niyogi, P., & Zhang, H. J. (2005). Face recognition using Laplacianfaces. *IEEE Transactions on Pattern Analysis and Machine Intelligence, 27*(3), 328–340. doi:10.1109/TPAMI.2005.55

Heikkilä, M., & Pietikäinen, M. (2006). A texture-based method for modeling the background and detecting moving objects. *IEEE Transactions on Pattern Analysis and Machine Intelligence, 28*(4), 657–662. doi:10.1109/TPAMI.2006.68

Heikkilä, M., Pietikäinen, M., & Schmid, C. (2009). Description of interest regions with local binary patterns. *Pattern Recognition, 42*(3), 425–436. doi:10.1016/j.patcog.2008.08.014

Heusch, G., Rodriguez, Y., & Marcel, S. (2006). *Local binary patterns as an image preprocessing for face authentication.* Paper presented at the 7th International Conference on Automatic Face and Gesture Recognition.

Huang, R., Liu, Q., Lu, H., & Ma, S. (2002). *Solving the small sample size problem of LDA.*

Hyvärinen, A., Karhunen, J., & Oja, E. (2001). *Independent component analysis.* Wiley-Interscience. doi:10.1002/0471221317

Jain, A. K., & Li, S. Z. (2005). *Handbook of face recognition.* New York, NY: Springer-Verlag, Inc.

Jing, F., Li, M., Zhang, H. J., & Zhang, B. (2004). An efficient and effective region-based image retrieval framework. *IEEE Transactions on Image Processing, 13*(5), 699–709. doi:10.1109/TIP.2004.826125

Joachims, T. (1999). *Transductive inference for text classification using support vector machines.* Paper presented at the Sixteenth International Conference on Machine Learning.

Joachims, T. (2003). *Transductive learning via spectral graph partitioning.* Paper presented at the International Conference on Machine Learning (ICML).

Jodogne, S. (2006). *Closed-loop learning of visual control policies.* PhD thesis, University of Liege. Retrieved from http://www.montefiore.ulg.ac.be/\~{}jodogne/jodogne-phd.pdf

Jodogne, S., & Piater, J. H. (2005). *Interactive learning of mappings from visual percepts to actions.* Paper presented at the 22nd International Conference on Machine Learning, Bonn, Germany.

Jodogne, S., & Piater, J. H. (2007). Closed-loop learning of visual control policies. *Journal of Artificial Intelligence Research, 28*, 349–391.

Kim, J., Choi, J., Yi, J., & Turk, M. (2005). Effective representation using ICA for face recognition robust to local distortion and partial occlusion. *IEEE Transactions on Pattern Analysis and Machine Intelligence, 27*(12), 1977–1981. doi:10.1109/TPAMI.2005.242

Kim, K. I., Jung, K., & Kim, H. J. (2002). Face recognition using kernel principal component analysis. *IEEE Signal Processing Letters, 9*(2), 40–42. doi:10.1109/97.991133

Kim, T.-K., Arandjelovic, O., & Cipolla, R. (2007). Boosted manifold principal angles for image set-based recognition. *Pattern Recogn., 40*(9), 2475-2484. doi: http://dx.doi.org/10.1016/j.patcog.2006.12.030

Kwak, K. C., & Pedrycz, W. (2007). Face recognition using an enhanced independent component analysis approach. *IEEE Transactions on Neural Networks, 18*(2), 530–541. doi:10.1109/TNN.2006.885436

Lee, K.-C., Ho, J., & Kriegman, D. J. (2005). Acquiring linear subspaces for face recognition under variable lighting. *IEEE Transactions in Pattern Analysis and Machine Intelligence, 27*(5), 684-698. doi: http://dx.doi.org/10.1109/TPAMI.2005.92

Leibe, B., & Schiele, B. (2003). *Analyzing appearance and contour based methods for object categorization.*

Li, F., & Wechsler, H. (2005). Open set face recognition using transduction. *IEEE Transactions on Pattern Analysis and Machine Intelligence, 27*(11), 1686–1697. doi:10.1109/TPAMI.2005.224

Li, S. Z., Lu, X. G., Hou, X., Peng, X., & Cheng, Q. (2005). Learning multiview face subspaces and facial pose estimation using independent component analysis. *IEEE Transactions on Image Processing, 14*(6), 705–712. doi:10.1109/TIP.2005.847295

Lian, H. C., & Lu, B. L. (2007). Multi-view gender classification using multi-resolution local binary patterns and support vector machines. *International Journal of Neural Systems, 17*(6), 479–487. doi:10.1142/S0129065707001317

Liu, C. (2004). Gabor-based kernel PCA with fractional power polynomial models for face recognition. *IEEE Transactions on Pattern Analysis and Machine Intelligence, 26*(5), 572–581. doi:10.1109/TPAMI.2004.1273927

Liu, C., & Wechsler, H. (2000). Evolutionary pursuit and its application to face recognition. *IEEE Transactions on Pattern Analysis and Machine Intelligence, 22*(6), 570–582. doi:10.1109/34.862196

Liu, C., & Wechsler, H. (2003). Independent component analysis of Gabor features for face recognition. *IEEE Transactions on Neural Networks, 14*(4), 919–928. doi:10.1109/TNN.2003.813829

Liu, Y., Wang, X. L., Wang, H. Y., Zha, H., & Qin, H. (2010). Learning robust similarity measures for 3D partial shape retrieval. *International Journal of Computer Vision, 89*(2-3), 408–431. doi:10.1007/s11263-009-0298-x

Lowe, D. G. (2004). Distinctive image features from scale-invariant keypoints. *International Journal of Computer Vision, 60*(2), 91–110. doi:10.1023/B:VISI.0000029664.99615.94

Lu, J., Plataniotis, K. N., & Venetsanopoulos, A. N. (2003). Face recognition using kernel direct discriminant analysis algorithms. *IEEE Transactions on Neural Networks, 14*(1), 117–126. doi:10.1109/TNN.2002.806629

Lu, J., Plataniotis, K. N., Venetsanopoulos, A. N., & Li, S. Z. (2006). Ensemble-based discriminant learning with boosting for face recognition. *IEEE Transactions on Neural Networks, 17*(1), 166–178. doi:10.1109/TNN.2005.860853

Lui, Y. M., Beveridge, J. R., Draper, B. A., & Kirby, M. (2008). *Image-set matching using a geodesic distance and cohort normalization.*

Mäenpää, T., & Pietikäinen, M. (2004). Classification with color and texture: Jointly or separately? *Pattern Recognition, 37*(8), 1629–1640. doi:10.1016/j.patcog.2003.11.011

Mikolajczyk, K., Leibe, B., & Schiele, B. (2005). *Local features for object class recognition.*

Mikolajczyk, K., & Schmid, C. (2005). A performance evaluation of local descriptors. *IEEE Transactions on Pattern Analysis and Machine Intelligence, 27*(10), 1615–1630. doi:10.1109/TPAMI.2005.188

Moghaddam, B. (2002). Principal manifolds and probabilistic subspaces for visual recognition. *IEEE Transactions on Pattern Analysis and Machine Intelligence, 24*(6), 780–788. doi:10.1109/TPAMI.2002.1008384

Monari, E., Maerker, J., & Kroschel, K. (2009). *A robust and efficient approach for human tracking in multi-camera systems.*

Nanni, L., & Lumini, A. (2008). Local binary patterns for a hybrid fingerprint matcher. *Pattern Recognition, 41*(11), 3461–3466. doi:10.1016/j.patcog.2008.05.013

Niblack, W., Barber, R., Equitz, W., Flickner, M. D., Glasman, E. H., Petkovic, D., et al. (1993). *QBIC project: Querying images by content, using color, texture, and shape.*

Norouzi, E., Nili Ahmadabadi, M., & Nadjar Araabi, B. (2010). Attention control with reinforcement learning for face recognition under partial occlusion. *Machine Vision and Applications, 22*(2), 1–12.

Ojala, T., Pietikainen, M., & Maenpaa, T. (2002). Multiresolution gray-scale and rotation invariant texture classification with local binary patterns. *IEEE Transactions on Pattern Analysis and Machine Intelligence, 24*(7), 971–987. doi:10.1109/TPAMI.2002.1017623

Paletta, L., Fritz, G., & Seifert, C. (2005). *Q-learning of sequential attention for visual object recognition from informative local descriptors.* Paper presented at the 22nd International Conference on Machine Learning, Bonn, Germany.

Ponce, J., Hebert, M., Schmid, C., & Zisserman, A. (2007). *Toward category-level object recognition.* Lecture Notes in Computer Science New York, NY: Springer-Verlag, Inc.

Proedrou, K., Nouretdinov, I., Vovk, V., & Gammerman, A. (2002). *Transductive confidence machines for pattern recognition.* Paper presented at the 13th European Conference on Machine Learning.

Rachev, S. T. (1985). The Monge--Kantorovich mass transference problem and its stochastic applications. *Theory of Probability and Its Applications, 29*(4), 647–676. doi:10.1137/1129093

Rubner, Y., Tomasi, C., & Guibas, L. J. (2000). Earth mover's distance as a metric for image retrieval. *International Journal of Computer Vision, 40*(2), 99–121. doi:10.1023/A:1026543900054

Serre, T., Wolf, L., Bileschi, S., Riesenhuber, M., & Poggio, T. (2007). Robust object recognition with cortex-like mechanisms. *IEEE Transactions on Pattern Analysis and Machine Intelligence, 29*(3), 411–426. doi:10.1109/TPAMI.2007.56

Shan, C., Gong, S., & McOwan, P. W. (2005). *Robust facial expression recognition using local binary patterns.* Paper presented at the IEEE International Conference on Image Processing, 2005. ICIP 2005.

Shechtman, E., & Irani, M. (2007). *Matching local self-similarities across images and videos.*

Sim, T., Baker, S., & Bsat, M. (2003). The CMU pose, illumination, and expression database. *IEEE Transactions in Pattern Analysis and Machine Intelligence, 25*(12), 1615-1618. doi: http://dx.doi.org/10.1109/TPAMI.2003.1251154

Sirovich, L., & Kirby, M. (1987). Low-dimensional procedure for the characterization of human faces. *Journal of the Optical Society of America. A, Optics and Image Science, 4*(3), 519–524. doi:10.1364/JOSAA.4.000519

Su, Y., Shan, S., Chen, X., & Gao, W. (2009). Hierarchical ensemble of global and local classifiers for face recognition. *IEEE Transactions on Image Processing, 18*(8), 1885–1896. doi:10.1109/TIP.2009.2021737

Sutton, R. S., & Barto, A. G. (1998). *Introduction to reinforcement learning.* MIT Press.

Swain, M. J., & Ballard, D. H. (1991). Color indexing. *International Journal of Computer Vision, 7*(1), 11-32. doi: http://dx.doi.org/10.1007/BF00130487

Tan, X., & Triggs, B. (2007). Enhanced local texture feature sets for face recognition under difficult lighting conditions. *LNCS, 4778*, 168–182.

Tenenbaum, J., Silva, V., & Langford, J. (2000). A global geometric framework for nonlinear dimensionality reduction. *Science, 290*(5500), 2319-2323. doi: citeulike-article-id:266187

Turaga, P., Veeraraghavan, A., & Chellappa, R. (2008). *Statistical analysis on stiefel and grassmann manifolds with applications in computer vision.*

Turk, M., & Pentland, A. (1991). Eigenfaces for recognition. *Journal of Cognitive Neuroscience, 3*(1), 71-86. doi: http://dx.doi.org/10.1162/jocn.1991.3.1.71

Vapnik, V. (2000). *The nature of statistical learning theory* (2nd ed.). New York, NY: Springer-Verlag, Inc.

Vasilescu, M. A. O., & Terzopoulos, D. (2005). *Multilinear independent components analysis.*

Vidal, R., Ma, Y., & Sastry, S. (2005). Generalized principal component analysis (GPCA). *IEEE Transactions on Pattern Analysis and Machine Intelligence, 27*(12), 1945–1959. doi:10.1109/TPAMI.2005.244

Wang, L., Wang, X., & Feng, J. (2006). Subspace distance analysis with application to adaptive Bayesian algorithm for face recognition. *Pattern Recognition, 39*(3), 456–464. doi:10.1016/j.patcog.2005.08.015

Wang, R., Shan, S., Chen, X., & Gao, W. (2008). *Manifold-manifold distance with application to face recognition based on image set.*

Wang, X., Gong, H., Zhang, H., Li, B., & Zhuang, Z. (2006). *Palmprint identification using boosting local binary pattern.*

Wang, X., & Tang, X. (2006). Random sampling for subspace face recognition. *International Journal of Computer Vision, 70*(1), 91–104. doi:10.1007/s11263-006-8098-z

Weinberger, K. Q., & Saul, L. K. (2009). Distance metric learning for large margin nearest neighbor classification. *Journal of Machine Learning Research, 10*, 207–244.

Wolf, L., & Shashua, A. (2003a). Learning over sets using kernel principal angles. *Journal of Machine Learning Research, 4*, 913–931.

Wolf, L., & Shashua, A. (2003b). Learning over sets using kernel principal angles. *Journal of Machine Learning Research, 4*, 913–931.

Xing, E., Ng, A., Jordan, M., & Russell, S. (2002). *Distance metric learning, with application to clustering with side-information.* Paper presented at the Advances in Neural Information Processing Systems 15.

Yamaguchi, O., Fukui, K., & Maeda, K. (1998a). *Face recognition using temporal image sequence.* Paper presented the 3rd International Conference on Face and Gesture Recognition.

Yamaguchi, O., Fukui, K., & Maeda, K. (1998b). *Face recognition using temporal image sequence.* Paper presented at the 3rd International Conference on Face & Gesture Recognition.

Yan, S., Xu, D., Zhang, B., Zhang, H. J., Yang, Q., & Lin, S. (2007). Graph embedding and extensions: A general framework for dimensionality reduction. *IEEE Transactions on Pattern Analysis and Machine Intelligence, 29*(1), 40–51. doi:10.1109/TPAMI.2007.250598

Yang, J., Frangi, A. F., Yang, J. Y., Zhang, D., & Jin, Z. (2005). KPCA plus LDA: A complete kernel fisher discriminant framework for feature extraction and recognition. *IEEE Transactions on Pattern Analysis and Machine Intelligence, 27*(2), 230–244. doi:10.1109/TPAMI.2005.33

Yang, J., Zhang, D., Frangi, A. F., & Yang, J. Y. (2004). Two-dimensional PCA: A new approach to appearance-based face representation and recognition. *IEEE Transactions on Pattern Analysis and Machine Intelligence, 26*(1), 131–137. doi:10.1109/TPAMI.2004.1261097

Yang, M. H., Ahuja, N., & Kriegman, D. (2000). *Face recognition using Kernel eigenfaces.*

Yu, H. (2001). A direct LDA algorithm for high-dimensional data — With application to face recognition. *Pattern Recognition, 34*(10), 2067-2070. doi: citeulike-article-id:5907405

Yuen, P. C., & Lai, J. H. (2002). Face representation using independent component analysis. *Pattern Recognition, 35*(6), 1247–1257. doi:10.1016/S0031-3203(01)00101-7

Zhang, H., Gao, W., Chen, X., & Zhao, D. (2006). Object detection using spatial histogram features. *Image and Vision Computing, 24*(4), 327–341. doi:10.1016/j.imavis.2005.11.010

Zhang, J., He, L., & Zhou, Z. H. (2006). Ensemble-based discriminant manifold learning for face recognition. *LNCS, 4221*, 29–38.

Zhang, J., Marszałek, M., Lazebnik, S., & Schmid, C. (2007). Local features and kernels for classification of texture and object categories: A comprehensive study. *International Journal of Computer Vision, 73*(2), 213–238. doi:10.1007/s11263-006-9794-4

Zhao, C., Shi, W., & Deng, Y. (2005). A new Hausdorff distance for image matching. *Pattern Recognition Letters, 26*(5), 581-586. doi: http://dx.doi.org/10.1016/j.patrec.2004.09.022

Zhao, G., & Pietikäinen, M. (2007). Dynamic texture recognition using local binary patterns with an application to facial expressions. *IEEE Transactions on Pattern Analysis and Machine Intelligence, 29*(6), 915–928. doi:10.1109/TPAMI.2007.1110

Zhao, Q., Yang, Z., & Tao, H. (2010). Differential earth mover's distance with its applications to visual tracking. *IEEE Transactions on Pattern Analysis and Machine Intelligence, 32*(2), 274–287. doi:10.1109/TPAMI.2008.299

Zhao, W., Chellappa, R., Phillips, P. J., & Rosenfeld, A. (2003). Face recognition: A literature survey. *ACM Computing Surveys, 35*(4), 399–458. doi:10.1145/954339.954342

Zhou, S., Krueger, V., & Chellappa, R. (2003). Probabilistic recognition of human faces from video. *Computer Vision and Image Understanding, 91*(1-2), 214-245. doi: http://dx.doi.org/10.1016/S1077-3142(03)00080-8

Zhu, X., Goldberg, A. B., Brachman, R., & Dietterich, T. (2009). *Introduction to semi-supervised learning.* Morgan and Claypool Publishers.

Zhuang, X. S., & Dai, D. Q. (2005). Inverse Fisher discriminate criteria for small sample size problem and its application to face recognition. *Pattern Recognition, 38*(11), 2192–2194. doi:10.1016/j.patcog.2005.02.011

Zhuang, X. S., & Dai, D. Q. (2007). Improved discriminate analysis for high-dimensional data and its application to face recognition. *Pattern Recognition*, *40*(5), 1570–1578. doi:10.1016/j.patcog.2006.11.015

ENDNOTE

[1]   Texture features are commonly defined by histograms of energy componcnt.

Chapter 8
Applications of Machine Learning for Linguistic Analysis of Texts

Rosemary Torney
University of Ballarat, Australia

John Yearwood
University of Ballarat, Australia

Peter Vamplew
University of Ballarat, Australia

Andrei Kelarev
University of Ballarat, Australia

ABSTRACT

This chapter describes a novel multistage method for linguistic clustering of large collections of texts available on the Internet as a precursor to linguistic analysis of these texts. This method addresses the practicalities of applying clustering operations to a very large set of text documents by using a combination of unsupervised clustering and supervised classification. The method relies on creating a multitude of independent clusterings of a randomized sample selected from the International Corpus of Learner English. Several consensus functions and sophisticated algorithms are applied in two substages to combine these independent clusterings into one final consensus clustering, which is then used to train fast classifiers in order to enable them to perform the profiling of very large collections of text and web data. This approach makes it possible to apply advanced highly accurate and sophisticated clustering techniques by combining them with fast supervised classification algorithms. For the effectiveness of this multistage method it is crucial to determine how well the supervised classification algorithms are going to perform at the final stage, when they are used to process large data sets available on the Internet. This performance may also serve as an indication of the quality of the combined consensus clustering obtained in the preceding stages. The authors' experimental results compare the performance of several classification algorithms incorporated in this multistage scheme and demonstrate that several of these classification algorithms achieve very high precision and recall and can be used in practical implementations of their method.

DOI: 10.4018/978-1-4666-1833-6.ch008

INTRODUCTION

The Internet and email have revolutionised both business and personal communication methods, negating the problems of distance and time-zones Alrawi & Sabry (2009). Although there have always been a small percentage of dubious enterprises that are prepared to prey on unsuspecting customers, in the real world it is usually possible to trace these unscrupulous establishments. The anonymity of the Internet makes this far more difficult. There is no physical location to return to and the victim has not seen or heard the perpetrator to give a description to law enforcement agencies. Criminal elements seem to be relying on the anonymity of cyberspace to protect them while they engage in illegal activities such as scams, phishing and predatory behavior Chaski (2008). However, they must make contact with their victims, and this is usually achieved with some form of text communication. This is where authorship analysis can be applied to extract some details about the identity or profile of the author on the basis of their use of language. It has been discovered, for example, in Abbasi & Chen (2008), Baayen et al. (2002), Chaski (2005), that authors leave a textual "fingerprint" behind in their choice of language. Stylometry or authorship analysis, has been used to determine the authenticity of evidence presented for both the prosecution and defense in USA courts, as reported in Chaski (2008).

The development of automated methods for various aspects of linguistic analysis based on machine learning techniques is one of the major research topics which has been very actively investigated. To illustrate let us refer to just a few recent articles Agarwal et al. (2009), Bao et al. (2009), Bian & Tao (2009), Ikeda et al. (2009), Long et al. (2009), Malik & Kender (2008), Momma et al. (2009), Nakajima et al. (2005), Negi et al. (2009), Ni et al. (2007), Park et al. (2009), Roth et al. (2009), Sindhwani et al. (2008). Clustering of documents based on similar linguistc features

often forms an early stage in these automated analysis methods.

Several authors have demonstrated that ensemble clustering approaches can be highly useful for solving various problems, as in Aho & Dzeroski (2009), Domeniconi et al. (2009), Lu et al. (2009), Read (2008). Highly sophisticated and effective consensus functions and heuristics for clustering ensembles have been developed, for example, by Ailon, Charikar and Newman (2005), Fern & Brodley (2004, 2004A), Goder & Filkov (2008), Strehl & Ghosh (2002). However such methods are not practically applicable to the very large number of documents that are often encountered in linguistic analysis tasks.

This article proposes a novel multistage method for linguistic clustering of very large collections of documents available on the Internet. The method is based on creating a multitude of independent initial clusterings of a randomized sample of texts from the International Corpus of Learner English. The ICLE corpus represents a unique collection of essays with detailed authorship information. Two substages of the method apply advanced consensus functions and sophisticated ensemble clustering algorithms to obtain final consensus clustering of the sample, which is then used to train fast supervised classifiers.

The sets of documents available on the Internet are huge and have many possible initial clusterings worth considering. It is computationally infeasible to apply highly sophisticated consensus ensemble clustering algorithms to these enormous data sets directly. Instead, we propose a novel more advanced multistage approach, as shown in Figure 1. First, a multitude of independent clustering algorithms were applied to a randomized sample from the International Corpus of Learner English (ICLE). Second, several consensus functions and sophisticated algorithms were used in two substages to combine these independent clusterings into one final consensus clustering. Third, several fast supervised classification algorithms were trained on the consensus clustering of the ran-

Figure 1. Overview of the multistage consensus clustering and classification approach to linguistic clustering

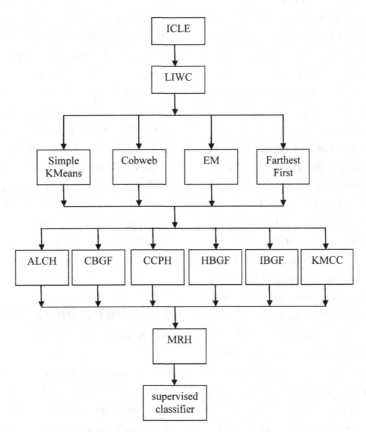

domized sample. This training enables these fast classification algorithms to be used for linguistic clustering or profiling of very large collections of documents available on the Internet.

For the effectiveness of this multistage method it is crucial to determine how well the supervised classification algorithms are going to perform at the final stage, when they are used to process large data sets available on the Internet. This performance may also serve as an indication of the quality of the combined consensus clustering obtained in the preceding stages. Accordingly, we have conducted experimental evaluation of the precision, recall and kappa statistics of several supervised classification algorithms after their training on the consensus clustering of the randomized sample.

The main idea of our novel approach is in replacing consensus clusterings of very large collections of text documents (which are computationally infeasible) by a combination of a consensus clustering of a small sample with fast supervised classification algorithms. This scheme is more computationally efficient.

INTERNATIONAL CORPUS OF LEARNER ENGLISH

Authorship analysis can use many different demographic characteristics to differentiate between authors, including age, gender, first language and educational level. This paper is using the ICLE corpus as a training set in order to obtain consensus clusterings for linguistic profiling of very large collections of documents available on the Internet. This corpus has been tagged with the relevant data for first language, age, gender, and other characteristics of the authors. It has been compiled for language research and has been previously used in similar studies (for example, in Argamon et al. (2009), Koppel et al. (2005), Tsur & Rappoport (2007).

The International Corpus of Learner English, ICLE, has been collated over more than 10 years by the Louvain Centre for English Corpus Linguistics at the Universite Catholique de Louvain in Belgium, see Granger et al. (2001). It is the result of more than a decade of collaboration between a number of international universities. It consists of essays written by English language students who are studying English in their third or fourth year at university. The corpus currently has over 3 million words from students from 16 different native languages. The target for each language corpus is 200,000 words from a minimum of 200 students. Essays consist of work on set topics of between 500 and 1000 words each. No student is permitted to submit more than 1000 words. While the Centre has a preference for all the essays for each language group coming from one university, this has not always been possible, and where more than one university is involved, this is indicated on the student profiles in the corpora. Each essay has a student profile that indicates considerable demographic data about the author, including first language, gender and age. It also includes information such as second and third languages, language spoken at home, time of residence in an English speaking country and resources used during essay writing (dictionaries, grammar books, etc). The instructions to universities submitting to the corpus request that the essays be submitted electronically on discs in plain text files. The essays are to be written from a list of topic choices supplied by the Centre, thus limiting the differences in style attributable to differences in genre. The instructions caution the universities to keep all errors in the texts, including spelling errors and to be careful not to add typographical errors while transcribing. All quotes and references have been removed by the Centre, being replaced with the symbols <*> and <R>, respectively, and illegible words with <?>. While the Louvain Centre for English Corpus Linguistics has endeavored to keep the corpus balanced, it is heavily skewed towards female authors. The Centre speculates that this is due to the higher number of female students interested and enrolled in humanities and soft sciences. There are also sub-corpora that consist of higher numbers of essays than others. For classification purposes, these numbers are usually limited to the maximum number of essays in the smallest sub-corpora being used.

LINGUISTIC INQUIRY AND WORD COUNT SOFTWARE

A key aspect of any automated linguistic analysis system is the choice of features used to represent and compare the similarity of documents. For this study the primary feature set which has been used are the attributes derived by the Linguistic Inquiry and Word Count software. LIWC was developed by Pennebaker et al. (2007) to aid in the study of various emotional, cognitive and structural components of individual's verbal and written speech, as part of an exploratory study of language. It quickly analyses either individual or multiple language files by comparing them, word by word to an internal dictionary. As each word is found in the dictionary, the appropriate scale or scales are incremented. Overall word count and punctuation counts are also incremented. The program produces approximately output variables that indicate either a count or the percentage of words in each category.

The output includes the name of the file checked, 4 general descriptor variables: the word count, sentence length and number of long words (more than 6 letters) in the file, as well as the percentage of words in the document found in the dictionary. It also includes 22 standard linguistic dimensions, 32 word categories tapping into psychological constructs, 7 personal concern categories, 3 paralinguistic dimensions and 12 punctuation categories. The dictionary has over 4,500 words and word stems, each one belonging to one or more categories or dimensions. For example the word 'cried' is included in 5 counts: sadness, negative emotion, overall affect, verb, and past tense verb. The categories are hierarchical, so that all negative emotion words are also counted as overall emotion words. The dictionary was developed using several word sources and up to 6 judges that compiled the initial word listings. The listings were then independently judged and tested to eliminate words that had poor reliability or very low rates of usage.

PREPROCESSING

We refer to Liu & Motoda (1988), Witten & Frank (2005) for theoretical background on preprocessing and more comprehensive bibliography. The ICLE data base allows the selection of specific essays, however they are all in one file. We separated the essays into separate files and removed all blank lines. The individual files were then processed using the LIWC system. The resultant.txt files were again preprocessed to add the features that are included in the file names: first language, gender and age. The resulting feature vectors were then combined with the TF-IDF scores and were then converted into attribute-relation file format.arff files used by the WEKA data mining software as described in Bouckaert et al. (2010), Hall et al. (2009) and Witten & Frank (2005). A Python module was written for the purpose of conversion of LIWC feature vectors in order to record them in the attribute-relation file format. Thus all features were assembled in an algebraic vector space model representing the data set.

Following Joachims (1997), we used the *term frequency-inverse document frequency* word weights, or TF-IDF weights, as additional features for the clustering. These weights are defined using the following concepts and notation. Suppose that we are extracting features from a data set E, which consists of |E| texts. For a word w and a text m, let N(w,m) be the number of times w occurs in m. Suppose that a collection T of terms is being looked at. The *term frequency* of a word w in T in a text m is denoted by TF(w,m) and is defined as the number of times w occurs in m, normalized over the number of occurrences of all terms in m. The *document frequency* of the word w is denoted by DF(w) and is defined as the number of texts in the given data set where the word w occurs at least once. The *inverse document frequency* is used to measure the significance of each term. It is denoted by IDF(w) and is defined by the following formula:

$$IDF(w) = \log (|E| / DF(w)).$$

The *term frequency-inverse document frequency* of a word w in text m, or TF-IDF weight of w in m, is defined by

$$TF\text{-}IDF(w,m) = TF(w,m)\, IDF(w,m).$$

We collected a small set of words with highest TF-IDF scores in all texts of the data set. For each text, the TF-IDF scores of these words in the text were determined. These weights and additional features were assembled in a vector and combined with other features produced by the LIWC software. In order to determine the TF-IDF scores we used Gensim, a Python and NumPy package for vector space modeling of text documents.

A number of independent initial clusterings were then obtained for the feature vectors of the texts in the sample using several clustering algorithms, as described in the next section.

INDEPENDENT INITIAL CLUSTERINGS

We refer to Bouckaert et al. (2010), Hall et al. (2009), Jain & Dubes (1988), Witten & Frank (2005) for preliminaries on clustering and further references. We obtained several independent initial clusterings of the feature vectors of the essays in a randomized sample of 3000 essays. For the purposes of this investigation we used the following clustering algorithms implemented in WEKA: SimpleKMeans, Cobweb, EM and FarthestFirst.

SimpleKMeans is the classical k-mean clustering algorithm described, for example, in Jain & Dubes (1988), Section 3.3.2, and Witten & Frank (2005), Section 4.8, see also Turaga et al. (2009). This algorithm randomly chooses k essays as centroids of clusters at the initialization stage. Every other essay is allocated to the cluster of its nearest centroid. After that each iteration finds new centroids of all current clusters as a mean of all members of the cluster. This is equivalent to finding the point such that the sum of all distances from the new centroid to all other sequences in the cluster is minimal. Then the algorithm reallocates all points to the clusters of the new centroids. It proceeds iteratively until the centroids stabilize. We used SimpleKMeans with the default Euclidean distance.

The outcomes of the k-means algorithm often depend on the initial selection of the very first centroids. The outcome of the SimpleKMeans in the WEKA implementation depends on the value of the input parameter "seed." To overcome the dependence of the outcome on the random choice of this parameter we run it with 30 random selections of the "seed," as recommended in Goder & Filkov (2008) and Jain et al. (1999).

Cobweb is the WEKA implementation of the Cobweb and Classit clustering algorithms described in Fisher (1987) and Gennari et al. (1990), respectively. EM is the expectation maximisation algorithm in WEKA. It determines the probability of each instance belonging to each of the clusters. It can be used to assign every instance to the cluster where it belongs with the highest probability. FarthestFirst is a WEKA implementation of the clustering algorithm described in Hochbaum (1985).

Cobweb, EM, FarthestFirst, and SimpleKMeans can produce clustering given a fixed number of clusters as an input parameter. All of them can process our data without any additional data transformations or encoding. The outcomes of all of these clustering algorithms often depend on the initial random selections made during the start of their iterations. A standard approach is to run them for several random selections of initial parameters, as in Goder & Filkov (2008) and Jain et al. (1999). In WEKA, the outcomes of these algorithms depend on their input parameter "seed." We run each of these algorithms for 30 random selections of the "seed" and obtained a total of 120 initial clusterings. This provided sufficient input for the consensus clustering algorithms considered in the next section.

We did not use other clustering algorithms implemented in WEKA not only because the four chosen algorithms produced enough initial clusterings, but also for the following reasons. The algorithms X-means and sIB could not process our data without some encoding of nominal attributes as numerical attributes. The algorithm CLOPE could not process our data set without some discretization of numerical attributes and their encoding as nominal attributes. We did not use the DBScan algorithm, since it does not produce meaningful clusterings for data sets of high dimension. Our data set has many attributes and for various selections of its input parameters DBScan could only discard some instances as noise and include all the remaining instances in only one class. Thus we have used multiple start versions of the Cobweb, EM, FarthestFirst and SimpleKMeans, which could process our sample directly and produced sufficient input for the next stage of our approach.

CONSENSUS FUNCTIONS FOR ENSEMBLE CLUSTERINGS

The process of finding the combined consensus clustering has also been divided into two substages. During the first substage several independent initial clusterings were ensembled using various consensus functions. This has produced a number of similar consensus clusterings. During the second substage a fairly simple and fast consensus heuristic was used to combine them all into one common final consensus clustering.

During the first substage, given an ensemble of several independent clusterings on one and the same data set, consensus functions were applied to form new common consensus clusterings. Here we use the methods described, for example, in Fern & Brodley (2004), Strehl & Ghosh (2002), Topchy (2003).

Looking at the features extracted as described above, we applied several different clustering algorithms to obtain initial clusterings. After that we used the following consensus functions and algorithms to combine the resulting cluster ensemble into one consensus clustering:

- **ALCH:** Average Link Consensus Heuristic
- **CBGF:** Cluster-Based Graph Formulation
- **CCPH:** Consensus Clustering Pivot Heuristic
- **HBGF:** Hybrid Bipartite Graph Formulation
- **IBGF:** Instance-Based Graph Formulation
- **KMCC:** k-Means Consensus Function
- **MRH:** Majority Rule Heuristic

Here we include only very brief information on these methods and refer to Ailon, Charikar and Newman (2005), Fern & Brodley (2004), Fern & Brodley (2004A), Filkov & Skiena (2004), Goder & Filkov (2008), Strehl & Ghosh (2002) for more details.

Average Link Consensus Heuristic, ALCH, is an agglomerative clustering algorithm described in Goder & Filkov (2008). It starts off with a partition where every element belongs to its own separate singleton cluster. For each pair of elements i, j, the proportion of the initial consensus clusterings which cluster i and j in different clusters is determined. Then the algorithm finds two clusters with the smallest average distance and merges them together into one new cluster. This is repeated until the two closest clusters have average distance greater than the set threshold 1/4.

Cluster-Based Graph Formulation, CBGF, is a graph-based consensus function. It defines a complete weighted undirected graph on the set of vertices consisting of all the given clusters. The weight of each edge of this graph is determined by a measure of similarity of the clusters corresponding to the vertices. Namely, for two clusters C' and C'' the weight of the edge (C',C'') can be set equal to

$$w((C',C'')) = |C' \cap C''| \, / \, |C' \cup C''|,$$

known as the *Jaccard index* or *Jaccard similarity coefficient*, see Tan et al. (2005), Chapter 2. In order to ensure that clusters which have a lot of elements in common are grouped together, the edges with lowest weights are then eliminated by applying a graph partitioning algorithm. Each element is then allocated to the new final cluster where it occurs most frequently.

Consensus Clustering Pivot Heuristic, CCPH, is an agglomerative clustering algorithm described in Ailon et al. (2005). It chooses a pivot element i uniformly at random from the unclustered elements. It finds all elements j such that the proportion of the given initial clusterings in the ensemble, which cluster i and j in different clusters, does not exceed the threshold value 1/2, and places all of these elements j in the same cluster with i. This continues until all elements are clustered.

Hybrid Bipartite Graph Formulation, HBGF, is a consensus function based on a bipartite graph. It has two sets of vertices: clusters and elements of the data set. A cluster C and an element d are connected by an edge in this bipartite graph if and only if d belongs to C. (The weights associated to these edges may have to be chosen as very large constants if the particular graph partitioning algorithm does not allow zero weights and can handle only complete graphs.) An appropriate graph partitioning algorithm is then applied to the whole bipartite graph, and the final clustering is determined by the way it partitions all elements of the data set. We used the METIS graph partitioning software described in Karypis & Kumar (1998).

Instance-Based Graph Formulation, IBGF, is also a consensus function based on a complete undirected weighted graph. Vertices of the graph are all elements of the data set. The edge (d',d") has weight equal to the proportion of clusterings where the clusters of d' and d" coincide. Then IBGF applies an appropriate graph partitioning algorithm to divide the graph into classes. These classes determine clusters of the final consensus clustering.

K-Means Consensus Function, KMCF, relies on the standard k-means algorithm to produce final clustering. A complete explanation of this method is given in Topchy (2003). KMCF uses the set of all clusters in all clusterings of the ensemble as features for its feature vectors. For each element d in D and each cluster C, the C-th component of the feature vector of d is set to 1 if d belongs to C, and it is set to 0 otherwise. The standard k-means clustering algorithm is then used to cluster this set of feature vectors in order to find the consensus clustering.

During the second substage all the resulting consensus clusterings described above have been combined into one common consensus clustering using a very simple *Majority Rule Heuristic*, MRH, described in Goder & Filkov (2008). It is also known as the quote rule, see Filkov & Skiena (2004). It is an agglomerative clustering algorithm, which starts with a partition where every element belongs to a separate singleton cluster. For each pair of elements i and j it computes the proportion p of the initial consensus clusterings which

cluster i and j in different clusters. If p is less than a threshold value t, then the current clusters containing i and j are combined together into one cluster. In our problem we used t equal to the half of the total number of the consensus clusterings being combined.

SUPERVISED CLASSIFICATION ALGORITHMS

The resulting consensus clustering described above was used to train supervised classification algorithms implemented in WEKA. We have investigated the performance of all classifiers implemented in WEKA and included in the tables of this paper the outcomes of the algorithms, which worked well in our scheme:

- AdaBoostM1 classifier boosting DecisionStump with AdaBoostM1 method, Freund & Schapire (1996).
- ADTree classifier using Alternating Decision Trees, Freund & Mason (1999).
- BayesNet—Bayes Network learning algorithm K2, Bouckaert et al. (2010).
- DecisionTable builds and uses a decision table majority classifier, Kohavi (1995).
- IBk is a k-nearest neighbours classifier selecting an appropriate value of k based on cross-validation, Aha & Kibler (1991).
- J48 classifier generating a C4.5 decision tree, Quinlan (1993).
- JRip classifier implementing a propositional rule learner RIPPER, Cohen (1995).
- HyperPipes is a very simple and fast classifier, Bouckaert et al. (2010).
- LibLINEAR is a library for large linear classification, Fan et al. (2008).
- LibSVM is a library for Support Vector Machines, Chang & Lin (2001). It implements an SMO-type algorithm proposed in Fan et al. (2005).

- MultilayerPerceptron using backpropagation to classify instances, Duda et al. (2001), Witten & Frank (2005).
- NaiveBayes classical algorithm, Duda et al. (2001), Witten & Frank (2005).
- PART classifier generating decision list based on partial C4.5 decision trees and separate-and-conquer, Frank & Witten (1998).
- RBFNetwork implementing a normalized Gaussian radial basis function network, Bouckaert et al. (2010).
- Ridor -- a ripple down rule classifier, Bouckaert et al. (2010).
- SMO classifier using Sequential Minimal Optimization for training a support vector classifier, Hastie & Tibshirani (1998), Keerthi et al. (2001), Platt (1998),
- VFI -- voting feature intervals classification due to Demiroz & Guvenir (1997).

More information on these algorithms can be found in Aha1991, Bouckaert et al. (2010), Demiroz & Guvenir (1997), Duda et al. (2001), Fan et al. (2005), Frank & Witten (1998), Freund & Mason (1999), Freund & Schapire (1996), Keerthi et al. (2001), Koknar & Latecki (2009), Liu et al. (2008), Min et al. (2009), Quinlan (1993), Ren (2009), Witten & Frank (2005). Experimental results on performance of these algorithms in our scheme are summarized in Tables 1 to 6. The tables include several algorithms from the list of top 10 algorithms in data mining, Wu et al. (2007). We have not included data for a few other classifiers which have turned out substantially less accurate in the scheme.

EXPERIMENTAL RESULTS

First, we found combined consensus clustering for a randomized sample of 3000 essays selected in the whole corpus. Second, this clustering was used as a benchmark to determine the precision and recall of several classification algorithms incorporated into the scheme. As recommended in Witten & Frank (2005), we used ten times tenfold cross validation and evaluated the weighted average precision and recall — standard measures of performance included in the WEKA outputs for these algorithms. We refer to Witten & Frank (2005) for background information on these notions.

The first three tables included in this paper deal with the SMO classifier, LibSVM and LibLINEAR. These tools depend on the kernels and methods used. For each of them, we used the optimization procedure outlined in the article Hsu et al. (2003). The performance of the SMO classifier depends on the kernel it is using. We investigated the performance of the SMO algorithm with the polynomial kernel, the normalized polynomial kernel, the RBF kernel, and the Pearson

Table 1. SMO, LibSVM, LibLINEAR: Weighted average precision

Number of clusters / SMO	2	3	5	10
- normalized polynomial	0.956	0.94	0.923	0.886
- polynomial kernel	**0.974**	**0.956**	**0.955**	**0.916**
- Pearson universal	0.963	0.933	0.911	0.883
- RBFKernel	0.94	0.89	0.833	0.798
LibSVM C-SVC				
- linear kernel	0.897	0.866	0.782	0.717
- polynomial kernel	0.902	0.869	0.795	0.723
- radial basis function	0.882	0.828	0.78	0.693
- sigmoid kernel	0.33	0.196	0.067	0.017
LibSVM nu-SVC				
- linear kernel	0.865	0.8	0.727	0.704
- polynomial kernel	0.872	0.827	0.752	0.633
- radial basis function	0.811	0.792	0.629	0.582
- sigmoid kernel	0.504	0.169	0.141	0.017
LibLINEAR				
- L2 loss svm (dual)	0.807	0.684	0.606	0.416
- L1 loss svm (dual)	0.794	0.659	0.59	0.429
- multi-class svm	0.793	0.762	0.729	0.633

Table 2. SMO, LibSVM, LibLINEAR: Weighted average recall

Number of clusters	2	3	5	10
SMO				
- normalized polynomial	0.956	0.938	0.92	0.879
- polynomial kernel	**0.974**	**0.955**	**0.954**	**0.916**
- Pearson universal	0.962	0.927	0.902	0.864
- RBFKernel	0.935	0.871	0.803	0.735
LibSVM C-SVC				
- linear kernel	0.897	0.866	0.811	0.724
- polynomial kernel	0.902	0.859	0.791	0.682
- radial basis function	0.712	0.612	0.509	0.438
- sigmoid kernel	0.574	0.443	0.259	0.131
LibSVM nu-SVC				
- linear kernel	0.885	0.79	0.724	0.682
- polynomial kernel	0.893	0.827	0.758	0.704
- radial basis function	0.717	0.617	0.515	0.438
- sigmoid kernel	0.505	0.248	0.19	0.131
LibLINEAR				
- L2 loss svm (dual)	0.804	0.648	0.575	0.368
- L1 loss svm (dual)	0.792	0.65	0.58	0.356
- multi-class svm	0.789	0.759	0.715	0.621

Table 3. SMO, LibSVM, LibLINEAR: Kappa statistic

Number of clusters	2	3	5	10
SMO				
- normalized polynomial	0.9093	0.9046	0.8979	0.8597
- polynomial kernel	**0.9474**	**0.9422**	**0.9319**	**0.9022**
- Pearson universal	0.9206	0.8873	0.8754	0.8414
- RBFKernel	0.8637	0.7999	0.7466	0.6889
LibSVM C-SVC				
- linear kernel	0.7897	0.7887	0.7621	0.6926
- polynomial kernel	0.8010	0.7771	0.7367	0.6457
- radial basis function	0.3660	0.3550	0.3538	0.3332
- sigmoid kernel	0.0085	0.0021	0.0019	0.0008
LibSVM nu-SVC				
- linear kernel	0.7635	0.6926	0.6573	0.6182
- polynomial kernel	0.7921	0.7653	0.7273	0.6346
- radial basis function	0.3673	0.3660	0.3620	0.3423
- sigmoid kernel	0.0154	0.0053	0.0032	0.0017
LibLINEAR				
- L2 loss svm (dual)	0.6029	0.4679	0.4608	0.2946
- L1 loss svm (dual)	0.5658	0.4720	0.4565	0.2823
- multi-class svm	0.6432	0.6257	0.5781	0.4739

VII function-based universal kernel described in Uestuen et al. (2006). The experimental results on the optimization of SMO are presented in Tables 1, 2 and 3. The best results were obtained with the polynomial kernel of SMO. The performance of LibSVM depends on the SVM type, the kernel and several numerical parameters, which can be optimized as explained in Hsu et al. (2003). We investigated the C-SVC and nu-SVC types of SVM, which are used for multiple classification. Each of these types of SVM was used with the linear kernel, polynomial kernel, radial basis function kernel and sigmoid kernel. The performance of LibLINEAR tool also depends on the SVM type and numerical parameters, which can be optimized. We investigated the L2 loss dual SVM type, L1 loss dual SVM type, and the multi-class SVM type. Some other types of SVMs and

kernels for SMO, LibSVM and LibLINEAR are also implemented in Weka but these could not be used for classification of our data.

The experimental results on the optimization of LibSVM and LibLINEAR are summarized in Tables 1, 2 and 3. These best outcomes of SMO, LibSVM and LibLINEAR have been included in Tables 4, 5 and 6 in order to compare them with the performance of other algorithms. Other tools incorporated in the LibSVM and LibLINEAR libraries could not be applied in our scheme. For example, the one-class SVM of LibLINEAR cannot handle multivalued nominal classes.

We ran the combined consensus clustering procedure on the training set to prepare input for training. After that several supervised classification algorithms were trained on the training set

Table 4. Accuracy of classifiers: Weighted average precision

	Number of clusters				
	2	3	5	10	20
Ada-BoostM1	0.901	0.771	0.248	0.091	0.029
BayesNet	0.916	0.858	0.791	0.778	0.724
DecisionT-able	0.887	0.823	0.802	0.704	0.656
IBk	0.913	0.886	0.879	0.845	0.842
J48	0.905	0.834	0.813	0.802	0.787
JRip	0.924	0.873	0.829	0.781	0.726
HyperPipes	0.806	0.699	0.591	0.573	0.522
LibLINEAR	0.807	0.762	0.729	0.633	0.558
LibSVM	0.902	0.859	0.795	0.723	0.694
NaiveBayes	0.902	0.823	0.699	0.687	0.597
PART	0.908	0.854	0.791	0.767	0.758
RBFNet-work	0.873	0.792	0.727	0.613	0.557
Ridor	0.885	0.844	0.76	0.668	0.594
SMO	**0.974**	**0.956**	**0.955**	**0.916**	**0.905**
VFI	0.809	0.771	0.7	0.648	0.644

Table 5. Accuracy of classifiers: Weighted average recall

	Number of clusters				
	2	3	5	10	20
AdaBoostM1	0.901	0.745	0.454	0.29	0.148
BayesNet	0.915	0.855	0.778	0.765	0.708
DecisionTable	0.887	0.815	0.792	0.699	0.649
IBk	0.912	0.884	0.877	0.844	0.84
J48	0.905	0.833	0.815	0.802	0.787
JRip	0.922	0.873	0.828	0.776	0.71
HyperPipes	0.763	0.622	0.498	0.491	0.48
LibLINEAR	0.804	0.759	0.715	0.621	0.567
LibSVM	0.902	0.866	0.811	0.724	0.643
NaiveBayes	0.9	0.818	0.733	0.679	0.585
PART	0.908	0.832	0.789	0.761	0.753
RBFNetwork	0.872	0.793	0.727	0.612	0.557
Ridor	0.885	0.843	0.763	0.668	0.594
SMO	**0.901**	**0.745**	**0.454**	**0.29**	**0.148**
VFI	0.915	0.855	0.778	0.765	0.708

Table 6. Kappa statistic in stratified cross validation

	Number of clusters				
	2	3	5	10	20
Ada-BoostM1	0.7971	0.6056	0.2674	0.1360	0.0591
BayesNet	0.8239	0.7770	0.7428	0.7010	0.6853
Deci-sionTable	0.7660	0.7339	0.7167	0.6475	0.6187
IBk	0.8534	0.8272	0.8211	0.8187	0.8124
J48	0.8043	0.7709	0.7696	0.7639	0.7471
JRip	0.8419	0.8062	0.7822	0.7404	0.6858
Hyper-Pipes	0.4812	0.4414	0.4231	0.4037	0.3305
LibLIN-EAR	0.6432	0.6257	0.5781	0.4739	0.4319
LibSVM	0.8010	0.7887	0.7621	0.6926	0.6432
Naive-Bayes	0.7930	0.7212	0.6443	0.5909	0.5537
PART	0.8112	0.7745	0.7389	0.7315	0.7221
RBFNet-work	0.7654	0.7324	0.6872	0.6032	0.5143
Ridor	0.7647	0.7598	0.7006	0.6341	0.5417
SMO	**0.9474**	**0.9422**	**0.9319**	**0.9022**	**0.8961**
VFI	0.6137	0.5919	0.5724	0.5696	0.5073

obtained. Our experimental results compare the performance of these classification algorithms presented after their training on the initial consensus clustering data.

We used ten times tenfold cross validation to evaluate the weighted average precision and recall of these classification algorithms in comparison with the classes of the combined overall total consensus clustering obtained previously. This was repeated ten times. Each time the data set was divides into ten equal parts, nine parts were used as a training set and one part was used as a testing set for the classification algorithm. Accordingly, the weighted average precision and recall were obtained as part of WEKA output. The results of our experiments are summarized in Tables 1 through to 6.

The results demonstrate that some of these classification algorithms achieve very high precision and recall and can be used in practical implementations of our scheme in order to obtain new clusterings for linguistic profiling of very large collections of texts available on the Internet. The best results were obtained by the SMO classifier using Sequential Minimal Optimization for training a Support Vector Machine with polynomial kernel. While SMO is only slightly better than the other classifiers when there are only two clusters, it scales up much better in terms of precision and kappa as the number of clusters increases.

CONCLUSION

This article investigated a novel approach to profiling very large collections of text documents on the basis of linguistic features. A two-stage approach based on advanced consensus functions and heuristics applied to ensemble clusterings of a randomized sample of essays selected from the International Corpus of Learner English. First, independent clustering algorithms were used to obtain a number of independent initial clusterings of the randomized sample of essays. Second, several consensus functions and sophisticated algorithms were applied in two substages to combine these independent clusterings into one final consensus clustering. Third, several fast supervised classification algorithms were trained on the consensus clustering of the randomized sample. Finally, these fast classification algorithms classified the whole data set.

We applied this approach to a randomized sample of 3000 essays selected and preprocessed. Our experimental results compare the performance of several classification algorithms incorporated in this scheme. They are included in Tables 1 through to 6. The results demonstrate that several classification algorithms achieve very high precision and recall and can be used in practical implementations of our method. The best results

have been obtained by the SMO classifier using Sequential Minimal Optimization for training a Support Vector Machine with polynomial kernel. Our multistage approach makes it possible to combine highly accurate consensus clustering techniques with fast classification algorithms in one scheme capable of obtaining consensus clusterings for linguistic profiling of very large collections of texts available on the Internet. The accuracy of the clusterings produced using this method is sufficiently high for them to provide a solid basis for further linguistic analysis to identify characteristics of the unknown authors of the documents.

REFERENCES

Abbasi, A., & Chen, H. (2008). Writeprints: A stylometric approach to identity-level identification and similarity detection in cyberspace. *ACM Transactions on Information Systems, 26*(2), 1–29. doi:10.1145/1344411.1344413

Agarwal, N., Liu, H., Subramanya, S., Salerno, J. J., & Yu, P. S. (2009). Connecting sparsely distributed similar bloggers. In *Proceedings 2009 Ninth IEEE International Conference on Data Mining, ICDM09* (pp. 11-20). Miami, Florida, USA.

Aha, D., & Kibler, D. (1991). Instance-based learning algorithms. *Machine Learning, 6,* 37–66. doi:10.1007/BF00153759

Aho, B. T., & Dzeroski, S. (2009). Rule ensembles for multi-target regression. In *Proceedings 2009 Ninth IEEE International Conference on Data Mining, ICDM09* (pp. 21-30). Miami, Florida, USA.

Ailon, N., Charikar, M., & Newman, A. (2005). Aggregating inconsistent information: ranking and clustering. In *Proceedings of 37th Annual ACM Symposium on Theory of Computing* (pp. 684-693).

Alrawi, K. W., & Sabry, K. A. (2009). E-commerce evolution: A Gulf region review. *International Journal of Business Information Systems, 4*(5), 509–526. doi:10.1504/IJBIS.2009.025204

Argamon, S., Koppel, M., Pennebaker, J. W., & Schler, J. (2009). Automatically profiling the author of an anonymous text. *Communications of the ACM, 52*(2), 119–123. doi:10.1145/1461928.1461959

Baayen, H., van Halteren, H., Neijt, A., & Tweedie, F. (2002). An experiment in authorship attribution. In *Proceedings 6th International Conference Statistical Analysis of Textual Data*, (pp. 1-7).

Bao, S. H., Xu, S. L., Zhang, L., Yan, R., Su, Z., Han, D., & Yu, Y. (2009). Joint emotion-topic modeling for social affective text mining. In *Proceedings 2009 Ninth IEEE International Conference on Data Mining*, ICDM09 (pp. 699-704). Miami, Florida, USA.

Bian, W., & Tao, D. C. (2009). Dirichlet mixture allocation for multiclass document collections modeling. In *Proceedings 2009 Ninth IEEE International Conference on Data Mining, ICDM09* (pp. 711-715). Miami, Florida, USA.

Bouckaert, R. R., Frank, E., Hall, M., Kirkby, R., Reutemann, P., Seewald, A., & Scuse, D. (2010). *WEKA manual for version 3-7-1*. Retrieved October 11, 2010, from http://www.cs.waikato.ac.nz/ml/weka/

Chang, C.-C., & Lin, C.-J. (2001). LIBSVM - A library for support vector machines. Retrieved June 10, 2010, from http://www.csie.ntu.edu.tw/~cjlin/libsvm/

Chaski, C. (2005). Who's at the keyboard? Authorship attribution in digital evidence investigations. *International Journal of Digital Evidence, 4*(1), 1–13.

Chaski, C. (2008). *Text and pretext on the internet: Recognizing problematic communications.* Retrieved May 5, 2010, from http://cyber.law.harvard.edu

Cohen, W. W. (1995). Fast effective rule induction. In *12th International Conference on Machine Learning*, (pp. 115-123).

Demiroz, G., & Guvenir, A. (1997). Classification by voting feature intervals. In *9th European Conference on Machine Learning*, (pp. 85-92).

Domeniconi, C., Gullo, F., & Tagarelli, A. (2009). Projective clustering ensembles. In *Proceedings of 2009 Ninth IEEE International Conference on Data Mining, ICDM09* (pp. 794-799). Miami, Florida, USA.

Duda, R. O., Hart, P. E., & Stork, D. G. (2001). *Pattern classification* (2nd ed.). Wiley-Interscience.

Fan, R.-E., Chang, K.-W., Hsieh, C.-J., Wang, X.-R., & Lin, C.-J. (2008). LIBLINEAR - A library for large linear classification. Retrieved May 10, 2010, from http://www.csie.ntu.edu.tw/~cjlin/liblinear/

Fan, R.-E., Chen, P.-H., & Lin, C.-J. (2005). Working set selection using second order information for training SVM. *Journal of Machine Learning Research, 6*, 1889–1918.

Fern, X. Z., & Brodley, C. E. (2004). Cluster ensembles for high dimensional clustering: An empirical study. *Journal of Machine Learning Research*, 2004.

Fern, X. Z., & Brodley, C. E. (2004A). Solving cluster ensemble problems by bipartite graph partitioning. In *Proceedings 21st International Conference on Machine Learning ICML'04*, Vol. 69. New York, NY: ACM.

Filkov, V., & Skiena, S. (2004). Heterogeneous data integration with the consensus clustering formalism. In *Proceedings of Data Integration in the Life Sciences*, (pp. 110-123).

Fisher, D. (1987). Knowledge acquisition via incremental conceptual clustering. *Machine Learning, 2*(2), 139–172. doi:10.1007/BF00114265

Frank, E., & Witten, I. H. (1998). Generating accurate rule sets without global optimization. In *15th International Conference on Machine Learning*, (pp. 144-151).

Freund, Y., & Mason, L. (1999). The alternating decision tree learning algorithm. In *Proceedings 16th International Conference on Machine Learning* (pp. 124-133). Bled, Slovenia.

Freund, Y., & Schapire, R. E. (1996). Experiments with a new boosting algorithm. In *Proceedings 13th International Conference Machine Learning* (pp. 148-156). San Francisco, USA.

Gennari, J. H., Langley, P., & Fisher, D. (1990). Models of incremental concept formation. *Artificial Intelligence, 40*, 11–61. doi:10.1016/0004-3702(89)90046-5

Goder, A., & Filkov, V. (2008). Consensus clustering algorithms: comparison and refinement. In *Proceedings Tenth SIAM Workshop on Algorithm Engineering and Experiments, ALENEX 2008,* (pp. 109-117). Retrieved from http://www.siam.org/proceedings/alenex/2008/alx08_011godera.pdf

Granger, S., Dagneaus, E., Meunier, F., & Paquot, M. (2009). *International corpus of learner English: The ICLE Project, Version 2*. Belgium: UCL Presses Universitaires de Lovain.

Hall, M., Frank, E., Holmes, G., Pfahringer, B., Reutemann, P., & Witten, I. H. (2009). The WEKA data mining software: An update. *SIGKDD Explorations, 11*(1), 10–18. doi:10.1145/1656274.1656278

Hastie, T., & Tibshirani, R. (1998). Classification by pairwise coupling. In *Advances in Neural Information Processing Systems*.

Hochbaum, S. (1985). A best possible heuristic for the k-center problem. *Mathematics of Operations Research, 10*(2), 180–184. doi:10.1287/moor.10.2.180

Hsu, C.-W., Chang, C.-C., & Lin, C.-J. (2003). *A practical guide to support vector classification*. Dept. Computer Science, National Taiwan University. Retrieved from http://www.csie.ntu.edu.tw/~cjlin

Ikeda, K., Yanagihara, T., Matsumoto, K., & Takishima, Y. (2009). Unsupervised text normalization approach for morphological analysis of blog documents. In A. Nicholson & X. Li (Eds.), *Advances in Artificial Intelligence, AI 2009, Lecture Notes in Artificial Intelligence, 5866*, 401-411.

Jain, A. K., & Dubes, R. C. (1988). *Algorithms for clustering data*. London, UK: Prentice Hall.

Jain, A. K., Murty, M. N., & Flynn, P. J. (1999). Data clustering: A review. *ACM Computing Surveys, 31*(3), 264–323. doi:10.1145/331499.331504

Joachims, T. (1997). A probabilistic analysis of the Rocchio algorithm with TF-IDF for text categorization. In *Proceedings 14th International Conference on Machine Learning*, (pp. 143-151).

Karypis, G., & Kumar, V. (1998). *METIS: A software package for partitioning unstructured graphs, partitioning meshes, and computing fill-reducing orderings of sparse matrices*. Technical Report, University of Minnesota, Department of Computer Science and Engineering, Army HPC Research Centre, Minneapolis.

Keerthi, S. S., Shevade, S. K., Bhattacharyya, C., & Murthy, K. R. K. (2001). Improvements to Platt's SMO algorithm for SVM classifier design. *Neural Computation, 13*(3), 637–649. doi:10.1162/089976601300014493

Kohavi, R. (1995). The power of decision tables. In *Proceedings 8th European Conference on Machine Learning* (pp. 174-189).

Koknar-Tezel, S., & Latecki, L. J. (2009). Improving SVM classification on imbalanced data sets in distance spaces. In *Proceedings 2009 Ninth IEEE International Conference on Data Mining, ICDM09* (pp. 259-267). Miami, Florida, USA.

Koppel, M., Schler, J., & Zigdon, K. (2005). Determining an author's native language by mining a text for errors. In *Proceedings 11th International Conference Knowledge Discovery and Data Mining, ACM SIGKDD* (pp. 624-628). Chicago, Illinois, USA.

Liu, B., Cao, L., Yu, P. S., & Zhang, C. (2008). Multi-space-mapped SVMs for multi-class classification. In *Proceedings Eighth IEEE International Conference on Data Mining, ICDM08* (pp. 911-916). Pisa, Italy.

Liu, H., & Motoda, H. (1988). *Feature extraction, construction and selection: A data mining perspective*. Dordrecht, The Netherlands: Kluwer.

Long, C., Huang, M. L., Zhu, X. Y., & Li, M. (2009). Multi-document summarization by information distance. In *Proceedings Ninth IEEE International Conference on Data Mining, ICDM09* (pp. 866-871). Miami, Florida, USA.

Lu, Z., Wu, X., & Bongard, J. (2009). Active learning with adaptive heterogeneous ensembles. In *Proceedings 2009 Ninth IEEE International Conference on Data Mining, ICDM09* (pp. 327-336). Miami, Florida, USA.

Malik, H. H., & Kender, J. R. (2008). Classifying high-dimensional text and web data using very short patterns. In *Proceedings 2008 Eighth IEEE International Conference on Data Mining, ICDM08* (pp. 923-928). Pisa, Italy.

Min, R., Stanley, D., Yuan, Z., Bonner, A., & Zhang, Z. L. (2009). A deep non-linear feature mapping for large-margin kNN classification. In *Proceedings Ninth IEEE International Conference on Data Mining, ICDM09* (pp. 357-366). Miami, Florida, USA.

Momma, M., Morinaga, S., & Komura, D. (2009). Promoting total efficiency in text clustering via iterative and interactive metric learning. In *Proceedings 2009 Ninth IEEE International Conference on Data Mining, ICDM09* (pp. 878-883). Miami, Florida, USA.

Nakajima, S., Tatemura, J., Hino, Y., Hara, Y., & Tanaka, K. (2005). Discovering important bloggers based on analyzing blog threads. In *Proceedings 2nd Annual Workshop on the Weblogging Ecosystem: Aggregation, Analysis and Dynamics*.

Negi, S., Joshi, S., Chalamalla, A. K., & Subramaniam, L. V. (2009). Automatically extracting dialog models from conversation transcripts. In *Proceedings Ninth IEEE International Conference on Data Mining, ICDM09* (pp. 890-895). Miami, Florida, USA.

Ni, X., Xue, G. R., Ling, X., Yu, Y., & Yang, Q. (2007). Exploring in the weblog space by detecting informative and affective articles. In *Proceedings of the 16th International World Wide Web Conference, WWW2007* (pp. 281-290).

Park, L. A. F., Leckie, C. A., Ramamohanarao, K., & Bezdek, J. C. (2009). Adapting spectral co-clustering to documents and terms using latent semantic analysis. In A. Nicholson & X. Li (Eds.), *Advances in Artificial Intelligence, AI 2009, Lecture Notes in Artificial Intelligence, 5866*, 301-311.

Pennebaker, J. W., Chung, C. K., Ireland, M., Gonzales, A., & Booth, R. J. (2007). *The development and psychometric properties of LIWC2007*. Retrieved October 20, 2010, from http://www.liwc.net

Platt, J. (1998). Fast training of support vector machines using sequential minimal optimization. In Schoelkopf, B., Burges, C., & Smola, A. (Eds.), *Advances in kernel methods - Support vector learning*.

Quinlan, R. (1993). *C4.5: Programs for machine learning*. San Mateo, CA: Morgan Kaufmann.

Read, J., Pfahringer, B., & Holmes, G. (2008). Multi-label classification using ensembles of pruned sets. In *Proceedings 2008 Eighth IEEE International Conference on Data Mining, ICDM08* (pp. 995-1000). Pisa, Italy.

Ren, J., Lee, S. D., Chen, X., Kao, B., Cheng, R., & Cheung, D. (2009). Naive Bayes classification of uncertain data. In *Proceedings Ninth IEEE International Conference on Data Mining, ICDM09* (pp. 944-949). Miami, Florida, USA.

Roth, D., & Tu, Y. C. (2009). Aspect guided text categorization with unobserved labels. In *Proceedings Ninth IEEE International Conference on Data Mining, ICDM09* (pp. 962-967). Miami, Florida, USA.

Sindhwani, V., & Melville, P. (2008). Document-word co-regularization for semi-supervised sentiment analysis. In *Proceedings Eighth IEEE International Conference on Data Mining, ICDM08* (pp. 1025-1030). Pisa, Italy.

Strehl, A., & Ghosh, J. (2002). Cluster ensembles — A knowledge reuse framework for combining multiple partitions. *Journal of Machine Learning Research, 3*, 583–617.

Tan, P. N., Steinbach, M., & Kumar, V. (2005). *Introduction to data mining*. London, UK: Addison Wesley.

Topchy, A., Jain, A. K., & Punch, W. (2003). Combining multiple weak clusterings. In *Proceedings IEEE Internat. Conf. on Data Mining* (pp. 331-338).

Tsur, O., & Rappoport, A. (2007). Using classifier features for studying the effect of native language on the choice of written second language words. In *Proceedings Workshop on Cognitive Aspects of Computational Language Acquisition* (pp. 9-16). Prague, Czech Republic.

Turaga, D. S., Vlachos, M., & Verscheure, O. (2009). On k-means cluster preservation using quantization schemes. In *Proceedings 2009 Ninth IEEE International Conference on Data Mining, ICDM09* (pp. 533-542). Miami, Florida, USA.

Uestuen, B., Melssen, W. J., & Buydens, L. M. C. (2006). Facilitating the application of support vector regression by using a universal Pearson VII function based kernel. *Chemometrics and Intelligent Laboratory Systems, 81*, 29–40. doi:10.1016/j.chemolab.2005.09.003

Witten, I. H., & Frank, E. (2005). *Data mining: Practical machine learning tools and techniques*. Amsterdam, The Netherlands: Elsevier/Morgan Kaufman.

Wu, X., Kumar, V., Quinlan, J. R., Ghosh, J., Yang, Q., & Motoda, H. (2007). Top 10 algorithms in data mining. *Knowledge and Information Systems, 14*(1), 1–37. doi:10.1007/s10115-007-0114-2

Chapter 9
An Automatic Machine Learning Method for the Study of Keyword Suggestion

Lin-Chih Chen
National Dong Hwa University, Taiwan

ABSTRACT

Keyword suggestion is an automatic machine learning method to suggest relevant keywords to users in order to help users better specify their information needs. In this chapter, the authors adopt two semantic analysis models to build a keyword suggestion system. The suggested keywords returned from the system not only with a certain semantic relationship, but also with a similarity measure. The benefit of the authors' method is to overcome the problems of synonymy and polysemy over the information retrieval field by using a vector space model. This chapter shows that using multiple semantic analysis techniques to generate relevant keywords can give significant performance gains.

INTRODUCTION

Meeting users' search requirement is always one of the most fundamental and challenging issues in the design of search engines. What makes this issue challenging is that most Internet users always give only short queries. According to the analysis of search engine transaction logs, the average length of queries is about 2.3 words (Silverstein, Henzinger, Marais, & Moricz, 1998; Spink, Wolfram, Jansen, & Saracevic, 2001). Thus, it is

not simple to find out real search goal from such short queries. In order to effectively deal with the problem of short query, incorporating some kind of the keyword suggestion mechanisms (Belkin, 2000) has become a commonly practice in the search engine design (Google, 2006; Microsoft, 2006; Yahoo, 2006).

Keyword suggestion is a kind of Information Retrieval (IR) technique that attempts to suggest relevant keywords to help the users formulate more effective queries and reduce unnecessary search steps. According to related research as seen in

DOI: 10.4018/978-1-4666-1833-6.ch009

(Abhishek & Hosanagar, 2007a; Yifan Chen, Xue, & Yu, 2008; Ferragina & Guli, 2008; Janruang & Kreesuradej, 2006; Joshi & Motwani, 2006; Wang, Mo, Huang, Wen, & He, 2008), this technique can be broadly classified into three categories: log analysis, proximity analysis, and snippet analysis. The category of log analysis analyzes the content of query logs to suggest relevant keywords (Abhishek & Hosanagar, 2007a; Bartz, Murthi, & Sebastian, 2006; Google, 2006; Lee, Huang, & Hung, 2007; Mei, Zhou, & Church, 2008; Yahoo, 2006). The category of proximity search sends the seed keyword to several search engines and expands new suggested keywords in its proximity range (Abhishek & Hosanagar, 2007b; Yifan Chen, et al., 2008; Joshi & Motwani, 2006). The category of snippet analysis first collects the snippets that are summarized by remote search engines; it then uses several snippet cleaning and pattern matching techniques to extract relevant keywords (Ferragina & Guli, 2008; Janruang & Kreesuradej, 2006; Wang, et al., 2008).

Two additional problems with most traditional keyword suggestion methods are the low coverage and the lack of disambiguation ability. In some cases, two relevant keywords never occur with each other. They will not be found by the traditional methods. In other cases, a keyword may have more than one meaning. A very famous example is that "apple" has at least two meanings: it can be either fruit or corporation. The relevant keywords of apple for these two meanings are obviously different. The traditional methods cannot distinguish between these two meanings and the suggested keywords may be a mixture of both meanings (Yifan Chen, et al., 2008).

The main purpose of our system is not only to suggest relevant and important keywords, but also to measure the degree of similarity between keywords. The screen dump of our system is shown in Figure 1. Our system is based on two semantic analysis models, including Latent Semantic Indexing (LSI) (Deerwester, Dumais, Furnas, Landauer, & Harshman, 1990) and Probabilistic LSI (PLSI) (Hofmann, 1999). The bases of these two semantic analysis models are based on the concept of automatic machine learning to

Figure 1. The screen dump of the authors' system in response to the search query is "mobile phone" (accessed from http://cayley.sytes.net/li_new)

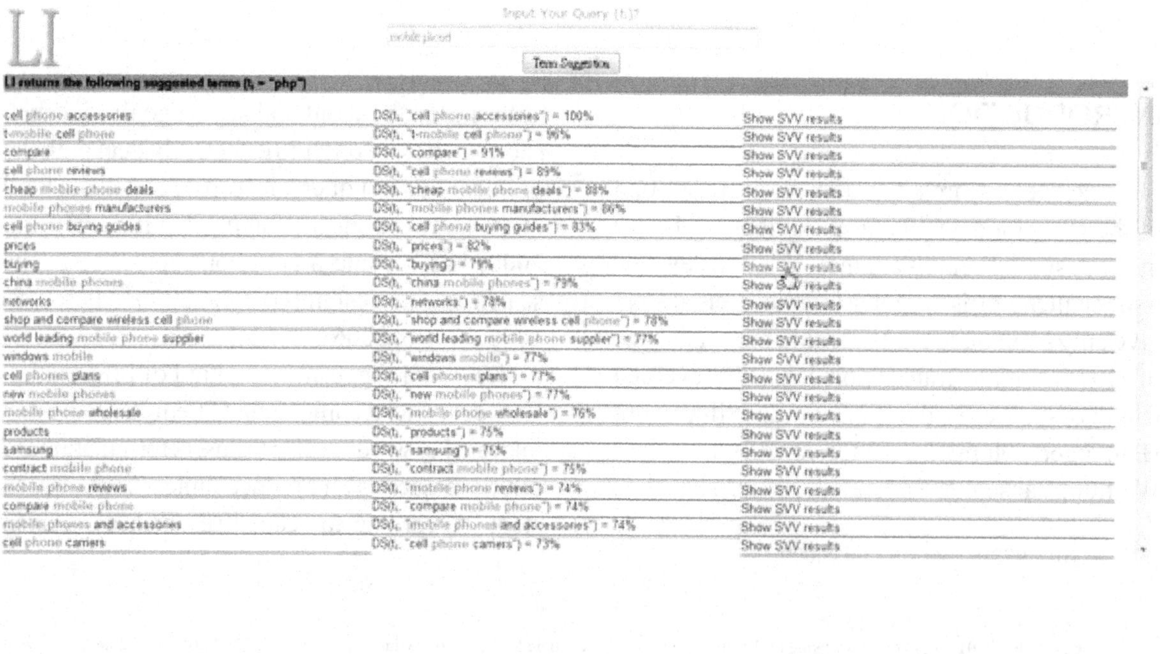

discover latent semantic relationships between query and document.

The main contribution of this chapter is the following. We implement a prototype system that runs on the Internet. Based on the characteristics of LSI and PLSI (Deerwester, et al., 1990; Hofmann, 1999), our system can gracefully deal with the problems of synonymy and polysemy.

RELATED WORK

In this section, we review two key concepts related to our work: LSI and keyword suggestion.

LSI

A classical way to represent the co-occurrences of terms and documents is term matching. There are two problems exist in this way. The first problem is synonymy implying that syntactically different but semantically interchangeable expressions. The second problem is polysemy, which means that a term has multiple meanings. LSI is an information retrieval technique to solve the first problem. In LSI, a document is represented as a mixture of latent topics instead of terms only (Brand, 2006; Deerwester, et al., 1990; Gorrell & Webb, 2005). LSI is a variant of the vector space model that converts a representative sample of documents to a term-document matrix in which each element indicates the frequency with which each term (row) occurs in each document (column). The advantage of LSI is that it allows coping with semantic issues such as synonymy and term dependence (Chakrabarti, 2005; Hand, Mannila, & Smyth, 2001; Kontostathis & Pottenger, 2002; Rosario, 2000). Another advantages of LSI are described in literature (Rosario, 2000).

Formally, the term-document matrix TD for a corpus of M terms and N documents is a $M \times N$ matrix as shown below, where $td(t_i, d_j)$ is the weight of term t_i in document d_j.

$$TD = [td(t_i, d_j)] \tag{1}$$

In the above matrix, $td(t_i, d_j)$ must always correctly reflect the significance of term t_i in document d_j. For example, a straightforward way is to set $td(t_i, d_j)$ equal to the number of times that term t_i appears in document d_j. More specially, it can use some more sophisticated weighting schemes to achieve better performance. Various weighting schemes are introduced in references (Kolda & O'Leary, 1998; Polettini, 2004).

Let us assume that the rank of TD is r and the singular values of TD are arranged in decreasing order $\sigma_i \geq \sigma_{i+1} > 0$. LSA uses Singular Value Decomposition (SVD) (Forsythe, 1977), a mathematical technique widely used in text analysis to extract higher-order semantic information from a large corpus, to decompose TD into the product of three other matrices, as shown in the following equation, where $\Sigma = \text{diag}(\sigma_1, \sigma_2, \ldots, \sigma_r)$ is a $r \times r$ diagonal matrix; $U = (u_1, u_2, \ldots, u_r)$ is a $M \times r$ matrix of left singular vectors; and $V = (v_1, v_2, \ldots, v_r)$ is a $N \times r$ matrix of right singular vectors.

$$TD = U\Sigma V^T \tag{2}$$

LSI then finds a low-rank approximation matrix $\sim TD$, which is smaller and less noisy than TD. For a fixed $k < r$, using a truncated SVD technique that conserves k largest singular values and set others to be zero to approximate TD, as shown in the following equation, where $\Sigma_k = \text{diag}(\sigma_1, \sigma_2, \ldots, \sigma_k)$ is a $k \times k$ diagonal matrix; $U_k = (u_1, u_2, \ldots, u_k)$ is a $M \times k$ matrix of left singular vectors; and $V_k = (v_1, v_2, \ldots, v_k)$ is a $N \times k$ matrix of right singular vectors.

$$TD \approx \sim TD = U_k \Sigma_k V_k^T \tag{3}$$

Keyword Suggestion

According to related researches (Yifan Chen, et al., 2008; Ferragina & Guli, 2008; Joshi & Motwani,

Table 1. The comparison of advantages and disadvantages between different categories

Category	Advantages	Disadvantages
Proximity search	It can generate a large number of suggested terms	It cannot produce relevant terms that do not contain the seed term
Query log analysis	It can generate the most popular search terms related to the seed term	It cannot produce relevant terms that do not contain the seed term
Web snippet analysis	It can suggest the terms with semantic relationships and variable word length	It fails to suggest such terms that do not appear on snippets

2006; Wang, et al., 2008), keyword suggestion can be broadly divided into three categories: proximity search, query log analysis, and Web snippet analysis. Table 1 shows the comparison of advantages and disadvantages between different categories.

For the first category, proximity search, it first sends the seed term to multiple search engines; then, it collects all important Web pages that are listed in the Search Engine Result Pages (SERPs). Finally, it expands new suggested terms in the proximity range of the seed term for all collected Web pages (Yifan Chen, et al., 2008; Joshi & Motwani, 2006). Since this category uses a proximity search method to implement it, a large number of suggested terms should be generated. However, it cannot produce relevant terms that do not contain the seed term (Abhishek & Hosanagar, 2007a). RapidKeyword (2006) proposed a Google Proximity Search (GPS) system, a commercial product that uses the proximity search technology to generate a large number of suggested terms. Metzler and Croft (2007) applied a latent concept expansion technology to expand the seed term in a gradual incremental way. Feuer et al. (2009) designed a keyword suggestion approach based on frequent phrase search. In the search stage, they arbitrarily chosen 32 terms as the size of proximity range to narrow or broaden original phrase.

For the second category, query log analysis, it analyzes the content of query logs to find out the co-occurrence relationships between terms and suggest similar terms starting from the seed

term (Google, 2006; Mei, et al., 2008; Yahoo, 2006). Since this category uses a term matching method to implement it, the most popular search terms related to the seed term should be suggested (Mei, et al., 2008). However, it also cannot produce relevant terms that do not contain the seed term (Abhishek & Hosanagar, 2007a). Google and Yahoo officially released Google AdWords (GAwords) (Google, 2006) and Yahoo Search Marketing (YSM) (Yahoo, 2006) systems, respectively, which are two famous commercial products that belong to this category. Chen and Zhang (2009) proposed a personalized query suggestion approach that uses the query-concept bipartite graphs and concept relation trees to update the weight of every candidate suggested terms.

For the third category, Web snippet analysis, it first sends the seed term to multiple search engines. Then, it collects all snippets that are summarized by remote search engines. Finally, it uses several document cleaning and pattern matching techniques to analyze snippets. All terms or phrases appeared on the results of document cleaning and pattern matching that can be considered as the candidate suggested terms (Ferragina & Guli, 2008; Wang, et al., 2008). Since this category uses a natural language processing method to implement it, it can suggest the terms with semantic relationships and variable word length (Ferragina & Gulli, 2004). However, it fails to suggest such terms that do not appear on snippets. Wu and Chen (2003) released a Highlight system that adopts a lexical analysis and a probabilistic analysis to construct a concept hierarchy for all relevant terms. Carpineto and Romano (2004) designed a Credo system that applies a formal concept analysis to construct all suggested terms in a hierarchy form that allows users to judge which one is appropriate. Osinski and Weiss (2005) proposed a Carrot2 system that uses the sentences with variable length words as the candidate suggested terms; then, it utilities a suffix tree clustering to identify which one should be suggested. Radovanović and Ivanović (2006) used a separate category tree to design a CatS system, which is based on the concept of dmoz taxonomy. Segev et al. (2007) proposed a Clusty system that adopts the concept of concise all pairs profiling to match all possible pairs of relevant terms. Ferragina and Guli (2008) built a SnakeT system that uses a frequent itemset-like approach to extract all candidate terms; then, it uses a bottom-up hierarchy construction process to suggest relevant terms in a hierarchy form.

In this chapter, we adopt two semantic analysis models, including LSI and PLSI, to implement a new keyword suggestion system. LSI uses a SVD technique to capture the synonym relationships between terms (Deerwester, et al., 1990). PLSI can deal with the problem of polysemy and can explicitly distinguish between different meanings and different types of term usage (Hofmann, 2004). In our system, we first use a graph search method to find some good candidate terms. Then, we use LSI and PLSI to identify the type of semantic relationships between terms and to calculate the similarity degree between terms.

METHOD

In this section, we present the system architecture of our proposed system, named Learning and Inference (LI), which involves two stages. The first stage is Learning, whose main task is continually to update the training parameter of our system. The second stage is Inference, whose main task is to rank all suggested terms according to the edge weight of the semantic graph derived from

the training parameter. The detail descriptions of Learning and Inference are presented in next two subsections.

Learning Stage

The main purpose of this stage is continually to update the training parameter, named the Probability of Query and Document (PQD) occurring in a mixture of latent topics, based on the models of LSI and PLSI. The system flow chart of the Learning stage is shown in Figure 2. First of all, in the Vector Space Model (VSM) step, we use a search engine to transform the query logs and Web pages into a VSM matrix. Secondly, in the LSI step, we use a truncated SVD technique to transform the VSM matrix into the LSI model. Thirdly, in the Dual Probability step, we use a dual probability model to transform the LSI model into the probability form of LSI. This step serves not only to transform the LSI model into the probability form, but also to obviate a problem of SVD that may introduce negative values in the decomposition process and such values cannot be treated as a probability distribution. Finally, in the PLSI step, we use an EM algorithm to transform the probability form of LSI into the PLSI model, which is final training parameter.

VSM Step

In this chapter, we use the VSM model to represent the similarity feature between terms that appears in a collection of documents. In this step, we use a search engine to transform all collected query logs and Web pages into a VSM matrix as shown in the following figure, where M is all collected terms in a log file and N is all collected Web pages in our search engine.

In our prototype system, we used the source of AOL Query Log (AOL, 2006), which consists of about 20 million instances of queries collected from about 650 thousand users, as our main collected terms, and the cached pages of our search

Figure 2. The system flow chart of the learning stage

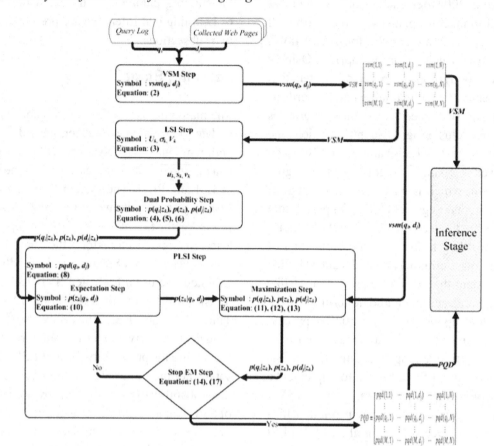

Figure 3. Organization of VSM matrix

$$VSM = \begin{bmatrix} vsm(1,1) & \cdots & vsm(1,d_j) & \cdots & vsm(1,N) \\ \vdots & \vdots & \vdots & \vdots & \vdots \\ vsm(q_i,1) & \cdots & vsm(q_i,d_j) & \cdots & vsm(q_i,N) \\ \vdots & \vdots & \vdots & \vdots & \vdots \\ vsm(M,1) & \cdots & vsm(M,d_j) & \cdots & vsm(M,N) \end{bmatrix}$$

engine, which consist of about 100 million Web pages collected from the Internet, as our collected Web pages.

For each entry of the VSM matrix, $vsm(q_i,d_j)$, we refer to our previous project (Chen & Luh, 2005). This project is based on the primacy effect of browsing behavior (Morris & Maisto, 2001); that is, users prefer top ranking items in the search results, and this preference always gradually decreases. Based on the primacy effect, we define a User Behavior Function (UBF) to express the behavior of human browsing as follows, where α is the degree of user preference for the first item; x_{obj} is the relative order of the object *obj* within an ordered item list x; and β is the decline degree of the user preference.

$$UBF(x, obj) = \alpha x_{obj}^{\beta} \text{ (where } 0<\alpha<1 \text{ and } \beta<0)$$

$$(4)$$

According to UBF's definition, we use the dot product between the UBF distributions of different search engines to calculate $vsm(q_i, d_j)$, as shown in the following equation, where $|se|$ is the number of search engines used in SVV; se is a search engine number; $\alpha_{se,qi}$ is the degree of user preference for the first listing returned from a search engine se in response to a given query q_i; and $x_{se,dj,qi}$ is the rank of a Web page d_j within the search listings x returned from se in response to q_i. More details of SVV are given in reference (Chen & Luh, 2005).

$$vsm(q_i, d_j) = \sum_{se=1}^{|se|} (\alpha_{se,q_i} x_{se,d_j,q_i}^{\beta})$$

$$(5)$$

LSI Step

The LSI model (Deerwester, et al., 1990) uses a dimensionality reduction technique to transform all collected terms and Web pages into a new VSM matrix with smaller dimensions that minimize the distance between the projected terms and the original terms. The dimensionality reduction technique reduces noise in original VSM matrix and has the potential benefit to detect synonyms as well as terms that refer to the same topic. In this step, we use a truncated SVD technique to transform the VSM matrix into the LSI model. For a fixed rank of k, it conserves the k largest singular values and set others to be zero to approximate the VSM matrix, as shown in Equation (3).

Dual Probability Step

The LSI model based on the SVD technique is a dimensionality reduction technique and as such does not have a probabilistic interpretation. In addition, the SVD technique may introduce negative values in the decomposition process and such val-

ues cannot be treated as a probability distribution. In this step, we adopt a dual probability model (Ding, 2005) to transform the LSI model into the probability form of LSI, as shown in the following equations, where $p(q_i|z_k)$, $p(z_k)$, and $p(d_j|z_k)$ are all PLSI parameters defined in section 3.1.4, and u_k, σ_k, and v_k are all LSI parameters previously defined in section 3.1.2.

$$U_k = p(q_i \mid z_k)$$
$$\approx \exp(q_i \times u_k)^2 / \sum_{i=1}^{M} \exp(q_i \times u_k)^2$$

$$(6)$$

$$\Sigma_k = p(z_k) \approx f(\sigma_k) / \sum_{k=1}^{k} f(\sigma_k)$$

$$(7)$$

$$V_k = p(d_j \mid z_k)$$
$$\approx \exp(d_j \times v_k)^2 / \sum_{j=1}^{N} \exp(d_j \times v_k)^2$$

$$(8)$$

PLSI Step

The LSI model explores the structure of term co-occurrence and solves the problem of synonym very well. However, it brings noise while reducing the dimensionality because it is unable to recognize the polysemy of a same term in different latent topics. Hofmann (1999) proposed a PLSI model to provide a probabilistic version of LSI that attempts to capture the polysemy terms from all collected terms and Web pages.

The PLSI model is based on a statistic model called aspect model, which can be utilized to identify the hidden semantic relationships among terms. For the given aspect model, PLSI supposes that a term q_i and a Web page d_j exist as a mixture of latent topics $Z=\{z_1,...,z_k\}$. PLSI then computes relevant probability distributions $pqd(q_i, d_j)$ by selecting the parameters of PLSI that maximize the probability of observed data, i.e., the likelihood function.

Figure 4. Organization of PQD matrix

$$PQD = \begin{bmatrix} pqd(1,1) & \cdots & pqd(1,d_j) & \cdots & pqd(1,N) \\ \vdots & \vdots & \vdots & \vdots & \vdots \\ pqd(q_i,1) & \cdots & pqd(q_i,d_j) & \cdots & pqd(q_i,N) \\ \vdots & \vdots & \vdots & \vdots & \vdots \\ pqd(M,1) & \cdots & pqd(M,d_j) & \cdots & pqd(M,N) \end{bmatrix}$$

Now, let us formally describe how to calculate the training parameter, called PQD matrix (Figure 4), by the PLSI model.

To calculate the entry of PQD matrix, $pqd(q_i,d_j)$, we first need to define the following probability notations:

- $p(q_i)$ denotes the probability that a particular term q_i will be selected.
- $p(z_k|q_i)$ denotes the posterior probability of a latent topic z_k given the observation q_i.
- $p(q_i|z_k)$ denotes the posterior probability of q_i given the observation z_k.
- $p(d_j|z_k)$ denotes the posterior probability of a particular Web page d_j given the observation z_k.

According to these definitions, PLSI first calculate the joint probability of an observed pair, $pqd(q_i,d_j)$, by summing over all possible choices of k from which the observation has been generated, as shown in the following equation:

$$pqd(q_i, d_j) = p(q_i)p(d_j \mid q_i)$$

where

$$p(d_j \mid q_i) = \sum_{k=1}^{k} p(d_j \mid z_k)p(z_k \mid q_i) \qquad (9)$$

PLSI then applies the Bayes rule to transform Equation (9) into the following form.

$$pqd(q_i, d_j) = \sum_{k=1}^{k} p(q_i \mid z_k)p(z_k)p(d_j \mid z_k) \qquad (10)$$

To calculate $pqd(q_i,d_j)$, PLSI follows the likelihood principle to estimate the parameters of PLSI, including $p(q_i|z_k)$, $p(z_k)$, $p(d_j|z_k)$, by maximum the likelihood function $L_n(q_i,d_j)$ at iteration n as shown in follows, where $vsm(q_i,d_j)$ is the entry of VSM matrix, which is the occurrence weight of q_i in d_j.

$$L_n(q_i, d_j) = \sum_{i=1}^{M} \sum_{j=1}^{N} vsm(q_i, d_j) \log(pqd(q_i, d_j)) \qquad (11)$$

The standard procedure for maximum likelihood estimation in the aspect model is the EM algorithm. Generally, two steps are needed to perform in this algorithm alternately: (1) Expectation step, where the posterior probability of z_k is calculated based on the current estimates of conditional probability; and (2) Maximization step, where the estimated conditional probabilities are updated and used to maximize the total likelihood function (Equation (11)) based on the posterior probability calculated in previous expectation step.

For a given initialization, the total likelihood function increases with each iteration of the EM algorithm, so that the quality of solution can be highly variable and depends on the initial values. In our PLSI model, we use a dual probability model as the initial values of PLSI. Let us now describe the EM algorithm in details.

1. First of all, in the initialize step, we use the results of dual probability step (Equations (6) to (8)) as the initial values of the PLSI model, including $p(q_i|z_k)$, $p(z_k)$, and $p(d_j|z_k)$.
2. Secondly, in the expectation step, PLSI again applies the Bayes rule to generate the latent variable z_k based on the current estimates of the parameters q_i and d_j as Equation 12.
3. Finally, in the maximization step, PLSI applies the Lagrange multipliers method (see (Hofmann, 2001) for details) to solve the constraint maximization problem to get the following equations for re-estimated the PLSI parameters as Equations 13, 14, and 15.

Now we can substitute equations (13) to (15) into Equations (10) and (11) that will result in the monotonically increasing of the total likelihood function $L_n(q_i, d_j)$ of the observation data. The executing of expectation and maximization steps are repeating until a stopping criterion is reached.

Inference Stage

The main purpose of this stage is to rank all suggested terms according to the edge weight of the KRG graph, which is derived from the training parameter of previous stage. The system flow chart of KRG is shown in Figure 5. First of all, in the KRG without Edge Weight step, we apply the Breadth First Search (BFS) algorithm and the concept of inverted index to build a KRG graph. Secondly, in the KRG with Edge Weight step, we measure the similarity degree between terms based on the edge weight of the KRG graph.

KRG without Edge Weight Step

KRG is a relatively new graph concept that is applied to filtering a large database (Yi Chen, Wang, Liu, & Lin, 2009; Zhou & Pei, 2009). In the concept of KRG graph, a node corresponds to a term and an edge indicates there is a relationship between terms present in the database. The weight of an edge is used to measure the importance of this relationship. Following the concept of KRG, we define our graph terminology as follows.

In our definition of KRG(V,E,W), based on a given query q_i, V is a set of nodes, each of which corresponding to a candidate term q_{ct} listed in the VSM matrix. E is a set of directed edges, an edge (q_i, q_{ct}) represents that these two terms exist in a semantic relationship and q_{ct} is suggested from q_i. W is a set of weight vectors, each of which using

Equation 12.

$$p(z_k \mid q_i, d_j) = p(q_i \mid z_k)p(z_k)p(d_j \mid z_k) \Big/ \sum_{k=1}^{k} p(q_i \mid z_k)p(z_k)p(d_j \mid z_k)$$

Equations 13, 14, and 15.

$$p(q_i \mid z_k) = \sum_{j=1}^{N} vsm(q_i, d_j)p(z_k \mid q_i, d_j) \Big/ \sum_{i=1}^{M}\sum_{j=1}^{N} vsm(q_i, d_j)p(z_k \mid q_i, d_j)$$

$$p(z_k) = \sum_{i=1}^{M}\sum_{j=1}^{N} vsm(q_i, d_j)p(z_k \mid q_i, d_j) \Big/ \sum_{i=1}^{M}\sum_{j=1}^{N} vsm(q_i, d_j)$$

$$p(d_j \mid z_k) = \sum_{i=1}^{M} vsm(q_i, d_j)p(z_k \mid q_i, d_j) \Big/ \sum_{i=1}^{M}\sum_{j=1}^{N} vsm(q_i, d_j)p(z_k \mid q_i, d_j)$$

Figure 5. The system flow chart of the inference stage

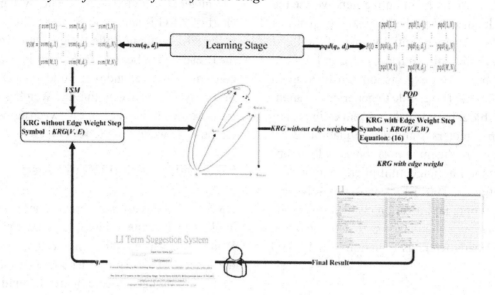

to measure the degree of similarity between the edge (q_i, q_{ct}).

Definition 1. The semantic relationship between q_i and q_{ct}

Two terms, q_i and q_{ct}, exist in a semantic relationship if and only if these two terms have at least one of the following relationships: equivalence, hierarchy, and association. First of all, if q_i and q_{ct} share a same concept, these two terms exist in an equivalence relationship. Secondly, if q_i and q_{ct} exist in a parent-child relationship through an intermediate term, these two terms exist in a hierarchy relationship. Finally, if q_i and q_{ct} exist in an ancestor-descendant relationship through a series of intermediate terms, these two terms exist in an association relationship.

Figure 6 shows an example of KRG graph without the edge weight. We will discuss about how to calculate the edge weight in next step.

For each pair of the equivalence relationship between q_i and q_{ct}, KRG uses the concept of inverted index to specify these two terms. That is,

Figure 6. An example of KRG graph without the edge weight

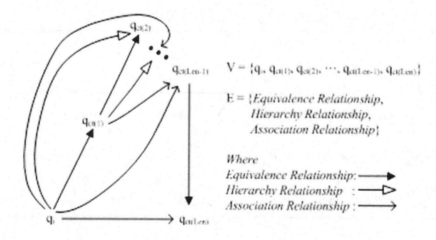

if q_i and q_{ct} are all indexed into a Web page $d_{i,ct}$, then we can use the inverted index of $d_{i,ct}$ listed in the VSM matrix to specify q_i and q_{ct}.

For each pair of the hierarchy and association relationships between q_i and q_{ct}, KRG uses a series of BFS (BuildKRG) calls to implement it. The pseudo code of BuildKRG is listed in Figure 7. In this pseudo code, q_i is a seed term, q_{ct} is any candidate term derived from this code, *Len* is the current path length between q_i and q_{ct}, and *MaxRunLen* is a maximum path length for q_i that is used to restrict the size of KRG.

KRG with Edge Weight Step

Although in the previous step, BuildKRG uses the parameter *MaxRunLen* to reduce the size of KRG, but we still need to prune the number of directed edges in advance. That is, if the edge weight of KRG is less than a relatively small edge weight, we do not further consider it in further recursive calls. In summary, the edge weight of KRG is not only used to determine the degree of similarity between terms, but also used to discard the candidate terms with a relatively small edge weight.

Let us now discuss how to calculate the edge weight of KRG (line 16 in the BuildKRG algorithm). In this step, we use the cosine similarity metric to transform the training parameter of the Learning stage, PQD matrix, into the edge weight of KRG by the following equation, where $pqd(q_m,d_j)$, $m \in \{i,ct\}$, is the entry of PQD matrix, which is the joint probability of an observed pair (q_m,d_j). For example, in Figure 1, the degree of similarity of the directed edge ("mobile phone", "samsung") is 75%.

$$Sim(q_i, q_{ct}) = \frac{\sum_{j=1}^{N} pqd(q_i, d_j) pqd(q_{ct}, d_j)}{\sqrt{\sum_{j=1}^{N} pqd(q_i, d_j)^2} \sqrt{\sum_{j=1}^{N} pqd(q_{ct}, d_j)^2}}$$

(16)

Figure 7. The pseudo code of BuildKRG

```
1      Algorithm BuildKRG (qi, qct, Len, MaxRunLen)
2      {
3          If (Len≥MaxRunLen)
4              Return(KRG(V<qct>, E<(qi,qct)>, W<(qi,qct)>);
5          Else
6          {
7              If (Len == 1)
8                  qct = qi;
9              <di,ct> = The list of web pages that are indexed by the query qct;
10             For each (<di,ct> as di,ct)
11             {
12                 V<qct> = Using the inverted index of di,ct that is listed in VSM matrix to identify all
                   candidate terms qcts;
13                 For each (<qct> as qct)
14                 {
15                     E<(qi,qct)> += Adding the pair of (qi,qct) as a directed edge of KRG;
16                     W<(qi,qct)> += Adding the pair of Sim(qi,qct) (discuss later) as an edge weight of KRG;
17                     BuildKRG (qi, qct, Len+1, MaxRunLen);
18                 } End of For each;
19             } End of For each;
20         } End of Else;
21     } End of Algorithm;
```

EXPERIMENT

In this section, we present a preliminary experiment result to compare the performance of keyword suggestion obtained from our system and other online systems. The compared systems are GPS, GAwords, YSM, Highlight, Credo, Carrot2, CatS, Clusty, SnakeT, and LI. All of abovementioned systems, except LI, are described in section 2.2.

In this experiment, we selected 32 of the most popular search queries on the Internet in 2008 from Yahoo (2009), Google (2009), AOL (2008), and Lycos (2008) that belonging to many different topics ("american idol", "angelina jolie", "barack obama", "beijing 2008", "britney spears", "clay aiken", "euro 2008", "facebook", "facebook login", "flat belly diet", "golf", "heath ledger", "holly madison", "iphone", "jessica alba", "jonas brothers", "lindsay lohan", "miley cyrus", "naruto", "nascar", "nasza klasa", "obama", "pamela anderson", "paris hilton", "poker", "presidential election", "runescape", "sarah palin", "tuenti", "wer kennt wen", "wwe", "youtube"), and asked to 35 undergraduate and 6 graduate students from our department. We use three well-known measures from information retrieval to evaluate the performance of different systems: Precision, Recall, and F-measure. Precision, Recall, and F-measure for the system i at the first 10 suggested terms are defined as Equations (17), (18), and (19), respectively (Baeza-Yates & Ribeiro-Neto, 1999; Chen, 2010; Wan, 2009), where $|M_i|$ is the number of suggested terms that have been manually tagged relevant among the 10 suggested terms computed by system i; $|\bigcup_{i=GPS}^{LI} M_i|$ is the number of labels such that the union of all M_is contains all suggested terms for all is.

$$Precision_i = |M_i|/10 \qquad (17)$$

$$Recall_i = \frac{|M_i|}{|\bigcup_{i=GPS}^{LI} M_i|} \qquad (18)$$

$$F - measure_i = 2 \times \frac{Precision_i \times Recall_i}{Precision_i + Recall_i} \qquad (19)$$

The second, third, and fourth columns of Table 2 show the average Precision, average Recall, and average F-measure, respectively. The average Precision value for LI is 0.737. Moreover, in Table 2, we also extend the Precision measure to other measures Recall and F-measure. According to the results of this table, our system has a better user perceived performance than other systems.

For all quantitative analyses, we used a SPSS statistical software and the level of statistical significance was set at $p < 0.05$. We first used the Analysis of Variance (ANOVA) test to determine whether there was a statistically significant difference in the performance of different systems. The results of one-way ANOVA test are presented in Table 3. According to the results of one-way ANOVA test shown in Table 3, the difference is statistically significant at the 95% confidence level. We then conducted a post host

Table 2. Average precision, recall, and F-measure for different systems

System Name	Average Precision$_i$	Average Recall$_i$	Average F-measure$_i$
GPS	0.504	0.117	0.190
GAwords	0.640	0.135	0.223
YSM	0.642	0.135	0.223
Highlight	0.576	0.126	0.207
Credo	0.453	0.114	0.182
Carrot2	0.621	0.131	0.216
CatS	0.362	0.108	0.166
Clusty	0.670	0.147	0.241
SnakeT	0.651	0.141	0.232
LI	0.737	0.151	0.251

Fisher's Least Significant Different (LSD) test for pair-wise comparison at the 5% significant level. Since the results of LSD are long-winded and complicated, we encourage the readers who are interesting to our full-length report (Cayley-Group, 2010). According to the results of LSD, our system is found to be significantly better than other systems.

For a large part of the evaluated queries, the evaluators did not like CatS since it only provides the category names, which is derived from the dmoz taxonomy, not any specific names as the suggested terms. Credo only suggests the terms with a single word. Highlight obtains the top-level suggested terms by using a classification technique, so that the results of suggested terms are few. GPS, GAwords, and YSM are failing to suggest any terms that do not contain the evaluated query. Although Carrot2, Clusty, and SnakeT can suggest the terms with semantic relationships and variable word length, but they only use a pattern matching technique to analyze snippets. That is, they fail to suggest such terms that do not appear on snippets. Our system uses the models of LSI and PLSI to construct latent topics from the VSM matrix, and the terms suggested by our

system are all based on the results of LSI and PLSI. Thus, our system can gracefully deal with the problems of synonymy and polysemy.

CONCLUSION

In this chapter, we have adopted two semantic analysis models, including LSI and PLSI, to implement a keyword suggestion system. Our system suggests relevant terms by the following two stages: Learning and Inference. In the Learning stage, we applied the models of LSI and PLSI to transform the VSM model into the training parameter. In the Inference stage, we applied a semantic graph to transform the training parameter into a list of suggested terms with a similarity measure.

The benefit of our semantic graph is easily to find the terms with semantic relationships by using a graph search. However, this graph lacks not only the ability to distinguish the type of semantic relationships, including synonymy and polysemy, but also the ability to calculate the similarity degree between terms. LSI and PLSI are designed to solve these two problems. That is, our mixed methods can be applied to solve the following

Table 3. The results of one-way ANOVA test

		Sum of Squares	df	Mean Square	F	Sig.
PR@3	Between Groups	3.714	9	0.413	378.144	0
	Within Groups	0.338	310	0.001		
	Total	4.052	319			
PR@5	Between Groups	3.758	9	0.418	405.525	0
	Within Groups	0.319	310	0.001		
	Total	4.077	319			
PR@7	Between Groups	3.752	9	0.417	398.321	0
	Within Groups	0.324	310	0.001		
	Total	4.077	319			
PR@10	Between Groups	3.713	9	0.413	372.197	0
	Within Groups	0.344	310	0.001		
	Total	4.057	319			

problem: finding any two objects with a semantic relationship and calculating the similarity degree between these two objects.

ACKNOWLEDGMENT

We would like to thank 41 students to evaluate the online questionnaire. We would also like to thank anonymous reviewers of the chapter for their constructive comments which help us to improve the chapter in several ways. This work was supported in part by National Science Council, Taiwan under Grant NSC 99-2221-E-259-023.

REFERENCES

Abhishek, V., & Hosanagar, K. (2007a). *Keyword generation for search engine advertising using semantic similarity between terms.* Paper presented at the Ninth International Conference on Electronic Commerce.

Abhishek, V., & Hosanagar, K. (2007b). *Keyword generation for search engine advertising using semantic similarity between terms.* Paper presented at the Ninth International Conference on Electronic Commerce.

AOL. (2006). *AOL search data.* Retrieved December 6, 2009, from http://www.gregsadetsky.com/aol-data/

AOL. (2008). *AOL search - 2008 year end hot searches.* Retrieved December 6, 2009, from http://about-search.aol.com/hotsearches2008/index.html

Baeza-Yates, R., & Ribeiro-Neto, B. (1999). *Modern information retrieval.* Addison Wesley Press.

Bartz, K., Murthi, V., & Sebastian, S. (2006). *Logistic regression and collaborative filtering for sponsored search term recommendation.* Paper presented at the Second Workshop on Sponsored Search Auctions.

Belkin, N. J. (2000). Helping people find what they don't know. *Communications of the ACM, 43*(8), 58–61. doi:10.1145/345124.345143

Brand, M. (2006). Fast low-rank modifications of the thin singular value decomposition. *Linear Algebra and Its Applications, 415*(1), 20–30. doi:10.1016/j.laa.2005.07.021

Carpineto, C., & Romano, G. (2004). Exploiting the potential of concept lattices for information retrieval with CREDO. *Journal of Universal Computer Science, 10*(8), 985–1013.

CayleyGroup. (2010). *VLDP_KRG's evaluation results.* Retrieved April 2, 2010, from http://cayley.sytes.net/vldp_krg/OUTPUT_VLDP_KRG.htm

Chakrabarti, S. (2005). *Mining the Web: Analysis of hypertext and semi structured data.* Morgan Kaufmann Press.

Chen, L.-C. (2010). Using a two-stage technique to design a keyword suggestion system. *Information Research: An International Electronic Journal, 15*(1).

Chen, L.-C., & Luh, C. J. (2005). Web page prediction from metasearch results. *Internet Research: Electronic Networking Applications and Policy, 15*(4), 421–446. doi:10.1108/10662240510615182

Chen, Y., Wang, W., Liu, Z., & Lin, X. (2009). *Keyword search on structured and semi-structured data.* Paper presented at the 2009 ACM SIGMOD International Conference on Management of Data.

Chen, Y., Xue, G.-R., & Yu, Y. (2008). *Advertising keyword suggestion based on concept hierarchy.* Paper presented at the International Conference on Web Search and Web Data Mining.

Chen, Y., & Zhang, Y.-Q. (2009). A personalised query suggestion agent based on query-concept bipartite graphs and concept relation trees. *International Journal of Advanced Intelligence Paradigms, 1*(4), 398–417. doi:10.1504/IJAIP.2009.026761

Deerwester, S., Dumais, S. T., Furnas, G. W., Landauer, T. K., & Harshman, R. (1990). Indexing by latent semantic analysis. *Journal of the American Society for Information Science American Society for Information Science, 41*(6), 391–407. doi:10.1002/(SICI)1097-4571(199009)41:6<391::AID-ASI1>3.0.CO;2-9

Ding, C. H. Q. (2005). A probabilistic model for latent semantic indexing. *Journal of the American Society for Information Science and Technology, 56*(6), 597–608. doi:10.1002/asi.20148

Ferragina, P., & Guli, A. (2008). A personalized search engine based on Web-snippet hierarchical clustering. *Software, Practice & Experience, 38*(1), 189–225. doi:10.1002/spe.829

Ferragina, P., & Gulli, A. (2004). *The anatomy of a hierarchical clustering engine for web-page, news and book snippets.* Paper presented at the Fourth IEEE International Conference on Data Mining.

Feuer, A., Savev, S., & Aslam, J. A. (2009). Implementing and evaluating phrasal query suggestion for proximity search. *Information Systems, 34*(1), 711–723. doi:10.1016/j.is.2009.03.012

Forsythe, G. E. (1977). *Computer methods for mathematical computations.* Prentice Hall Press.

Google. (2006). *Google AdWords: Keyword tool.* Retrieved April 2, 2010, from https://adwords.google.com/select/KeywordToolExternal

Google. (2009). *2008 year-end Google zeitgeist.* Retrieved April 2, 2010, from http://www.google.com/intl/en/press/zeitgeist2008/index.html

Gorrell, G., & Webb, B. (2005). *Generalized Hebbian algorithm for incremental latent semantic analysis.* Paper presented at Interspeech 2005.

Hand, D. J., Mannila, H., & Smyth, P. (2001). *Principles of data mining.* MIT Press.

Hofmann, T. (1999). *Probabilistic latent semantic indexing.* Paper presented at the 22th Annual International SIGIR Conference on Research and Development in Information Retrieval.

Hofmann, T. (2001). Unsupervised learning by probabilistic latent semantic analysis. *Machine Learning, 42*(1), 177–196. doi:10.1023/A:1007617005950

Hofmann, T. (2004). Latent semantic models for collaborative filtering. *ACM Transactions on Information Systems, 22*(1), 89–115. doi:10.1145/963770.963774

Janruang, J., & Kreesuradej, W. (2006). *A new Web search result clustering based on true common phrase label discovery.* Paper presented at the International Conference on Computational Inteligence for Modelling Control and Automation and International Conference on Intelligent Agents Web Technologies and International Commerce.

Joshi, A., & Motwani, R. (2006). *Keyword generation for search engine advertising.* Paper presented at the Sixth IEEE International Conference on Data Mining.

Kolda, T. G., & O'Leary, D. P. (1998). A semidiscrete matrix decomposition for latent semantic indexing in information retrieval. *ACM Transactions on Information Systems, 16*(4), 322–346. doi:10.1145/291128.291131

Kontostathis, A., & Pottenger, W. M. (2002). *Detecting patterns in the LSI term-term matrix.* Paper presented at the ICDM'02 Workshop on Foundations of Data Mining and Discovery.

Lee, H. M., Huang, C. C., & Hung, W. T. (2007). Mining navigation behaviors for term suggestion of search engines. *Journal of Information Science and Engineering, 23,* 387–401.

Lycos. (2008). *Top search terms for 2008.* Retrieved April 2, 2010, from http://www.lycos.com

Mei, Q., Zhou, D., & Church, K. (2008). *Query suggestion using hitting time.* Paper presented at the 17th ACM Conference on Information and Knowledge Mining.

Metzler, D., & Croft, W. B. (2007). *Latent concept expansion using Markov random fields.* Paper presented at the 30th Annual International ACM SIGIR Conference on Research and Development in Information Retrieval.

Microsoft. (2006). *Microsoft adCenter.* Retrieved April 2, 2010, from http://adcenter.microsoft.com/

Morris, C. G., & Maisto, A. A. (2001). *Psychology: An introduction.* Prentice Hall Press.

Osinski, S., & Weiss, D. (2005). A concept-driven algorithm for clustering search results. *IEEE Intelligent Systems, 20*(3), 48–54. doi:10.1109/MIS.2005.38

Polettini, N. (2004). *The vector space model in information retrieval - Term weighting problem.* Department of Information and Communication Technology, University of Trento.

Radovanović, M., & Ivanović, M. (2006). CatS: A classification-powered meta-search engine. *Advances in Web Intelligence and Data Mining, 23*(1), 191–200. doi:10.1007/3-540-33880-2_20

RapidKeyword. (2006). *Rapid keyword -Keyword research software and keyword generator tools.* Retrieved April 2, 2010, from http://www.rapid-keyword.com/

Rosario, B. (2000). *Latent semantic indexing: An overview.* Retrieved April 2, 2010, from http://people.ischool.berkeley.edu/~rosario/projects/LSI.pdf

Segev, A., Leshno, M., & Zviran, M. (2007). Context recognition using Internet as a knowledge base. *Journal of Intelligent Information Systems, 29*(3), 305–327. doi:10.1007/s10844-006-0015-y

Silverstein, C., Henzinger, M., Marais, H., & Moricz, M. (1998). Analysis of a very large AltaVista query log. Retrieved July 1, 2010, from http://www.hpl.hp.com/techreports/Compaq-DEC/SRC-TN-1998-014.pdf

Spink, A., Wolfram, D., Jansen, M. B. J., & Saracevic, T. (2001). Searching the Web: The public and their queries. *Journal of the American Society for Information Science and Technology, 52*(3), 226–234. doi:10.1002/1097-4571(2000)9999:9999<::AID-ASI1591>3.0.CO;2-R

Wan, X. (2009). Combining content and context similarities for image retrieval. *Lecture Notes in Computer Science, 5478*(1), 749–754. doi:10.1007/978-3-642-00958-7_79

Wang, J., Mo, Y., Huang, B., Wen, J., & He, L. (2008). Web search results clustering based on a novel suffix tree structure. *Lecture Notes in Computer Science, 5060*(1), 540–554. doi:10.1007/978-3-540-69295-9_43

Wu, Y.-F., & Chen, X. (2003). *Extracting features from Web search returned hits for hierarchical classification.* Paper presented at the International Conference on Information and Knowledge Engineering.

Yahoo. (2006). *Start advertising with Yahoo! Search marketing.* Retrieved 2 April, 2010, from https://signup13.marketingsolutions.yahoo.com/signupui/signup/loadSignup.do

Yahoo. (2009). *Top 10 - Yahoo! 2008 year in review - Top 10 searches for 2008.* Retrieved April 2, 2010, from http://buzz.yahoo.com/yearinreview2008/top10/

Zhou, B., & Pei, J. (2009). *Answering aggregate keyword queries on relational databases using minimal group-bys.* Paper presented at the 12th International Conference on Extending Database Technology: Advances in Database Technology.

KEY TERMS AND DEFINITIONS

Keyword Suggestion: An algorithm to suggest relevant keywords to Internet users.

LSI: Latent Semantic Indexing.

Machine Learning: It is a scientific discipline that is concerned with the design and development of algorithms that allow computers to evolve behaviors based on empirical data.

PLSI: Probabilistic Latent Semantic Indexing.

Polysemy: A term has multiple meanings.

Semantic Analysis: Two terms have at least one of the following relationships: equivalence, hierarchy, and association.

Synonymy: Two terms are syntactically different but semantically interchangeable expressions.

Vector Space Model: It is an algebraic model for representing text documents as vectors of identifiers.

Section 2
Computational Intelligence Techniques and Applications

Chapter 10
Emergence Phenomenon and Fuzzy Logic in Meaningful Image Segmentation and Retrieval

Sagarmay Deb
Central Queensland University, Australia

Siddhivinayak Kulkarni
University of Ballarat, Australia

ABSTRACT

Content-based image retrieval is a difficult area of research in multimedia systems. The research has proven extremely difficult because of the inherent problems in proper automated analysis and feature extraction of the image to facilitate proper classification of various objects. An image may contain more than one object, and to segment the image in line with object features to extract meaningful objects and then classify it in high-level like table, chair, car and so on has become a challenge to the researchers in the field. The latter part of the problem, the gap between low-level features like colour, shape, texture, spatial relationships, and high-level definitions of the images is called the semantic gap. Until this problem is solved in an effective way, the efficient processing and retrieval of information from images will be difficult to achieve. In this chapter, the authors explore the possibilities of how emergence phenomena and fuzzy logic can help solve these problems of image segmentation and semantic gap.

INTRODUCTION

Research on multimedia systems and content-based image retrieval has gained momentum during the last decade. Content-based image retrieval (CBIR) is a very difficult area in the access of multimedia databases simply because there still exist vast differences in the perception capacity between a human and a computer. There are two basic problems that still remain unresolved in the area although some progresses have been made (Zhau, Grosky, 2002). The first one is the problem of efficient and meaningful image segmentation

DOI: 10.4018/978-1-4666-1833-6.ch010

where we break-up a particular image into meaningful parts based on low-level features like colour, texture, shape and spatial locations. In computer vision, segmentation refers to the process of partitioning a digital image into multiple segments (sets of pixels, also known as superpixels). The goal of segmentation is to simplify and/or change the representation of an image into something that is more meaningful and easier to analyze. Image segmentation is typically used to locate objects and boundaries (lines, curves, etc.) in images. More precisely, image segmentation is the process of assigning a label to every pixel in an image such that pixels with the same label share certain visual characteristics (Wikipedia, 2008). Developing a segmentation algorithm which will meaningfully segment all images is yet an open problem in image analysis (Mehta, Diwakar, Jawahar, 2003). The second one is the vast gap existing for an image between low-level features mentioned earlier and high-level or semantic expressions contained in the image like the image of a car, a house, a table and so on (Zhau, Grosky, 2002). To develop efficient indexing techniques for the retrieval of enormous volumes of images being generated these days, we need to achieve reasonable solutions to these above-mentioned two problems. But only in very limited and selected cases, some kinds of solutions have been achieved with apparently promising experimental results. In this chapter we focus our attention on the first problem. The research identifies few issues causing this gap, for example, failure to capture local image details with low level features, unavailability of semantic representation of images, inadequate human involvement in the retrieval, and ambiguity in query formulation (Islam, 2006). We offer future directions of research in solving this difficult problem using emergence phenomena.

The remaining book chapter has been organized as follows. Section Emergence Phenomenon provides a definition of emergence phenomenon, structure, behaviour and function. Section Use of Emergence Phenomenon details about the use of

emergence phenomenon in extracting meanings in image segmentation. Next section deals with neural networks for image classification and implementation of fuzzy logic based similarity measure. Finally chapter is concluded in Conclusion Section.

EMERGENCE PHENOMENON

Definition of Emergence Phenomenon

A feature of an image which is not explicit would be emergent feature if it can be made explicit. There are three types of emergence: computational emergence, thermodynamic emergence and emergence relative to a model (Cariani, 1992). In computational emergence, it is assumed computational interactions can generate different features or behaviors (Forrest, 1991), (Langton, 1989). This is one of the approaches in the field of artificial life. Thermodynamic emergence is of the view that new stable features or behaviors can arise from equilibrium through the use of thermodynamic theory. In emergence relative to a model, deviation of the behavior from the original model gives rise to emergence. We will use this latter view in our work.

In computational emergence, new shapes or images develop but within certain limit as programmed by the computer programmers. No new shape can emerge beyond the logic of the program. In thermodynamic emergence, emergence can be defined as emergence of order from noise. Stochastic processes at micro-level form discrete macro-level structures or behaviors. The example of this type of emergence is gas where stochastic movements of atoms or molecules within the gas create the ordered properties of temperature, pressure and volume at a higher level.

Example of emergence relative to a model is where changes in internal structure and consequently in its behavior occur and we as observers will need to change our model to track the device's behavior in order to successfully continue to predict actions. The example of a square having two triangles hidden in it as given below is of this type. Whenever we shift our focus on an existing shape in other words an image, new shape emerges. The representation of the new shape is based upon view of the original shape. The new shape emerges as we change our view of the original shape. This is the fundamentally most important idea of emergence.

Two classes of shape emergence have been identified: embedded shape emergence and illusory shape emergence. In embedded shape emergence all the emergent shapes can be identified by set theory kind of procedures on the original shape under consideration. For example, in a set $S = \{a, b, c, d, e\}$, we can find subsets like $S1 = \{a, b, c\}$, $S2 = \{c, d, e\}$, $S3 = \{a, c, e\}$ and so on. But in illusory shape emergence, where contours defining a shape are perceived even though no contours are physically present, this kind of set theory procedures are not enough and more effective procedures have to be applied to find these hidden shapes (Gero, Maher,1994), (Gero, 1993). These procedures could be based on geometrical, topological or dimensional studies of the original shape.

Structure, Behaviour, and Function of Emergence

Structure of a shape is the physical definition of the shape. For example, a box could be rectangular in shape, its length, width and height as well as colour, substance like wood, metal or hard chapter would define the structure of the shape. Behavior of the box could be to contain certain stuffs in it and the function could be to carry stuff from one place to another using the box as a container, which is the purpose for which the box is used. Emergence of new structure, behavior or function takes place when these descriptions are interpreted

in ways not anticipated in the original description (Gero and Maher, 1994).

Examples of Emergence

Shape emergence is associated with emergence of individual or multiple shapes. The following figures are examples of shape emergence.

Definition of Emergence Index

Image retrieval where the hidden or emergence meanings of the images are studied and based on those hidden meanings as well as explicit meanings, an index of search is defined to retrieve images is called emergence index. When images are retrieved based on textual information, various parameters and descriptions might define the input and the images of the database. Whenever there would be symmetry of parameters and descriptions, the image could be retrieved. In CBIR, colour, texture and shape are widely used as index to retrieve images. But in this study, the hidden meanings of the images could be found and whenever those hidden meanings match with

Figure 1. Two emergent shapes derived from the existing one (Gero, 1993)

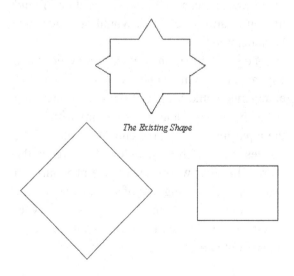

The Existing Shape

Figure 2. Example of emergence where diagonal generates two triangles

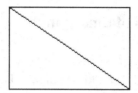

the input given, although the original image may not match at all with the input, could be retrieved.

To describe in detail, as we have mentioned, emergence is a phenomenon where we bring out the shapes, which are not explicit but implicit. The following Figure shows a simple example of emergence where an apparently square shape has two triangles hidden in it as discussed earlier.

When an input would come in the form of an image, the image could be studied based on features, constraints, variables, domains and emergence and converted into parametric form. Then the image database would be accessed and each image would be interpreted considering the items mentioned above and converted into parametric form like the input image. Whenever there would be a match between parameters of the input and the images of the database, those records would be selected. In other words, indexing would be decided by the outcome of emergence which means more meaningful images could be found hidden in an image which would otherwise not be understood.

Many images in the database may not have any apparent similarities with the input, but emergence could bring out the hidden meaning of the image and could establish similarities with the input image. So emergence outcomes of the images would form the index structure of the search. In other words emergence phenomenon can generate meanings out of a segmented image where apparently no meaning exists. That way it can help in the definition of meanings out of segmented images.

Structure of Emergence Index

Parameter Definitions

To make an effective query, the images in the query or database must be analysed so that we know what we are looking for and where to look for. Features, domains, variables, constraints, similarities, indexing are the parameters, which play very important role in similarity searching. Hence they constitute the structure of the emergence index.

Features

Input, could come in the form of text. For example, the text may indicate we have to pick up all the images of a database that contains the image of a particular person or an object. In this case, nothing much could be done on input side in the sense that we cannot study the input's features etc. We have to go through the images and pick up the image records. But if the query is posted in the form of an image of a person then we have to analyse it before accessing the database images. Features would tell us about a few important characteristics of the input image. To start up, our query could be an image where a particular person is sitting on a chair. Then obviously there are two important features in the query image - the particular person and the chair. We have to locate these two features in the database image while searching for similarities.

Colour plays a very important role in the definition of features. Quite often a query might mention an object with certain specified colour to be picked up from the databases. Besides, colour is being used extensively in various models as a tool in finding symmetry with the input image. Sometimes the input may be in the form of a sketch. In that case, a similar kind of image should be selected from the image database. The selection should be made on the basis of few dominant characteristics of the input and image and finding similarities in those characteristics.

Texture is another part of the feature where the general alignment of the image like the background part of the image is considered where the image of a person or an object could be the dominant part. There would be some global features of an image like area, perimeters and a set of rectangles or triangles that cover the entire shape and there would be some local features, which can be obtained from the image's local region.

When we retrieve images by browsing, then in most cases the user does not have clear idea about what he or she is looking for. In this case, there would not be input image and the search through browsing would be manual. The user would have vague idea about the features of the images to be retrieved like the picture of a particular person with certain specified background. In the objective features based queries, the retrieval is performed on an exact match of attribute values whereas in the subjective features, query is specified by features, which could be interpreted differently by different users. Retrieval by motion facilitates retrieving spatio-temporal image sequence depicting a domain phenomenon that varies in time or geographic space. Sometimes images are retrieved, as we mentioned earlier, by text. In other words, text defines the features of the images to be selected. Then the database is searched based on those features defined in the input (Gudivada and Raghavan, 1995).

Domain

We now proceed to discuss the domain. Domain is a sort of classification of the images into certain categories. Domain is a way for a class of objects to present knowledge representing a certain concept held by objects (Yoshitaka, Kishida, Hirakawa, 1994).

It is vital to make use of the various properties of the features of an image to define the domain in which the image concerned would lie. For example, from an image we can understand whether the image is that of a geographical location of a certain area of the earth or the image is that of a person or object with certain background like a screen or a landscape behind. This kind of classification at the initial stage of search should enable us to access the image database rapidly and more efficiently. Also in a multimedia database, the database might contain various kinds of records like the images, the data in figures, the documents, audios, videos and so on. The concept of domain would classify them according to their categories.

The domain could also be formulated based on the length of the certain features of the image like finding the images of a particular person or object where the length is of certain range value. Colour could also define a domain where the images having a particular colour or a combination of colours lie in one domain. Domain could be defined on the basis of objects only. For example, we can pick up image where the images of a triangle and square would be present. We can make it more specific by mentioning colour and length or size of the triangle and the rectangle to pick up images like where the triangle is red coloured and sides of length, say, *(3, 3, 3)* and rectangle of colour white and sides of length, say, *(4, 2)*.

Variables

Since in our research we are considering a multimedia database where a particular record in the database could be an image or a data record or a document and so on, the definition of variables would vary depending upon the type of records we are considering. In an image database, where we would consider two-dimensional pictures, the image of an object or a person has to be measured. If we try to measure it graphically, then the size could be measured in terms of x and y coordinates. Therefore, size would be a very important variable in our research.

Colour could be another very important variable. There are, as we know many colours available and for specific definition of the image, the colour would play a very vital role. It is possible to define colours digitally in the sense that each colour could be given a digital number like red $= 1$, blue $= 2$ and so on. Location would point towards where a particular object of interest is situated. If we were interested in finding the image of a person with a certain background at a particular point of the image, then location would tell us about where it is present. In a graphically defined image, the coordinate of the center of the image would give information about the location of the object. Distance between two particular objects of interest is a variable to be considered. Sometime in an image depicting a geographic picture, the distance between two points is very important. Here also we should be able to measure the distance between two objects by applying graphical methods.

Motion of objects, like storm or cloud moving in a satellite picture, is also an important variable. We have to measure the distance travelled by the object in the picture and then convert it into kilometers and notice the time difference. From these we can measure the speed, velocity and so on of the object.

Constraints

It could be a very good idea to define an image in terms of various constraints in the sense that constraints help define the image more specifically.

In our case of multimedia database, where various kinds of data could be there, the concept of constraints is very important. For example, if the image is that of a rectangle, we know one of the constraints would be that the number of sides of the object is *4*. Then the second constraint would be opposite sides are parallel. The third one would be opposite sides are equal. If we include the emergence phenomenon, then if there is a diagonal drawn on it, this would give rise to two triangles. These constraints together could define the image successfully.

In an image of a geographical map of any part of the world, the concept of constraint would be effective in finding the location. If we are interested in finding a place, for example, an island with triangular shape, then obviously the constraint would be number of sides is *3*. If we have more information about sides like whether any two sides are same or all sides are same or all sides are of different size, then this kind of information should help us identify the object more accurately.

Similarities

In a database containing only data, the input may be a query with certain constraints like to pick up records from a SALARY database where salary is greater than, say, *30000*. In relational database, as we know, this can be accomplished by a SQL command with the following kind of statement:

SEL * FROM SALARY_DB WHERE SALARY *> 30000*.

This would pick up all the records with salary *> 30000*.

In our multimedia database system, this kind of queries could also be made and we can handle them with this kind of or more complicated SQL statements.

But when the input is in the form of image, then we have to find the similarities of the input in the image part of the database. The basic approach to the problem of similarity is to find certain parametric values as well as some coordinates of the input image. Then we find the same for various image of the image database and pick up records where some matching occurs. Of course, we study the emergence phenomenon in both input and images of an image database while calculating parameters. For example, if we want to find similarities involving a triangular figure as input, then some of the parametric values could be defined like, number of sides which is 3, lengths of each sides, colour of the triangle. Based on these values and constraints, we can find out similarities in the image database. But in the image database, there could be figures like squares or rectangles with a diagonal drawn on them. Then obviously this diagonal gives rise to two triangles according to emergence. So we have to study these cases too, find out the parameters of these triangles to see whether they match our parameters from the input.

Indexing

In the early stage of data processing, there was no established conception of indexing. Most of the data files were accessed sequentially. This was pretty slow and inefficient particularly when the data file is big enough. To get rid of this problem, the concept of indexing came to the picture. At the initial stage, a number is used to be given against each record by the system in a file created on disk. We could specify these numbers to access any record randomly. Then came the concept of Indexed Sequential Access Method where instead of assigning separate number against each record, a field or a combination of fields were started being used as key. There could be two kinds of indexing, one where the key value in a particular file is unique and the other where the key value could be a duplicate. The search method is called Binary Search where to find a particular key value, the whole file is divided into two halves and the part, which contains the particular key value we are searching, is taken and then divided into two halves again. The part here which contains the key value is again taken and divided into two halves. This process continues until it finds the match against the key value.

Nowadays an old file system is hardly used in maintaining computer records. Instead, a database system has been developed. The latest development in this field is Relational Database System, which contains tables to store data. In our problem of dealing with multimedia databases, which would contain images, the concept of indexing is very important. We are trying to develop a more sophisticated method of indexing where there won't be any clear-cut definition of index against the images, but indexes would be defined based on our study of emergence phenomenon of each of the image.

Sometime to locate a particular spot in the geographic map of a part of the world, an input image would point to a particular part and that particular part in one or more than one image could be the outcome of emergence or it could be straight away present in the map without any emergence. In either case, input image refers to an index, which is nothing but that particular spot of the map.

Model of the Emergence Index

Emergence indexes can be defined out of five factors as discussed in above.

$$EI = f(D, F, V, C, E) \qquad (1)$$

Where *EI* stands for emergence index, *D* for domain where the image belongs, *F* for features, *V* for variables which can define the feature's constraints under which the features are defined, *C* for constraints and *E* for emergence characteristics of images.

We believe any image, static or in motion, could be expressed semantically in terms of the above mentioned five parameters.

Construction

We take the case of a square with a diagonal, as mentioned earlier, to build up an emergence index. If this is an image in the database, then firstly we have to put it under certain domain *D* for the ease of accessing. Since images are generated in enormous volume, we have to put them in various separate entities or tables according to certain classification rather than in one table which could be extremely time consuming to access. The table that would contain this square image record would define the domain of the image. We can term it as *TAB1*.

To define the second factor *F*, we find the number of maximum sides present would be *5*, where there are *4* regular sides and *1* diagonal.

The variables are *a, b, c, d, e* where first four define the perimeter of the square and *e* the diagonal.

The constraints *c* are $a = b = c = d$ since it is a square.

The emergence *E* is composed of two triangles with sides *a, b, e* and c, d, e.

Hence Emergence Index

EI = {TAB1; 5; a, b, c, d, e; a = b = c = d; (a, b, e and c, d, e)}

USE OF EMERGENCE PHENOMENON

We provide a very simple example of how emergence phenomenon can give rise to meanings for a segmented image where apparently no meaning exists.

Here we see in Figure 4 the image is very clearly of a tiger. We segment the picture and get the image of the tiger in Figure 5. But we note that the figure does not clearly point to the image of the tiger but indicates an animal. So we can interpret the image of the tiger in Figure 5 as that of an animal instead of a tiger. This is the outcome of emergence phenomenon where we are able to

Figure 3. Flow chart

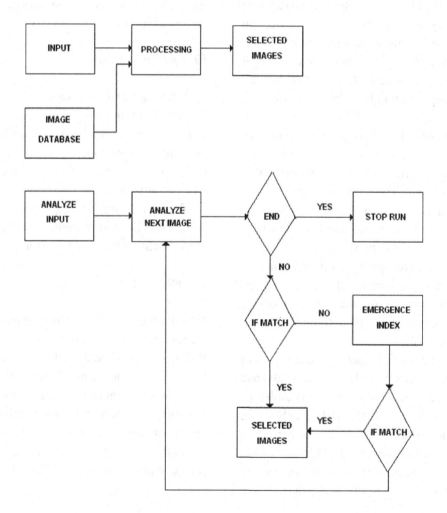

Figure 4. The image of a tiger in a picture before segmentation (Jepson, Fleet, 2007)

Figure 5. The image of the tiger after segmentation (Jepson, Fleet, 2007)

interpret the segmented image in a different way than original picture shows or in other words we extract different meaning of the segmented image. This would enable us to ascribe some meanings to segmented image which otherwise after segmentation may not deliver any meaning. This way through emergence phenomenon we interpret segmented image in a meaningful way.

NEURAL NETWORKS FOR IMAGE CLASSIFICATION

There are various attempts made to extract semantic meanings from an image to fill-in the semantic gap between low-level features and high-level semantic meanings which can arise from image segmentation. These include Latent Semantic Indexing (LSI), contextual search, user feedback, data clustering in the extraction of perceptual concepts, content-based soft annotation (CBSA), image classifications, ontology, top-down, ontologically driven approaches and bottom-up, automatic-annotation approaches, using machine learning methods to associate low-level features with query concepts, using relevance feedback to learn users' intention, generating semantic template to support high-level image retrieval, fusing the evidences from HTML text and the visual content of images for WWW image retrieval, use of ontology which represent task-specific

attributes, objects, and relations, and relate these to the processing modules available for their detection and recognition, use of context-awareness for identifying image semantics and relationships to contribute to closing the semantic gap between user information requests and the shortcomings of current content-based image retrieval techniques, enhanced ICBIR system which allows users to input partial relevance which includes not only relevance extent but also relevance reason for a multi-phase retrieval where partial relevance can adapt to the user's searching intention in a from-coarse-to-fine manner (Deb, 2010).

Although these are good, constructive progresses in solving the problem of semantic gap in CBIR, they cannot define the semantic meanings of an image specifically. They can contribute to some broad classification of the image in certain groups. To solve this problem we have to develop devices to define the semantic meanings of an image very specifically from low-level features and that should be done automatically without users' interaction. We seem to be still far away from this objectivity.

As we have shown in Section Use of Emergence Phenomenon, emergence phenomenon can bring meanings out of a segmented image where apparently no meaning could be found. We work on the theory of emergence index as described in Section Emergence Phenomenon to generate software to provide the assistance in identifying the images from segmentation. Our approach would be to apply Artificial Neural Networks which have been employed for many years in many different application areas such as speech recognition and pattern recognition. In general, these models are composed of many nonlinear computational elements operating in parallel and arranged in patterns reminiscent of biological neural nets. Similar to pattern recognition, there exist two types of modes for neural networks – unsupervised and supervised. The unsupervised type of these networks, which possesses the self-organizing property, is called competitive learning networks. A competitive learning provides a way to discover the salient, general features which can be used to classify a set of patterns. Because of the variations of object characteristics, atmosphere condition, and noise, remotely sensed images may be regarded as samples of random processes. Thus, each pixel in the image can be regarded as a random variable. It is extremely difficult to achieve high classification accuracy for most per-pixel classification algorithms (classifiers). Photo interpreters have had pre-eminence in the use of context-dependent information for remote sensing mapping. Neural networks have been recognized as an important tool for constructing membership functions, operations on membership functions, fuzzy inference rules, and other context-dependent entities in fuzzy set theory (Chavoshi, Amiri, Amini, 2007).

In supervised modes many adaptive, non-parametric neural-net classifiers have been proposed for real-world problems. These classifiers show that they are capable of achieving higher classification accuracy than conventional pixel-based classifiers; however, few neural net classifiers which apply spatial information have been proposed. The feed-forward multilayer neural network has been widely used in supervised image classification of remotely sensed data. A back propagation Feed forward multilayer network is an interconnected network in which neurons are arranged in multilayer and fully connected. There is a value called weight associated with each connection. These weights are adjusted using the back propagation algorithm or its variations, which is called train-

ing the neural networks. Once the network is well trained, it can be used to perform the image classification (Chavoshi, Amiri, Amini, 2007).

FUZZY LOGIC AS SIMILARITY MEASURE

A particular image in a database is segmented based on the colour regions and then interpreted using emergence index technique. The colour features are extracted from the image using colour histogram technique. N_p represents the total number of pixels in an image. For each colour value (red, green, blue etc.) the number of the pixels that belong to the value are recorded and denoted by N_f where $f \in F_u$. That way we segment the image and then interpret each segmented image using emergence phenomenon as shown Figures 4 and 5 (Deb, Kulkarni, 2007).

Once the image is segmented based on colours each segmented image of that particular image would be up for similarity measures with the input for retrieval. For image retrieval based on similarity measure, the fuzzy distance between the two images should be calculated. This distance is used to retrieve and index images based on the similarity.

Let us consider the extracted features for each image in the form of:

$$I_1 = [I_1C_1, I_1C_2 ... I_1C_i ... I_1C_n],$$

where I_1 is the first segmented image of a particular image and C indicates the colour extracted from that image. Similarly, these colour features are extracted from each segmented image. For each segmented image we could have a prime colour and few subordinate colours which lie within the threshold limit of the prime colour.

The segmented images are represented by an n-dimensional feature vectors. The similarity is calculated for each component of the feature vectors. Hence for each pair of images, we have n similarity measures. The global similarity is given by:

FuzzyAND = Min [(Q₁, T₁), (Q₂, T₂)…(Qₙ, Tₙ)]

FuzzyOR = Max [(Q₁, T₁), (Q₂, T₂)…(Qₙ, Tₙ)],

where Q_1 represents the first colour vector for the query image, similarly T_1 represents first colour vector for the segmented image.

The global similarity measure is calculated by:

$$F.D. = \sum_{j=0}^{k} \sum_{i=0}^{n} \frac{FuzzyOR - FuzzyAND}{FuzzyOR}$$

An F.D. standS for Fuzzy Distance, n is the colour feature vectors and k is the number of images in database. The similarity measure for each segmented image is calculated in accordance with the query image. Whenever a query image finds similarity with a segmented image of a particular image that image is selected for retrieval (Deb, Kulkarni, 2007).

In unsupervised feature selection and learning for image segmentation, feature clustering is a popular approach for segmentation and grouping. For image segmentation, clustering is performed in order to subdivide the feature space into dense clusters which (presumably) correspond to homogeneous regions in the image. Finite Mixture models (FMM) has been proved as a powerful technique for clustering. It has been successfully used for segmentation. FMM try to model the distribution of each cluster in the data using a probability density function. Feature selection is important for mitigating over-segmentation due to uniform (non-relevant) features (Allili, Ziou, Bouguila, Boutemedjet, 2010). We would continue with these experiments to provide more accurate segmentations based on emergence index.

CONCLUSION

This chapter provides the problem of extracting meaningful image segmentation using emergence phenomenon. It also describes with basics of emergence index, definitions and its performance on various images. Chapter also explains how we can use emergence phenomenon in meaningful image segmentation. This is very important to reduce the semantic gap between low level features and high level queries. Experiments are performed on different sets of image to calculate emergence index. It requires continuation of work for extracting more useful information from the set of complex images which contains fundamental image features such as colour, texture and advanced features like shapes and meaningful objects. Computational Intelligence techniques such as artificial neural networks and fuzzy logic are proposed for identifying the problem of image classification and similarity measure. Artificial neural networks have been proposed to classify images based on their structure, features and objects. Fuzzy logic has been used to calculate the similarity between segmented objects and shapes and their colours. Since this is a very important area of research with major implications in all spheres of life beginning with medical images, the necessity of this study cannot be overestimated.

REFERENCES

Allili, M. S., Ziou, D., Bouguila, N., & Boutemedjet, S. (2010). Unsupervised feature selection and learning for image segmentation. Retrieved from http://www.computerrobotvision.org/2010/talks/Allili_CRV2010.pdf

Cariani, P. (1992). Emergence and artificial life. In Langton, C., Taylor, C., Farmer, J. D., & Rasmussen, S. (Eds.), *Artificial life II* (pp. 775–797). Reading, MA: Addision-Wesley.

Chavoshi, S. H., Amiri, A., & Amini, J. (2007). *Supervised classification in high resolution images (Quikbird) using neural network, fuzzy sets and minimum distance*. Presented at the Map Asia 2007 Conference, August 14 - 16, 2007, Kuala Lumpur, Malaysia.

Deb, S. (2010). *Using relevance feedback in bridging semantic gaps in content-based image retrieval.* The Second International Conference on Advances in Future Internet (AFIN2010), Venice/Mestre, Italy, July 18 - 25, 2010

Deb, S., & Kulkarni, S. (2007). Human perception based image retrieval using emergence index and fuzzy similarity measure. *The Third International Conference on Intelligent Sensors, Sensor Networks and Information Processing (ISSNIP07),* Melbourne, Australia, December 3-6, 2007, (pp. 359-363).

Forrest, S. (Ed.). (1991). *Emergent computation.* New York, NY: Elsevier.

Gero, J. S. (1993). Visual emergence in design collaboration. *International Journal of CADCAM and Computer Graphics, 8*(3), 349–357.

Gero, J. S., & Maher, M. L. (1994). *Computational support for emergence in design.* Information Technology in Design Conference, Moscow, September 1994.

Gudivada, V. N., & Raghavan, V. V. (1995). *Content-based image retrieval systems.* IEEE, September 1995.

Islam, M. (2006). *Reducing semantic gap in content based image retrieval using region based relevance feedback techniques.* Retrieved from http://www.gscit.monash.edu.au/gscitweb/seminar.php?id=41

Jepson, A. D., & Fleet, D. J. (2007). *Image segmentation.* Retrieved from www.cs.toronto.edu/~jepson/csc2503/segmentation.pdf

Langton, G. L. (1989). *Artificial life.* Addision-Wesley.

Mehta, D., Diwakar, E. S. V. N. L. S., & Jawahar, C. V. (2003). *A rule-based approach to image retrieval.* Retrieved from www.iiit.net/techreports/2003_8.pdf

Wikipedia. (n.d.). *Segmentation (image processing).* Retrieved from http://en.wikipedia.org/wiki/Segmentation

Yoshitaka, A., Kishida, S., & Hirakawa, M. (1994). Knowledge-assisted content-based retrieval for multimedia databases. *IEEE MultiMedia,* (Winter): 12–21. doi:10.1109/93.338682

Zhau, R., & Grosky, W. I. (2002). *Bridging the semantic gap in image retrieval.* Retrieved from http://citeseer.ist.psu.edu/497446.html

KEY TERMS AND DEFINITIONS

Content-Based Image Retrieval: Retrieving images from image database by checking their contents.

Emergence Phenomenon: To find out hidden meanings from an image or from various parts of it.

Fuzzy Logic: To make a judgement on a problem on the basis of various different possibilities that could have arisen.

High-Level Features: Any object which has a definition like table, chair, car and so on.

Image Segmentation and Retrieval: Breaking a particular image into various meaningful parts where each part would be an object and retrieving it if input matches to it.

Low-Level Features: In image retrieval we define colour, texture, spatial relationship, shape as low-level features.

Semantic Gap: Low-level features can define an object in terms of colour, texture, spatial relationship, shape whereas high-level features define the same object in terms of what it is like table, chair, car and so on.

Chapter 11
Predicting Adsorption Behavior in Engineered Floodplain Filtration System Using Backpropagation Neural Networks

Eldon Raj Rene
University of La Coruña, Spain

Shishir Kumar Behera
University of Ulsan, South Korea

Hung Suck Park
University of Ulsan, South Korea

ABSTRACT

Engineered floodplain filtration (EFF) system is an eco-friendly low-cost water treatment process wherein water contaminants can be removed, by adsorption and-or degraded by microorganisms, as the infiltrating water moves from the wastewater treatment plants to the rivers. An artificial neural network (ANN) based approach was used in this study to approximate and interpret the complex input/ output relationships, essentially to understand the breakthrough times in EFF. The input parameters to the ANN model were inlet concentration of a pharmaceutical, ibuprofen (ppm) and flow rate (md⁻¹), and the output parameters were six concentration-time pairs (C, t). These C, t pairs were the times in the breakthrough profile, when 1%, 5%, 25%, 50%, 75%, and 95% of the pollutant was present at the outlet of the system. The most dependable condition for the network was selected by a trial and error approach and by estimating the determination coefficient (R^2) value (>0.99) achieved during prediction of the testing set. The proposed ANN model for EFF operation could be used as a potential alternative for knowledge-based models through proper training and testing of variables.

DOI: 10.4018/978-1-4666-1833-6.ch011

INTRODUCTION

Neural Computing

Artificial neural networks are non-linear mathematical models capable of learning the arbitrary and complex physico-chemical process of a system from observed input variables and desired outputs of the system. The primary advantage of ANN over phenomenological/conceptual models is that, it does not require information about the complex nature of the underlying process to be explicitly described in mathematical form (Sahoo et al., 2005).

ANNs consists of a system of simple interconnected processing element called neurons. This gives the ability to model any non-linear process through a set of unidirectional weighted connections (Simpson, 1990). Multi-layer perceptron (MLP) belongs to the class of supervised feed-forward networks in which the processing elements are arranged in a multi-layered structure; as an input layer, one or more hidden layers, and an output layer, as illustrated in Figure 1.

The input layer consists of a set of neurons N_I, each representing an input parameter and propa-

gates the raw information to the neuron in the hidden layer (N_H), which in turn transmits them, to the neurons in the output layer (N_O). Each layer consists of several neurons and the layers are connected by the connection weights (W_{ij}^1 and W_{ij}^2). The most commonly used transfer function is the sigmoid function that produces output in the range of 0 to 1, as described by;

$$f(x) = \frac{1}{1 + e^{-x}} \tag{1}$$

The back propagation network is the most prevalent supervised ANN learning model (Rumelhart et al., 1986). It uses the gradient descent algorithm to correct the weights between interconnected neurons (Maier and Dandy, 2001). During the learning process of the network, the algorithm computes the error between the predicted and specified target values at the output layer. The error function (E) at the output layer can be defined by;

$$E = \frac{1}{2} \sum \left(O_d - O_p \right)^2 \tag{2}$$

Figure 1. Schematic of a multi-layered perceptron

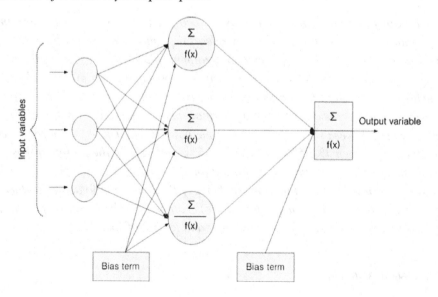

where, O_d is the desired (experimental) value, and O_p is the model predicted value.

ANNs have already been applied to solve, predict and optimize a variety of environmental and biotechnological problems: wastewater treatment plant performance, effectiveness of riverbank filtration, biodegradation kinetics of organic compounds, and air-pollution related problems.

Wastewater Treatment Processes

According to Qasim (1999), any wastewater treatment plant would necessarily comprise of a number of unit operations and processes in order to achieve the required degree of physico-chemical or biological treatment. The schematic shown in Figure 2 is called a process flow diagram, wherein many unit processes are combined to achieve the desired treatment efficiency of polluted water. Many of these treatment processes, physical, chemical, or biological, however, are used to treat the liquid and solid portions of the wastewater simultaneously. Some typical examples are; stabilization ponds, aerated lagoons, land treatment, and constructed wet lands. The principal types of reactors used for wastewater treatment are; (i) batch reactors, (ii) plug-flow or tubular-flow reactors, (iii) completely mixed or continuous flow stirred tank reactor (CFSTR), and (iv) arbitrary-flow reactors. The basic criteria for developing a process scheme, amongst others, depends on the following factors, (i) characteristics of the wastewater, (ii) require-ment of the regulatory authorities, (iii) proximity to the build-up areas, (iv) topography and site characteristics, (v) plant economics (vi) quantity and quality of sludge generated from each process, and (vii) minimal environmental consequence, and maximal environmental benefits/improvements.

Flood Plain Filtration (FPF) for Wastewater Treatment

There are conventional approaches, as explained above, as well as non-conventional approaches for wastewater treatment. For waters, already subjected to primary and secondary treatment steps, land treatment systems such as overland flow system, rapid infiltration system, sand filter, wetland, soil aquifer etc. are considered as promising and sustainable tertiary treatment technologies. In wetlands, a wide range of physical, chemical and biological processes are involved in the removal of contaminants from wastewaters. In soil aquifer treatment of wastewater, sewage effluent is degraded or treated by both biodegradation and sorption in soil (Wilson et al., 1995). The reclaimed water obtained after soil treatment can be used in agricultural, industrial, municipal, and recreational facilities (Kanarek and Micheal, 1996; Bdour et al., 2009; Pedrero et al., 2010).

The land treatment can remove most of the contaminants to a certain level from the waste-waters, thereby increasing the quality of the water, which, in turn, improves the receiving

Figure 2. Typical treatment scheme for wastewater treatment systems

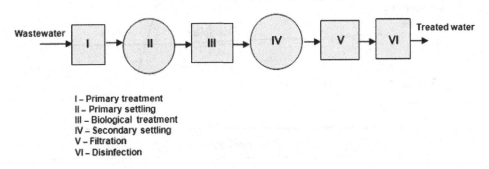

I – Primary treatment
II – Primary settling
III – Biological treatment
IV – Secondary settling
V – Filtration
VI – Disinfection

surface water quality. However, land availability for treatment is scarce in many developing countries, which mainly face the problems with wastewaters. However, wide floodplains, low – lying areas on either sides of rivers and streams, predominantly made up of permeable materials, mostly sandy alluvial sediments can contribute to the substantial natural polishing of secondarily treated wastewater through sorption, trapping or biological transformations during residence in the floodplains (Venterink et al., 2003; Kunjikutty et al., 2007). Therefore, floodplains could be very well used as a soil – filter for wastewater treatment and the FPF technique may be viewed as a low – cost, and technically and environmentally favourable treatment option.

Mechanism and Usefulness of FPF

The floodplains associated with most rivers and streams, inundate only during rainy season, and are uncultivated and weedy for most part of the year. In tropical developing countries like India and Korea, seasonal patterns of rainy season, $\leq 3{\sim}4$ months in a year, (Kumar, 2003; Kim et al., 2003) allow floodplains to be used for treating wastewaters during a major part of the year. The vegeta-

tion in the floodplains develop a rhizosphere, an excellent habitat of microbes and worms, with the supply of organic matter and oxygen in the top soil zone, thereby enhancing the biochemical reactions which remove most of the contaminants from the wastewaters. The schematic of the FPF system is shown in Figure 3.

FPF systems can be used as an engineered system by maximizing the exploitation of the natural conditions to get water of reasonably better quality (Chung et al., 2004). Since the amount of clay in floodplain sediment is very less, $\leq 2\%$ (Jeong et al., 2003; Kunjikutty et al., 2007), removal of emerging micro – pollutants such as pharmaceuticals and personal care products (PPCPs) from secondarily treated municipal wastewater can be enhanced if the floodplains available nearby wastewater treatment facilities be amended by some suitable sorbents and used as an engineered system. The FPF system can be modified to an *"engineered floodplain filtration"* (EFF) system, essentially a modified slow sand filter, by placing a layer of sorbent, *e.g.*:- activated carbon, sandwiched between two sand layers. The amendment of sorbent layer is aimed at making it a bio – barrier to remove or degrade all the pollutants including the micro – pollutants

Figure 3. Schematic of the floodplain filtration system (adapted from Behera, 2010)

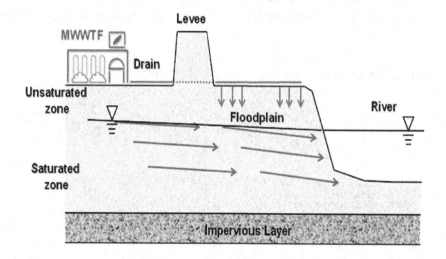

by a combination of adsorption and biological processes, wherein surface water contaminants particularly micro – pollutants can be removed or degraded as the infiltrating water moves from the wastewater treatment plants to the rivers.

ADSORPTION PROCESS

Adsorption operations exploit the ability of certain solids preferentially to concentrate specific substances from solution onto their surfaces. In the field of gaseous separations, adsorption is used to dehumidify air and other gases, to remove objectionable odors and impurities from industrial gases. Liquid separations include the removal of objectionable taste and odor.

In environmental and chemical engineering applications, adsorption is considered as a process by which a component moves from one phase to another across a surface. The driving forces that control adsorption include electrical attraction, chemical affinity of a particular adsorbate for the adsorbent, van der Waal forces (weak attractive forces acting between molecules), and the hydrophobic nature of adsorbate (LaGrega et al., 2001).

The adsorption capacity of an adsorbent is calculated using the following equation;

$$q = \frac{(C_i - C_e) \times V}{M} \tag{3}$$

where, q is the mass of contaminant adsorbed (mg g^{-1}), C_i is the initial concentration of contaminant in solution (mgL^{-1}), C_e is the equilibrium or final concentration of contaminant in solution (mgL^{-1}), V is the volume of solution (L) and M is the mass of adsorbent (g).

Conventional Isotherm Models in Adsorption

Adsorption is usually described through isotherms, *i.e.,* the amount of adsorbate on the adsorbent as a function of its pressure (if gas) or concentration (if liquid) at constant temperature.

According to Nemr (2009), there are different mathematical forms of isotherms. The analysis of isotherm data is important to develop equation, which can accurately represent the results of the column, and could be used for column design purposes in practical situations. Besides, adsorption isotherm could also be used to describe how solute interacts with the adsorbent and so is critical in optimizing the use of adsorbent.

Nemr (2009) also outlines the different forms of the most commonly used isotherm models, *viz.,* Langmuir, Freundlich, Tempkin, Dubinin – Radushkevich (D – R), and the generalized isotherm equations, which are mentioned below.

When the sorbent surface is homogeneous, isotherm data may be approximated by the Langmuir equation. This equation represents one of the first theoretical treatments of non – linear sorption and suggests that uptake occurs on a homogenous surface by monolayer sorption without interaction between the adsorbed molecules. The Langmuir equation takes the form;

$$q_e = \frac{Q_m K_L C_e}{(1 + K_L C_e)} \tag{4}$$

where, C_e is the equilibrium concentration (mgL^{-1}), qe is the amount of pollutant adsorbed (mgg^{-1}), Q_m is the complete monolayer (mgg^{-1}), and K_L is the adsorption equilibrium constant (Lmg^{-1}). Equation 4 can be linearized into four different forms, which then provides information on other parameters, as shown by Equations 5 – 8.

$$\frac{C_e}{Q_e} = \frac{1}{K_L Q_m} + \frac{1}{Q_m} C_e \qquad (5)$$

$$\frac{1}{Q_e} = \frac{1}{K_L Q_m}\left(\frac{1}{C_e}\right) + \frac{1}{Q_m} \qquad (6)$$

$$Q_e = Q_m - \frac{1}{K_L}\frac{Q_e}{C_e} \qquad (7)$$

$$\frac{Q_e}{C_e} = K_L Q_m - K_L Q_e \qquad (8)$$

The Freundlich isotherm is an empirical model based on sorption heterogeneous energetic distribution of active sites accompanied by interactions between adsorbed molecules. Usually, it assumes that a logarithmic decrease in the enthalpy of sorption occurs with an increase in the fraction of occupying sites and is given by the following non – linear equation;

$$q_e = K_F C_e^{1/n} \qquad (9)$$

where, K_F is the adsorption capacity (mgg^{-1}), and n is the adsorption intensity of the pollutant on the sorbent. Equation 9 can be linearized to give the following form;

$$\log Q_e = \log K_F + \frac{1}{n}\log C_e \qquad (10)$$

Tempkin isotherm model considers the effects of indirect adsorbate – adsorbate interaction isotherms which explains the fact that, the heat of adsorption of all the molecules on the adsorbent surface layer would decrease linearly with coverage area due to adsorbate – adsorbate interactions. This isotherm assumes that the fall in heat of adsorption is linear rather than logarithmic, and takes the form as shown here.

$$Q_e = \frac{RT}{b}\ln(A_T C_e) \qquad (11)$$

Equation 10 can be further simplified as,

$$Q_e = B_T \ln A_T + B_T \ln C_e \qquad (12)$$

where, $B_T = RT/b$, and A_T (Lg^{-1}) are the Tempkin constant, T is the absolute temperature in Kelvin, and R is the universal gas – constant. The constant b is related to the heat of adsorption.

The Dubinin – Radushkevich isotherm does not assume a homogenous surface or a constant sorption potential. The D – R model estimates the characteristic porosity, and the apparent free energy of adsorption, given b;

$$q_e = Q_m \exp(-K_{D-R}\varepsilon^2) \qquad (13)$$

$$\ln q_e = \ln Q_m - K_{D-R}\varepsilon^2 \qquad (14)$$

where, K_{D-R} is a constant related to the adsorption energy, Q_m is the theoretical monolayer saturation capacity (mgg^{-1}), and ε is the Polanyi potential, calculated as follows;

$$\varepsilon = RT\ln\left(1 + \frac{1}{C_e}\right)$$

The generalized form of the isotherm is given by;

$$\log\left[\frac{Q_m}{q_e} - 1\right] = \log K_G - N_b \log C_e \qquad (15)$$

where, K_G is the saturation constant (mgL^{-1}), N_b is the cooperative binding constant, Q_m is the maximum adsorption capacity of the adsorbent (mgg^{-1}), and q_e (mgg^{-1}), and C_e (mgL^{-1}) are the equilibrium pollutant concentrations in the solid and liquid phases, respectively.

Role of Adsorption in FPF

Adsorption is a predominant mechanism in the EFF system for the removal of liquid phase pollutants. The pharmaceutical, ibuprofen was chosen as the main pollutant in this study. In order to enhance the sorption potential of FPF, a small layer of activated carbon possessing high surface area can also be added. These commercially available activated carbons are usually derived from natural materials such as wood, coconut shell, lignite or coal. In a recently published review article, Crini (2006) explains that *"the adsorption capacities of a carbon depend on the different sources of raw materials, the history of its preparation and treatment conditions such as pyrolysis temperature and activation time. Many other factors can also affect the adsorption characteristics, such as surface chemistry, surface charge and pore structure"*. For long passage times within the FPF, the adsorbent closer to the inlet of the fluid becomes saturated with the contaminant at a given influent concentration of ibuprofen. Consequently, breakthrough is likely to be attained and the first emergence of the contaminant (usually at very low concentration) would take place. Contaminants that are chemically adsorbed within the stabilized matrix are less likely to be released into the environment than those that are not fixed.

EXPERIMENTAL

Column Configuration and Operation

In order to assess the behaviour of ibuprofen in the floodplain sediment, lysimeter studies were undertaken. The parameters examined were initial pharmaceutical concentration, *i.e.,* initial concentration of ibuprofen, and flow rate. For this purpose, columns were made up of borosilicate glass with dimensions 30 cm length and 6.5 cm (ID). A schematic of the column set up is presented in Figure 4, while the conditions of the column

experiments are listed in Table 1. Six columns were run in parallel, at their respective conditions, in order to envisage the breakthrough profiles, which usually occurred between 40 and 80 days. To ensure abiotic condition, the floodplain sediment was sterilized at 100 °C for 1 hour and 100 ppm of sodium azide (NaN_3) was added to the contaminated solution prepared by spiking desired compounds in deionized water. The pH of the solution was maintained at ~7. The columns were filled with floodplain sediment with a 1 cm layer of activated carbon (16 g), 14 cm from the top of the column. All the columns were pre – wetted with double distilled water from the bottom to prevent the formation of air bubbles and to reduce the risk of channelling and then left to equilibrate for 2 days. The experiments took place at a room temperature of ~20 °C and all parts of the column experiment, including the tanks, were protected against exposure to light.

Analytical Techniques

An HPLC system (Ultimate® 3000) (Dionex, Sunnyville, CA, USA) equipped with a Discovery® RP-Amide C-16 (4.6 mm×150 mm, 5μm) column (Supelco, Bellefonte, PA, USA) and an UV-Vis detector was used to measure the ibuprofen concentration at a detection wavelength of 230 nm. The mobile phase used for elution was 25 mM KH_2PO_4 at a pH value of 3.0 (40%), and acetonitrile (60%) delivered at 1 mL min⁻¹ through the column. A sample injection volume of 100 μL was used. The column temperature was maintained at 30 °C. For quantification purposes, a calibration plot was performed within the range of experimental concentrations used.

Results from Lysimeter Experiments

Continuous lysimeter tests were carried out under abiotic conditions at three different initial concentrations and flow – rates, in different combinations, leading to five different experimental conditions

Figure 4. Schematic diagram of the column experimental set-up (adapted from Behera, 2010)

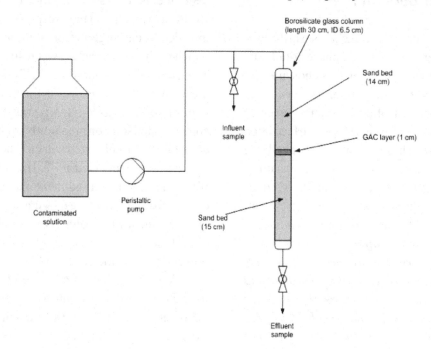

Table 1. Column conditions – C/C_o at different operational times for ibuprofen

Run No	Conc, ppm	Flow rate, md⁻¹	C/C_o - 40 d	C/C_o - 60 d	C/C_o - 80 d
1	0.1	1	0	0	0.99
2	1	1	0.0099	0.65	0.99
3	0.1	5	0.4181	0.98	0.98
4	1	5	0.98	0.98	0.98
5	0.55	3	0.163	0.87	0.99

(Table 1). The inlet and outlet concentration of ibuprofen was measured every day, and the results were interpreted in terms of the trend of C/C_o, to achieve breakthrough. In order to understand the main and interaction effects during the course of the experiments, C/C_o values observed at the end of 60th experimental day was used. For instance, if the experimental data on the 80th day were to be used, the possibility of understanding these effects were significantly nil, under the tested experimental conditions, because breakthrough was visualized in all the experiments by the end of the 80th day, and C/C_o values were basically the same (0.99).

The time course C/C_o profile of ibuprofen at all the tested conditions is illustrated in Figure 5. From this figure, it can be clearly elucidated that, the onset of breakthrough condition differed depending on the initial setting of flow rate (Q) and concentration (C_o). It is clear that the breakthrough time decreased with an increase of C_o and Q. Expectedly, at lower C_o and Q settings, breakthrough occurred slower. This result demonstrates that the change of both concentration and flow rate affects the saturation rate of sorbent and the breakthrough time. As the C_o and Q increases, the loading rate of ibuprofen increases, and consequently the fixed-bed EFF column became saturated with the ibuprofen concentration as the effluent approached the C_o. Ibuprofen was able to realize its first breakthrough within 40 days, and run no 4, *i.e.,* high flow rate and high concentration, favoured this phenomenon.

Figure 5. Breakthrough profiles of ibuprofen at different initial concentration and flow rate

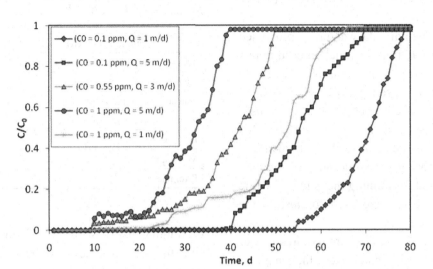

The variation in the adsorption capacity at various C_o and Q can be explained by the basic fundamentals of mass transfer, as explained in many chemical and environmental engineering books. The breakthrough time at $Q = 1$ md^{-1} is longer than that at $Q = 5$ md^{-1} because it takes a longer time to reach its effective bed load when the other operating conditions are constant. Therefore, as Q increases, the breakthrough curve becomes steeper because of the shorter time required to attain its effective bed load. On the other hand, a close examination of Figure 5 reveals that at same Q, the value of breakthrough time decreased with an increase in C_o. The larger the C_o, the steeper is the slope of the breakthrough curve and smaller is the breakthrough time. This can also be explained by the fact that more adsorption sites are being occupied with increase in C_o. As the C_o increased, loading rate of ibuprofen increased, so does the driving force or mass transfer, which results in a decrease in the adsorption zone length. This result is in agreement with the works reported previously on various fixed-bed adsorption systems with a variety of contaminants (Lua and Jia, 2009; Singh et al., 2009; Ahmad and Hamid, 2010). Also, as evident, among the linear effects, flow rate appears to play a significant role for achieving quicker breakthrough, than the initial concentration and their chances for interactions were negative.

PREDICTION OF ADSORPTION BEHAVIOUR IN EFF USING NEURAL NETWORKS

Model Development Procedure

The input vectors to the network were the easily monitored parameters namely; inlet concentration (X_1) and flow rate (X_2) from these five experiments. The output to the ANN model was the times (day) corresponding to the six concentration levels. The six concentration levels considered are those corresponding to the non–dimensional parameter (C/C_o) values of 1%, 5%, 25%, 50%, 75% and 95%. These outputs are denoted as T1, T5, T25, T50, T75 and T95, respectively. Ibuprofen concentrations below $C = 0.01$ C_o and the concentrations of $C = C_o$ are practically difficult to detect in fixed– bed experiments. The six– point method proposed here is assumed to be sufficient to sketch an approximate, yet a close enough breakthrough curve. Besides, breakpoints at 1% and 5% are commonly used in water and wastewater treatment applications.

The experimental data was pre – processed to suit the sigmoid transfer function used in this study, and scaled to values varying between 0 and 1. The back – propagation neural network developed by Rumelhart et al. (1986) that uses the gradient descent algorithm was used in this study. The processed data was later divided into two sets; training and testing. 80% of the data points were used for training the network, while the remaining 20% were used for testing the developed network.

A good network architecture requires proper selection of sensitive parameters like: number of hidden layers, the number of neurons in the hidden layer (N_H), the activation function f(x), the learning rate of the network (η), epoch size (ε), momentum term (α) and training cycles (T_C). The network architecture has to be optimized to reduce computer processing, achieve good predictability and avoid over fitting. More information concerning the influence of internal parameters, and methods used to estimate these values can be found elsewhere (Maier and Dandy, 1998; Maier and Dandy, 2001; Rene et al., 2009). The performance of the training and test data set were evaluated in terms of the correlation coefficient values (R^2), which substantially determines the closeness of prediction between the desired and predicted output from the network.

ANN– based predictive modeling was carried out using the shareware version of the neural network and multivariable statistical modeling software–NNMODEL (version 1.4, neural fusion, NY). The same software was also used to generate contour plots and carrying out sensitivity analysis.

Model Architecture Analysis

The number of neurons in the input layer ($N_I = 2$) and output layer ($N_0 = 6$) were chosen based on the number of input and output variables to the network. However in order to get the best /

Table 2. Best values of network parameters used for training the network

Training parameters	Value
Training count (Iterations)	20000
Number of neurons in input layer	2
Number of neurons in hidden layer	4
Number of neurons in output layer	6
Learning rate	0.9
Momentum term	0.8
Error tolerance	0.00001

optimum network parameters, in most instances, literature suggests the use of a trial and error approach where the performance goal is set by the user. The best network architecture was chosen (Table 2) based on the maximum predictability of the network for the test data by analyzing the correlation coefficient values (R^2).

The model was trained using different combinations of these network parameters, *viz.*, by altering the learning rate, momentum term and number of neurons in the hidden layer, so as to achieve maximum correlation coefficient values (target value $= 1$, *i.e.*, 100% correlation between measured and predicted variables). This was achieved by a vigorous trial and error approach by keeping some training parameters constant and by slowly moving the other parameters over a wide range of values. During this process, it was observed that, increasing the number of neurons from 2 to 4 in the hidden layer (N_H), increased the R^2 value, while values larger than 4 did not show any improvement in the predictive ability of the developed model. Due to the high R^2 observed under this particular setting of network parameters ($R^2 > 0.95$), this value of N_H was kept constant at 4. Thus, by keeping the number of neurons in the hidden layer constant, the values of both learning rate and momentum term was slowly changed from 0.1 to 0.95, through a series of trial and errors, and by observing the changes of R^2, in the training data set. It was observed that, lower

Table 3. Coefficient of regression (R^2) values obtained during training and testing

Run No	Run - 1	Run - 2	Run - 3	Run - 4
Training	0.999	0.984	0.9938	0.9994
Testing	0.993			

values of these parameters decreased the R^2, from 0.98 to 0.87, while higher values showed maximum predictive potential for the developed model. Thus these values were then set at 0.9 and 0.8, respectively. The R^2 values obtained during model training and testing are given in Table 3.

Predictive Capability of the Model

The model predicted breakthrough profiles, during training, for ibuprofen from various experiments are shown in Figure 6. It can be seen that some data points show deviancy between the measured and predicted C/C_o profiles. This is probably due to the fact that different conditions exhibited different onset times for reaching breakthrough. The delay in achieving breakthrough, *i.e.,* at low flow rates and concentrations would have caused an impact

in the neural networks learning/generalization pattern while predicting the performance parameter.

The neural network predicted breakthrough curves are very close to the experimental profiles. Although the developed neural network is specific, more general networks using wider ranges and variety of input parameters can be developed using the procedure adopted in this work. Using sensitivity analysis, the degree of influence of the various input parameters was determined. This was performed according to the standard procedure outlined by Zurada (1994), by varying the value of one parameter over a certain range and by observing the associated effect on the desired outcome. For the ibuprofen adsorption profile studied in this paper using EFF, the two input parameters were checked for their sensitivity to the breakthrough curve. The four– hidden nodes network was used for this test. However, to avoid any bias, a representative set was selected by taking the average of each input parameter from the training and testing databases. The two parameters in the average set are $C_o = 0.55$ mg L^{-1} and $Q = 3$ m d^{-1}. The value of each of these two parameters is perturbed about its mean and the output breakthrough curve is determined using the predictive network. It is to be mentioned here

Figure 6. Training data for Ibuprofen (Run 1 – 4/p: model predicted/e: experimental)

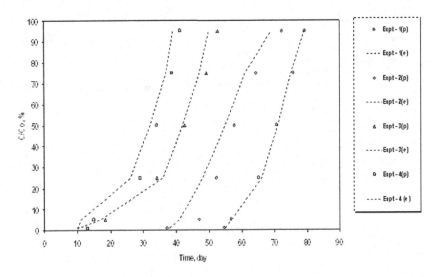

that all perturbations were made within the limits of the applicability of each input parameter. A new, by estimating the absolute average sensitivity (AAS), a sensitivity analysis was carried out using the software NNMODEL to identify the most influential parameter that affects the reactor performance. The sensitivity is calculated by summing the changes in the output variables caused by moving the input variables by a small amount over the entire training set. The absolute average sensitivity matrix, $S_{ki,abs}$ can be defined as follows:

$$S_{ki, abs} = \frac{\sum_{p=1}^{p} \left| S_{ki}^{(p)} \right|}{p} \qquad (16)$$

where, P is the number of patterns presented to the network.

The higher AAS values for flow rate (0.7586) than concentration (0.2414) suggest that flow change has a significant and greater influence on the C/C_o values than concentration. In general, the predictive ability of the proposed model using the concepts of artificial intelligence and the back propagation algorithm was high at the 95% confidence interval and meaningfully significant, as ascertained from the correlation coefficient values between the measured and predicted outputs in the training and test data.

Figures 7 and 8 depicts the contours of adsorption times corresponding to two of the outputs of the developed model (T5, T25, T50, and T75 data not shown). These contour plots reveal the ANN model predicted times for each of the output, due to changes in both flow rate and ibuprofen concentration. These contours reveal sufficient information about the range of conditions required to achieve the desired T1 to T 95. One of the contour plot could be interpreted as follows (Figure 8): low flow rate (< 1.2 m d⁻¹) and low concentrations (< 0.5 ppm) would envisage more than 79.6 days for achieving 95% removal of ibuprofen, while higher flow rates and concentrations would lead to a decrease in the time required to achieve 95% removal.

Application of ANNs in hydrology and water – resource problems has been gaining tremendous momentum only since the early 2000's, as it has provided promising results for many non – linear and complex systems that pose a difficult task for any physically based conceptual model. ANNs may not be a good substitute to conceptually model the adsorption process in EFF system, yet it can be used in a meaningful and intelligent way

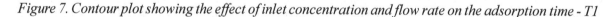

Figure 7. Contour plot showing the effect of inlet concentration and flow rate on the adsorption time - T1

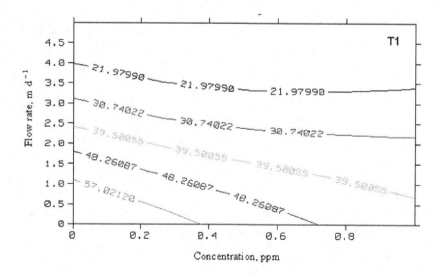

Figure 8. Contour plot showing the effect of inlet concentration and flow rate on the adsorption time – T95

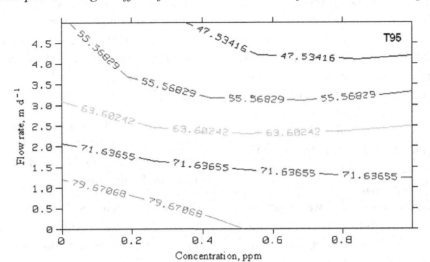

in EFF, when the process requires an efficient estimation of the breakthrough times, using only the available minimal cause – effect time series data, *i.e.,* concentration – time data. Anew, the determination of breakthrough times by ANN (predictive modeling) would, in particular, be very helpful during the design stages of an EFF system. The model developed in this study can be easily extended or – redeveloped to suit biotic conditions by incorporating some easily measurable state parameters such as oxygen utilization rate and specific activity of the microorganisms to the model inputs. The breakthrough profiles can be assessed on a long – term, for different pollutants, and under different physico – chemical conditions prevailing in EFF system.

CONCLUSION

The following conclusions were made based on the experimental results and neural networks model developed for the EFF system (lysimeters):

(i) The linear effects of the process variables, *i.e.,* flow rate and initial ibuprofen concentration played a major role in controlling

the dynamics of ibuprofen removal process within the EFF system, while the effects due to their interactions was observed to be minimal.

(ii) The results from ANN– based data– driven modeling shows that the EFF system performance, in terms of C/C_o values, can be predicted with high confidence level (95%) using easily measurable operational parameters, namely, inlet concentration and flow rate. The model was adequately trained with the lab– scale EFF column data and tested with a separate data set.

(iii) A three– layered MLP was sufficient to describe the breakthrough using connection weights and bias terms (thresholds). The suitable network architecture of the model was determined through a vigorous trial and error approach. The computed determination coefficient (R^2) values for the test data set show high correlation between the predicted and measured performance values. The best topology was found to be a simple three– layered network, 2–4–6, achieved at the following settings of internal network parameters: learning rate (0.9), momentum

(0.8) and a training count (epoch size) of 20,000.

(iv)   From practical application view point, if the pollutants and their concentration are known in the inlet stream, they can be added to the network and can be trained easily. Consequently, the time for removing 1%, 5%, 25%, 50%, 75%, and 95% of the target pollutants in the EFF system by adsorption can be evaluated, which indicates the versatility of the model.

(v)   The robustness of the ANN was further explored with a sensitivity analysis of the input parameters, which showed that flow rate was a more critical factor affecting EFF system performance, than the inlet concentration.

ACKNOWLEDGMENT

This research work was supported by the research funds obtained from University of Ulsan in South Korea. ERR thanks the Ministry of Science and Innovation, Spain, for his *"Juan de La Cierva"* – research grant. SKB thankfully acknowledges the Brain Korea 21 Post Doctoral fellowship from Ministry of Education, Science and Technology through Environmental Engineering Program at University of Ulsan.

REFERENCES

Ahmad, A. A., & Hameed, B. H. (2010). Fixed-bed adsorption of reactive azo dye onto granular activated carbon prepared from waste. *Journal of Hazardous Materials*, *175*, 298–303. doi:10.1016/j.jhazmat.2009.10.003

Bdour, A. N., Hamdi, M. R., & Tarawneh, Z. (2009). Perspectives on sustainable wastewater treatment technologies and reuse options in the urban areas of the Mediterranean region. *Desalination*, *237*, 162–174. doi:10.1016/j.desal.2007.12.030

Behera, S. K. (2010). *Removal of triclosan and ibuprofen by engineered floodplain filtration system*. Unpublished Ph.D. dissertation, University of Ulsan, South Korea.

Chung, J. B., Kim, S. H., Jeong, B. R., & Lee, Y. D. (2004). Removal of organic matter and nitrogen from river water in a model floodplain. *Journal of Environmental Quality*, *33*, 1017–1023. doi:10.2134/jeq2004.1017

Crini, G. (2006). Non-conventional low-cost adsorbents for dye removal: A review. *Bioresource Technology*, *97*, 1061–1085. doi:10.1016/j.biortech.2005.05.001

Jeong, B. R., Chung, J. B., Kim, S. H., Lee, Y. D., Cho, H. J., & Baek, N. J. (2003). Rhizosphere enhances removal of organic matter and nitrogen from river water in floodplain filtration. *Korean Journal of Soil Science and Fertilizer*, *36*, 8–15.

Kanarek, A., & Micheal, M. (1996). Groundwater recharge with municipal effluent: Dan region reclamation project, Israel. *Water Science and Technology*, *34*, 227–233. doi:10.1016/S0273-1223(96)00842-6

Kim, S.-H., Chung, J.-B., Lee, Y.-D., & Prasher, S. O. (2003). Electron affinity coefficients of nitrogen oxides and biodegradation kinetics in denitrification of contaminated stream water. *Journal of Environmental Quality*, *32*, 1474–1480. doi:10.2134/jeq2003.1474

Kumar, C. P. (2003). *Fresh water resources: A perspective, international year of fresh water - 2003*. Roorkee, India: National Institute of Hydrology. Retrieved August 10, 2010, from http://www.angelfire.com/bc/nihhrrc/documents/fresh.html

Kunjikutty, S. P., Prasher, S. O., Patel, R. M., Barrington, S. F., & Kim, S. H. (2007). Simulation of nitrogen transport in soil under municipal wastewater application using LEACHN. *Journal of the American Water Resources Association, 43*, 1097–1107. doi:10.1111/j.1752-1688.2007.00086.x

LaGrega, M. D., Buckingham, P. L., & Evans, J. C. (2001). *Hazardous waste management* (2nd ed.). Singapore: McGraw Hill.

Lua, A. C., & Jia, Q. (2009). Adsorption of phenol by oil-palm-shell activated carbons in a fixed bed. *Chemical Engineering Journal, 150*, 455–461. doi:10.1016/j.cej.2009.01.034

Maier, H. R., & Dandy, G. C. (1998). The effect of internal parameters and geometry on the performance of back-propagation neural networks: An empirical study. *Environmental Modelling & Software, 13*(2), 193–209. doi:10.1016/S1364-8152(98)00020-6

Maier, H. R., & Dandy, G. C. (2001). Neural network based modelling of environmental variables: A systematic approach. *Mathematical and Computer Modelling, 33*, 669–682. doi:10.1016/S0895-7177(00)00271-5

Nemr, A. E. (2009). Potential of pomegranate husk carbon for Cr(VI) removal from wastewater: Kinetic and isotherm studies. *Journal of Hazardous Materials, 161*, 132–141. doi:10.1016/j.jhazmat.2008.03.093

Pedrero, F., Kalavrouziotis, I., José Alarcón, J., Koukoulakis, P., & Asano, T. (2010). Use of treated municipal wastewater in irrigated agriculture-Review of some practices in Spain and Greece. *Agricultural Water Management, 97*, 1233–1241. doi:10.1016/j.agwat.2010.03.003

Qasim, S. R. (1999). *Wastewater treatment plants: Planning, design, and operation* (2nd ed.). CRC Press.

Rene, E. R., Veiga, M. C., & Kennes, C. (2009). Experimental and neural model analysis of styrene removal from polluted air in a biofilter. *Journal of Chemical Technology and Biotechnology (Oxford, Oxfordshire), 84*, 941–948. doi:10.1002/jctb.2130

Rumelhart, D. E., Hinton, G. E., & Williams, R. J. (1986). Learning internal representations by error propagation. In Rumelhart, D. E., & McClelland, J. L. (Eds.), *Parallel distributed processing* (pp. 318–362). Cambridge, UK: MIT Press.

Sahoo, G. B., Ray, C., Wang, J. Z., Hubbs, S. A., Song, R., Jasperse, J., & Seymour, D. (2005). Use of artificial neural networks to evaluate the effectiveness of riverbank filtration. *Water Research, 39*, 2505–2516. doi:10.1016/j.watres.2005.04.020

Simpson, P. (1990). *Artificial neural systems: Foundations, paradigms, applications, and implementations.* New York, NY: Pergamon Press.

Singh, S., Srivastava, V. C., & Mall, I. D. (2009). Fixed-bed study for adsorptive removal of furfural by activated carbon. *Colloids and Surfaces A: Physicochemical and Engineering Aspects, 332*, 50–56. doi:10.1016/j.colsurfa.2008.08.025

Venterink, H. O., Wiegman, F., Van der Lee, G. E. M., & Vermaat, J. E. (2003). Role of active floodplains for nutrient retention in the river Rhine. *Journal of Environmental Quality, 32*, 1430–1435. doi:10.2134/jeq2003.1430

Wilson, L. G., Amy, G. L., Gerba, C. P., Gordon, H., & Johnson, M. (1995). Water quality changes during soil aquifer treatment of tertiary effluent. *Water Environment Research, 67*, 371–376. doi:10.2175/106143095X131600

Zurada, J. M., Malinowski, A., & Cloete, I. (1994). Sensitivity analysis for minimization of input data dimensions for feed forward neural network. In *IEEE International Symposium on Circuits and Systems*, (pp. 447-450). London.

KEY TERMS AND DEFINITIONS

Adsorption Isotherm: Adsorption isotherm is a plot of the amount of contaminant sorbed per unit mass of sorbent against the concentration of contaminant in the bulk fluid at constant temperature.

Back Propagation Algorithm: A set of learning rules in a generalized feed – forward network, where the error term propagates backward during training, looking for a global minimum of the error function in weight space using the method of gradient descent.

Breakthrough Curve: Refers to the concentration versus time profile of the effluent and describes the performance of the floodplain columns.

Engineered Floodplain Filtration (EFF): EFF is the modified floodplain filtration technique that resembles to a slow sand filter, and is designed by placing a layer of sorbent sandwiched between two sand layers. The amendment of sorbent layer is primarily aimed at making it a bio – barrier to remove or degrade all the pollutants including micro – pollutants by a combination of sorption and biological processes when the infiltrating water moves from the wastewater treatment plants to the rivers.

Lysimeter: In this study, lysimeters refers to a cylindrical vessel containing floodplain soil as the filtration media. It was saturated by water and stabilized for few days so that it can mimic the real world floodplain environment.

Multilayer Perceptron (MLP): MLP refers to a simple network of interconnected neurons. These neurons perceptron computes a single output from multiple inputs by forming a linear combination according to its input weights and then possibly putting the output through some nonlinear activation function. A typical MLP consists of one input layer, one or more hidden layer and an output layer.

Network Internal Parameters: Refers to a set of internal parameters of the back propagation algorithm that can be adjusted to improvise the speed of training and convergence. These include epoch size, learning rate, momentum, activation function, error function and initial weight distribution.

Chapter 12

Computational Intelligence Techniques for Pattern Recognition in Biomedical Image Processing Applications

D. Jude Hemanth
Karunya University, India

J. Anitha
Karunya University, India

ABSTRACT

Medical image classification is one of the most widely used methodologies in the biomedical field for abnormality detection in the anatomy of the human body. Image classification belongs to the broad category of pattern recognition in which different abnormal images are grouped into different categories based on the nature of the pathologies. Nowadays, these techniques are automated and high accuracy combined with low convergence rate has become the desired features of automated techniques. Artificial Intelligence (AI) techniques are the highly preferred automated techniques because of superior performance measures. In this chapter, the application of AI techniques for pattern recognition is explored in the context of abnormal Magnetic Resonance (MR) brain image classification. This chapter illustrates the theory behind the AI techniques and their effectiveness for practical application in medical image classification. Few experimental results are also provided to aid the conclusions. Algorithmic approach of the AI techniques such as neural networks, fuzzy theory, and genetic algorithm are also dealt in this chapter.

DOI: 10.4018/978-1-4666-1833-6.ch012

INTRODUCTION

Computational applications are becoming increasingly important in day-to-day life. But the complexity and the practical difficulties involved in these applications are significantly high. Several techniques are being developed to counter these drawbacks to make them suitable for real-time applications. Again, the pros and cons of these techniques are considerably different which lay an emphasis to highlight the optimal problem solving techniques. Among the problem solving techniques, machine learning algorithms are highly preferred because of its high accuracy. The technique of incorporating intelligence in these machine learning algorithms have yielded significantly superior results. In this chapter, the theory and the applications of some of the Artificial Intelligence (AI) techniques are explained in the context of solving the practical problems in medical image classification.

Medical image classification is one of the primary computational applications in the biomedical field. This process involves the categorization of abnormal images into different groups. This process is extremely important for diagnosing the nature of abnormalities in the human body. Since the subsequent treatment planning is purely based on the disease identification technique, the accuracy of this process must be exceedingly high. Another significant requirement of this image classification technique is the low computational speed. Even though many automated techniques are available, machine intelligence techniques are holding a significant position because of its superior performance measures. The commonly used AI techniques are Artificial Neural Networks (ANN), Fuzzy theory, Genetic Algorithm (GA), etc.

One of the significant machine learning approaches is the Artificial Neural Networks. These are developed based on natural behaviour of the human beings. The performance measures of these techniques are good enough for real-time applica-

tions. The structural and functional operations of the ANN are similar to the natural neurons which are completely computational in nature. Another approach namely, fuzzy theory is a recent version of AI techniques which is used to improve the accuracy of the inputs. This technique is a rule based system which ultimately improves the accuracy of the output. The combination of fuzzy theory and neural networks possess the advantages of both the techniques. A third approach such as GA is used to enhance the performance of the conventional AI techniques. This technique is used to eliminate the irrelevant inputs which significantly improve the quality of the outputs. This technique is based on the natural theory of evolution. The dimensionality of the input vectors is significantly reduced which enhances the accuracy besides improving the convergence rate. All these techniques have been successfully used for practical applications including the biomedical applications.

In this chapter, two algorithms of ANN, one algorithm of fuzzy theory and the concept of GA are explained with mathematical expressions. The basic theoretical background of these algorithms is also dealt in this chapter. The application of these algorithms is explained in the context of medical image classification. Abnormal Magnetic Resonance (MR) brain tumor images are used as the representative of medical images. A suitable methodology for image classification is proposed and these AI algorithms are tested with the input images. Experimental results are analyzed in terms of classification accuracy and convergence rate. A comparative analysis is performed to highlight the significant algorithm for MR brain tumor image classification. Thus this chapter deals with the problem solving AI algorithms for computational applications such as medical image classification.

BACKGROUND

Modern medical imaging technology such as MRI has given physicians a non-invasive means to visualize internal anatomical structures and diagnose a variety of diseases. MR images are typically interpreted visually and quantitatively by radiologists. The need for quantitative information is becoming increasingly important in clinical and surgical environment. Brain tumors are the leading cause of cancer death among humans. Hence early detection and correct treatment based on accurate diagnosis are important steps to avoid any fatal results.

Classification is the grouping of tumors on the basis of their characteristics. Classification of brain MR images has important research and clinical applications. Brain classification methods can be broadly categorized as manual methods and computer-aided semi automated or automated methods. In recent years, computer-aided classification methods have been developed at a rapid pace to overcome the disadvantages of the manual classification methods. These methods are more automatic, objective and the results are highly reproducible. Various computational algorithms, ranging from semi automated (requiring user interactions) to fully automated have been developed. An important application of classification is in detecting the type of the tumor as it responds to treatment. Therefore an automatic and reliable method for classifying tumor would be a useful tool.

Many efforts have exploited MRI's multi-dimensional data capability through multi-spectral analysis for brain tumor classification. Brain tumor classification has been performed using long echo proton MRS signals (Lukas et al., 2004). The major limitation is the limited number of available spectra for the tumor types which results in inferior classification accuracy. Brain tumor classification has also been implemented using wavelets (Chaplot et al., 2006). But the major drawback is the low convergence rate. Expectation-maximization techniques are also used for brain tumor classification (Prastawa et al., 2003). But the major limitation is the requirement of a spatial probabilistic atlas that contains expert prior knowledge about the brain structures. Statistical classifiers, Probabilistic classifiers, AI techniques are some of the widely used image classifiers (Egmont-Petersona et al., 2002). The major drawback of the statistical classifiers is its inability to classify accurately. On the other hand, probabilistic classifiers suffer from the setback of difficulty in estimating the conditional probabilities. But AI outperforms the other classifiers because of its flexibility, scalability, tolerance to faults, accuracy, learning (Fausett, 2002). AI includes ANN, fuzzy theory and GA methodologies.

In general, artificial neural networks are composed of many non-linear computational elements operating in parallel and arranged in patterns reminiscent of biological neural nets. There exists two modes of training for neural networks-supervised and unsupervised. The various training algorithms of ANN are proposed in (Haykin, 1999 ; Freeman & Skapura, 2002). A number of designs have been proposed.One among them is the MAXNET scheme which is a simple network used to find node with largest initial input value (Wilson, 1977). But it suffers from the disadvantage of non-flexibility. The clustering Kohonen layer which follows the unsupervised algorithm is also widely used for classification (Kohonen, 1989). But it is less accurate in classification problems. On the other hand, Counter propagation networks enjoy the advantages of both supervised and unsupervised paradigms but it is computationally heavy. The feed-forward multilayer back propagation network has been widely used for supervised image classification and Kohonen network has been widely used for unsupervised image classification. (Arora & Foody, 1997) concluded that the supervised neural networks would produce the most accurate classification results. (Hosseini et al., 2003) revealed the high convergence rate of the back propagation neural network for image classification. (Hemanth et al., 2010) have illustrated the application of Adaptive networks for MR brain tumor image classification.

On the other hand, several researches based on fuzzy logic techniques are also reported in the literature. (Denkowski et al., 2004) used rule based fuzzy logic inference for MR brain image classification. Experiments based on fuzzy C-means algorithm are also proposed in the literature (Song et al., 2006). (Yang & Zheng, 2005) implemented a modified fuzzy C-means algorithm for image classification. The fuzzy set theoretic models try to mimic human reasoning and the capability of handling uncertainty, whereas the neural network models attempt to emulate the architecture and information representation schemes of the human brain. Integration of the merits of the fuzzy set theory and neural network theory promises to provide, to a great extent, more intelligent systems to handle real life problems.

The dependence on the input training vectors for high classification accuracy which results in computational complexity is the major disadvantage of these techniques. By optimizing the input training vectors, this problem can be minimized. Several optimization algorithms are available in the literature. The significant optimization algorithm for image classification system is genetic algorithm. Genetic algorithm is used for optimizing the similarity measures of the K-Nearest Neighbour classifier (Peterson et al., 2005). The application of genetic algorithm for selecting the K value in the K-NN classifier is reported in (Nath et al., 2005). GA approaches are also widely used for other medical applications such as brain image segmentation (Yeh et al., 2008). Apart from the statistical classifiers, GA approach is also widely used for artificial neural networks. (Abbas et al., 2009) successfully implemented a GA based multilayer perceptron for aircraft applications. (Hemanth et al., 2010) have used other optimization techniques for performance enhancement of the neural classifiers. (Palaniappan et al., 2009) proposed an advanced Adaptive theory resonance network based on genetic algorithm.

In this chapter, the representatives of ANN such as Back propagation network (BPN) & Kohonen

network are dealt in detail. A fuzzy classifier such as fuzzy nearest centre classifier is demonstrated to explore the suitability of fuzzy techniques for MR brain image classification. Finally, the usage of GA for performance enhancement of these AI techniques is also illustrated with experimental results.

AI BASED MR BRAIN IMAGE CLASSIFICATION

Proposed Methodology

A suitable system based on AI techniques is proposed for MR brain image classification which is shown in Figure 1. The various stages involved in this process are illustrated in the diagram. Much emphasis is laid on the AI techniques whereas other pre-processing steps such as feature extraction are also dealt in this chapter. The subsequent sections clearly illustrate the theoretical and the mathematical background of AI techniques and their application for MR brain image classification. Finally, a comparison between the various techniques is performed to show the best technique for real-time application.

MR Image Database and Feature Extraction

A set of MR brain tumor images comprising of the four tumor types namely meningioma, astrocytoma, glioma and metastase are collected from radiologists. The images used are 256*256 gray level images with intensity value ranges from (0 to 255). Initially, these MRI images are normalized to gray level values from (0 to 1) and the features are extracted from the normalized images. Since normalization reduces the dynamic range of the intensity values, feature extraction is made much simpler. Some samples of the MRI database have been displayed in Figure 2.

Figure 1. Framework of the automated image classification system

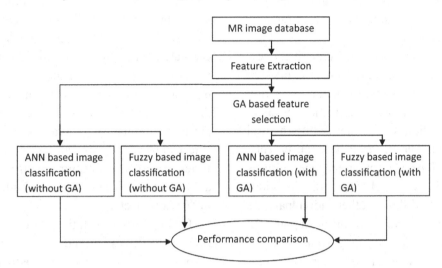

Figure 2. Sample data set: (a)Metastase (b)Glioma (c) Astrocytoma (d) Meningioma

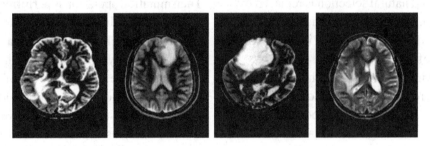

The purpose of feature extraction is to reduce the original data set by measuring certain properties, or features, that distinguish one input pattern from another pattern. The extracted feature should provide the characteristics of the input type to the classifier by considering the description of the relevant properties of the image into a feature space. In this experimental analysis, twelve features based on the first order histogram and the gray level co-occurrence matrices (GLCM) are extracted from the data set images and used for image classification. The features used are Mean, Standard deviation, Energy, Entropy, Correlation, Skewness, Kurtosis, Contrast, Variance, Inverse difference moment, Sum average and Difference variance. A detailed explanation and their mathematical formulae can be obtained in (Haralick, 1979).

Feature Selection (Genetic Algorithm)

All the extracted features do not guarantee high accuracy. Some of the features besides degrading the output results also increase the convergence time period. These insignificant features must be eliminated to enhance the performance of the classifiers. Thus the objective of the feature selection is twofold: (a) improving the classification accuracy & (b) feature dimensionality reduction which improves the convergence rate. Several algorithms have been proposed for feature selection among which optimization algorithms holds a significant position for practical applications. Some of the algorithms are PSO (Tu et al., 2008), SVM, etc. One such optimization algorithm is

Genetic Algorithm (GA). A detailed analysis of optimization algorithms is given in (Jain & Zongker, 2002).

Genetic algorithms (GA) are a relatively new paradigm for a search, based on principles of natural selection. They employ natural selection of fittest individuals as optimization problem solver. Optimization is performed through natural exchange of genetic material between parents. Offsprings are formed from parent genes. Fitness of offsprings is evaluated. The fittest individuals are retained while the other individuals are eliminated. GA is proven to be the most powerful optimization technique in a large solution space. They are used where exhaustive search for solution is expensive in terms of computation time. In computer world, genetic material is replaced by strings of bits and natural selection is replaced by fitness function. Mating of parents is represented by crossover and mutation. Figure 3 illustrates the flow diagram of genetic algorithm.

In this experimental analysis, each of the twelve features are represented by a chromosome (string of bits) with 12 genes (bits) corresponding to the number of features. An initial random population of 20 chromosomes is formed to initiate the genetic optimization. A suitable fitness function is estimated for each individual. The fittest individuals are selected and the crossover and the mutation operations are performed to generate the new population. This process continues for a particular number of generations and finally the fittest chromosome is calculated based on the fitness function. The features with a bit value "1" are accepted and the features with the bit value of "0" are rejected.

In this work, a solution is represented by a finite sequence of 0's and 1's (chromosome).the chromosomes are allowed to 'crossover', i.e. two chromosomes exchange their parts at a randomly chosen point to create two new chromosomes. Then mutation operation is performed by flipping the bits in the chromosome. In each generation, only the fittest chromosomes are allowed to survive and finally an optimized chromosome is estimated. There are several ways of optimization. One method is to define a threshold error rate t, and to find the string with the lowest number of selected features that leads to an error rate e, lower than t. A fitness function is defined that takes this into account:

Figure 3. Flow diagram of genetic algorithm

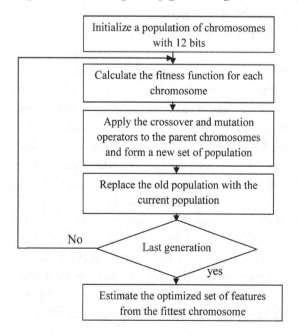

$$f\left(a_i\right) = J\left(a_i\right) - \left(\left\langle J\left(a_i\right)\right\rangle - c\Delta J\left(a_i\right)\right) \qquad (1)$$

where $\left\langle . \right\rangle$ and Δ are the mean and standard deviation over the population and c is a small positive constant which assures that min $f\left(a_i\right) > 0$, i.e. even the least fit chromosome is given a chance to reproduce. The score $J\left(a\right)$ of a string a is given by

$$J\left(a\right) = l\left(a\right) + p\left(e\left(a\right)\right) \qquad (2)$$

where $l(a)$ is the length (number of '1') of string a and $p(e)$ is a penalty function for the obtained error rate e. If e is below the threshold error rate t, $p(e)$ is negative and if e grows larger than t, $p(e)$ grows rapidly.

$$p(e) = \frac{\exp(e-t)/(m-1)}{\exp(1)-1} \qquad (3)$$

where m is a small scaling parameter (about 1%). The classification error rate e for each individual chromosome a is calculated by training the artificial neural network with the features corresponding to '1' in the chromosome. Hence, the value e is different for all the 2^{12} combination of the chromosomes. Finally an optimized chromosome is obtained which yield the optimal set of features.

Classifiers

Two set of features are used for image classification. One set is the complete feature set and another set is the optimized feature set. Based on these, the following classifiers are analyzed in this book.

(a) ANN based image classification (without GA)
(b) Fuzzy based image classification (without GA)
(c) ANN based image classification (with GA)
(d) Fuzzy based image classification (with GA)

ANN Based Image Classification (without GA)

The features extracted from the raw images are directly fed to the ANN for image classification. Artificial Neural Networks are relatively crude electronic models based on the neural structure of the brain. This brain modelling also promises a less technical way to develop machine solutions.

This new approach to computing also provides a more graceful degradation during system overload than its more traditional counterparts. The brain stores information in the form of patterns. Some of these patterns are very complicated and allow us the ability to recognize individual faces from many different angles. This process of storing information as patterns, utilizing those patterns, and then solving problems encompasses a new field in computing. This field does not utilize traditional programming but involves the creation of massively parallel networks and the training of those networks to solve specific problems. This field also utilizes words which are very different from traditional computing words like behave, react, self-organize, learn, generalize and forget. ANN is a collection of neurons arranged in an orderly fashion.

Once a network has been structured for a particular application, that network is ready to be trained. To start this process, a parameter called as "weights" are chosen randomly. Then, the training begins. There are two approaches to training - supervised and unsupervised. Supervised training involves a mechanism of providing the network with the desired output either by manually "grading" the network's performance or by providing the desired outputs with the inputs. Unsupervised training is where the network has to make sense of the inputs without outside help.

In supervised training, both the inputs and the outputs are provided. The network then processes the inputs and compares its resulting outputs against the desired outputs. Using the error value obtained, the system adjusts the weights which control the network. This process occurs over and over as the weights are continually tweaked. The set of data which enables the training is called the "training set". During the training of a network, the same set of data is processed many times as the connection weights are ever refined. The other type of training is called unsupervised training.

In unsupervised training, the network is provided with inputs but not with desired outputs.

The system itself must then decide what features it will use to group the input data. This is often referred to as self-organization or adaption. In this chapter, one supervised neural network namely, Back propagation neural network (BPN) and one unsupervised neural network namely, Kohonen network are dealt in detail.

Back Propagation Neural Network

Back propagation network is the primarily used supervised artificial neural network. Prior to training, the selection of architecture plays a vital role in determining the classification accuracy.

Network Design

In this work, a three layer network is developed. An input vector and the corresponding desired output are considered first. The input is propagated forward through the network to compute the output vector. The output vector is compared with the desired output, and the errors are determined. The errors are then propagated back through the network from the output to input layer. The process is repeated until the errors being minimized. The input layer of network contains 12 neurons, corresponding to 12 features of each MR image. The output layer contains 4 neurons corresponding to 4 predefined tumor categories in the classification. When designing a neural network, one crucial and difficult step is determining the number of neurons in the hidden layers. The hidden layer is responsible for internal representation of the data and the information transformation input and output layers. If there are too few neurons in the hidden layer, the network may not contain sufficient degrees of freedom to form a representation. If too many neurons are defined, the network might become over trained. Therefore, an optimum design for the number of neurons in the hidden layer is required. In this research, one hidden layer with a number of different neurons is used to determine the suitable network.

Initially, images from all the four classes are used to train the BPN with 5 neurons in the hidden layer. The network is trained with few images from each class and the rest are used for the testing phase. The number of misclassifications in each class is observed individually and the classification error in percent is calculated. This procedure is repeated with different neurons (5 to 20) in the hidden layer of the BPN. The average error value for all the classes with different neurons in the hidden layer is calculated. The error values for BPN with 5,10,15,20 hidden neurons are observed and the minimum error value is taken as the best case. In this research, a network with 15 neurons yielded the minimum error value and hence architecture of 12-15-4 is used in this work.

Training Algorithm

There are several training algorithms for feed forward networks. All these algorithms use the gradient of the performance function to determine how to adjust the weights to minimize performance. The weight vectors are randomly initialised to trigger the training process. During training, the weights of the network are iteratively adjusted to minimize the network performance function in the sense of sum of squared error.

$$E= \sum (T-Y)^2 \tag{4}$$

where

T=target vector
Y=output vector

Equation (4) can be easily expressed in terms of the input training vector X, the weight vectors and the activation function. Such a learning algorithm uses the gradient of the performance function with a view to determine how to adjust the weights in order to minimize the error. The gradient is determined using a technique called back propagation, which involves performing computational backwards through the network. Back propagation learning updates the network weights in the direction where the performance function decreases most rapidly, the gradient being negative. Such an iterative process can be expressed as

$$W_{k+1} = W_k - \alpha \cdot g_k \qquad (5)$$

where

W_k = weight vector (includes U and V)

α = learning rate ; g_k = current gradient.

The gradient vector is the derivative of the error value with respect to the weights. Hence, the weight updation criterion of the BPN network is given by

$$W_{k+1} = W_k - \alpha \cdot \frac{\partial E}{\partial w_k} \qquad (6)$$

where

k = iteration counter

E = difference between the target and the output
    values of the network.

When the weight vectors (U and V) of the network remain constant for successive iterations, then the network is said to be stabilized. These weight vectors are the finalised vectors which represent the trained network. The testing images are then given as input to the trained network and the performance measures are analysed. The same architecture and training algorithm is used for the optimized and the unoptimized BPN neural network. The number of features used for training and hence the number of neurons in the input layer differs for both the network

Kohonen Self-organizing Map

One type of the unsupervised neural networks, which posses the self-organizing property, is called Kohonen self-organizing map. Similar to statistical clustering algorithms, these Kohonen networks are able to find the natural groupings from the training data set. As the training algorithm follows the "winner take-all" principle, these networks are also called as competitive learning networks.

Network Design

The topology of the Kohonen self-organizing map is represented as a 2-Dimensional, one-layered output neural net. Each input node is connected to each output node. The dimension of the training patterns determines the number of input nodes. There is no particular geometrical relationship between the output nodes in the competitive learning networks. During the process of training, the input patterns are fed into the network sequentially. Output nodes represent the 'trained' classes and the center of each class is stored in the connection weights between input and output nodes. The architecture used in this work is 12-4. If more number of output nodes is used, then more than one neuron represents the same class. The implementation is made simpler when the number of output nodes is the multiples of the number of output classes. This imparts equal emphasis for all the classes. For example, if 8 nodes are used, then 2 nodes represent each class.

Training Algorithm

The kohonen self-organizing map uses the competitive learning rule for training the network. It uses the "winner- take all" principle in which a winner neuron is selected based on the performance metrics. The weight adjustment is performed only for the winner neuron and the weights of all other neurons remain unchanged. A detailed training algorithm has been furnished below.

STEP 1: Initialize weights w_{ij}

STEP 2: While stopping condition is false, do steps 3 to 7.

STEP 3: For each J (output layer neurons), compute

$$D(J) = \sum_i \left(w_{ij} - x_i\right)^2 \qquad (7)$$

STEP 4: Find index J such that $D(J)$ is a minimum.

STEP 5: Update the winner neuron's weight using the rule

$$w_{ij}\left(new\right) = w_{ij}\left(old\right) + \alpha\left[x_i - w_{ij}\left(old\right)\right] \qquad (8)$$

x_i denotes the intensity values of input data set.

α denotes the learning rate.

STEP 6: Test for stopping condition. (Maximum number of iterations).

Fuzzy Based Image Classification (without GA)

The features extracted from the raw images are directly fed to the fuzzy technique for image classification. Fuzzy Logic is a departure from classical two-valued sets and logic, that uses "soft" linguistic (e.g. large, hot, tall) system variables and a continuous range of truth values in the interval [0,1], rather than strict binary (True or False) decisions and assignments. Formally, fuzzy logic is a structured, model-free estimator that approximates a function through linguistic input/output associations. Fuzzy rule-based systems apply these methods to solve many types of "real-world" problems, especially where a system is difficult to model, is controlled by a human operator or expert, or where ambiguity or vagueness is common. The algorithm used in this work for classification is the fuzzy nearest center classifier.

Fuzzy Nearest Center Classifier

Methodology

The data set is divided into two categories: training data and testing data. The training data set consists of images from all the four tumor types. These training samples are clustered into four different regions namely white matter, grey matter, cerebrospinal fluid and the abnormal tumor region using the fuzzy C-means (FCM) algorithm. The cluster center of the tumor region for all the four classes are observed and stored. In the testing process, the Euclidean distance between the testing data and the cluster centers of the trained samples are calculated. The testing data is assigned to the class with the cluster center whose distance is minimum.

Algorithm

Fuzzy c-means algorithm is based on minimization of the following objective function:

$$J(U, c_1, c_2, ..., c_c) = \sum_{i=1}^{c} J_i = \sum_{i=1}^{c}\sum_{j=1}^{n} u_{ij}^{m} d_{ij}^{2} \qquad (9)$$

u_{ij} is between 0 and 1;

c_i is the centroid of cluster i;

d_{ij} is the Euclidian distance between i_{th} centroid (c_i) and j^{th} data point.

$m \in [1,\infty]$ is a weighting exponent.

Step 1

Fuzzy partitioning of the known data sample is carried out through an iterative optimization of the objective function shown in eqn (13), with the update of membership u_{ij} and the cluster centers c_i by:

$$u_{ij} = \frac{1}{\sum_{k=1}^{c} \left(\frac{d_{ij}}{d_{kj}} \right)^{2/(m-1)}} \; ; \; c_i = \frac{\sum_{j=1}^{n} u_{ij}^{m} x_j}{\sum_{j=1}^{n} u_{ij}^{m}}$$

$$(10)$$

At the $(k+1)^{th}$ iteration, if $\|u(k+1) - u(k)\| < \varepsilon$, then the classifier is assumed to have reached the stabilized condition.

Step 2

Observe the cluster center of the tumor region for all the training samples. Store the cluster centers A_1, A_2, A_3 and A_4 which corresponds to the four tumor types namely metastase, meningioma, glioma and astrocytoma.

Step 3

For a new data, calculate the Euclidean distance between the data and all the cluster centers of the training samples.

Step 4

Assign the data to the class with the cluster center whose Euclidean distance is minimum.

$$d(X, A_i) = \min_{1 \leq k \leq 4} \{ d(X, A_k) \}$$

$$(11)$$

The threshold value (ε) used in this work is 0.01. This algorithm associates the image into any one of the four different tumor types based on the cluster center of the tumor region.

ANN and Fuzzy Based Image Classification (with GA)

The same algorithms dealt in the previous sections are used in this category. But the only difference in the implementation lies in the input feature set. The inputs for these algorithms are the optimal feature set selected from the GA technique instead

of the entire data set. Thus the number of input features are significantly minimized which aid in improving the convergence time period besides enhancing the classification accuracy. But the architectural design of the ANN and the fuzzy algorithm has to be re-modified to account for the difference in the input data set.

Thus, there are totally six techniques analyzed in this chapter among which three are based on GA and three without the concept of GA. Among the three, two are based on ANN and one based on fuzzy theory. Experiments are conducted on these six techniques with the images collected from the scan centres and the results are analyzed to highlight the optimal method for image classification.

EXPERIMENTAL RESULTS AND DISCUSSIONS

In the following section, the classification performance of the three classifiers is reported. The performance criterion used in this work is the classification accuracy and the convergence rate. Classification accuracy is the ratio of the number of images correctly classified to the total number of images. In this experimental analysis, 470 images from four classes are used. Convergence rate is the time period taken for the training and testing of the corresponding algorithm. Initially the results of the GA process are analyzed followed by the performance measure analysis of the optimized and unoptimized AI classifiers.

Feature Dimensionality Reduction Using GA

All the extracted features do not contribute for high classification accuracy. The presence of insignificant features accounts for high computational complexity (high convergence time period) besides yielding inferior classification accuracy. Hence, an extensive feature selection process based on genetic algorithm is performed to

Table 1. Optimized classifiers vs. unoptimized classifiers

Parameters	GA Optimized AI classifiers	Unoptimized AI classifiers
Features used	Energy, Kurtosis, Skewness, Entropy, Correlation, Inverse Difference Moment.	All the features (12)
Number of input neurons for neural classifiers	6	12
Input layer weight matrix for neural classifier	6×15	12×15

determine the optimum number of features which yield high classification accuracy besides reducing the dimensionality problem. The results obtained from the genetic algorithm shows the following optimal features: Energy, Entropy, Correlation, Inverse difference moment, skewness and entropy. Thus the number of features selected by GA is only 6. These features show a bit value "1" while the other features show a bit value "0" in the final optimized chromosome. These optimized features are used for training the optimized AI classifiers. A comparison is made between the optimized AI classifiers and the unoptimized classifiers to

analyze the feature dimensionality problem. Table 1 shows the parameters used for these classifiers.

From the above table, it is evident that the architecture of GA optimized AI classifiers is less complex than the unoptimized classifiers. Approximate 50% reduction in the complexity is achieved with the genetic algorithm. Since the size of the weight matrix is small for the optimized classifiers, the training time period is also reduced. Thus, the effectiveness of the genetic algorithm in terms of computational complexity is proved. Further analysis is performed on the classifiers based on classification accuracy and convergence rate.

Classification Accuracy Results

In this work, both bi-level classification and multilevel classification are carried out with the classifiers. The classification accuracy of the three classifiers for the binary classification is as shown in Table 2.

The binary classification is performed using all the three networks with two neurons in the output layer. Since there is high correlation between the astrocytoma and the glioma images, the neural networks find the classification process

Table 2. Classification accuracy for binary classification of the classifiers

CLASSES	BPN (with GA)	Kohonen (with GA)	Fuzzy approach (with GA)	BPN (without GA)	Kohonen (without GA)	Fuzzy approach (without GA)
Meningioma vs. Astrocytoma	93.4%	82.7%	91.5%	90%	79%	90%
Meningioma vs.Metastas	94.6%	84.5%	92%	92%	81.5%	91%
Meningioma vs.Glioma	88%	79%	93%	85.5%	77%	89%
Astrocytoma vs.Metastas	94.7%	81.2%	92.5%	93%	80%	92%
Astrocytoma vs.Glioma	85.5%	72.2%	91%	82.5%	71.5%	89.5%
Metastase vs. Glioma	90.7%	79.5%	94.4%	90%	78%	92%

Table 3. Classification accuracy for multiclass classification of the classifiers

CLASSES	BPN (with GA)	Kohonen (with GA)	Fuzzy approach (with GA)	BPN (without GA)	Kohonen (without GA)	Fuzzy approach (without GA)
Meningioma vs. Astrocytoma vs Glioma vs Metastase	94%	84.5%	92%	91%	81%	90.5%

very difficult which results in inferior results. On the contrary, the correlation between metastas and meningioma images are very less which results in high classification accuracy. Thus there is an inconsistency among the classifiers in classifying the images. This analysis has also shown that the Kohonen neural network yields inferior results even for two input cases. From the above table, the inferior nature of the unsupervised neural networks in terms of accuracy is proved. The classification accuracy is also calculated for the multiclass classification of the brain tumors. Table 3 shows the classification accuracy of the three classifiers in the multiclass approach.

In the multiclass classification, quantitative analysis is performed with four neurons in the output layer. The overall classification accuracy is less for multiclass classification because the probability of an image being successfully classified is less (only 25%).But in binary classification, the probability of an image being successfully classified is high (50%).All the AI techniques have yielded comparably better results. The Kohonen neural network yields inferior results than the other two techniques because it works in an unsupervised manner where no target vector is available for training. Thus from the above analysis, it is evident that Kohonen neural network is inferior to BPN and the fuzzy theory. Also, the fuzzy algorithm is purely based on the intensity of the input images where there is no iterative procedure to correct the output results and hence it is inferior to BPN. Thus, BPN is a better ap-

proach than the other techniques in terms of classification accuracy.

The performance of the three classifiers is further analyzed on the basis of the convergence rate i.e., the training time and the testing time. Training time refers to the time required by the classifier to derive classification rules that will allow it to classify the images. Testing time refers to the time required by a trained classifier to classify the untrained images. Since GA technique, reduces the size of the feature set, the AI techniques with GA are superior to the AI techniques without GA. Also, fuzzy theory and Kohonen network consumes less time period than the BPN since fuzzy is devoid of training and Kohonen is a single layer network. But the time period varies with respect to the number of input images/features and the processing speed of the computational device. Thus this work highlights BPN with GA technique as a better option for practical applications since BPN improves the accuracy and GA minimizes the computational time period.

CONCLUSION

This chapter mainly focuses on the importance of AI techniques for computational applications in the biomedical field. Several AI techniques are analyzed both theoretically and experimentally. Real time MR brain images are used for the experiments and the performance measures of the AI techniques are estimated in terms of accuracy and time period. It has been noted that the AI techniques such as ANN perform considerably better than any other approaches. Also, the inclusion of GA into ANN has enhanced the performance of the classifier to higher extent. This chapter also suggest the application of BPN for medical applications. It also opens new avenues for research in the area of soft computing techniques for biomedical applications.

FUTURE WORK

Different AI techniques can be tested with the same set of input images. The nature and the number of input features may be changed to yield better results. A different optimization algorithm may be tried out instead of GA. Suitable modifications in the existing techniques may be incorporated to enhance the performance of the AI techniques.

REFERENCES

Abbas, Y., & Aqel, M. (2003). Pattern recognition using multilayer neural-genetic algorithm. *Neurocomputing, 51*, 237–247. doi:10.1016/S0925-2312(02)00619-7

Arora, M. K., & Foody, G. M. (1997). An evaluation of some factors affecting the accuracy of classification by an artificial neural network. *International Journal of Remote Sensing, 18*(4), 799–810. doi:10.1080/014311697218764

Chaplot, S., Patnaik, L. M., & Jaganathan, N. R. (2006). Classification of MR brain images using wavelets as input to SVM and neural network. *Biomedical Signal Processing and Control, 1*, 86–92. doi:10.1016/j.bspc.2006.05.002

Denkowski, M., Chlebiej, M., & Mikołajczak, P. (2004). Segmentation of human brain MR images using rule-based fuzzy logic inference. *Studies in Health Technology and Informatics, 105*, 264–272.

Egmont-Petersena, M., Ridderb, D., & Handelsca, H. (2002). Image processing with neural networks-A review. *Pattern Recognition, 35*.

Fausett, L. (2002). *Fundamentals of neural networks: Architectures, algorithms and applications*. Englewood Cliffs, NJ: Prentice Hall.

Freeman, J. A., & Skapura, D. M. (2002). *Neural networks, algorithms, applications and programming techniques*. Addison –Wesley Publication Company.

Haralick, R. M. (1979). Statistical and structural approaches to texture. *IEEE Transactions on Systems, Man, and Cybernetics, 67*, 786–804.

Haykin, S. S. (1999). *Neural networks: A comprehensive foundation*. Upper Saddle River, NJ: Prentice Hall.

Hemanth, D. J., Selvathi, D., & Anitha, J. (2010). Application of adaptive resonance theory neural network for MR brain tumor image classification. *International Journal of Healthcare Information Systems and Informatics, 5*(1), 61–75. doi:10.4018/jhisi.2010110304

Hemanth, D. J., Vijila, C. K. S., & Anitha, J. (2010). Performance improved PSO based modified counter propagation neural network for abnormal MR brain image classification. *International Journal of Advances in Soft Computing and its Applications, 2*(1).

Hosseini, A. E., Amini, J., & Saradjian, M. R. (2003). Back propagation neural network for classification of IRS-1D satellite images. *Proceedings of the Conference of High Resolution Mapping from Space*, Hanover, Germany.

Jain, A., & Zongker, D. (2002). Feature selection: Evaluation, application, and small sample performance. *IEEE Transactions on Pattern Analysis and Machine Intelligence, 19*(2), 153–158. doi:10.1109/34.574797

Kohonen, T. (1989). *Self organization and associative memory*. New York, NY: Springer – Verlaag Publication.

Lukas, L., Devos, A., & Suykens, A. K. (2004). Brain tumor classification based on long echo proton MRS signals. *Artificial Intelligence in Medicine, 31*, 73–89. doi:10.1016/j.artmed.2004.01.001

Nath, A. K., Rehman, S. M., & Salah, A. (2005). An enhancement of k-nearest neighbour classification using genetic algorithm. *Proceedings of the MICS*, (pp. 1-12).

Palaniappan, R., & Eswaran, C. (2009). Using genetic algorithm to select the presentation order of training patterns that improves simplified fuzzy ARTMAP classification performance. *Applied Soft Computing, 9*, 100–106. doi:10.1016/j.asoc.2008.03.003

Peterson, M. R., Doom, T. E., & Raymer, M. L. (2005). GA-facilitated classifier optimization with varying similarity measures. *Proceedings of the IEEE Conference on Genetic and Evolutionary Computation*, (pp. 2514-2525).

Prastawa, M., Bullit, E., & Moon, N. (2003). Automatic brain tumor segmentation by subject specific modification of atlas priors. *Medical Image Computing, 10*, 1341–1348.

Song, Y. S. (2006). Lecture Notes in Computer Science: *Vol. 4223. Fuzzy c-means algorithm with divergence-based kernel* (pp. 99–108). Berlin, Germany: Springer-Verlag.

Tu, C. J., et al. (2008). Feature selection using PSO-SVM. *IAENG International Journal of Computer Science, 33*(1).

Wilson, A. (1977). Architecture for a self organizing neural pattern recognition machine. *Computer Vision. Image Processing, 37*, 104–115.

Yang, Y., & Zheng, C. (2005). Fuzzy C-means clustering algorithm with a novel penalty term for image segmentation. *Opto-Electronics Review, 13*(4), 309–315.

Yeh, J. Y., & Fu, J. C. (2008). A hierarchical genetic algorithm for segmentation of multi-spectral human brain MRI. *Expert Systems with Applications, 34*, 1285–1295. doi:10.1016/j.eswa.2006.12.012

Chapter 13

A PSO–Based Framework for Designing Fuzzy Systems from Noisy Data Set

Satvir Singh
Shaheed Bhagat Singh College of Engineering & Technology, India

J. S. Saini
Deenbandhu Chhotu Ram University of Science & Technology, India

Arun Khosla
Dr. B. R. Ambedkar National Institute of Technology, India

ABSTRACT

In most of Fuzzy Logic System (FLS) designs, human reasoning is encoded into programs to make decisions and/or control systems. Designing an optimal FLS is equivalent to an optimization problem, in which efforts are made to locate a point in fitness search-space where the performance is better than that of other locations. The number of parameters to be tuned in designing an FLS is quite large. Also, fitness search space is highly non-linear, deceptive, non-differentiable, and multi-modal in nature. Noisy data, from which to construct the FLS, may make the design problem even more difficult. This chapter presents a framework to design Type-1 (T1) and Interval Type-2 (IT2) FLSs (Liang and Mendel, 2000c, Mendel, 2001, 2007, Mendel et al., 2006) using Particle Swarm Optimization (PSO) (Eberhart and Kennedy, 1995, Kennedy and Eberhart, 1995). This framework includes the use of PSO based Nature Inspired (NI) Toolbox discussed in the chapter titled, "Nature-Inspired Toolbox to Design and Optimize Systems."

INTRODUCTION

FLSs are being used successfully in an increasing number of application areas where system response can be described far easily using linguistic variables and rules than using their mathematical models. One of the most important considerations in designing any FLS is the generation of the fuzzy rules and Membership Function (MF) for each involved Fuzzy Set (FS). In most existing applications, the fuzzy rules are extracted from the experts' knowledge (Mendel, 2001, Khosla et al., 2005). With an increasing number of variables, the

DOI: 10.4018/978-1-4666-1833-6.ch013

possible number of rules for the system increases exponentially, which makes it difficult for experts to define a complete rule set for modeling a system with good performance. An automated way to design fuzzy systems might be preferable (Shi et al., 1999, Saini et al., 2004, Khosla et al., 2005).

The design of an FLS can be formulated as a search problem in high-dimensional search-space where each point is an FLS, i.e., collection of FSs, and rulebase, etc. Given some performance measurement criteria, the performance of the system forms a hyper-surface in the space. Developing the optimal FLS design is equivalent to finding the optimal location of this hyper-surface. The hyper-surface can be (Shi et al., 1999):

- *infinitely large* since the number of possible FSs for each variable can be unbounded.
- *non-differentiable* since changes in the FSs can be discrete and can have a discontinuous effect on the fuzzy systems performance.
- *complex* and *noisy* since the mapping from a fuzzy rule set to its performance is indirect and dependent on the evaluation method used.
- *multi-modal* since different fuzzy rule sets and/or membership functions may have similar performance.
- *deceptive* since almost similar fuzzy rule sets and membership functions may have quite different performances.

All these characteristics make evolutionary algorithms a better option to search optimal designs from the hyper-surface search-space than the conventional hill-climbing search methods.

FUZZY SETS AND SYSTEMS

Each input is expressed linguistically and depicted in graphical shapes (S, Z, Triangular, Trapezoidal, and Gaussian, etc.) called FSs or MFs. If membership value for a particular FS is crisp (certain) for some crisp input over the Universe of Discourse (UOD), the FS is called T1 FS and denoted as A. It may be expressed in two different mathematical formats as in (1) and (2)

$$A = \{(x, \mu_A(x)) \mid x \in X\} \tag{1}$$

$$A = \int_X \mu_A(x) \, / \, x; \, x \in X \tag{2}$$

If the membership value for a particular FS is not one crisp value for a crisp input from the UOD X, i.e., $x = x' \in X$, but is another single FS or are multiple FSs (called secondary MFs) of any shape, then such an FS is called T2 FS. Figure 1 shows a T2 FS, with all triangular secondary MFs, in 3D and 2D representations. Such a T2 FS is denoted, by $\tilde{A}$, and is characterized by a T2 MF as $\mu_A(x, u)$, where $x \in X$ and $u \in J_x \subseteq [0, 1]$, where J_x is the primary membership of x where $J_x \subseteq [0, 1]$ for all $x \in X$. $\tilde{A}$ can be expressed mathematically in either of the following forms, i.e., (3) and (4).

$$A = \{(x, u), (\mu_A(x, u)) \mid \forall x \in X, u \in J_x \subseteq [0, 1]\} \tag{3}$$

$$A = \int_{x \in X} \mu_A(x, u) \, / \, (x, u)$$
$$= \int_{x \in X} \left[\int_{u \in J_x} f_x(u) \, / \, u \right] \Big/ x; \, J_x \subseteq [0, 1] \tag{4}$$

Here, secondary MF $\mu_A(x, u)$ is such that $0 \leq \mu_A(x, u) \leq 1$. Domain of a secondary MF is called the primary membership of x. The amplitude of secondary MF is called a secondary grade. In (4), $f_x(u)$ is a secondary grade and in (3), $\mu_A(x', u')$ for a particular $x' \in X$ and $u' \in J_{x'}$ is a secondary grade.

Figure 1. Typical general T2 FS with Triangular secondary MFs in 3D and 2D

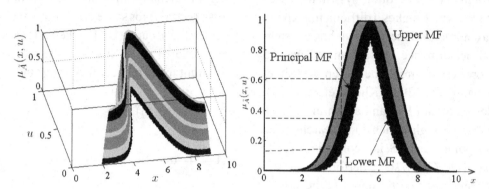

For discrete UOD, $\int$ is replaced by $\sum$ and (4) is re-expressed in (5) for discrete X and J_x

$$A = \sum_{x \in X} \left[f_x(u) \, / \, u \right] \Big/ x \quad (5)$$

Assume that each of secondary MFs of T2 FS has only one secondary grade equal to 1. A *principal membership function* is the union of all such points at which this occurs (as shown in Figure 1), i.e.,

$$A = \int_{x \in X} u \, / \, x$$

where

$$f_x(u) = 1 \quad (6)$$

Uncertainty in the primary memberships of a T2 FS, $\tilde{A}$, consists of a bounded region called the Footprint of Uncertainty (FOU) and is the union of all primary memberships, i.e.,

$$FOU(\tilde{A}) = \bigcup_{x \in X} J_x \quad (7)$$

The term FOU is very useful, as it not only focuses our attention on the uncertainties inherent in the specific T2 FS, whose shape is a direct consequence of the nature of these uncertainties, but also provides a very convenient verbal description of the entire domain of support for all the secondary grades of a T2 FS.

As a special case, if a GT2 FS has all secondary grades as equal to an interval set, i.e., $J_x = 1$ for $x \in X$, then it is called an IT2 FS. A 3D view of such an IT2 FS is shown in Figure 2 with all secondary grades equal to unity. The FOU interval is shaded uniformly to indicate secondary grade equal to 1 for representing IT2 FSs in 2D as in Figure 2.

There are many ways to express FOU (Liang and Mendel, 2000c, Mendel, 2001, 2007, Mendel et al., 2006), and hence, approaches to describe IT2 FS and the ones implemented in GFS Toolbox are discussed in the following subsections:

Lower MF + Upper MF

FOU of any IT2 FS, say $\tilde{A}$, can be expressed using lower and upper bounds of uncertainty involved that are termed as Lower Membership Function (LMF) and Upper Membership Function (UMF) and are denoted as $\underline{\mu}_{\tilde{A}}(x)$ and $\overline{\mu}_{\tilde{A}}(x)$. Mathematically,

$$\underline{\mu}_{\tilde{A}}(x) \equiv \underline{FOU(\tilde{A})}; \, \forall x \subseteq X \quad (8)$$

and

Figure 2. Typical 3D and 2D representations of IT2

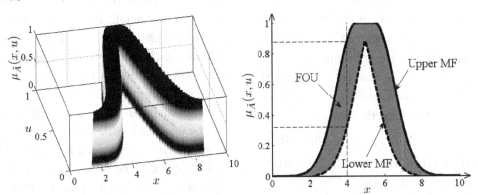

$$\overline{\mu_{\tilde{A}}}(x) \equiv \overline{FOU(\tilde{A})};\; \forall x \subseteq X \qquad (9)$$

In line with (7), $\underline{FOU(\tilde{A})} = \bigcap_{x \in X} \underline{J_x}$ and $\overline{FOU(\tilde{A})} = \bigcap_{x \in X} \overline{J_x}$, where $\underline{J_x}$ and $\overline{J_x}$ denote the lower and upper bounds on J_x, respectively. Therefore, (4) can be modified to express IT2 FS in terms of LMF and UMF, as

$$A = \int_{x \in X} \left[\int_{u \in [\underline{\mu_{\tilde{A}}}(x),\, \overline{\mu_{\tilde{A}}}(x)]} f_x(u)\, /\, u \right] \Big/ x \qquad (10)$$

As shown in Figure 2 (darkened region), all the secondary membership grades within the FOU interval are unity for IT2 FS, i.e.,

$$\int_{u \in [\underline{\mu_{\tilde{A}}}(x),\, \overline{\mu_{\tilde{A}}}(x)]} f_x(u)\, /\, u = 1 \qquad (11)$$

This further simplifies (10) to:

$$A = \int_{x \in X} \left[\int_{u \in [\underline{\mu_{\tilde{A}}}(x),\, \overline{\mu_{\tilde{A}}}(x)]} 1\, /\, u \right] \Big/ x \qquad (12)$$

Figure 2 is a 2D graphical representation of (12) where LMF and UMF are shown with dashed and solid lines respectively. Note that if $\underline{\mu_{\tilde{A}}}(x) = \overline{\mu_{\tilde{A}}}(x)$, i.e., all secondary uncertainties disappear, then IT2 FS reduces to T1 FS. Stated mathematically,

$$\mu_{\tilde{A}}(x) \Big|_{\underline{\mu_{\tilde{A}}}(x) = \overline{\mu_{\tilde{A}}}(x)} = \overline{\mu}_{\tilde{A}}(x) = \mu_A(x) \qquad (13)$$

In most of research papers IT2 FSs have been described in terms of LMF and UMF, discussed in this section. The other variants to this specification proposed by us in this chapter (again LMF & UMF) are discussed in the following subsections.

Left T1 FS + Right T1 FS

Uncertainty about the T1 FSs, can be expressed with the help of two similar FSs, i.e., left and right T1 FSs. For example, a gaussian shaped T1 FS is specified using two parameters namely, mean (m) and standard deviation (σ); uncertainties about such a T1 FS can be expressed if mean (m) has a range of values, i.e., $[m_1, m_2]$, rather than a single value. Such an IT2 FS can be expressed mathematically using *Left T1 FS* and *Right T1 FS* as follows:

$$\mu_{A_{Left}}(x) = \exp\left[-\frac{1}{2}\left(\frac{x - m_1}{\sigma} \right)^2 \right] \qquad (14)$$

$$\mu_{A_{Right}}(x) = \exp\left[-\frac{1}{2}\left(\frac{x - m_2}{\sigma} \right)^2 \right] \qquad (15)$$

In continuous UOD, total number of T1 and/or T2 sub FSs, termed as Embedded FSs and denoted as A_e and $\tilde{A}_e$ respectively, are uncountable. However, for the case of discrete UODs of X and U (each having N elements), there exist a finite number of Embedded FSs. Each Embedded T2 FS, $\tilde{A}_e$, contains exactly one element from $J_{x_1}, J_{x_2}, ..., J_{x_N}$ namely $u_1, u_2, ..., u_N$ each with its associated secondary grade, namely $f_{x_1}(u_1), f_{x_2}(u_2), ..., f_{x_N}(u_N)$, i.e.,

$$\tilde{A}_e = \sum_{i=1}^{N}\left[f_{x_i}(u_i)\,/\,u_i\right]\!/x_i \;\; ; \;\; u_i \in J_{x_i} \subseteq [0,1] \tag{16}$$

However, for similar discrete UODs of X and U, each Embedded T1 FS, A_e, has one element from $J_{x_1}, J_{x_2}, ..., J_{x_N}$, namely $u_1, u_2, ..., u_N$, i.e.,

$$A_e = \sum_{i=1}^{N} u_i\big/x_i \;\; ; \;\; u_i \in J_{x_i} \subseteq [0,1] \tag{17}$$

A T2 FS $\tilde{A}$, is the union of all its Embedded FSs. Alternatively, extreme left and extreme right T1 FSs can directly express IT2 FSs, in terms of LMF and UMF with the following simple MATLAB algorithm:

```
L = Left T1 FS ;
R = Right T1 FS ;
LMF = min(L, R);
UMF = max(L, R);
indices = find(L == max(L)): find(L == max(R));
UMF(indices) = 1;
```

Here, LMF and UMF are two T1 FSs, same as specified in (8) and (9).

Principal T1 FS + FOU

T1 FLS, derived from data, may not be appropriate if the data are noisy. However, one may improve upon the response of the FLS if the involved FSs are enabled to handle these uncertainties. T1 FSs can be upgraded to T2 FSs by shifting MFs towards left and right by equal or unequal amounts depending upon the pattern of the noise present in the data. For example, an arbitrary gaussian shaped T1 FS with mean m and standard deviation, σ, can be upgraded to T2 FS by blurring the T1 FS towards left and right side uniformly if the noise is considered to be uniform, i.e., m may range from $m - r$ to $m + r$, where r is the measure of FOU. Such a blurred T1 FS may be expressed in a MATLAB algorithm, in terms of LMF and UMF as follows:

```
L = T1 FS – r;
R = T1 FS + r;
LMF = min(L, R);
UMF = max(L, R);
indices = find(L == max(L)): find(L == max(R));
UMF(indices) = 1;
```

Fuzzy Operators

Operations of crisp set theory viz. union, intersection and complement, are also applicable in FS theory. These operations are computationally much easier for the case of IT2 FSs (Liang and Mendel, 2000c, Mendel et al., 2006) as compared to the case of T2 FSs (Karnik and Mendel, 2001b). Consider two T2 FSs $\tilde{A}$ and $\tilde{B}$ over a UOD of X. Let $\mu_{\tilde{A}}(x) = \int_u f_x(u)\,/\,u$ and $\mu_{\tilde{B}}(x) = \int_w g_x(w)\,/\,w$ for $J_x \in [0, 1]$ be the membership grades, where u, $w \in J_x$ indicate the primary membership of x while $f_x(u)$, $g_x(w) \in [0, 1]$, indicate the secondary membership grade of x. Using Zadeh's Extension Principle (Dubois and Prade, 1980, Zadeh, 1975), the membership grades for the union, intersection and complement of T2 FSs $\tilde{A}$ and $\tilde{B}$ have been defined as follows (Karnik and Mendel, 2001b, Mizumoto and Tanaka, 1976):

$$\mu_{\tilde{A}} \sqcup \mu_{\tilde{B}} = \int_u \int_w (f_x(u) \star g_x(w)) / (u \vee w) \quad (18)$$

$$\mu_{\tilde{A}} \sqcap \mu_{\tilde{B}} = \int_u \int_w (f_x(u) \star g_x(w)) / (u \star w) \quad (19)$$

$$\neg \mu_{\tilde{A}} = \int_u f_x(u) / (1 - u) \quad (20)$$

However, for two IT2 FSs, $\tilde{A} = 1 / FOU(\tilde{A}) = 1 / [\underline{\mu}_{\tilde{A}}(x), \overline{\mu}_{\tilde{A}}(x)]$ and $\tilde{B} = 1 / FOU(\tilde{B}) = 1 / [\underline{\mu}_{\tilde{B}}(x), \overline{\mu}_{\tilde{B}}(x)]$, $\forall x \in X$, thus above fuzzy operators are modified to computationally much simpler expressions listed in Box 1 (Mendel et al., 2006) for $x \in X$.

Here, $\star$ and $\vee$ denote the t-norm and t-conorm respectively. $\sqcup$, $\sqcap$ and $\neg$ are referred to as *join*, *meet* and *negation* respectively, to distinguish them from the corresponding operators used in T1 FLSs, i.e., *union*, *intersection* and *complement*, respectively.

Rulebase

Rules are the kernel of every FLS, and may be provided by experts or extracted from numerical data. In either case, rules can be expressed as a collection of IF-THEN statements. A multi-input multi-output (MIMO) rulebase can be considered as a group of multi-input single-output (MISO) rulebases; hence, it is sufficient to concentrate on a MISO rule base (Mendel, 2007). Consider an FLS having p antecedents $x_1 \in X_1$, $x_2 \in X_2$,...,

$x_p \in X_p$ (denoted as $\langle x \rangle$ collectively) and one consequent $y \in Y$. Assume there are M rules and ith rule has the form:

$$R^i : IF\ x_1\ is\ \tilde{F}_1^i\ AND\ x_2\ is\ \tilde{F}_2^i\ AND\ ...$$
$$AND\ x_p\ is\ \tilde{F}_p^i\ \ THEN\ y\ is\ \tilde{G}^i;\ i = 1, 2, ..., p \quad (24)$$

This rule represents a T2 relation between the input space, $X_1 \times X_2 \times ... \times X_p$ and the output space, Y, of the IT2 FLS. $\tilde{F}_k^i$ represent the antecedent FSs with associated $\mu_{\tilde{F}_k^i}(x_k)$ MFs $(k = 1, 2, ..., p)$ and $\tilde{G}^i$ represents consequent FS of ith rule with associated MF $\mu_{\tilde{G}^i}(y)$. For a crisp input vector, i.e., $\langle x \rangle = \langle x_1', x_2', ..., x_p' \rangle$, to an IT2 FLS:

(a) The result of the input and antecedent operations, is an IT1 set, called *firing set* (see Equation 25).

(b) The ith rule R^i fired output consequent set, $\mu_{\tilde{B}^i}(y)$, is an IT2 FS:

$$\mu_{\tilde{B}^i}(y) = \int_{b^i \in [\underline{f}^i \star \underline{\mu}_{\tilde{G}^i},\ \overline{f}^i \star \overline{\mu}_{\tilde{G}^i}]} (1/b^i);\ y \in Y \quad (26)$$

where $\underline{\mu}_{\tilde{G}^i}(y)$ and $\overline{\mu}_{\tilde{G}^i}(y)$ are the lower and upper membership grades of $\mu_{\tilde{G}^i}(y)$.

Box 1.

$$\mu_{\tilde{A}} \sqcup \mu_{\tilde{B}} = 1 / [\underline{\mu}_{\tilde{A}}(x) \vee \underline{\mu}_{\tilde{B}}(x),\ \overline{\mu}_{\tilde{A}}(x) \vee \overline{\mu}_{\tilde{B}}(x)] \quad (21)$$

$$\mu_{\tilde{A}} \sqcap \mu_{\tilde{B}} = 1 / [\underline{\mu}_{\tilde{A}}(x) \star \underline{\mu}_{\tilde{B}}(x),\ \overline{\mu}_{\tilde{A}}(x) \star \overline{\mu}_{\tilde{B}}(x)] \quad (22)$$

$$\neg \mu_{\tilde{A}} = 1 / [1 - \underline{\mu}_{\tilde{A}}(x),\ 1 - \overline{\mu}_{\tilde{A}}(x)] \quad (23)$$

Equation 25.

$$F^i(x') = [\underline{f}^i(x'), \overline{f}^i(x')] \equiv [\underline{f}^i, \overline{f}^i]$$
$$= [\underline{\mu}_{\tilde{F}_1}(x'_1)\star\cdots\star\underline{\mu}_{\tilde{F}_p}(x'_p), \ \overline{\mu}_{\tilde{F}_1}(x'_1)\star\cdots\star\overline{\mu}_{\tilde{F}_p}(x'_p)]$$

Equation 27.

$$\mu_{\tilde{B}}(y) = \int_{b\in\left[[\underline{f}^1\star\underline{\mu}_{\tilde{G}^1}(y)]\vee\cdots\vee[\underline{f}^N\star\underline{\mu}_{\tilde{G}^N}(y)],[\overline{f}^1\star\overline{\mu}_{\tilde{G}^1}(y)]\vee\cdots\vee[\overline{f}^N\star\overline{\mu}_{\tilde{G}^N}(y)]\right]} 1/b; \quad y\in Y$$

Equation 28.

$$Y_{TR}(x') = [Y_l(x'), Y_r(x')] = [y_l, y_r]$$
$$= \int_{y^1\in[y_l^1,y_r^1]}\cdots\int_{y^M\in[y_l^M,y_r^M]}\int_{f^1\in[\underline{f}^1,\overline{f}^1]}\cdots\int_{f^M\in[\underline{f}^M,\overline{f}^M]} 1 \left/ \frac{\sum_{i=1}^M f^i y^i}{\sum_{i=1}^M f^i}\right.$$

(c) Suppose that N out of M rules in the IT2 FLS get fired, where $N \le M$, and the combined output set, $\mu_{\tilde{B}}(y)$, is obtained by combining the output consequent FSs, with the help of t-conorms, of all the fired rules. This is expressed mathematically in Equation 27.

Type-Reductions and Defuzzification

There are five different TR methods (Karnik et al., 1999, Mendel, 2001); (1) Centroid, (2) Height, (3) Modified Height, (4) Center-of-sums, and (5) Center-of-sets, that provide an interval of uncertainty for the output of an IT2 FLS. Each is inspired by what we do in T1 FLSs and are based on computing the centroid of an IT2 FS (Karnik and Mendel, 2001a). This was possible as the centroid of an IT2 FS is an IT1 FS, and such sets are completely characterized by their left- and right-end points; hence, computing the centroid of an IT2 FS set requires computing only those two end-points. Center-of-sets, centroid, center-of-sums, and height TR can all be expressed mathematically as in Equation 28. The integral signs denote the union operation rather than arithmetic integration; y_l^i and y_r^i are left- and right- end points of the centroid of the consequent of the ith rule; $\underline{f}^i$, $\overline{f}^i$ are the lower and upper firing levels of the ith rule, computed using (25) for M fired fuzzy rules. Further, the defuzzified crisp output of an IT2 FLS is simply the average of y_l and y_r, calculated using KM algorithm (Karnik and Mendel, 2001a), and expressed mathematically in (29),

$$y(\langle x'\rangle) = \frac{1}{2}\left[y_l(\langle x'\rangle) + y_r(\langle x'\rangle)\right] \qquad (29)$$

PSO FRAMEWORK FOR EVOLVING FLS FROM NOISY DATA SET

The following framework is proposed by us for designing FLSs using PSO-based NI Toolbox:

i.   List FLS features to be evolved within respective UODs and resolution in MS Excel file/sheet.

ii. Identify PSO model, topology, strategy parameters, population, and neighborhood sizes, etc., and specify in the NIT Editor window.

iii. Identify error-based fitness function based on available Input-Output data specified in another MS Excel file/sheet.

iv. Start the process of evolution, using NI Toolbox, where each particle in the swarm is updated, validated, and evaluated, repeatedly, till any of the termination criterions is met.

v.   Get valuations for finally evolved various FLS parameters from the MS Excel file/sheet that contains the string format and simulate it for actual response verification.

Following sub-sections discuss the major points of consideration while designing FLSs using NI Toolbox, in detail.

Particle String Encoding of FLSs

To completely represent an MISO FLS as a particle, all of its features are required to be specified in the form of a string using some encoding mechanism. Here, we refer to each component (feature) in the particle string as an element. It is also suggested to evolve the FSs and rulebase, simultaneously, since they are co-dependent in an FLS (Khosla et al., 2005, Saini et al., 2004, Shi et al., 1999).

String Encoding of T1 FSs and FLSs

Following is the groundwork to encode singleton and non-singleton MISO FLSs:

i.   FLS has n antecedents and $(n+1)$ corresponds to the single consequent.

ii. Let ith antecedent be fuzzified using m_i FSs, where $i = 1, 2, ..., n$.

iii. The consequent is fuzzified using m_{n+1} either singleton (Sugeno) or non-singleton (Mamdani) FSs.

iv. Each non-singleton T1 FS of the antecedents can be represented with $p_a = 3$ elements in the string; two elements for supports, i.e., first (x_1), and second (x_2), and one element for shape of the MF (Shi et al., 1999).

Various shapes of the FSs are represented with corresponding integer numbers in the particle string, e.g., Z-shape (1), Triangle (2), Gaussian (3), and S-shape (4), etc.

v.   Consequent FSs can be either singleton or non-singleton. Every singleton FS is represented with single element ($p_c = 1$) in the particle string, however, each non-singleton FS requires three elements ($p_c = 3$), as stated in (iv) above.

vi. The heart of an FLS is its rulebase, where every fuzzy rule is represented by $(n+1)$ elements. The values of these elements can be integer numbers within $[-m_i, +m_i]$, where $i = 1, 2, ..., n+1$. The magnitude corresponds to the index of the FS in the respective input/output variable.

Minus sign (–) encodes the NOT operation on antecedent/consequent FS and '0' represents the missing antecedent FS. It is important to note that a fuzzy rule with no consequent part, i.e., '0' value, is not a valid rule. A fuzzy rule with four

Figure 3. UMF, LMF, Right T1, Left T1 FSs, and FOU in an IT2 FS

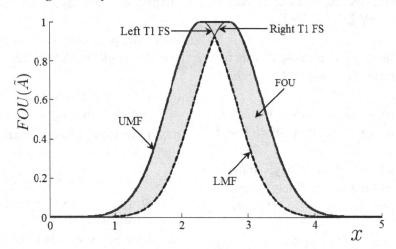

antecedents and single consequent, e.g., IF *input1* is not FS2 and *input2* is not FS3 and *input4* is FS4, THEN *output* is FS5, can be encoded with 5 digits as -2-3045. Maximum number of such possible rules are $\prod_{i=1}^{n} m_i$ and string length for encoding of complete rule base is $(n+1)\prod_{i=1}^{n} m_i$

In general, the total length the particle string for any FLS (Sugeno or Mamdani) may be determined by (30)

$$Particle\ Size = \prod_{i=1}^{n} p_a m_i + p_c m_{n+1} + (n+1)\prod_{i=1}^{M} m_i$$
(30)

where $\prod_{i=1}^{n} p_a m_i$, $p_c m_{n+1}$ and $(n+1)\prod_{i=1}^{M} m_i$ are segment sizes, in the particle string, used for encoding of antecedent, consequent FSs and rule base of the FLS, respectively. From simulations, it is experienced that smaller number of rules, than the maximum possible one, not only requires less computational time but helps in faster convergence also, provided that the rules are well framed and truly capture the entire knowledge of the system. The total particle string lengths for Sugeno (e.g., *IRIS Data Classifier*) and Mamdani (e.g., *Single-stage Mackey-Glass Time Series*

Forecaster) FLSs implemented by us with four antecedents, single consequent, and 20 rules are 165 and 175, respectively, as given by (30).

Encoding of IT2 FSs

An IT2 FS $\tilde{A}$ is represented with two T1 MFs, i.e., LMF and UMF, that bound the FOU (as shown in Figure 3). T1 FS mathematics is sufficient for implementing IT2 FLSs (Mendel et al., 2006), but IT2 FLSs are is computationally more complex than T1 FLSs.

Strategic planning for encoding and evolution of IT2 FLS using PSO is similar to the encoding scheme discussed above for T1 FLSs, except for the FS representation. Many papers (Liang and Mendel, 2000b, Mendel, 2000, 2001, Mendel et al., 2006, Mendez and Castillo, 2005) have described IT2 FLSs in terms of LMF and UMF. However, there are a few more approaches (including the one proposed by us) to represent FOU as discussed in the previous chapter. We suggest below how to use them in particle strings encoding.

Table 1. String lengths for FLSs with 4 inputs, 1 output & 20 rules

FS Types & Approaches	String Length for		
	Single FS	Singleton FLS	Non-singleton FLS
T1 FS	3	165	175
IT2 (LMF + UMF)	7	250	275
IT2 (Left T1 FS + Right T1 FS)	6	250	250
IT2 (Principal T1 FS + FOU)	4	190	200

LMF + UMF Approach

As LMF and UMF are T1 FSs, they can be encoded with the scheme discussed above, however, an additional element is required for LMF encoding as its peak value can be less than unity. Hence, an IT2 FS can be encoded using $p_a = 7$ (and $p_c = 7$) elements as follows:

UMF: S_1(support 1), S_2(support 2), S_3(shape)
LMF: S_4(support 1), S_5(support 2), S_6(shape), S_7(peak of LMF)
IT2 FS: $S_1 S_2 S_3 S_4 S_5 S_6 S_7$

The total length of the particle of an FLS, in which each non-singleton IT2 FS is expressed using LMF + UMF approach, is 275 as given by (30).

Left T1 FS + Right T1 FS Approach

The FOU in an IT2 FS can be approached using two extreme left and right T1 FSs. Hence, we can encode every IT2 FS using $p_a = 6$ (and $p_c = 6$) elements, one lesser compared to LMF + UMF approach as peak value in each LMF is unity, as follows:

Left T1 FS: S_1(support 1), S_2(support 2), S_3(shape)
Right T1 FS: S_4(support 1), S_5(support 2), S_6(shape)
IT2 FS: $S_1 S_2 S_3 S_4 S_5 S_6$

The total length of the particle, that encodes a non-singleton IT2 FSs using Left T1 FS + Right T1 FS approach, is 250 as given by (30).

Principal T1 FS + FOU Approach

FOU of an IT2 FS is proportional to the noise, i.e., uncertainty addition, in the system. In this last approach to represent an IT2 FS, the amount of uncertainty (FOU) about the principal MF is expressed directly. The FOU will require only one element in particle string if it is expressed as some percentage of UOD. Hence, we encode every IT2 FS using $p_a = 4$ (and $p_c = 4$) elements, as follows:

Principal T1 FS: S_1(support 1), S_2(support 2), S_3(shape)
FOU: S_4(FOU about principal MF)
IT2 FS: $S_1 S_2 S_3 S_4$

The total length of the particle, that encodes a non-singleton IT2 FSs using Principal T1 FS+ FOU approach, is the minimum among the cases of IT2 FLSs, i.e., 200 as per (30). Particle string lengths for various FLSs are summarized in Table 1. In each case, there are four input variables and one output variable, and number of rules in rule base are restricted to 20 only.

Particle String Validation

Usually, shapes of FSs and antecedent/consequent parts of fuzzy rules are represented as integer numbers, and UODs of input-output variables are limited and discretized into specific number of intervals. However, during the process of evolution, particle string elements may attain real-number values, values beyond respective UODs, or even violate some of constraints specified during the process of particle string encoding due to analog nature of PSO. Such particles with invalid strings are of no use and have to be validated before their fitness evaluation.

There are two approaches to handle particles with invalid strings: Firstly, do not validate them but assign minus infinity fitness value to such particles, and they will return soon into valid search-space as the process of evolution iterates. Secondly, validate them intentionally by (i) rounding-off element values to make them valid integer values, (ii) shift arbitrarily within respective UOD, and/or (iii) exchange the element values in case they do not match the constraints of being less/greater than their counterparts.

This process of validation may quite sometimes be disturbed during the optimization flow. However, as PSO itself is stochastic in nature and particles remember the best locations visited in the past, these disturbances do not create any problem.

Fitness Function

The particle representation encodes candidate solutions into strings, however, fitness function determines their rank within the swarm of particles. Finding a good fitness measurement function, that is problem-dependent, can make it easier for the PSO to evolve a useful system. Fitness function can have single-objective or multiple-objective function (Deb, 2001, Deb et al., 2002).

For prediction and estimation problems most suitable and commonly used fitness functions are either based on absolute error or relative error, discussed in the previous chapter. In classification problems, the number of misclassified classes and the number of correctly classified classes are used in the error function and, therefore, fitness functions.

PSO MODEL AND STRATEGY PARAMETERS

The fitness search-space is high nonlinear, multimodal, non-differentiable and deceptive in nature

due to its large number of independent parameters with different UODs. Finding a near optimal FLS design is always doubtful with gbest PSO model as it is highly prone to be trapped in local optima. On the other hand, lbest PSO model is capable of escaping from the local optima trap, however, it suffers from much slower rate of evolution. A new model, i.e., hbest PSO model, is proposed to be used that is blended with both capabilities of faster evolution rate and avoids pre-mature convergence.

Another important thing is to decide PSO strategy parameters, e.g., population size, constriction factor, acceleration parameters, and connection weight, etc., that govern the process of evolution. Following are typical recommendations, based on experimental studies (discussed in the chapter titled, "Nature-Inspired Toolbox to Design and Optimize Systems"), to plan PSO evolution for FLS designing:

- *hbest* PSO Model with Ring swarm topology
- Populations Size (P_{size}) = 30
- Neighborhood Size (N_{size}) = 3 (1 each side)
- Inertia Weight (w) = 0.5
- Maximum Velocity (V_{max}) = 1 (silent as Constriction Factor is used)
- Acceleration Parameters ($\phi_1 = \phi_2 = \phi_3$) = 2.1
- Constriction Factor (χ) = 0.729

APPLICATION: DESIGNING FUZZY LOGIC SYSTEMS FROM NOISY DATA

The application of designing FLSs for forecasting of time-series is taken up in this chapter. The most popular, Mackey-Glass time-series data sets, corrupted with various noise levels, are used for training and testing of designed FLSs. The framework presented above is used to evolve T1 FLSs, however, with less number of FLS features.

The uncertainties in a T1 FLS may arise from noisy training data and/or noisy measurements that activate the FLS (Liang and Mendel, 2000c, Mendel, 1999, 2001). It is now a well established notion that T2 FSs are capable of dealing with all such uncertainties as they are three-dimensional in nature (Liang et al., 2000, Liang and Mendel, 2000a,d, 2001). To contain the uncertainties present in the training data, T1 FLSs are then upgraded to IT2 FLSs.

MACKEY-GLASS TIME SERIES FORECASTING

Mackey-Glass chaotic time-series (Mackey and Glass, 1987) can be represented, mathematically, as

$$\frac{ds(t)}{dt} = \frac{0.2s(t-\tau)}{1+s^{10}(t-\tau)} - 0.1s(t) \qquad (31)$$

Such a system, with $\tau \leq 17$ exhibits deterministic/periodic behavior, however, it turns chaotic with $\tau > 17$. For our simulations of (31), we convert it to a discrete-time equation by using Euler's method (Quinney, 1985):

$$f(s,n) = \frac{0.2s(n-\tau)}{1+s^{10}(n-\tau)} - 0.1s(n) \qquad (32)$$

$$s(n+1) = s(n) + hf(s,n) \qquad (33)$$

where h is a small number and the initial values of $s(n) \ \forall n \leq \tau$ are set randomly.

The typical noise-less Mackey-Glass time-series data set, obtained using $h = 1$ and $\tau = 30$, is tabulated in Table 2 and shown, graphically, in Figure 4. The training data set of 200 points (solid line) are then used to evolve FLSs, how-

ever, test data set of next 200 points (dotted line) are used to evaluate them, after corruption with different noise levels of uniform noise.

Particle String Encoding of T1 FLS

After some preliminary experimental studies, we decided to evolve FLSs that will have only five FSs to express fuzzily every input/output variable and a small rulebase comprised of only ten fuzzy rules. Further, only the locations of the FSs (i.e., supports) and fuzzy rules (i.e., antecedent and consequent parts) are evolved, simultaneously, using *hbest* PSO. However, the shape of each FS, t-norm and t-conorm operators, and defuzzification methods are kept fixed as symmetrical-triangular, min, max, and centroid, respectively, and are not evolved.

Particle String Validation

Particle strings whose elements have attained invalid values, during the process of evolution, have to be validated before their fitness evaluations. During the process of string validation for FLSs, one must take care of the followings:

(i)   Supports of each FS have to be restricted within the UOD of respective input/output variable. So, if they cross the limits, they are truncated to the extreme values or shifted, arbitrarily, within the UOD.

(ii) String elements which represent first supports of the FSs have to have values smaller than those of the second supports, else their values may be swapped.

(iii) Each element, in string-segments meant for fuzzy rules, has to attain an integer value only (either positive or negative) as its magnitude represents the index number of the respective antecedent/consequent FS. In the process of optimization, the attained real values are, therefore, to be rounded-off to the nearest integers.

Table 2. Mackey-Glass time-series using $h = 1$ and $\tau = 30$

S. No.	Training Data Set					Test Data Set				
	1-40	41-80	81-120	121-160	161-200	201-240	241-280	281-320	320-360	361-400
1.	0.665	1.277	0.754	1.146	0.518	0.845	1.340	0.223	0.722	1.136
2.	0.663	1.222	0.810	1.171	0.484	0.829	1.341	0.220	0.779	1.101
3.	0.679	1.160	0.851	1.197	0.454	0.813	1.342	0.224	0.842	1.066
4.	0.714	1.095	0.881	1.221	0.428	0.797	1.345	0.237	0.902	1.028
5.	0.762	1.028	0.899	1.243	0.406	0.780	1.351	0.261	0.953	0.987
6.	0.819	0.962	0.909	1.263	0.388	0.762	1.359	0.298	0.989	0.942
7.	0.878	0.897	0.912	1.279	0.374	0.745	1.367	0.349	1.013	0.894
8.	0.934	0.834	0.908	1.291	0.364	0.728	1.369	0.415	1.027	0.843
9.	0.985	0.774	0.899	1.298	0.356	0.712	1.356	0.491	1.036	0.792
10.	1.030	0.718	0.885	1.301	0.350	0.700	1.328	0.575	1.044	0.741
11.	1.068	0.665	0.868	1.300	0.344	0.693	1.287	0.658	1.052	0.691
12.	1.102	0.618	0.848	1.295	0.336	0.694	1.241	0.737	1.063	0.644
13.	1.132	0.574	0.825	1.286	0.326	0.706	1.191	0.806	1.079	0.601
14.	1.160	0.535	0.802	1.274	0.314	0.730	1.142	0.863	1.099	0.560
15.	1.186	0.500	0.778	1.261	0.302	0.769	1.094	0.907	1.122	0.524
16.	1.211	0.467	0.753	1.246	0.292	0.819	1.047	0.939	1.149	0.491
17.	1.235	0.437	0.728	1.233	0.286	0.876	1.000	0.959	1.176	0.463
18.	1.255	0.408	0.703	1.223	0.287	0.933	0.952	0.970	1.202	0.438
19.	1.272	0.381	0.678	1.219	0.295	0.982	0.904	0.972	1.227	0.416
20.	1.283	0.356	0.654	1.224	0.316	1.019	0.855	0.967	1.247	0.397
21.	1.290	0.333	0.630	1.236	0.352	1.045	0.806	0.956	1.264	0.380
22.	1.293	0.313	0.607	1.255	0.405	1.063	0.757	0.941	1.275	0.363
23.	1.294	0.295	0.587	1.274	0.476	1.076	0.709	0.922	1.281	0.347
24.	1.297	0.279	0.571	1.283	0.558	1.086	0.662	0.900	1.283	0.330
25.	1.303	0.265	0.560	1.277	0.643	1.098	0.617	0.875	1.282	0.314
26.	1.313	0.252	0.559	1.256	0.723	1.111	0.574	0.850	1.277	0.299
27.	1.325	0.239	0.570	1.223	0.793	1.126	0.534	0.823	1.271	0.287
28.	1.337	0.228	0.596	1.181	0.849	1.145	0.497	0.796	1.265	0.279
29.	1.345	0.217	0.637	1.134	0.891	1.165	0.462	0.768	1.261	0.277
30.	1.348	0.208	0.693	1.083	0.921	1.187	0.430	0.740	1.262	0.281
31.	1.347	0.202	0.758	1.028	0.940	1.209	0.401	0.712	1.268	0.294
32.	1.343	0.202	0.824	0.972	0.950	1.230	0.374	0.685	1.280	0.314
33.	1.339	0.211	0.886	0.915	0.951	1.251	0.351	0.661	1.296	0.343
34.	1.339	0.233	0.940	0.857	0.947	1.270	0.329	0.639	1.309	0.383
35.	1.343	0.273	0.983	0.801	0.938	1.288	0.309	0.623	1.311	0.433
36.	1.351	0.334	1.018	0.746	0.925	1.303	0.291	0.613	1.298	0.495
37.	1.361	0.415	1.048	0.694	0.910	1.316	0.274	0.611	1.273	0.567
38.	1.363	0.508	1.074	0.645	0.894	1.326	0.258	0.620	1.240	0.645
39.	1.350	0.600	1.098	0.599	0.877	1.333	0.244	0.641	1.205	0.724
40.	1.321	0.684	1.122	0.557	0.861	1.337	0.232	0.675	1.170	0.796

Fitness Function

There are many suitable error-functions to describe fitness functions (discussed in the previous chapter) for the applications where input-output training data are available. In this case, for grading performance of each candidate solution during the process of evolution we treated the minimization of Root Mean Square Error or RMSE, in short, as single-objective fitness function. Mathematically,

$$E = \sqrt{\frac{1}{N} \sum_{i=1}^{N} (C_i - T_i)^2} \qquad (34)$$

Figure 4. Time-series data sets used for training (solid) and testing (dotted) of FLSs

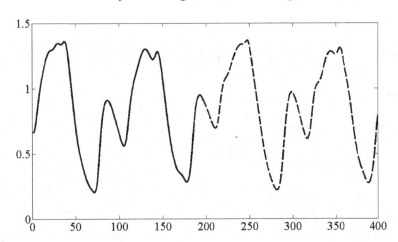

where C_i and T_i are the ith computed and target output values from total, N, training data points.

SIMULATION RESULTS

Evolved T1 FLSs

All four T1 FLSs, evolved from differently corrupted data sets (i.e., SNRs = 15dB, 20dB, 25dB, and 30dB), are tabulated in Table 3 along with their RMSE and MSE. These T1 FLSs are then upgraded to IT2 FLSs by adding FOU in each FS to study improvements. In an another analysis, depicted in Figure 5, we are spurred to fix FOU equal to 0.25 that seems to be the best performing FOU in all cases.

Up-Gradation to IT2 FLSs

For overall comparative evaluations, each set of FLSs (i.e., T1 and IT2 FLSs) is tested 50 times using test data (listed in Table 2) with different corruption levels, i.e., SNR = 15dB, 20dB, 25dB, and 30dB. The forecasted outputs of T1 FLSs (Red) and IT2 FLSs (Blue) are plotted, separately for each noise level, in Figures 6-9. It can be observed from these plots that the envelops of blue traces

are narrower and closer to the desired noise-less output than the red traces, indicating superiority of IT2 FLS over T1 FLS. The mean RMSE corresponding to multiple forecast runs (tabulated in Table 4) depict that all IT2 FSs, with FOU = 0.25, perform better than the respective T1 FLSs.

CONCLUSION

In this chapter, four T1 FLSs for forecasting of Mackey-Glass time-series are evolved, using *hbest* PSO algorithm, from the input-output training data corrupted with different noise levels, i.e., SNR = 15dB, 20dB, 25dB, and 30dB. To match the uncertainties added due to noise, each T1 FLS is upgraded to IT2 FLS by adding certain FOU in all FSs. It is observed from the simulation results that IT2 FLSs give marginally better forecasts even in the presence of noise than T1 FLSs. However, one can design even better FLSs, using this framework, if the process of evolution is made to run for a larger number of iterations with more number of FSs and fuzzy rules. Finally, this chapter concludes that IT2 FLSs, which can outperform T1 FLSs, can be designed/evolved easily using the framework presented in this chapter, even if the designer does not possess considerable domain expertise.

Table 3. Evolved T1 FLSs, with all Triangular FSs, from noisy data with SNR = 15dB, 20dB, 25dB, and 30dB

Variables	Names	FS Parameters (SNR = 15dB)	FS Parameters (SNR = 20dB)	FS Parameters (SNR = 25dB)	FS Parameters (SNR = 30dB)
Input1	mf1	[1.1 1.775 2.45]	[1.1, 1.86, 2.62]	[0.2, 1.6, 3]	[-0.16, 0.88, 1.92]
	mf2	[-0.23 1.3 2.83]	[1.05, 2.025, 3]	[0.05, 1.41, 2.77]	[1.07, 2.03, 2.99]
	mf3	[0.58 1.465 2.35]	[-1.13, 0.935, 3]	[-1.52, 0.485, 2.49]	[2.12, 2.19, 2.26]
	mf4	[0.11 1.555 3]	[1.19, 2.095, 3]	[2.44, 2.57, 2.7]	[-0.54, 1.23, 3]
	mf5	[-1.25 0.73 2.71]	[2.15, 2.575, 3]	[2.85, 2.925, 3]	[-0.46, -0.24, -0.02]
Input2	mf1	[-0.24 0.58 1.4]	[1.73, 2.005, 2.28]	[1.89, 2.445, 3]	[1.65, 2.195, 2.74]
	mf2	[1 1.92 2.84]	[-0.14, 0.52, 1.18]	[0.91, 1.6, 2.29]	[-1.2, 0.165, 1.53]
	mf3	[-0.15 1.325 2.8]	[0.09, 1.535, 2.98]	[0.79, 1.475, 2.16]	[1.07, 2.035, 3]
	mf4	[1.03 2.015 3]	[-0.51, 0.71, 1.93]	[0.41, 0.975, 1.54]	[-1.18, 0.91, 3]
	mf5	[0.39 1.66 2.93]	[-0.61, 0.865, 2.34]	[-0.63, 0.815, 2.26]	[0.11, 1.435, 2.76]
Input3	mf1	[0.25 0.765 1.28]	[1.63, 2.24, 2.85]	[2.28, 2.64, 3]	[1.76, 2.015, 2.27]
	mf2	[0.44 1.705 2.97]	[-0.55, 0.785, 2.12]	[-0.43, 1.285, 3]	[-0.51, -0.165, 0.18]
	mf3	[-0.62 0.6 1.82]	[0.33, 1.1, 1.87]	[0.03, 0.85, 1.67]	[-1.22, 0.89, 3]
	mf4	[-1.03 0.985 3]	[0.43, 1.715, 3]	[-0.79, 0.895, 2.58]	[-1.06, 0.52, 2.1]
	mf5	[0.1 1.55 3]	[-0.57, 0.785, 2.14]	[0.13, 1.565, 3]	[-0.78, 0.285, 1.35]
Input4	mf1	[1.31 2.155 3]	[-0.88, 0.18, 1.24]	[-1.4, -0.32, 0.76]	[1.45, 2.225, 3]
	mf2	[-0.97 0.31 1.59]	[0.39, 1.11, 1.83]	[-0.21, 1.01, 2.23]	[-1.26, 0.15, 1.56]
	mf3	[-1.26 0.87 3]	[1.23, 2.115, 3]	[2.51, 2.755, 3]	[0.25, 1.625, 3]
	mf4	[-0.78 0.505 1.79]	[-0.38, 0.58, 1.54]	[-0.03, 1.485, 3]	[-2, 0.045, 2.09]
	mf5	[1.2 2.1 3]	[0.08, 0.93, 1.78]	[-0.45, 0.455, 1.36]	[-1.6, 0.285, 2.17]
Output	mf1	[-0.62 0.6 1.82]	[0.33, 1.1, 1.87]	[0.03, 0.85, 1.67]	[-1.22, 0.89, 3]
	mf2	[-1.03 0.985 3]	[0.43, 1.715, 3]	[-0.79, 0.895, 2.58]	[-1.06, 0.52, 2.1]
	mf3	[0.1 1.55 3]	[-0.57, 0.785, 2.14]	[0.13, 1.565, 3]	[-0.78, 0.285, 1.35]
	mf4	[1.31 2.155 3]	[-0.88, 0.18, 1.24]	[-1.4, -0.32, 0.76]	[1.45, 2.225, 3]
	mf5	[-0.97 0.31 1.59]	[0.39, 1.11, 1.83]	[-0.21, 1.01, 2.23]	[-1.26, 0.15, 1.56]
Rulebase		5, 4, 5, 5, 5 5, 5, 4, 5, 5 4, 4, 4, 4, 5 4, 5, 5, 3, 4 5, 3, 4, 4, 5 5, 5, 5, 5, 5 5, 4, 5, 5, 4 4, 5, 5, 5, 4 3, 2, 4, 5, 5 4, 5, 5, 5, 4	3, 5, 5, 5, 5 5, 5, 5, 5, 4 5, 5, 5, 5, 3 4, 5, 5, 5, 3 5, 5, 4, 3, 5 3, 5, 5, 4, 4 5, 4, 5, 4, 5 2, 4, 5, 5, 5 3, 5, 4, 5, 5 3, 3, 4, 2, 2	3, 5, 5, 4, 3 5, 4, 5, 5, 4 5, 5, 5, 5, 3 5, 5, 5, 5, 5 5, 5, 4, 4, 4 3, 5, 4, 5, 4 3, 3, 5, 5, 5 3, 5, 3, 4, 5 5, 4, 5, 3, 5 5, 4, 5, 4, 5	4, 4, 4, 4, 3 5, 5, 3, 5, 5 3, 4, 4, 5, 2 5, 5, 3, 5, 3 4, 5, 3, 3, 4 5, 2, 3, 5, 5 5, 5, 5, 2, 3 4, 4, 5, 5, 5 5, 4, 5, 5, 5 5, 5, 5, 3, 5
RMSE		0.21968	0.14684	0.09655	0.05737
MSE		0.04826	0.02156	0.00932	0.00329

Figure 5. FOU vs. comparative mean performance for 50 Monte-Carlo runs

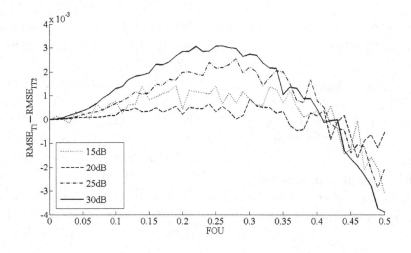

Figure 6. Performance with SNR = 15dB (red: T1 & blue: IT2 FLSs)

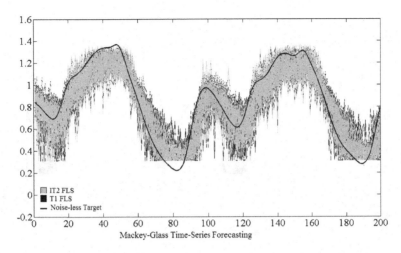

Figure 7. Performance with SNR = 20dB (red: T1 & blue: IT2 FLSs)

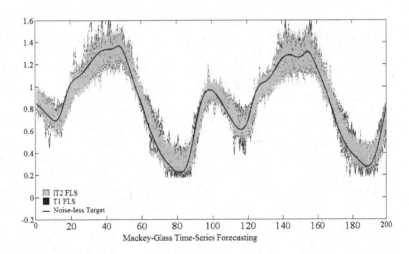

Figure 8. Performance with SNR = 25dB (red: T1 & blue: IT2 FLSs)

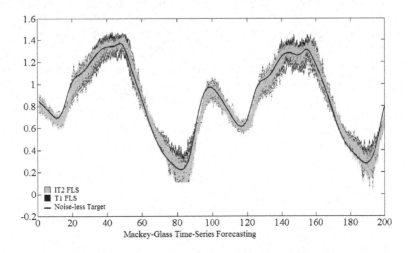

Figure 9. Performance with SNR = 30dB (red: T1 & blue: IT2 FLSs)

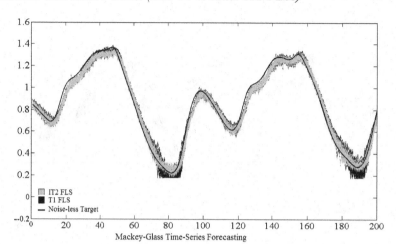

Table 4. Performance T1 vs. IT2 FLSs for 20 Monte-Carlo simulations

S. No.	15dB		20dB		25dB		30dB	
	T1 FLS	IT2 FLS	T1 FLS	T1 FLS	T1 FLS	IT2 FLS	T1 FLS	IT2 FLS
1	0.24131	0.24028	0.14163	0.14110	0.09260	0.09040	0.06041	0.05713
2	0.24285	0.24170	0.13922	0.13913	0.09310	0.09070	0.05946	0.05632
3	0.24058	0.23993	0.13732	0.13708	0.09510	0.09240	0.05951	0.05626
4	0.23661	0.23525	0.14002	0.13982	0.09520	0.09320	0.06035	0.05724
5	0.23815	0.23720	0.13996	0.13945	0.09360	0.09140	0.05949	0.05707
6	0.23672	0.23586	0.13865	0.13829	0.09220	0.09030	0.06018	0.05725
7	0.23984	0.23969	0.13797	0.13794	0.09340	0.09110	0.06061	0.05726
8	0.23861	0.23750	0.13760	0.13742	0.09430	0.09200	0.06060	0.05764
9	0.23758	0.23672	0.13901	0.13894	0.09280	0.09070	0.05866	0.05596
10	0.23965	0.23825	0.13875	0.13871	0.09270	0.09020	0.05937	0.05628
11	0.24043	0.23821	0.13704	0.13647	0.09270	0.09050	0.06108	0.05820
12	0.23553	0.23474	0.13552	0.13550	0.09260	0.09030	0.06073	0.05768
13	0.23430	0.23320	0.13768	0.13755	0.09290	0.09080	0.05968	0.05686
14	0.23858	0.23798	0.13772	0.13711	0.09330	0.09080	0.05920	0.05621
15	0.23543	0.23484	0.13831	0.13766	0.09330	0.09130	0.05924	0.05629
16	0.23950	0.23905	0.13824	0.13786	0.09350	0.09170	0.06029	0.05725
17	0.23687	0.23557	0.13923	0.13894	0.09270	0.09000	0.05990	0.05719
18	0.23520	0.23449	0.14013	0.13999	0.09240	0.09010	0.05924	0.05631
19	0.23824	0.23601	0.13926	0.13884	0.09270	0.09020	0.06053	0.05766
20	0.23683	0.23663	0.13882	0.13857	0.09380	0.09120	0.05968	0.05708
Mean RMSE	0.23814	0.23716	0.13860	0.13832	0.09324	0.09096	0.05991	0.05696
Improved	0.00098		0.00028		0.00228		0.00295	

REFERENCES

Deb, K. (2001). *Multi-objective optimization using evolutionary algorithms*. New York, NY: John Wiley & Sons, Inc.

Deb, K., Pratap, A., Agarwal, S., & Meyarivan, T. (2002). A fast and elitist multiobjective genetic algorithm: NSGA-II. *IEEE Transactions on Evolutionary Computation*, *6*(2), 182–197. doi:10.1109/4235.996017

Dubois, D., & Prade, H. (1980). *Fuzzy sets and systems: Theory and applications*. New York, NY: Academic Press.

Eberhart, R., & Kennedy, J. (1995). A new optimizer using particle swarm theory. In *Proceedings of the Sixth International Symposium on Micro Machine and Human Science*, (pp. 39-43).

Karnik, N. N., & Mendel, J. M. (2001a). Centroid of a type-2 fuzzy set. *Information Sciences*, *132*(6), 195–220. doi:10.1016/S0020-0255(01)00069-X

Karnik, N. N., & Mendel, J. M. (2001b). Operations on type-2 fuzzy sets. *International Journal on Fuzzy Sets & Systems*, *122*, 327–348. doi:10.1016/S0165-0114(00)00079-8

Karnik, N. N., Mendel, J. M., & Qilian, L. (1999). Type-2 fuzzy logic systems. *IEEE Transactions on Fuzzy Systems*, *7*(6), 643–658. doi:10.1109/91.811231

Kennedy, J., & Eberhart, R. (1995). Particle swarm optimization. In *Proceedings of International Conference on Neural Networks (ICNN'95)*, Vol. 4, (pp. 1942-1948). Perth, Australia.

Khosla, A., Kumar, S., & Aggarwal, K. K. (2005). A framework for identification of fuzzy models through particle swarm optimization algorithm. In *Proceedings of IEEE Indicon 2005 Conference*, Chennai, India.

Liang, Q., Karnik, N. N., & Mendel, J. M. (2000). Connection admission control in ATM networks using survey-based type-2 fuzzy logic systems. *IEEE Transactions on Man, Cybernetics Part C. Applications and Reviews*, *30*, 329–339.

Liang, Q., & Mendel, J. M. (2000a). Equalization of nonlinear time-varying channels using type-2 fuzzy adaptive filters. *IEEE Transactions on Fuzzy Systems*, *8*, 551–563. doi:10.1109/91.873578

Liang, Q., & Mendel, J. M. (2000b). Interval type-2 fuzzy logic systems. In *Proceeding of FUZZ IEEE'00*, San Antonio, TX.

Liang, Q., & Mendel, J. M. (2000c). Interval type-2 fuzzy logic systems: Theory and design. *IEEE Transactions on Fuzzy Systems*, *8*(5), 535–550. doi:10.1109/91.873577

Liang, Q., & Mendel, J. M. (2000d). Overcoming time-varying co-channel interference using type-2 fuzzy adaptive filter. *IEEE Transactions on Circuits and Systems-II: Analog and Digital Signal Processing*, *47*(12), 1419–1428. doi:10.1109/82.899635

Liang, Q., & Mendel, J. M. (2001). MPEG VBR video traffic modeling and classification using fuzzy techniques. *IEEE Transactions on Fuzzy Systems*, *9*(1), 183–193. doi:10.1109/91.917124

Mackey, M. C., & Glass, L. (1987). Oscillation and chaos in physiological control systems. *Science*, *197*, 287–289. doi:10.1126/science.267326

Mendel, J. M. (1999). Computing with words, when words can mean different things to different people. In *Proceedings of Third International ICSC Symposium on Fuzzy Logic and Applications*, Rochester University, Rochester, NY.

Mendel, J. M. (2000). Uncertainty, fuzzy logic, and signal processing. *Signal Processing*, *80*(6), 913–933. doi:10.1016/S0165-1684(00)00011-6

Mendel, J. M. (2001). *Uncertain rule-based fuzzy logic systems: Introduction and new directions.* Upper Saddle River, NJ: Prentice-Hall.

Mendel, J. M. (2007). Computing with words and its relationships with fuzzistics. *Information Science, 177*(4), 988–1006. doi:10.1016/j.ins.2006.06.008

Mendel, J. M., John, R. I., & Liu, F. (2006). Interval type-2 fuzzy logic systems made simple. *IEEE Transactions on Fuzzy Systems, 14*(6), 808–821. doi:10.1109/TFUZZ.2006.879986

Mendez, G., & Castillo, O. (2005). Interval type-2 TSK fuzzy logic systems using hybrid learning algorithm. In *Proceeding of IEEE FUZZ Conference*, (pp. 230-235). Reno, NV.

Mizumoto, M., & Tanaka, K. (1976). Some properties of fuzzy sets of type-2. *Information and Control, 31*, 312–340. doi:10.1016/S0019-9958(76)80011-3

Quinney, D. (1985). *An introduction to the numerical solution of differential equation.* Hertforshire, UK: Research Studies.

Saini, J. S., Gopal, M., & Mittal, A. P. (2004). Evolving optimal fuzzy logic controllers by genetic algorithms. *Journal of the Institution of Electronics and Telecommunication Engineers, 50*(3), 179–190.

Shi, Y., Eberhart, R., & Chen, Y. (1999). Implementation of evolutionary fuzzy systems. *IEEE Transactions on Fuzzy Systems, 7*(5), 109–119. doi:10.1109/91.755393

Zadeh, L. A. (1975). The concept of a linguistic variable and its application to approximate reasoning. *Information Sciences, 8*, 199–249. doi:10.1016/0020-0255(75)90036-5

Chapter 14
Neural Network Based Classifier Ensembles:
A Comparative Analysis

B. Verma
Central Queensland University, Australia

ABSTRACT

This chapter presents the state of the art in classifier ensembles and their comparative performance analysis. The main aim and focus of this chapter is to present and compare the author's recently developed neural network based classifier ensembles. The three types of neural classifier ensembles are considered and discussed. The first type is a classifier ensemble that uses a neural network for all its base classifiers. The second type is a classifier ensemble that uses a neural network as one of the classifiers among many of its base classifiers. The third and final type is a classifier ensemble that uses a neural network as a fusion classifier. The chapter reviews recent neural network based ensemble classifiers and compares their performances with other machine learning based classifier ensembles such as bagging, boosting, and rotation forest. The comparison is conducted on selected benchmark datasets from UCI machine learning repository.

INTRODUCTION

Classifier ensembles, also known as fusion of classifiers, hybrid systems, mixture of experts, multiple classifier systems, combination of multiple classifiers and committee of classifiers, are approaches which train multiple classifiers and fuse their decisions to produce the final decision. The recent research results show that classifier ensembles can produce better classification accuracy than an individual classifier and they can be powerful tools for solving many real world problems.

The history of first classifier ensemble dates back to 1979 (Polikar, 2006) although in early days it was not called a classifier ensemble. According to a review paper (Polikar, 2006), Dasarathy and Sheela (1979) proposed a system that used two or more classifiers. The history of first neural network based classifier ensemble dates back to

DOI: 10.4018/978-1-4666-1833-6.ch014

1990. Hansen and Salamon (1990) showed that the generalization performance of a neural network can be improved using an ensemble of similarly configured neural networks.

The research in classifier ensembles have significantly grown in the past two decades and many classifier ensemble techniques have been applied to solve a number of real world problems (Aviden, 2007, Ma et al., 2007, Wei et al., 2010, Takemura et al., 2010, Su et al., 2009, Silva, 2010, and Kuncheva, et al., 2010) particularly by computational intelligence research community. Many new classifier ensembles have been proposed and some promising results have been published in the literature. Windeatt (2006) proposed and investigated a Multilayer Perceptron based classifier ensemble. A new measure is described that can predict the number of training epochs for achieving optimal performance in an ensemble of MLP classifiers. The measure is computed between pairs of patterns on the training data and it is based on a spectral representation of a boolean function. This representation characterizes the mapping from classifier decisions to target label and allows accuracy and diversity to be incorporated within a single measure. Rodriguez et al. (2006) proposed a classifier ensemble based on rotation forest. The base classifiers are trained by randomly splitting feature data into K subsets and principal component analysis is applied to each subset. They compared the results with other existing ensembles and showed a significant improvement in accuracy. Maclin et al. (1995) proposed a neural network based ensemble classifier where different network weights are used to initialise the base neural network's learning process in order to diversify the base classifiers. Yamaguchi et al. (2009) proposed an ensemble approach which used neural networks with different initial weights to classify land surface images obtained from the sensors. The approach achieved better generalisation in comparison to other existing approaches.

Wiering and van Hasselt (2008) investigated several ensemble approaches that combine multiple reinforcement learning algorithms in a single agent. They wanted to enhance learning speed and final performance by combining the chosen actions or action probabilities of different reinforcement learning algorithms. Liu and Yao (1999) presented a new cooperative ensemble learning system for designing neural network ensembles. The idea was to encourage different individual networks in an ensemble to learn different parts or aspects of a training data so that the ensemble can learn the whole training data better. The individual networks are trained simultaneously rather than independently or sequentially. It can create negatively correlated neural networks using a correlation penalty term in the error function. Islam et al. (2008) proposed two cooperative ensemble learning algorithms. The proposed algorithms use the negative correlation learning algorithm and train different neural networks in an ensemble. Bagging and boosting algorithms are used in NegBagg and NegBoost, respectively, to create different training sets for different neural networks in the ensemble. Parikh and Polikar (2007) introduced an ensemble of classifiers based on incremental learning for data fusion. Their approach sequentially generates an ensemble of classifiers that specifically seek the most discriminating information from each data set. They observed and documented that their approach for data fusion consistently outperforms a similarly configured ensemble classifier trained on any of the individual data sources across several applications.

Hernandez-Lobáto et al. (2009) proposed statistical instance-based pruning in ensembles of independent classifiers. They argue that it is possible to estimate with a given confidence level the prediction of the complete ensemble by querying only a subset of classifiers. They have conducted a number of experiments and shown that their instance-based ensemble pruning method is very effective. Muhlbaier et al. (2009) proposed a new approach for combining ensemble of classifiers with dynamically weighted consult-and-vote for efficient incremental learning of new classes. They introduced a novel voting mechanism which works as follows: individual classifiers consult with each other to determine which ones are most qualified to classify a given instance, and decide how much weight, if any, each classifier's decision should carry. They presented a number of experiments on benchmark datasets and showed that their new algorithm performs quite well in comparison to other methods. Topchy et al. (2005) extended work on clustering ensembles and demonstrated the efficacy of combining partitions generated by weak clustering algorithms that use data projections and random data splits. The results on several benchmark datasets demonstrated the effectiveness of their approach. Chen et al. (2009) proposed a new approach based on a generalized adaptive ensemble generation and aggregation for multiple classifier systems. In their approach, base classifiers are generated by fitting the validation data globally with different degrees. They have tested their approach on benchmark datasets and claim that it outperforms other methods in terms of average accuracy. Garcia-Pedrajas (2009) has constructed an ensemble by using means of weighted instance selection. An instance selection was used for obtaining a subset of the instances available for training capable of achieving at least the same performance as the whole training set. The experiments showed that the approach is able to produce better and simpler ensembles than random subspace for NN and standard ensemble for C4.5 and SVMs. Verma and Rahman (2011) proposed a neural based ensemble "cluster oriented ensemble classifier" and showed the impact of multi-cluster characterisation on ensemble classifier learning. Their approach has achieved improved accuracy on benchmark datasets. Researchers (Aviden, 2007, Ma et al., 2007, Wei et al., 2010, Takemura et al., 2010, Su et al., 2009, Silva, 2010, and Kuncheva, et al., 2010) have applied ensemble classifiers to many real world applications such as visual tracking, spoken language recognition, cancer classification, face recognition and text classification and reported improved accuracies.

A comparison of various ensemble methods has also been reported in (Polikar, 2006, Dietterich, 2000a, Dietterich, 2000b Bauer & Kohavi, 1999, and Quinlan, 1996).

As it can be seen from the literature review presented above that many classifier ensembles have been proposed and evaluated on benchmark datasets, however it is hard to say which ensemble is the best. This chapter presents and compares three types of recently developed neural network based classifier ensembles with some well-known ensembles on five benchmark datasets. The comparative analysis provides a fair evaluation and helps in finding which classifier ensemble is the best.

The remainder of this chapter consists of 4 sections. Section 2 "Classifier Ensembles" describes three neural network based classifier ensembles and three other classifier ensembles used for comparison in this chapter. Section 3 "Experimental Datasets and Parameters" describes the UCI benchmark datasets and parameters used for experiments and analysis in this chapter. A comparative analysis of obtained results on 5 UCI benchmark datasets is presented in Section 4 "Experimental Performances and Analysis". Finally, Section 5 "Conclusions" concludes the chapter.

CLASSIFIER ENSEMBLES

Neural Network Based Classifier Ensembles

Neural networks have been very attractive and powerful classifiers for application in many real world problems because of their generalisation abilities. However, it is well known to neural network community that neural network classifiers with even similar accuracy on training data may have different accuracy on test data (generalisation). This is the main reason why neural network researchers turned to ensembles which means combining various neural network classifiers.

The classifier ensemble may or may not improve the accuracy but it certainly minimises the risk of selecting a poor classifier. There are many ways a neural network can be incorporated into classifier ensembles. Some of the most common approaches are described below. The first way (see Figure 1) is to have a classifier ensemble that uses a neural network for all its base classifiers. Second way (see Figure 2) is to have a classifier ensemble that uses a neural network as one of the classifiers among many of its base classifiers. Third and final way (see Figure 3) is to have a classifier ensemble that uses a neural network as a fusion classifier.

Classifier Ensemble-All Neural Classifiers (CE-ANC)

A classifier ensemble with all its base classifier as a neural network based classifier is shown in Figure 1.

This type of classifier ensembles have been presented and investigated in the literature. An ensemble using Multilayer Perceptrons is described in Windeatt (2006). A slight modified version using layer wise clustering and atomic and non-atomic cluster based philosophy, has been investigated recently by our research group. In such ensembles,

the training data set is clustered in N separate layers. At each layer, the data is segmented into K clusters based on clustering parameters and a cluster analyser identifies atomic and non–atomic clusters. A neural network is trained on patterns from non–atomic clusters and class number is memorised for atomic clusters. During the testing, a test pattern is passed through a clustering algorithm and cluster for the test pattern is identified at each layer. If the selected cluster is atomic the memorised class is recorded. If the cluster is non-atomic then the test pattern is fed to the corresponding neural network and the output is recorded. Once the output from all the N layers is received then the final decision is obtained by using the majority voting.

Classifier Ensemble-One Neural Classifier (CE-ONC)

A classifier ensemble with only one neural network as a base classifier is shown in Figure 2.

In such classifier ensembles, three individual classifiers are trained with the training data and the decision is fused with majority voting or some other fusion methods. A modified version of such ensemble classifier by incorporating clustering has

Figure 1. Classifier ensemble with all neural network classifiers

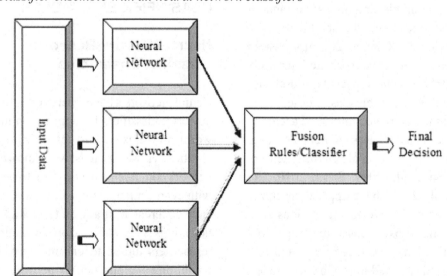

Figure 2. Classifier ensemble with one neural network classifier

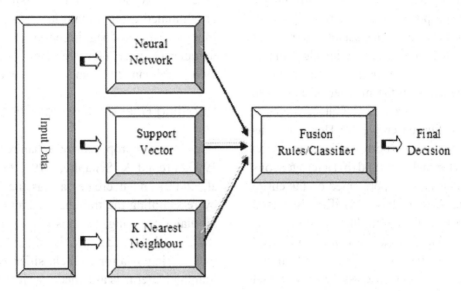

Figure 3. Classifier ensemble with a neural network as a fusion classifier

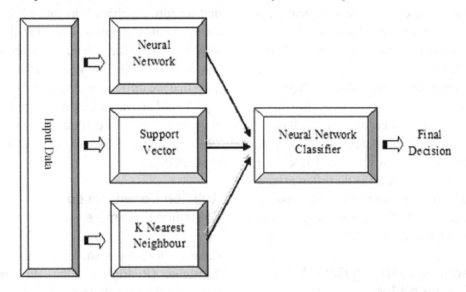

been discussed in Verma & Rahman (2011). A fusion method "majority voting" can be replaced by a neural network and such classifier ensemble is presented and discussed in the following section.

Classifier Ensemble- Neural Fusion Classifier (CE-NFC)

The classifier ensemble with a neural network based fusion has been shown in Figure 3. A slightly modified version of this classifier ensemble with a clustering approach "Cluster Oriented Ensemble Classifier" is described in Verma & Rahman (2011). In this ensemble, the learning process starts by partitioning the training data into multiple clusters. The purpose of the clustering algorithm is to partition the training dataset into a number of clusters. The output of the clustering algorithm is the modified data set. The output of the clustering algorithm depends on the number of classes in the training data so two types of clustering have been used in this ensemble (a) Homogeneous clustering: clustering is performed separately on training data for each class and (b) Heterogeneous clustering: clustering is performed on the entire training data. A set of base classifiers is trained with new clustered data as produced by the clustering algorithm. The confidence matrices produced by the base classifiers are combined to form the input to the neural fusion classifier. The target matrix is composed of class confidence vectors that are set according to the proportion of class instances within the cluster. The parameters for fusion classifier are optimized to fit input-output pattern produced by the training examples. At the completion of training, a model for the ensemble classifier is obtained. During testing, a test pattern is presented to each of the base classifiers. Each base classifier produces different confidence values that indicate the possibility of the pattern belonging to the different clusters. The cluster confidence vectors produced by the different base classifiers are combined to produce the input to the fusion classifier. The fusion classifier produces the class confidence values.

Other Machine Learning Based Classifier Ensembles

Bagging Based Classifier Ensemble

Bagging (bootstrap aggregating) is a simple ensemble technique and it was first introduced by Breiman (Polikar 2006, Breiman, 1998, Breiman, 1996, Breiman, 2001, and Fumera et al., 2008). In bagging, subsets of training data are randomly created from the entire training data. Each subset is used to train a different classifier of the same type. The decision of trained classifiers is fused or combined using a majority voting approach. Many variations of bagging ensembles exist in the literature (Polikar 2006, Breiman, 1998, Breiman, 1996, Breiman, 2001, and Fumera et al., 2008).

Boosting Based Classifier Ensemble

Boosting was proposed by Schapire (Schapire, 1990, Freund & Schapire, 1997, Friedman et al., 2000) and it creates a classifier ensemble by re-sampling the training data and combined by majority voting. In boosting, re-sampling is strategically geared to provide the most informative training data for each classifier. Each of the training patterns is assigned a weight that determines how well the pattern was classified in the previous iteration. A subset of the training data that is badly classified is included in the training set for the next iteration. This way the different base classifier errors are made uncorrelated. The subsets in boosting not necessarily contain patterns that are difficult to classify when combined together. Many variations of boosting ensembles exist in the literature [Polikar 2006, Schapire, 1990, Freund & Schapire, 1997 and Friedman et al., 2000).

Rotation Forest Based Classifier Ensemble

Rotation forest ensemble was introduced by Rodrıguez (Rodrıguez, 2006). In rotation forest ensemble, classifiers are generated based on feature data subsets and analysis. The base classifiers are trained by randomly splitting feature data into K subsets and principal component analysis is applied to each subset. All principal components are retained in order to preserve the variability information in the data. Thus, K axis rotations take place to form the new features for a base classifier. The idea of the rotation approach is to have both accuracy and diversity within the classifier ensemble. Diversity is obtained through the feature extraction for each base classifier and decision trees are used because they are sensitive to rotation of the feature axes. A detailed description of rotation forest can be found in Rodrıguez, (2006).

EXPERIMENTAL DATASETS AND PARAMETERS

The benchmark datasets for this research are obtained from UCI machine learning repository. The datasets have already been processed and available as training and test datasets. The performance of classifier ensembles are evaluated using test datasets. The training and test datasets such as Iris, Segment, Wisconsin breast cancer, Pima-diabetes and Vehicle are selected and used in this chapter. The main criteria for selecting these datasets were (a) diverse parameters such as small number of patterns, inputs and outputs as well as large number of patterns, inputs and outputs (b) availability of results in published papers.

Experimental Performances and Analysis

Neural network based classifier ensembles were evaluated and compared with other ensembles and two individual classifiers on 5 benchmark datasets. The datasets were randomly selected and the main intention was to have diverse range of parameters and availability of results. The parameters such as inputs, outputs and total number of patterns are described in Table 1. The accuracies for each ensemble were taken from recent literature except the accuracies of neural fusion based classifier ensemble. The experiments for neural fusion ensembles were conducted recently by our research group and have not been published yet. The accuracies of each classifier ensemble and each individual classifier have been averaged for 5 datasets and the average is shown

for comparison. A full performance comparison is shown in Table 2.

As seen in Table 2, the classifier ensemble with all neural network based classifiers has achieved the highest average accuracy on 5 datasets. It should be noted that this classifier ensemble incorporates multi-clustering characteristics idea introduced in Verma & Rahman (2011) which is major reason for improvement in accuracy. The second best ensemble classifier is bagging and the third best is rotation forest based classifier ensemble from Rodrıguez, (2006). We have also included the results of two individual classifiers such as support vector machine (SVM) and neural network (NN) to make a point that no matter which classifier ensemble is considered, it is always better than an individual classifier.

CONCLUSION

We have presented three types of neural network based classifier ensembles and compared them with bagging, boosting, and rotation forest classifier ensembles. We have also compared the results of classifier ensembles with two well-known individual classifiers used in classifier ensembles discussed in this chapter. The accuracies on 5 benchmark datasets from machine learning repository have been considered for comparison. The experimental accuracies and analysis presented in this chapter show that the classifier ensemble

Table 1. Datasets from UCI repository for comparative analysis

Dataset	#Patterns	#Inputs	#Outputs
Iris	150	4	3
Segment	2310	19	7
Breast Cancer	699	9	2
Diabetes	768	8	2
Vehicle	946	18	4

Table 2. Performance comparison of neural ensembles on 5 UCI repository datasets

Classifier Ensemble	Accuracy on Iris dataset (%)	Accuracy on Segment dataset (%)	Accuracy on Breast cancer dataset (%)	Accuracy on Pima-diabetes dataset	Accuracy on Vehicle dataset (%)	Average accuracy (%)
CE-ANC (Windeatt, 2006)	95.2	95.4	96.5	75.7	76.5	88.784
CE-ANC (Our Experiments)	96.93	97.80	97.50	72.71	83.60	89.708
CE-ONC (Verma & Rahman, 2011)	95.33	96.36	97.61	70.46	70.86	86.124
CE-NFC (Verma & Rahman, 2011)	96	95.97	97.72	71.08	71.77	86.508
Bagging (Rodrıguez, 2006)	94.67	97.49	95.99	75.65	74.45	87.650
Bagging (Our Experiments)	96	96.88	96.12	72.45	85.14	89.318
Boosting (Rodrıguez, 2006)	94.27	98.14	96.06	71.96	75.78	87.242
Boosting (Our Experiments)	96	96.58	95.80	71.71	83.17	88.652
Rotation Forest (Rodrıguez, 2006)	95.73	98.05	97.04	76.48	78.05	89.070
SVM (Verma & Rahman, 2011)	94.67	93.33	92.02	71.74	70.15	84.382
NN (Verma & Rahman, 2011)	96	95.46	95.09	68.62	72.26	85.486

which consists of all neural classifier with clustering is the best. It has achieved slightly better average accuracy than the bagging ensemble which is the second best. The rotation forest ensemble was the third best. Finally, we can conclude that no matter which classifier ensemble is used, it is always better than an individual classifier and a classifier ensemble with all its base classifiers using a neural network performs better than bagging, boosting and rotation forest.

REFERENCES

Aviden, S. (2007). Ensemble tracking. *IEEE Transactions on Pattern Analysis and Machine Intelligence*, *29*(2), 261–271. doi:10.1109/TPAMI.2007.35

Bauer, E., & Kohavi, R. (1999). An empirical comparison of voting classification algorithms: Bagging, boosting and variants. *Machine Learning*, *36*(2), 105–142. doi:10.1023/A:1007515423169

Breiman, L. (1996). Bagging predictors. *Machine Learning*, *24*(2), 123–140. doi:10.1007/BF00058655

Breiman, L. (1998). Arcing classifiers. *Annals of Statistics*, *26*(3), 801–849.

Breiman, L. (2001). Random forests. *Machine Learning*, *45*(1), 5–32. doi:10.1023/A:1010933404324

Chen, L., & Kamel, M. S. (2009). A generalized adaptive ensemble generation and aggregation approach for multiple classifier systems. *Pattern Recognition*, *42*(5), 629–644. doi:10.1016/j.patcog.2008.09.003

Dasarathy, B. V., & Sheela, B. V. (1979). Composite classifier system design: Concepts and methodology. *Proceedings of the IEEE, 67*(5), 708–713. doi:10.1109/PROC.1979.11321

Dietterich, T. G. (2000a). Ensemble methods in machine learning. In J. Kitler & F. Roli (Eds.), *1st International Workshop on Multiple Classifier Systems, Lecture Notes in Computer Science, 1857,* (pp. 1–15).

Dietterich, T. G. (2000b). Experimental comparison of three methods for constructing ensembles of decision trees: Bagging, boosting, and randomization. *Machine Learning, 40*(2), 139–157. doi:10.1023/A:1007607513941

Freund, Y., & Schapire, R. E. (1997). A decision-theoretic generalization of on-line learning and an application to boosting. *Journal of Computer and System Sciences, 55*(1), 119–139. doi:10.1006/jcss.1997.1504

Friedman, J., Hastie, T., & Tibshirani, R. (2000). Additive logistic regression: A statistical view of boosting. *Annals of Statistics, 28*(2), 337–374. doi:10.1214/aos/1016218223

Fumera, G., Roli, F., & Serrau, A. (2008). A theoretical analysis of bagging as a linear combination of classifiers. *IEEE Transactions on Pattern Analysis and Machine Intelligence, 30*(7), 1293–1299. doi:10.1109/TPAMI.2008.30

Garcia-Pedrajas, N. (2009). Constructing ensembles of classifiers by means of weighted instance selection. *IEEE Transactions on Neural Networks, 20*(2), 258–277. doi:10.1109/TNN.2008.2005496

Hansen, L. K., & Salamon, P. (1990). Neural network ensembles. *IEEE Transactions on Pattern Analysis and Machine Intelligence, 12*(10), 993–1001. doi:10.1109/34.58871

Hernandez-Lobáto, D., Martinez-Muñoz, G., & Suárez, A. (2009). Statistical instance-based pruning in ensembles of independent classifiers. *IEEE Transactions on Pattern Analysis and Machine Intelligence, 31*(2), 364–369. doi:10.1109/TPAMI.2008.204

Islam, M. M., Yao, X., Shahriar, S. M., Islam, M. A., & Murase, K. (2008). Bagging and boosting negatively correlated neural networks. *IEEE Transactions on Systems, Man, and Cybernetics. Part B, 38*(3), 771–784.

Jacobs, R. A., Jordan, M. I., Nowlan, S. J., & Hinton, G. E. (1991). Adaptive mixtures of local experts. *Neural Computation, 3,* 79–87. doi:10.1162/neco.1991.3.1.79

Kuncheva, L. I., Rodríguez, J. J., Plumpton, C. O., Linden, D. E. J., & Johnston, S. J. (2010). Random subspace ensembles for fMRI classification. *IEEE Transactions on Medical Imaging, 29*(2), 531–542. doi:10.1109/TMI.2009.2037756

Kuncheva, L. I., & Whitaker, C. J. (2003). Measures of diversity in classifier ensembles and their relationship with the ensemble accuracy. *Machine Learning, 51*(3), 181–207. doi:10.1023/A:1022859003006

Liu, Y., & Yao, X. (1999). Simultaneous training of negatively correlated neural networks in an ensemble. *IEEE Transactions on Systems, Man, and Cybernetics. Part B, 29*(6), 716–725.

Ma, B., Li, H., & Tong, R. (2007). Spoken language recognition using ensemble classifiers. *IEEE Transactions on Audio, Speech, and Language Processing, 15*(7), 2053–2062. doi:10.1109/TASL.2007.902861

Maclin, R., & Shavlik, J. W. (1995). Combining the predictions of multiple classifiers: Using competitive learning to initialize neural networks. *International Joint Conference on Artificial Intelligence,* (pp. 524–531).

Muhlbaier, M. D., Topalis, A., & Polikar, R. (2009). Learn++. NC: Combining ensemble of classifiers with dynamically weighted consult-and-vote for efficient incremental learning of new classes. *IEEE Transactions on Neural Networks, 20*(1), 152–168. doi:10.1109/TNN.2008.2008326

Parikh, D., & Polikar, R. (2007). An ensemble-based incremental learning approach to data fusion. *IEEE Transactions on Systems, Man, and Cybernetics. Part B, 37*(2), 437–450.

Polikar, R. (2006). Ensemble based systems in decision making. *IEEE Circuits and Systems Magazine, 6*(3), 22–44. doi:10.1109/MCAS.2006.1688199

Quinlan, J. R. (1996). Bagging, boosting and C4.5. *13th International Conference on Artificial Intelligence*, (pp. 725–730).

Rodriguez, J. J. (2006). Rotation forest: A new classifier ensemble method. *IEEE Transactions on Pattern Analysis and Machine Intelligence, 28*(10), 1619–1630. doi:10.1109/TPAMI.2006.211

Schapire, R. E. (1990). The strength of weak learnability. *Machine Learning, 5*(2), 197–227. doi:10.1007/BF00116037

Silva, C., Lotrič, U., Ribeiro, B., & Dobnikar, A. (2010). Distributed text classification with an ensemble kernel-based learning approach. *IEEE Transactions on Systems, Man and Cybernetics. Part C, Applications and Reviews, 40*(3), 287–297. doi:10.1109/TSMCC.2009.2038280

Su, Y., Shan, S., Chen, X., & Gao, W. (2009). Hierarchical ensemble of global and local classifiers for face recognition. *IEEE Transactions on Image Processing, 18*(8), 1885–1896. doi:10.1109/TIP.2009.2021737

Takemura, A., Shimizu, A., & Hamamoto, K. (2010). Discrimination of breast tumors in ultrasonic images using and ensemble classifier based on the adaboost algorithm with feature selection. *IEEE Transactions on Medical Imaging, 29*(3), 598–609. doi:10.1109/TMI.2009.2022630

Topchy, A., Jain, A. K., & Punch, W. (2005). Clustering ensembles: models of consensus and weak partitions. *IEEE Transactions on Pattern Analysis and Machine Intelligence, 27*(12), 1866–1881. doi:10.1109/TPAMI.2005.237

Verma, B., & Rahman, A. (2011). Cluster oriented ensemble classifier: Impact of multi-cluster characterisation on ensemble classifier learning. *IEEE Transactions on Knowledge and Data Engineering, 24*(4).

Wei, J., Wang, S., & Yuan, X. (2010). Ensemble rough hypercuboid approach for classifying cancers. *IEEE Transactions on Knowledge and Data Engineering, 22*(3), 381–391. doi:10.1109/TKDE.2009.114

Wiering, M. A., & Hasselt, H. (2008). Ensemble algorithms in reinforcement learning, *IEEE Transactions on Systems, Man, and Cybernetics. Part B, 38*(4), 930–936.

Windeatt, T. (2006). Accuracy/diversity and ensemble MLP classifier design. *IEEE Transactions on Neural Networks, 17*(5), 1194–1211. doi:10.1109/TNN.2006.875979

Yamaguchi, T., Mackin, K. J., Nunohiro, E., Park, J. G., Hara, K., & Matsushita, K. (2009). Artificial neural network ensemble-based land-cover classifiers using MODIS data. *Artificial Life and Robotics, 13*(2), 570–574. doi:10.1007/s10015-008-0615-4

KEY TERMS AND DEFINITIONS

Bagging: Generation of a classifier ensemble in which subsets of training data are randomly created from the entire training data and each subset is used to train a different classifier of the same type. The decision of trained classifiers is fused using a majority voting approach.

Boosting: Generation of a classifier ensemble by re-sampling the training data and combining the decisions using majority voting.

Classifier Ensembles: A combination of multiple classifiers by training them and fusing their decisions to produce the final decision.

Neural Fusion: A fusion technique that uses a neural network for combining outputs of multiple classifiers.

Rotation Forest: Generation of a classifier ensemble by training the base classifiers using randomly splitting feature data into K subsets and principal component analysis is applied to each subset.

Chapter 15

Development of an Intelligent Neural Model to Predict and Analyze the VOC Removal Pattern in a Photocatalytic Reactor

Jagannathan Krishnan
Universti Teknologi MARA, Malaysia

Eldon Raj Rene
University of La Coruña,, Spain

Artem Lenskiy
University of Ulsan, South Korea

Tyagarajan Swaminathan
Indian Institute of Technology Madras, India

ABSTRACT

Volatile organic compounds (VOCs) belong to a new class of air pollutant that causes significant effect on human health and environment. Photocatalytic oxidation is an innovative, highly efficient, and promising option to decontaminate air polluted with VOCs, at faster elimination rates. This study pertains to the application of artificial neural networks to model the removal dynamics of an annular type photoreactor for gas – phase VOC removal. Relevant literature pertaining to the experimental work has been reported in this chapter. The different steps involved in developing a suitable neural model have been outlined by considering the influence of internal network parameters on the model architecture. Anew, the neural network modeling results were also subjected to sensitivity analysis in order to identify the most influential parameter affecting the VOC removal process in the photoreactor.

DOI: 10.4018/978-1-4666-1833-6.ch015

INTRODUCTION

The rapid growth of small – medium – large scale polluting industries and the arising trend in urbanization has led to large scale emission of both point and non – point source air pollutants, particularly in developing countries. Besides, the increasing development of synthetic chemicals, particularly the petrochemicals, a new class of air pollutants, called the volatile organic compounds (VOCs) have become a matter of concern in recent years. The Clean Air Act of 1990 (CAA – 90), proposed by the United States Environmental Protection Agency (US – EPA), classifies the different organic and inorganic chemical species present in the atmosphere, that are likely to cause significant effect on human health and the environment, based on their inherent toxicity and physico – chemical properties. VOCs can be defined as "any compound of carbon, excluding CO, CO_2, carbonic acid, metallic carbides or carbonates, which participates in atmospheric photochemical reactions" (Nunez, 1998). According to the US – EPA website, VOCs are emitted as gases from certain solids or liquids that are usually chemicals, some of which might pose short – and long – term adverse health effects. The US – EPA further clarifies that the concentrations of many VOCs are consistently higher indoors ($\times$10) than outdoors. Some typical examples are as follows: paints and lacquers, paint strippers, cleaning supplies, pesticides, building materials and furnishings, emissions from fine chemical, pharmaceutical and petroleum related industries.

Toluene is a VOC, most commonly used as a raw material for the synthesis of compounds such as tri-nitro toluene (TNT), chloroamine-T, saccharin and many dyestuffs (Rene et al., 2005). Toluene has shown to cause serious adverse human health effects. Even at low concentrations, toluene has been found to be carcinogenic, cause damage to the liver and kidney and paralyze the central nervous system (Martin et al., 1998). In human studies, the uptake of gas – phase toluene

has been estimated by different authors to be 40-60% of the total amount inhaled (WHO, 1993). The results of some studies suggests that low levels of toluene exposure ($3.75\ mg/m^3$) may have behavioural effects (Horiguchi and Inoue, 1977), electroencephalogram (EEG) changes and sleep rhythm in mice (Takeuchi and Hisanaga, 1977). The widespread use of toluene in various industrial operations, its high vapour pressure (28.6 mmHg at 25 °C) and high polarity characterized by its water solubility (0.53 g/l at 25 °C) warrants their removal before its emission into the natural environment (Spicer et al., 2002).

PHOTOREACTOR FOR VOC REMOVAL AND WORKING MECHANISM

Among the different techniques, chemical and – or biological, used for the removal of gas – phase VOCs, photocatalytic oxidation process can be considered as ''an innovative and promising technology to completely oxidize high concentrations of VOCs to harmless end – products such as H_2O and CO_2, at ambient temperatures''. Titanium dioxide (TiO_2) irradiating with UV or near UV light, results in the formation of 'electron – hole pairs' on the catalyst surface. These electrons and holes interact with the adsorbed species producing highly reactive hydroxyl radicals, which in turn initiate redox reactions to decompose VOCs. In some cases, it has been proved that the activity of TiO_2 could be greatly enhanced by modifying the catalyst properties. Zuo et al. (2006) gave sufficient information on the benefits of modifying a photocatalyst, as; (i) inhibiting electron–hole recombination by increasing the charge separation, (ii) increasing the wavelength response range, and (iii) changing the selectivity or yield of a particular product.

According to Wang and Ray (2000), the application of photo oxidation technique for gas – phase VOC removal is more appealing due to the following reasons: (i) lower UV absorption by air than water; (ii) higher mobility of dissociated species which prevents the reverse process of recombination of the radicals; (iii) higher UV –absorbance of the organics in the gas – phase compared to that in the liquid phase, (iv) presence of excess oxygen in the gas – phase promotes oxidation by producing reactive species such as ozone, and (v) the absence of scavengers such as bicarbonate and carbonate ions.

Photoreactors of various configurations have been developed; however, annular fixed-bed reactors with TiO_2 coated on the surface of reactor wall (Figure 1) is the most commonly employed photoreactor for their ease of construction and operation.

Ku et al. (2005) studied the removal of gas – phase acetone by a combined UV/TiO_2 process using an annular type reactor, operated in continuous mode, at inlet acetone concentrations varying between 80 to 350 ppmv. It was reported that, the conversion of acetone to carbon dioxide (an innocuous end – product during decomposition experiments) depended on three major factors,

viz., the UV light intensity applied, the gas – retention time (9 to 81.3 min), and when experiments were conducted below relative humidity values of 20%. Zuo et al. (2006) studied the photolytic and photocatalytic reactions of two aromatics and four chlorohydrocarbons under the same irradiation intensity of germicidal lamp, and by using a modified TiO_2 (commercially available in the market as Degussa P25) catalyst coating. Among the organics, benzene elimination was only 25% during the 2 h irradiation, and 40% of gas – phase benzene was converted to carbon dioxide. In comparison, toluene, the other organic compound used in that study, mineralized faster, reaching more than 90% removal in 2 h, and with about 16% mineralization to carbon dioxide. It was later presumed that, the better removal of toluene in gas – phase was due to the presence of a methyl group (- CH_3) in toluene that enhanced the reactivity of that molecule and for the fact that the methyl group was easily destroyed through photocatalytic oxidation than the aromatic cycle. Momani (2007) investigated the decomposition of gas – phase toluene by UV, ozone/UV, $TiO_2/$

Figure 1. Schematic of the photoreactor used for VOC removal

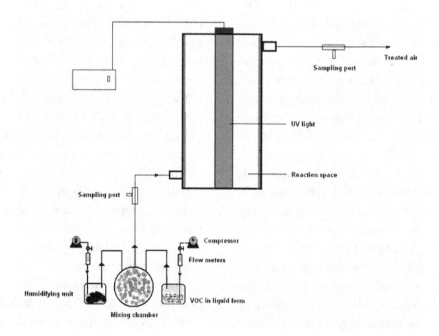

UV, and ozone/TiO_2/UV, and compared the removal efficiency of each of these systems. Experiments were performed in the concentration range of 2 to 20 ppmv, at different humidity conditions, and at a gas – flow rate of 2 ml/min in an annular type photoreactor. The authors reported that, 100% toluene conversion for the combined ozone/TiO_2/UV process, and 70% removal for the UV process. Besides, the ozone/ UV process was found to be affected more by the relative humidity values, with higher performance at a relative humidity value of 50%.

More details concerning the experimental and process details involved in the preparation and coating of various photo-catalysts, a comparison of different photocatalytic reactors, their advantages and limitations, the different kinetic experiments performed in photoreactors, novel methods for measuring kinetic parameters, a summary of different kinetic models used to describe the behaviour of photoreactors, reaction pathways of a wide variety of industrial chemicals, and the different intermediates generated by PCO are collectively, yet systematically described in a recent review article on photocatalytic purification of volatile organic compounds in indoor air (Mo et al., 2009).

BACKGROUND TO ARTIFICIAL NEURAL NETWORKS (ANNS)

Conventional kinetic and phenomenological modeling of photocatalytic reactors are based on several complex physico – chemical factors, interactions amongst factors, reactor type, coating thickness, hydrophilic or hydrophobic nature of the gas – phase pollutant, properties of the catalyst, amongst others. In a recent report, it was assumed that the gas – phase concentrations over the catalyst surface are uniform throughout the system and same as the gas – phase of the airflow in the bulk, which may be a very rough assumption if the boundary layer diffusion is the rate limiting factor (Zhong et al., 2010). Knowledge driven

models can easily explain the underlying phenomenon of the system, with a prior knowledge of its sensitive parameters. However, the accurate measurement of these sensitive variables in a photoreactor, operating at any industrial scale, involves elaborate experimentation that is not only complex, but also difficult to determine. Recently, several mathematical and empirical models have been proposed by researchers, some of them however fail to predict the data of other researchers as they were originally developed / validated with the experimental data from a particular photocatalytic reactor.

The impetus of employing ANNs to model dynamic systems is due to their advantages over other non – linear modeling paradigms. A typical heterogeneous photocatalytic process can have characteristics including non – linearity, which render conventional mathematical models difficult to predict the performance. Moreover, changing reactor kinetics, along with other factors such as catalyst thickness, type and properties of catalyst used and the composition of pollutants (individual or as mixtures) can strongly affect the performance characteristics of any photocatalytic reactor, which makes some of the conventional photocatalytic reactor models difficult to predict. Thus there exist good prospects to model a photocatalytic process using ANNs, due to their process complexity, dynamic behaviour and persistence of uncertainty due to changing pollutant loads and process parameters.

Biological Background

The inspiration and quest for computing with artificial neural networks (ANNs) came from studies on the structure and functioning of the brain and nerve systems as well as the biological mechanisms of learning and responding. Neural networks take their name from the simple processors in the brain, called neurons, which are interconnected by a network that transmits signals between them. The major components of a biological neuron are shown in Figure 2. It consists of dendrites, soma, axon and synapses. Dendrites are the receptive zones which constitute the major part of the input surface of the neuron, and the axon is the transmission (output) line. Synapses are elementary structural and functional units that connect the axon of one neuron to various parts of other neurons. When the input signals (nerve impulse) come into these synapses, it results in local changes in the input potential in the cell body of receiving neurons. These potentials are spread through the main body of the cell, and are weighted since some are stronger than others. The ability of the nervous system to adjust to signals is a mechanism of learning, and the rate of firing an output (response) is altered by the activity in the nervous system. In a similar way, ANNs possess characteristics which are common with the biological system - they consist of numerous simple processing elements (neurons) joined together by variable strength connections (synaptic weights) to form a massively parallel and highly interconnected information processing system (Simpson,

1990). This gives ANNs several characteristics which are appealing and proven for the modeling and control of non-linear systems (Cybenko, 1989; Hornik et al., 1989).

Typical Applications of Neural Models: Waste-Gas Treatment Processes and Other Familiar Applications

It is noteworthy to highlight that, the fundamental concepts of ANNs to model waste-gas treatment systems was initiated only recently, in the mid 2000's, when a continuously operated biotrickling filter and biofilter were modelled for their removal performance to handle BTX and hydrogen sulphide vapours (Rene et al., 2006; Elias et al., 2006). Rene et al. (2006) investigated the removal of benzene, toluene and xylene (collectively called as BTX) in a lab-scale biotrickling filter inoculated with well-acclimated mixed culture, and modelled the removal performance using neural networks. The authors developed two models, using inlet

Figure 2. A typical biological neuron

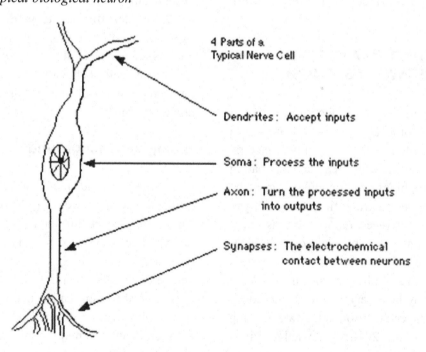

BTX concentration, inlet loading rate, gas-flow rate, and pressure drop information to obtain prior information on the outlet concentrations, removal efficiency and pollutant elimination capacity in the biotrickling filter. Regard the effect of network parameters, the following observations were made by the authors; (i) increasing the number of neurons in the hidden layer and the learning rate decreased the model predictability (high error between he model predictions and the experimental observations), and (ii) increasing the training count and momentum term from high to low values increased the model predictions, thus yielding high correlation coefficient values. Elias et al. (2006) operated a lab-scale biofilter, packed with pig manure and saw dust, to treat hydrogen sulphide vapours. The raw data consisting of start-up, intermittent fluctuation, steady-state and shut-down information was pre-processed and divided into training and test sets using cluster analysis in combination with a genetic algorithm. The authors used inlet H_2S concentration and unit flow values (Q/V, h^{-1}) as the input to the ANN model, for predicting the removal efficiency of the biofilter (RE, %). The best multi layer perceptron (MLP) was decided by trial and error, by testing nearly 10,000 different combinations of MLPs, and it was observed that a 2-2-1 network architecture was able to predict the RE well, with relatively high correlation coefficient values (0.92). Results from sensitivity analysis showed that flow rate affected the biofilter performance more strongly than inlet H_2S concentrations, and these findings were similar to the actual experimental data collected from the biofilter during 3 years of continuous operation. In a recent biofiltration work, Rene et al. (2009) modelled the performance of a biofilter (RE, %) using a back propagation algorithm for a reactor inoculated with a mixed culture taken from the wastewater sludge of a petrochemical refinery and treating gas-phase styrene. A log-sigmoid transfer function was used with inlet styrene concentration and unit flow as the inputs, and the best network topology obtained through trial and error was

found to be 2-4-1. Sensitivity analysis, in terms of absolute average sensitivity (AAS) was carried out for the developed model, to estimate the most influencing input parameter for the model, and it was observed that these values were 0.5250 and 0.4249 for unit flow and inlet styrene concentration, respectively. This higher AAS values for unit flow reported by the authors suggested that the biofilter performance highly depended on the gas-flow rate, and that the effects due to the pollutant, gas-phase styrene, was only minimal. Ravi et al. (2010) operated a compost biofilter for 9 months at different gas-flow rates (0.024-0.144 m^3h^{-1}), with dichloromethane (DCM) concentrations varying between 0.05 to 1.1 gm^{-3}. The authors divided the data points into training (75%) and testing (25%) sets, before formulating a 2-4-1 network topology using inlet DCM concentration and gas-flow rate as the input variables for the ANN model. The authors used a trial-and error approach to identify the best values of different network parameters, and found that a training count of 9000, with learning rate and momentum term values of 0.1, and 0.9 were able to map the behaviour of the biofilter with high correlations (R^2=0.944).

Prior to their recent applications to waste-gas (environmental) systems, ANNs have also been widely studied and successfully employed in diverse applications, such as pattern recognition (Gatts et al., 2005), fault detection (Sharma et al., 2004), weather forecasting (Ramirez et al., 2005), natural language interpretation (Selman, 1989) and image analysis (Nattkemper, 2004). In addition to this, ANNs have also been widely used for prediction (Sozen et al., 2005), and forecasting purposes (Kulkarni and Haidar, 2009). The prevalence of the MLP is due to its multi-dimensional nonlinear approximation abilities. It has been proved that, given sufficient hidden layer nodes, a MLP incorporating one hidden layer can approximate any continuous non-linear function to a higher degree of accuracy.

FEED-FORWARD NEURAL NETWORKS

A feed forward MLP consists of two – or more layers of processing elements which are linked by weighted connections. Neural networks can be thought of as "black box" devices that accept inputs and produces the desired outputs. A typical architecture of a three layered ANN, assuming to have four input and two output parameters, is shown in Figure 3. It consists of; (a) *Input Layer*: that receives information from external sources, and passes this information to the network for processing. (b) *Hidden Layer*: that receives information from the input layer and processes them in a hidden way (c) *Output Layer*: that receives processed information and signals of the desired output and (d) *Bias term*: that acts on a neuron like an offset. The function of the bias is to provide a threshold for the activation of neurons. The bias input is connected to each of the hidden and output neurons in a network.

A predictor based on MLP offers few advantages: instead of computing distances between an input vector and all features from the training set, the MLP learns to transform training vectors into matrices of interlayer weight coefficients. The total number of coefficients is usually substantially less than the number of training samples. As a consequence fast computation can be achieved with less memory consumption.

The training process consists in turning coefficients of interlayer W^{Hi} and output W^{O} matrices, and correspondent bias vectors b^{Hi} and b^{O}. It has been proved that three layers feed forward neural networks are capable of approximating any smooth transform with multiple inputs and outputs. In the case of two layers neural network with linear action function in output neurons (Figure 3), the decision function can be written as follows:

$$y_l = \sum_{i=0}^{N3} w_{l,i}^{(3)} f \left(\sum_{j=0}^{N2} w_{i,j}^{(2)} f \left(\sum_{k=0}^{N1} w_{j,k}^{(1)} x_k \right) \right) \quad (1)$$

where, x is an input vector corresponding to the time – series samples, and f is a sigmoid function. The following hyperbolic sigmoid function is commonly used:

Figure 3. Schematic of a three-layered perceptron

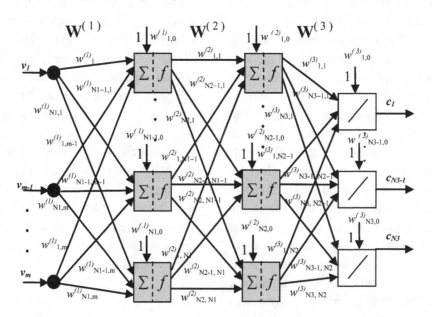

$$f(x) = \frac{2}{\left(1 + e^{-2 \cdot x}\right)} - 1 \qquad (2)$$

The training set contains pairs of input x and known target vectors t. The number of network inputs corresponds to the length a running window and the number of outputs is equal to the number of predicted samples.

The goal of the learning procedure is to find weights W that minimize the following criterion obtained by substituting (3) into (1), given as follows;

$$\varepsilon(w) =$$
$$\sum_{m=1}^{M}\left(\sum_{i=0}^{N3}w_{l,i}^{(3)}f\left(\sum_{j=0}^{N2}w_{i,j}^{(2)}f\left(\sum_{k=0}^{N1}w_{j,k}^{(1)}x_k\right)\right) - t_m\right)^2 \to min \qquad (3)$$

The most popular method for learning in multilayer networks is called the Back-propagation. The idea of the learning algorithm is the repeated application of the chain rule which allows finding how much each of the weights contributes to the network error (Rumelhart et al., 1986):

$$\frac{\partial \varepsilon}{\partial w_{i,j}} = \frac{\partial \varepsilon}{\partial f_i}\frac{\partial f_i}{\partial u_i}\frac{\partial u_i}{\partial w_{i,j}}, \qquad (4)$$

Then, the calculated errors modify each weight in order to minimize the error (Maier and Dandy, 1998):

$$w_{i,j}(t+1) = w_{i,j}(t) - \mu\frac{\partial \varepsilon}{\partial w_{i,j}}(t). \qquad (5)$$

The ordinary "gradient decent" by back propagation is slow and often ends far from the optimal solution. To improve the quality of minimum search a number of modifications have been proposed. One is called RPROP, or 'resilient propagation' (Riedmiller and Braun, 1993). The idea behind this algorithm is to introduce for each weight its individual update-value $\Delta_{i,j}$ which determines the size of the weight-update. Every time the partial derivative of the corresponding weight $w_{i,j}$ changes its sign, which indicates that the last update was too big and the algorithm has jumped over a local minimum, the update-value $\Delta_{i,j}$ is decreased by the factor $\mu-$. If the derivative retains its sign, $\Delta_{i,j}$ is slightly increased in order to accelerate convergence in shallow regions. After all update-values are adapted, neural weights are adjusted as follows:

$$\Delta w_{i,j}(t) = \begin{cases} -\Delta_{i,j}(t) & if\ \dfrac{\partial \varepsilon}{\partial w_{i,j}}(t) > 0 \\ +\Delta_{i,j}(t) & if\ \dfrac{\partial \varepsilon}{\partial w_{i,j}}(t) < 0, \\ 0 & else \end{cases} \qquad (6)$$

$$w_{i,j}(t+1) = w_{i,j}(t) - \Delta w_{i,j}(t). \qquad (7)$$

Probably, the most successful and widely used learning algorithm is the Levenberg – Marquardt algorithm (Levenberg, 1944; Marquardt, 1963). The Quasi – Newton methods are considered to be more efficient than gradient decent methods, but their storage and computational requirements go up as the square of the size of the network. Levenberg – Marquardt algorithm (LMA) is taking advantages of both Gauss–Newton algorithm and the method of gradient descent.

If the error function is simply written as;

$$\varepsilon(w) = \sum_{m=1}^{M}\left(e_m(w)\right)^2 \qquad (8)$$

and,

$$e_m(w) = y_i(w) - t_i \qquad (9)$$

Thus by using the following notation:

$$e(w) = \begin{bmatrix} e_1(w) \\ e_2(w) \\ \cdots \\ e_M(w) \end{bmatrix},$$

$$J(w) = \begin{vmatrix} \dfrac{\partial e_1}{\partial w_1} & \dfrac{\partial e_1}{\partial w_2} & \cdots & \dfrac{\partial e_1}{\partial w_n} \\ \dfrac{\partial e_2}{\partial w_1} & \dfrac{\partial e_2}{\partial w_2} & \cdots & \dfrac{\partial e_2}{\partial w_n} \\ \cdots & \cdots & \cdots & \cdots \\ \dfrac{\partial e_M}{\partial w_1} & \dfrac{\partial e_M}{\partial w_2} & \cdots & \dfrac{\partial e_M}{\partial w_n} \end{vmatrix} \qquad (10)$$

Gradient vector and Hessian approximation can be defined as;

$$g(w) = \left[J(w) \right]^T e(w), \qquad (11)$$

$$G(w) = \left[J(w) \right]^T J(w) + R(w), \qquad (12)$$

where, $R(w)$ contains Hessian components of higher order derivatives.

The main idea of the LMA consists in approximating $R(w)$ with regularized parameter $v_k I$, so that Hessian can be approximated as;

$$G(w_k) = [J(w_k)]^T J(w_k) + v_k I. \qquad (13)$$

Then, at the beginning of learning procedure, when w_k is far from the optimal solution, v_k is substantially higher than Eigen values of

$[J(w_k)]^T J(w_k)$. In this situation the Hessian matrix is replaced with:

$$G(w_k) = v_k I, \qquad (14)$$

The minimization direction is chosen using the method of gradient descent, given by:

$$p_k = -\frac{g(w_k)}{v_k}. \qquad (15)$$

One of the advantages of the LMA is that it usually converges in less number of iterations than when resilient propagation is used.

NEURAL MODELING PROCEDURE

The modeling methodology adopted in this study, *i.e.,* to model the performance of the photoreactor for gas – phase toluene removal is illustrated in Figure 4 (modified from Kulkarni and Haidar, 2009). It consists of the following sequence of steps;

Step 1: Choosing the Activation Function

The activation function denoted by $f(\chi)$, defines the output of a neuron in terms of the induced local field χ. The most commonly used activation function, the hyperbolic sigmoid function (Equation 2) or the logistic sigmoid function used in this study, takes the form as shown in Equation 16.

$$f(x) = \frac{1}{1 - e^{-x}} \qquad (16)$$

Figure 4. Steps involved in ANN model development (after Kulkarni and Haidar, 2009)

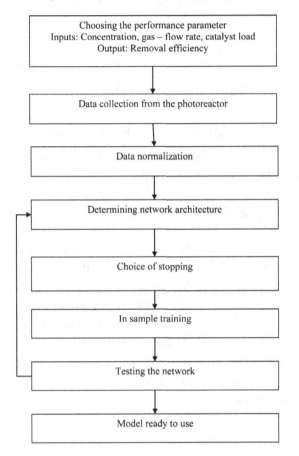

Step 2: Choosing the Appropriate Training Algorithm

The standard back propagation neural network (BPNN) developed by Rumelhart et al. (1986) was used. It is considered as the most popular method of optimizing the connection weights during network training. The software used for developing the neural model in this study is the shareware version of the ANN software NNMODEL, which limits itself to the back propagation algorithm.

Step 3: Data Pre-Processing and Randomization

The experimental data was randomized to obtain a spatial distribution of the data. Besides, the data was also scaled to the range of 0 to 1 using Equation 17, so as to suit the transfer function in the hidden (sigmoid) and output layer (linear).

$$\hat{X} = \frac{X - X_{min}}{X_{max} - X_{min}} \tag{17}$$

where, $\hat{X}$ is the normalized value, X_{min} and X_{max} are the minimum and maximum values of X, respectively.

Step 4: Data Division

The experimental data, consisting of results from 20 experimental sets, was divided into training and testing sets. 75% of the data points were used for training the network, whereas the remaining 25% was used for testing the developed neural based models.

Step 5: Network Training and Testing

The network was operated in two distinct phases called training and testing. During training, a set of (training) data was repeatedly presented to the ANN, which processes each data vector according to its architecture and adjusts its weights, and in some cases also adjusts some processing element parameters according to a training rule. The purpose of the training rule was to adapt the network weights so that the network processes the batch of training data to achieve some specified result, which is usually the minimization of some objective function of the training data.

This transfer function produces output in the range of 0–1 and introduces certain amount of non – linearity into the output.

Step 6: Internal Parameters of the Network

The internal network parameters such as number of neurons in the hidden layer (N_H), training count (T_c), learning rate (η) and momentum term (μ) should also be varied and optimized, in order to obtain smooth convergence and a good network topology. The minimum number of neurons (nodes) in the hidden layer can be equal to or greater than the number of inputs to the network. However the optimum number of neurons is generally estimated by trial and error. If the learning rate is too low (say 0.01), the network learns the pattern very slowly. On the contrary, too high learning rate (0.99) makes the weights and objective function diverge, so there is no learning at all. The amount of a particular weight connection changed is proportional to the learning rate, η which in turn affects the size of steps taken in weight space (Maier and Dandy, 1998). If η is too small, the algorithm will take a long time to converge and conversely, if η is too large, the network would go through large oscillations during training and never converge. The momentum term μ accelerates the convergence of the error during the learning process and is the most popular extension of the back propagation algorithm. This term simply adds a fraction to the previous weight update to the current one and is often related to the learning rate. High η and μ values can rush convergence towards a local minimum with huge steps, whereas small η values with high μ can lead to divergent behaviour during training (Maier and Dandy, 1998 and 2001).

Step 7: Error Index

The coefficient of determination (R^2) between the experimental and predicted values was used as an error – estimating index to evaluate the accuracy of the developed ANN model (Equation 18). The network configuration yielding the best value of

R^2, in the testing data was then chosen as the best / optimal setting of the network topology.

$$R^2 = \frac{\sum (x - \bar{x})(y - \bar{y})}{\sqrt{\sum (x - \bar{x})^2 \sum (y - \bar{y})^2}} \qquad (18)$$

where, x and y are the sample data of experimental and predicted values; $\bar{x}$ and $\bar{y}$ are the means of the samples respectively.

Step 8: Sensitivity Analysis

Sensitivity analysis, as absolute average sensitivity (AAS), was calculated by summing the changes in the output variables caused by moving the input variables by a small amount over the entire training set. The different sensitivity indices described by Zurada et al. (1994), for a specific training pattern (P) can be given as follows;

The mean square average sensitivity $S_{ki,avg}$ is defined as;

$$S_{ki,avg} = \sqrt{\frac{\sum_{P=1}^{P} [S_{ki}^{(P)}]^2}{P}} \qquad (19)$$

The absolute value average sensitivity matrix $S_{ki,abs}$ is defined as;

$$S_{ki,abs} = \sum_{P=1}^{P} \frac{\left| S_{ki}^{(P)} \right|}{P} \qquad (20)$$

where, $S_{ki}^{(p)}$ is the sensitivity of a trained output O_k and P is the number of training patterns.

PHOTO OXIDATION EXPERIMENTS: GAS-PHASE TOLUENE REMOVAL

Photoreactor Configuration

The annular photoreactor, as shown earlier in Figure 1, consisted of a cylindrical tube, 3.7 cm inner diameter and 43 cm long, coated on the inner surface with titanium dioxide (TiO_2). The UV irradiation was provided by a 15 Watt tubular UV lamp, 2.6 cm in diameter and 43.5 cm long, mounted centrally in the reactor using the light fitting end caps, giving an effective annular volume of 234 ml. The UV lamp emitted predominantly at 254 nm and its intensity measured by Lutran digital radiometer was found to be 7 μ Einstein/m^2s.

Catalyst Coating

The TiO_2 catalyst was coated on the inner surface of the tubular reactor by introducing 10 ml of ultra – sonicated slurry containing 20% TiO_2 (weight basis), closing both the ends and rotating the tube through a specially designed rotary mechanism, maintained at 10 rpm. Hot air blown through the end caps facilitated uniform drying. After 10 minutes, the coated TiO_2 film was calcined in an oven for 8 h, at 200 °C.

Photoreactor Operation

Gas – phase toluene vapor was generted by passing air through mini diaphragm pumps into troughs containing toluene (in liquid form). The vapour thus generated was passed into a mixing chamber, where another larger humidified stream, generated independently by passing air through a trough containing water, enters to produce a well mixed humidified gas – phase toluene stream. The inlet gaseous stream was passed through the reactor without illumination till an equilibrium adsorption is attained. After ensuring steady state, the lamp was turned on and gaseous samples from the inlet and outlet sampling port were analyzed at regular intervals. All the experiments were carried out at ambient temperatures (28±2°C) and at a relative humidity of 55%.

The performance of the photoreactor was evaluated in terms of its removal efficiency which is the fraction of gas – phase toluene removed by the system, as mentioned in Equation 20.

$$\text{Removal efficiency} = \frac{(C_i - C_o)}{C_i} \times 100 \quad (21)$$

where, C_i and C_o, are the inlet and outlet toluene concentrations, respectively.

Photoreactor Performance Results for Gas – Phase Toluene Removal

Experiments in continuous gas – phase were conducted under the following conditions; catalyst load: 5 to 20 g/m^2, inlet toluene concentration: 0.2 to 6 g/m^3, and gas – flow rate: 0.2 to 1 l/min. The removal efficiency (RE) of toluene was ascertained to be in the range of 15.7% to 99.7%. The RE was affected strongly, antagonistically and synergistically, by the changes in toluene concentration compared to changes in catalyst load and gas – flow rate. The RE of toluene increased directly with an increase in the catalyst load, while the RE decreased with an increase in toluene concentration, as well as gas – flow rate. The increase in RE due to increasing catalyst loading rate can be attributed to the absorption of radiation energy into the catalyst, and hence the potential of photo – catalysis increases as the catalyst loading increases to a critical value. However, retardation of gas – phase toluene degradation by excessive catalyst coating also occurs as the upper layer of the catalyst coating alone is effectively utilized for adsorption of toluene and the lower layer is left unused or hindered. Bouzaza et al. (2006) have also observed similar decrease in degradation of toluene with the initial concentration in an annular photocatalytic reactor. The effect of flow rate on the removal of toluene in an annular photoreactor has also been reported in the literature, with similar results (Jeong et al., 2004).

ANN MODEL FOR A PHOTOCATALYTIC REACTOR

The critical parameters that are most likely to affect the performance parameter, *i.e.,* removal efficiency, of any photo oxidation process are catalyst load, inlet pollutant concentration and gas – residence time or gas – flow rate. These parameters are easily measurable and are common to any photoreactor. Hence these parameters were taken as inputs to the network and RE values

were used as the outputs, according to the network topology illustrated in Figure 4. The schematic of the network designated for this study is shown in Figure 5.

The range of inputs and output parameter used for training and testing the ANN model formulated for the photoreactor treating gas – phase toluene are given in Table 1. The 20 experimental data points, each data set corresponding to steady – state toluene removal profiles at the respective condition of gas – flow rate, catalyst load and inlet toluene concentration, were divided as training set (N_{Tr}) = 15, and test set (N_{Te}) = 5.

Figure 5. Schematic of the network topology developed for gas – phase VOC removal in the photoreactor

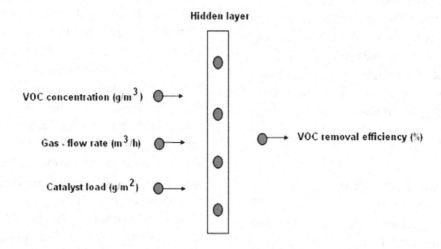

Table 1. Range of input and output parameters used for training and testing the ANN model

Parameter	Training, N_{Tr}-15			Testing, N_{Te}-5		
	Min	Max	Mean	Min	Max	Mean
Input						
Catalyst load (g/m²)	2.75	22.25	12.50	5.00	20.00	12.50
Toluene initial concentration (g/m³)	0.14	7.06	3.33	0.17	6.34	3.23
Flow rate (lpm)	0.08	1.12	0.60	0.20	1.00	0.60
Output						
Toluene removal efficiency, %	15.69	99.68	35.01	18.34	80.09	39.99

Effect of Internal Network Parameters on the Network Architecture

In order to obtain the best network topology that possess the ability to map the removal efficiency of the photoreactor, the number of neurons in the hidden layer (N_H), the training count (T_c), the learning rate (η), and the momentum term (μ) were varied through a series of trial and error procedure, and the closeness of model prediction were ascertained by the R^2 values. After this initial trial and error approach, the range of these parameters that affected the performance of the model was found to vary over a wider range, *i.e.,* $N_H - 4$ to 12, $T_c - 1000$ to 9000, $\eta_{ih} - 0.1$ to 0.9, $\eta_{ho} - 0.1$ to 0.9, and $\mu - 0.1$ to 0.9. The best network topology was then determined by performing simulations designed by the 2^k – full factorial design of experiments, as described elsewhere (Montgomery, 2005). Table 2 shows the determination coefficient values of both training and testing, using different combinations of these network parameters.

The results from factorial plots (main effects) shown in Figure 6 could be interpreted as follows;

(i)   Increasing the number of neurons (N_H) in the hidden layer increases the R^2 value.

(ii) An increase in all other parameters significantly decreased the R^2 value, and these effects were more pronounced for η_{ih} (learning rate between the input and hidden layer) and the momentum term (μ).

The results were further confirmed with a statistical analysis of significance, the Analysis of Variance (ANOVA). The main effects of the internal network parameters showed higher significance than the interaction effects. This was manifested in the high F and low P values obtained for the main effect in comparison to those for interaction effects as shown in Table 3. The T and P values of the main effects of the network are given in Table 4. Among these, the momentum term appears to play a major role (T = -11.4, P = 0.008), followed by the input-hidden layer learning rate (T = -0.073, P = 0.011). The factorial design table with responses obtained for training and test data is shown in Table 2. The best network for ANN model for the toluene removal was obtained with the following conditions of the internal network parameters: $N_H = 4$, $T_c = 9000$, $\eta_{ih} = 0.90$, $\eta_{ho} = 0.1$ and $\mu = 0.1$. With this best network conditions, the ANN model predictions were high for both training ($R^2 - 0.9621$) and testing ($R^2 - 0.9922$), compared to other network combinations, as shown in Table 2.

Predictive Capability of the Model

The removal efficiency predicted by ANN model for photo oxidation of gas – phase toluene is illustrated for the training data in Figure 7 and compared with the experimentally determined values. The testing of the ANN model with the best network architecture and its comparison with experimental values is shown in Figure 8. The close matching between the RE values predicted by the models with the experimental values reveals the predictive capability of the models. The model was able to adequately identify the low and high peaks in the RE values. The relative deviations between the experimental and model predicted values of RE are shown as a function of the experimental RE in Figures 9 and 10, respectively. It could be distinctly seen that the points predicted by the models were homogenously distributed within the experimentally observed domain. Except a few data points, most of them converged smoothly within the 10% error margin, in the error graph, indicating the goodness of fit of the models to predict the performance of photoreactor.

The weights and biases assigned for the developed model are shown in Table 5. These weights, W_{ih} and W_{ho}, determine which input neuron dominates the contribution to a hidden neuron, while the sign (+, –) suggests the nature of correlation between an input to a neuron and

Table 2. Full 2^5 - factorial design for estimating the best network architecture along with their determination coefficients values

Run Order	Neurons, N_H	Training count, T_c	Learning rate, η_{ih}	Learning rate, η_{ho}	Momentum term, μ	Determination coefficient	
						Train	Test
1	4	1000	0.10	0.10	0.10	0.2885	0.8750
2	12	1000	0.10	0.10	0.10	0.3910	0.9250
3	4	9000	0.10	0.10	0.10	0.8380	0.9556
4	12	9000	0.10	0.10	0.10	0.7911	0.9586
5	4	1000	0.90	0.10	0.10	0.7517	0.9116
6	12	1000	0.90	0.10	0.10	0.7311	0.9303
7	**4**	**9000**	**0.90**	**0.10**	**0.10**	**0.9621**	**0.9922**
8	12	9000	0.90	0.10	0.10	0.9245	0.9616
9	4	1000	0.10	0.90	0.10	0.6874	0.8979
10	12	1000	0.10	0.90	0.10	0.6721	0.9038
11	4	9000	0.10	0.90	0.10	0.9136	0.9165
12	12	9000	0.10	0.90	0.10	0.8482	0.9404
14	12	1000	0.90	0.90	0.10	0.8221	0.9397
13	4	1000	0.90	0.90	0.10	0.7772	0.9438
15	4	9000	0.90	0.90	0.10	0.9381	0.8064
16	12	9000	0.90	0.90	0.10	0.9431	0.7767
17	4	1000	0.10	0.10	0.90	0.8262	0.9477
18	12	1000	0.10	0.10	0.90	0.7801	0.9564
19	4	9000	0.10	0.10	0.90	0.9396	0.8039
20	12	9000	0.10	0.10	0.90	0.9594	0.8339
21	4	1000	0.90	0.10	0.90	0.9228	0.8066
22	12	1000	0.90	0.10	0.90	0.9017	0.9568
23	4	9000	0.90	0.10	0.90	0.9818	0.7346
24	12	9000	0.90	0.10	0.90	0.9815	0.7385
25	4	1000	0.10	0.90	0.90	0.8428	0.9649
26	12	1000	0.10	0.90	0.90	0.8888	0.9342
27	4	9000	0.10	0.90	0.90	0.9707	0.8600
28	12	9000	0.10	0.90	0.90	0.9652	0.8366
29	4	1000	0.90	0.90	0.90	0.9403	0.7396
30	12	1000	0.90	0.90	0.90	0.9420	0.6950
31	4	9000	0.90	0.90	0.90	0.9912	0.6863
32	12	9000	0.90	0.90	0.90	0.9868	0.7154
33	8	5000	0.50	0.50	0.50	0.9344	0.9007

Figure 6. The main effects plot of network internal parameters on the R^2 value during training of ANN model for the photo oxidation of gas-phase toluene

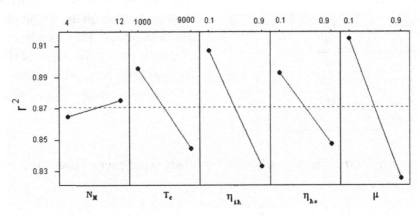

Table 3. ANOVA for the network parameters of ANN model

Source	DF	Seq SS	Adj SS	Adj MS	F	P
Main Effects	5	0.1447	0.1447	0.0289	59.32	0.017
2-Way Interactions	10	0.0696	0.0696	0.0070	14.27	0.067
3-Way Interactions	10	0.0369	0.0369	0.0037	7.57	0.122
4-Way Interactions	5	0.0112	0.0112	0.0022	4.59	0.189
5-Way Interactions	1	0.0025	0.0025	0.0025	5.14	0.151
Residual Error	2	0.0010	0.0010	0.0005		
Lack of Fit	1	0.0002	0.0002	0.0002	0.33	0.670
Pure Error	1	0.0007	0.0007	0.0007		
Total	33	0.2659				

Figure 7. Comparison of experimental and predicted values of gas-phase toluene removal efficiency during model training

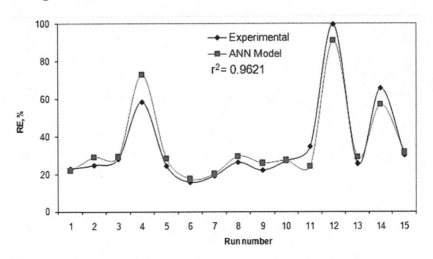

Table 4. T and P values for identifying the main effects of the network parameters

Term	Effect	T	P
N_H	0.011	1.350	0.311
T_c	-0.051	-6.490	0.023
η_{ih}	-0.073	-9.410	0.011
η_{ho}	-0.046	-5.850	0.028
μ	-0.089	-11.400	0.008

the output from the neuron. The results from sensitivity analysis reveal the influence of process input parameters on the output of the network as shown in Table 6. These results indicate that inlet concentration plays a major role in predicting the removal efficiency, while flow rate appears to have a slightly larger effect than catalyst load.

Figure 8. Comparison of experimental and predicted values of gas-phase toluene removal efficiency in the test data

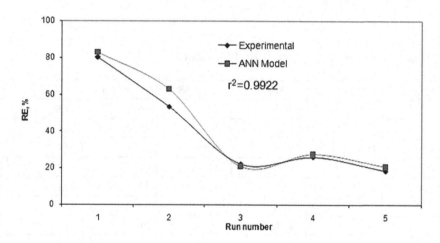

Figure 9. Relative deviations between predicted (RE$_{pred}$) and experimental (RE$_{exp}$) values of gas-phase toluene removal efficiency during model training

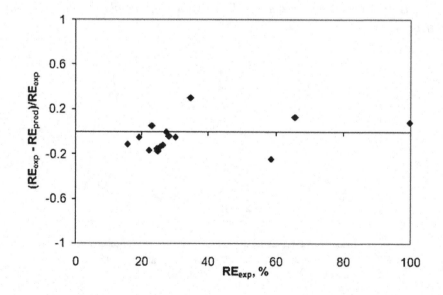

Figure 10. Relative deviations between predicted (RE_{pred}) and experimental (RE_{exp}) values of gas-phase toluene removal efficiency during model testing

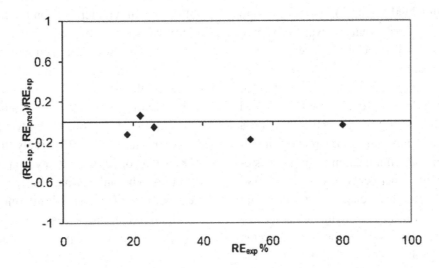

Table 5. Weights ascertained after neural network training

Neurons	W_{ih}				W_{ho}	
	x_1	x_3	x_4	Bias	Neurons	Y
1	2.6147	8.3603	2.4067	-3.7331	1	-2.2933
2	0.7625	-7.5383	-3.0076	2.7571	2	2.2426
3	-1.3257	-0.8944	1.5394	0.1076	3	-0.6843
4	-0.9774	-7.8635	-2.5758	2.9718	4	2.2647
					Bias	1.8205

Table 6. Sensitivity analysis of process input variables after network training (N_{Tr} -15)

Order	Parameter	AAS[a]	AS[b]	PS[c]	Peak row
1	Toluene concentration	0.5408	-0.5408	0.0118	11
2	Flow rate	0.4071	-0.4071	0.0098	3
3	Catalyst load	0.0521	0.0043	0.0014	3

Note: a - Absolute Average Sensitivity; b - Average Sensitivity; c - Peak Sensitivity

There are only a few reports that apply the concept of artificial neural networks to model the performance of gas – phase reactors, for the sole purpose of pollution abatement, and these studies were initiated only very recently. Elías et al. (2006) obtained start–up, intermittent fluctuation, steady – state and shut – down data from a lab – scale biofilter packed with pig manure and saw dust, handling hydrogen sulphide vapours. Data divi-

sion was done using cluster analysis in combination with a genetic algorithm, and the data were divided as training (50%), testing (40%) and validation (10%). Inlet hydrogen sulphide concentration and unit flow values (Q/V, per hour) were used as the input to the model, for predicting the removal efficiency of the biofilter (RE, %). The best MLP was decided by trial and error, by testing nearly 10,000 different combinations of

MLPs, and it was observed that a 2 – 2 – 1 network architecture was able to predict RE well with relatively high R^2 values (0.92). Furthermore, in that study, a sensitivity analysis was performed and it was observed that the biofilter performance was largely affected by the gas – flow rate, *i.e.*, unit flow, and not by the inlet concentration of hydrogen sulphide. Rene et al. (2009) modelled the performance of a biofilter (RE, %) using a back propagation algorithm, for a reactor inoculated with a mixed culture taken from the wastewater sludge of a petrochemical refinery and treating gas – phase styrene. A log – sigmoid transfer function was used with inlet styrene concentration and unit flow as the inputs, and the best network topology obtained through trial and error was found to be 2 – 4 – 1. During regular experiments, greater than 92% styrene removal was achievable for loading rates up to 250 g/m³h, and the critical load to the system was found to depend highly on the gas – flow rate. A sensitivity analysis, in terms of absolute average sensitivity (AAS) was carried out for the developed model, to estimate the most influencing input parameter for the model, and it was observed that these values were 0.5250 and 0.4249 for unit flow and inlet styrene concentration, respectively. This higher AAS values for unit flow suggested that the BF performance highly depended on the flow rate, and that the effects due to the pollutant, gas – phase styrene, was only minimal. The result from this study, where, gas – phase toluene concentration was shown to affect the performance of the photoreactor, is different from those observed for other gas – phase bioreactors reported in the literature. This is presumably due to the difference in the reactor configuration, and the mechanism of pollutant removal within the reactor, *i.e.*, photo – chemical oxidation technique in a photoreactor *vs* biodegradation in a bioreactor. The performance of biological reactors are often limited when the reactors are subjected to harsher operating conditions, *i.e.*, high loading rates, shock – loads and starvations, and the pattern of pollutant removal depends on the activity of the microbial species present, prevailing nutrient concentrations, operating temperature, pH, other physico – chemical conditions, amongst others. However, this is certainly not the case with the photoreactor, as the whole mechanism itself depends on the ability of the catalyst to create hydroxyl radicals for effectively decomposing VOCs, at a convenient rate even at ambient temperatures. The only setback of this technique is the generation of undesirable intermediates during the photo oxidation process, some of which can be more toxic than the parent compound.

CONCLUSION

The results from this study show that high gas – phase toluene removal efficiencies (98.8%) can be achieved in a photoreactor under the following condition: catalyst load – 5 g/m²; toluene concentration – 0.2 g/m³, and gas – flow rate – 0.2 l/min. The performance of the photoreactor was modelled using a three – layered feed forward network with back propagation algorithm. The best network for ANN model was obtained with the following conditions of the internal network parameters: $N_H = 4$, $T_c = 9000$, $\eta_{ih} = 0.90$, $\eta_{ho} = 0.1$ and $\mu = 0.1$, *i.e.*, network with the topology 3 – 4 – 1. The ANN model predictions were high for both training ($R^2 – 0.9621$) and testing ($R^2 – 0.9922$), and results from sensitive analysis showed that toluene concentration was the most influential parameter affecting the performance of the photoreactor. For future research, the combined advantages of the photoreactor and the neural model should be explored and understood for other gas – phase pollutants (hydrophobic and hydrophilic), and other photoreactor types, *viz.*, slurry, flat – plate, rotating disc, and falling film.

ACKNOWLEDGMENT

JK thanks the Universti Teknologi MARA, Malaysia, for their kind cooperation in publishing this research work. ERR thanks the Spanish Ministry of Science and Innovation, Spain, for his *Juan de La Cierva* research contract. The authors extend their appreciation for the experimental and modeling support received from EMRL, IIT Madras, India.

REFERENCES

Bouzaza, A., Vallet, C., & Laplanche, A. (2006). Photocatalytic degradation of some VOCs in the gas phase using an annular flow reactor: Determination of the contribution of mass transfer and chemical reaction steps in the photo degradation process. *Journal of Photochemistry and Photobiology A Chemistry, 177*, 212–217. doi:10.1016/j.jphotochem.2005.05.027

Cybenko, G. (1989). Continuous value neural networks with two hidden layers are sufficient. *Mathematics of Control, Signals, and Systems, 2*, 303–314. doi:10.1007/BF02551274

Elías, A., Ibarra-Berastegi, G., Arias, R., & Barona, A. (2006). Neural networks as a tool for control and management of a biological reactor for treating hydrogen sulphide. *Bioprocess and Biosystems Engineering, 29*, 129–136. doi:10.1007/s00449-006-0062-3

Gatts, C. E. N., Ovalle, A. R. C., & Silva, C. F. (2005). Neural pattern recognition and multivariate data: Water typology of the Paraíba do Sul River, Brazil. *Environmental Modelling & Software, 20*(7), 883–889. doi:10.1016/j.envsoft.2004.03.018

Horiguchi, S., & Inoue, K. (1977). Effects of toluene on the wheel-turning activity and peripheral blood findings in mice: An approach to the maximum allowable concentration of toluene. *The Journal of Toxicological Sciences, 2*(4), 363–372. doi:10.2131/jts.2.363

Hornik, K., Stinchcombe, M., & White, H. (1989). Multilayer feedforward networks are universal approximators. *Neural Networks, 2*, 359–366. doi:10.1016/0893-6080(89)90020-8

Jeong, J., Sekiguchi, K., & Sakamoto, K. (2004). Photochemical and photocatalytic degradation of gaseous toluene using short-wavelength UV irradiation with TiO2 catalyst: Comparison of three UV sources. *Chemosphere, 57*, 663–671. doi:10.1016/j.chemosphere.2004.05.037

Ku, Y., Tseng, K. Y., & Wang, W. Y. (2005). Decomposition of gaseous acetone in an annular photoreactor coated with TiO2 thin film. *Water, Air, and Soil Pollution, 168*, 313–323. doi:10.1007/s11270-005-1778-4

Kulkarni, S., & Haidar, I. (2009). Forecasting model for crude oil price using artificial neural networks and commodity future prices. *International Journal of Computer Science and Information Security, 2*(1), 1–8.

Levenberg, K. (1944). A method for the solution of certain non-linear problems in least squares. *Quarterly of Applied Mathematics, 2*, 164–168.

Maier, H. R., & Dandy, G. C. (1998). The effect of internal parameters and geometry on the performance of back-propagation neural networks: An empirical study. *Environmental Modelling & Software, 13*(2), 193–209. doi:10.1016/S1364-8152(98)00020-6

Maier, H. R., & Dandy, G. C. (2001). Neural network based modelling of environmental variables: A systematic approach. *Mathematical and Computer Modelling, 33*(6-7), 669–682. doi:10.1016/S0895-7177(00)00271-5

Marquardt, D. (1963). An algorithm for least-squares estimation of nonlinear parameters. *SIAM Journal on Applied Mathematics, 11*, 431–441. doi:10.1137/0111030

Martin, M. A., Keuning, S., & Janssen, D. B. (1998). *Handbook on biodegradation and biological treatment of hazardous organic compounds* (2nd ed.). Dordrecht, The Netherlands: Academic Press.

Mo, J. H., Zhang, Y. P., Xu, Q., Lamson, J. J., & Zhao, R. (2009). Photocatalytic purification of volatile organic compounds in indoor air: A literature review. *Atmospheric Environment, 43,* 2229–2246. doi:10.1016/j.atmosenv.2009.01.034

Momani, F. A. (2007). Treatment of air containing volatile organic carbon: Elimination and post treatment. *Environmental Engineering Science, 24,* 1038–1047. doi:10.1089/ees.2006.0162

Montgomery, D. C. (2005). *Design and analysis of experiments* (5th ed.). New York, NY: Wiley.

Nattkemper, T. W. (2004). Multivariate image analysis in biomedicine. *Journal of Biomedical Informatics, 37*(5), 380–391. doi:10.1016/j.jbi.2004.07.010

Nunez, C. (1998). VOCs: Sources, definitions and considerations for recovery. In *EPA, Volatile Organic Compounds (VOC) Recovery Seminar,* September 16-17, Cincinnati, OH, (pp. 3-4).

Ramírez, M. C. V., Velho, H. F. de C., & Ferreira, N. J. (2005). Artificial neural network technique for rainfall forecasting applied to the São Paulo region. *Journal of Hydrology (Amsterdam), 301*(1-4), 146–162. doi:10.1016/j.jhydrol.2004.06.028

Ravi, R., Philip, L., & Swaminathan, T. (2010). An intelligent neural model for evaluating performance of compost biofilter treating dichloromethane vapors. In *Proceedings of the 2010 Duke-UAM Conference on Biofiltration for Air Pollution Control,* (pp. 49-58).

Rene, E. R., Maliyekkal, S. M., Swaminathan, T., & Philip, L. (2006). Back propagation neural network for performance prediction in trickling bed air biofilter. *International Journal of Environment and Pollution, 28,* 382–401. doi:10.1504/IJEP.2006.011218

Rene, E. R., Murthy, D. V. S., & Swaminathan, T. (2005). Performance evaluation of a compost biofilter treating toluene vapors. *Process Biochemistry, 40,* 2771–2779. doi:10.1016/j.procbio.2004.12.010

Rene, E. R., Veiga, M. C., & Kennes, C. (2009). Experimental and neural model analysis of styrene removal from polluted air in a biofilter. *Journal of Chemical Technology and Biotechnology (Oxford, Oxfordshire), 84,* 941–948. doi:10.1002/jctb.2130

Riedmiller, M., & Braun, H. (1993). A direct adaptive method for faster backpropagation learning: The RPROP algorithm. In *Proceedings of the IEEE International Conference on Neural Networks 1993* (ICNN – 93).

Rumelhart, D. E., Hinton, G. E., & Williams, R. J. (1986). Learning internal representations by error propagation. In Rumelhart, D. E., & McClelland, J. L. (Eds.), *Parallel distributed processing* (pp. 318–362). Cambridge, MA: MIT Press.

Selman, B. (1989). Connectionist systems for natural language understanding. *Artificial Intelligence Review, 3,* 23–31. doi:10.1007/BF00139194

Sharma, R., Singh, K., Singhal, D., & Ghosh, R. (2004). Neural network applications for detecting process faults in packed towers. *Chemical Engineering and Processing, 43*(7), 841–847. doi:10.1016/S0255-2701(03)00103-X

Simpson, P. (1990). *Artificial neural systems: Foundations, paradigms, applications, and implementations.* New York, NY: MPergamon Press.

Sözen, A., Arcaklioglu, E., Özalp, M., & Çaglar, N. (2005). Forecasting based on neural network approach of solar potential in Turkey. *Renewable Energy, 30*(7), 1075–1090. doi:10.1016/j.renene.2004.09.020

Spicer, C. W., Gordon, S. M., Holdren, M. W., Kelly, T. J., & Mukund, R. (2002). *Hazardous air pollutant handbook. Measurements, properties and fate in ambient air.* Boca Raton, FL: CRC Press. doi:10.1201/9781420032352

Takeuchi, Y., & Hisanaga, N. (1977). The neurotoxicity of toluene. EEG changes in rats exposed to various concentrations. *British Journal of Industrial Medicine, 34*(4), 314–324.

Wang, J. H., & Ray, M. B. (2000). Application of ultraviolet photooxidation to remove organic pollutants in the gas phase. *Separation and Purification Technology, 19*, 11–20. doi:10.1016/S1383-5866(99)00078-7

WHO. (1981). Recommended health-based limits in occupational exposure to selected organic solvents, Geneva, World Health Organization. In *Technical Report Series 664.*

Zhong, L., Haghighat, F., Blondeau, P., & Kozinski, J. (2010). Modeling and physical interpretation of photocatalytic oxidation efficiency in indoor air applications. *Building and Environment, 45*(12), 2689–2697. doi:10.1016/j.buildenv.2010.05.029

Zuo, G. M., Cheng, Z. X., Chen, H., Li, G. W., & Miao, T. (2006). Study on photocatalytic degradation of several volatile organic compounds. *Journal of Hazardous Materials, B128*, 158–163. doi:10.1016/j.jhazmat.2005.07.056

Zurada, J. M., Malinowski, A., & Cloete, I. (1994). Sensitivity analysis for minimization of input data dimensions for feed forward neural network. In *IEEE International Symposium on Circuits and Systems*, London, May 30- June 1, (Vol. 6, pp. 447-450).

KEY TERMS AND DEFINITIONS

Back Propagation Algorithm: A set of learning rules in a generalized feed – forward network, where the error term propagates backward during training, looking for a global minimum of the error function in weight space using the method of gradient descent.

Elimination Capacity: The amount of pollutant removed in a biological treatment equipment per unit bed volume, usually represented as g/m^3h.

Factorial Design of Experiments: Factorial design of experiment, or simply factorial design, is a systematic method for formulating the steps needed to successfully implement a factorial experiment. Factorial Experiments are experiments that investigate the effects of two or more factors or input parameters on the output response of a process. An experiment using factorial design allows one to examine simultaneously the effects of multiple independent variables and their degree of interaction with a minimal number of observations enabling optimization of the output of the process.

Multilayer Perceptron (MLP): MLP refers to a simple network of interconnected neurons. These neurons perceptron computes a single output from multiple inputs by forming a linear combination according to its input weights and then possibly putting the output through some nonlinear activation function. A typical MLP consists of one input layer, one or more hidden layer and an output layer.

Network Internal Parameters: Refers to a set of internal parameters of the back propagation algorithm that can be adjusted to improvise the speed of training and convergence. These include epoch size, learning rate, momentum, activation function, error function and initial weight distribution.

Photo Oxidation: Oxidation reaction carried out under the influence of light or some other radiant energy.

Photoreactor: A reactor in which illumination or light source or some other source of radiant energy is provided to carry out photo oxidation.

Section 3
Miscellaneous Techniques in Machine Learning

Chapter 16
An Introduction to Pattern Classification

Tomoharu Nakashima
Osaka Prefecture University, Japan

Gerald Schaefer
Loughborough University, UK

ABSTRACT

In this chapter the authors present an overview of pattern classification. In particular, they focus on the mathematical background of pattern classification rather than discussing the practical analysis of various pattern classification methods, and present the derivation of classification rules from a mathematical aspect. First, the authors define the pattern space without the loss of generality. Then, the categorisation of pattern classification is presented according to the design of classification systems. The mathematical formulation of each category of pattern classification is also given. Theoretical discussion using mathematical formulations is presented for distance-based pattern classification and statistical pattern classification. For statistical pattern classification, the standard assumption is made where patterns from each class follow normal distributions with different means and variances.

INTRODUCTION

Many problems can be seen as pattern classification problems (Duda, Hart, and Stork, 2001). There are a lot of approaches to pattern classification such as Bayesian (Gelman, Carlin, Stern, and Rubin, 2003), fuzzy (Ishibuchi, Nakashima, and Nii, 2004), neural networks (Bishop, 1995), and support vector machines (Abe 2010). These are only a part of various approaches to pattern classification. Pattern classification is a process of mapping from an observed pattern into one of pre-specified concepts. A concept here is called a "class". For example, in the case of medical diagnosis, the classes are often "benign" and "malignant". A general framework of pattern classification is shown in Figure 1. Raw input data is first collated. From this information, a raw input vector is then generated. Often, efficient classification cannot be performed using such raw input patterns. Thus, it is necessary to reduce the dimensionality of patterns into a reasonably small

DOI: 10.4018/978-1-4666-1833-6.ch016

number. The actual input vector to a classification system is generated by reducing the number of dimensionalities of pattern vectors. Relevant features for classification are extracted by using some feature selection method such as sequential feature selection (Kohavi and John, 1996) and principal component analysis (Fukunaga, 1990). A normalisation process can be also performed to generate pattern vectors for classification systems. For example, in Figure 1, a normalisation process is performed so that attribute values range in a unit interval of [0.0, 1.0] after the number of features is reduced to five. A classification system then decides which class an input vector belongs to. This chapter describes elements of pattern classification. Specifically, the fundamentals of distance-based and statistical pattern classification are given.

PATTERN SPACE

Let us denote that an input pattern for classification systems is an n-dimensional numerical vector. Without loss of generality, we also assume

Figure 1. A general framework of classification for medical imaging

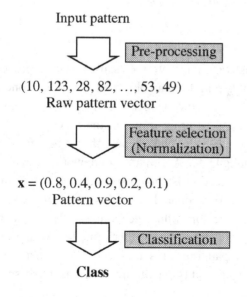

that each element of the n-dimensional vector is normalised into a unit interval [0.0, 1.0]. In this case, any n-dimensional input patterns reside in an n-dimensional hypercube $[0.0, 1.0]^n$. We refer to this hypercube as pattern space. The task of classification systems is then to divide the pattern space into a number of regions that correspond to pre-specified classes. For example, in Figure 2, the two-dimensional pattern space for a three-class problem is divided into three regions with each region corresponding to one of the three classes. A representation that divides the pattern space is called a hypothesis. Thus, classification systems generate a hypothesis that is consistent with a given set of training patterns. The hypothesis is also called classification rule.

CATEGORISATION OF CLASSIFICATION SYSTEMS

There are several types of classification systems. Three major types are described below:

1. Distance-based type: An input pattern is classified as the class with the nearest training

Figure 2. Division of pattern space (two-dimensional case)

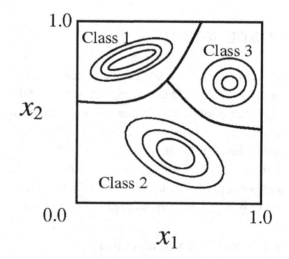

pattern in terms of a pre-defined distance measure.

2. Statistical type: An input pattern is classified based on the statistical property that is derived from a given set of training patterns.

3. Structure-based type: An input pattern is classified by using structural information of features. Structural information of features is usually defined by a human expert.

Distance-based type classification systems are suitable when clusters of training patterns for each class are isolated from each other. In this case, simple classification systems are likely to perform sufficiently well. However, if multiple classes overlap each other in the pattern space, it is impossible to generate a perfect hypothesis without error. In this case, statistical type classification systems should be used in order to minimise misclassification. Since statistical type classification systems need an assumption that pattern vectors follow some probabilistic distribution for each class, they do not perform well when the assumption does not conform to the true distribution of pattern vectors. The idea of structure-based type classification systems is to incorporate as much domain knowledge as possible to generate informative structure of features. In this chapter, we describe distance-based type and statistical type classification.

DISTANCE-BASED CLASSIFICATION

Let us assume that we have an n-dimensional pattern classification problem. We also assume that a set of training patterns are given beforehand. Usually, a training pattern is a typical pattern of a certain class. Given that the given training patterns $\boldsymbol{x}_c = (x_{c_1}, x_{c_2}, \ldots, x_{cn})$, $c = 1, 2, \ldots, C$ include only one training pattern from each class, distance-based classification systems use a distance measure between an unseen input pattern

vector. The distance between an unseen pattern $\boldsymbol{x}$ and a training pattern $\boldsymbol{x}_c$ is written as a norm of two vectors as

$$d_c(\boldsymbol{x}) = \mid \boldsymbol{x} - \boldsymbol{x}_c \mid, \; c = 1, 2, \ldots, C, \tag{1}$$

where $d_c(\boldsymbol{x})$ is the norm between $\boldsymbol{x}$ and $\boldsymbol{x}_c$. Euclidean distance is one of the well-known measures as a norm. The unseen pattern $\boldsymbol{x}$ is classified as Class $c*$ with the minimum distance measure that is determined by

$$d_{c*}(\boldsymbol{x}) = \min_{c=1,\ldots,C} d_c(\boldsymbol{x}). \tag{2}$$

Here, let us calculate the square of the distance measure defined in Equation (1),

$$d_c^2(\boldsymbol{x}) = \mid \boldsymbol{x} - \boldsymbol{x}_c \mid^2 = \mid \boldsymbol{x} \mid^2 - 2\boldsymbol{x} \cdot \boldsymbol{x}_c + \mid \boldsymbol{x}_c \mid^2. \tag{3}$$

Since the square calculation $d_c^2(\boldsymbol{x})$ does not change the order of the distance $d_c(\boldsymbol{x})$, $d_{c*}^2(\boldsymbol{x})$ is also the smallest among $c = 1, 2, \ldots, C$ if $d_c(\boldsymbol{x})$ is the smallest. After omitting irrelevant terms in Equation (3) reformulating the equation, we have the following hypothesis (i.e., classification rule) as follows:

$$d_{c*}(x) = \max_{c=1,\ldots,C} d_c'(x), \tag{4}$$

where

$$d_c' = \boldsymbol{x} \cdot \boldsymbol{x}_c - \tfrac{1}{2} \mid \boldsymbol{x}_c \mid^2. \tag{5}$$

The derived metric $d_c'(\boldsymbol{x})$ in Equation (5) is called a discrimination function for Class c.

Let us consider the classification boundary generated by distance-based classification systems. Since it is assumed that each of C training patterns represents a class, a classification boundary between Class i and j is obtained as follows:

$$d_i(\boldsymbol{x}) = d_j(\boldsymbol{x}), \tag{6}$$

$$d_i(\mathbf{x}) - d_j(\mathbf{x}) = 0, \tag{7}$$

$$\mathbf{x} \cdot \mathbf{x}_i - \tfrac{1}{2}|\mathbf{x}_i|^2 - \mathbf{x} \cdot \mathbf{x}_j - \tfrac{1}{2}|\mathbf{x}_j|^2 = 0, \tag{8}$$

$$\mathbf{x} \cdot (\mathbf{x}_i - \mathbf{x}_j) - \tfrac{1}{2}(|\mathbf{x}_i|^2 - |\mathbf{x}_j|^2) = 0, \tag{9}$$

$$\mathbf{x} \cdot (\mathbf{x}_i - \mathbf{x}_j) - \tfrac{1}{2}(\mathbf{x}_i + \mathbf{x}_j) \cdot (\mathbf{x}_i - \mathbf{x}_j) = 0, \tag{10}$$

$$(\mathbf{x}_i - \mathbf{x}_j)\{\mathbf{x} - \tfrac{1}{2}(\mathbf{x}_i + \mathbf{x}_j) \cdot (\mathbf{x}_i - \mathbf{x}_j)\} = 0. \tag{11}$$

That is, the classification boundary between Class i and j is a set of points $\mathbf{x}$ that satisfy Equation (11). From Equation (11), we can see that the classification boundary is a hyper-plane that is perpendicular to the vector $(\mathbf{x}_i - \mathbf{x}_j)$. We can also see that the intersection point of the vector $(\mathbf{x}_i - \mathbf{x}_j)$ with the classification boundary is the middle point between $\mathbf{x}_i$ and $\mathbf{x}_j$ (see Figure 3). Thus, the classification boundary is a set of perpendicular bisectors between two different training patterns in the case of two-dimensional pattern classification problems.

STATISTICAL CLASSIFICATION

In statistical classification systems, pattern classification is performed based on statistical decision theory or information theory called Bayesian theory. The basic idea is to minimise cost incurred by misclassification (or even correct classification). In statistical classification systems, a set of training patterns is considered as a set of sample patterns that are drawn from a population with a certain form of probabilistic distribution. Let us consider that we have C populations, $\omega_1, \omega_2, \ldots, \omega_C$, with different probabilistic distributions, which represent a class. Let us also define the probability that an unseen pattern $\mathbf{x}$ comes from ω_i as $P(\omega_i \mid \mathbf{x})$. In the simplest form of statistical classification, an unseen pattern $\mathbf{x}$ is classified as Class c* with the maximum probability $P(\omega_{c*} \mid \mathbf{x})$:

Figure 3. Classification boundary by a distance-based classification system. Classification boundary is represented by a hyper-plane.

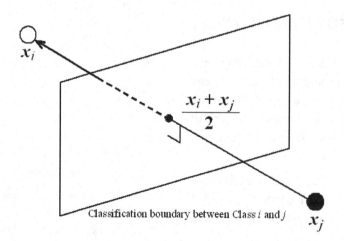

Classification boundary between Class i and j

$$P(\omega_{c*} \mid \mathbf{x}) = \max_{c=1,\ldots,C} P(\omega_c \mid \mathbf{x}). \qquad (12)$$

Since $P(\omega_i \mid \mathbf{x})$ is a posteriori probability that is not available in the phase of classification, Bayesian theory is used to calculate it from the a priori probability $P(\omega_i)$ of Class i, the unconditional probability $P(\mathbf{x})$ of an unseen pattern $\mathbf{x}$, and the class-conditional probability $P(\mathbf{x} \mid \omega_i)$ of Class *i*:

$$P(\omega_i \mid \mathbf{x}) = \tfrac{P(\omega_i)P(\mathbf{x}\mid\omega_i)}{P(\mathbf{x})}. \qquad (13)$$

Since $P(\mathbf{x})$ in Equation (13) is independent of Class *i*, the classification of an unseen pattern $\mathbf{x}$ in Equation (12) is to find Class *c** with the maximum numerator in the right side of Equation(13) as follows:

$$P(\omega_{c*})P(\mathbf{x} \mid \omega_{c*}) = \max_{c=1,\ldots,C} P(\omega_c)P(\mathbf{x} \mid \omega_c). \qquad (14)$$

It is natural to say that classifying an input pattern involves some amount of cost. For example, in the case of cancer diagnosis, diagnosing a malignant tumor as benign will pose a serious risk to the patient. Let L_{ij} be the cost of classifying an input pattern from Class i as Class j. We can formulate a cost function $r_j(\mathbf{x})$ as

$$r_j(\mathbf{x}) = \sum_{i=1}^{C} L_{ij} P(\omega_i \mid \mathbf{x}), \qquad (15)$$

where $r_j(\mathbf{x})$ is a cost of classifying an input pattern $\mathbf{x}$ as Class j. That is, the cost function is the average cost of classifying an input pattern from Class j as Class i for $i = 1, 2, \ldots, C$. Thus, the best decision making is to classify an input pattern as the class with the smallest value of the cost function.

For example, let us consider a two-class pattern classification problem. The cost function for each class is written by using Bayes theorem in Equation (13) as follows:

$$r_1(\mathbf{x}) = L_{11}P(\mathbf{x} \mid \omega_1)p(\omega_1) + L_{21}P(\mathbf{x} \mid \omega_2)P(\omega_2), \qquad (16)$$

$$r_2(\mathbf{x}) = L_{12}P(\mathbf{x} \mid \omega_1)p(\omega_1) + L_{22}P(\mathbf{x} \mid \omega_2)P(\omega_2), \qquad (17)$$

The denominator in Equation (13) was omitted as it is common for both classes. Thus the classification of an input pattern x is determined as

$$\mathbf{x} \text{ belongs to } \begin{cases} \text{Class 1,} & \text{if } r_1(\mathbf{x}) \leq r_2(\mathbf{x}), \\ \text{Class 2,} & \text{otherwise.} \end{cases} \qquad (18)$$

This classification rule of $\mathbf{x}$ can be rewritten from Equation (16) and Equation (17) as Equation 19.

Let $l_{12}(\mathbf{x}) = \tfrac{P(\mathbf{x}\mid\omega_1)}{P(\mathbf{x}\mid\omega_2)}$ be the likelihood ratio of $\mathbf{x}$. Since it is natural to assume that $L_{12} - L_{11} > 0$ and $L_{21} - L_{22} > 0$, the classification rule of $\mathbf{x}$ can be further rewritten as

Equation 19.

$$\begin{cases} \text{Class 1,} & \text{if } (L_{21} - L_{22})P(\mathbf{x} \mid \omega_2)P(\omega_2) \leq (L_{12} - L_{11})P(\mathbf{x} \mid \omega_1)P(\omega_1), \\ \text{Class 2,} & \text{otherwise.} \end{cases}$$

$$\mathbf{x} \text{ belongs to} \begin{cases} \text{Class 1,} & \text{if } l_{12}(\mathbf{x}) > \theta_{12}, \\ \text{Class 2,} & \text{otherwise.} \end{cases} \quad (20)$$

where

$$\theta_{12} = \frac{P(\omega_2)(L_{21}-L_{22})}{P(\omega_1)(L_{12}-L_{11})} . \quad (21)$$

The above principle can also be applied to multi-class pattern classification problems. Let us formulate the cost function $r_i(\mathbf{x})$ of classifying an input pattern $\mathbf{x}$ as Class i for a C-class pattern classification problem. The cost function $r_i(\mathbf{x})$ is defined as

$$r_i(\mathbf{x}) = \sum_{k=1}^{C} L_{ki} P(\mathbf{x} \mid \omega_k) P(\omega_k) . \quad (22)$$

Thus, the input pattern x is classified as Class i if the following equation holds:

$$r_i(\mathbf{x}) < r_j(\mathbf{x}), \text{ for all } j = 1,2,\ldots,C, j \neq i . \quad (23)$$

For simplicity, let us assume that $L_{ii} = 0$ for $i = 1,\ldots,C$ and $L_{ij} = 1$ for $i \neq j$. Then, the cost function for multi-class pattern classification problems in (22) is rewritten as

$$r_i(x) =$$
$$\sum_{k=1,k\neq i}^{C} P(\mathbf{x} \mid \omega_k) P(\omega_k) = P(\mathbf{x}) - P(\mathbf{x} \mid \omega_i) P(\omega_i) \quad (24)$$

Extending the classification rule for the two-class case in Equation (18), the input pattern $\mathbf{x}$ is classified as Class i if the following equation holds:

$$P(\mathbf{x} \mid \omega_i) P(\omega_i) > P(\mathbf{x} \mid \omega_j) P(\omega_j), \text{ for all } j \neq i \quad (25)$$

In Equation (25), $P(\mathbf{x} \mid \omega_i) P(\omega_i)$ can be seen as the discrimination function for Class i. Since the joint probability is by definition

$$P(\mathbf{x}, \omega_i) = P(\mathbf{x} \mid \omega_i) P(\omega_i) = P(\omega_i \mid \mathbf{x}) P(\mathbf{x}), \quad (26)$$

and $P(\mathbf{x})$ is independent of ω_i, $P(\omega_i \mid \mathbf{x})$ can also be used as the discrimination function of $\mathbf{x}$.

STATISTICAL PATTERN CLASSIFICATION FOR NORMAL DISTRIBUTIONS

From the classification rule in Equation (25), it can be seen that a prior distribution $P(\mathbf{x} \mid \omega_i)$ for Class i is necessary to classify an input pattern. It is, however, very difficult to correctly estimate the probabilistic distribution $P(\mathbf{x} \mid \omega_i)$. Alternatively, an assumption on the distribution of input patterns is employed in statistical classification. One of the well-known forms of pattern distribution is normal distribution, where the probability density function is defined, for the one-dimensional case, as follows:

$$P(x) = \frac{1}{\sqrt{2\pi}\sigma} \exp\{-\frac{1}{2}\left(\frac{x-m}{\sigma}\right)^2\}, \quad (27)$$

where

$$m = E[x] = \int_{-\infty}^{+\infty} xp(x)dx, \quad (28)$$

$$\sigma^2 = E[(x-m)^2] = \int_{-\infty}^{+\infty} (x-m)^2 p(x)dx . \quad (29)$$

In the case of multi-dimensional problems, the probability density function of input pattern $\mathbf{x} = (x_1, x_2, \ldots, x_n)$ is written as

$$p(x) = \frac{1}{(2\pi)^{n/2}|\mathbf{C}|^{1/2}} \exp\{-\tfrac{1}{2}(\mathbf{x}-\mathbf{m})\mathbf{C}^{-1}(\mathbf{x}-\mathbf{m})\},$$
(30)

where

$$m = E[\mathbf{x}],$$
(31)

and $\mathbf{C}$ is a positive semidefinite matrix called covariance matrix, which is defined as

$$\mathbf{C} = E[(\mathbf{x}-\mathbf{m})'(\mathbf{x}-\mathbf{m})].$$
(32)

The i-th diagonal element C_{ii} of $\mathbf{C}$ represents the deviation in the i-th element of input patterns, and the element C_{ij} the covariance between the i-th and j-th elements of input patterns. The value of C_{ij} is zero when the *i*-th and *j*-th elements of input patterns are independent from each other. We show two-dimensional examples of normal distribution in Figure 4. For distribution A in Figure 4, the two variables x_1 and x_2 are independent from each other (i.e., the diagonal elements C_{12} and C_{21} are both zero). On the other hand, there is a correlation between the two variables in distribution B.

The probabilistic distribution $P(\mathbf{x})$ becomes the simple multiplication of $P(x_i)$ when $C_{ij} = 0$ for $i, j = 1, 2, \ldots, n$, $i \neq j$. The discrimination function $d_i(\mathbf{x})$ for Class i under the assumption that each class follows a normal distribution is calculated in the same way as in Equation (25). Given the above assumption, the probability distribution of $\mathbf{x}$ for Class i is formulated as

$$P(\mathbf{x} \mid \omega_i) = \frac{1}{(2\pi)^{n/2}|\mathbf{C}_i|^{1/2}} \exp\{-\tfrac{1}{2}(\mathbf{x}-\mathbf{m}_i)\mathbf{C}_i^{-1}(\mathbf{x}-\mathbf{m}_i)\},$$
(33)

where $\mathbf{m}_i$ and $\mathbf{C}_i$ is the mean vector and covariance matrix of Class i, $i = 1, 2, \ldots, C$. Thus, the

Figure 4. Examples of normal distribution in a two-dimensional pattern space. There is no correlation between x_1 and x_2 in distribution A while there is a correlation between them in distribution B.

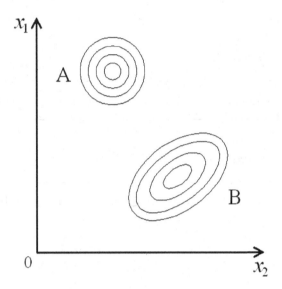

input pattern $\mathbf{x}$ is classified as the class with the maximum multiplication of $P(\omega_i)$ and $P(\mathbf{x} \mid \omega_i)$. Instead, the classification of an input pattern $\mathbf{x}$ can also be performed by comparing the natural logarithm of $P(\mathbf{x} \mid \omega_i)$. In this case, $d_i(\mathbf{x})$ is defined as Equation 34.

Removing irrelevant terms that do not involve class information such as $\mathbf{C}_i$ and $\omega_i, i = 1, 2, \ldots, C$ produces the modified discriminating function in Equation 35.

The classification rule in this case is

$\mathbf{x}$ belongs to Class i if $d_i'(\mathbf{x}) > d_j'(\mathbf{x})$ for all $j \neq i$.
(36)

Let us now consider the classification boundary between Class *i* and Class *j*. The classification boundary is obtained by

$$d_i'(\mathbf{x}) = d_j'(\mathbf{x}).$$
(37)

Equation 34.

$$d_i(\mathbf{x}) = \ln\{P(\mathbf{x} \mid \omega_i)P(\omega_i)\}$$
$$= \ln P(\mathbf{x} \mid \omega_i) + \ln P(\omega_i)$$
$$= \ln P(\omega_i) - \tfrac{1}{2}\ln 2\pi - \tfrac{1}{2}\ln |\mathbf{C}_i| - \tfrac{1}{2}\{(\mathbf{x} - \mathbf{m}_i)\mathbf{C}_i^{-1}(\mathbf{x} - \mathbf{m}_i)'\}.$$

Equation 35.

$$d_i'(\mathbf{x}) = \ln P(\omega_i) - \tfrac{1}{2}\ln |\mathbf{C}_i| - \tfrac{1}{2}\ln |\mathbf{C}_i| - \tfrac{1}{2}\{(\mathbf{x} - \mathbf{m}_i)\mathbf{C}_i^{-1}(\mathbf{x} - \mathbf{m}_i)\}$$

Equation 39.

$$(\mathbf{m}_i - \mathbf{m}_j)\mathbf{C}^{-1}\mathbf{x}' - \tfrac{1}{2}\mathbf{m}_i\mathbf{C}^{-1}\mathbf{m}_i' + \tfrac{1}{2}\mathbf{m}_j\mathbf{C}^{-1}\mathbf{m}_j' + \ln P(\omega_i) - \ln P(\omega_j) = 0$$

From Equations (35) and (37), we can see that the classification boundary is represented by a quadratic function. Let us consider a special form of the classification boundary where the covariance matrices are exactly the same for all classes (i.e., $\mathbf{C}_i = \mathbf{C}$ for $i = 1, 2, \ldots, C$). Then, the classification boundary is represented by Equation 38 and Equation 39.

$$d_i'(\mathbf{x}) - d_j'(\mathbf{x}) = 0, \qquad (38)$$

In Figure 5, we show an example of classification boundary in a two-dimensional two-class pattern classification problem. It is assumed that the covariance matrix is exactly the same (i.e., $\mathbf{C}_1 = \mathbf{C}_2$). The classification boundary is a line that has the same gradient as the probabilistic distributions. It also bisects the line that connects the centres of the two distributions.

Let us also consider another special case of the classification boundary where the covariance matrices are the identity matrix (i.e., $\mathbf{C}_i = \mathbf{I}$ for

Figure 5. Classification boundary between Class 1 and Class 2. The covariance between the two variables (i.e., $\mathbf{X}_1$ and $\mathbf{X}_2$) is the same for the two classes. The classification boundary is a line in two-dimensional pattern classification problems.

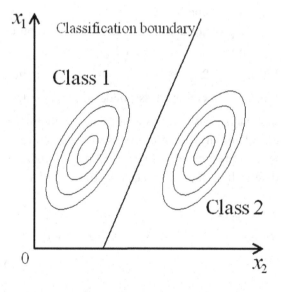

$i = 1, 2, \ldots, C$ and $P(\omega_i) = P(\omega_j)$) for all $i, j = 1, 2, \ldots, C$. The classification boundary in this case is derived from Equation (38) as

$$(\mathbf{m}_i - \mathbf{m}_j)\mathbf{x}' - \tfrac{1}{2}\mathbf{m}_i\mathbf{m}_i' - \tfrac{1}{2}\mathbf{m}_j\mathbf{m}_j' = 0. \quad (40)$$

The classification boundary in Equation (40) is exactly the same as the one that is obtained by the nearest neighbour classification (compare Equations (11) and (40)). We show an example of this special case in Figure 6, where both probabilistic distributions have no correlation between the two variables x_1 and x_2. That is, the value of non-diagonal elements in the covariance matrix is zero (i.e., $C_{12} = C_{21} = 0$ for both classes). We can see from Figure 6 that the classification boundary is a bisecting perpendicular line to the line that connects the centre of the probabilistic distribution of each class.

CONCLUSION

In this chapter, classical pattern classification methods are reviewed. Especially distance-based and statistical pattern classification is described. We also described the general flow of pattern classification. Pre-processing and normalisation is often necessary in order to reduce the number of features and use only salient features that are important for classification. It is generally assumed that a set of training patterns is given for constructing a hypothesis. In distance-based pattern classification systems, a simple metric such as Euclidean distance between a training pattern and an unseen pattern is used to classify the unseen pattern. On the other hand, probabilistic assumption for patterns and classes are used in statistical pattern classification systems. This chapter also discussed statistical pattern classification from the view point of minimising classification costs. The property of classification boundaries were also explained for both distance-based and statistical pattern classification.

Figure 6. Classification boundary between Class 1 and Class 2. The distribution of both Class 1 and Class 2 has no correlation between the two variables (i.e., $\mathbf{X}_1$ and $\mathbf{X}_2$). The classification boundary is perpendicular to the line connecting the centres of the two distributions. It also bisects the line.

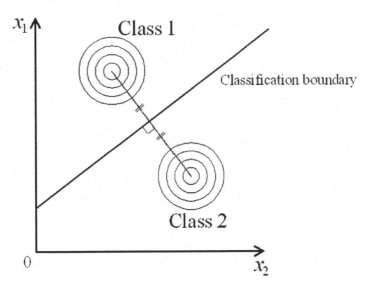

REFERENCES

Abe, S. (2010). *Support vector machines for pattern classification* (2nd ed.). London, UK: Springer.

Bishop, C. M. (1995). *Neural networks for pattern recognition*. New York, NY: Oxford University Press.

Duda, R. O., Hart, P. E., & Stork, D. G. (2001). *Pattern classification*. New York, NY: Wiley.

Fukunaga, K. (1990). *Introduction to statistical pattern recognition*. San Diego, CA: Academic Press.

Gelman, A., Carlin, J. B., Stern, H. S., & Rubin, D. B. (2003). *Bayesian data analysis* (2nd ed.). Boca Raton, FL: Chapman and Hall/CRC.

Ishibuchi, H., Nakashima, T., & Nii, M. (2004). *Classification and modeling with linguistic information granules: Advanced approaches to linguistic data mining*. Berlin, Germany: Springer.

Kohavi, R., & John, G. (1996). Wrappers for feature subset selection. *Artificial Intelligence, 97*(1-2), 273–324. doi:10.1016/S0004-3702(97)00043-X

Chapter 17
Nature–Inspired Toolbox to Design and Optimize Systems

Satvir Singh
Shaheed Bhagat Singh College of Engineering & Technology, India

Arun Khosla
Dr. B. R. Ambedkar National Institute of Technology, India

J. S. Saini
Deenbandhu Chhotu Ram University of Science & Technology, India

ABSTRACT

Nature-Inspired (NI) Toolbox is a Particle Swarm Optimization (PSO) based toolbox which is developed in the MATLAB environment. It has been released under General Public License and hosted at SourceForge.net (http://sourceforge.net/projects/nitool/). The purpose of this toolbox is to facilitate the users/designers in design and optimization of their systems. This chapter discusses the fundamental concepts of PSO algorithms in the initial sections, followed by discussions and illustrations of benchmark optimization functions. Various modules of the Graphical User Interface (GUI) of NI Toolbox are explained with necessary figures and snapshots. In the ending sections, simulations results present comparative performance of various PSO models with concluding remarks.

INTRODUCTION

Since early 90's, investigations on new optimization techniques, based on the analogy of social behavior of swarms of natural creatures, have been started. Dorigo introduced Ant Colony Optimization (ACO) (Colorni et al., 1991) based on the social behavior of insects, especially ants where each individual exchanges information implic-

itly through pheromone. Eberhart and Kennedy developed PSO (Kennedy and Eberhart, 1995) based on the analogy of bird flock and fish school where each individual is allowed to learn from the experiences of its own and others.

PSO is a swarm based optimization tool which is useful, like other evolutionary algorithms, to evolve near-optimum solution to a problem. The evolution is initialized with a set of randomly generated potential solutions and then is allowed to search for the optimum one, iteratively. It

DOI: 10.4018/978-1-4666-1833-6.ch017

searches the optimum solution by observing the best performing particles. As compared to Genetic Algorithms, the PSO has much better intelligent background and could be performed more easily (Shi et al., 2007). Due to its advantages, the PSO is not only suitable for scientific research, but also engineering applications. PSO has attracted broad attention in the fields of evolutionary computing, optimization and many others (Angeline, 1998, Chang et al., 2005, Clerc and Kennedy, 2002, Trelea, 2003). Although the PSO is developed for continuous optimization problems, however, investigational studies have been reported that are focused on discrete problems as well (Kennedy and Eberhart, 1997).

ADDING NI TOOLBOX IN THE MATLAB ENVIRONMENT

Download NIT.zip folder from SourceForge. net (http://sourceforge.net/projects/nitool/) and follow these steps to embed it in the MATLAB environment:

1. Unzip the downloaded NIT.zip file. This contains two folders (a) nitool folder – copy into the /matlab/toolbox and (b) NI Toolbox folder – contains demo and make it your Work Directory.
2. In the MATLAB environment click Start → Desktop Tools → Path → Add Folder
3. Specify the nitool folder path as /matlab/ toolbox/nitool, Save and Close.
4. Now, NI Toolbox is ready to use. Type nitool in the MATLAB Command Window to run NI Toolbox for a fresh system description.

PARTICLE SWARM OPTIMIZATION

PSO belongs to the category of Swarm Intelligence (Kennedy and Eberhart, 2001) tool and is useful in solving global optimization problems. It was originally proposed by James Kennedy, as a simulation of social behavior, and was introduced as an optimization method in 1995 (Eberhart and Kennedy, 1995, Kennedy and Eberhart, 1995). PSO is an evolutionary computing technique related to artificial life, specifically to swarming bodies, as it involves simulation of social behaviors.

PSO implementation is easy and computationally inexpensive, since its memory and CPU speed requirements are low (Eberhart et al., 1996). Moreover, it does not require gradient information of the fitness function but only its values. PSO has been proved to be an efficient method for many global optimization problems and, in some cases, it does not suffer from the difficulties experienced by other evolutionary algorithms (Eberhart and Kennedy, 1995).

What differentiates the PSO paradigm from other instances of evolutionary computing is memory and social interaction among the individuals. In the other paradigms, the important information an individual possesses, usually called genotype, is its current position, however, in PSO, really important asset is the previous best experience. Each individual stores the best position, found so far, that drives the evolution toward better solutions.

PSO algorithm has originated as a simplified simulation of a social system. The first program was a graphical simulation of a bird flock (Heppner and Grenander, 1990, Reynolds, 1987). In this simulation, a point on the screen was defined as food, called the cornfield vector (Kennedy and Eberhart, 1995); the idea was to allow birds to find food through social learning, by observing the behavior of nearby birds, who seemed nearer to the food source. The optimization potential was realized in the initial experiments and the algorithm was modified to incorporate topological rather than Euclidean neighborhoods and multi-dimensional search was attempted successfully (Eberhart and Kennedy, 1995, Eberhart et al., 1996, Kennedy and Eberhart, 1995).

PSO usually initializes the population by assigning each particle a random starting position in the solution space and a randomized velocity. Genetic Algorithms use selection, crossover and mutation to replace less fit individuals by combining the traits of high performing ones. However, in PSO, members of the particle swarm persist over time, retaining their identities and improving through imitation and interactions with their neighbors.

Each individual, *i*, in a particle swarm is composed of three vectors, with a dimensionality equal to that of the problem space. These are the current position, previous best position and associated velocity denoted as x_i, p_i, and v_i, respectively. The position, x_i, represents a set of coordinates describing a point in solution space. In each iteration, the current position is evaluated as a problem solution and if found better than the previous best one, then it substitutes the one stored in p_i. The best fitness results found are stored in *pbest*$_i$ to use for comparisons in later iterations. Each particle belongs to a social neighborhood and, therefore, its social behavior will result from the observation of its neighbors. It means that a particle will be affected by the best point found by any member of its topological neighborhood. If we consider *g*th particle to be the best individual in whole swarm, we call it global best position and denote it as p_g.

The definition of a neighborhood topology is simply the characterization of a social network, represented as a graph, where each individual is represented as a vertex and an edge exists between two individuals if they can in hence one another. Neighbors and neighborhoods don't change during a run. There is an infinite number of neighborhood topologies. However, only two types have been frequently used: the *gbest* (global best) topology – where each particle influences every other one, i.e., a fully connected case, and the *lbest* (local best) topology – where each particle is connected to *k* of its adjacent neighbors and *k* is a parameter. Most applications include particle, *i*, itself as a member

of its own neighborhood, so a neighborhood of *k* = 2 really has 3 members. The velocity of each particle is iteratively adjusted so that it oscillates around p_i and p_g. Acceleration is weighted by a random coefficient, with separate random numbers being generated for each dimension. The original algorithm to implement PSO is as follows:

1. Initialize a population of particles with random positions and velocities. Initialize p_i and *pbest*$_i$ to store the starting position and fitness, respectively.
2. For each particle, evaluate its fitness at the present position, x_i.
3. Compare the particle's fitness with *pbest*$_i$. If the current value is better, copy it to *pbest*$_i$ and set p_i equal to the current position, x_i.
4. Identify the most successful particle in the neighborhood and store it as p_g.
5. Update the velocity and position of the particle as follows:

$$v_i = v_i + U[0, \phi_1](p_i - x_i) + U[0, \phi_2](p_g - x_i) \quad (1)$$

$$x_i = x_i + v_i \quad (2)$$

6. Loop to step ii. until a termination criterion is met, usually a sufficiently good fitness over a number of iterations, or a maximum number of iterations.

U[lower, upper] represents a vector of random variables following the uniform distribution between lower and upper limits. The acceleration constants φ_1 and φ_2 in (1) represent the stochastic pulls that each particle experiences towards p_i and p_g, respectively. Adjustment of these constants alters the relative effects of p_i and p_g; higher values result in abrupt movement toward, or away from the target, or may lead to a skip over the targets. All such parameters which govern the process

Figure 1. PSO Topologies gbest, lbest, and wheel, respectively

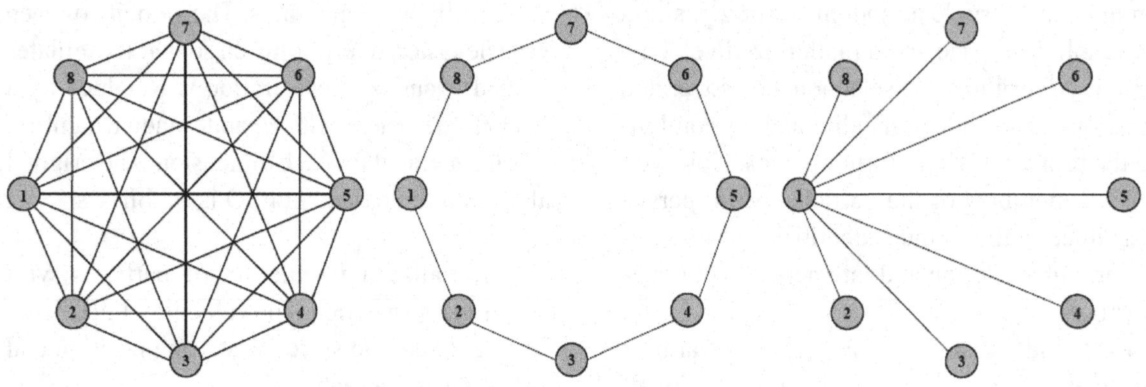

of evolution need to be specified carefully, as discussed in the next section.

PSO MODELS AND TOPOLOGIES

After observing the detrimental effect of using *gbest* PSO, Kennedy (Kennedy, 1999) conducted the first study on other sociometries besides *gbest*, to observe their influence on the performance. In these experiments, following topologies were investigated (shown in Figure 1):

1. *gbest* – where every particle is connected to every other
2. *lbest* – where every particle is connected to two others
3. *wheel* – where every particle was connected to a central one

The main conclusions of this study were that *gbest* seemed to be faster but more vulnerable to local optima whilst *lbest* was much slower but more robust if the maximum number of iterations was increased. The *lbest* topology, as extreme vertices are interconnected, is also termed as *Ring* topology. *Wheel* performed badly except on one of the functions, however, these results were deemed somewhat inconclusive.

Figure 2. The linear topologies with only one path between two vertices

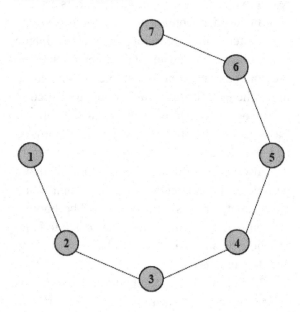

In (Mendes, 2004), Mendes has investigated another topology, namely, *wheel* – there is only one possible path between two vertices, as shown in Figure 2. It is noticed that that particles with higher indices take longer to converge. The reason for this behavior is the fact that information takes time to travel along the graph from one individual to the next.

The next logical step was to generalize *lbest* by using a bigger neighborhood adjacency. Figure

Figure 3. The ring topologies with neighborhood sizes 1, 2, and 3, respectively

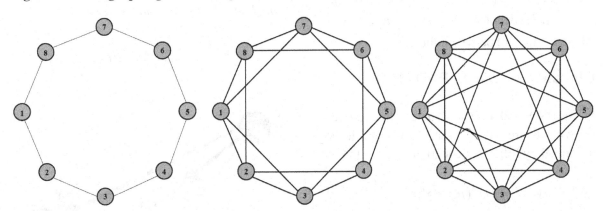

3 shows how this is performed: instead of being connected to just one neighbor on each side, each individual is connected to several. Several researchers have used a neighborhood of size two on each side.

The increase of robustness of *lbest* over *gbest* indicated that a more thorough study of the effect of sociometries in PSO performance was needed. An attempt to study the influence of neighborhoods on PSO performance is described in (Kennedy and Mendes, 2002). They have reported considerable influence of different topologies on the behavior of the algorithm.

These are a few variants of PSO algorithms and similar other variants may be investigated for avoiding premature convergence and for obtaining faster evolutionary rate. Designing a Fuzzy Logic System (FLS) requires considerable expertise in the domain of Fuzzy Logic and application area, however, one can investigate to facilitate the process FLS designing using PSO.

PSO is a sociologically inspired optimization technique, since it was initially developed as a tool by Reynolds (Kennedy and Eberhart, 2001, Reynolds, 1987) for simulating the flight patterns of bird flocks, which was mainly governed by three major concerns: *collision avoidance*, *velocity matching* and *flock centering*. On the other hand, the main reasons presented for the flocking behavior observed in nature are: *protection* from

predator and *gaining-food* from a large effective search-space. The latter reason assumes a great importance, when the food is unevenly distributed over the search-space. It was realized by Kennedy and Eberhart that the bird flocking behavior can be adopted to be used as an optimizer and resulted in the first simple version of PSO (Eberhart and Kennedy, 1995, Kennedy and Eberhart, 1995) that has been recognized as one of the computational intelligence techniques intimately related to evolutionary algorithms. Like evolutionary algorithms, it uses a population of potential solutions called particles that are own through the search-space with adaptable velocities that determines their movements. Each particle also has a memory and hence it is capable of remembering the best position, in the search-space, ever visited by it. The position corresponding to the best fitness is known as *pbest* and the overall best out of all the particles in the population is called *gbest*.

Consider that the search space is d-dimensional and ith particle in the swarm can be represented by $X_i = (x_{i1}, x_{i2}, ..., x_{id})$ and its velocity can be represented by another d-dimensional vector $V_i = (v_{i1}, v_{i2}, ..., v_{id})$. Let the best position ever visited in the past by ith particle be denoted by $P_i = (p_{i1}, p_{i2}, ..., p_{id})$. Many a times, the whole swarm is subdivided into smaller groups and each group/sub-swarm has its own local best particle, denoted as $P_{ld} = (p_{l1}, p_{l2}, \ldots, p_{ld})$, and an overall best particle, denoted as $P_{gd} = (p_{g1}, p_{g2}, \ldots, p_{gd})$, where g and l are particle indices.

Global-Best (*gbest*) PSO Model

In this PSO model, each particle is free to interact with its present *pbest* and *gbest* particles as described by following equations (3) and (4):

$$v_{id}^{n+1} = \chi(wv_{id}^n + \phi_1 r_1^n (p_{id}^n - x_{id}^n) \\ + \phi_2 r_2^n (p_{gd}^n - x_{id}^n)) \tag{3}$$

$$x_i^{n+1} = x_i^n + v_i^n \tag{4}$$

The PSO parameters, viz., inertia weight (w), cognitive acceleration φ_1, social acceleration φ_2, along-with $v_{id} \in [-V_{\max}, +V_{\max}]$ are known as the strategy/operating parameters of PSO algorithm that are specified by the user before the evolution starts (Parsopoulos and Vrahatis, 2002). The parameter $V_{\max}$ is the maximum velocity along any dimension, which implies that, if the velocity along any dimension exceeds $V_{\max}$, it shall be clamped to this value to avoid search explosion. The inertia weight, w, governs how much of the velocity should be retained from the previous time step. Generally, the inertia weight is not kept fixed and is varied as the algorithm progresses so as to allow the PSO to explore a large area at the start of simulation run and to refine the search later by a smaller inertia weight (Eberhart and Shi., 2001, Parsopoulos and Vrahatis, 2002). The parameters φ_1 and φ_2 determine the relative pulls of *pbest* and *gbest*. Random numbers r_1 and r_2 help in, stochastically, varying these pulls, which also account for slightly unpredictable natural swarm behavior. This is depicted, graphically, in two-dimensional search-space in Figure 4.

Figure 4. Attractions experienced, in gbest PSO model, in two-dimensional search-space

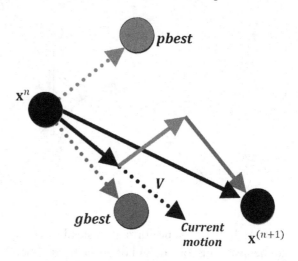

Local-Best (*lbest*) PSO Model

In this model, the whole swarm is subdivided into sub-swarms. The model is termed as *lbest* PSO model if each particle in the swarm experiences attractions due its present *pbest* particle, P_i, and *lbest* particle, P_l. Mathematically,

$$v_{id}^{n+1} = \chi(wv_{id}^n + \phi_1 r_1^n (p_{id}^n - x_{id}^n) \\ + \phi_3 r_3^n (p_{ld}^n - x_{id}^n)) \tag{5}$$

$$x_i^{n+1} = x_i^n + v_i^n \tag{6}$$

The neighborhood acceleration parameter, φ_3, determines the relative pull of *lbest* particle, whereas random numbers, r_1 and r_3, varies these pulls, stochastically, as shown in Figure 5.

Hybrid-Best (*hbest*) PSO Model

This is a newly proposed PSO variant where each particle belongs to a sub-swarm and feels collective attraction towards its present *pbest* particle, P_i, the *lbest* particle, P_l, and the *gbest* particle, P_g, as expressed mathematically,

Figure 5. Particle attractions experienced in the lbest PSO model represented in two-dimensional search-space

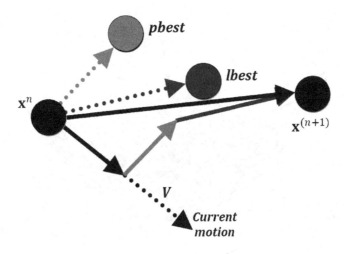

Figure 6. Particle attractions experienced in hbest PSO model represented in two-dimensional search-space

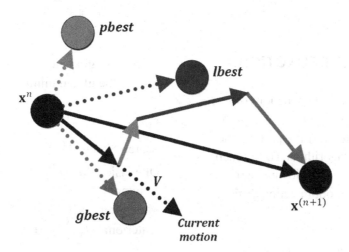

$$v_{id}^{n+1} = \chi(wv_{id}^n + \phi_1 r_1^n(p_{id}^n - x_{id}^n)$$
$$+\phi_2 r_2^n(p_{gd}^n - x_{id}^n) + \phi_3 r_3^n(p_{ld}^n - x_{id}^n)) \quad (7)$$

$$x_i^{n+1} = x_i^n + v_i^n \quad (8)$$

These collective pulls that govern the movement of each particle in the swarm are depicted, in two dimensional search-space, in Figure 6.

The *gbest* PSO model is endowed with the quality of faster evolution due to involvement of less number of computations but prone to be trapped into local optima. The second model, i.e., *lbest* PSO is slower as it involves more calculation, however, capable of escaping local optima and, therefore, avoids premature convergence. In our proposed *hbest* PSO model, these both capabilities, i.e., faster evolution and matured convergence, are embedded together. The comparative studies for performances all these PSO models are presented in ending sections.

Figure 7. Graph of sphere function in two dimensions (i.e., n = 2)

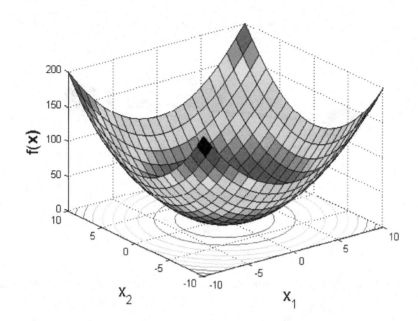

BENCHMARK TEST FUNCTIONS

There is a suite of benchmark functions (Mendes, 2004, Shi and Eberhart, 1999) which are commonly used to critically test the performance of numeric optimization algorithms. These functions are chosen because of their following particularities, which render their optimization difficult:

- Multi-modality
- Deceptive gradient information
- The curse of dimensionality

Sphere/DeJong

This function is very simple. Any algorithm capable of numeric optimization should solve it without any problem. Its simplicity helps to focus on the effects of dimensionality in optimization algorithms. It is uni-modal, with its global minimum located at $\langle x \rangle = \langle 0,...0 \rangle$, with $f(\langle x \rangle) = 0$. This function has no interaction between its variables and gradient information always points toward the global minimum.

Function: $f(\langle x \rangle) = \sum_{i=1}^{n} x_i^2$

Search Space: $\{\langle x \rangle | \forall i = -100 \leq x_i \leq +100\}$

Dimensionality (n): 30

Minimum: 0

Maximum: 3×10^5

Criterion: $f(\langle x \rangle) \leq 0.1$

Rosenbrock

Not all uni-modal functions are simple to optimize. The fitness landscape is simple from afar but banana shaped when close to the minimum. Rosenbrock's variables are strongly dependent and gradient information often misleads algorithms. Its global minimum of $f(\langle x \rangle) = 0$ is located at $\langle x \rangle = \langle 1,...1 \rangle$.

Figure 8. Graph of Rosenbrock function in two dimensions

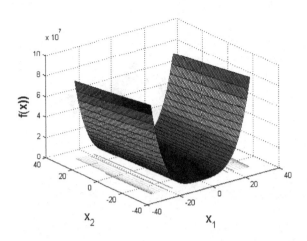

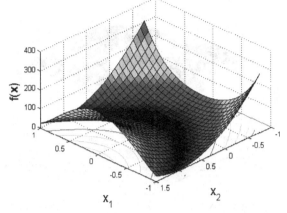

Function: $f(\langle x \rangle) = \sum_{i=1}^{n-1} 100(x_{i+1} - x_i^2)^2 + (x_i - 1)^2$

Search Space: $\{\langle x \rangle | \forall i = -30 \leq x_i \leq +30\}$

Dimensionality (n): 30

Minimum: 0

Maximum: 2508237869

Criterion: $f(\langle x \rangle) \leq 100$

Ackley

Ackley is a multi-modal function with many local optima. The global minimum is $f(\langle x \rangle) = 0$, where $\langle x \rangle = \langle 0,...0 \rangle$. This function is difficult because optimization algorithm can easily be trapped in a local minimum on its way to the global minimum.

Function: $f(\langle x \rangle) = 20 + e - 20e^{-0.2\sqrt{\frac{\sum_{i=1}^{n} x_i^2}{n}}} - e^{\frac{\sum_{i=1}^{n} \cos 2\pi x_i}{n}}$

Search Space: $\{\langle x \rangle | \forall i = -30 \leq x_i \leq +30\}$

Dimensionality (n): 30

Minimum: 0

Maximum: 22.35040

Criterion: $f(\langle x \rangle) \leq 0.01$

Rastrigin F1

This function is a multi-modal version of the Spherical function, characterized by deep local minima arranged as sinusoidal bumps. The global minimum is $f(\langle x \rangle) = 0$, where $\langle x \rangle = \langle 0,...0 \rangle$. An optimization algorithm can easily become trapped in a local minimum on its way to the global minimum.

Function: $f(\langle x \rangle) = \sum_{i=1}^{n} x_i^2 - 10 \cos 2\pi x_i 20 + 10$

Search Space: $\{\langle x \rangle | \forall i = -5.12 \leq x_i \leq +5.12\}$

Dimensionality (n): 30

Minimum: 0

Maximum: 1210.6

Criterion: $f(\langle x \rangle) \leq 100$

MATLAB-BASED NATURE INSPIRED TOOLBOX

The NI Toolbox is a GUI-based general purpose optimization tool, developed in MATLAB environment, that is useful in evolution of solution to any general NP-complete problem, e.g., valuations

Figure 9. Graph of Ackley function in two dimensions

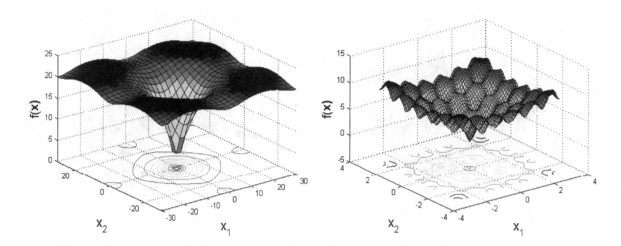

Figure 10. Graph of Rastrigin function in two dimensions

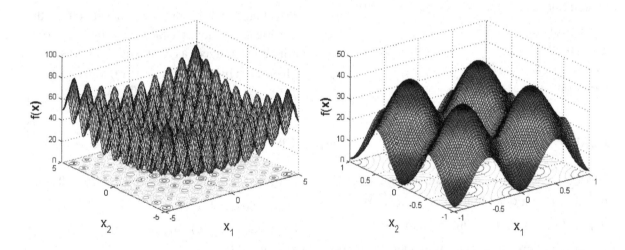

of fuzzy models, traveling salesman problem, load-scheduling, training of neural networks, etc.

NIT Editor and Plots

NI Toolbox is a GUI-based optimization toolbox that is comprised of two different windows, namely, NIT Editor window and NIT Plots window. User can tick/untick any of fitness plots (Global Best, Average, and/or Local Best) in the NIT Editor window (See Figure 11) before the start of evolution. The plots can be observed in

NIT Plots window (See Figure 12) throughout the run. Various other sub-modules of the GUI-based NI Toolbox are discussed as follows.

Menu Organization

Most options, available in the GUI, are also available in duplicate in the Menu as a quick facility to users. This Menu of the NIT Editor Window is organized as shown in Table 1.

Figure 11. NIT GUI for PSO module

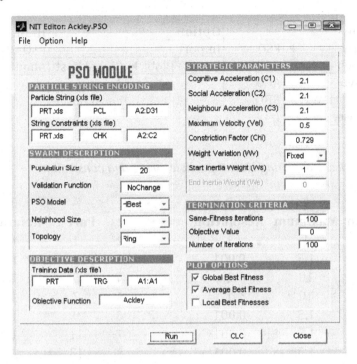

Figure 12. Typical fitness plots in NIT plots window

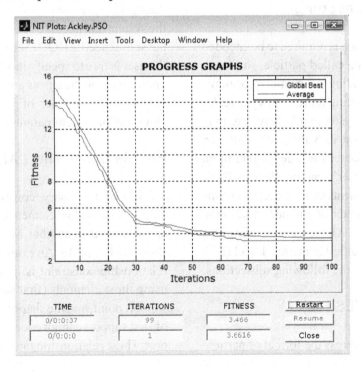

Table 1. NIT menu organization

File		Option		Help
New ▶	PSO	Import		PSO
Open	GA	Fitness Plots ▶	Global Best	About
Save	ACO		Average	
Export to WS	BBO		Local Best	
Close				

Figure 13. MS Excel sheets depicting typical particle string and constraints

	B	C	D
1	Minimum	Maximum	Resolution
2	0	1	1
3	0	1.5	0.001
4	0	10	1
5	-10	10	1
6	0.2	1.5	0.001
7	0.2	1.5	0.001
8	0.2	1.5	0.001

	A	B	C
1	Part 1	Relation	Part 2
2	1	1	2
3	3	1	4
4	5	1	6
5	7	1	8
6	9	1	10
7	11	1	12
8	13	1	14

Particle String Encoding

Each candidate solution is required to be encoded in the form of a string called particle, similar to the chromosome encoding in Genetic Algorithms. Each element in the string represents a particular characteristic of the system and, therefore, may observe restrictions on its values, e.g., integer, floating point or binary values depending upon the application and user's choice. Besides these restrictions, some elements may have relationships for attaining only greater or smaller values than those of other elements. All these characterizations of the system are specified in the MS Excel files/ sheets as discussed in the following subsections.

Particle String (.XLS File)

User is required to express the format of particle string in an external MS Excel (most often used) file/sheet which is then called into NI Toolbox as the process of evolution starts. Every element of the string represents a particular characteristic of the system that needs to be evolved and, therefore, has some specific UOD (See Figure 13). However, the user is free to specify its resolution depending upon time constraints as smaller resolution may lead to more number of iterations but precise valuation of system parameters.

Particle Constraints (.XLS File)

Additional necessary constraints between the values of individual elements of the particle string are described in another MS Excel file/sheet as shown in Figure 13. An example of such required relationship/constraint is: if a T1 FS is encoded using three elements (first support point, second support point, and the shape of FS), then the value of first support cannot exceed that of second support. These relationships are numerically symbolized as: 1-less than, 2-greater than, 3-less than equal to, 4-greater than equal to, 5-equal to, and 6-not equal to. The first row of editable textboxes in Particle String Encoding module (In the NIT Editor window as shown in Figure 11), describes how to specify particulars of the MS Excel file that contains particle string format. Here, PRT.xls, PCL and A2:D31 are file name, sheet name, and range of cells, respectively. However, in editable textboxes of second row, CHK represents another sheet name, in the same MS Excel file and A2:C2 is the range of cells describing relationship(s) between string elements; only one in this case.

Swarm Description

Various swarm aspects, e.g., population size, topology, and neighborhood size, etc., are specified in this module of NIT Editor window. If the size of population is too small, it does not create enough interactions among particles, thus leading to early convergence, however, larger swarm size leads to more number of function evaluations that take longer time to converge.

There are a host of PSO models and their variants that are studied by the researchers. In our NI Toolbox, we have incorporated the most popular ones – Global-Best Model (*gbest* Model), Local-Best Model (*lbest* Model), and the one proposed by us, i.e., Hybrid-Best Model (*hbest* Model).

Further, if *lbest* or *hbest* model is chosen, then Neighborhood Size and Topology pop-up options become enabled, otherwise remain disabled. There are many possible topologies in PSO models where whole swarm is subdivided into smaller ones and the most popular topologies, e.g., *Ring, Linear*, and *Wheel*, have been incorporated into this toolbox, with different neighborhood size options.

Objective/Fitness Function Description

The fitness function, that is also essential in other evolutionary algorithms, measures the performance of the individual candidate solutions. Unlike traditional gradient-based methods, evolutionary algorithms can be used to evolve systems

with any kind of fitness functions, including non-differentiable, deceptive, and discontinuous ones, etc. Finding a good fitness function enables the evolutionary algorithms to evolve a useful system in the end.

How to define the fitness function for a system to be evolved is problem-dependent. For prediction and estimation problems, a few commonly used error functions are (Shi et al., 1999):

1. Mean Square Error (MSE)

$$E = \frac{1}{N} \sum_{i=1}^{N} (C_i - T_i)^2 \qquad (9)$$

2. Mean Absolute Difference Error

$$E = \frac{1}{N} \sum_{i=1}^{N} |C_i - T_i| \qquad (10)$$

3. Mean Relative Square Error

$$E = \frac{1}{N} \sum_{i=1}^{N} \left(\frac{C_i - T_i}{T_i} \right)^2 \qquad (11)$$

4. Mean Relative Absolute Difference Error

$$E = \frac{1}{N} \sum_{i=1}^{N} \left| \frac{C_i - T_i}{T_i} \right| \qquad (12)$$

where N is the number of training data points, and T_i and C_i are ith computed and target outputs, respectively. Any one from the above error functions can itself be treated as a fitness function to be minimized. Another one possible fitness function, to be maximized, is

$$F = E_{max} - E \qquad (13)$$

Figure 14. Input-output training data set in MS Excel

	A	B	C	D	E
1	**Antecedent1**	**Antecedent2**	**Antecedent3**	**Antecedent4**	**Consequent**
2	0.27037	0.62937	0.25509	0.4823	0.73775
3	0.27461	0.8329	0.1379	0.51398	0.3928
4	0.46881	0.45426	0.39881	0.29005	0.4416
5	0.76384	0.33454	0.12046	0.42863	0.90065
6	0.59762	0.45086	0.40226	0.76037	0.2462
7	0.17608	0.10462	0.31699	0.027522	0.62478
8	0.86864	0.87607	0.96422	0.88479	0.30094
9	0.69169	0.35372	0.71205	0.013729	0.3982

where E_{max} is the maximum error value. With the use of error functions (i) and (ii) to calculate the fitness, the obtained system will have better accuracy for large valued outputs. For a system to have similar accuracy for any ranged output relative error, (iii) and (iv) can be introduced.

This section of NIT Editor window (Figure 11) is dedicated to specify the collection of input-output training data, in the form of an MS Excel file/sheet as shown in Figure 14. The name of m-file, describing the fitness function, is to be specified in the respective editable textbox.

Strategic Parameters

The user can specify the PSO strategic parameters in this sub-module which govern the evolution throughout, viz. Cognitive Acceleration (φ_1), Social Acceleration (φ_2), Local Acceleration (φ_3), Maximum Velocity (V_{max}), and Constriction Factor (χ). These are renamed as C1, C2, C3, Vel, and Chi, respectively, as shown in Figure 11. User can opt to have Inertia Weight as fixed or variable for system convergence and if user chooses variable weight then end weight, w_e, is required to be specified along with starting weight, w_s.

Termination Criteria

Evolutionary algorithms do not guarantee the best solution; rather yield near about the best one. The process of evolution is a long and sometimes never ending one as the scope of improvements always exists. Hence, these evolutionary algorithms are terminated intentionally based on any of the following three criteria, and so are incorporated in the toolbox:

1. *Same-Fitness Iterations* – It is observed whether *gbest* solution offers any improvement or not over user-specified number of successive iterations. The algorithm is terminated if no improvement is forthcoming.
2. *Objective Value* – The algorithm terminates upon achievement of a desired level of fitness value.
3. *Number of Iterations* – It is the maximum number of iterations for which the algorithm is planned to run and terminates upon reaching this number.

The process of evolution may sometimes collapse before actual convergence or the termination may occur due to unforeseen problems, e.g., power failure, or computer malfunctioning, etc. To overcome such exigencies, a special feature has been built into this toolbox that enables this toolbox to resume simulation from the point of collapse or restart the evolution afresh, on user's choice.

Plot Options

To observe the performance of the algorithms, the fitness plots are necessary throughout the run. This toolbox facilitates the user with such plots as *Global Best Fitness*, *Average Fitness* and *Local Best Fitness* with respect to number of iterations as shown in Figure 12. User can select or deselect any plot option before staring the evolution process.

NIT Structure Variable and File

Every system, created in the NIT Editor window, can be exported to or imported from the MALTAB Workspace, through menu operations, in the form of an NIT structure variable. This can further be used as an interface for MATLAB Simulink, and other Toolboxes or Blocksets. Various fields / sub-fields in the NIT structure variable can be seen in the following typical example file 'Ackley.PSO'.

```
[NI SYSTEM]
nit.Name = 'Ackley.PSO'
nit.Type = 'PSO'
 [PARTICLE STRING ENCODING]
nit.String.File = 'PRT.xls'
nit.String.Sheet = 'PCL'
nit.String.Range = 'A2:D31'
 [STRING ENCODING CHECKS]
nit.Checks.File = 'PRT.xls'
nit.Checks.Sheet = 'CHK'
nit.Checks.Range = 'A2:C2'
 [SWARM DESCRIPTION]
nit.Swarm.PSize = 20
nit.Swarm.VFunction = 'NoChange'
nit.Swarm.Model = 'HBest'
nit.Swarm.NSize = 1
nit.Swarm.Topology = 'Ring'
 [OBJECTIVE DESCRIPTION]
nit.Objective.File = 'PRT'
```

```
nit.Objective.Sheet = 'TRG'
nit.Objective.Range = 'A1:A1'
nit.Objective.Function = 'Ackley'
 [STRATEGIC PARAMETERS]
nit.Parameter.C1 = 2.1
nit.Parameter.C2 = 2.1
nit.Parameter.C3 = 2.1
nit.Parameter.MaxVelocity = 0.5
nit.Parameter.Chi = 0.729
nit.Parameter.WeightOption = 'Fixed'
nit.Parameter.StartWeight = 1
nit.Parameter.EndWeight = 0
 [TERMINATION CRITERIA]
nit.Terminate.NoChange = 100
nit.Terminate.Goal = 0
nit.Terminate.MaxIterations = 100
 [PLOT OPTIONS]
nit.Plot.GBest = 1
nit.Plot.Average = 1
nit.Plot.LBest = 0
```

This file, at any point of time, can be saved as a text file with '.PSO' extension and reloaded as and when required through File menu in the NIT Editor window.

SIMULATION RESULTS FOR BENCHMARK OPTIMIZATION TEST FUNCTIONS

All three PSO models are tested with four benchmark optimization test functions, viz. DeJong, Ackley, Rastrigin, and Rosenbrock, whose respective global minima lie at $\langle x \rangle = \langle 0, ... 0 \rangle$. With the help of this comparative study, we validate these PSO models and their use through NI Toolbox.

As PSO is stochastic in nature, these test evolutions are run multiple times (seven) for each PSO model and then for overall assessment, their mean values are plotted, simultaneously, with respect to number of iterations. To allow a common compari-

Figure 15. Mean comparative performance plots for DeJong function

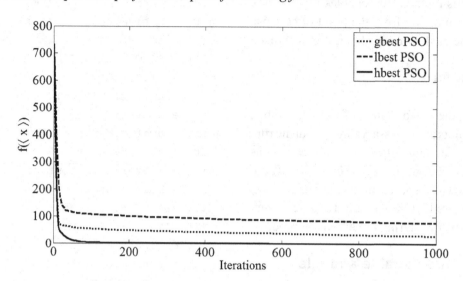

son yard stick, in all PSO evolutions, following test conditions are made common:

- Dimensional Size (n) = 30
- UOD for each element = 10
- Swarm Size = 10
- Neighborhood Size = 1
- Topology = Ring
- Acceleration Parameters = 2.1 each
- Constriction Factor = 0.729
- Maximum Velocity = 1
- Inertia Weight = 0.5
- Number of Iterations = 1000

DeJong Function

This function is uni-modal optimization test function that is also named as Sphere function and is the simplest among all the test functions. Mathematically,

$$f(\langle x \rangle) = \sum_{i=1}^{n} x_i^2 \tag{14}$$

In a limited number of 1000 iterations, the hbest PSO has evolved close to the optimal solution, i.e., particle with all zero element values. It

can be observed in Figure 15 that the fitness in other PSO models also improves with number of iterations and may evolve optimal solutions if run for large number of iterations.

Ackley Function

This function is an optimization test function which involves multiple local optima. Mathematically,

$$f(\langle x \rangle) = 20 + e - 20e^{-0.2\sqrt{\frac{\sum_{i=1}^{n} x_i^2}{n}}} - e^{\frac{\sum_{i=1}^{n} \cos 2\pi x_i}{n}} \tag{15}$$

Comparative global fitness plots for various PSO models are shown in Figure 16, when evolved for Ackley test function. In a limited number of 1000 iterations, none of the PSOs could turn out with global minimum solution, i.e., particle with all zero element values. However, *hbest* PSO approached nearer the best solution among all PSO models. The *lbest* PSO may approach the optimum solution if the process of evolution is made to run for much longer time.

Figure 16. Mean comparative performance plots for Ackley function

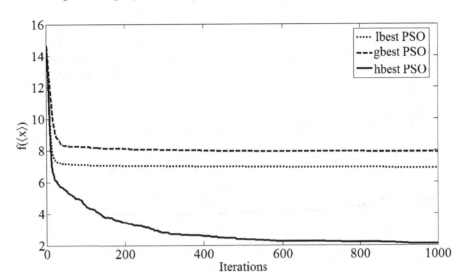

Figure 17. Mean comparative performance plots for Rastrigin function

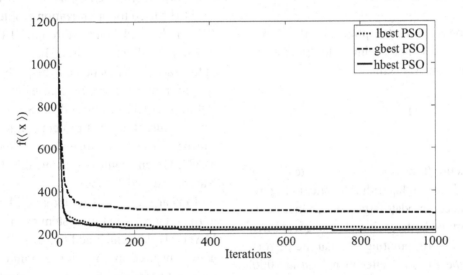

Rastrigin Function

This function is multi-modal optimization test function. Mathematically,

$$f(\langle x \rangle) = \sum_{i=1}^{n} x_i^2 - 10\cos 2\pi x_i \, 20 + 10$$

(16)

Due to multiple local optima, this function is deceptive for the gbest PSO and, therefore, gets trapped in local optima. However, lbest and hbest PSO algorithms are capable of escaping from local optima, hence, evolved much fitter solutions than those of gbest PSO, as shown in Figure 17. Once again, the hbest PSO outperformed, marginally, over the lbest PSO.

Figure 18. Mean comparative performance plots for Rosenbrock function

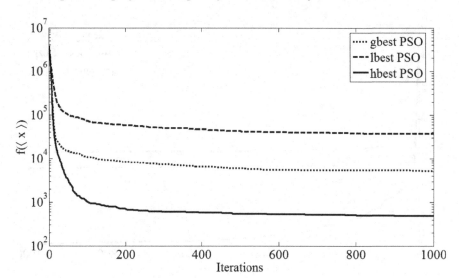

Rosenbrock Function

This function is uni-modal optimization test function, however, it is not as simple to optimize as DeJong function. Mathematically,

$$f(\langle x \rangle) = \sum_{i=1}^{n-1} 100(x_{i+1} - x^2)^2 + (x_i - 1)^2 \qquad (17)$$

The function/fitness values are plotted along with vertical axis on logarithmic scale, in Figure 18, so as to accommodate large values. Once gain, *hbest* performed better than *lbest* and *gbest* PSO models. It is worth pointing out that the performance of *gbest* is still better than *lbest* in 1000 iterations due to uni-modal nature of the function.

CONCLUSION AND FUTURE SCOPE

In this chapter, a PSO-based versatile toolbox to evolve any general system, including T1 and T2 FLS (discussed in the next chapter), is presented. In this toolbox, along with most of the popular variants of PSO, a new PSO model (named as *hbest* PSO), proposed by us, is embedded in its GUI to be used for optimization problems. These PSO models and their use through NI Toolbox are tested and validated with the help of benchmark optimization test functions. To help other researchers, this toolbox has been released under General Public License and hosted on SourceForge.net (http://sourceforge.net/projects/ nitool). Users can design and optimize their systems, in the MATLAB environment, using this PSO-based Nature Inspired Toolbox.

In near future, this toolbox will be upgraded to run on any operating system even without the MATLAB platform. In addition to PSO, a few more nature-inspired optimization techniques, e.g., Ant Colony Optimization, Genetic Algorithms, Biogeography Based Optimization, etc. will also be embedded into this toolbox.

REFERENCES

Angeline, P. J. (1998). Evolutionary optimization versus particle swarm optimization: Philosophy and performance differences. *Evolutionary Programming*, 7, 601–610. doi:10.1007/BFb0040811

Chang, J. F., Chu, S. C., Roddick, J. F., & Pan, J. S. (2005). A parallel particle swarm optimization algorithm with communication strategies. *Journal of Information Science and Engineering, 4*(21), 809–818.

Clerc, M., & Kennedy, J. (2002). The particle swarm: Explosion, stability, and convergence in a multi-dimensional complex space. *IEEE Transactions on Evolutionary Computation, 6*(1), 58–73. doi:10.1109/4235.985692

Colorni, A., Dorigo, M., & Maniezzo, V. (1991). Distributed optimization by ant colonies. In *Proceedings of First European Conference on Artificial Life*, (pp. 132-142). Cambridge, MA: MIT Press.

Eberhart, R., & Kennedy, J. (1995). A new optimizer using particle swarm theory. In *Proceedings of the Sixth International Symposium on Micro Machine and Human Science*, (pp. 39-43).

Eberhart, R., & Shi, Y. (2001). Particle swarm optimization: Developments, applications and resources. In *Proceedings of Congress on Evolutionary Computation*, (pp. 81-86). Seoul, Korea.

Eberhart, R., Simpson, P., & Dobbins, R. (1996). *Computational intelligence PC tools*. Boston, MA: Academic Press Professional.

Heppner, F., & Grenander, U. (1990). A stochastic nonlinear model for coordinated bird flocks . In *The ubiquity of chaos*. Washington, DC: AAAS Publications.

Kennedy, J. (1999). Small worlds and mega-minds: Effects of neighborhood topology on particle swarm performance. In *Proceedings of the 1999 Conference on Evolutionary Computation*, (pp. 1931-1938).

Kennedy, J., & Eberhart, R. (1995). Particle swarm optimization. In *Proceedings of ICNN '95- International Conference on Neural Networks*, Vol. 4, (pp. 1942-1948). Perth, Australia.

Kennedy, J., & Eberhart, R. (2001). *Swarm intelligence*. Morgan Kaufmann Publishers.

Kennedy, J., & Eberhart, R. C. (1997). A discrete binary version of the particle swarm algorithm. In *IEEE International Conference on Systems, Man and Cybernetics*, Vol. 5, (pp. 4104-4108). Orlando, Florida, USA.

Kennedy, J., & Mendes, R. (2002). Topological structure and particle swarm performance. In *Proceedings of the Fourth Congress on Evolutionary Computation* (CEC-2002).

Mendes, R. (2004). *Population topologies and their influence in particle swarm performance*. PhD thesis, University of Minho.

Parsopoulos, K. E., & Vrahatis, M. N. (2002). Natural computing . In *Recent approaches to global optimization problems through particle swarm optimization* (pp. 235–306). Kluwer Academic Publishers.

Reynolds, C. W. (1987). Flocks, herds and schools: A distributed behavioral model. *Computer Graphics, 21*(4), 25–34. doi:10.1145/37402.37406

Shi, X. H., Liang, Y. C., Lee, H. P., Lu, C., & Wang, Q. X. (2007). Particle swarm optimization-based algorithms for TSP and generalized TSP. *Information Processing Letters, 103*, 169–176. doi:10.1016/j.ipl.2007.03.010

Shi, Y., & Eberhart, R. (1999). Empirical study of particle swarm optimization. In *Proceedings of Congress on Evolutionary Computation*, (pp. 1945-1950).

Shi, Y., Eberhart, R., & Chen, Y. (1999). Implementation of evolutionary fuzzy systems. *IEEE Transactions on Fuzzy Systems, 7*(5), 109–119. doi:10.1109/91.755393

Trelea, I. C. (2003). The particle swarm optimization algorithm: Convergence analysis and parameter selection. *Information Processing Letters, 85*, 317–325. doi:10.1016/S0020-0190(02)00447-7

Chapter 18

Adaptive Intelligent Systems for Recognition of Cancerous Cervical Cells Based on 2D Cervical Cytological Digital Images

Bernadetta Kwintiana Ane
Institute of Computer-aided Product Development Systems, Universitaet Stuttgart, Germany

Dieter Roller
Institute of Computer-aided Product Development Systems, Universitaet Stuttgart, Germany

ABSTRACT

To date, cancer of uterine cervix is still a leading cause of cancer-related deaths in women in the world. Papanicolau smear test is a well-known screening method of detecting abnormalities of the cervix cells. Due to scarce number of skilled and experienced cytologists, the screening procedure becomes time consuming and highly prone to human errors that leads to inaccurate and inconsistent diagnosis. This condition increases the risk of patients who get HPV infection not be detected and become HPV carriers. Coping with this problem, an adaptive intelligent system is developed to enable automatic recognition of cancerous cells from. Here pattern recognition is done based on three morphological cell characteristics, i.e. size, shape, and color features, and measured as numerical values in terms of N/C ratio, nucleus perimeter, nucleus radius, cell deformity, texture heterogeneity, wavelet approximation coefficients, and gray-level intensity. Through a supervised learning of multilayer perceptron network, the system is able to percept abnormality in the cervix cells, and to assign them into a predicted group membership, i.e. normal or cancerous cells. Based on thorough observation upon the selected features and attributes, it can be recognized that the cancerous cells follow certain patterns and highly distinguishable from the normal cells.

DOI: 10.4018/978-1-4666-1833-6.ch018

INTRODUCTION

Cervix cancer is a malignant cancer of the cervix uteri or cervical area. This is considered as the second most common form of cancer in women in the world (Cotrans et al., 1999; WHO, 2010). In 2008, it is recorded 529,828 incidences and 275,128 deaths due to cervix cancer, with 68 per cent of the cases occurs in the poorest regions of the world; i.e. South Asia, sub-Saharan Africa, and parts of Latin America. The majority of cases are squamous cell carcinoma (WHO: Human Papillomavirus, 2007; Reproductive Health Technologies Project, 2008), while the adenocarcinomas are less common. This number is estimated to increase by 35.90 per cent worldwide in year 2025 with 720,060 incidences and 395,095 deaths (WHO: HPV and Related Cancers, 2010).

The pathogenesis of cervical cancer is pointed to Human Papillomavirus (HPV). Papillomavirus are icosahedral DNA viruses, non-enveloped with diameter of 52-55 nm. It belongs to the family of Papovaviridae. The viral particles consists of a single double-stranded DNA molecule of about 8000 base-pairs that is bound to cellular histones and contained in a protein capsid composed of 72 pentametric capsomers (WHO: Human Papillomavirus, 2007).

HPV infection is associated with malignancies of urogenital tract and anus. It is also related to disorder of skin and the upper respiratory system. To date, more than 100 HPV types are acknowledged to exist. There 15 types are classified as high-risk (16, 18, 31, 33, 35, 39, 45, 51, 52, 56, 58, 59, 68, 73, and 82), 3 types as probable high-risk (26, 53, and 66), and 12 types as low-risk (6, 11, 40, 42, 43, 44, 54, 61, 70, 72, 81, and CP6108). Almost 85 per cent of invasive squamous cell cancer is infected by types 16 and 18, and less common by types 31, 33, 35, and 51 (Prayitno, 2006; Kumar et al., 2007).

Unlike many cancers, actually cervix cancer can be prevented. By providing women with proper screening tests and when necessary medical treatment, this devastating disease can be cured. Papanicolau smear, or so-called Pap smear, test is one of screening methods commonly used for detecting abnormalities in the uterine cervix cells, including the changes in the cells when they evolve into cancerous cells. The result of Pap smear test provides information on the characteristics of cervix cells, that valuable for cytologists to diagnose whether a cell is normal or cancerous.

Today, many parts of the world are still mostly doing the screening and diagnosis of Pap smear test conventionally. Due to scarce number of skilled and experienced cytologists, the screening procedure becomes time consuming and highly prone to human errors that leads to inaccurate and inconsistent diagnosis. Meanwhile, early cervical pre-cancers or cancers often have no physical signs or symptoms. In most cases, symptoms do not appear until the cancer is further along and has spread to nearby areas (American Cancer Society, 2010). This condition increases the risk of patients who get HPV infection not to be detected and become HPV carriers while the virus spread out and turns into malignant in the cervix uteri.

In order to overcome this problem, standardization and automation of the screening process seems to be a solution. As regards machines, we might say, very broadly, that a machine learns whenever it changes its structure, program, or data in such a manner that its expected future performance improves. Machine learning, as a branch of artificial intelligence, concerns with the design and development of algorithms that allow computing to evolve such behaviors based on empirical data. A major focus of machine learning is to automatically learn to recognize complex patterns and make intelligent decisions based on data. The goals in machine learning are primarily to make predictions as accurately as possible and to understand the behaviour of learning algorithms (Rasmussen and Williams, 2006).

Therefore, an adaptive intelligent system is being developed to enable automatic recognition of the cancerous cells from the Pap smear specimens. The intelligent system is built by adopting and embodying expert knowledge of the cytologists. It is designed through a supervised learning to automatically recognize abnormality in the cervix cells, and to assign them into a predicted group membership, i.e. normal cells or cancerous cells. Here the term 'adaptive' represents an ability of the intelligent agent to adapt with changes in its environment that commonly sources from changes of structure, program, or data (i.e. based on its input or in response to external information) in such a manner that the expected future performance will improve. Using a standardized decision making rule, the adaptive intelligent system is able to recognize and generate perception used for detecting abnormality in the cervix cells, which is objective, more accurate and consistent. Thus, it can solve the problem of lack of skilled and experienced cytologists. This system does not mean to replace the cytologists' role, instead to become an aid tool for cytologists to make better diagnosis for the patients.

RELATED STUDIES

Prior studies have been devoted to eliminate inaccuracy and inconsistency problems in the cervix cancer screening. In the beginning, image analysis of the structural organization of cells in histological sections has been shown to be useful for the quantitative characterization of cervical tissue. As medical science advances, the method of cervical cancer screening has evolved. Using specimens derived from histological section, Pap smear, spectroscopy, or HPV-DNA, abnormality in the uterine cervix cells can be recognized.

In 1988, Chaudhuri et al. introduces techniques to express the cervical cells structure in the form of a tree or a graph, and to derive features from them. Information derived from the graph along with the cell features can be effectively used for cervical cells classification and diagnosis. A decade later, Tumer et al. (1998) introduces the

use of radial basis function (RBF) networks to extract clinically useful information of cervical tissue spectra produced by in vivo fluorescence spectroscopy used to discriminate healthy tissue from precancerous tissue samples.

During 1990s, computational techniques in Image Processing, Computer Vision, Soft-Computing, and Machine Learning are fast progressing and establishing new approaches and algorithms. Since then studies on cervical cancer detections are more focus on the development of efficient computational techniques that can produce more accurate and consistent diagnosis.

Mitra et al. (2000) develops a hybrid decision support system using a rough set theory based Genetic Algorithm and an Interactive Dichotomizer 3 (ID3) algorithm. The system evolution is designed using a restricted mutation operator that utilizes knowledge of the modular structure, which can lead to faster convergence. Liu et al. (2002) applies Soft-Computing techniques for automatic cancer cells detection in multispectral microscopic thin Pap smear images. From each pixel, various types of image features are extracted in a fix-sized block. This procedure is applied to every band that results in a very high dimensional multispectral texture, which sensitive to discriminate cancerous cells from normal cells. Continuing Liu et al. (2002), Zhao et al. (2002) improves the performance of the approach of multispectral texture (MST) features by carrying out pairwise comparison between MST versus average spectral texture features (AST, without spectral information), and MST versus multispectral intensity features (MSI, without texture information). The results demonstrate that well-selected MST features combining both multispectral and texture information can achieve better classification for cervical cancer detection. Coombes and Culverhouse (2003) applies an Atrous wavelet transformation to identify the maximum hue on the cervical cytological slides derived from Pap smear test. The hue is relatively stable while saturation depends upon the amount of illumination used, hence, hue becomes a superior measure for the discrimination of cells between groups.

In the following years, Machine Learning theory and algorithms are becoming well-established. Many studies are then more focus on the development of efficient algorithms that are sensitive to discrimination of cervical cells characteristics. In 2003, Mat-Isa et al. presents the use of Hybrid Multilayered Perceptron (HMLP) network to diagnose cervical cancer in the early stage by classifying cells into three classes, i.e. normal, LSIL (low grade squamous intraepithelial lesion), and HSIL (high grade squamous intraepithelial lesion). Here the ability of neural network to produce a good performance is analyzed using two measures, i.e. the diagnosis confidence percentage and diagnosis confidence level. Afterwards, Zhang & Liu (2004) introduce a novel feature screening algorithm by deriving relevance measures from the decision boundary of Support Vector Machines. The algorithm is applied for automatic cervical cancer detection in multispectral microscopic thin Pap smear images. It alleviates the "independence" assumption of traditional screening methods, e.g. those based on Information Gain and Augmented Variance Ratio, without sacrificing computational efficiency. Lassouaoui et al. (2005) applies an unsupervised Genetic Algorithm for the diagnosis of malignancy based on the set of atypical morphological details of cell components, i.e. nucleus and cytoplasm. The morphological characteristics of cells are analyzed referring to the nucleus-to-cytoplasm ratio, cell deformity, and texture heterogeneity. Thangavel et al. (2006) applies K-means algorithm to identify clusters of cervical cancer patients from a given database. The results are shown to be consistent with traditional medical diagnosis and are useful in prediction of non-linear groups, which are essentially different risk groups. Feng et al. (2007) develops an improved Cosine Correlation Analysis (CCA) algorithm to extract multispectral features from each pixel derived from the microscopic cervical cells images. By combining the characteristics

of cell area, the identification of abnormality as well as lower false negative rate (FNR) and false positive rate (FPR) can be made efficiently.

Recently, Mustafa et al. (2008) has improved the work of Mat-Isa et al. (2003) by improving the application of HMLP for cervical cancer diagnosis using ThinPrep® images. By employing a new set of cell features, i.e. size, grey-level, perimeter, red, green, blue, intensity, and saturation, the hierarchical HMLP can produce suitable cells classification for the cervical cancer diagnostic. Respectively, De Marchi Triglia et al. (2009) applies the Mann-Whitney and Fisher tests to compare and classify membership of cervical cells into the specified groups, i.e. patients without progression and with progression. Data and analysis is based on HPV-DNA, it is one factor for malignant transformation of cervical cells that can only be identified using in situ hybridization (ISH). The results indicate good recognition of punctate nuclei patterns in the basal region for both groups.

This research is done in favor for improving the sensitivity of hierarchical MLP algorithm in recognizing abnormality of cervical cells based on a new set of atypical morphological characteristics, i.e. size, shape, and color. Here, the cells size is measured using parameters nucleus-to-cytoplasm (N/C) ratio, nucleus perimeter, and nucleus radius. The cells shape is identified through cells deformity, texture heterogeneity, and wavelet approximation coefficients. Then, the cells color is identified through the gray-level intensity. Data used in this research comes from the Euthman's database, which consists of 967 cervical cell images derived from worldwide women suspects. The database is divided into seven groups, i.e. normal, mild dysplasia, severe dysplasia, CIS (carcinoma in situ), CIN-I (cervical intraepithelial neoplasia level 1), CIN-II (CIN level 2), and CIN-III (CIN level 3) cells. Evaluation on the performance of the proposed MLP algorithm is done in two stages. First, the algorithm is trained through a supervised learning to recognize cells abnormality and assign them into a predicted group membership. In this stage, the database is regrouped into two groups, i.e. normal cells and cancerous cells. The normal cells group consists of images randomly selected from the normal, mild dysplasia, and severe dysplasia cells. While, the cancerous cells group contains random images from the CIS, CIN-I, CIN-II, and CIN-III cells. In the second stage, the algorithm obtained from prior stage is trained in a higher-level sensitivity to discriminate cells for recognizing cervix cancer staging. In this chapter, we would only like to discuss about machine learning process of the first stage.

MACHINE LEARNING

Many tasks such as recognition, diagnosis, planning, robot control, and prediction apply machine learning methods. Basically, machine learning refers to the changes in systems that perform tasks associated with artificial intelligence (AI). The changes might be either enhancements to already performing systems or *ab initio* synthesis of new systems (Nilson, 1998).

Analogy to human visual perception, the electromagnetic radiation in the optical band generated from the visual environment enters the human's visual system through eyes and is incident upon the sensitive cells of the retina. The activities start in the retina, where the signals from neighboring receivers are compared and a coded message dispatched on the optic nerves to the cortex. Then, the perceptual recognition and interpretation of vision takes place in human's brain. The objects and different regions in an image are recognized in the brain from the edges or boundaries that encapsulate the objects or the regions inside the scene. The process of recognition is a result of learning that takes place in the neural organization.

Adopting human's neural system, the learning process is designed as an artificial neural network (ANN) that resembles the mechanism of neurons in human's brain. ANN is a computational model

with learning, or adaptive, characteristics (Jang, Sun & Mizutani, 1997). It consists of large set of interconnected neurons, which execute in parallel to perform the task of learning. Generally, learning process can be classified into two category, i.e. supervised and unsupervised. In the case of supervised ANN, the learning process uses input-output training data to model the dynamic system. On the other hand, in unsupervised ANN only the input data is given.

Here the learning task is to classify cervical cells into the predicted group membership based on the specified input-output features. The learning process is performed by an intelligent agent, which is built in the adaptive intelligent system. Meanwhile, the learning network model applies the multilayer perceptron (MLP) with 2 hidden layers that is an extension of the single-layer perceptron model of Rosenblatt (Rosenblatt, 1958; Rumelhart and McClelland, 1986).

The Adaptive Intelligent System

According to the Knowledge System Laboratory at Stanford University (2003), an adaptive intelligent system refers to an AI system that coordinates perception, reasoning and action to pursue multiple goals while functioning autonomously in dynamic environments. Principally, AI agent is composed by perception, modeler, planning and reasoning, and action computation subsystems. Figure 1 depicts the architecture of AI agent applied in this research. The AI agent perceives and models its environment based on the sensory signals input, then reasons the impulse and plans according to the learning goal, and finally computes appropriate action that might also inherently anticipates impacts of the action. Changes applied in one or more subsystems induce machines to learn. Different learning mechanism can be employed suitable to the subsystem behavior where changes are taking place.

The adaptive intelligent system embodies an MLP model with 2 hidden layers to classify the

Figure 1. Architecture of adaptive intelligent agent

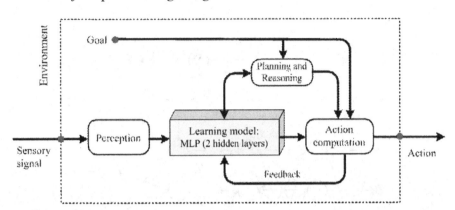

unknown pattern of cervical cells through a supervised learning. Here as done mostly in parametric supervised classification, the classifier is trained with a large set of labeled training pattern samples in order to estimate the statistical parameters of each class of patterns, e.g. N/C ratio, nucleus perimeter and radius, and so forth. In this regard, the 'labeled pattern samples' mean the set of patterns whose class memberships are known in advance. The input feature vectors obtained during the training phase of the supervised classification are assumed to be Gaussian in nature. Using the weights (w_i) of neuron generated from the training process, classification can be applied for the test pattern data. Figure 2 describes the block diagram of MLP classifier.

Using pairs of input-output features, the MLP network model can adjust the internal structure and construct functions to approximate the implicit input-output relationship. In the case of

important relationships are hidden amongst large amount of data, the MLP model can extract those relationships and make them transparently recognizable. It is important to understand process of learning in machine. The following subsections describe the MLP model and its learning process in the neural network.

Multilayer Perceptron

Generally speaking, multilayer perceptrons are a feedforward network having distinct input, output, and hidden layers. The basic architecture of an MLP network consists of layers of structurally identical computing nodes, or neurons, arranged so that the output of every neuron in one layer feeds into the input of every neuron in the next layer (Gonzales and Woods, 2002) as described in Figure 3. The number of neurons in the first layer, called layer A, is N_A. Often $N_A = n$, the

Figure 2. The block diagram of multilayer perceptron classifier

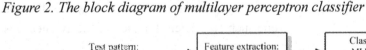
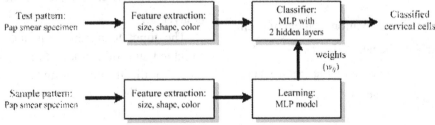

Figure 3. Basic architecture of multilayer perceptron network model (Source: Gonzales and Woods, 2002)

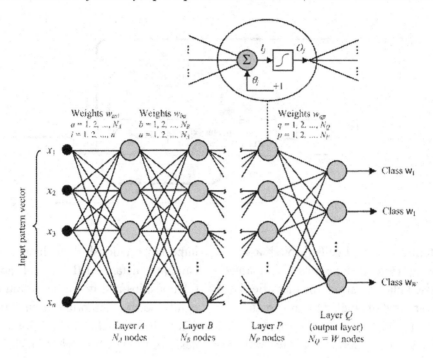

dimensionality of the input pattern vectors. The number of neurons in the output layer, called layer Q, is N_Q. The number N_Q equals W, the number of pattern classes that the MLP network will be trained to recognize.

As depicted at the upper part of Figure 3, each neuron has the same form with a soft-limiting *sigmoid* function. In this regard, differentiability along all path of the MLP network is required for the development of the training rule. The following sigmoid activation function has the necessary differentiability,

$$h_j\left(I_j\right) = \frac{1}{1 + e^{-(I_j + \theta_j)/\theta_o}} \qquad (1)$$

where I_j: input to the activation element of each neuron in layer j of the network, j: 1, 2, ..., N_j, θ_j: an offset, and θ_o: parameter that controls the shape of the sigmoid function.

Plotting Equation (1) along with the limits for the "high" and "low" responses out of each neuron, the sigmoid activation function can be derived as illustrated in Figure 4. It is shown, the sigmoid activation function is always positive, and it can reach its limiting values of 0 and 1 only if the input to the activation element is infinitely negative or positive, respectively. In principle, different types of activation functions can be used for different layers or even for different neurons in the same layer of a network. For practical reason, this chapter applies the same form of activation function throughout the network. The inputs and its modifying weight θ_j are integral parts of the networks neurons. As noted in Figure 3, there is one such coefficient for each of the N_j neurons in layer J.

The input to a neuron in any layer is the weighted sum of the outputs from the previous layer. For illustration, letting layer K denote the layer preceding layer J gives the input to the

Figure 4. The sigmoid activation function (Source: Gonzales and Woods, 2002)

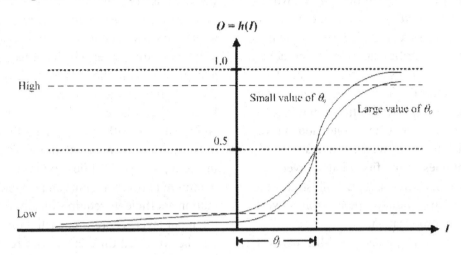

activation element of each neuron in layer J, then I_j can be represented as

$$I_j = \sum_{k=1}^{N_k} w_{jk} O_k \qquad (2)$$

where N_j: the number of neurons in layer J, N_k: the number of neurons in layer K, and w_{jk}: the weights modifying the outputs O_k of the neurons in layer K before fed into the neurons in layer J, and $j = 1, 2, ..., N_j$. Then, the outputs of layer K are

$$O_k = h_k\left(I_k\right) \qquad (3)$$

for $k = 1, 2, ..., N_k$. Substituting Equation (2) into (1) yields

$$h_j\left(I_j\right) = \frac{1}{1 + e^{-\left(\sum_{k=1}^{N_A} w_{jk} O_k + \theta_j\right)/\theta_o}} \qquad (4)$$

which is the form of activation function applied in the proposed MLP network model.

In this chapter, the MLP network is designed as a 2-class problem (i.e. normal and cancerous groups) with 3-dimensional patterns, where the input layer consists of three neurons (i.e. N/C ratio, nucleus perimeter, and nucleus radius) and the output layer consists of two neurons. Between the input and the output layers, there are two hidden layers that consist of four neurons (i.e. cell deformity, texture heterogeneity, wavelet approximation coefficients, and gray-level intensity). The output from each neuron in the input layer is fed to the neurons in the hidden layers. No computations are performed at the input layer neurons. The hidden layer neurons sum up the inputs, passes them through the sigmoid non-linearity function and fan-out multiple connections to the output layer neurons.

In feed-forward activation, neurons of the first hidden layer compute their activation and output values, and fed them as inputs to the neurons in the second hidden layer. The similar computation is done by neurons of the second layer for activation and generating output values, and passes them to the neurons in the output layer. The feed-forward from the second hidden layer to the output layer generates the network's actual response towards the input being presented by neurons in the input layer. Once the activation proceeds forward from the input to the output neurons, the network's response is compared to the desired output corresponding to each set of labeled pattern samples belong to each specific class. Often the actual response at the output layer will deviate from the desired output that may result in an error at the output layer. The error at the output layer is used to compute error at the second hidden layer that immediately preceding the output layer. This process continues to the first hidden layer and, then, to the input layer. Figure 5 illustrates the architecture of the multilayer perceptron network with error backpropagation.

As it has been mentioned, the MLP network in Figure 5 uses a similar activation function throughout the network. The activation function applies two types of relation of input and output. First, (1:1) relation refers to a relation between output from a single neuron in the preceding layer that is fed as input to a single neuron in the next layer. Second, ($M:1$) relation represents to a relation between outputs from several neurons in the preceding layer which are fed as inputs to a single neuron in the next layer. As illustration, there are three inputs to every neuron in the first hidden layer, where each individual input can be weighted differently. For instance, the cell deformity neuron requires three inputs from neurons in the input layer. While, texture heterogeneity neuron requires two inputs and wavelet approximation coefficients requires only one input from the input layer. Therefore, each individual input will be weighted differently with respect to the neuron which they are fed as input.

Figure 5. Architecture of backpropagation multilayer perceptron network

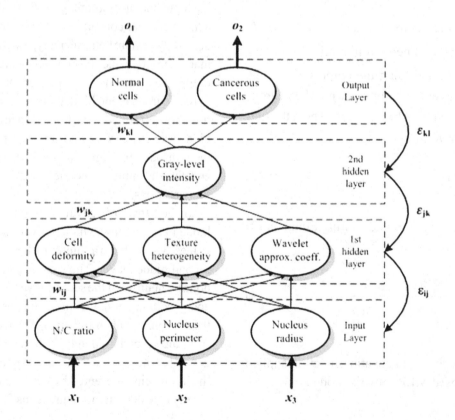

Backpropagation Multilayer Perceptron Learning Algorithm

Generally, the term "backpropagation" refers to the procedure for finding a gradient vector in a network structure that is calculated in the direction opposite to the flow of the output of each neuron (Melin and Castillo, 2005). In this regard, a backpropagation multilayer perceptron is an adaptive network whose neurons, or neurons, perform a similar function on the incoming signals. This neuron function is usually a composite of the weighted sum and a differentiable non-linear activation function, which is also known as "transfer function".

Suppose that a given feed-forward adaptive network has L layers and layer $l(l = 0, 1, ..., L)$ has $N(l)$ neurons. Then, the output and function of neuron $i[i = 1, ..., N(l)]$ in layer l can be represented as $x_{l,i}$ and $f_{l,i}$ respectively. Since the output of a neuron depends on the incoming signals and the parameter set of the neuron, then the neuron function, $f_{l,i}$, is expressed as

$$X_{l,i} = f_{l,i}\left(x_{i-1,1}, ..., x_{l-1,N(l-1)}, \alpha, \beta, \gamma, ...\right) \qquad (5)$$

where α, β, γ, etc. are the parameters of neuron.

Assuming that the given training data has P entries, the error (E_p) measure for the p-th $(1 \leq p \leq P)$ entry of the training data can be defined as the sum of the squared errors

$$E_p = \sum_{k=1}^{N(l)}\left(d_k - x_{L,k}\right)^2 \qquad (6)$$

where d_k: the k-th neuron of the p-th desired output vector, $x_{L,k}$: the k-th neuron of the actual output vector produced by presenting the p-th input vector to the network.

In feed-forward activation, the net input to the i-th hidden neuron at layer l can be computed as

$$I_{l,i} = \sum_{i=1}^{N(l)} x_i w_{l,i} + \theta_i \qquad (7)$$

where x_i: input pattern vector, $w_{l,i}$: weight between the l-th hidden layer and the input layer, and θ_i: bias term associated with each neuron in the hidden layer. While, the output of the i-th hidden layer neuron is

$$x_{l,i} = f\left(I_{l,i}\right) = \frac{1}{1 - exp\left(-I_{l,i}\right)} . \qquad (8)$$

The Equation (7)-(8) are known as forward pass calculation. The error $\left(d_k - x_{L,k}\right)$ between the desired output and the actual output is propagated backward through the backward pass. The calculations governing the backward pass are used to correct the weights. Thus, the network learns the desired mapping function by backpropagating the error between layers.

In this framework, the Delta rule (δ) is applied for minimizing the sum of squared error between the actual network output and the desired output responses overall the patterns. Then, the average error can be re-written as a function of the weights

$$E\left(w_{l,i}\right) = \frac{1}{2} \sum_{l=1}^{N(l)}\left(d_k - x_{l,k}\right)^2 . \qquad (9)$$

Obviously, when E_p is equal to zero, the network is able to reproduce exactly the desired output in the p-th training data pair. Thus, here the task is to minimize an overall error measure

$$E = \sum_{p=1}^{P} E_p = 0 \tag{10}$$

that can be done by finding the root of the partial derivatives of Equation (9)

$$\sum_{l=1}^{N(l)} \frac{\partial E}{\partial w_{l,i}} = 0. \tag{11}$$

Under the Delta rule (δ), the error can be minimized by taking incremental steps to correct the weights by

$$\nabla w_{l,i}(t) = -\eta \frac{\partial E}{\partial w_{l,i}} + \alpha \nabla w_{l,i}(t-1). \tag{12}$$

where η : learning rate of the hidden layer neurons. Then, the partial derivative $\dfrac{\partial E}{\partial w_{l,i}}$ for the output layer can be obtained through a Chain Rule as

$$\frac{\partial E}{\partial w_{l,i}} = x_{L,k}(1 - x_{L,k})(d_k - x_{L,k}) \tag{13}$$

$$w_{l,i}^{(new)} = w_{l,i}^{(old)} + \eta \delta_i x_{L,k} \tag{14}$$

Similarly, δ_j can be denoted as

$$\delta_j = x_j (1 - x_j)(d_j - x_j) \tag{15}$$

where d_j is the ideal response. Following the Chain Rule, δ_j for the other layers can be obtained using the similar rule.

The elegance of the equation δ_j emanates from the differentiable characteristic of the sigmoidal function. Thus, when the errors are propagated backwards, a formulation in terms of the expected and calculated output patterns is obtained.

Herein lies the power and simplification of backpropagation, which makes this function versatile.

It is important to note that the backpropagation performs gradient descent in the errors. By adjusting the weights after each sample patterns is presented, the network converges to a fixed weight vector. As proven by Rumerlhart and McClelland (1986), by selecting small learning rate a good approximation of gradient descent can be achieved through the sequence of small movements.

Referring to Equation (6), by taking both direct and indirect paths into consideration an error signal ($\varepsilon_{l,i}$) can be defined as the derivative of error (E_p) with respect to the output of neuron i in layer l

$$\varepsilon_{l,i} = \frac{\partial^+ E_p}{\partial x_{l,i}} \tag{16}$$

According to Werbos (1974), the Equation (16) is mathematically called the "ordered derivative". The difference between the ordered derivative and the ordinary partial derivative lies in the way of the function to be differentiated. For an internal neuron output $x_{l,i}$, the partial derivative $\partial^+ E_p / \partial x_{l,i}$ is equal to zero, since E_p does not depend on $x_{l,i}$ directly. However, it is obvious that E_p depends on $x_{l,i}$ indirectly, since a change in $x_{l,i}$ will propagate through indirect paths to the output layer and, thus, produces a corresponding change in the value of E_p.

Afterwards, the error signal for the i-th output at layer l can be calculated directly

$$\varepsilon_{L,i} = \frac{\partial^+ E_p}{\partial x_{L,i}} = \frac{\partial E_p}{\partial x_{L,i}}. \tag{17}$$

This is equal to $\varepsilon_{L,i} = -2(d_i - x_{L,i})$ if E_p is defined as in the Equation (6). For the internal neuron at the i-th position of layer l, the error signal can be derived by the Chain Rule of differential calculus (see Equation 18) where $0 \leq l \leq L-1$. The error signal of an internal neuron at layer l can be expressed as a linear combination of the error signal of the neurons at layer $l+1$. Therefore, for any l and i, the error signal $\varepsilon_{l,i}$ can be found by at first applying Equation (17) to get error signals at the output layer, and then applying Equation (18) iteratively until the desired layer l is reached.

Under the Chain Rule, the recursive formula for ε_i can be written as Equation 19 where d_i: the desired output of neuron i, O_i and O_i: the actual output of neurons i and j, ε_j: error signal of neuron j, and w_{ij}: connection weight from neuron i to j. If w_{ij} is zero, means no direct connection.

The gradient vector can be defined as the derivative of the error measure with respect to each parameter. If α is a parameter of the i-th neuron at layer l, then

$$\frac{\partial^+ E_p}{\partial \alpha} = \frac{\partial^+ E_p}{\partial x_{l,i}} \cdot \frac{\partial f_{l,i}}{\partial \alpha} = \varepsilon_{l,i} \frac{\partial f_{l,i}}{\partial \alpha}. \tag{20}$$

The derivative of the overall error measure E with respect to α is

$$\frac{\partial^+ E}{\partial \alpha} = \sum_{p=1}^{P} \frac{\partial^+ E_p}{\partial \alpha} \tag{21}$$

Accordingly, in simple steepest descent applied for a minimization problem, the generic parameter α can be corrected as

$$\Delta \alpha = -\eta \frac{\partial^+ E}{\partial \alpha}, \tag{22}$$

which can be further expressed as

$$\eta = \frac{k}{\sqrt{\sum_{\alpha} (\partial E / \partial \alpha)^2}} \tag{23}$$

Equation 18.

$$\varepsilon_{l,i} = \underbrace{\frac{\partial^+ E_p}{\partial x_{l,i}}}_{\substack{\square error\ signal \\ \square at\ layer\ l}} = \underbrace{\sum_{m=1}^{N(l+1)} \frac{\partial^+ E_p}{\partial x_{l+1,m}} \cdot \frac{\partial f_{l+1,m}}{\partial x_{l,i}}}_{\substack{\square error\ signal \\ \square at\ layer\ l+1}} = \sum_{m=1}^{M(l+1)} \epsilon_{l+1,m} \frac{\partial f_{l+1,m}}{\partial x_{l,i}}$$

Equation 19.

$$\varepsilon_i = \begin{cases} if\ "i"\ is\ an\ output: & -2(d_i - O_i)\frac{\partial O_i}{\partial O_i} = -2(d_i - O_i)O_i(1 - O_i) \\ otherwise: & \frac{\partial O_i}{\partial O_i} \sum_{j,i<j} \frac{\partial^+ E_p}{\partial O_j} \cdot \frac{\partial O_j}{\partial O_i} = O_i(1 - O_i)\sum_{j,i<j} \varepsilon_j w_{ij} \end{cases}$$

where k: the "step size", i.e. the length of each transition along the gradient direction in the parameter space.

Generally speaking, there are two types of learning paradigms that are available to suit the needs for various applications. First, it is called "off-line learning" or "batch learning", the correction of parameter α is generated based on Equation (21) and the update action takes place only after the whole training data set has been presented, that is only after each *epoch* or *sweep*. Second, it is called "on-line learning" or "pattern-by-pattern learning", the parameter α is determined based on Equation (20) and the parameters are updated immediately after each input-output pair has been presented. In their application, it is possible to combine these two learning modes and to correct the parameter after k training data entries have been presented. Here k is between 1 and P that refers to epoch size.

In the on-line learning, the connection weight w_{ki} from neuron k to i is corrected through

$$\Delta w_{ki} = -\eta \frac{\partial^+ E_p}{\partial w_{ki}} = -\eta \frac{\partial^+ E_p}{\partial O_i} \cdot \frac{\partial O_i}{\partial w_{ki}} = -\eta \varepsilon_i O_k$$

(24)

where η as a learning rate will affect the convergence speed and stability of the weights during learning. On the other hand, in the off-line learning the weight w_{ki} is corrected only after presentation of the entire data set, or only after an epoch as

$$\Delta w_{ki} = -\eta \frac{\partial^+ E}{\partial w_{ki}} = -\eta \sum_p \frac{\partial^+ E_p}{\partial w_{ki}}$$

(25)

or, in vector form is

$$\Delta w = -\eta \frac{\partial^+ E}{\partial w} = -\eta \nabla w E$$

(26)

where $E = \sum_{p=1}^{P} E_p$ as defined in Equation (10). This corresponds to the way of using the true gradient direction based on the entire data set.

This backpropagation MLP algorithm is applied into the intelligent agent, which is inherently built in the adaptive intelligent system. The design of the intelligent system itself involves seven respective stages that will be explained in section 4.

Non-Linear Separability

In its most basic form, a perceptron learns a linear decision function that dichotomizes two linearly separable training sets. Thus, for more than two inputs a single layer perceptron implements a hyperplane decision surface. This is called *linear separation*. However, a single layer perceptron cannot classify the input patterns that are not linearly separable such as an *exclusive-OR* (XOR) problem. XOR is the same as OR logic operator, but is false when both inputs are true, thus, *exclusive*.

The XOR problem can be solved by using three well-arranged perceptrons and splitting up the problem into three different parts in terms of Boolean operation,

```
y = (x₁ AND NOT(x₂)) OR (NOT(x₁) AND
x₂)
or
y = (x₁ OR x₂) AND NOT(x₁ AND x₂)
thus,
y₁ = x₁ OR x₂
y₂ = NOT(x₁ AND x₂)
y  = y₁ AND y₂
```

As resultant, the perceptrons y_1, y_2, and y will be interconnected as depicted in Figure 6.

The XOR problem may be considered as a special case of a more general non-linear mapping problem, namely, classification of points in the *unit hypercube*. Each point in the hypercube is

Figure 6. Multiperceptron interconnection in the XOR problem (Source: Matthew, 2004)

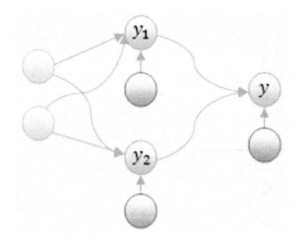

either class 0 or class 1. In the XOR problem, there are only four corners of a unit square that correspond to the input pattern (0,0), (0,1), (1,1), and (1,0), need to be considered. Moving from one corner to the next represents a single bit (i.e., binary digit) changes.

The first and third input patterns are in class 0, hence,

$$0 \oplus 0 = 0$$

and

$$1 \oplus 1 = 0 \tag{27}$$

where $\oplus$ denotes the *exclusive-OR* Boolean function operator. The input patterns (0,0) and (1,1) are at the opposite corners of the unit square that produce the identical output 0. On the other hand, the input (0,1) and (1,0) are also at the opposite corners, but they are in class 1, then

$$0 \oplus 1 = 1$$

and

$$1 \oplus 0 = 1 \tag{28}$$

As stated by Touretzky and Pomerleau (1989), the *XOR* problem can be solved using multiperceptron under the following assumptions:

Each neuron is represented by a McCulloch-Pitts (1943) model, which uses a threshold function for its activation function.

Bits 0 and 1 are represented by the level 0 and +1, respectively.

Using a single hidden layer with two neurons, the top neuron, labeled as "Neuron 1" in the hidden layer, is characterized as

$$w_{11} = w_{12} = +1 \tag{29}$$

$$b_1 = -\frac{3}{2} \tag{30}$$

The slope of the decision boundary constructed by this hidden neuron is equal to -1 as. The bottom neuron, labeled as "Neuron 2" in the hidden layer, is characterized as

$$w_{21} = w_{22} = +1 \tag{31}$$

$$b_2 = -\frac{1}{2} \tag{32}$$

The output neuron, labeled as "Neuron 3, is characterized as

$$w_{31} = w_{22} = -2 \tag{33}$$

$$w_{32} = w_{22} = +1 \tag{34}$$

$$b_3 = -\frac{1}{2} \tag{35}$$

Figure 7 describes the orientation and position of the decision boundary constructed by the hidden neurons in the signal-flow graph of the network.

Figure 7. Multiperceptron network for solving the XOR problem: (a) architectural graph, (b) signal-flow graph (Source: Haykin, 2009)

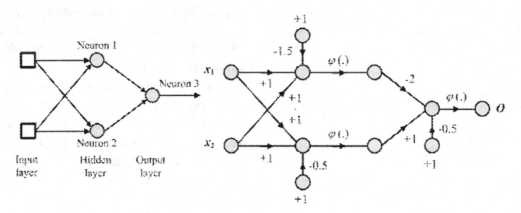

The function of the output neuron is to construct a linear combination of the decision boundaries formed by the two hidden neurons. As depicted in Figure 7, the bottom hidden neuron has an excitatory (positive) connection to the output neuron, whereas the top hidden neuron has an inhibitory (negative) connection to the output neuron. When both hidden neurons are "off", which occurs when the input pattern is (0,0), the output neuron remains off. When both hidden neurons are "on", which occurs when the input pattern is (1,1), the output neuron is switched off again because the inhibitory effect of the larger negative weight connected to the top hidden neuron overpowers the excitatory effect of the positive weight connected to the bottom hidden neuron. When the top hidden neuron is "off" and

the bottom hidden neuron is "on", which occurs when the input pattern is (0,1) or (1,0), the output neuron is switched on because of the excitatory effect of the positive weight connected to the bottom hidden neuron (Haykin, 2009). Thus, the network does indeed solve the XOR problem. Figure 8 illustrates the output of decision boundaries.

The same mechanism can be extended for solving more complex problems with two or higher number of hidden layers. A multiperceptron network with two hidden layers implements decision surfaces of arbitrary complexity. The number of neurons used in each layer determines the complexity of the problem. While, the number of classes is arbitrary, since the number of output neurons can be selected to fit the problem at hand.

Figure 8. Decision boundary of the XOR problem constructed by: (a) neuron 1, (b) neuron 2, (c) complete network in Figure 7

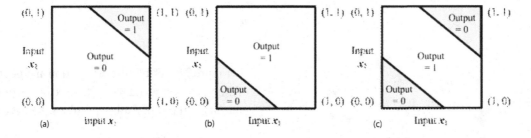

ANALYTICAL FRAMEWORK

According to Karp (2005), there are three critical characteristics can be observed using human vision during the development of cancerous cells in the cervix, i.e. size, shape, and color. Cancerous cells commonly have larger nucleus and smaller cytoplasm. They have abnormal morphological shape and tend to lump together as colony. Their color is relatively darker in comparison with normal cells. These characteristics are applied for pattern recognition and classification of cervical cells.

In order to achieve the aforementioned objective, the design of the adaptive intelligent system begins by designing the database of Pap smear specimen.

Data Construction

Database of Pap smear specimens used in this research is taken from the Euthman's images collection (2010). It consists of 967 cervical cytological images with composition of 74 normal (db1), 70 mild dysplasia (db2), 98 severe dysplasia (db3), 182 CIS (db4), 146 CIN-1 (db5), 197 CIN-II (db6), and 200 CIN-III (db7) cells. Images db1, db2 and db3 are grouped into normal cells, and images db4, db5, db6 and db7 are grouped into cancerous cells. This regrouping is done suitable to the first stated goal that is to develop a classification algorithm for recognizing cells abnormality and assign them into a predicted group, i.e. normal cells or cancerous cells. The classifier is developed to be adaptive, that means it can do self-adjustment when the input data and structure are changes in order to attain the system ability to discriminate cervix cancer staging.

The Pap smear specimens are diagnosed and have been classified by human cytologists. The classification is then confirmed by the cell characteristics in another database derived from authors' prior research (Suryatenggara et al., 2009). The cell characteristics in those two databases show similarity. Therefore, the specimens are regarded to be valid and can be used for analysis.

Preprocessing

In order to obtain valuable information from the Pap smear specimens, the two-dimensional (2D) cervical cytological images are preprocessed and converted to binary images. Preprocessing begins by picking single cell up individually from the thin-layered cytological specimen. This process selects only single cells in non-depraved shapes, either in circular or non-circular shape.

The preprocessing is important since most digital cytological images contain noises and may not have adequate contrast. This condition creates difficulty for edge detection, which may leads to inaccurate image segmentation and false feature extraction. While, conversion to binary images is also important. Working on binary scale, i.e., "0" as absolute black and "1" as absolute white, provides an advantage, where the system is able to recognize the edges and boundaries clearly and not to be confused by the differences in the specimen staining, either in red or blue color.

In the preprocessing, in the first stage the cytological images are converted to grayscale. This conversion is necessary in order to avoid problems due to color differences. During the laboratory process, the cytological specimens have been processed using the red and blue staining reagents. In color vision, blue is designated to specific wavelength (λ) values 435.9-490 nm and red to 635-700 nm with the electromagnetic energy (υ_b) spectrum spans from 1.43 μm^{-1} (red) to 2.13 μm^{-1} (blue) (The International Commission on Illumination, 2011). This fact causes that two different cytological specimens illuminated with the same amount of radiance will reflect light at two different primary wavelengths and absorb most of the energy at other wavelengths. This mechanism reflects in the digital images and will be represented by different RGB values of pixels.

Therefore, the color images need to be converted to grayscale and transformed the gray-level onto a uniform distribution interval. The term *gray-level* is generally used to describe monochromatic intensity that ranges from black to white, i.e., from 0 to 255 values. Hence, the cytological images will have similar image attributes that is valid as a basis for further preprocessing. Afterwards, the grayscale images are resized to 400*x*400 pixels and duplicated. One set is stored as original images will be used for feature extraction, and the other one is preprocessed for conversion to binary images.

In the second stage, the grayscale image is filtered using the Wiener filter, i.e. a discrete time linear FIR (finite impulse response) filter (Andrews and Hunt, 1977). This filter has been widely used in the reconstruction of 1D signals and 2D images. It is sensitive to noise. The elegance of Wiener filter lies in its ability to incorporate the prior knowledge about the noise embedded in the signal and the spectral density of the object being imaged. Hence, it provides a better and improved restoration of original signal. The discrete version of Wiener filter applied onto 2D images is a straightforward extension to the continuous Wiener filter (Acharya and Ray, 2005).

Filtering an image in the presence of blur and noise, both the image $f(x, y)$ and the noise $\eta(x, y)$ are considered as zero mean random processes.

Here the objective is to obtain an estimate $\hat{f}(x, y)$ of the original image $f(x, y)$ with minimum mean squared of error (MMSE),

$$e^2 = E\left\{ \left[f(x, y) - \hat{f}(x, y) \right]^2 \right\}. \tag{36}$$

If the image and the noise are written in a mathematical relation

$$g(x, y) = h(x, y) * f(x, y) + \eta(x, y) \tag{37}$$

and asssuming linear shift invariance with $\left(1 - \eta(x, y)^{-1} \right) = w(x, y)$, then

$$\hat{f}(x, y) = w(x, y) * g(x, y) \tag{38}$$

where $g(x, y)$: the original object being imaged, $w(x, y)$: Wiener filter, and

$\hat{f}(x, y) = w(x, y) \{ h(x, y) * f(x, y) \}$. As a result, the image $\hat{f}(x, y)$ has been filtered from noise, but the presence of blur still remains. Therefore, the cytological images need to be further preprocessed to enhance the contrast.

Image enhancement is a set of techniques for improving the subjective quality of an image and for enhancing the accuracy rate in automated object detection and picture interpretation (Acharya and Ray, 2005). In a poorly contrasted image a large number of pixels occupy only a small portion of the available range of intensities. Through histogram modification, the frequency of the pixels intensity can be redistributed and each pixel can be reassigned to a new intensity value so that the dynamic range of gray-levels is increased. Here the principle is to stretch the dynamic range of the pixel values in such a way, hence, the lighter pixels may turn still lighter and comparatively the darker pixels may be still darkened.

In this stage, image enhancement is done using the contrast-limited adaptive histogram equalization. Generally speaking, histogram equalization is a technique for adjusting the grayscale of the image so that the gray-level histogram of the input image is mapped onto a uniform histogram (Rosenfeld and Kak, 1982; Pratt, 1991; Gonzales and Woods, 1992). This technique is based on a transformation using the histogram of a complete image. The goal is to obtain a uniform histogram for the output image. Assuming r is a random variable which indicates the gray-level of an image. Variable r is continuous and lies within the closed interval [0:1] with $r = 0$ representing black and $r = 1$ representing white. Thus, any r in the specified interval will be transformed as

$$s = T(r) \qquad (39)$$

and the inverse transform from s to r is

$$r = T(s)^{-1} \qquad (40)$$

where s is the transformed gray-level for every pixel value r in the original image. During the transformation, T should satisfy the following criteria:

$T(r)$ is a single valued function that monotonically increasing in the interval [0:1],
$T(r)$ lies between 0 and 1.

In comparison with histogram equalization, the contrast-limited adaptive histogram equalization operates on small regions in the image, called 'tiles', instead of the entire image. The contrast is enhanced on each tile so that the histogram of the output region approximately matches the desired histogram shape as specified by the distribution parameter, i.e. uniform, Rayleigh, or exponential distribution. In this preprocessing, the uniform distribution is applied. Using this technique, the contrast in homogenous areas can be limited to avoid amplification of any noise that might be present in the image. The neighboring tiles are then combined using bilinear interpolation to eliminate artificially induced boundaries.

Finally, the enhanced images are converted to binary images and standardized to the output type of unsigned 8-bit-integer (uint8), which has output range of pixel intensity between 0 to 255. Figure 9 describes the results from the image preprocessing.

Image Morphology

An image is defined by a set of regions that are connected and non-overlapping. In the context of mathematical morphology, morphological image processing refers to a procedure for extracting image components that are useful in the representation and description of region shape, such as boundaries, skeletons, and the convex hull (Gonzales and Woods, 2002). Sets in mathematical morphology represent objects in an image. In the cervical cytological image, the set of all white pixels in a binary image is a complete morphological description of a boundary or a region of the cell, cytoplasm, or nucleus. In binary images, the sets of objects of interest are members of the Z^2 (2D integer) space, where each element of a set is a tuple (i.e. 2D vector) whose coordinates are the (x, y) coordinates of a white pixel in the image.

Extracting the boundary and region of a cell requires an image should go through the

Figure 9. Image preprocessing: (a) original RGB image, (b) grayscale image, (c) filtered image, d) enhanced image, and (e) binary image

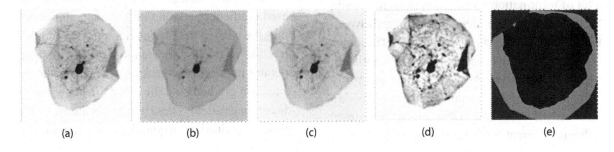

(a)　　　　(b)　　　　(c)　　　　(d)　　　　(e)

segmentation process. Segmentation involves partitioning an image into a set of homogeneous and meaningful regions, such that the pixels in each partitioned region possess an identical set of properties or attributes (Rosenfeld and Kak, 1982; Pratt, 1991; Gonzales and Woods, 1992). The result of segmentation is a number of homogenous regions, each having an unique label. Each pixel in an image acquires a unique region label that indicates the region where it belongs to.

Segmentation algorithms are based on one of the two basic properties of gray-level values, i.e. discontinuity and similarity of the pixels. In the pixels discontinuity category of algorithms, partition of an image is based on abrupt changes in gray-level. The principal areas of interest within this category are the detection of lines and edges in an image. Thus, the edges can be extracted and linked. The connected set of pixels of the edges has more or less the same homogenous intensity that forms the regions. Then, the region is described by the edge contour that contains it.

The second category of algorithms is based on the similarity amongst the pixels within a region. Segmenting an image requires various local properties of the pixels should be utilized. In this stage, the boundary and regions of cervical cells is identified using edge detection that is coupled with image dilation and erosion.

Edge Detection

The edge detection is essentially an operation to detect significant local changes in the intensity level in an image. In this process, edges, lines and points are usually termed as local features that carry a lot of information about the various regions in the image. An edge essentially demarcates between two distinctly different regions, hence, it becomes the border between two regions. On the other hand, a line may be embedded inside a single uniformly homogenous region. A point is embedded inside a uniformly homogenous region and its gray-level value is different from the average gray-level of the region in which it is embedded. In this stage, the goals are to derive the boundaries of nucleus and cytoplasm. Therefore, all detected lines and points inside a region will be closed using the filling hole operation.

In the pixels discontinuity algorithm, the change in intensity level is measured by the gradient of the image. Since an image $f(x, y)$ is a 2D function, then the gradient can be represented as a vector

$$\begin{bmatrix} G_x \\ G_y \end{bmatrix} = \begin{bmatrix} \dfrac{df}{dx} \\ \dfrac{df}{dy} \end{bmatrix}. \tag{41}$$

The magnitude of the gradient is

$$G\big[f(x, y)\big] = \sqrt{G_x^2 + G_y^2} \tag{42}$$

and the direction of the gradient is

$$\theta\big(x, y\big) = tan^{-1}\big(G_y \, / \, G_x\big) \tag{43}$$

where the angle θ is measured with respect to the x-axis.

The decision regarding the existence of an edge point is based on a threshold. If the gradient magnitude is greater than a threshold, then an edge point exists at that point, else there is no edge point. In this process, Sobel operator-based edge detector is applied.

The Sobel operator is a 3×3 neighborhood based gradient operator. Gradient operator computes the change in gray-level intensities and the direction in which the change occurs. Gradient operator requires two masks, one to derive the x-direction gradient and the other to obtain the y-direction gradient. These two gradients are combined to obtain a vector quantity whose magnitude

Table 1. Sobel mask to compute (a) gradient G_x and (b) gradient G_y

1	2	1		1	0	-1
0	0	0		2	0	-2
-1	-2	-1		1	0	-1
	(a)				*(b)*	

represents the strength of the edge gradient at a point in the image and whose angle represents the gradient angle, θ.

The convolution masks for the Sobel operator are defined by the two kernels described in Table 1. The two masks are separately applied on the input image to yield two gradient components G_x and G_y in the horizontal and vertical orientations respectively.

$$G_x =$$
$$\left[f(i-1, j-1) + 2(i-1, j) + f(i-1, j+1) \right] -$$
$$[f(i+1, j-1) + 2f(i+1, j) + f(i+1, j+1)] \tag{44}$$

and

$$G_y =$$
$$\left[f(i-1, j-1) + 2(i, j-1) + f(i+1, j-1) \right] -$$
$$[f(i-1, j+1) + 2f(i, j+1) + f(i+1, j+1)] \tag{45}$$

In edge detection, the fudge factor applied for detecting the edge points are respectively 0.8 and 0.3 for the cytoplasm and nucleus boundaries. The results demonstrate some gaps, or non smooth, between edge points. Therefore, image dilation is applied for bridging the gaps.

Dilation

Given A is a binary image of cervical cell and B is the inversed binary image. Assuming A and

B as sets in 2D integer space, Z^2, the dilation of A by B can be defined as

$$A \oplus B = \{ z \mid (\hat{B})_z \cap A \neq \varnothing. \tag{46}$$

Set B refers to as the structuring element in dilation, at the same time, is also viewed as a convolution mask. Equation (11) represents the reflection of B about its origin and shifting this reflection by z. Then, the dilation of A by B is the set of all displacements, z, such that $\hat{B}$ and A overlap by at least one element. Based on this interpretation, equation (11) can be rewritten as

$$A \oplus B = \{ z \mid (\hat{B})_z \cap A \subseteq A. \tag{47}$$

As a resultant, the boundary or cytoplasm and nucleus are obtained. All points inside a boundary constitute the dilation of A by B. In order to obtain region inside the boundary, image erosion is applied.

Erosion

For sets A and B in Z^2, the erosion of A by B can be denoted as

$$A \ominus B = \{ z \mid (\hat{B})_z \subseteq A. \tag{48}$$

Equation (13) indicates that the erosion of A by B is the set of all points z such that B, translated by z, is contained in image A. Erosion method erodes the white parts of the binary image using an eroding unit with determinable shape and size. Here image erosion is done using a 1×1 structuring element. The process is to translate an input image in Z^2 space by an integer number of pixels as described in Figure 10. In binary image, black has value of 0 (zero), thus not considered as an object. By eroding all objects with sufficient

Figure 10. Image erosion with 1×1 structuring element

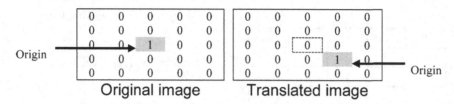

erosion, the small noisy pieces will be totally annihilated masks, while larger pieces, i.e. the cell region, still have some remains.

As a resultant, the areas of cytoplasm and nucleus can be derived. Figure 11 describes respectively the results of edge detection, dilation, and erosion on the binary image.

Cell Segmentation

In this stage, the cervical image undergoes to segmentation process in order to extract the area that contains the target features. Segmentation is done by adding the binary image and the grayscale image using a linear combination operation. Image linear combination provides an advantage as compared to the arithmetic image addition. The function computes linearly each element of the output Z individually, in element-by-element basis in double-precision floating point. In the 'uint8' numeric data type, the linear combination truncates elements of Z that exceeds the range of the integer type (i.e. between 0-255) and rounds off the fractional values. Overflow is handled automatically. The function saturates the final return values only, instead of rounds and saturates the result at the end of each step that can significantly reduce the precision of the computation. Figure 12 describes segmentation of a cytoplasm. A similar process can also be applied for segmenting the nucleus.

The segmentation begins by marking boundary of the target feature (i.e. cytoplasm) on the grayscale image using the computed cell boundary. Then, creating an inverse binary image of the target feature as a mask. Finally, performing linear combination to the marked feature and the mask in order to extract the area of target feature. In this process, there are three target features are being derived from a cervical cell, i.e. whole cell, cytoplasm, and nucleus. These features needs to be further processed through feature extraction process in order to extract relevant information about the cervical cells.

Figure 11. Cell morphologies: (a) detected edge, (b) cell boundary, (c) cytoplasm area, (d) nucleus area

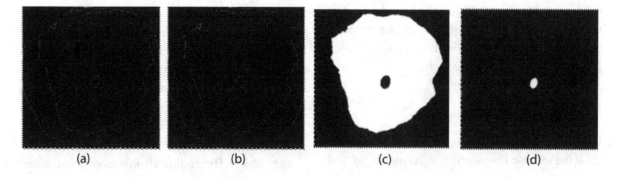

Figure 12. Image segmentation: (a) cell boundary on binary image, (b) cell boundary on grayscale image, (c) mask, and (d) segmented cytoplasm

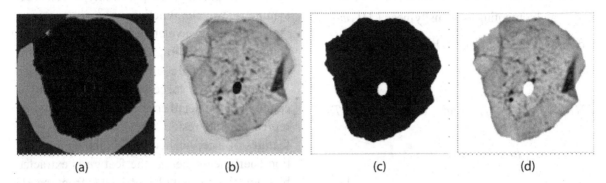

(a)   (b)   (c)   (d)

Feature Extraction

Generally speaking, feature extraction is understood as the transformation of input image into a set of features. Here the input is images but the outputs are attributes, which can be in numeric or graphic formats. Using these attributes, more relevant and more accurate data can be obtained to perform classification and analysis of the cervical cells. In this stage, three atypical morphological characteristics of cervical cells are extracted, i.e. size, shape, and color. Those features are extracted in both numerical and graphical formats.

Feature

The cells size is measured using three parameters, i.e., N/C ratio, nucleus perimeter, and nucleus radius, in unit pixels. The nucleus perimeter, or edges, is extracted as an interconnected pixels which have lower (i.e., lighter) abrupt changes in gray-level in the binary images. Afterwards, assuming the nucleus is in a circular shape, then, the radius can be approximated as

$$r = P / 2\pi = \sqrt{A / \pi} \tag{49}$$

where P : nucleus perimeter, and A : nucleus area in unit pixels.

Shape Feature

The cells shape is identified using parameters cell deformity, cell heterogeneity, and wavelet approximation coefficients. The first parameter, the degree of deformity of cervical cells is measured using the circularity factor, f_c, which lies within a range of $0 \leq f_c \leq 1$. The closer f_c value to "0" (zero) means the nucleus more deformed, and vice versa, the closer f_c value to "1" (one) represents more circular the nucleus. The circularity factor (Lassouaoui et al. 2005) can be calculated as

$$f_c = P^2 / A. \tag{50}$$

where P : nucleus perimeter, and A : nucleus area in unit pixels.

The second parameter, the cell heterogeneity is measured in terms of

$$\text{intensity mean}: \ MI = \sum_{i=1}^{s} I(i) / S \tag{51}$$

$$\text{variance}: \ \sigma^2 = \sum_{i=1}^{s} \left[I(i) - MI \right]^2 / S \tag{52}$$

where $I(i)$: intensity of pixel i, and S : the number of pixels.

Measuring the heterogeneity is done by dividing the cell feature into window (wi) of size $n \times m$ and computing its intensity mean $\left(MI\left[wi\right] \right)$ and variance $\left(\sigma^2\left[wi\right] \right)$ on each window, wi. Then, a cell is heterogeneous if

$$
\begin{cases}
\left| MI\left[wi\right] - MI \right| > T_1 \quad and \quad \left| \sigma^2\left[wi\right] - \sigma^2 \right| > T_2 \\
\\
otherwise,\ homogenous
\end{cases}
$$

$$(53)$$

where T_1 and T_2 are thresholds.

The third parameter, it is based on wavelet approximation coefficient. For analysis using wavelet transform, the segmented image needs to be further processed by converting the 2D digital image into 1D wavelet plot. Here the 2D image is decomposed using wavelet Biorthogonal 3.7 level 3 that satisfies the biorthogonality condition,

$$
\sum_{n\in\mathbb{Z}} a_n\, a_{n+2m} = 2\delta_{m,0}
$$

$$(54)$$

where a and a: scaling sequences, n and m: the number of coefficients; and δ: Kronecker delta (1 if $m = 0$, otherwise 0 if $m \neq 0$). Then, the wavelet sequences can be determined as

$$
b_n = (-1)^n\, a_{M-1-n}, \cdots n = 0,1,\ldots,M-1,
$$

$$(55)$$

$$
b_n = (-1)^n\, a_{M-1-n}, \cdots n = 0,1,\ldots,N-1 \qquad (56)
$$

where M and N are coefficients in the scaling sequences.

A biorthogonal wavelet is a wavelet where the associated wavelet transform is invertible, but not necessarily orthogonal. Designing a biorthogonal wavelet allows more degrees of freedom than orthogonal wavelets. The one additional degree of freedom provides the possibility to construct symmetric wavelet functions.

The result of wavelet transform is as array that contains a vector of approximation coefficients and a vector of detail coefficients. The information lost between two successive decompositions is captured in the detail coefficients, which mainly represents the residuals. Since the important features of a cervical cell lie on the approximation coefficients, hence, the feature is extracted by truncating the detail coefficients from the 1D wavelet plot.

Color Feature

During preprocessing, the original color image of cervical cells has been converted to grayscale image and standardized into 'uint8' type which has output range of pixel intensity between 0 to 255. Therefore, it is valid to measure the cells color based on the gray-level intensity.

Pattern Recognition

Each object (e.g. cell, cytoplasm, or nucleus) is a pattern and the measured values are the features of the pattern. Recognizing objects in the image from a set of measurements (e.g. N/C ratio, perimeter, radius, etc.) of the objects is the objective of pattern recognition. A set of similar objects possessing more or less identical features are classified belong to a certain pattern class.

In this stage, all features related to the size, shape, and color are undergoing to a recognition process to discover the patterns of normal cells and cancerous cells. Recognition is done at first based on human visual eye-tracking system in order to identify certain unique patterns of the cervical cells. Using prior knowledge of the cytologist (Elit, 2008; Suryatenggara et al., 2009), empirical observation is performed to recognize the cancerous cells based on its size, nucleus deformity, texture heterogeneity, and changing color. After a thorough observation, the following important patterns can be identified that is able to provide a measure for a cell to which predicted group membership it should be classified.

Patterns Related to Cell Size

It is visually tracked that cancerous cells have larger nucleus, as well as smaller cytoplasm, than normal cells. The distance between cancerous cells is very close. They tend to lump together as colony as depicted in Figure 13.

Patterns Related to Cell Shape

It can be recognized that the nucleus of cancerous cells is deformed from circular shape. According to the cell texture, the cancerous cells are more heterogeneous than normal cells. Figure 14 and 15 demonstrate the cell patterns based on cell deformity and texture heterogeneity. Meanwhile, based on wavelet characteristics the cancerous cells have wider interval of low-frequency values within the approximation coefficients, than normal cells. This pattern is well-described on the 1D wavelet plot as illustrated in Figure 16.

Figure 13. Cervical cells pattern based on size: (a) normal cell, (b) cancerous cell (source: Klinik Kloster Paradise - Germany, 2009)

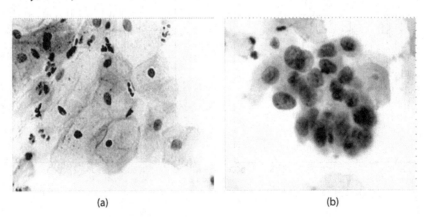

(a)   (b)

Figure 14. Pattern based on cell deformity: (a) normal cell, (b) cancerous cell (source: Euthman's images collection, 2010)

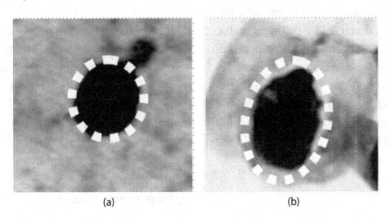

(a)   (b)

Figure 15. Pattern based on texture heterogeneity: (a) normal cell, (b) cancerous cell

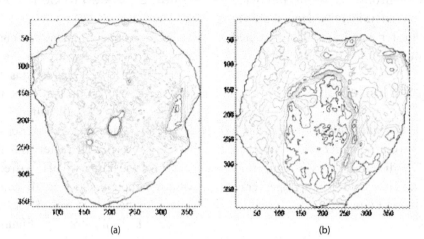

(a)   (b)

Figure 16. Pattern based on wavelet approximation coefficient: (a) normal cell, (b) cancerous cell

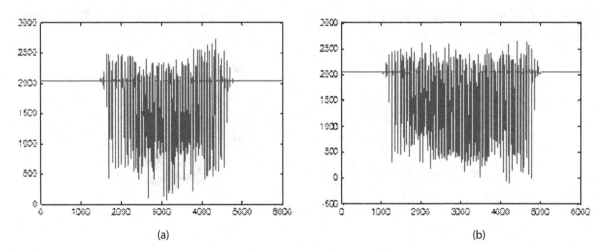

(a)   (b)

Patterns Related to Cells Color

The cancerous cells have relatively darker color intensity than normal cells. The distinguishable pattern can be analyzed using the corresponding pixel intensity histogram as described in Figure 17.

Finally, the last condition that has to be satisfied by a pattern is it has to be measurable and classifiable by a specified classifier, or machine learning process. This process is described in the following paragraphs.

Machine Perception and Classification

Unlike human being, a machine can only comprehend information in a well-defined exact format, such as numbers (0, 1,..., 9), binary code (0 or 1), and rules (e.g. IF-THEN). Therefore, all of the unique patterns recognized from the human's visual eye-tracking should be translated into a set of codes, where each unique only to its own kind.

In this stage, to enable a machine recognizes and percepts a cell belongs to a certain predicted group membership (i.e. normal or cancerous

Figure 17. Pattern based on wavelet approximation coefficient: (a) normal cell, (b) cancerous cell

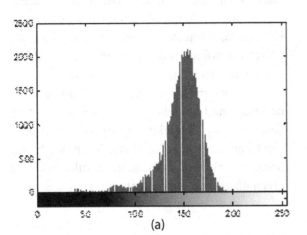
(a)

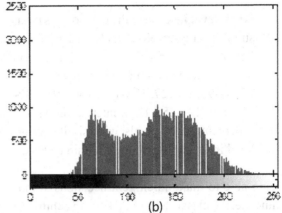
(b)

group), the related patterns are translated into numbers in terms of integer, real numbers, ratio, and intervals as follows.

Size Feature

- **Nucleus and cytoplasm sizes:** the N/C ratio is defined as a fraction of nucleus area to cytoplasm area.
- **Nucleus perimeter:** the nucleus boundary is measured as integer numbers in unit pixels. It ranges on a continuum between 63 to 953 pixels.
- **Nucleus radius:** the radius is computed from the nucleus perimeter under an assumption that in common nucleus has circle shape. The radius is derived as real numbers that ranges on a continuum between 10.03 to 228.39 pixels.

Shape Feature

- **Cell deformity:** the cell deformity is recognized from the nucleus shape and measured as circularity factor (f_c) that is a fraction of the squared nucleus perimeter to nucleus area as given in Equation (50).

- **Texture heterogeneity:** the heterogeneity of cell texture is measured using parameters given in Equation (51)-(52). The parameter of intensity mean (MI) is measured as a total fraction of the intensity of pixel i to the number of pixels. The second parameter is variance (σ^2) that is a total fraction of (intensity of pixel $i - MI$) to the number of pixels.

- **Wavelet approximation coefficients:** the wavelet approximation coefficients are classified into 12 uniform class-intervals based on the frequency values, i.e.: intervals (-1400 to -1000), (-999.99 to -600), (-599.00 to -200), (-199.99 to -+200), (+200.01 to +600), (+600.01 to +1000), (+1000.01 to +1400), +1400.01 to +1800), (+1800.01 to +2200), (+2200.01 to +2600), (+2600.01 to +3000), and (+3000.01 to +3400). Each interval represents a percentage of the approximation coefficients distribution within a certain class. The percentage of approximation coefficients amongst the details coefficients ranges on a continuum between 39.45% to 60.41%.

Color Feature

• **Gray-level intensity:** the cell color is measured in gray-level intensity that is classified into 8 uniform class-intervals based on the intensity values, i.e.: intervals 0-31, 32-63, 64-95, 96-127, 128-159, 160-191, 192-223, and 224-255. Each interval represents a percentage of pixels with similar gray-level intensity distribution within a class.

Being able to make intelligent decisions, a machine, i.e. the classifier, should have the ability to recognize complex patterns and deduce a correct perception of the pattern. To do this, a classifier needs to be trained to recognize the expected patterns and make a decision on to which predicted group an observed pattern should be assigned.

Generally, the classification algorithms work based on the similarity principle. A perceptron can perform linear classification. While, multiperceptrons can classify the non-linearly separable classification problems (Konar, 2005). Applying the MLP network model in Figure 5, the classification is performed based on given cell size, shape and color features. Once the settings complete, the machine (i.e., intelligent system) will access the training database for every single pattern values. Then, the machine learns by investigating each pattern value and build perception for the observed cells by comparing them with the relevant pattern values from the database.

Automation and Prototyping

Finally, the whole processes are aligned and verified, then, built into the adaptive intelligent system to function as an automated recognition system. The system prototype is developed using C++ language and M-file format of Matlab 7.6.0.

The prototype is designed user-friendly with GUI windows, which consists of different frames. The first frame is to visualize the diagnostic cervix cell image, i.e.: respectively a whole cell, the nucleus, and the cytoplasm. The second frame is visualizing the diagnostic graphs and histograms, i.e.: 1D plot of wavelet approximation coefficients, wavelet coefficients distribution, and gray-level histogram. The third frame visualizes the diagnostic pattern values, i.e.: N/C ratio, nucleus perimeter and boundary, cell deformity, texture heterogeneity, wavelet approximation coefficients, and gray-level intensity. Then, the fourth frame visualizes the diagnostic results based on given diagnostic pattern values.

SIMULATION AND DISCUSSION

In this section, the simulation design will be presented based on the developed MLP model and given features dataset. Following the simulation, discussion on the findings and analysis is provided.

Simulation Design

In order to show learning process that occurs in the MLP network, here the simulation is designed through three steps, i.e. data training, validation, and testing, respectively. Data training is performed using 100 samples from both normal and abnormal cells. The MLP model runs in the combination of learning rate (L) 0.3, momentum (M) 0.2, validation threshold (E) 20, and training time (N) 500. Meanwhile, 10-fold cross validation is performed at 10, 20, and 25 epoch respectively.

Afterwards, data testing is performed using 20 samples in the same combination of learning rate, momentum, and threshold by applying weights generated at the last stage of data validation. The results of data training, validation, and testing are provided in Table 2, 2, and 3. Table 2 describes the simulation results in terms of the mean absolute error (MAE), root mean squared error (RMSE), relative absolute error (RAE), true positive (TP), false positive (FP), true negative (TN), false negative (FN), Cohen's Kappa (κ) coefficient, the

Table 2. The results of data training, validation, and testing (α = 0.05)

Parameters	Testing (100 samples)	Validation (10-folds)	Testing (20 samples)
Mean absolute error (MAE)	0.0035	0.004	0.0033
Root mean squared error (RMSE)	0.0039	0.0046	0.0035
Relative absolute error (RAE)	0.6918%	0.8007%	0.6547%
True positive (TP)	100% (50)	100% (50)	100% (10)
False positive (FP)	0%	0%	0%
True negative (TN)	100% (50)	100% (50)	100% (10)
False negative (FN)	0%	0%	0%
Cohen's Kappa coefficient (κ)	0.999	0.999	0.999
Coefficient of determination (R^2)	0.999	0.989	0.989
Time taken to build model	1.43 seconds	1.41 seconds	1.42 seconds

coefficient of determination (R^2), and the time taken to build the network model. Table 3 demonstrates the weights generated during the data training, validation and testing.

In statistics, the mean absolute error (MAE) is a measure of accuracy for continuous variables. It measures the average magnitude of the errors (e_i), or differences, between prediction (y_i) and the true values (y_i). The MAE is given by

$$MAE = \frac{1}{n}\sum_{i=1}^{n}\left|\hat{y}_i - y_i\right| = \frac{1}{n}\sum_{i=1}^{n}\left|e_i\right| \qquad (57)$$

The root mean squared error (RMSE) is a good measure of precision. It is a frequently-used measure of the differences between values predicted by a model and the actually observed values. The RMSE is defined as

$$RMSE = \sqrt{MSE\left(e_i\right)} = \sqrt{\sum_{i=1}^{n}\left(\hat{y}_i - y_i\right)^2} \qquad (58)$$

The relative absolute error (RAE) is a relative measure to a simple predictor $\hat{y}_i$. The RAE takes the total absolute error and normalizes it by dividing by the mean absolute error

$$RAE = \frac{\sum_{i=1}^{n}\left|\hat{y}_i - y_i\right|}{\sum_{i=1}^{n}\left|y_i - \overline{y}_i\right|} \qquad (59)$$

Cohen's Kappa coefficient (κ), or simply Kappa statistic, is a statistical measure of inter-rater or inter-annotator agreement for qualitative categorical items (Cohen, 1968). Generally, it is thought to be a more robust measure than simple percent agreement calculation since κ takes into account the agreement occurring by chance. The Cohen's kappa measures the agreement between two raters who each classify N items into C mutually exclusive categories

$$\kappa = \frac{PR\left(a\right) - \Pr(b)}{1 - \Pr(b)} \qquad (60)$$

Table 3. The weights generated during learning process

Neurons	Weights		
	Training	**Validation**	**Testing**
Size feature:			
N/C ratio	0.828	0.828	0.828
nucleus perimeter	0.853	0.853	0.853
nucleus radius	0.850	0.850	0.850
Shape feature:			
cell deformity	-0.875	-0.875	-0.875
texture heterogeneity:			
mean intensity	-0.052	-0.052	-0.052
variance	0.131	0.131	0.131
Wavelet approximation coefficients:			
class-1 (-1400,00 to -1000,00)	0.004	0.004	0.004
class-2 (-999,99 to -600,00)	-0.104	-0.104	-0.104
class-3 (-599,99 to -200,00)	-0.184	-0.184	-0.184
class-4 (-199,99 to +200,00)	-0.113	-0.113	-0.113
class-5 (+200,01 to +600,00)	0.242	0.242	0.242
class-6 (+600,01 to +1000,00)	0.212	0.212	0.212
class-7 (+1000,01 to +1400,00)	-0.195	-0.195	-0.195
class-8 (+1400,01 to +1800,00)	-0.015	-0.015	-0.015
class-9 (+1800,01 to +2200,00)	0.146	0.146	0.146
class-10 (+2200,01 to +2600,00)	-0.048	-0.048	-0.048
class-11 (+2600,01 to +3000,00)	-0.085	-0.085	-0.085
class-12 (+3000,01 to +3400,00)	-0.199	-0.199	-0.199
Color feature:			
interval-1 (0 -31)	-0.230	-0.230	-0.230
interval-2 (32 - 63)	0.005	0.005	0.005
interval-3 (64 - 95)	0.209	0.209	0.209
interval-4 (96 - 127)	0.059	0.059	0.059
interval-5 (128 - 159)	-0.286	-0.286	-0.286
interval-6 (160 - 191)	0.076	0.076	0.076
interval-7 (192 - 223)	-0.058	-0.058	-0.058
interval-8 (224 - 255)	0.042	0.042	0.042

where $Pr(a)$: the relative observed agreement among raters, and $Pr(e)$: the hypothetical probability of chance agreement. If the raters are in complete agreement, then $\kappa = 1$. If there is no agreement among the raters, other than what would be expected by chance, then $0 \leq \kappa < 1$.

The coefficient of determination (R^2) is a representation of the percent of the variation that can be explained by the independent variables in the regression function. It is a measure of how well future outcomes are likely to be predicted by the MLP network model (Gujarati, 1995). The R^2 is computed as

$$R^2 = 1 - \frac{SSE}{SS_{yy}} = 1 - \frac{\sum_{i=1}^{n}\left(y_i - \hat{y}_i\right)^2}{\sum_{i=1}^{n}\left(y_i - \hat{y}\right)^2} \qquad (61)$$

where SSE : deviations of the observations from the predicted values, and SS_{yy} : deviations of the observations from the average.

Findings and Discussion

Examining the simulation results in Table 2, it is evident that the learning process through the MLP network runs effectively. The learning effectiveness is represented by the very low error measurements for all errors statistic, in terms of the MAE (0.003 and 0.004), RMSE (0.004 and 0.005), and RAE (0.655%, 0.692%, and 0.801%). It can also be observed the decrease in the RAE from 0.692% in the training to 0.655% in the testing, shows an increasing capability of the machine to better recognize the explained variability, i.e., $(1 - SSE \,/\, SS_{yy})$, amongst variables in the

network and to generate prediction more closer to the true values.

During learning, weights are generated for each neuron in the input layer and hidden layers that represent their contribution to the actual output ($x_{L,k}$). In each run, the weights are changing in each epoch and gradually converge to the optimal weights in the last epoch. Figure 18 depict the best validation performance that is achieved with the mean squared error (MSE) = 0.007 at epoch 4. From Table 3, it can be observed that the training, validation and testing through the network bring the learning process to converge into the same weights, means the optimal.

The simulation is performed at the level of significance (α) 0.05. Using the 26 attributes, the simulation provides evidences on the Kappa (κ) coefficients as the inter-rates agreement statistics "1". The coefficients of determination for data training ($R^2_{training}$) 0.999, while, for validation ($R^2_{validation}$) and testing (R^2_{test}) are 0.989. Figure 19 depicts the regression functions and their fitness, i.e., training $\hat{y}_i = y_i + 4.3^{-14}$, validation $\hat{y}_i = y_i + 0.047$, testing $\hat{y}_i = y_i + 0.053$, and

Figure 18. The best validation performance 0.0070394 at epoch 4

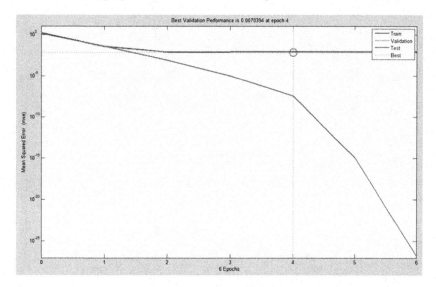

overall $y_i = y_i + 0.011$. Meanwhile, the time taken to build the model does not exhibit significant differences between time needed for training (1.43 seconds), validation (1.41 seconds), and testing (1.42 seconds). These results provide support on the reliability of the proposed MLP network model for recognizing the pattern of cervix cells and to produce the desired outputs (d_k).

The observation of normal cells and abnormal cells shows quite distinctive patterns that are visually distinguishable by human's visual tracking system. Computationally, these patterns can be further analyzed using the 26 variables given in Table 3. Comparative study on the size feature produces distinguish patterns behavior between normal cells and abnormal cells, which can be demonstrated using the N/C ratio, nucleus perim-

eter, and nucleus radius attributes as depicted in Figure 20, 21, and 22. It can be observed on these attributes, the abnormal cells always form patterns with higher values and behave above on the normal cells. These patterns emerge from the morphology of cancerous cells, which have larger nucleus in comparison with normal cells. The N/C ratio is the most common measure used for distinguishing the characteristic of normal cells and cancerous cells. Prior to knowledge, the nucleus size of a cancerous cell is significantly larger than in a normal cell. Vice versa, the cytoplasm size of a cancerous cell is a few times smaller than in a normal cell. Then, it is found the N/C ratio for normal cells ranges between 0.40% – 2.67% and for cancerous cells between 222.67% – 988.77%, at the significance level $\alpha = 0.05$. While, the N/C ratio between both classifications, i.e. 2.68% –

Figure 19. Regression functions and their fitness: (a) training, (b) validation, (c) testing, and (d) overall

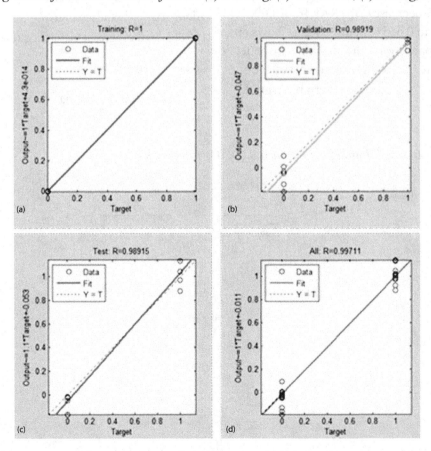

222.66%, is temporarily labeled as dysplasia. For nucleus perimeter, the pattern values range between 63–188 pixels for normal cells and 341–953 pixels for abnormal cells. While, for the nucleus radius the pattern values range between 11–30 pixels for normal cells and 55–152 pixels for abnormal cells. Table 4 summarizes the decision boundary of the attributes belong to the size feature.

According to the shape feature, the cell deformity pattern behaves similarly that the circularity factor (f_c) of the abnormal cells always ranges in higher values than the normal cells as illustrated in Figure 23. This pattern behavior emerges due to the measurement of f_c is based on the nucleus perimeter and area, as similarly applied in the measurement of attributes belong to the size feature. It is found that the circularity factor of normal cells ranges between 9.82–23.16 pixels and 11.74–20.99 pixels for abnormal cells. Meanwhile, the attribute of mean intensity (MI) behave differently where the mean intensity of normal cells ranges in higher values than the abnormal cells as depicted in Figure 24. This pattern emerges due to the fact that normal cells have brighter color, means higher pixels intensity, than abnormal cells. Hence, when the color images are converted to the grayscale images (i.e. 0-255 scale), it results in higher gray-level intensity as well. It is found that the pattern of mean intensity ranges between 155.62–213.57 pixel

Figure 20. Cervix cells patterns based on N/C ratio

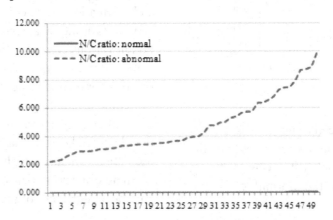

Figure 21. Cervix cells patterns based on nucleus perimeter

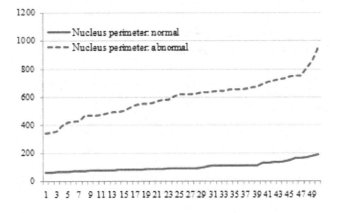

Figure 22. Cervix cells patterns based on nucleus radius

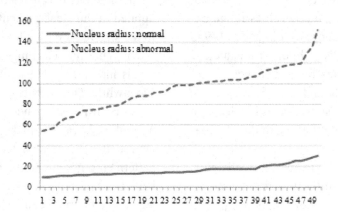

Table 4. Decision boundary based on N/C ratio, nucleus perimeter, and radius

Labels	N/C Ratio	Nucleus Perimeter	Nucleus Radius
N-DB$_L$	0.40%	63 pixels	11 pixels
N-DB$_U$	2.67%	188 pixels	30 pixels
C-DB$_L$	222.67%	341 pixels	55 pixels
C-DB$_U$	988.77%	953 pixels	152 pixels

Note: *N*: normal cells; *C*: cancerous cells, *DB$_L$*: lower decision boundary; *DB$_U$*: upper decision boundary.

intensity for normal cells and 150.22–202.09 pixel intensity for abnormal cells. While, the variation of the mean intensity occurs between 2231.00–6071.28 for the normal cells and

1976.26–6809.10 pixel intensity for the abnormal cells.

According to the wavelet approximation coefficients, it mentions macro information of the cell morphology such as the cell basic shape, position and orientation, basic color, etc. After some observations on the behavior of wavelets approximation in various cells, it is found that the approximation coefficients always have a sharp dive towards low-values in the frequency domain after sometime oscillating in high-values intervals. Soon after past a certain interval, the wavelet rises back in the same manner up, and continues oscillating normally in high-values interval. These sharp dive and rise exist corresponds to the morphological attributes of the nucleus. Apparently,

Figure 23. Cervix cells patterns based on cell deformity

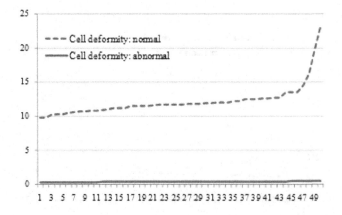

Figure 24. Cervix cells patterns based on mean intensity

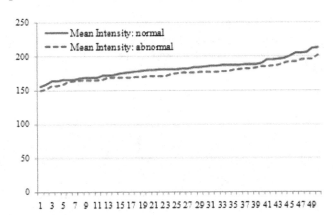

this dive and rise behavior is affected by the size, position, and the number of nucleus that exist as the dark-colored objects within the cell image. Larger nucleus size results in wider interval of low-values in the frequency domain that happens immediately after the wave dives down. When the position of the nucleus changes, the location where the wave dives and rises will also change in the time domain. Then, when the number of nucleus in a cancerous cell increase, so does the number of dives and rises in the wavelet approximation coefficients, which represents the 'occurrence' is not limited to once. Based on these three characteristics, the pattern of normal cells and cancerous cells can be recognized as depicted in Figure 25. Table 5 summarizes the decision boundary of attributes belong to the shape feature, i.e., the cell deformity and texture heterogeneity. Meanwhile, the decision boundary of the Wavelet approximation coefficient is described in Table 6. The wavelet characteristics, in terms of the distribution of the approximation coefficients, demonstrates the coefficients of abnormal cells that is intensively distributed within class-4 to class-8, i.e. between frequency domain -199.99 to +1800.00 (at $\alpha = 0.05$). For the normal cells, the coefficients are well-distributed into all classes, i.e. between frequency domain -1400.00 to +3400.00. Furthermore, it can be observed that the coefficients of normal cells and abnormal cells

follows the same pattern between class-1 to class-3, then behave vary between class-4 to class-8, and converge to follow the same pattern again in the class-8 to diminish together at class-12.

According to the color feature, using human vision one can realize that the distribution of total gray-level intensity in normal cells and cancerous cells are distinctively different. In order to recognize the differences accurately, the cell patterns is observed in the form of gray-level intensity histogram. Here, the histogram counts the number of pixels in the image on a similar scale between "0", i.e. zero intensity or absolute black, to "255", i.e. full intensity or absolute white. From the 2D cervical cell image, it can be identified that in a cancerous cell image there are more pixels with relatively lower gray-level intensity, i.e. darker pixels, due to the large size of the nucleus. In contrary, in normal cells there is abundance of brighter pixels due to the overwhelming proportion of cytoplasm in comparison with a very small proportion of nucleus. Hence, the pattern inside a cervix cell can be recognized on the basis of the gray-level intensity distribution as illustrated in Figure 26.

Based on thorough observation, it is confirmed that the distribution of gray-level intensity between normal and cancerous cells follows certain patterns and highly distinguishable as described in Table 7. The gray-level intensity of normal cells are indeed greater distributed in the higher inten-

Figure 25. Cervix cells patterns based on Wavelet approximation coefficient

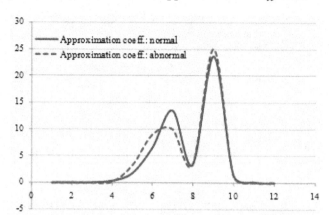

Table 5. Decision boundary based on circularity factor, mean intensity, and variance

Labels	Cell Deformity	Texture Heterogeneity	
	Circularity Factor (f_c)	Mean Intensity (MI)	Variance (σ^2)
N-DB$_L$	9.82	155.62	2231.00
N-DB$_U$	23.16	213.57	6071.28
C-DB$_L$	11.74	150.22	1976.26
C-DB$_U$	20.99	202.09	6809.10

Note: N: normal cells; C: cancerous cells, DB_L: lower decision boundary; DB_U: upper decision boundary.

Table 6. Decision boundary based on Wavelet approximation coefficients

Labels	Wavelet Approximation Coefficients (in percentage)											
	Class 1	Class 2	Class 3	Class 4	Class 5	Class 6	Class 7	Class 8	Class 9	Class 10	Class 11	Class 12
N-DB$_L$	0.00	0.00	0.00	0.00	0.17	1.12	5.05	0.61	18.00	1.02	0.00	0.00
N-DB$_U$	0.02	0.08	0.25	1.37	5.56	13.22	26.45	10.48	27.41	1.65	0.36	0.02
C-DB$_L$	0.00	0.00	0.00	0.00	0.33	3.99	3.02	0.54	18.38	0.84	0.00	0.00
C-DB$_U$	0.02	0.02	0.20	0.74	8.04	15.08	18.09	10.78	27.76	1.70	0.38	0.02

Note: N: normal cells; C: cancerous cells, DB_L: lower decision boundary; DB_U: upper decision boundary.

sity interval, i.e. averagely 40.51% between intervals 5 to 8 (i.e., gray-level 128–255) (at α = 0.05). Meanwhile, cancerous cells have greater distribution in the lower intensity interval, i.e. averagely 33.56% between intervals 3 to 6 (i.e., gray-level 64-191) at α = 0.05. Furthermore, it can be observed that the gray-level intensity of normal cells and abnormal cells behave vary between interval-2 to interval-6, then, converge at interval-6 and goes to follow a similar pattern to diminish together at interval-8 as depicted in Figure 26a. Meanwhile, Figure 26b shows the

Figure 26. Cervix cells patterns based on gray-level intensity: (a) behavior, (b) majority dominance

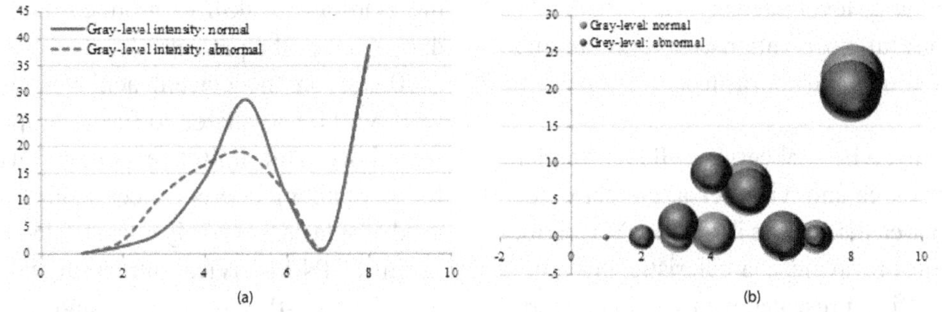

(a)

(b)

majority dominance of the abnormal cells in the lower intervals of gray-level intensity.

During the simulation, an additional analysis is performed to select attributes that have the most significant effect to the output. A similar analysis is applied in the data training, validation, and testing and generating similar results on the selected 6 attributes, i.e., N/C ratio, nucleus perimeter, nucleus radius, cell deformity, color-1 (interval 0-31 on 0-255 gray-scale), and color-3 (interval 64-95 on 0-255 gray-scale).

Conforming to Siebert et al. (2006) who worked on the development and validation of a decision-analytic model for cervical cancer screening, the aforementioned results are to assure that the adaptive intelligent system performs well suitable to how it is designed to function. Hence, the intelligent system is able to generate prognosis on the condition of the observed cervix cells correctly, which are robust, objective, more accurate, and consistent.

CONCLUSION

Today, coping with problems of inaccuracy and inconsistency in the Pap smear diagnosis, an adaptive intelligent system can be developed as a tool for early detection of cervical cancer. The intelligent system applies learning mechanism of multilayer perceptron network to enable the machine to learn and percept patterns of 2D cervical cytological digital images. Through a supervised learning, the system is able to recognize patterns of cervical cells as desired and achieves the optimal performance level at learning rate 0.2 and momentum 0.3.

Here the recognition of cervix cells pattern is performed on the basis of three characteristics of the cell morphology, i.e. size, shape, and color features. These three features are materialized and measured as numerical values in terms of the N/C ratio, nucleus perimeter, nucleus radius, cell deformity, texture heterogeneity (mean intensity

Table 7. Decision boundary based on gray-level intensity

Labels	Gray-level Intensity (in percentage)							
	Interval-1	Interval-2	Interval-3	Interval-4	Interval-5	Interval-6	Interval-7	Interval-8
N-DB$_L$	0.00	0.02	0.28	0.41	6.85	0.06	0.00	21.61
N-DB$_U$	0.62	6.27	19.64	32.55	46.47	27.42	18.70	69.45
C-DB$_L$	0.00	0.00	1.85	8.67	6.15	0.17	0.00	19.70
C-DB$_U$	0.15	10.14	27.50	29.67	36.04	41.02	9.97	64.24

Note: *N*: normal cells; *C*: cancerous cells, *DB$_L$*: lower decision boundary; *DB$_U$*: upper decision boundary.

and its variance), wavelet approximation coefficients, and gray-level intensity.

After careful observations, several unique patterns are found and confirmed:

- generally, a normal cervix cell has smaller nucleus area and, vice versa, greater cytoplasm area that results in smaller N/C ratio. In terms of wavelet characteristic, this morphology is represented by a specific pattern of the approximation coefficients where it has narrower interval of low-values in the frequency domain. In the meantime, based on gray-level intensity a normal cell has greater distribution within the higher gray-level intensity intervals, which represents larger proportion of brighter pixels in the image.

- in contrary, a cancerous cell has greater N/C ratio which is in fact derived from a proportion of greater nucleus and smaller cytoplasm areas. Due to the morphological shape of the nucleus, the wavelet approximation coefficients of a cancerous cell has wider interval of low-values in the frequency domain. Hence, the coefficients are more distributed in the lower values intervals. Furthermore, in terms of color intensity a cancerous cell has mainly greater distribution in the lower gray-level intensity interval, which means larger proportion of darker pixels in the image.

The adaptive intelligent system is developed by adopting the cytologists' knowledge and build them into an intelligent agent that performs pattern recognition through a multilayer perceptron network The system is designed to automatically recognize and generate perception used to detect abnormality in the cervix cells, which is objective, more accurate and consistent using a standardized decision making rule. Therefore, it is expected can eventually replace the diagnosis made by human cytologists. Nevertheless, it is not intended to replace the cytologists' role, instead to leverage the cytologists' skill to produce more accurate diagnosis for the patient.

Based on the current achievements, future work will be organized to further improving the sensitivity of the multilayer perceptron algorithm for recognizing cervix cancer staging at normal, mild dysplasia, severe dysplasia, CIS (carcinoma in situ), CIN-I (cervical intraepithelial neoplasia level 1), CIN-II (CIN level 2), and CIN-III (CIN level 3) stages.

REFERENCES

Acharya, T., & Ray, A. K. (2005). *Image processing: Principles and applications*. New Jersey, USA: John Wiley & Sons, Inc. doi:10.1002/0471745790

American Cancer Society. (2010). *Cervical cancer overview*. Atlanta, GA: Author.

Andrews, H. C., & Hunt, B. R. (1977). *Digital image restoration*. Baltimore, MD: The Johns Hopkins University Press.

Chaudhuri, B. B., Rodenacker, K., & Burger, G. (1988). Characterization and featuring of histological section images. *Pattern Recognition Letters*, 7, 245–252. doi:10.1016/0167-8655(88)90109-2

Cohen, J. (1968). Weighed kappa: Nominal scale agreement with provision for scaled disagreement or partial credit. *Psychological Bulletin*, 70(4), 213–220. doi:10.1037/h0026256

Coombes, L. R., & Culverhouse, P. F. (2003). Pattern recognition in cervical cytological slide images. In D. P. Mukherjee & S. Pal (Eds.), *The 5th International Conference on Advances In Pattern Recognition (ICAPR) 2003* (pp. 227-230). New Delhi, India: Allied Publishers Pvt. Ltd.

Cotrans, R. S., Kumar, V., & Robbins, S. L. (1999). *Robbins pathologic basis of disease* (6th ed.). London, UK: W. B. Saunders Co.

De Marchi Triglia, R., Metze, K., Zeferino, L. C., & De Angelo Andrade, L. A. C. (2009). HPV in situ hybridization signal patterns as a marker for cervical intraepithelial neoplasia progression. *Gynecologic Oncology, 112*, 114–118. doi:10.1016/j.ygyno.2008.09.047

Elit, L. (2008). Cervical cancer. In Elit, L. (Ed.), *Resource compendium available for cervical and breast cancer control and prevention in the majority world*. New York, NY: Nova Science Publisher, Inc.

Euthman's Images Collection. (2010). *Pathology cases*. Retrieved from http://www.flickr.com/photos/euthman/collections/72157603641714831

Feng, C., Shuzhen, C., & Libo, Z. (2007). New abnormal cervical cell detection method of multi-spectral Pap smear. *Wuhan University Journal of Natural Sciences, 12*(3), 476–480. doi:10.1007/s11859-006-0108-z

Gonzales, R. C., & Woods, R. E. (2002). *Digital image processing* (2nd ed.). New Jersey, USA: Prentice-Hall, Inc.

Gonzalez, R. C., & Woods, R. C. (1992). *Digital image processing*. Boston, MA: Addison-Wesley Publishing Company.

Gujarati, D. N. (1995). *Basic econometrics* (3rd ed.). New York, NY: McGraw-Hill.

Haykin, S. (2009). *Neural networks and learning machines* (3rd ed.). New Jersey, USA: Pearson Education Inc.

International Commission on Illumination (CIE). (2011). *Selected colorimetric tables*. Vienna, Austria: CIE Central Bureau. Retrieved March 14, 2011, from http://www.cie.co.at/index.php/LEFTMENUE/ index.php?i_ca_id=298

Jang, J.-S. R., Sun, S.-T., & Mizutani, E. (1997). *Neuro-fuzzy and Soft-computing: A computational approach to learning and machine intelligence*. New Jersey, USA: Prentice-Hall Inc.

Karp, G. C. (2005). *Cell and molecular biology: Concepts and experiments* (4th ed.). Jefferson City, MO: Von Hoffman Press.

Knowledge System Laboratory at Stanford University. (2003). *The BB1 Blackboard control architecture*. Retrieved from http://www.ksl.stanford.edu/projects/BB1/bb1.html

Konar, A. (2005). *Computational intellingence: Principles, techniques and applications*. Heidelberg, Germany: Springer-Verlag.

Kumar, V., Abbas, A., Fausto, N., & Mitchell, R. (2007). *Robbins basic pathology*. Philadelphia, PA: Saunders Publishing Co.

Lassouaoui, N., Hamami, L., & Nouali, N. (2005). Morphological description of cervical cell images for the pathological recognition. *World Academy of Science. Engineering and Technology, 5*, 49–52.

Liu, Y., Zhao, T., & Zhang, J. (2002, November). *Learning multispectral texture features for cervical cancer detection*. Paper presented at the IEEE Symposium on Biomedical Imaging: SBI 02. Macro to Nano. Retrieved from IEEE Xplore: http://ieeexplore.ieee.org/ xpl/freeabs_all.jsp?arnumber=1029220

Mat-Isa, N. A., Mashor, M. Y., & Othman, N. H. (2003). Classification of cervical cancer cells using HMLP network with confidence percentage and confidence level analysis. *International Journal of The Computer. The Internet and Management, 11*(1), 17–29.

Matthew, J. (2004). *Perceptrons*. Generation5.org website. Retrieved March 16, 2011, from http://www.generation5.org/ content/1999/ perceptron.asp

McCulloch, W., & Pitts, W. (1943). A logical calculus of the ideas immanent in nervous activity. *The Bulletin of Mathematical Biophysics, 7*, 115–133. doi:10.1007/BF02478259

Melin, P., & Castillo, O. (2005). *Hybrid intelligent systems for pattern recognition using soft computing: An evolutionary approach for neural networks and fuzzy systems*. Heidelberg, Germany: Springer-Verlag.

Mitra, P., Mitra, S., & Pal, S. K. (2000). Staging of cervical cancer with soft computing. *IEEE Transactions on Bio-Medical Engineering, 47*(7), 934–940. doi:10.1109/10.846688

Mustafa, N., Mat-Isa, N. A., Mashor, M. Y., & Othman, N. H. (2008). Capability of new features of cervical cells for cervical cancer diagnostic system using hierarchical neural network. *International Journal of Simulation, Systems. Science & Technology, 9*(2), 56–64.

Nilsson, N. J. (1998). *Introduction to machine learning*. Stanford, CA: Stanford University, Department of Computer Science.

Pratt, W. K. (1991). *Digital image processing*. New York, NY: John Wiley & Sons.

Prayitno, A. (2006). Cervical cancer with Human Papilloma Virus and Epstein Barr virus positive. *Journal of Carcinogenesis, 5*(13), 1–4.

Rasmussen, C. E., & Williams, C. K. I. (2006). *Gaussian processes for machine learning*. Cambridge, MA: MIT Press.

Reproductive Health Technologies Project. (2008). *HPV vaccine update*. Retrieved from http://www.rhtp.org/fertility/cervix/documents/HPVVaccineUpdateFinal.pdf

Rosenblatt, F. (1958). The perceptron: A probabilistic model for information storage in the brain. *Psychological Review, 65*, 365–408. doi:10.1037/h0042519

Rosenfeld, A., & Kak, A. C. (1982). *Digital picture processing* (*Vol. 2*). New York, NY: Academic Press.

Rumelhart, D. E., & McClelland, J. L.PDP Research Group. (1986). *Parallel and distributed processing* (*Vol. I-II*). Cambridge, USA: MIT Press.

Siebert, U., Sroczynski, G., Hillemanns, P., Engel, J., Stabenow, R., & Stegmaier, C. (2006). The German cervical cancer screening model: Development and validation of a decision-analytic model for cervical cancer screening in Germany. *European Journal of Public Health, 16*(2), 185–192. doi:10.1093/eurpub/cki163

Suryatenggara, J., & Ane, B. K. Pandjaitan, & M., Steinberg, W. (2009, December). *Pattern recognition on 2D cervical cytological digital images for early detection of cervix cancer*. Paper presented at the World Congress on Nature & Biologically Inspired Computing (NaBIC 2009). Retrieved from http://ieeexplore.ieee.org/xpl/ freeabs_all.jsp?arnumber=5393710

Thangavel, K., Jaganathan, J. P., & Easmi, P. O. (2006). Data mining approach to cervical cancer patients analysis using clustering technique. *Asian Journal of Information Technology, 5*(4), 413–417.

Touretzky, D. S., & Pomerleau, D. A. (1989). What's hidden in the hidden layer? *Byte, 14*(8), 227–233.

Tumer, K., Ramanujam, N., Ghosh, J., & Richards-Kortum, R. (1998). Ensembles of radial basis function networks for spectroscopic detection of cervical precancer. *IEEE Transactions on Bio-Medical Engineering, 45*(8), 953–961. doi:10.1109/10.704864

Werbos, P. J. (1974). *Beyond regression: New tools for prediction and analysis in the behavioral sciences*. (Unpublished PhD thesis). Harvard University, Cambridge, USA.

World Health Organization. (2007). IARC monographs on the evaluation of carcinogenic risks to humans: *Vol. 90. Human Papillomaviruses*. Lyon, France: International Agency for Research on Cancer.

World Health Organization. (2010). *Human Papillomavirus and related cancers*. Geneva, Switzerland: WHO/ICO HPV Information Centre.

World Health Organization. (2010). *World Health Report 2010: The path to universal coverage*. Geneva, Switzerland: WHO Media Center.

Zhang, J., & Liu, Y. (2004). Cervical cancer detection using SVM based feature screening. In Barillot, C., Haynor, D. R., & Hellier, P. (Eds.), *Medical Image Computing and Computer-assisted Intervention - MICCAI 2004* (pp. 873–880). Heidelberg, Germany: Springer-Verlag. doi:10.1007/978-3-540-30136-3_106

Zhao, T., Zhang, J., & Liu, Y. (2002, August). *Does multispectral texture features really improve cervical cancer detection*? Paper presented at the International Conference on Diagnostic Imaging and Analysis (ICDIA 2002). Retrieved from http://www.ri.cmu.edu/ publication_ view.html?pub_id=4034

KEY TERMS AND DEFINITIONS

Adaptive Intelligent System: Adaptive intelligent system refers to an AI system that coordinates perception, reasoning and action to pursue multiple goals while functioning autonomously in dynamic environments.

Adaptive: Adaptive represents an ability of the intelligent agent to adapt with changes in its environment that commonly sources from changes of structure, program, or data (i.e. based on its input or in response to external information) in such a manner that the expected future performance will improve.

Artificial Neural Network (ANN): Artificial neural network is a computational model with learning, or adaptive, characteristics that consists of large set of interconnected neurons, which execute in parallel to perform the task of learning.

Backpropagation: Backpropagation refers to the procedure for finding a gradient vector in a network structure that is calculated in the direction opposite to the flow of the output of each neuron.

Multilayer Perceptrons: Multilayer perceptrons is a feed-forward network having distinct input, output, and hidden layers.

Supervised Artificial Neural Network: Supervised ANN represents neural network based learning process that uses input-output training data to model the dynamic system.

Unsupervised Artificial Neural Network: Unsupervised ANN represents neural network based learning process where only the input data is given.

Chapter 19
Ontology–Based Clustering of the Web Meta–Search Results

Constanta-Nicoleta Bodea
Academy of Economic Studies, Romania

Adina Lipai
Academy of Economic Studies, Romania

Maria-Iuliana Dascalu
Academy of Economic Studies, Romania

ABSTRACT

The chapter presents a meta-search tool developed in order to deliver search results structured according to the specific interests of users. Meta-search means that for a specific query, several search mechanisms could be simultaneously applied. Using the clustering process, thematically homogenous groups are built up from the initial list provided by the standard search mechanisms. The results are more user oriented, as a result of the ontological approach of the clustering process. After the initial search made on multiple search engines, the results are pre-processed and transformed into vectors of words. These vectors are mapped into vectors of concepts, by calling an educational ontology and using the WordNet lexical database. The vectors of concepts are refined through concept space graphs and projection mechanisms, before applying the clustering procedure. Implementation details and early experimentation results are also provided.

INTRODUCTION

Information retrieval refers to the "representation, storage, organization and access to information items" and its success is strongly related to users' needs (Baeza-Yates & Ribeiro-Neto, 1999), (Heisig, Caldwell, Grebici, & Clarkson, 2010),

DOI: 10.4018/978-1-4666-1833-6.ch019

(Domingo-Ferrer, Bras-Amorós, Wu, & Manjón, 2009). Nevertheless, defining users' needs is not a straightforward issue. Building a query with a set of keywords, as an expression of users' needs and applying that query to a large set of data is not enough. The users have to receive the most relevant results, according to the query. The task became more challenging once the World Wide Web came into scene: "The Web is becoming a universal repository of human knowledge and culture which has allowed unprecedented sharing of ideas and information in a scale never seen before" (Baeza-Yates & Ribeiro-Neto, 1999). Trying to keep up with the continuous growth of the World Wide Web (WWW), the retrieval tools are engaged in a permanent race for faster development in order to reach better performances (Ajayi, Aderounmu, & Soriyan, 2010), (Wang, Tsai, & Hsu, 2009), (Tu & Seng, 2009). Information retrieval doesn't just mean information access (summarization, filtering, search, categorization), but also knowledge acquisition (visualization, mining, extraction, clustering). Thus, besides simple retrieval application, mining and learning applications are needed. Many operations in information retrieval can be automated, such as document indexing or query refinement, but classifications are more often performed manually. For saving time, algorithms were developed for mining documents (Qiu, 2010), (Jeng, Chuang, & Tao, 2010) (Chen, Tseng, & Liang, 2010). These algorithms are based on machine learning," a dynamic, burgeoning area of computer science which is finding application in domains ranging from 'expert systems', where learning algorithms supplement—or even supplant—domain experts for generating rules and explanations (Langley, & Simon, 1995), to 'intelligent agents', which learn to play particular, highly-specialized, support roles for individual people and are seen by some to herald a new renaissance of artificial intelligence in information technology (Hendler, 1997)" (Cunningham, Littin, & Witten, 2001). A good example of machine learning algorithm used in information retrieval is the case in which knowledge bases are built as mirrors of WWW in local computer, thus optimizing the search process (Craven, et al., 2000).

Langley & Simon (1995) identify five major paradigms in machine learning research: rule induction, instance-based learning, neural networks, genetic algorithms and analytic learning. First four of them can be applied in information

retrieval: their mechanism is based on learning from information with very simple structure, such as lists of symbolic or numeric attributes. Genetic algorithms are applied to generate structures that represent relationships implicit in the data. According to Lewis (1991), the information retrieval process can be divided into four distinct stages: indexing, query Equationtion, comparison and feedback. Usually, when a researcher tries to improve the retrieval process, one focuses on one of these stages. In clustering techniques links are built between related documents so that indexing becomes more effective (Martin, 1995).

THE RESEARCH CONTEXT

A common way of dealing with efficient information retrieval in web environments is using an ontology approach (Yang, 2010), (Segura, Sánchez, García-Barriocanal, & Prieto, 2011), (Park, Cho, & Rho, 2010). In clustering, the methods which use the ontology approach identify the concepts instead of the index words occurring in web documents (Hotho, Staab, & Stumme, 2003), (Bloehdorn, & Hotho, 2004). The corresponding concepts are identified with the aid of ontology class labels and the WordNet lexical database. In WordNet the terms are organized in synsets, which are sets of synonyms. Using concepts instead of index words reduces the clustering dimensionality, considering that we can have multiple index words replaced by the same concept. Some methods recommend adding the identified concepts to the index words list, and increasing the dimensionality of the process (Jing, Zhou, Ng, & Huang, 2006). As a consequence, it is not possible to consider the concept-based clustering as an implicit solution for the dimensionality issue. The clustering solution proposed in this paper is based on the concepts' identification, via WordNet and the replacement of the index words by the corresponding concepts.

For clustering purpose, a document is represented as a vector of index words in a vector space model. The vector components are weights of the correspondent index words showing their relative importance in the document and the entire set of documents. Having the vector collection (all the documents represented as vectors), the Euclidean distance, Minkowski distance, Manhatten distance, and other distance measures could be used in order to compute the distance or similarity between documents, as part of the clustering algorithms, such as k-means. In order to take into consideration the document semantic, different ontology-based measure were defined (Hotho, Maedche & Staab, 2001). Considering the semantic relationship between each pair of words, as mutual information between terms, Jing, Zhou, Ng, & Huang(2006) proposed the extension of the vector space model with a mutual information matrix and an Euclidian distance measure considering the correlation between each pair of terms. Using this modeling framework a clustering method, named FW-Kmeans, was defined, performing better than classical methods.

Hotho, Maedche & Staab(2001) proposed the COSA (Concept selection and aggregation) clustering method. The COSA approach uses a core ontology for restricting the document features used by aggregation process. The aggregation result is exploited by K-means algorithm, in order to produce a set of clustering results, considered as a set of views.

An ontology-based clustering framework is proposed by Lula & Paliwoda-Pekosz(2008), giving the possibility of incorporating various kinds of measures to determine similarity between objects and sets of objects in the following three dimensions: taxonomic, relationship and attribute. Kogilavani & Balasubramanie(2009) developed a system which revises the user query by mapping it with synonyms and semantically related concepts using MeSH ontology knowledge source. First, the system clusters terms using a term semantic similarity measure. Then the term is re-weightedto increase the weight of the terms which are more

semantically similar. The similarity measures are defined based on the information content.

PURPOSE OF THE RESEARCH

The chapter presents an ontology-based clustering procedure defined by the authors in order to deliver meta-search results structured according to user's interests. Meta-search means that for a specific query, several search mechanisms could be applied. The lists of results delivered by the standard search mechanisms are used to build up thematically homogenous groups using an ontology-based clustering algorithm, without any predefined categories.

Organizing search results in clusters is not meant to replace the classical way of presenting results in ranked lists. Its purpose is to provide supplementary organization for those results. The clustering method will provide a series of search results clusters, with the property that the pages inside one cluster are similar to each other, and the pages belonging to different clusters differ from one another. Inside each cluster the initial ranking order provided will be preserved.

THE RESEARCH METHODOLOGY

The chapter describes the theoretical bases of the approach and the clustering algorithm, then the application of it – the clustering tool itself. Finally, the chapter presents the experimentation results.

Clustering the search results means grouping them into object classes which are developed using the search results characteristics, with the purpose of simplifying the user work to retrieve the relevant results.

Generally, the list of results provided by a search engine is composed of the link to the site that meet the query criteria, a brief description of the page (usually the selection of the page) and the page title. Some search engines return additional information such as: the page size, the connection to similar pages, the connection to the pages in cash, the page indexing date. Using this information, the user usually goes through the entire list of results to find relevant pages. Even if the results list is sorted by a rank which gives a score of importance of the site, there are cases where the user will have to go through a high number of results (20 to 100 sites) in order to find the desired pages.

In order to make the user's job easier, the clustering algorithm will divide the list of results in homogenous groups. The user will have to identify the cluster in which his pages are most likely to be and only search through that cluster, ignoring the other clusters. In Figure 1, we have represented schematically the basic principles of how clustering method operates. The initial results $R_1, R_2, ..., R_n$ form a list, which after clustering will become part of one cluster $C_1, ..., C_n$. The cluster can differ in size accordingly to what web pages meet the subject criteria of that cluster. The

search results' clusters have the property that the pages inside one cluster are similar to each other, and the pages belonging to different clusters differ from one another. Inside each cluster the initial ranking order provided will be preserved.

The results' clustering module has a unique user interface to take over the search keywords for querying different search engines (Google, Yahoo, MSN search, and so on). The search module will send keywords to different search engines which will retrieve the results and send them to the clustering module. The clustering algorithm is run on the local machine. The clustering results are presented to the user, together with all web documents (the link and the description) included in those clusters. Figure 1 presents the integration of the clustering module in a meta-search process. The ontology used for results' clustering is an educational one. For these ontologies, an important relationship type is *requires(Ci, Cj)*, meaning "Ci requires Cj as prerequisite", where Ci and Cj are two learning

Figure 1. The Web search results clustering process

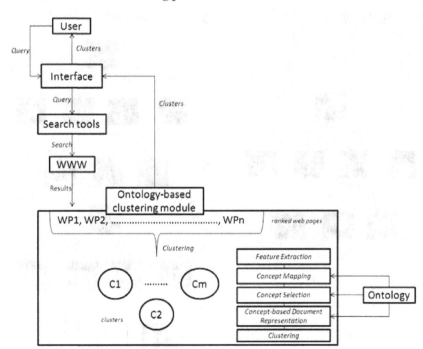

concepts. Each concept class of the ontology has its self-weight as class attribute. The attribute value is set using expert opinion.

The *space graph* of concept Ci is the graph which has Ci as the root node and all other concepts directly or indirectly connected to Ci with "requires" links as graph nodes. The relevance of the concept Ci with respect to its prerequisites is measured by $W_s(i)$, *the self weight* of the concept. The *prerequisite weight* of concept Ci, $W_p(i)$ is the relative semantic relevance of the prerequisite topics and *the link weight* $l(i,j)$ represents the relative importance of learning concept Cj for learning Ci. For all nodes of the concept space graph, the sum of self-weight and prerequisite weight is 1. The sum of all prerequisite link weights to the child nodes is also 1.

$$W_s(i) + W_p(i) = 1, \forall i \qquad (1)$$

$$\sum_{j=1}^{n} l(C_0, C_j) = 1 \qquad (2)$$

Figure 2 shows an example of concept space graph (for concept C1.19), with $W_p(i)$ shown on the right side of node and $W_s(i)$ on the left side.

Given a root concept C_0 and a projection threshold coefficient λ, *a projection graph* is defined as a sub-graph with root C_0 and all nodes C_t, where there is at least one path from C_0 to C_t such that node path weight $\eta(C_0, C_t)$ satisfies the condition: $\eta(C_0, C_t) >= \lambda$, where node path weight between C_0 and C_t for the path $[C_0, C_1, \dots, C_t]$ is:

$$\eta(C_0, C_t) = W_s(t) \prod_{m=n}^{1} l(C_{m-1}, C_m) * W_p(m-1) \qquad (3)$$

We consider as an example the concept space graph shown on the upper part of Figure 2. A small value for λ parameter has as result a larger projection graph, as shown in Table 1.

The results from Table 1 are also presented in graphical format in Figure 2. The white nodes of the concept space graph are not included in the projection graphs.

Figure 2. The projection graphs for different values of the λ parameter

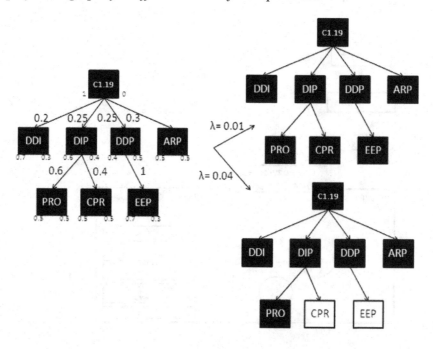

Table 1. The projection results for different values of the λ parameter, for root node C1.19

Concept	ŋ	ŋ>=λ (λ=0.01)	ŋ>=λ(λ=0.04)
ARP	0.15	TRUE	TRUE
DDP	0.125	TRUE	TRUE
DIP	0.1	TRUE	TRUE
DDI	0.06	TRUE	TRUE
PRO	0.045	TRUE	TRUE
CPR	0.03	TRUE	FALSE
EEP	0.03	TRUE	FALSE

The projection graphs are used during the concept selection process, in order to reduce the dimension of the extended index concept vector. The result of the concept selection process is the reduced index vector list.

Each concept class has lexical instances, in addition to usual concept instances. The lexical instances are created using the synonym classes of the WordNet and represent synonyms for the concept label. The number of lexical instances is related to the concept self-weight measure. In our experiments, we applied relation (4) to set the lexical instance number for each ontology concept.

$$Li_i = \gamma \cdot e^{W_s(i)} \qquad (4)$$

where: Li_i is the number of lexical instances for concept class I, γ is a positive parameter, greater than 1 (we used γ =10), and $W_s(i)$ is the self-weight of the concept Ci.

The synonyms of ontology concepts are used on the concept mapping process, to find the corresponding ontological class for each index word. A direct matching between the concept labels and index words is not recommended, because most of the ontologies have a very limited lexicon, comparing to the web content, so there is a small chance to find concept labels in the index words' list.

THE CLUSTERING ALGORITHM

The main steps of the search results clustering are the following:

- Obtaining the web page list
- Pre-processing of the documents
- Transforming the documents into vector representation
- K-means clustering, with adequate adaptations for web pages
- Designing the cluster representation for final results

Obtaining the Web Page List

The initial web page list is obtained putting all the results delivered by all the search tools in a single list. This list will be used to cluster the results. In order to obtain the web page list the next steps have to be done:

a) **Performing simultaneous queries** on multiple search engines through a meta-search interface.

b) **Elimination of the multiple links:** because the results are obtained from more search tools it's more than likely the same site will be returned by more than one tool.

c) **Calculating the new rank:** the Equation below will be used.

$$\text{Rank}_{new} = I_M * \text{NrRez} + I_{Rez} \qquad (5)$$

where:

Rank_{new}: the new rank calculated for each web page

I_M : the index of the search engine which provided this page

NrRez: total number of results after the duplicates were eliminated

I_{Rez}: the index of the page in the I_M search tool

d) **Duplicate web pages** will receive the rank from the search tool with the lowest index

Pre-Processing of the Documents

The clustering algorithm uses information from the pages in order to determine its subject or characteristics. Most document clustering algorithms use the whole document for this process, but such approach would slow our web page clustering algorithm too much. Therefore the algorithm will only use the snippets provided by the initial search tools. Previous work has showed that snippets provide good quality description of web pages, and this aspect justifies their use (Leuski, & Allan, 2000). The title of the web page will also be used, if there is one. Title words will become more important for classification than snippet words. Web pages processing is made up by the following operations:

a) *The tag cleaning;* It will eliminate the portions of the web document which are strictly related to the text formatting.
b) *The lexical analysis;* the purpose of the analysis is to identify distinct words. The process implies eliminating useless characters such as comma, punctuation marks, sometimes numbers, or characters like: #, $..
c) *The word root extraction;* the goal is to obtain a homogenous one-word description of similar but not identical words. The word obtained in the end doesn't have to have a meaning, nor be grammatically correct, but it will contain the description and similarity with all the other words that it represents. For example: *implementing, implementation, implemented* will be described by the root word *implement*.
d) *The stop word elimination;* a stop word is a word that does not have an informational value. In all languages there are a series of words which are considered stop words. For example: "on", "and", "the", "in", etc.
e) *Establishing the index words;* an index word, is a word that is representative in the context of the document.

The Figure 3 presents the pre-processing steps. In the upper part of the image, one can see the query results provided by Google on "knowledge management": the list of web documents is sorted by rank. The documents' information (such as title, snippet) will be further used for processing the results. The results' processing is showed in the lower part of the Figure 3: part (a) shows the beginning of the lexical analysis (the snippet's separation in words) and part (b) shows the beginning of the removal of stop words and other characters which are useless in the processing phase.

Transforming the Documents into a Concept Vector Representation

In order to use the k-means clustering algorithm we need to transform each document into a concept vector. The vectors will have the same size, turning our result list into an M*N matrix. A line represents one web page and each column represents a concept. The N dimension represents the total number of concepts that will be used for document clustering, from all documents. The dimension M represents the remaining number of web pages after the duplicate eliminations, the final search result list.

Supposing we have:

*   M web pages: d_1, d_2,.., d_M and
*   N indexed concepts from 1 to N

A web page will be represented in concept vector space using the following Equation:

$$d_i = \left[W'_{i1}, W'_{i2}, \ldots, W'_{iN} \right] \qquad (6)$$

Figure 3. Web pages pre-processing steps

where $W_{ij}^{'}$ represents the weight of concept j for document d_i

Transforming the documents into concept vector space representation requires the following steps:

a) ***Index word vector identification and vector space representation;*** It implies joining together in one vector all the index words from all the documents. For each document and each index word we will count the number of times one word appears in the same page.

b) ***Word weight calculation for each document;*** In order to calculate each word weight, the frequency of word in document and the inverted document frequency are used.

c) ***The concept mapping;*** each index word is checked against the lexical instances, for all ontology concept classes, starting with those having the greatest W_s. The first successful matching will indicate the parent class of the concept to be assigned to the index word.

Having the list of the index words as input data of the concept mapping process, an extended index concept list will be produced as a result of this process.

d) ***The concept selection;*** projection graphs of the concepts included in the extended index concept list are used to reduce the dimension of the extended index concept vector during the concept selection process. The result is a reduced index concept vector list.

e) ***Concept weight calculation for each document and the concept-based representation of documents;*** the concept weight for a document is the weight of the corresponding word adjusted with the concept's self weight.

We start the concept vector space representation of documents with the index word vector identification. The words 1.L are usually the index words, and they are obtained after the pre-processing the documents. Assigning each word a weight it's crucial in order to distinguish the more relevant words from the less important ones. In the end we will quantify the importance that each concept has for a given web page.

The weight of word t_j for a specific document d_i is calculated using the Equation (7):

$$w_{ij} = fT_{ij} * \log(n \, / \, fd_j) \qquad (7)$$

where:

- w_{ij} is the weight of word t_j for document d_i
- fT_{ij} is the frequency of word t_j in d_i document
- fd_i is the total number of web pages in which the word t_j appears.

The term $\log(n \, / \, fd_j)$ is also called *inverted document frequency*. The words that have a higher frequency in a page will most likely be a better description than the words that have low frequency. But also, the terms that have high frequency in all documents, will not make good description for differences that appear between pages. The term inverted document frequency intends to minimize the importance of the words that appear frequently in all documents (Chi, 2003).

The weight of concept C_k for the document d_i, W'_{ik} is calculated using the following Equation (8):

$$W'_{ik} = W_{ik} * \log\left(\frac{1}{W_s(k)}\right) \qquad (8)$$

where:

- W_{ik} is the weight of corresponding word for document d_i
- $W_s(k)$ is the self weight of the concept k.

K-Means Clustering, with Adequate Adaptations for Web Pages

Classical K-means clustering algorithm uses numerical input to build up distinct clusters. It splits the total data set into exclusive clusters using a measure called "distance". The distance can be calculated using many Equations, but basically having the meaning of metric distance. Just as in traditional k-means clustering, a cluster K will be represented by its centre or centroid (Baeza-Yates & Ribeiro-Neto, 1999). For web page clustering this centroid will represent a weighted concept document within the vector space documents. This centroid will be called "the representative of cluster K_k" noted R_k.

In order for R_k to be equivalent with the centre of clusters from the traditional k-means clustering, it must meet the following conditions:

- Each document d_i from K_k has joined concepts with R_k
- The concepts in R_k also appear in the most documents in K_k
- Not all the concepts from R_k have to appear in all the documents from K_k
- The weight of concept C_j from R_k is calculated as an average weight of all the concepts present in all documents of K_k (Chi, 2003).

After determining the representatives of the cluster, the web meta-search results clustering algorithm is as follows:

- *Input data:*
  Di are the web pages/documents provided by the initial search.
  l is the number of clusters, accordingly to k-means traditional algorithm.
- *Output data:*

l clusters with documents (the clusters can overlap, meaning the same page can be assigned to more than just one cluster, for each distribution there will be a weight assigned to the document)

Step 1: *l documents from the web page list are randomly selected.* These l documents will form the starting representatives of the clusters. We have $K_1, K_2, ..., K_l$ clusters and $R_1, R_2, ..., R_k$ as clusters representatives.

Step 2: *For each web page from D:* $d_i \in D$ and each cluster K_k, k = 1, ..., l we calculate the similarity between the web page and the representative of the cluster $S(d_i, R_k(K_k))$.

Step 3: *If the similarity is bigger than a given threshold* $S(d_i, R_k(K_k)) > \delta$, than the document d_i will be assigned to cluster K_k with a weight attached, the weight being calculated based upon the similarity value:

$$m(d_i, K_k) = S(d_i, R_k(K_k)) \tag{9}$$

Step 4: For each cluster the representative is re-calculated taking into account the new documents that were assigned to that particular cluster.

Step 5: The process is re-started from step 2 until the new changes are below a given threshold.

Step 6: *For each web page* d_n which is not assigned to any cluster the closest neighborhood will be calculated $V(d_u)$. The neighborhood must not contain documents that have similarity measure zero. The d_n web page will be assigned to the cluster to which the neighborhood $V(d_u)$ belongs to. The weight for d_n assignation to K_k is calculated:

$$m(d_n, K_k) = m(V(d_u), K_k) * S(d_n, (V(d_u))) \tag{10}$$

Step 7: *For each cluster* K_k the representative of the cluster R_k is recalculated.

Similarity is calculated using the following Equation, also named as Salton's cosine coefficient (Salton, 1989):

$$s(x, y) = \frac{\sum_{i=1}^{t} x_i y_i}{\sqrt{\sum_{i=1}^{t} x_i^2 + \sum_{i=1}^{t} y_i^2}} \tag{11}$$

Developing the Cluster-Like Representation for the Final Results

a) **Label extraction;** For each clusters the sequence of words with the highest frequency will be assigned as label for that class. If a sequence of words is not found then a single word will be used instead.

b) **Creating the cluster structure;** It will be done using both the size of the clusters and the weight of the pages inside the cluster. A measure of the cluster quality will be calculated.

c) **Results delivery;** During the pre-processing phase, we extracted the root for the similar words and we eliminated the stop words, and some other changes took place in order to make the document suitable for clustering. In order for the user to understand what a page is about it must be presented with a short relevant description of that web page. In almost all cases the initial search results' list provides a short description (the snippet). That description can be kept, and delivered to the user after clusters are developed, but it can also be enhanced with particular characteristics of the cluster.

The Figure 4 presents the results of the query "Knowledge management", delivered as clusters.

Figure 4. Search results delivered as clusters

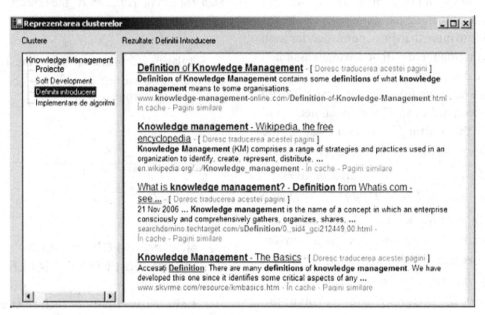

On the left side, there are mentioned four clusters induced for this search. On the right side, we can see the links and the related snippets, for the selected cluster (in our case, "Definitii introducere" – "Definition introduction").

IMPLEMENTATION OF THE ONTOLOGY-BASED SEARCH CLUSTERING SOLUTION

Clustering solutions for web documents which query search engines must meet the following functions: acquisition of queries from the user, providing one or more query search engines, results acquisition, processing of web documents, web documents' clustering and results' display. The proposed application respects the general expectations of a clustering solution. The overall functioning of the application is the following:

- the user inserts search words, selects the search engines and other preferences (for languages, displaying, clustering), if wanted;

- the search engines are interrogated and the results are retrieved (using the internet); these results are web pages;

- the retrieved web pages are processed (HTML tags and stop words are eliminated, texts are processed);

- the processed web pages are transformed into vectors of words;

- implement the space vector model (build the vector of indexed terms, calculate the weights of indexed terms in documents, map the indexed terms into ontological concepts, build reduced index concepts list, calculate concepts' weights in documents, build the "documents-concepts" matrix);

- implement clustering process (select the cetroids, build the clusters, calculate the similarity and distribute a document into clusters, recalculate the centroids and so on and so forth); the algorithm used for clustering is "k-means" (Franstrom, & Lewis, 2000) and it is customized for calculating the similarity between documents; by default, it will build 6 clusters, but it can build between 2 and 10 clusters;

• display results in user interface;

The functional components that perform the above described tasks are presented below.

User Interface

The user interface has the role of taking the words which have to be searched, the search engines on which queries will be executed and users' display and clustering preferences, if any. The application interface is represented in Figure 5.

Selecting search engines is made using the right tab. The search begins when all engines were selected and loaded by inserting the keywords and when the button "Initiate Search" is pressed. The browsers within the application are fully functional, so if a search is performed in the browser, it will be taken by the processing module. The disadvantage of using this method of query (by browsers) is that the browsers will not be synchronized. Thus if one wants one meta-search on multiple search engines using the same keywords and same parameters, it is recommended to use the searching and viewing facilities

offered by the application. If one wants special preferences offered by a certain search engine, which aren't implemented in the application, then it is best to access the browsers.

The application allows the possibility of inserting user-specific preferences for viewing the results and for establishing clustering parameters, such as: search by language, processing a given number of results and choosing a visualization level. Each of these preferences will be further described.

a. Language preferences

The application has the possibility of searching documents in Romanian and in English. The default option is Romanian: so, if one searches for documents in any other language, the results will contain Romanian web pages. A set of processing are specific to Romanian language: it is expected that the search algorithms will achieve better results on documents written in Romanian, because the preprocessing stage is more detailed. However, there are many situations that will get poor results due particularities of the Romanian language to use accents. There are several web sites which don't display correctly these accents,

Figure 5. Ontology-based search clustering application: User interface

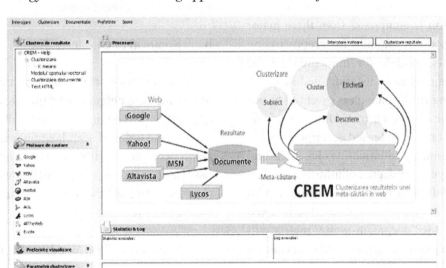

so the snippet displayed after processing the search will be grammatically wrong.

b.   Results number to be processed

The application has the possibility of introducing the number of results that are intended to be used. By default, the maximum number of results provided by an engine on first page will be considered, but one can choose a smaller number of results.

c.   Visualization level

The user is allowed to see, at runtime, certain steps of the clustering process. Default viewing level is 5, which means that the whole process is invisible to the user. Finally, only the obtained clusters are presented to the user. Using a low-level view is not recommended, since it slows down the computing process. This option is useful when one wants to estimate the performance obtained in the clustering process. When restarting a search, we have the option to keep and use the old results. This option is useful when the user wants an in-depth search for the same keywords. By default, the data is reset for every search.

Processing Modules

The application is comprised from three major processing modules: module for preprocessing the documents, module for implementing the vector space model and clustering module itself. The processing of documents is essential to obtain qualitative results. The main function of this module is to form a condensed description of the web search results, by eliminating characters and words that have a low degree of information. The description will be used in the construction of the vector of indexed terms. Using the indexed terms' vector, the "document-terms" matrix will be built, which will be further used to clustering

composition. These results are obtained by taking the results from all the search engines and eliminating identical ones. The properties of an indexed terms' vector are:

- it does not contain duplicate words;
- it does not contain stop words;
- it does not contain figures or special characters;
- it is composed of all the words from unique results;

Documents Preprocessing

Search results are obtained by performing a query on multiple engines. The selection of the engines is made before making the actual search. By default, the system uses Google search.

a.   HTML Tag Removal

Search results are retrieved from search engines via a browser, by extracting useful content from the HMTL document body. The first step in processing this document is to remove the sequences of letters which have the purpose of formatting the pages in standard HTML, for example, "head", "script" or "style" tags. A removal procedure is used, in order to keep the information between tags for further processing.

b.   Removal of Duplicate Sites

Since multiple search engines are used, it is inevitable the emergence of duplicate results. The application will retain only one result, taking into account the order of search engines in which the result occurred. Finally, we have a concatenated list of unique results, which will be clustered. Each result has attached the following attributes: title, description, link and rank.

c.   Removal of Stop Words and Characters

The stop words don't bring any information in text processing: they are eliminated from the vector of indexed terms. Some examples of stop words are: „end", „with", „in". Stop words are removed entirely from the vector of indexed terms. Still, stop words might bring information about the text structure. This is the reason for which their position in the text is memorized when documents' description is processed. When determining the frequent phrases in the text, this position will be used. A frequent phrase is a pair of two consecutive terms or two consecutive terms separated by the same sequence of stop words. Stop characters are considered any character that delimits a word. These are: { ' ', ',', ';', '.', '-', '/', '|', '\\', '%', '#', '@', '!', '~', '$', '^', '(', ')', '+', '[', ']', '{', '}', '""', ':', '<', '>', '?', '\r', '\n', '*' }.

d.   Words Root Extraction and Language Processing

Root extraction module has been developed entirely in C #, using basic grammatical rules. The module makes only minimal extraction of roots' level. We believe that more complex processing would be inefficient to implement in terms of computing time, and not justified by the added quality. For extracting the root level, the following rules have been used: removal of plural forms, removal of standard suffixes and removal of verbal suffixed. The module is available only for Romanian language.

Implementing Vector Space Model

The vector space model of documents' processing consists of transforming the string of words from a snippet into a vector of numbers: a document will be represented by a numerical vector of n elements, where n represents the number of unique words in the document. The value of each element of the vector is given by the number of occurrence of that word in the document.

a.   Building the vector of index terms

Building the vector of index terms is the first step in implementing the vector space model. The vector of index terms is built from individual words contained by the page title or the page description. The entire list of pages/documents is browsed in order to build the vector. The vector of index terms doesn't contain: stop words, stop characters, single-letter words, numbers of one or two digits and the keywords used to process the search, because these keywords are presented in all the documents.

b.   Building the reduced concept lists

Each element of the index terms vector is mapped to the educational ontology and then projections are applied to obtain the most relevant lists of concepts for each document.

c.   Vectoring the Documents

Vectoring the documents is the step in which numerical vectors are built for each document. In the vector space model, each document is represented by a numerical vector of n elements, where n is the number of indexed terms. The value of each word in the numerical vector is calculated using two Equations: word frequency-inverted document frequency and linear inverted document frequency. (Wróblewski, 2003)

Vectoring procedure can be described as:

Step 1: Each document will have an array of null values associated with it.

Step 2: For each result:

    Step 2.1: The result is decomposed in individual words using the words' delimiters.

    Step 2.2: The presence of each word is tested in the index vector

Step 2.3: The occurrence of each word from document d_i is counted into the index vector f++.

Step 2.4: The indexed term- frequency of occurrence in the document is built.

Step 3: For each indexed term, the inverted document frequency in which it appears is calculated.

Step 4: Using the matrix of indexed terms and frequency of word c_j and the vector of indexed terms t_j among all results, we calculate the weight of the word c_j in document D_i.

Step 5: All indexed terms are mapped into ontological concepts and the extended index concepts' list is obtained.

Step 6: The extended index concepts' list is transformed into reduced index concepts' list, through projection.

Step 7: Concept weight is calculated for each document, using the weight of the corresponding word (from Step4) adjusted with the concept's self weight.

After vectoring the documents and calculating the frequency of words in documents we will remove the index words that appear in a single document.

Clustering Algorithm Implementation

a. Determining the Initial Cluster's Centroids

A major disadvantage of k-means method (Franstrom, & Lewis, 2000) is the high number of iterations. When clustering results of a search in a network, a high number of iterations means a high computing time. In current study, we implemented three methods for calculating the initial centroids, following to determine experimentally which of the methods is more successful. The three methods are described below.

- The documents with the highest number of concepts

In this method, the initial centroids are the documents with the highest frequency of occurrence of the index concepts. Based on the method of approximate tolerant sets, our hypothesis is that a document containing a large number of words will be an approximate representation for documents that contain only one set of those concepts.

- The documents with the highest weight of concepts

Initial centroids will consist of documents that have concepts with the highest weight. Such documents will be representative for a limited set of documents, resulting in compact clusters, with high similarity between clusters.

- Segmented algorithm

The algorithm consists of dividing the dataset into k groups where k is the number of clusters we want to get. For each of the k groups we calculate the group average. This vector of averages will form the initial centroids. The algorithm is based on the assumption that results will be ranked by page rank. Thus the first group will be a centroid containing the averages of highly ranked pages. The algorithm is based on clustering by partitioning.

b. Clustering Algorithm

Basically, clustering means calculating the similarity between each instance and the centroids of each cluster. The main adjustments of k-means algorithm for web documents are: calculating the similarity as a measure of distance and use a software assignment to obtain clusters. In the end, we will have a set of k+1 overlapping clusters, where the last cluster contains the unclassified documents.

Clustering will be realized after a predefined number of iterations. This number will be determined experimentally in order to find a compromise between computing time and quality of clusters obtained. By default, we make 6 clusters, the 7th cluster representing unclassified documents and we use a threshold value of 0.3 for classification of instances in clusters. After each clustering, we recalculate the centroids and we reset the clusters' components. The new centroids are calculated using the average weigh of words reached in that cluster.

The source code for the clustering procedure, developed in C#, is shown in Code 1.

c.   Clusters Representation

After determining the composition of clusters by successive assignment as stated by the k-means algorithm, clusters are displayed. The first step in clusters display is determining clusters label. Clusters label may consist of one, two or three representative words for that cluster. The label will be chosen according to the centroid's weight for that cluster.

EXPERIMENTATION AND EVALUATION

The current experimentation has several major aims, namely:

- determining the performance of the proposed solution;
- determining the best parameters for certain situations;
- determining the degree of performance for the Romanian language compared with English;
- comparison with other clustering methods;

Preliminary Stages of Preprocessing

The removal of HTML tags was always successful. For four queries ("management", "proiect", "eficient", "succes"), we obtained an indicator of stop words removal having the value of 0.11. Using as a comparison measure the frequency of stop words in an unprocessed document, which ranges between 0.3-0.6, we can say there has been a satisfactory removal of stop words. The calculation of the indicator of stop words removal is presented in Table 2 and uses the following Equation (Equation 12):

$$IICstop = \frac{\sum_{i=1}^{n} \frac{NoStopWords_i}{TotalNoIndexWords_i}}{n}$$

(12)

where

- $IICstop$ represents the of the indicator of stop words removal;
- i represents a query;
- n represents the total number of queries;
- $NoStopWords_i$ represents the number of stop words removed for query i;
- $TotalNoIndexWords_i$ represents the total number of index words for query i;

Table 2. The calculation of the indicator of stop words removal for 4 queries

Query No	No Stop Words	Total No Index Words	Stop Words in Index Words
1	9	88	0.1
2	6	56	0.1
3	11	88	0.13
4	7	58	0.12
Sum of stop words in index words			0.45
IICstop			0.11

Code 1.

```
private void ClusteringProcedure()
{
int mDistanceCols = dimAllResults;
int mDistanceRows = noClusters;
double[,] distance = new double[mDistanceCols, mDistanceRows];
for (int i = 0; i < mDistanceRows; i++) {
for (int j = 0; j < mDistanceCols; j++) { distance [j, i] = Similarity(j, i);
}
}
int indexComponent = 0;
for (int j = 0; j < mDistanceCols; j++) {
for (int k = 0; k < noClusters; k++) {
indexComponenta = dimClustere[k];
if (distance[j, k] > threshold) {
indexComponent ++;
ClustersComponent[k, indexComponent] = j;
dimClusters[k]++;
}
}
}
//building the k+1 cluster of unclassified instances
int finalClusters = noClusters;
int instUnclassified = 0;
int found = 0;
for (int i = 0; i < dimAllResults; i++) {
found = 0;
for (int k = 0; k < noClusters; k++) {
for (int j = 0; j < dimClusters [k]; j++) {
if (ClustersComponent [k, j] == i){
 found = 1;
}
}
if (found == 0) {
ClustersComponent [finalClusters, instUnclassified] = i;
instUnclassified ++;
}
}
dimClusters[finalClusters] = instUnclassified;
                }
}
```

Clustering Results

For testing the clustering algorithms, we use ten queries, with the following features:

- Query 1: query string: "Inteligenţă artificială", query language: Romanian, query specificity: low, number of tested results: 90;
- Query 2: query string: "Data miningquery language: English, query specificity: high, number of tested results: 100;
- Query 3: query string: "Indice refracţie", query language: Romanian, query specificity: high, number of tested results: 82;
- Query 4: query string: "Salariu net", query language: Romanian, query specificity: low, number of tested results: 90;
- Query 5: query string: "Knowledge management", query language: English, query specificity: low, number of tested results: 100;
- Query 6: query string: "Proiect", query language: Romanian, query specificity: high, number of tested results: 90;
- Query 7: query string: "Competenţe", query language: Romanian, query specificity: medium, number of tested results: 80;
- Query 8: query string: "Cunoştinţe", query language: Romanian, query specificity: medium, number of tested results: 100;
- Query 9: query string: "Eficient", query language: Romanian, query specificity: high, number of tested results: 95;
- Query 10: query string: "Succes", query language: Romanian, query specificity: high, number of tested results: 90;

It should be noted that the evaluation was made using a group of 20 users. The parameters used in queries are the following:

- Search engines: Google, Yahoo!
- Number of used results: maximum
- Language preferences: Romanian (1,3,4,6,7,8,9) and Default (2,5)
- Similarity threshold: 0,3
- Number of clusters: 4
- Method of calculating the weight: inverted document frequency
- Method of calculating the initial centroids: documents with the highest number of word
  a. Results obtained in evaluating the quality of the cluster label

In our tests, the quality of the cluster label range between 0.6 and 0.95, with the observation that the quality is higher for queries with low specificity. The quality of the cluster label is calculated as a ratio between the average number of useful clusters and the total number of clusters. The average number of useful clusters range between 2.1 and 3.8, which is a very good result, considering the fact that we had only 4 clusters, as shown in Table 3. The average number of useful clusters is given, for each query, by the average number of clusters considered by our group of users.

Table 3. Evaluation of the quality of the cluster label

Q No	Average number of useful clusters	Total number of clusters	The quality of the cluster label
1	3.4	4	0.85
2	2.8	4	0.7
3	2.4	4	0.6
4	3.8	4	0.95
5	3.5	4	0.88
6	2.1	4	0.53
7	2.6	4	0.65
8	2.7	4	0.68
9	2.4	4	0.6
10	3.1	4	0.78

b. Results obtained in evaluating the quality of documents' distribution

In Table 4, the indicators of correctly, medium or incorrectly classified documents, for all queries and clusters, are illustrated. The Equations used for calculating them are the following:

$$DocsCorrectlyClassifiedInK=NoDocsCorrectlyClassifiedInK / TotalNoDocsInK \qquad (13)$$

$$DocsMediumClassifiedInK=NoDocsMediumClassifiedInK / TotalNoDocsInK \qquad (14)$$

$$DocsIncorrectlyClassifiedInK=NoDocsIncorrectlyClassifiedInK / TotalNoDocsInK \qquad (15)$$

After analyzing the results from Table 4, one can notice that the indicator for correctly classified documents is always greater than 0.5 and the other two indicators (for medium and incorrectly classified documents) are lower than 0.5. This result is underlined, for Query 5, in Figure 6.

Table 4. Indicators of correctly, medium or incorrectly classified documents

No Query	Indicator of docs correctly classified in K				Indicator of docs medium classified in K				Indicator of docs incorrectly classified in K			
Query 1	0.64	0.61	0.68	0.67	0.20	0.23	0.05	0.27	0.16	0.16	0.27	0.07
Query 2	0.57	0.69	0.77	0.73	0.22	0.08	0.10	0.15	0.22	0.23	0.13	0.12
Query 3	0.65	0.48	0.53	0.61	0.17	0.33	0.35	0.30	0.17	0.19	0.12	0.09
Query 4	0.72	0.68	0.65	0.75	0.14	0.21	0.21	0.11	0.14	0.11	0.15	0.14
Query 5	0.74	0.75	0.69	0.73	0.13	0.08	0.17	0.15	0.13	0.17	0.14	0.12
Query 6	0.76	0.69	0.83	0.78	0.17	0.14	0.10	0.19	0.07	0.17	0.07	0.04
Query 7	0.69	0.71	0.75	0.79	0.23	0.14	0.18	0.11	0.08	0.14	0.07	0.11
Query 8	0.74	0.72	0.72	0.70	0.15	0.20	0.14	0.15	0.11	0.08	0.14	0.15
Query 9	0.59	0.76	0.77	0.72	0.22	0.08	0.15	0.17	0.19	0.16	0.08	0.10
Query 10	0.75	0.69	0.66	0.73	0.11	0.17	0.19	0.13	0.14	0.14	0.16	0.13
Cluster	k1	k2	k3	k4	k1	k2	k3	k4	k1	k2	k3	k4

Figure 6. Clustering results for query 5

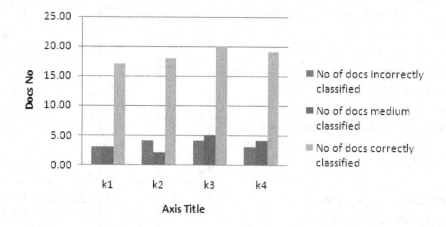

Figure 7. Indicators of documents classification: Empirical results

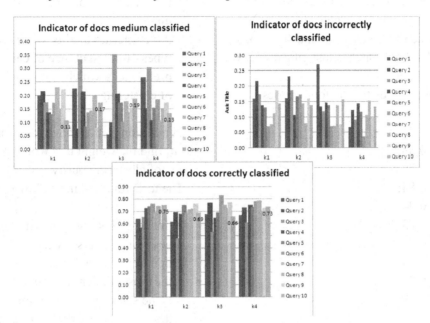

The graphical representation of the indicators is visible in Figure 7.

Based on the above indicators, another two quality indicators were defined. The following Equations were used and some empirical results are available in Figure 8.

Qstrict = ∑ DocsCorrectlyClassifiedInK/ k

Qtolerant = ∑ (DocsCorrectlyClassifiedInK + DocsMediumClassifiedInK)/ 2k

where

- k represents the number of clusters;
- DocsCorrectlyClassifiedInK represents the indicator of correctly classified documents in cluster K;
- DocsMediumClassifiedInK represents the indicator of medium classified documents in cluster K;

Figure 8. Quality indicators of clusters: Empirical results

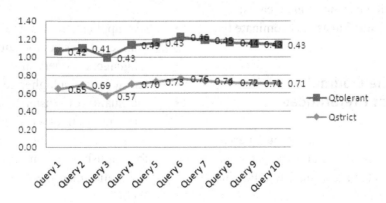

The bigger the Qstrict is, the better the clustering process was. Taking into consideration that Qstrict has values between 0.57 and 0.76, our empirical results show that the clustering process was a successful one.

The coverage degree for the four queries is:

- Query 1: 0.96;
- Query 2: 0.88;
- Query 3: 0.89;
- Query 4: 0.84;
- Query 5: 0.94;
- Query 6: 0.85;
- Query 7: 0.89;
- Query 8: 0.83;
- Query 9: 0.81;
- Query 10: 0.91;

The coverage degree represents the classified documents, because there are documents which can't be classified. Given the fact that, in our cases, the coverage degrre is above 0.8 (almost 1), one can say that the clustering process is a meaningful one.

Taking into account the above results and the charts from Figure 8, one can draw the following conclusions:

- The number of incorrectly classified instances is less than the number of correctly classified instances, in all cases;
- The number of partial/medium classified instances is less than the number of correctly classified instances, in all cases;
- Correctly classified instances dominate the clusters;

Determining the Optimal Combination of Preferences

Resuming testing on the same set of four queries, an expert test was performed on various combinations available in the program. The following parameters were tested:

- the ideal number of clusters to achieve quality;
- the clustering quality when using the three types of initial choice of centroids;
- preferences which have the lowest speed of clustering;

In addition to the above aims, another target was to find the weight that would provide a high degree of clustering purity.

The tests revealed the following:

- the best clustering in terms of the usefulness of clusters, will be obtained for a number of 4 clusters;
- the most efficient choice of initial centroids is the segmented algorithm;
- the two Equations for calculating the weights induce the same performance;
- the clustering average speed is 10 seconds, for 50 results;
- the components that have the greatest effect on clustering are the root extraction modules and replacement of stop words;

Comparison with Other Similar Applications

After comparing the performance of our solution to other three similar applications, available on the market (Carrot: see Table 5, Clusty: see Table 6 and WebClust: see Table 7), we came to these conclusions:

- our application has the highest average number of clusters for a query in Romanian language; for query in English, Carrot system will have a higher performance;
- the quality of cluster label is higher than the one from other implementations for the Romanian language and is comparable for English to the one from Carrot engine; it is better than the ones from Clusty and WebClust;

Table 5. Estimation of performances obtained by Carrot

Query No	Average no of useful clusters	Quality of cluster label	Indicator of correctly classified docs (avg)	Indicator of incorrectly classified docs (avg)	Coverage degree
1	4.3	0.86	0.66	0.22	0.98
2	6.1	0.92	0.87	0.1	0.87
3	2	0.56	0.33	0.2	0.78
4	3	0.6	0.45	0.5	0.77
5	3	0.6	0.51	0.45	0.81
6	2	0.55	0.53	0.4	0.83
7	4	0.7	0.55	0.53	0.87
8	5	0.6	0.57	0.34	0.78
9	6.1	0.61	0.62	0.3	0.79
10	4.3	0.63	0.64	0.23	0.78

Table 6. Estimation of performances obtained by Clusty

Query No	Average no of useful clusters	Quality of cluster label	Indicator of correctly classified docs (avg)	Indicator of incorrectly classified docs (avg)	Coverage degree
1	4.1	0.78	0.59	0.33	0.68
2	5.5	0.77	0.7	0.12	0.88
3	2.1	0.55	0.25	0.66	0.78
4	2.2	0.45	0.31	0.42	0.82
5	2.6	0.6	0.51	0.45	0.81
6	2.8	0.78	0.53	0.12	0.88
7	2.9	0.77	0.59	0.66	0.78
8	4.1	0.55	0.7	0.34	0.82
9	3.9	0.45	0.25	0.12	0.79
10	4.3	0.63	0.31	0.66	0.78

Table 7. Estimation of performances obtained by WebClust

Query No	Average no of useful clusters	Quality of cluster label	Indicator of correctly classified docs (avg)	Indicator of incorrectly classified docs (avg)	Coverage degree
1	3.3	0.67	0.45	0.43	0.83
2	1	0.8	0.79	0.12	0.75
3	1.9	0.5	0.22	0.52	0.78
4	2.4	0.55	0.23	0.43	0.6
5	3	0.67	0.79	0.45	0.81
6	2	0.8	0.22	0.4	0.83
7	1.9	0.5	0.23	0.43	0.75
8	2.4	0.55	0.45	0.12	0.78
9	1	0.61	0.79	0.52	0.6
10	1.9	0.63	0.64	0.41	0.78

- we will have a lower number of correctly classified documents than Carrot system for queries in English; in the same time, we will have a lower number of incorrectly classified documents for English;
- for queries in Romanian we will get the largest number of correctly classified documents and the lowest number of incorrectly classified documents;
- the coverage degree is lower than at Carrot system, being higher in one example out of four queries;

In conclusions, we can say that the proposed system has a very high performance of clustering documents in Romanian language and an acceptable performance of clustering English documents.

FUTURE DEVELOPMENT

Although using ontological approaches brings more refined clustering results, our application currently uses only the educational ontology. A module which permits the connection to any ontology would be a nice improvement: after the user inserts the features of the ontology, the application should be able to map the indexed words to the concept structure from that particular ontology. Another targeted improvement is to be able to use multiple ontological representations, in the same time: the value of the results would be considerably increased. In order to increase the usability of the solution, we should migrate the clustering process on the web and go for a distributed architecture: the ontology can stay on a machine, the clustering process on other machine and so on.

CONCLUSION

The chapter proposes a clustering solution for web search. The chapter presents the characteristics that a clustering module needs to meet in order to be efficient. Then, the classical k-means clustering algorithm is presented, and the changes to which it was undertaken in order to be adapted to a web page clustering process. The web page clustering process was then described in detail starting with the initial document processing steps, and moving to the clustering process itself. In the end, the representation requirements that the clustering module must meet in order to be efficient in a web search were highlighted.

REFERENCES

Baeza-Yates, R., & Ribeiro-Neto, B. (1999). *Modern information retrieval.* New York, NY: Addison Wesley; ACM Press.

Chi, N. L. (2003). *A tolerance rough set approach to clustering web search results.* Master thesis, Faculty of Mathematics, Informatics and Mechanics, Warsaw University.

Craven, M., DiPasquo, D., Freitag, D., McCallum, A., Mitchell, T., & Nigam, K. (2000). Learning to construct knowledge bases from the World Wide Web. *Artificial Intelligence, 118*(1-2), 69–113. doi:10.1016/S0004-3702(00)00004-7

Cunningham, S. J., Littin, J., & Witten, I. H. (2001). *Applications of machine learning in information retrieval.* Hamilton, New Zealand: University of Waikato.

Franstrom, F., & Lewis, J. (2000). *Fast, single-pass K-means algorithms.* Retrieved December 27, 2009, from http://citeseerx.ist.psu.edu/viewdoc/summary?doi=10.1.1.36.7008

Hendler, J. (1997). Intelligent agents: Where AI meets information technology. *IEEE Expert, 11*(6), 20–23. doi:10.1109/MEX.1996.546578

Hotho, A., Maedche, A., & Staab, S. (2001). *Ontology-based text clustering. Text Learning: Beyond Supervision.* Seattle, Washington: IJCAI.

Jing, L., Zhou, L., Ng, M., & Huang, J. Z. (2006). *Ontology-based distance measure for text mining.* Sixth SIAM International Conference on Data Mining (SDM), Bethesda, Maryland.

Kogilavani, A., & Balasubramanie, P (2009). Ontology enhanced clustering based summarization of medical documents. *International Journal of Recent Trends in Engineering, 1.*

Langley, P., & Simon, H. (1995). Applications of machine learning and rule induction. *Communications of the ACM, 38*(11), 55–64. doi:10.1145/219717.219768

Leuski, A., & Allan, J. (2000). Improving interactive retrieval by combining ranked list and clustering. *Proceedings of RIAO,* College de France, (pp. 665-681). Paris.

Lewis, D. (1991). Learning in intelligent information retrieval. *Proceedings of the International Workshop on Machine Learning,* (pp. 235–239). Evanston, Illinois.

Lula, P., & Paliwoda-Pekosz, G. (2008). An ontology-based cluster analysis framework. *Proceedings of the First International Workshop on Ontology-Supported Business Intelligence,* (pp.1-6), Karlsruhe, Germany.

Martin, J. (1995). Clustering full text documents. *Proceedings of the IJCAI Workshop on Data Engineering for Inductive Learning at IJCAI-95.* Montreal, Canada.

Salton, G. (1989). *Automatic text processing: the transformation, analysis and retrieval of information by computer.* Addison-Wesley Longman Publishing.

Wróblewski, M. (2003). *A hierarchical WWW pages clustering algorithm based on the vector space model.* Master thesis, Department of Computing Science, Poznań University of Technology.

ADDITIONAL READING

Ajayi, A., Aderounmu, G., & Soriyan, H. (2010). An adaptive fuzzy information retrieval model to improve response time perceived by e-commerce clients. *Expert Systems with Applications, 37*(1), 82–91. doi:10.1016/j.eswa.2009.05.071

Chen, C.-L., Tseng, F. S., & Liang, T. (2010). An integration of WordNet and fuzzy association rule mining for multi-label document clustering. *Data & Knowledge Engineering, 69*(11), 1208–1226. doi:10.1016/j.datak.2010.08.003

Domingo-Ferrer, J., Bras-Amorós, M., Wu, Q., & Manjón, J. (2009). User-private information retrieval based on a peer-to-peer community. *Data & Knowledge Engineering, 68*(11), 1237–1252. doi:10.1016/j.datak.2009.06.004

Heisig, P., Caldwell, N. H., Grebici, K., & Clarkson, P. J. (2010). Exploring knowledge and information needs in engineering from the past and for the future – Results from a survey. *Design Studies, 31*(5), 499–532. doi:10.1016/j.destud.2010.05.001

Jeng, J.-T., Chuang, C.-C., & Tao, C. (2010). Interval competitive agglomeration clustering algorithm. *Expert Systems with Applications, 37*(9), 6567–6578. doi:10.1016/j.eswa.2010.02.129

Park, J., Cho, W., & Rho, S. (2010). Evaluating ontology extraction tools using a comprehensive evaluation framework. *Data & Knowledge Engineering, 69*(10), 1043–1061. doi:10.1016/j.datak.2010.07.002

Qiu, D. (2010). A comparative study of the K-means algorithm and the normal mixture model for clustering: Bivariate homoscedastic case. *Journal of Statistical Planning and Inference, 140*(7), 1701–1711. doi:10.1016/j.jspi.2009.12.025

Segura, N. A., Sánchez, S., García-Barriocanal, E., & Prieto, M. (2011). An empirical analysis of ontology-based query expansion for learning resource searches using MERLOT and the gene ontology. *Knowledge-Based Systems, 24*(1), 119–133. doi:10.1016/j.knosys.2010.07.012

Tu, Y.-N., & Seng, J.-L. (2009). Research intelligence involving information retrieval – An example of conferences and journals. *Expert Systems with Applications, 36*(10), 12151–12166. doi:10.1016/j.eswa.2009.03.015

Wang, Y.-C., Tsai, R. T.-H., & Hsu, W.-L. (2009). Web-based pattern learning for named entity translation in Korean–Chinese cross-language information retrieval. *Expert Systems with Applications, 36*(2), 3990–3995. doi:10.1016/j.eswa.2008.02.067

Yang, S.-Y. (2010). Developing an ontology-supported information integration and recommendation system for scholars. *Expert Systems with Applications, 37*(10), 7065–7079. doi:10.1016/j.eswa.2010.03.011

KEY TERMS AND DEFINITIONS

Cluster Centroid: The concept or word which appears in all the documents from the same cluster.

Clustering Algorithms: Methods through which a set of entities are grouped into subsets, called clusters, so that observations in the same cluster are similar, according to some predefined criteria.

Documents Vectoring: The method by which numerical vectors are built for each document, according to the frequency of each word in a document; stop words (such as "and", "or", "in") and characters are not included.

Information Retrieval: The science of searching for documents, for information within documents, and for metadata about documents.

Machine Learning: An area of computer science which allows computers to evolve behaviors based on empirical data.

Meta-Search: The use of more search tools simultaneously for the same query.

Ontology: A formal representation of the knowledge by a set of concepts within a domain and the relationships between those concepts.

Chapter 20
A Beam Search Based Decision Tree Induction Algorithm

Márcio Porto Basgalupp
Federal University of Sao Paulo (UNIFESP), Brazil

Rodrigo Coelho Barros
University of Sao Paulo (ICMC-USP), Brazil

André C. P. L. F. de Carvalho
University of Sao Paulo (ICMC-USP), Brazil

Alex A. Freitas
University of Kent, UK

ABSTRACT

Decision tree induction algorithms are highly used in a variety of domains for knowledge discovery and pattern recognition. They have the advantage of producing a comprehensible classification model and satisfactory accuracy levels in several application domains. Most well-known decision tree induction algorithms perform a greedy top-down strategy for node partitioning that may lead to sub-optimal solutions that overfit the training data. Some alternatives for the greedy strategy are the use of ensemble of classifiers or, more recently, the employment of the evolutionary algorithms (EA) paradigm to evolve decision trees by performing a global search in the space of candidate trees. Both strategies have their own disadvantages, like the lack of comprehensible solutions (in the case of ensembles) or the high computation cost of EAs. Hence, the authors of this chapter present a new algorithm that seeks to avoid being trapped in local-optima by doing a beam search during the decision tree growth. In addition, their strategy keeps the comprehensibility of the traditional methods and is much less time-consuming than evolutionary algorithms.

DOI: 10.4018/978-1-4666-1833-6.ch020

INTRODUCTION

Decision tree induction has been widely applied to a broad range of areas, such as medical diagnosis and assessment of credit risk. The induction of optimal decision trees, however, has been proven to be NP-Hard (Tan *et* al., 2005). Consequently, heuristics methods are required for solving the problem.

There is a clear preference in the literature for algorithms that rely on a greedy, top-down, recursive partitioning strategy for the growth of the tree. These algorithms use variants of impurity measures like information gain (Quinlan, 1986), gain ratio (Quinlan, 1993), gini-index (Breiman *et* al., 1984), distance-based measures (Mántaras, 1991), etc.

The greedy partitioning strategy has the advantage of having inexpensive cost, producing decision trees quite rapidly, even for large data sets. Notwithstanding, it presents two major drawbacks: (i) produces locally (rather than globally) optimal solutions, (ii) iteratively degrades the quality of the data set for the purpose of statistical inference, because the larger the number of times the data is partitioned, the smaller the data sample that fits the current split becomes, making such results statistically insignificant and thus contributing to a model that overfits the data.

Two main threads in the literature addressed the mentioned problems. The first one focused on building ensemble methods (see, for instance, Quinlan (1996)). These methods aim at building different decision trees by sampling the training data and using a majority voting scheme to decide the classification. A downside of this approach, from the user's perspective, is that the simplicity of analyzing a single decision tree is lost. The second thread focused on using evolutionary algorithms to evolve decision trees in an attempt to find globally optimal solutions (see Barros *et* al. (2010) and Basgalupp *et* al. (2009) for successful examples). Nonetheless, evolutionary algorithms are time-consuming, mainly because the fitness component has to evaluate repeatedly the set of candidate solutions. Fitness evaluation is particularly costly when dealing with classifiers (more details in Espejo *et* al. (2010)).

In this work, we present a different approach for building decision trees. Instead of a greedy search, we use a beam search method in an attempt to avoid being trapped in local-optima. Beam search is a more efficient version of the well-known best-first search that reduces its memory requirements. Instead of keeping track of all possible states, beam search stores a predetermined number of states, namely the beam width (w), according to their heuristic values. Actually, beam search with $w = 1$ is equivalent to the greedy search, and $w = \infty$ is equivalent to breadth search.

Our new approach, namely Beam Classifier, uses a fixed beam width to reduce the chance of getting trapped into local optima. In addition, our strategy keeps the advantage of producing a single decision tree (easier to be interpreted than an ensemble of trees) and is much less time-consuming than evolutionary algorithms. Experimentation shows that our approach presents good results in several public data sets.

This work is organized as follows. We review classification and decision tree induction methods and then we detail our approach. Next, we present our experiments and we conclude this work with a summarized discussion of the results and future work.

CLASSIFICATION

Classification aims at building a concise class distribution model taking into account a set of predictive attributes. The outcome of such a model is used for assigning class labels to new examples whose only known information are the values of the predictive attributes (Ye, 2003).

The set of records whose class distribution is known is called the training set, and it can be described by a set of examples of the form (X, y), where X is the vector of predictive attributes $X = (x_1, x_2, x_3,...,x_n)$ and y is the class label to which this example belongs. Table 1 illustrates a data set that classifies whether a particular day is suitable for playing tennis from Quinlan (1986). In this table, each row represents a data set example and each column represents a predictive attribute that describes a particular aspect of the examples. The *PlayTennis* attribute holds the class label for each example, i.e., if the weather is suitable for playing tennis or not.

Figure 1 presents a diagram of how a classifier is induced and further applied to classify unseen data. First, the training set - in which the class label of each example is known a priori - is used by a learning algorithm to induce the classification model. Then, the classifier is used for predicting the class label of each example in the test set, a set in which the class labels are used to evaluate the classifier's predictive performance on new data. The accuracy or error rate computed from the test set can also be used to compare the relative performance of different classifiers on the same application domain.

This work is concerned to a simple yet widely used classifier: decision trees. We briefly present the basics of decision trees as well as the most popular methods used for decision tree induction in the next section.

DECISION TREE INDUCTION METHODS

A decision tree (DT) is a classifier depicted in a flowchart-like tree structure, with two kinds of nodes. Non-terminal nodes denote a test on an attribute, with each branch representing a possible outcome of the test. The terminal nodes hold a class label indicating the class to which the examples that fall within that node belong (Han, 2001) (Figure 2). DT induction is a powerful and widely-used technique for data mining classification tasks. This is due to several reasons, among them Tan *et al.* (2005): (i) produce a classification model that is easy to understand, due to the knowledge representation structure; (ii) robustness to the presence of noise; (iii) low computational cost,

Table 1. Data attributes

Day	Outlook	Temperature	Humidity	Wind	PlayTennis
D1	Sunny	Hot	High	Weak	No
D2	Sunny	Hot	High	Strong	No
D3	Overcast	Hot	High	Weak	Yes
D4	Rain	Mild	High	Weak	Yes
D5	Rain	Cool	Normal	Weak	Yes
D6	Rain	Cool	Normal	Strong	No
D7	Overcast	Cool	Normal	Strong	Yes
D8	Sunny	Mild	High	Weak	No
D9	Sunny	Cool	Normal	Weak	Yes
D10	Rain	Mild	Normal	Weak	Yes
D11	Sunny	Mild	Normal	Strong	Yes
D12	Overcast	Mild	High	Strong	Yes
D13	Overcast	Hot	Normal	Weak	Yes
D14	Rain	Mild	High	Strong	No

Figure 1. General approach for building a classification model (Adapted from Tan et al., 2005)

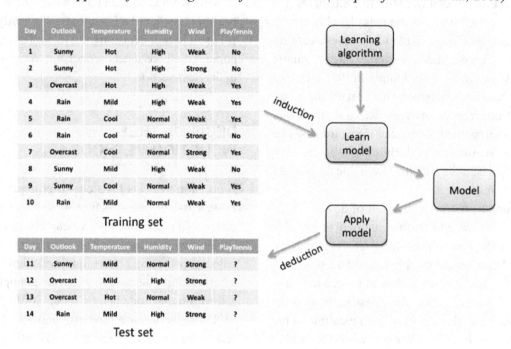

Figure 2. A decision tree for the mammal classification problem (Adapted from Tan et al., 2005)

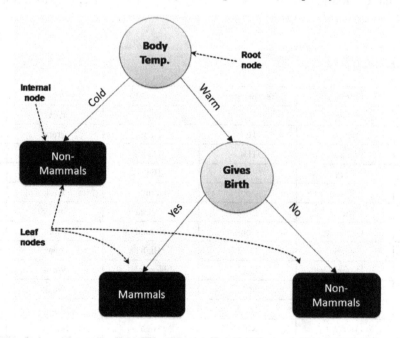

even for very large training data sets; and (iv) able to deal with redundant attributes.

Different algorithms for the induction of decision trees have been proposed in the literature. The most popular algorithms are ID3 (Quinlan, 1986) and C4.5 (Quinlan, 1993) proposed by Quinlan and CART (Classification and Regression Trees) proposed by Breiman and colleagues in Breiman *et* al. (1984). The approach used by these algorithms is usually greedy and based on a top-down recursive partitioning strategy for the tree construction. It should be observed that the use of a greedy algorithm usually lead to sub-optimal solutions. Moreover, recursive partitioning of the data set may result in very small data sets for the attribute selection in the deepest nodes of a tree, which may result in overfitting. Several alternatives have been proposed to overcome these problems, like using evolutionary algorithms (EAs) to evolve decision trees or building an ensemble of classifiers.

Evolutionary algorithms (EAs) are well explored in the context of decision trees induction. Works like Cantú-Paz & Kamath (2000) and Kretowski (2004) use EAs to induce Oblique Decision Trees. This type of tree, however, differs from traditional decision trees in the sense that each non-terminal node considers a linear combination of attributes, and not a single one, for partitioning the set of objects. As it is known, finding the best oblique decision tree is a NP-Complete problem (Tan *et* al., 2005), motivating the authors of Cantú-Paz & Kamath (2000) and Kretowski (2004) to propose EAs in order to select the best combination of attributes for each split, avoiding the greedy strategy.

One branch of EA, Genetic Programming (GP), has also been widely used as an induction method for decision trees, in works such as Koza (1991), Tür & Güvenir (1996), Zhao (2007), Zhao & Shirasaka (1999), Estrada-Gil *et* al. (2007), Bot & Langdon (2000), and Loveard & Ciesielski (2001, 2002). The work of Koza (Koza, 1991) was pioneering in inducing decision trees with

GP, converting the attributes of Quinlan's weather problem Quinlan (1986) into functions, described in LISP S-expressions. In Zhao (2007), it is proposed a tool which allows the user to set different parameters for generating the best computer program to induce a classification tree. The authors of Zhao (2007) take into account the cost-sensitivity of misclassification errors, in a multi-objective approach to define the optimal tree. In Estrada-Gil *et* al. (2007), it was implemented an algorithm of tree induction in the context of bioinformatics, in order to detect interactions in genetic variants. In Bot & Langdon (2000) is proposed a solution for linear classification tree induction through GP, where an intermediate node is a linear combination of attributes. In Loveard & Ciesielski (2001) the authors proposed different alternatives to represent a multi-class classification problem through GP, and later extended their work (Loveard & Ciesielski, 2002) for dealing with nominal attributes. In Zhao & Shirasaka (1999), the authors proposed the design of binary classification trees through GP, and in Tür & Güvenir (1996) it is described a GP algorithm for tree induction which considers only binary attributes.

Evolutionary algorithms, however, suffer from an important drawback - high computational cost due to time-consuming operations. In particular, fitness evaluation is quite costly when evolving classifiers, since it implies the application of the classifier encoded by each individual in the population to all the data examples in the training set Espejo *et* al. (2010). This indicates that the cost of the algorithm is strictly related to the training set size, and as a practical consequence, large-sized data sets may take several hours (or even days) to be processed.

The new algorithm we present in this work seeks to avoid being trapped in local-optima by doing a beam search during the decision tree growth. Additionally, this approach is much less time-consuming than evolutionary algorithms, since it does not need to continuously evolve and evaluate a population of decision trees. We detail our approach in the next section.

THE PROPOSED BEAM CLASSIFIER

In an attempt to decrease the problems intrinsic to the greedy search used in many algorithms for decision tree induction (C4.5, CART, etc.), and also to provide comprehensible models without requiring such a long training time as EAs, we propose a new decision tree induction algorithm called Beam Classifier.

According to Russel & Norvig (2003), a beam search algorithm keeps track of w states rather than just one. It begins with w randomly generated states (candidate solutions). At each step, all the successors of the w states are generated. If any successor is a goal state, the algorithm halts. Otherwise, it select the w best successors from the complete list, discards the other states in the list, and repeats this loop until the quality of the best current tree cannot be improved.

A well-known search strategy for generating decision trees is the greedy strategy, which is a particular case of beam search with $w = 1$. By using different values of w, we allow other candidate solutions to be explored in the search space, since w candidate solutions are explored instead of just one, at any given iteration.

Beam Classifier starts with n empty decision trees (root nodes), where n is the number of data set attributes, and each root node represents an attribute. Then, the algorithm selects the best w trees according to a given criterion (see later), and each one is expanded. For each expansion, the algorithm performs an adapted pre-order tree search method, expanding recursively (for each attribute) the leaf nodes from left to right. Thus, this expansion results in t new trees,

$$\sum_{i=1}^{w}\sum_{j=1}^{l_i} m_{ij}$$

where l_i is the number of leaf nodes of the ith tree and m_{ij} is the number of available attributes (nominal attributes are not used more than once in a given subtree) at the jth leaf node of the ith tree. Then, the algorithm selects once again the best w trees considering a pool of p trees, $p = w + t$. This process is repeated until a stop criterion is satisfied.

Algorithm 1. Beam classifier algorithm

```
Input: a data set data, a list of expanded trees e, a list of the best w trees bestW, a boolean
        value expansible
Output: a list of all intermediate trees h
    expansible = true
    e = createInicialTrees(data)
    h.add(e)
    bestW = theBestWTrees(e)
    expansible = isExpansible(bestW)
    while expansible do
        e = expand(bestW);
        bestW = theBestWTrees(e);
        h.add(e);
        expansible = isExpansible(bestW);
    end while
    h.add(bestW)
    return h
```

Even though the number of expansions grows proportionally to the number of leaves, which in turn is closely related to the number of categories of nominal attributes, the expansion process does not become exponential nor factorial, because the parameter w is fixed and limits the number of trees to be expanded. More specifically, after each round of expansion the algorithm will have many trees to analyze, but it will only expand w of these trees. Although Beam Classifier follows a relatively greedy strategy to explore the search space, it analyzes many alternatives in the search space, avoiding many cases of local optima. Beam Classifier works according to Algorithm 1.

Figure 3 depicts an example of Beam Classifier's execution considering the well-known *Play Tennis* data set and $w = 2$. The algorithm starts generating one tree for each data set attribute (4 initial trees) and selects the best two trees according to the validation accuracy, i.e., the performance of the tree when classifying examples from the validation set. The two selected trees are thus expanded by exploring all possibilities of attributes to fit each current leaf node. The next step is to select once again the best two trees among those generated in the expansion step. In the example, 15 trees were generated during expansion and 17 trees are considered in the selection of the two best trees (15 that were generated through expansion plus the previous best two trees). The expansion step only occurs when there is significant gain (see later) on partitioning the nodes. The algorithm ends its execution when the expansion of the best trees do not result in significant gain (determined by the isExapansible() method in Algorithm 1).

Beam Classifier uses two impurity-based measures for calculating the worthiness of expansions. The first measure is entropy Quinlan (1986) and the second is the Gini measure (Breiman *et al.*, 1984):

$$Entropy = -\sum_{j=1}^{n}\left(\frac{M\left(v_{j}\right)}{m} * \log_2 \frac{M\left(v_{j}\right)}{m}\right)$$

$$Gini = 1 - \sum_{j=1}^{n}\left(\frac{M\left(v_{j}\right)}{m}\right)^{2}$$

where m is the total number of examples at the parent node, n is the number of attribute values and $M(v_j)$ is the number of examples associated with the child node v_j. Entropy-based gain is called Information Gain and Gini-based gain is called Gini Index.

The choice of which impurity measure will be used is a user-defined parameter. The worthiness of a candidate tree expansion is calculated by associating these measures to the Gain calculation, given by

$$Gain = I\left(parent\right) - \sum_{j=1}^{n}\frac{M\left(v_{j}\right)}{m} I\left(v_{j}\right)$$

where $I(.)$ is the impurity measure of a given node. Entropy-based gain is called Information Gain and Gini-based gain is called Gini Index.

In the next section we present experiments in order to compare Beam Classifier with a traditional greedy approach, J48 (Witten & Frank, 1999) (Weka's implementation of the well-known C4.5 Quinlan (1993)) and also with an evolutionary approach called GALE (Llora & Garrell, 2001).

EXPERIMENTS

We have applied the proposed approach of inducing decision trees through a beam search based algorithm to 16 classification data sets available in the UCI machine learning repository (Newman *et* al., 1998) (Table 2). We have selected two base-

Figure 3. Beam search algorithm

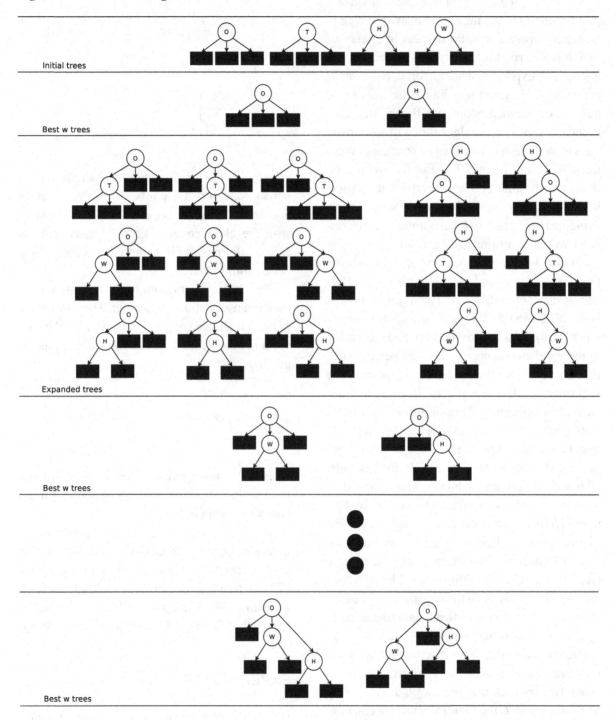

Table 2. Data sets specification

Data set	# examples	# Numeric Atributes	# Nominal Attributes	# Classes
anneal	898	6	32	6
audiology	226	0	69	24
autos	205	15	10	7
balance-scale	625	4	0	3
colic	368	7	15	2
credit-g	1000	7	13	2
diabetes	768	8	0	2
glass	214	9	0	7
heart-c	303	6	7	5
heart-statlog	270	13	0	2
hepatitis	155	6	13	2
iono-sphere	351	34	0	2
iris	150	4	0	3
labor	57	8	8	2
lymph	148	3	15	4
primary-tumor	339	0	17	22

lines algorithms for comparison purposes: J48 and GALE, an evolutionary algorithm used to evolve decision trees. We have chosen J48 because it is, to date, the most efficient and effective greedy approach for decision tree induction, whereas GALE is a popular publicly available evolutionary algorithm for decision tree induction.

The J48 and GALE parameter settings used are the default ones and we have used 10-fold cross-validation, a widely disseminated approach for validating prediction models. In each of the ten iterations of the cross-validation procedure, the training set is divided into sub-training and validation sets for the Beam Classifier algorithm. Sub-training set is used to tree partitioning and validation set to evaluate the trees and select the w best ones. Each set represents 50% of the full training set. This split is intended to avoid overfitting of a decision tree to the training data. We

have used a beam-search width $w = 4$, defined empirically in previous experiments.

We have calculated test set accuracy and tree size for each method, based on their performance in each fold, and report the average values of these measures over the 10 folds. We have also calculated the standard deviations of each measure. Finally, we have executed a corrected paired t-test (Nadeau & Bengio, 2003) with $\alpha = 0.05$ and 9 degrees of freedom (n - 1 degrees of freedom, where $n = 10$ folds) to assess the statistical significance of the presented results.

In Table 3, we present the test set accuracy for the three methods. We can see that J48 provides the best accuracy values in 10 out of 16 data sets, whereas GALE is better in 5 out of 16 data sets and Beam Classifier (from now on referred as BC) in 3 out of 16. Note that in some cases there are more than one method tied-up with the best accuracy values. Also, notice that even though GALE seems to be a better option than BC (5 vs 3), the direct comparison between them shows that BC is a better choice in 9 out of 16 data sets and GALE only in 4 (in the remaining 3 data sets they perform similarly).

In Table 4, we provide tree size of each method in terms of node counting. In this scenario, we can see that J48 never provides the smallest tree among the methods, and that GALE clearly produces the smallest tree in most cases (13 out of 16 data sets), whereas Beam Classifier produces the smallest tree in 3 data sets.

To assess if there is a statistic significance regarding the absolute values we have presented, we have applied the corrected paired t-test, that makes a paired comparison between methods. We present the results computed by this test in Table 5. By looking at this table, we can see that J48 performance regarding test set accuracy was not as significant as it seemed in absolute values. Actually, J48 significantly outperforms Beam Classifier in only 3 out of 16 data sets. For the remaining sets, J48 and BC did not differ statistically in terms of accuracy. On the other hand, BC

Table 3. Test set accuracy of GALE, J48 and Beam Classifier. In bold the best methods regarding accuracy are highlighted in terms of absolute values

Data set	GALE	J48	Beam Classifier
anneal	0.84 ±± 0.03	**0.98 ±0.01**	0.96 ±0.02
audiology	0.44 ±0.09	**0.78 ±0.08**	0.65 ±0.08
autos	0.51 ±0.07	**0.82 ±0.07**	0.64 ±0.10
balance-scale	**0.79 ±0.04**	0.77 ±0.04	0.74 ±0.06
colic	0.82 ±0.02	**0.85 ±0.05**	0.83 ±0.05
credit-g	**0.71 ±0.03**	**0.71 ±0.03**	0.70 ±0.04
diabetes	**0.74 ±0.02**	0.74 ±0.05	0.74 ±0.05
glass	0.59 ±0.09	0.67 ±0.08	**0.68 ±0.07**
heart-c	0.77 ±0.06	**0.78 ±0.08**	**0.78 ±0.08**
heart-statlog	**0.79 ±0.05**	0.77 ±0.09	0.73 ±0.07
hepatitis	0.80 ±0.05	**0.84 ±0.07**	0.77 ±0.09
ionosphere	0.89 ±0.03	**0.91 ±0.03**	0.90 ±0.05
iris	0.95 ±0.03	**0.96 ±0.05**	0.95 ±0.05
labor	0.68 ±0.19	0.74 ±0.21	**0.80 ±0.19**
lymph	**0.77 ±0.07**	0.77 ±0.10	0.77 ±0.11
primary-tumor	0.31 ±0.04	**0.40 ±0.05**	0.39 ±0.05

was capable of producing significantly smaller trees than J48 in 10 out of 16 data sets, whilst J48 only produced smaller trees in 2 data sets (for the remaining 4 data sets, the tree sizes produced by J48 and BC did not differ significantly).

Now comparing BC and GALE, we can see that BC was capable of inducing significantly more accurate trees in 5 data sets, while GALE did it only twice. Regarding tree size, GALE indeed provided smaller-sized trees, even though in most cases it was in detriment of accuracy. For instance, consider the first three data sets (anneal, audiology and autos). Even though GALE has induced significantly smaller trees than BC, we can see that the accuracy of BC was remarkably higher (96% vs 84%, 65% vs 44% and 64% vs 51%). The choice for smaller trees only pays off when the difference in accuracy between two methods is small. Even though there is no consensus in the literature on which would be the ideal difference threshold, we can assume as common sense that the differences in accuracy previ-

Table 4. Tree size of GALE, J48 and beam classifier. In bold the best method regarding tree size is highlighted in terms of absolute values.

Data set	GALE			J48			BeamClassifier		
anneal	5.42	±	1.93	50.10	±	**5.30**	66.40	±	12.29
audiology	**7.17**	±	**3.36**	48.90	±	3.65	37.80	±	4.13
autos	**12.73**	±	**4.70**	62.00	±	6.72	52.80	±	8.28
balance-scale	29.93	±	10.78	78.20	±	11.39	**15.80**	±	**3.55**
colic	**4.00**	±	**1.10**	8.10	±	2.02	36.60	±	5.15
credit-g	**22.09**	±	**13.11**	117.40	±	28.20	111.30	±	57.93
diabetes	**11.41**	±	**6.96**	37.40	±	12.39	13.00	±	3.53
glass	**4.05**	±	**5.26**	44.20	±	5.23	24.20	±	3.43
heart-c	**1.71**	±	**1.40**	43.30	±	11.33	27.90	±	5.45
heart-statlog	21.78	±	9.63	33.80	±	3.71	**13.60**	±	**4.53**
hepatitis	**6.71**	±	**3.03**	17.80	±	4.40	14.80	±	3.05
ionosphere	12.31	±	5.23	27.40	±	3.56	**12.00**	±	**4.14**
iris	**6.43**	±	**1.73**	8.40	±	0.92	6.60	±	0.84
labor	**2.91**	±	**1.30**	5.90	±	2.34	5.60	±	0.97
lymph	**12.95**	±	**6.17**	28.30	±	3.49	21.60	±	4.17
primary-tumor	**8.48**	±	**4.65**	83.70	±	6.65	55.60	±	5.04

Table 5. Statistical analysis of significance through the corrected paired t-test [15]. Symbols: ✓ means Beam Classifier (BC) outperforms the corresponding method with statistical significance; ✗ means BC is outperformed by the corresponding method with statistical significance; and – means that there is no statistical significantly difference.

Data set	BeamClassifer VS J48		BeamClassifier VS GALE	
	Accuracy	Tree Size	Accuracy	Tree Size
anneal	✗	✗	✓	✗
audiology	✗	✓	✓	✗
autos	✗	-	✓	✗
balance-scale	-	✓	✗	✓
colic	-	✗	-	✗
credit-g	-	-	-	✗
diabetes	-	✓	-	-
glass	-	✓	✓	✗
heart-c	-	✓	-	✗
heart-statlog	-	✓	✗	✓
hepatitis	-	-	-	✗
ionosphere	-	✓	-	-
iris	-	✓	-	-
labor	-	-	-	✗
lymph	-	✓	-	✗
primary-tumor	-	✓	✓	✗

ously mentioned (12%, 21% and 13%) are not acceptable, and thus it would not make sense to choose the smaller tree.

Finally, we can point out that BC is a better option than GALE specially considering execution time. We have compared the execution time of the three methods (we will not present these results due to space constraints). We can point out that J48 is clearly the faster algorithm, though BC is frequently only a few seconds slower. GALE, on the other hand, may take several minutes to

induce a decision tree, especially due to the fact it is a non-deterministic approach and thus demands several executions to provide a reliable result.

CONCLUSION AND FUTURE WORK

Decision trees are highly used in a variety of domains for knowledge discovery and pattern recognition. This is mainly because decision trees assemble the advantages of producing comprehensible outputs as well as satisfactory levels of accuracy in several real-world scenarios.

Most well-known decision tree induction algorithms (like C4.5 and CART) perform a greedy top-down strategy for node partitioning. It should be observed that the use of a greedy algorithm usually leads to sub-optimal solutions. Moreover, recursive partitioning of the data set may result in very small data sets for the attribute selection in the lowest nodes of a tree, which may result in overfitting. Some alternatives for the greedy strategy are the use of ensemble of classifiers or, more recently, the employment of the evolutionary algorithms paradigm (EAs) to evolve decision trees globally. Both strategies have advantages and disadvantages, like the lack of comprehensible solutions (in the case of ensembles) or the high computational cost of EAs.

In an attempt to decrease the problems intrinsic to the greedy search used in many algorithms for decision tree induction and also to provide comprehensible models that are not as costly as those evolved by EAs, we have proposed a new decision tree induction algorithm called Beam Classifier. It seeks to avoid being trapped in local-optima by doing a beam search during the decision tree growth. Additionally, it is much less time-consuming than evolutionary algorithms, since it does not need to continuously evolve and evaluate a population of trees.

We have tested our novel algorithm in 16 public UCI data sets. Experimentation shows that our approach provides a good trade-off between accuracy and simplicity, usually providing smaller trees (and thus less prone to overfitting) than J48 with similar accuracy levels, and also providing more accurate trees than GALE being, at the same time, much less time-consuming.

Our future research is twofold: (i) focusing on the use of different measures to select the *w* best trees during the expansion rounds of the classifier; (ii) conducting a detailed investigation on parameter optimization (finding optimal values of *w* and the impurity measure threshold for different data sets).

Regarding (i), we believe we can supply different measures for tree selection according to the domain at hand. For instance, in scenarios where interpretability is a decisive factor for determining a good decision tree, a multi-objective evaluation can be done taking into account tree complexity (e.g. number of nodes, number of leaves, number of attributes being tested, etc.). Similarly, for imbalanced problems in which the rare class is of great interest, cost-sensitive measures can be applied to select decision trees robust to imbalance problems. Multi-objective evaluation and cost-sensitive classification are common issues when dealing with decision tree induction. For more information on how to design multi-objective evaluation for decision trees please refer to the works of Basgalupp *et al.* (2009), Barros *et al.* (2010) and Barros *et al.* (2011). We also recommend reading the work of Zhao (2007) on how to incorporate cost-sensitive analysis to decision tree induction in an evolutionary framework.

In (ii), our goal is to perform a comprehensive study on the effects of parameter tuning in our proposed algorithm. More specifically, the beam width *w* can greatly influence the outcome of the algorithm, and it is not trivial to set its value in order to achieve an optimal response. Another important parameter is the threshold that defines whether the tree will be expanded in a particular node. By increasing this value, it may prevent the tree of being expanded, resulting in smaller trees that may underfit the data. Conversely, de-creasing this threshold may result in very large trees that overfit the training data. For parameter tuning, we suggest designing an evolutionary algorithm for performing a global search on the optimal parameter values for each data set at hand. The downside of this approach is regarding time constraints. Evolutionary algorithms are time-consuming and their application in certain scenarios may not be affordable.

ACKNOWLEDGMENT

This work was carried out during the tenure of an ERCIM "Alain Bensoussan" Fellowship Programme, and was partially funded by *Fundação de Amparo à Pesquisa do Estado de São Paulo* (FAPESP). We would also like to thank the authors of GALE, Mr. Xavier Llorà and Mr. Joseph M. Garrell, for kindly making available its source code, allowing for a fair comparison among the methods.

REFERENCES

Barros, R. C., Basgalupp, M. P., Ruiz, D. D., de Carvalho, A. C. P. L. F., & Freitas, A. A. (2010) Evolutionary model tree induction. In *SAC '10: Proceedings of the 2010 ACM Symposium on Applied Computing,* (pp. 1131–1137). New York, NY: ACM.

Barros, R. C., Ruiz, D. D., & Basgalupp, M. P. (2011). Evolutionary model trees for handling continuous classes in machine learning. *Information Sciences, 181*(5), 954–971. doi:10.1016/j. ins.2010.11.010

Basgalupp, M., de Carvalho, A., Barros, R., Ruiz, D., & Freitas, A. (2009). Lexicographic multi-objective evolutionary induction of decision trees. *International Journal of Bio-Inspired Computation, 1*(1/2), 105–117. doi:10.1504/IJBIC.2009.022779

Bot, M. C. J., & Langdon, W. B. (2000). Application of genetic programming to induction of linear classification trees. In Poli, R., Banzhaf, W., Langdon, W. B., Miller, J. F., Nordin, P., & Fogarty, T. C. (Eds.), *Genetic Programming, Proceedings of EuroGP'2000* (*Vol. 1802*, pp. 247–258). Edinburgh, UK: Springer- Verlag. doi:10.1007/978-3-540-46239-2_18

Breiman, L., Friedman, J. H., Olshen, R. A., & Stone, C. J. (1984). *Classification and regression trees*. Wadsworth.

Cantu-Paz, E., & Kamath, C. (2000). Using evolutionary algorithms to induce oblique decision trees. In D. Whitley, D. Goldberg, E. Cantu-Paz, L. Spector, I. Parmee, & H.G. Beyer (Eds.), *Proceedings of the Genetic and Evolutionary Computation Conference (GECCO-2000)*, (pp. 1053–1060)., Las Vegas, NV: Morgan Kaufmann.

De Mántaras, R. L. (1991). A distance-based attribute selection measure for decision tree induction. *Machine Learning*, *6*(1), 81–92. doi:10.1023/A:1022694001379

Espejo, P. G., Ventura, S., & Herrera, F. (2010). A survey on the application of genetic programming to classification. *Transactions on Systems, Man, and Cybernetics. Part C*, *40*(2), 121–144.

Estrada-Gil, J. K., Fernandez-Lopez, J. C., Hernandez-Lemus, E., & Silva-Zolezzi, I., Hidalgo- Miranda, A., Jimenez-Sanchez, G., & Vallejo-Clemente, E. E. (2007). GPDTI: A genetic programming decision tree induction method to find epistatic effects in common complex diseases. *Bioinformatics (Oxford, England)*, *23*(13), i167–i174. doi:10.1093/bioinformatics/btm205

Han, J. (2001). *Data mining: Concepts and techniques*. San Francisco, CA: Morgan Kaufmann Publishers Inc.

Koza, J. R. (1991). Concept formation and decision tree induction using the genetic programming paradigm. In *PPSN I: Proceedings of the 1st Workshop on Parallel Problem Solving from Nature*, (pp. 124–128). London, UK: Springer-Verlag.

Kretowski, M. (2004). An evolutionary algorithm for oblique decision tree induction. In *International Conference on Advances in Soft Computing*, (pp. 432–437).

Llora, X., & Garrell, J. M. (2001) Evolution of decision trees. In *Proceedings of the 4th Catalan Conference on Artificial Intelligence*, (pp. 115–122). ACIA Press.

Loveard, T., & Ciesielski, V. (2001). Representing classification problems in genetic programming. *Evolutionary Computation*, 2.

Loveard, T., & Ciesielski, V. (2002) Employing nominal attributes in classification using genetic pro- gramming. In L. Wang, K.C. Tan, T. Furuhashi, J.H. Kim, & X. Yao (Eds.), *Proceedings of the 4th Asia-Pacific Conference on Simulated Evolution And Learning (SEAL'02)*, (pp. 487–491). IEEE, Orchid Country Club, Singapore.

Nadeau, C., & Bengio, Y. (2003). Inference for the generalization error. *Machine Learning*, *52*(3), 239–281. doi:10.1023/A:1024068626366

Newman, D., Hettich, S., Blake, C., & Merz, C. (1998). *UCI repository of machine learning databases*. Retrieved from http://www.ics.uci.edu/~mlearn/mlrepository.html

Quinlan, J. R. (1986). Induction of decision trees. *Machine Learning*, *1*, 81–106. doi:10.1007/BF00116251

Quinlan, J. R. (1993). *C4.5: Programs for machine learning*. San Francisco, CA: Morgan Kaufmann Publishers Inc.

Quinlan, J. R. (1996). Bagging, boosting, and c4.5. In *Proceedings of the Thirteenth National Conference on Artificial Intelligence*, (pp. 725–730). AAAI Press.

Russell, S. J., & Norvig, P. (2003). *Artificial intelligence: A modern approach* (2nd ed.). Prentice Hall.

Tan, P. N., Steinbach, M., & Kumar, V. (2005). *Introduction to data mining* (1st ed.). Boston, MA: Addison-Wesley Longman Publishing Co., Inc.

Tür, G., & Güvenir, H. A. (1996). Decision tree induction using genetic. In *Proceedings of the Fifth Turkish Symposium on Artificial Intelligence and Neural Networks*, (pp. 187–196).

Witten, I. H., & Frank, E. (1999). *Data mining: Practical machine learning tools and techniques with Java implementations*. Morgan Kaufmann.

Ye, N. (2003). *The handbook of data mining*. Lawrence Erlbaum Human Factors and Ergonomics Series.

Zhao, H. (2007). A multi-objective genetic programming approach to developing pareto optimal de-cision trees. *Decision Support Systems, 43*(3), 809–826. doi:10.1016/j.dss.2006.12.011

Zhao, Q., & Shirasaka, M. (1999) A study on evolutionary design of binary decision trees. In P. J. Angeline, Z. Michalewicz, M. Schoenauer, X. Yao, & A. Zalzala (Eds.), *Proceedings of the Congress on Evolutionary Computation*, Vol. 3, (pp. 1988–1993). Washington, DC: IEEE Press.

KEY TERM AND DEFINITION

Validation Set: A subset of the training set that is not used for training the trees.

Chapter 21
Learning with Querying and its Application in Network Security

Liang-Bin Lai
National Taiwan University, Taiwan, ROC

Shu-Yu Lin
National Taiwan University, Taiwan, ROC

Ray-I Chang
National Taiwan University, Taiwan, ROC

Jen-Shiang Kouh
National Taiwan University, Taiwan, ROC

ABSTRACT

Understanding the ability of learning in both humans and non-humans is an important research crossing the boundaries between several scientific disciplines from computer science to brain science and psychology. In this chapter, the authors first introduce a query based learning concept (learning with query) in which all the minds' beliefs and actions will be revised by observing the outcomes of past mutual interactions (selective-attention and self-regulation) over time. That is, moving into an active learning and aggressive querying method will be able to focus on effectiveness to achieve learning goals and desired outcomes. Secondly, they show that the proposed method has better effectiveness for several learning algorithms, such as decision tree, particle swarm optimization, and self-organizing maps. Finally, a query based learning method is proposed to solve network security problems as a sample filter at intrusion detection. Experimental results show that the proposed method can not only increase the accuracy detection rate for suspicious activity and recognize rare attack types but also significantly improve the efficiency of intrusion detection. Therefore, it is good to design and to implement an effective learning algorithm for information security.

DOI: 10.4018/978-1-4666-1833-6.ch021

INTRODUCTION

Understanding the ability of learning in both humans and non-humans is an important research crossing the boundaries among several scientific disciplines from computer science to brain science and psychology. That capability from experience is one fundamental skill for the survival and evolution of life beings. Neuroscientists believed that human brain memorizes not just the perceived sensorial information of objects or events but also the interaction behavior occurred among the entity and the external environment (Damasio, 2000). In the past decades, cognitive psychologists have proposed a great variety of methods to account for the different aspects of human behavior. These models represent the theoretical idea about the process or the representation underlying the observed behavior. Rumelhart and Norman (1978) suggested that the procedure accounts for the minor schema modifications that come with new exemplars of concepts and principals. Learning in humans characterized in three different types of procedures: accretion, tuning, and restructuring.

- *Accretion* is a procedure that processes the importing knowledge into an already existing concept or schema.
- *Tuning* consists of revising the old schemata to acquire the new knowledge. It adjusts existing schemas incrementally to reflect variable circumstances.
- *Restructuring* involves changing an existing schema to map onto a novel and unfamiliar event. It requires exploration, comparison, and integration of concepts.

The learning machine consists of a learning protocol to specify the method of achieving accumulation of information, and a deduction procedure to learn the correct concept (Valiant, 1984). For learning protocol, the input information can be examples that exemplify the concept to be learned, or *oracles* that tell whether the

data exemplify the concept when presented with data. In an interactive environment, we assume that the learner starts with an initial set of positive and negative examples, and then he/she asks an oracle for membership classification of new examples which are selected according to some interactive guided learning strategies. In Figure 1, the procedures for querying oracle clearly differentiate from the different scenarios. In a common scenario, such an oracle can answer and correct the concept each time the learner makes an error what we shall call correction queries.

Machine learning is typically defined as a problem of function approximation from a fixed set of training examples. Most of the machines learning algorithms are based on the principles of similarity and contrast. Unsupervised learning methods are algorithms to search for similarities among objects. Supervised learning methods, especially classification algorithms, try to maximize the contrast between the classes. Current machine learning techniques do not totally use these types of learning. Most learning algorithms do not endorse the accretion mode of learning either. The worst portion of current machine learning techniques is the lack of restructuring capability. The real accretion in human learning is a long lasting process of accumulation of knowledge. Although there were some conceptual learning systems proposed over the past many years, they did not break through because of their poor performance. Connectionist models that simulate brain activity at a neuron level have provided important insights into pattern learning. However, they mostly focus on the tuning mode of learning.

Active learning (also called "query learning" or "optimal experimental design") is a subfield of machine learning in which the learning program has some control over the inputs it trained. The learner can control to ask an oracle, typically a human with extensive knowledge of the domain at hand, about the classes of the instances for which the model learned so far makes unreliable predic-

Figure 1. Diagram illustrating the different scenarios

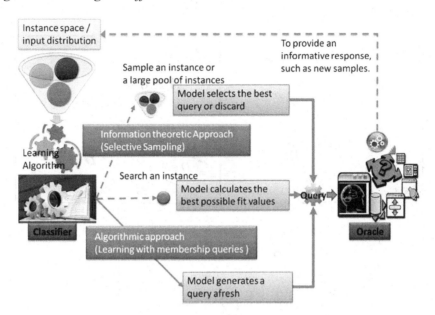

tions. Query-based learning (QBL) is famous as an active learning technique (Cohn, 1996). It starts by roughly training a system using the relatively small training data set. An inversion algorithm is exploited to offer input patterns depending on the decision boundary. Then querying the oracle is to give the correct output for each input pattern. The new set of true output pairs (the query data) used as the training data for the learning algorithms. Baum (1991) had shown that the QBL paradigm corresponded more closely to the way humans learned. This method does not only look at the original training examples, but also exploit queries to provide supplemental training samples and is then told which output the input vector is assigned. The presented supernumerary query capability is practical in many classification problems where the algorithm cans create additional inputs and an external supervisor instructed by to what classification outputs they correspond. Thus, the classification system refined further the queried samples in the *restructuring mode* of learning.

A simple example with two different input samples is shown in Figure 2 to illustrate the operations of QBL. As shown in Figure 2(a), the

presented input samples and are linear-separable as the bold dash-line, but the real classification boundary is not (see the dot-line). Thus, although training time is unlimited and training error for these input samples is down to zero, the classification error for test data is still very large. As shown in Figure 2(c), the linear-separated classification boundary is refined as an S-type boundary when the boundary point and the two additional queried samples and shown in Figure 2(b) are presented. Comparing the original classifier with a linear-separated boundary, the obtained classification accuracy is further increased.

BACKGROUND

A large number of computational techniques have been proposed for data analysis and pattern recognition. Statistical and intelligence techniques largely applied to these areas. The developing algorithms for complex problem solving have been inspired by these natural phenomena. Parts of the achievements to design new computational algorithms to solve intricate problems are based

Figure 2. A simple example with two different input samples is presented to demonstrate the operation flow of this QBL method

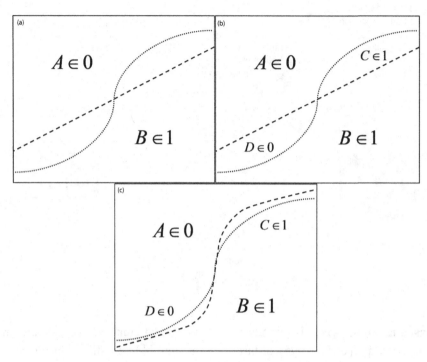

on the comprehension of mechanisms, behaviors and dynamics of natural (biological, agricultural, machinery and physical) systems. Therefore, to learn more efficient ways of moving if we can energetically select particularly prominent examples.

Learning from examples is not, however, a universal model. Many learning systems are not simply passive, but instead provide some kind of forms of active learning to examine the problem domain. We need to distinguish among "original" machine learning and query learning, the former often called passive learning or learning by random sampling from the available set of labeled training data. In contrast to passive learning, active learning is based on example-driven means to incorporate the teacher into the learning process; the instances that the learner asks (queries) the teacher to classify all unlabeled data. In the following, we describe the concept-learning problem in detail and give a formal definition of query learning.

Let X refer to the set of all possible instances over which target functions may be defined.

Moreover, we define a concept c to be some subset of points in the domain. Each concept c corresponds to some subset of X, or equivalently to some binary function $c: X \rightarrow \{0, 1\}$. We assume to generate some instances at random from X according to the probability distribution D. In general, D may be any distribution, and it will generally be unknown to the learner. All that is required is that D must be stationary; the distribution must not change over time. Training examples are generated by drawing an instance x at random according to D, then presenting x along with its target value, $c(x)$, to the learner. For target concept t, a training example is a pair $(x, t(x))$ consisting of a point x (usually drawn from some distribution D, and the point's classification $t(x)$). If x is a positive example of c, then we will write $t(x) = 1$; Otherwise, if x is a negative example, $t(x) = 0$. A concept c is consistent with an example $(x, t(x))$ if $c(x) = t(x)$, that is, if the concept produces the same classification of point x as the target. The error of c, with respect to t and distribution D, is the probability that c and t will be inconsistent with a random example drawn from D. We write this as

$$Error(c, t, D) = \text{Probability } [c(x) \neq t(x)],$$

Given a random example x drawn according to a probability distribution D. Angluin (1988) proposed the learning model of exact identification using queries. The learning algorithm allows the learner to ask questions about a language from an oracle and halts in polynomial time with a correct description of the language. To formalize the communication protocol between the learner and the oracle, one has to specify the allowed types of queries. Let c be a target concept. In the following $c \oplus c^*$ denote the symmetric difference between c and c^* that is $c \oplus c^* = (c \cup c^*) - (c \cap c^*)$.

- *Membership Queries*. In a membership query, the oracle is required to classify an instance provided by the learner. The input is an instance $x \in X$ and the output is *yes* if $x \in c^*$ and *no* if $x \notin c^*$.
- *Equivalence Queries*. In an equivalence query, the oracle is required to check the validity of a hypothesis provided by the learner. The input is a concept c and the output is *yes* if $c = c^*$ and *no* otherwise. If the answer is *no*, a counterexample is returned.
- *Subset Queries*. In a subset query, the oracle is required to check whether a hypothesis is included in the target concept c. The input is a concept c and the output is *yes* if $c^* \subseteq c$ and *no* otherwise. If the answer is no, an element $x \in c - c^*$ is returned.
- *Superset Queries*. In a superset query, the oracle is required to check whether a hypothesis is included in the target concept c. The input is a concept c and the output is *yes* if $c^* \supseteq c$ and *no* otherwise. If the answer is no, an element $x \in c^* - c$ is returned.

- *Stochastic Equivalence*. In a stochastic equivalence, the oracle is required to return an example classified by the target concept c. If c is compatible with all the samples drawn, then the identification method proceeds as though the equivalence query had returned the answer *yes*. Otherwise, there is an example which is misclassified by c, and the identification method proceeds as though the equivalence query had returned the answer *no*.

Recent research on query learning has led to a variety of approaches for the active selection of queries. For example, in (Atlas, Cohn, & Ladner, 1990; Cohn, 1994; Chang & Hsiao, 1997) several approaches to learning by queries described that both use a neural network model of the learner's uncertainty. A correctly trained neural network is not only capable of emulating the process responsible for generating the training data, but the inverse process as well. The inversion of neural networks procedures are looking for one or more input values that obtain a desired output response for an adjusted set of synaptic weights. There are several intentions, which one may expect to achieve using query learning. One is the optimization; the learner performs experiments to find a set of inputs that maximize some response variable. In learning settings where there is a fixed budget on gathering data, it is advantageous to approximate the objective function for data selection, because it guarantees near-optimal results with significantly less computational effort. The effectiveness of query learning is clarity: both aim to maximize some objective functions while minimizing data acquisition costs (and remaining within a budget).

Regions of Ambiguity

A QBL differs from selective sampling in that it generates new training data in the region of decision boundary. A decision boundary is a partition in N-dimensional space that divides the underlying vector space into two or more response regions. The objective of QBL is not necessarily to look for the target relation, but just to obtain the best output prediction for an individual input. Cohn (1994) proposed a concept of "region of uncertainty" which is the area in a problem domain where the learner's misclassiõcation is more likely to occur, and can be described as:

$$R(S^m) = \{x: \exists\, c_1, c_2 \in C, c_1(x) \neq c_2(x)\}$$

where S^m is a set of m examples and classifier c_1, c_2 are consistent with all $x \in S^m$.

The region of uncertainty is the set of all points x in the domain such that there are two concepts that are consistent with all training examples in S^m. For an arbitrary distribution D, we can define the size of this region as

$$\alpha = \text{Probability}[x \in R(S^m)]$$

Let us consider an active learning process and determine how much information each sequential example gives us. If we draw examples directly by randomly querying points according to D that lie strictly inside $R(S^m)$, then the probability that an individual sample will reduce our size is α, as defined above, which decreases to zero as we draw more and more examples. Frequently, however, the sample distribution D is unknown or is large-scale but only less information. In this case, we can take advantage of the QBL, the problem of using queries to learn an unknown concept considered. Considering multilayer propagation (MLP) with the backpropagation (BP) algorithm proposed by Rumelhart, Hinton, & Williams (1986), in which the neuron's output is binary trained to be either zero or one. Presenting a set of training samples with prespecified labels, the classification boundary of the neural system is defined as the set of points, which produces an output of using the points on the classification boundary, called boundary points; a set of conjugate input pairs

with significant boundary information can easily be generated to refine the classification result.

Assume we are able to calculate a subset $R^*(S^m) \subseteq R(S^m)$. Since any point in $R^*(S^m)$ will also be in the superset, we can selectively sample inside $R(S^m)$ and be assured that we will exclude any part of the regions of boundary. The efficiency of this approach can be measured as the ratio

$$Probability[x \in R^*(S^m)]/Probability[x \in R(S^m)]$$
where $R^*(S^m)$ is the regions of ambiguity.

In Baum (1991), the boundary point that has the maximum ambiguity was simply produced by the interpolation process between positive and negative examples. Besides, the inversion method, which allows a user to find one or more input vectors, yields a specific output vector and generates these boundary points (Hwang et. al., 1991). Since the inversion algorithm is a time-consuming iterative procedure, Eberhart (1992) presented a genetic algorithm to search for the decision surface as a means for achieving neural network inversion.

Query Based Learning with Selective-Attention and Self-Regulation

There are many theories that have been presented by various psychologists and social scientists about the regulation of internal states and perceptual experiences. This approach has been tried to model human behavior for the preprocessing of input stimulus from the external world by Newell and Simon (1961). The information processing theory within cognitive psychology provides a useful framework for how humans can be cognitive to transform sense data from their internal mental and external environment into information that enables adaptive processes to occur (Newell, 1990). Nadler (1977) pointed out the learning function of feedback not only the choice of whether or not to feed back relevant information, but also the extent to which information and feedback to be sought. Berelson and Steiner (1973) concluded that people tend to see and hear communications/media content that are favorable or congenial to their wants or desires. For example, hungry persons can report more food patterns in recognizing vague pictures than less hungry persons. Carver and Scheier (1981) reported that the human nervous system is not only learned from environment-focus (external-input samples), but also self-focus (queries of internal desires). Carver and Scheier (1998) further suggested that self-focus plays a self-regulatory role that helps people in the pursuit of goals. Self-focus directs attention toward discrepancy between desired and actual goals. For example, in this self-regulatory process, people compare their current standing with self-standards and determine whether they are meeting this standard. If the current self matches the desired standard, the person terminates the regulatory process.

Perceptual Control Theory (PCT) is a close loop of behavior as a control system making continual adjustments based upon feedback from the environment developed by William T. Powers, 1973. As well, PCT also is a unified integrative interdisciplinary theory of self-regulation within psychology. It is a dynamic working model based on the principle that goal directed activity arises from a hierarchy of negative feedback loops that control perception through control of the environment. The concepts of feedback and systems analysis are compatible with a control system model of human behavior. PCT referred to a hierarchical structure of neurological control system, in which each control system specifies the behavior of lower level systems and thus controls its own perceptions, goal seeking and feedback at different levels of organization. The perceptions are constructed and controlled at the lower levels to be passed along as the perceptual inputs at the higher levels. That is to say, inputs from lower-level perceptions combined to form higher-level, then outputs from higher levels sent to levels as

reference levels (goals). This theory suggests that our brain can realize our want and desire, so the nervous system will try to control external stimulus with selective-attention and direct to our internal desires under some self-regulation behaviors. In which, selectively attending to information originating from within and concerning the internal self is referred to as self-focus. Selectively attending to information that originates from the external environment is termed as environment-focus. To sum this theory, human behavior is less static and stable than the behavior of lower animals. Thus, it is not only under the control of physiological factors, but also under the control of some psychological factors.

Nosofsky's (1986) generalized context model (GCM) of perceptual categorization was derived from Medin and Schaffer's (1978) context model. GCM assumes that the new instances are classified depending on its similarity to stored category exemplars. Classification decisions are based on the similarities of objects to these memorized exemplars. For example, consider quantitative prediction for phenomena such as distance from boundary effects. Such that stimuli close to the decision boundary tended to be judged more ambiguously than were stimuli far from the boundary. The selective attention is described in terms of realizing and clarifying of distances in psychological space, which were located in the most ambiguous region of the stimulus space relative to the prior training exemplars. In particular, the field of category learning has had some significant successes using neural network learning mechanisms to classify stimuli. One of the best-known neural network exemplar models is the Kruschke's (1992) ALCOVE model. This model can be functionally approximated by a neural network that uses back-propagation to learn which attributes of a stimulus to attend to make a proper classification. ALCOVE can learn to shift attention to stimulus dimensions that are most relevant to the category and away from irrelevant dimensions. It assumes that category decisions are made by computing the similarity of the stimulus to memory representations of all previously seen exemplars. The classification tasks are those that provide trial-by-trial feedback just like the algorithms used for supervised learning. Next, Gluck et al. (2001) developed a connectionist-level model based on the Rescorla-Wagner model, a most successful trial-level behavioral formulation of classical conditioning. The Rescorla-Wagner model is a special case of the delta rule, also called the Least Mean Square (LMS) method (Widrow & Hoff, 1960), which is closely related to the error back-propagation training procedure found in many recent connectionist network models (Rumelhart et al., 1986). They argued that the model was able to produce behavior similar to that predicted by GCM, but without computing distances between stimuli in similarity with distance in the psychological space.

According to PCT, the behaviour of organisms is affected by how we perceive the effects of our actions in relation to our intents. Thus, when we learn, we continually try to evaluate how our brain perceives what we learn and adjust our future behaviour to address this feedback. With the behavior control theory, the proposed QBL framework can be applied to generate the query samples from the external-input samples (environment-focus) and the internal-desired samples (self-focus) as shown in Figure 3. Considering a learning system with the QBL, we can ask the oracle to respond to its internal-desired samples under some self-regulation or external-input samples with goal-directed selective-attention. In supervised learning, the query oracle is defined as a prespecified supervisor. The correctness of the queried samples can be checked and guaranteed by an external supervisor. However, the prespecified external supervisor is not existent in unsupervised learning. Note that the unsupervised learning method has the advantage that it can automatically classify input vectors without specifying their output labels. Based on a PCT property of selective-attention and self-regulation

is presented to design an unsupervised learning. We try to combine the effect from the external stimulus and the internal desires, and have shown that both the external stimulus and the internal desires are important and decisive for system learning. By considering the internal-desired sample, what is selected for attention may change from moment to moment and only depends on the system's current setting. The produced query sample has a queried output label for selective-attention.

In supervised learning, one of the most informative features of the classification model is the decision boundary. Reed et al. (1995) showed that information from the evenly distributed points on the decision boundary be able to generate the best training results. In other words, it would search among the input pieces of information for the points whose output value is 0.5 (the neuron output is between 0 and 1). Given $a(y) = 0.5$, we need to decide the point y. According to Hwang et al. (1991), we first employ the inversion algorithm to gain the points that could erase errors. Like the backpropagation algorithm, the inversion algorithm propagates the error signal backward to the input layer to update the activation value of the input units and eventually to lower the rate at which an error happens to the output value. In conjugate gradient approach, one picks the first descent direction and moves along that direction until the local minimum in error is reached. The second direction is then computed: This conjugate direction is the one along which the gradient does not change its direction, but merely its magnitude during the next descent. Descending along this direction does not spoil the contribution made from previous iterations. As shown in Figure 4, the conjugate training data pair is extracted along the reverse boundary. This is accomplished by inverting the MLP output function to compute decision boundaries. The inverted boundary point P (where the MLP output $a(p) = 0.5$) calculate the mutual of the magnitude of the gradient. New data in the neighborhood of boundaries are generated. Then along the magnitude of the gradient,

Figure 3. The query based learning framework

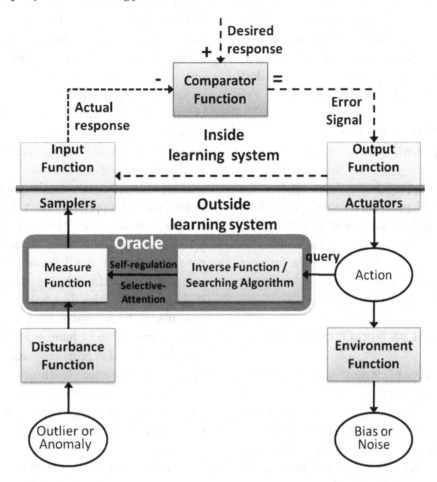

we would pick up two information points (P^+ and P^-) in symmetry and add to the training set.

However, without experts or simulators, or the oracle for specifying the correct output, this may be unrealistic or extremely expensive. To overcome the challenge, we have proposed a simplified approach to resolve this problem (Lai et al, 2006). First, we divide the training samples into one training set and one query set. In particular, these approaches have assumed that, for each point, the MLP output known and the input-output pattern existed. Secondly, an oracle is designed to follow the self-regulation rule to select samples (environment-focus) that are close to the conjugate data pair (self-focus). Thirdly, the oracle is required to examine non-trained samples in the query set

to detect whether they are put in the right class. As the output also indicates the probability of making a correct prediction to the samples, these correct samples were stored in a priority queue (max-heap). Finally, the stored points that are the

Figure 4. Conjugate data pairs

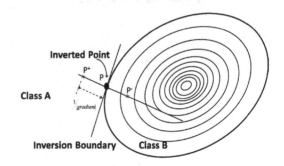

most correct predictions are picked as the extra training samples. It provides the learning algorithm with the ability to interact with the environment to train by queried samples. Thus, learning performance is improved by labeling only those data that are expected to be informative.

Learning with Querying and its Applications

The proposed approach has been applied for many real-world problem domains in machine learning, such as disease diagnosis (Chang, 2005), census income (Lai et al, 2006), and time-series predicative (Lai et al, 2007). QBL is the focus of this chapter and the details of issues and solutions will present in the following.

Query-Based Learning Decision Tree

Decision tree is one of the most significant classifiers. A classifier assigns one class to each point of the input space. The input space is thus partitioned into disjoint subsets, called decision regions, each associated with a class. The way a classifier classifies inputs is defined by its decision regions. In practice, input vectors of different classes are rarely so neatly distinguishable. Samples in different classes may have same input vectors. Due to such an uncertainty, areas of input space can be

clouded by a mixture of samples of different classes as shown in Figure 5(a). The optimal classifier is the one expected to produce the least number of misclassifications. Such misclassifications are due to uncertainty in the problem rather than a deficiency in the decision regions. A designed classifier is said to generalize well if the classifier achieves similar classification accuracy to both training samples and real world samples.

The decision tree's aim was to minimize the number of expected misclassifications by placing boundaries appropriately in the input space. However, an important disadvantage of straightforward implementation of the technique is its time consumption. It will spend a high computation cost when performing the large-scale data set in the real world. This drawback causes the decision tree to be ineligible in operating the time critical applications. Chang et al. (2006) applied the QBL concept to propose an efficient method, named query-based learning decision tree (QBLDT), to construct a decision tree classifier and can still benefit significantly from a training set constructed by an active learner using selective sampling.

According to QBL, this method needs to choose some significant extra learning data to strengthen the decision ability. Notably, after doing the classification, test data will obtain one of these three kinds of results:

Figure 5. Different learning points are pointed out

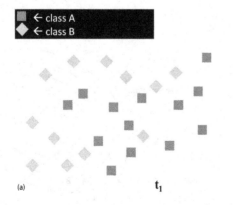
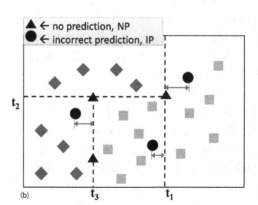

- Accuracy - assigned class is correct (Correct Prediction, CP)
- Uncertainty - cannot be assigned to any class (No Prediction, NP)
- Inaccuracy - assigned class is misclassification. (Incorrect Prediction, IP)

As shown in Figure 5(b), comparing with no prediction points (triangles), the incorrect prediction points (circles) may have a longer distance. Based on the QBL concept, QBLDT can add NP points (as extra learning data) as well as remove CP points from our consideration. Learning from composite points can let the boundary make fine-tuning and be able to get a better boundary. The initial decision tree may not have a good classification result. However, with more queried data added in, curve grows up and shows a better classification result in some cases.

Improving PSO Algorithm by Query-Based Learning

Recently, the particle swarm optimization (PSO) is well researched as one of the most important fields in evolution computing. PSO algorithm is not only a tool for optimization, but also a tool for representing socio-cognition of human and artificial agents, based on principles of social psychology. In PSO, every one of the feasible solutions is assigned a randomized velocity, and the potential solutions, called particles, fly through the problem space by following the current best particles. All the particles use the information related to the most successful particle to improve them. Thereby, information sharing plays a central role to coordinate learning experiences. That means the particles should actively select the evolution direction to enforce them learning smartly.

PSO also has the same drawbacks as other optimization algorithms despite its predominance in some fields. Particles may fall into local optima and this cause a premature convergence. Therefore, the algorithm fails on searching for the global optimal solution. Thus, Chang and Lin (2006) explore the query learning to redirect some particles into ambiguous solution space based on the oracle. The approach not only increases the searching diversity and accuracy but also prevents the premature convergence to improve the performance. The proposed framework of query-based learning PSO is illustrated in Figure 6.

Chang and Lin (2006) presented a novel and efficient approach, named particle swarm optimization with crowd redistribution (PSOCR), to exploit QBL concept based on redistributing particles into ambiguous solution space. PSOCR intelligently divided the solution space into some sub-spaces, and this helps PSOCR knowing well for the confused solution space. Then, the particles spread into those areas and enhance the searching diversity and accuracy. The CR mechanism also helps PSO jump out of redundant searching limited in a small area. The CR mechanism flowchart is shown in Figure 7. To apply this mechanism into PSOCR and model the oracle based on the frequency of sub-space being searched and the average of fitness value by every sub-space. To put it more concretely, average fitness value was calculated as the experience of the solution space to redirect some of the particles in regions of the state space. On the other hand, there are two thresholds in this model: Slope fitness value that is the threshold represent expression level change and is the iterations that remain for the same level. The main purpose of which is to control by the changing rate of fitness value. According to the experimental results, PSOCR can be able to strike a balance between exploration and exploitation. It not only extends diversity of PSO, but also improves the precision of solution.

Gene Clustering by Using Query-Based Self-Organizing Maps

In the bioinformatics domain, gene clustering is very important for extracting underlying biological information of gene expression data. SOM

Figure 6. The framework of a query-based learning PSO

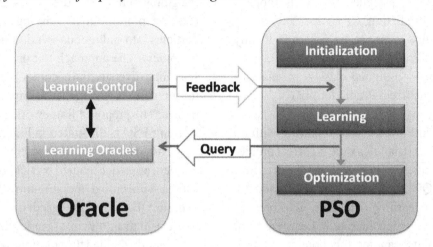

Figure 7. Flowchart of CR mechanism

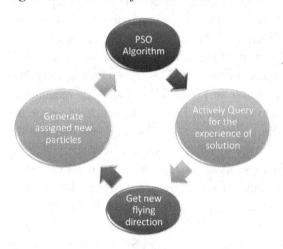

(self-organizing maps) is known as not only one of the most popular neural networks applied for gene clustering, but also it is shown to have some unique features that especially make it suitable to gene clustering. However, SOM has many limitations. One of the most serious drawbacks of SOM is that the clustering results are still dependent on initialization (Wu et al., 2004). This is because SOM randomly initializes the weight vector (network topology) and randomly imports the input vector. Better initial circumstances will produce better clustering results and vice versa. In practice, biologists usually need to spend a lot

of time to repeat several experiments until the satisfactory results are obtained.

Chang et al. (2009) proposed a more holistic approach to, called the query based self-organizing maps (QBSOM), to tackle the drawback, which is sensitive to the initialization of neurons' weights. A comparison between the conventional SOM and the proposed QBSOM is represented in Figure 8. QBSOM and related technologies (Chang and Hsiao, 1993; Chang and Hsiao, 1997b) have been previously applied to solve various problems. The geometric meaning of query-based learning is shown in Figure 8. The learning process of QBSOM could be divided into three phases. Phase I and phase II correspond to the right side of Figure 8. In these two phases, the winner neuron and the moving direction of the winner neuron are decided by both external-input-sample and internal-desired-sample. The left side of Figure 9 can be mapped into phase III, which is the same as SOM. Here, the network topology is disordered by SOM learning mechanism.

QBSOM considered both the external-input-samples (need) and the internal-desired-samples (want). The learning behavior is more similar to human behavior than the conventional SOM. QBSOM inherited the advantages from SOM, such as accuracy and ease of implementation and

Figure 8. A comparison between the conventional SOM and the proposed QBSOM

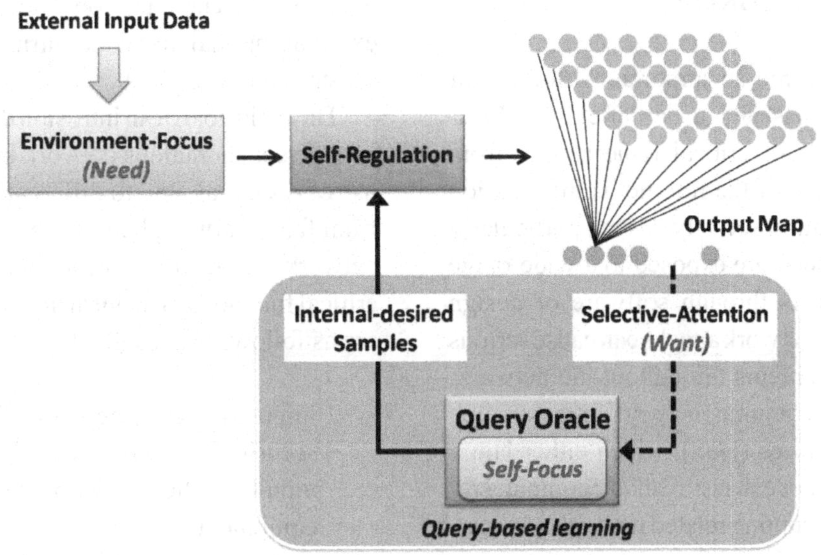

Figure 9. The geometric meaning of the conventional SOM and the proposed QBSOM

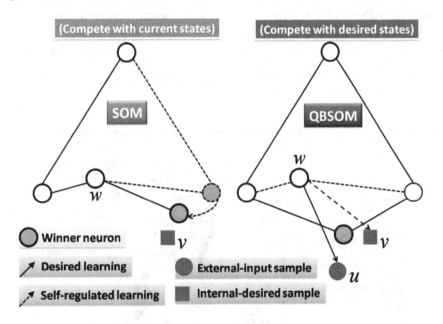

visualization. Moreover, as shown in our experiments, other advantages of QBSOM include, more stable (robust properties for different initialized configurations), more scalable (adapted for clustering from the higher dimensional data) and reasonably fast (faster convergence). Due to the properties of robustness and faster convergence, in practice, biologists would save significant time and effort by using QBSOM to cluster from the gene expression data, not needing to repeat the same experiments.

APPLICATION IN NETWORK SECURITY

Internet has become an important resource for information access and a battlefield for business competition. A critical issue arising from the rapid advance of the Internet is information and communication security. Users, particularly high volume users, are exposed to a wide range of security threats through software or design vulnerabilities. Network attacks can cause serious performance problems throughout the network. These include common network attacks such as Denial-of-Service (DoS), which either jam a network pathway or exhaust available computer resources, thus disrupting related network services. To respond to this increasing threat, information security technology provides a range of tools known as Intrusion Detection Systems (IDS). In its latest development, IDS attempts to stop these attacks by scanning network traffic for signatures; for policy anomalies, such as variations in traffic or network protocol that can signal impending illegal activity; and for signs of unwarranted activity

that could point to attacks from inside or outside the network. The intrusion detection system and external/internal network intrusion attacks are illustrated in Figure 10.

The main goal of an intrusion detection system is to detect anomalous network behavior or misuse of resources, and to differentiate true attacks from false alarms. Then, it subsequently notifies network administrators of the activity. The major critical functions of an intrusion detection system are as follows (Vacca, 2009):

- impose a greater degree of flexibility to the security infrastructure of the network
- monitor the functionality of critical equipments
- trace user activity from the network point of entry to the point of exit
- report on file integrity checks
- detect whether a system has been reconfigured by any an attack
- recognize a potential attack and generate an alert

Figure 10. The intrusion detection system and external/internal network intrusion attacks

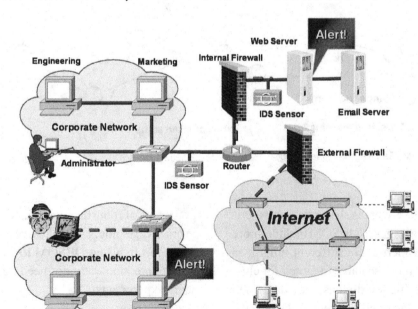

Active learning is a process whose objective is to make the optimal use of the given training data through query of the most informative samples. It has been explored for different applications, including feature selection, data sampling, and generalization improving. In the area of intrusion detection, applying techniques of active learning has become a new field of research in recent years. Li and Guo (2007) present a network anomaly detection method based on improved TCM-KNN machine learning algorithm, and using an active learning to select training data. Seliya and Khoshgoftaar (2010) present a neural-network-based active learning strategy for training intrusion detection dataset. Those proposed methods work well with reduced training data set. However, to reduce training data size can only improve the learning speed but cannot enhance whole system performance.

Effective intrusion detection should happen in real-time, as intrusions take place, to minimize compromises of security. Therefore, their success usually depends on the quality of the training data. If the data contains extraneous and irrelevant information, machine-learning algorithms may produce less accurate and understandable of results. To address this shortcoming, Lai, Chang, and Kouh (2009) applied the concepts of data quantization to signal processing to develop a sample filter using back propagation neural networks, named query-based sample filter (QBS Filter). The proposed framework of QBS filter is illustrated in Figure 10. The method has an enormous capacity to classify extraneous and irrelevant data as noisy data and to filter them out.

Pulse code modulation (PCM) is a digital technique that consists of three stages, sampling of the analog signal, quantization, and binary encoding. A quantization error is apparent when the signal is reconverted to analog form as distortion, a loss in audio quality, and it can be reduced by increasing the sample size; as allowing more bits per sample will improve the accuracy of the approximation. The approximation introduced by quantization

manifests itself as a noise. QBS filter exploits an oracle regarded as a compounded quantizer, which simulates the non-uniform quantization. It is designed using the approximation by quantization of the filter processes to achieve appropriate samples for the training procedure. Thus, learning performance is improved by labeling only those data that are expected to be informative (excluding noise). The method was tested with a benchmark intrusion data set (the KDD Cup 1999 network intrusion data) to verify its performance and effectiveness. Results show that selecting qualified training data will have an impact not only on the performance but also on overall execution (to reduce distortion).

Intrusion detection systems must be capable of distinguishing between normal (not security-critical) and abnormal user activities, to discover malicious attempts in time. However, translating user behavior (or a complete user-system session) in a consistent security-related decision is usual not that simple. Many behavior patterns are indistinguishable and unclear. It is more difficult to detect an invalid intrusion attempt if a signature alerts regularly on valid network activity. False alarms will rapidly gain the distrust of both users and system administrators, much in the same way that the "boy who cried wolf" lost the trust of his villager, and often ignore alarms. Consequently, the proposed method can significantly increase the accuracy detection rate for suspicious activity and recognize rare attack types. It can also improve the efficiency of a real-time intrusion detection model.

FUTURE RESEARCH DIRECTIONS

In this chapter, a wide variety of approaches using query learning for solving classification, cluster, and optimization problems are presented. It can effectively improve some drawbacks of the traditional algorithms, such as long running time and being trapped in local optima. When applying

Figure 11. The framework of QBS filter

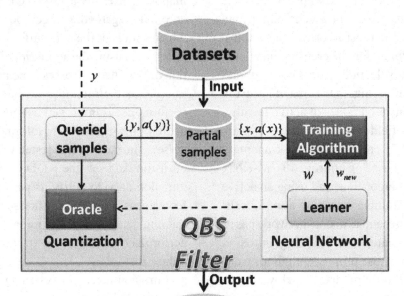

on the decision tree, this approach can benefit significantly from a training set constructed by an active learner using selective sampling. Moreover, it can tackle the drawback of self-organizing maps which is sensitive to the initialization of neurons' weights. Additionally, by redirecting some particles into ambiguous solution space in PSO, QBL can reach to prevent the local optimization problem and improve the performance. In the network security field, the proposed method can not only increase the accuracy detection rate for suspicious activity and recognize rare attack types but also significantly improve the efficiency of intrusion detection. Our future works are to extend this concept to develop other learning methods and to resolve various problems.

CONCLUSION

In this chapter, a framework of QBL concept for different models of supervised and unsupervised learning has been presented. According to Pe-

ter Drucker (1954), an influential management expert, stated that it is more important to do the right thing than to do things right. Moving into an active learning and aggressive querying method will be able to focus on effectiveness to achieve learning goals and desired outcomes. Query-based learning differs from traditional methods in that the samples could be selected out of its will for training, instead of accepting whatever information it is fed. The objective of learning is to produce a training sample that is comprehensive and educative. In consequence, the proposed framework can enhance the availability, effectiveness, and flexibility of different learning algorithms.

REFERENCES

Abe, N., Mamitsuka, H., & Nakamura, A. (1998). Empirical comparison of competing query learning methods. In *Proceedings of Discovery Science*, (pp. 387-388).

Angluin, D. (1987). Learning regular sets from queries and counterexamples. *Information and Computation*, *75*(2), 87–106. doi:10.1016/0890-5401(87)90052-6

Angluin, D. (1988). Queries and concept learning. *Machine Learning*, *2*(4), 319–342. doi:10.1007/BF00116828

Atlas, L., Cohn, R., & Ladner, R. (1990). Training connectionist networks with queries and selective sampling. In *Advances in neural information processing systems* (*Vol. 2*). MIT Press.

Baum, E. (1991). Neural net algorithms that learn in polynomial time from examples and queries. *IEEE Transactions on Neural Networks*, *2*, 5–19. doi:10.1109/72.80287

Berelson, B., & Steiner, G. (1973). *Human behavior: An inventory of scientific findings*. Orlando, FL: Harcourt Brace World.

Carver, C. S., & Scheier, M. F. (1981). *Attention and self-regulation: A control theory approach to human behavior*. New York, NY: Springer-Verlag.

Carver, C. S., & Scheier, M. F. (1998). *On the self-regulation of behavior*. New York, NY: Cambridge University Press.

Chang, R. I. (2005). Disease diagnosis using query-based neural networks. *Lecture Notes in Computer Science*, *3498*, 767–773. doi:10.1007/11427469_122

Chang, R. I., Chu, C. C., Wu, Y. Y., & Chen, Y. L. (2010). Gene clustering by using query-based self-organizing maps. *Expert Systems with Applications*, *37*(9), 6689–6695. doi:10.1016/j.eswa.2010.03.050

Chang, R. I., & Hsiao, P. Y. (1997). Unsupervised query-based learning of neural networks using selective-attention and self-regulation. *IEEE Transactions on Neural Networks*, *8*(2), 205–217. doi:10.1109/72.557657

Chang, R. I., Lai, L. B., Su, W. D., Wang, J. C., & Kouh, J. S. (2007). Intrusion detection by back-propagation neural networks with sample-query and attribute-query. *International Journal of Computational Intelligence Research*, *3*(1), 6–10. doi:10.5019/j.ijcir.2007.76

Chang, R. I., & Lin, S. Y. (2006). *Improving PSO algorithm by query-based learning*. Soft Computing and Technology Trends Workshop, Taiwan.

Chang, R. I., Lo, C. Y., Su, W. D., & Wang, J. C. (2006). *Query-based learning decision tree and its applications in data mining*. The 9th International Conference on Computer Science and Informatics (CSI).

Cohn, D. A. (1996). Neural network exploration using optimal experiment design. *Neural Networks*, *9*(6), 1071–1083. doi:10.1016/0893-6080(95)00137-9

Damasio, A. R. (2000). *The feeling of what happens: Body and emotion in the making of consciousness*. Fort Washington, PA: Harvest Books.

Drucker, F. P. (1954). *The practice of management: An introductory view of management*. New York, NY: Harper & Row.

Eberhart, R. C. (1992). The role of genetic algorithms in neural network QBL and explanation facilities. In *Proceedings of the international Workshop Combinations of GA and NN*, (pp. 169-183).

Gluck, M., & Myers, C. (2001). *Gateway to memory: An introduction to neural network models of the hippocampus in learning*. Cambridge, MA: MIT Press.

Hwang, J. N., Choi, J. J., Oh, S., & Marks, R. (1991). Query-based learning applied to partially trained multilayer perceptrons. *IEEE Transactions on Neural Networks*, *2*(1), 131–136. doi:10.1109/72.80299

Kruschke, J. K. (1992). ALCOVE: An exemplar-based connectionist model of category learning. *Psychological Review, 99*, 22–44. doi:10.1037/0033-295X.99.1.22

Lai, L. B., Chang, R. I., & Kouh, J. S. (2006). Mining data by query-based error-propagation. *Lecture Notes in Computer Science, 3610*, 1224–1233. doi:10.1007/11539087_162

Lai, L. B., Chang, R. I., & Kouh, J. S. (2007). *A time-series predicative model using query-based backpropagation neural networks*. Asia Pacific Industrial Engineering & Management System and 2007 Chinese Institute of Industrial Engineers Conference.

Lai, L. B., Chang, R. I., & Kouh, J. S. (2009). Detecting network intrusions using signal processing with query-based sampling filter. *EURASIP Journal on Advances in Signal Processing*, 2009.

Li, Y., & Guo, L. (2007). An active learning based TCM-KNN algorithm for supervised network intrusion detection. *Computers & Security, 26*, 459–467. doi:10.1016/j.cose.2007.10.002

Linden, A., & Kindermann, J. (1989). Inversion of multilayer nets. In *Proceedings of the International Joint Conference on Neural Networks*, (pp. 425-430).

MacKay, D. (1992). Information-based objective functions for active data selection. *Neural Computation, 4*, 590–604. doi:10.1162/neco.1992.4.4.590

Medin, D. L., & Schaffer, M. M. (1978). Context theory of classification learning. *Psychological Review, 85*, 207–238. doi:10.1037/0033-295X.85.3.207

Nadler, D. A. (1977). *Feedback and organization development: Using data based methods*. Reading, MA: Addison-Wesley.

Newell, A. (1990). *Unified theories of cognition*. Cambridge, MA: Harvard University Press.

Newell, A., & Simon, H. A. (1961). Computer simulation of human thinking. *Science, 134*, 2011–2017. doi:10.1126/science.134.3495.2011

Nosofsky, R. M. (1986). Attention, similarity, and the identiõcation-categorization relationship. *Journal of Experimental Psychology. General, 115*(1), 39–57. doi:10.1037/0096-3445.115.1.39

Powers, W. T. (1973). *Behavior: The control of perception*. New York, NY: Wiley.

Reed, R., Marks, R. J., & Oh, S. (1995). Similarities of error regularization, sigmoid gain scaling, target smoothing, and training with jitter. *IEEE Transactions on Neural Networks, 6*, 529–538. doi:10.1109/72.377960

Rumelhart, D. E., & Norman, D. A. (1978). Accretion, tuning, and restructuring: Three modes of learning. In Cotton, J. W., & Klatzky, R. L. (Eds.), *Semantic factors in cognition*. Hillsdale, NJ: Lawrence Erlbaum Associates.

Rumelhart, E., Hinton, G. E., & Williams, R. J. (1986). *Learning internal representations by error propagation in parallel distributed processing* (*Vol. 1*, pp. 318–362). Cambridge, MA: MIT Press.

Seliya, N., & Khoshgoftaar, T. M. (2010). Active learning with neural networks for intrusion detection. In *Proceedings of the 11th IEEE International Conference on Information Reuse and Integration*, Las Vegas.

Vacca, J. R. (2009). *Computer and information security handbook*. Morgan Kaufmann.

Widrow, B., & Hoff, M. E., Jr. (1960). Adaptive switching circuits. In *1960 IRE WESCON Convention Record*, Part 4, (pp. 96–104). New York, NY: IRE.

Compilation of References

Abbasi, A., & Chen, H. (2008). Writeprints: A stylometric approach to identity-level identification and similarity detection in cyberspace. *ACM Transactions on Information Systems, 26*(2), 1–29. doi:10.1145/1344411.1344413

Abbas, Y., & Aqel, M. (2003). Pattern recognition using multilayer neural-genetic algorithm. *Neurocomputing, 51*, 237–247. doi:10.1016/S0925-2312(02)00619-7

Abe, N., Mamitsuka, H., & Nakamura, A. (1998). Empirical comparison of competing query learning methods. In *Proceedings of Discovery Science*, (pp. 387-388).

Abe, S. (2010). *Support vector machines for pattern classification* (2nd ed.). London, UK: Springer.

Abhishek, V., & Hosanagar, K. (2007a). *Keyword generation for search engine advertising using semantic similarity between terms.* Paper presented at the Ninth International Conference on Electronic Commerce.

Abido, M. A. (2001). Particle swarm optimization for multimachine power system stabilizer design. In *Proceedings of IEEE Power Engineering Society Summer Meeting*.

Aboulmagd, H., Gayar, N., & Onsi, H. (2009). A new approach in content-based image retrieval using fuzzy logic. *Journal of Telecommunication Systems, 40*(1-2), 55–66. doi:10.1007/s11235-008-9142-9

Acharya, T., & Ray, A. K. (2005). *Image processing: Principles and applications.* New Jersey, USA: John Wiley & Sons, Inc.doi:10.1002/0471745790

Adini, Y., Moses, Y., & Ullman, S. (1997). Face recognition: The problem of compensating for changes in illumination direction. *IEEE Transactions in Pattern Analysis in Machine Intelligence, 19*(7), 721-732. doi:http://dx.doi.org/10.1109/34.598229

Agarwal, N., Liu, H., Subramanya, S., Salerno, J. J., & Yu, P. S. (2009). Connecting sparsely distributed similar bloggers. In *Proceedings 2009 Ninth IEEE International Conference on Data Mining, ICDM09* (pp. 11-20). Miami, Florida, USA.

Agrawal, M., & Doermann, D. (2009). Clutter noise removal in binary document images. *International Conference on Document Analysis and Recognition*, (pp. 556-560).

Aha, D., & Kibler, D. (1991). Instance-based learning algorithms. *Machine Learning, 6*, 37–66. doi:10.1007/BF00153759

Ahmad, A. A., & Hameed, B. H. (2010). Fixed-bed adsorption of reactive azo dye onto granular activated carbon prepared from waste. *Journal of Hazardous Materials, 175*, 298–303. doi:10.1016/j.jhazmat.2009.10.003

Aho, B. T., & Dzeroski, S. (2009). Rule ensembles for multi-target regression. In *Proceedings 2009 Ninth IEEE International Conference on Data Mining, ICDM09* (pp. 21-30). Miami, Florida, USA.

Ahonen, T., Hadid, A., & Pietikainen, M. (2006). Face description with local binary patterns: Application to face recognition. *IEEE Transactions in Pattern Analysis in Machine Intelligence, 28*(12), 2037-2041. doi: http://dx.doi.org/10.1109/TPAMI.2006.244

Ailon, N., Charikar, M., & Newman, A. (2005). Aggregating inconsistent information: ranking and clustering. In *Proceedings of 37th Annual ACM Symposium on Theory of Computing* (pp. 684-693).

Akiyama, T. (2004). Handwritten address interpretation system allowing for non-use of postal codes and omission of address elements. *International Workshop on Frontiers in Handwriting Recognition*, (pp. 527-532).

Alginahi, Y. (2009). A proposed hybrid OCR system for Arabic and Indian numerical postal codes. *International Conference on Computer Technology and Development*, (Vol. 2, pp. 400-404).

Allili, M. S., Ziou, D., Bouguila, N., & Boutemedjet, S. (2010). Unsupervised feature selection and learning for image segmentation. Retrieved from http://www.computerrobotvision.org/2010/talks/Allili_CRV2010.pdf

Al-Omari, F., & Al-Jarrah, O. (2004). Handwritten Indian numerals recognition system using probabilistic neural networks. *Advanced Engineering Informatics*, *18*(1), 9–16. doi:10.1016/j.aei.2004.02.001

Alrawi, K. W., & Sabry, K. A. (2009). E-commerce evolution: A Gulf region review. *International Journal of Business Information Systems*, *4*(5), 509–526. doi:10.1504/IJBIS.2009.025204

Amari, S.-I. (1999). Natural gradient learning for over- and under-complete bases in ICA. *Neural Computation*, *11*(9), 1875–1883. doi:10.1162/089976699300015990

American Cancer Society. (2010). *Cervical cancer overview*. Atlanta, GA: Author.

Andrews, H. C., & Hunt, B. R. (1977). *Digital image restoration*. Baltimore, MD: The Johns Hopkins University Press.

Angeline, P. J. (1998). Evolutionary optimization versus particle swarm optimization: Philosophy and performance differences. *Evolutionary Programming*, *7*, 601–610. doi:10.1007/BFb0040811

Angluin, D. (1987). Learning regular sets from queries and counterexamples. *Information and Computation*, *75*(2), 87–106. doi:10.1016/0890-5401(87)90052-6

Angluin, D. (1988). Queries and concept learning. *Machine Learning*, *2*(4), 319–342. doi:10.1007/BF00116828

AOL. (2006). *AOL search data*. Retrieved December 6, 2009, from http://www.gregsadetsky.com/aol-data/

AOL. (2008). *AOL search - 2008 year end hot searches*. Retrieved December 6, 2009, from http://about-search.aol.com/hotsearches2008/index.html

Argamon, S., Koppel, M., Pennebaker, J. W., & Schler, J. (2009). Automatically profiling the author of an anonymous text. *Communications of the ACM*, *52*(2), 119–123. doi:10.1145/1461928.1461959

Arica, N., & Yarman-Vural, F. (2001). An overview of character recognition focused on off-line handwriting. *IEEE Transactions on Systems, Man and Cybernetics. Part C, Applications and Reviews*, *31*(2), 216–233. doi:10.1109/5326.941845

Arimura, H., Katsuragawa, S., Suzuki, K., Li, F., Shiraishi, J., Sone, S., & Doi, K. (2004). Computerized scheme for automated detection of lung nodules in low-dose computed tomography images for lung cancer screening. *Academic Radiology*, *11*, 617–629. doi:10.1016/j.acra.2004.02.009

Arora, M. K., & Foody, G. M. (1997). An evaluation of some factors affecting the accuracy of classification by an artificial neural network. *International Journal of Remote Sensing*, *18*(4), 799–810. doi:10.1080/014311697218764

Ashley, K. D. (1992). Case-based reasoning and its implications for legal expert systems. *Artificial Intelligence and Law*, *1*(2), 113–208. doi:10.1007/BF00114920

Atlas, L., Cohn, R., & Ladner, R. (1990). Training connectionist networks with queries and selective sampling. In *Advances in neural information processing systems* (*Vol. 2*). MIT Press.

Aviden, S. (2007). Ensemble tracking. *IEEE Transactions on Pattern Analysis and Machine Intelligence*, *29*(2), 261–271. doi:10.1109/TPAMI.2007.35

Baayen, H., van Halteren, H., Neijt, A., & Tweedie, F. (2002). An experiment in authorship attribution. In *Proceedings 6th International Conference Statistical Analysis of Textual Data*, (pp. 1-7).

Baeza-Yates, R., & Ribeiro-Neto, B. (1999). *Modern information retrieval*. New York, NY: Addison Wesley; ACM Press.

Bagirov, A. M., Rubinov, A. M., & Yearwood, J. (2002). A global optimization approach to classification. *Optimization and Engineering*, *3*, 129–155. doi:10.1023/A:1020911318981

Bagirov, A. M., & Yearwood, J. L. (2006). A new nonsmooth optimization algorithm for minimum sum-of-squares clustering problems. *European Journal of Operational Research*, *170*, 578–596. doi:10.1016/j.ejor.2004.06.014

Baldi, P., & Brunak, S. (2001). *Bioinformatics: The machine learning approach*. Cambridge, MA: MIT Press.

Bao, S. H., Xu, S. L., Zhang, L., Yan, R., Su, Z., Han, D., & Yu, Y. (2009). Joint emotion-topic modeling for social affective text mining. In *Proceedings 2009 Ninth IEEE International Conference on Data Mining*, ICDM09 (pp. 699-704). Miami, Florida, USA.

Barros, R. C., Basgalupp, M. P., Ruiz, D. D., de Carvalho, A. C. P. L. F., & Freitas, A. A. (2010) Evolutionary model tree induction. In *SAC '10: Proceedings of the 2010 ACM Symposium on Applied Computing*, (pp. 1131–1137). New York, NY: ACM.

Barros, R. C., Ruiz, D. D., & Basgalupp, M. P. (2011). Evolutionary model trees for handling continuous classes in machine learning. *Information Sciences*, *181*(5), 954–971. doi:10.1016/j.ins.2010.11.010

Bartlett, M. S., Movellan, J. R., & Sejnowski, T. J. (2002). Face recognition by independent component analysis. *IEEE Transactions on Neural Networks*, *13*(6), 1450–1464. doi:10.1109/TNN.2002.804287

Bartz, K., Murthi, V., & Sebastian, S. (2006). *Logistic regression and collaborative filtering for sponsored search term recommendation*. Paper presented at the Second Workshop on Sponsored Search Auctions.

Baruch, O. (1988). Line thinning by line following. *Pattern Recognition Letters*, *8*(4), 271–276. doi:10.1016/0167-8655(88)90034-7

Basgalupp, M., de Carvalho, A., Barros, R., Ruiz, D., & Freitas, A. (2009). Lexicographic multi-objective evolutionary induction of decision trees. *International Journal of Bio-Inspired Computation*, *1*(1/2), 105–117. doi:10.1504/IJBIC.2009.022779

Basu, S., Das, N., Sarkar, R., Kundu, M., Nasipuri, M., & Basu, D. (2010). A novel framework for automatic sorting of postal documents with multi-script address blocks. *Pattern Recognition*, *43*(10), 3507–3521. doi:10.1016/j.patcog.2010.05.018

Bauer, E., & Kohavi, R. (1999). An empirical comparison of voting classification algorithms: Bagging, boosting and variants. *Machine Learning*, *36*(2), 105–142. doi:10.1023/A:1007515423169

Baum, E. (1991). Neural net algorithms that learn in polynomial time from examples and queries. *IEEE Transactions on Neural Networks*, *2*, 5–19. doi:10.1109/72.80287

Bdour, A. N., Hamdi, M. R., & Tarawneh, Z. (2009). Perspectives on sustainable wastewater treatment technologies and reuse options in the urban areas of the Mediterranean region. *Desalination*, *237*, 162–174. doi:10.1016/j.desal.2007.12.030

Beckmann, N., Kriegel, H.-K., Schneider, R., & Seeger, B. (1990). The R*-tree: An efficient and robust access method for points and rectangles. *Proceedings of the ACM SIG-MOD International Conference on Management of Data*, (pp. 322-331).

Behera, S. K. (2010). *Removal of triclosan and ibuprofen by engineered floodplain filtration system*. Unpublished Ph.D. dissertation, University of Ulsan, South Korea.

Belhumeur, P. N., Hespanha, J. P., & Kriegman, D. J. (1997). Eigenfaces vs. fisherfaces: Recognition using class specific linear projection. *IEEE Transactions on Pattern Analysis and Machine Intelligence*, *19*(7), 711–720. doi:10.1109/34.598228

Belkin, N. J. (2000). Helping people find what they don't know. *Communications of the ACM*, *43*(8), 58–61. doi:10.1145/345124.345143

Bell, A. J., & Sejnowski, T. J. (1995). An information-maximization approach to blind separation and blind deconvolution. *Neural Computation*, *7*(6), 1129–1159. doi:10.1162/neco.1995.7.6.1129

Bench-Capon, T. J. M. (1993). Neural networks and open texture. In the *Proceedings of the Fourth International Conference on Artificial Intelligence and* Law (pp. 292-297). Amsterdam, The Netherlands: ACM Press.

Benouareth, A., Ennaji, A., & Sellami, M. (2008). Semi-continuous HMMs with explicit state duration for unconstrained Arabic word modeling and recognition. *Pattern Recognition Letters*, *29*(12), 1742–1752. doi:10.1016/j.patrec.2008.05.008

Berelson, B., & Steiner, G. (1973). *Human behavior: An inventory of scientific findings*. Orlando, FL: Harcourt Brace World.

Berman, D. H., & Hafner, C. D. (1988). Obstacles to the development of logic-based models of legal reasoning. In Walter, C. (Ed.), *Computer power and legal reasoning* (pp. 183–214). New York, NY: Quorum Books.

Bian, W., & Tao, D. C. (2009). Dirichlet mixture allocation for multiclass document collections modeling. In *Proceedings 2009 Ninth IEEE International Conference on Data Mining, ICDM09* (pp. 711-715). Miami, Florida, USA.

Bishop, C. M. (1995). *Neural networks for pattern recognition*. New York, NY: Oxford University Press.

Blumenstein, M., & Verma, B. (2001). Analysis of segmentation performance on the CEDAR benchmark database. *Sixth International Conference on Document Analysis and Recognition* (pp. 1142-1146).

Boersma, L., van den Brink, M., Bruce, A., Shouman, T., Gras, L., te Velde, A., & Lebesque, J. (1998). Estimation of the incidence of late bladder and rectum complications after high-dose (70-78Gy) conformal radiotherapy for prostate cancer, using dose-volume histograms. *International Journal of Radiation Oncology • Biology • Physics, 41*, 83-92.

Bofill, P. (2000). *Blind separation of more sources than mixtures using sparsity of their short-time Fourier transform*. Helsinki, Finland.

Bofill, P., & Zibulevsky, M. (2001). Underdetermined blind source separation using sparse representations. *Signal Processing, 81*(11), 2353–2362. doi:10.1016/S0165-1684(01)00120-7

Borji, A., Ahmadabadi, M. N., Araabi, B. N., & Hamidi, M. (2010). Online learning of task-driven object-based visual attention control. *Image and Vision Computing, 28*(7), 1130–1145. doi:10.1016/j.imavis.2009.10.006

Bortolozzi, F., Britto, A., Oliveira, L. S., & Morita, M. (2005). Recent advances in handwriting recognition. *Proceedings of the International Workshop on Document Analysis* (pp. 1-30).

Bot, M. C. J., & Langdon, W. B. (2000). Application of genetic programming to induction of linear classification trees. In Poli, R., Banzhaf, W., Langdon, W. B., Miller, J. F., Nordin, P., & Fogarty, T. C. (Eds.), *Genetic Programming, Proceedings of EuroGP'2000* (*Vol. 1802*, pp. 247–258). Edinburgh, UK: Springer- Verlag. doi:10.1007/978-3-540-46239-2_18

Bouckaert, R. R., Frank, E., Hall, M., Kirkby, R., Reutemann, P., Seewald, A., & Scuse, D. (2010). *WEKA manual for version 3-7-1*. Retrieved November 15, 2010, from http://www.cs.waikato.ac.nz/ml/weka/

Bouzaza, A., Vallet, C., & Laplanche, A. (2006). Photocatalytic degradation of some VOCs in the gas phase using an annular flow reactor: Determination of the contribution of mass transfer and chemical reaction steps in the photo degradation process. *Journal of Photochemistry and Photobiology A Chemistry, 177*, 212–217. doi:10.1016/j.jphotochem.2005.05.027

Brand, M. (2006). Fast low-rank modifications of the thin singular value decomposition. *Linear Algebra and Its Applications, 415*(1), 20–30. doi:10.1016/j.laa.2005.07.021

Breiman, L. (1996). Bagging predictors. *Machine Learning, 24*(2), 123–140. doi:10.1007/BF00058655

Breiman, L. (1998). Arcing classifiers. *Annals of Statistics, 26*(3), 801–849.

Breiman, L. (2001). Random forests. *Machine Learning, 45*(1), 5–32. doi:10.1023/A:1010933404324

Breiman, L., Friedman, J., Stone, C., & Olshen, R. A. (1984). *Classification and regression trees*. Chapman and Hall/CRC.

Brüninghaus, S., & Ashley, K. D. (2001). Improving the representation of legal case texts with information extraction methods. In H. Prakken & R. Loui (Eds.), *Proceedings of the Seventh International Conference on Artificial Intelligence and Law (ICAIL-2001)*, St. Louis, MO

Buettner, F., Gulliford, S., Webb, S., & Partridge, M. (2009). Using Bayesian logistic regression with high-order interactions to model radiation-induced toxicities following radiotherapy. *Proceedings of 8th International Conference on Machine Learning and Applications*, (pp. 451-456).

Byrne, K., & Klein, E. (2003). Image retrieval using natural language and content-based techniques. *Proceedings of the 4th Dutch-Belgian Information Retrieval Workshop*, (pp. 57-62).

Cai, D., He, X., Han, J., & Zhang, H. J. (2006). Orthogonal laplacianfaces for face recognition. *IEEE Transactions on Image Processing*, *15*(11), 3608–3614. doi:10.1109/TIP.2006.881945

Calinon, S., & Billard, A. (2005). *Recognition and reproduction of gestures using a probabilistic framework combining PCA, ICA and HMM.* Paper presented at the ICML '05: 22nd International Conference on Machine Learning.

Camastra, F. (2007). A SVM-based cursive character recognizer. *Pattern Recognition*, *40*(12), 3721–3727. doi:10.1016/j.patcog.2007.03.014

Cantu-Paz, E., & Kamath, C. (2000). Using evolutionary algorithms to induce oblique decision trees. In D. Whitley, D. Goldberg, E. Cantu-Paz, L. Spector, I. Parmee, & H.G. Beyer (Eds.), *Proceedings of the Genetic and Evolutionary Computation Conference (GECCO-2000)*, (pp. 1053–1060)., Las Vegas, NV: Morgan Kaufmann.

Cardoso, J. F. (1997). Infomax and maximum likelihood for blind source separation. *IEEE Signal Processing Letters*, *4*(4), 112–114. doi:10.1109/97.566704

Cardoso, J., & Souloumiac, A. (1996). Jacobi angles for simultaneous diagonalization. *SIAM Journal on Matrix Analysis and Applications*, *17*(1), 161–164. doi:10.1137/S0895479893259546

Cariani, P. (1992). Emergence and artificial life. In Langton, C., Taylor, C., Farmer, J. D., & Rasmussen, S. (Eds.), *Artificial life II* (pp. 775–797). Reading, MA: Addision-Wesley.

Carpineto, C., & Romano, G. (2004). Exploiting the potential of concept lattices for information retrieval with CREDO. *Journal of Universal Computer Science*, *10*(8), 985–1013.

Carson, C., Belongie, S., Greenspan, H., & Malik, J. (1998). Blobworld: Image segmentation using expectation-maximization and its application to image querying. *Journal of Pattern Analysis and Machine Intelligence*, *24*(8), 1026–1038. doi:10.1109/TPAMI.2002.1023800

Carson, C., & Ogle, V. (1996). Storage and retrieval of feature data for a very large online image collections. *Bulletin of the IEEE Computer Society Technical Committee on Data Engineering*, *19*(4), 19–27.

Carver, C. S., & Scheier, M. F. (1981). *Attention and self-regulation: A control theory approach to human behavior.* New York, NY: Springer-Verlag.

Carver, C. S., & Scheier, M. F. (1998). *On the self-regulation of behavior.* New York, NY: Cambridge University Press.

Cayley Group. (2010). *VLDP_KRG's evaluation results.* Retrieved April 2, 2010, from http://cayley.sytes.net/vldp_krg/OUTPUT_VLDP_KRG.htm

Chakrabarti, S. (2005). *Mining the Web: Analysis of hypertext and semi structured data.* Morgan Kaufmann Press.

Chang, C.-C., & Lin, C.-J. (2001). LIBSVM - A library for support vector machines. Retrieved June 10, 2010, from http://www.csie.ntu.edu.tw/~cjlin/libsvm/

Chang, R. I., & Lin, S. Y. (2006). *Improving PSO algorithm by query-based learning.* Soft Computing and Technology Trends Workshop, Taiwan.

Chang, R. I., Lo, C. Y., Su, W. D., & Wang, J. C. (2006). *Query-based learning decision tree and its applications in data mining.* The 9th International Conference on Computer Science and Informatics (CSI).

Chang, J. F., Chu, S. C., Roddick, J. F., & Pan, J. S. (2005). A parallel particle swarm optimization algorithm with communication strategies. *Journal of Information Science and Engineering*, *4*(21), 809–818.

Chang, R. I. (2005). Disease diagnosis using query-based neural networks. *Lecture Notes in Computer Science*, *3498*, 767–773. doi:10.1007/11427469_122

Chang, R. I., Chu, C. C., Wu, Y. Y., & Chen, Y. L. (2010). Gene clustering by using query-based self-organizing maps. *Expert Systems with Applications*, *37*(9), 6689–6695. doi:10.1016/j.eswa.2010.03.050

Chang, R. I., & Hsiao, P. Y. (1997). Unsupervised query-based learning of neural networks using selective-attention and self-regulation. *IEEE Transactions on Neural Networks*, *8*(2), 205–217. doi:10.1109/72.557657

Chang, R. I., Lai, L. B., Su, W. D., Wang, J. C., & Kouh, J. S. (2007). Intrusion detection by backpropagation neural networks with sample-query and attribute-query. *International Journal of Computational Intelligence Research, 3*(1), 6–10. doi:10.5019/j.ijcir.2007.76

Chao, K., Deasy, J., Markman, J., Haynie, J., Perez, C., Purdy, J., & Low, D. (2001). A prospective study of salivary function sparing in patients with head-and-neck cancers receiving intensity-modulated or three-dimensional radiation therapy: Initial results. *International Journal of Radiation Oncology • Biology • Physics, 49*, 907-916.

Chaplot, S., Patnaik, L. M., & Jaganathan, N. R. (2006). Classification of MR brain images using wavelets as input to SVM and neural network. *Biomedical Signal Processing and Control, 1*, 86–92. doi:10.1016/j.bspc.2006.05.002

Chaski, C. (2008). *Text and pretext on the internet: Recognizing problematic communications.* Retrieved May 5, 2010, from http://cyber.law.harvard.edu

Chaski, C. (2005). Who's at the keyboard? Authorship attribution in digital evidence investigations. *International Journal of Digital Evidence, 4*(1), 1–13.

Chatzichristos, S., & Boutalis, Y. (2010). Content based radiology image retrieval using a fuzzy rule based scalable composite descriptor. *Journal of Multimedia Tools and Applications, 46*(2-3), 493-519.

Chaudhari, S., & Gravano, L. (1996). Optimizing queries over multimedia repositories. *Bulletin of the IEEE Computer Society Technical Committee on Data Engineering,* (pp. 45-52).

Chaudhuri, B. B., Rodenacker, K., & Burger, G. (1988). Characterization and featuring of histological section images. *Pattern Recognition Letters, 7*, 245–252. doi:10.1016/0167-8655(88)90109-2

Chavoshi, S. H., Amiri, A., & Amini, J. (2007). *Supervised classification in high resolution images (Quikbird) using neural network, fuzzy sets and minimum distance.* Presented at the Map Asia 2007 Conference, August 14 - 16, 2007, Kuala Lumpur, Malaysia.

Chen, L.-C. (2010). Using a two-stage technique to design a keyword suggestion system. *Information Research: An International Electronic Journal, 15*(1).

Chen, Y., Wang, W., Liu, Z., & Lin, X. (2009). *Keyword search on structured and semi-structured data.* Paper presented at the 2009 ACM SIGMOD International Conference on Management of Data.

Chen, Y., Xue, G.-R., & Yu, Y. (2008). *Advertising keyword suggestion based on concept hierarchy.* Paper presented at the International Conference on Web Search and Web Data Mining.

Cheng, J., Liu, Q., Lu, H., & Chen, Y. W. (2006). Ensemble learning for independent component analysis. *Pattern Recognition, 39*(1), 81–88. doi:10.1016/j.patcog.2005.06.018

Chen, L. F., Liao, H. Y. M., Ko, M. T., Lin, J. C., & Yu, G. J. (2000). New LDA-based face recognition system which can solve the small sample size problem. *Pattern Recognition, 33*(10), 1713–1726. doi:10.1016/S0031-3203(99)00139-9

Chen, L.-C., & Luh, C. J. (2005). Web page prediction from metasearch results. *Internet Research: Electronic Networking Applications and Policy, 15*(4), 421–446. doi:10.1108/10662240510615182

Chen, L., & Kamel, M. S. (2009). A generalized adaptive ensemble generation and aggregation approach for multiple classifier systems. *Pattern Recognition, 42*(5), 629–644. doi:10.1016/j.patcog.2008.09.003

Chen, S., Zhou, S., Yin, F., Marks, L., & Das, S. (2007b). Investigation of the support vector machine algorithm to predict lung radiation-induced pneumonitis. *Medical Physics, 34*, 3808–3814. doi:10.1118/1.2776669

Chen, S., Zhou, S., Zhang, J., Yin, F., Marks, L., & Das, S. (2007a). A neural network model to predict lung radiation-induced pneumonitis. *Medical Physics, 34*, 3420–3427. doi:10.1118/1.2759601

Chen, Y., & Wang, J. (2002). A region based fuzzy feature matching approach to content based image retrieval. *IEEE Transactions on Pattern Analysis and Machine Intelligence, 24*(9), 1252–1267. doi:10.1109/TPAMI.2002.1033216

Chen, Y., & Zhang, Y.-Q. (2009). A personalised query suggestion agent based on query-concept bipartite graphs and concept relation trees. *International Journal of Advanced Intelligence Paradigms, 1*(4), 398–417. doi:10.1504/IJAIP.2009.026761

Cheriet, M. (1995). A formal model for document processing of business forms. *International Conference on Document Analysis and Recognition,* (Vol. 1, p. 210).

Chi, N. L. (2003). *A tolerance rough set approach to clustering web search results.* Master thesis,Faculty of Mathematics, Informatics and Mechanics, Warsaw University.

Chung, J. B., Kim, S. H., Jeong, B. R., & Lee, Y. D. (2004). Removal of organic matter and nitrogen from river water in a model floodplain. *Journal of Environmental Quality, 33,* 1017–1023. doi:10.2134/jeq2004.1017

Ciaccia, P., Montesi, D., Penzo, W., & Trombetta, A. (2001). Fuzzy query languages for multimedia data. In Syed, M. R. (Ed.), *Design and management of multimedia information systems: Opportunities and challenges.* Hershey, PA: Idea Group Publishing. doi:10.4018/978-1-930708-00-6.ch010

Cichocki, A., & Amari, S.-I. (2002). *Adaptive blind signal and image processing: Learning algorithms and applications.* John Wiley & Sons, Inc.doi:10.1002/0470845899

Clerc, M. (1999). The swarm and the queen: Towards a deterministic and adaptive particle swarm optimization. In *Proceedings of IEEE International Conference on Evolutionary Computation* (ICEC'99).

Clerc, M., & Kennedy, J. (2002). The particle swarm: Explosion, stability, and convergence in a multi-dimensional complex space. *IEEE Transactions on Evolutionary Computation, 6*(1), 58–73. doi:10.1109/4235.985692

Cohen, W. W. (1995). Fast effective rule induction. In *12th International Conference on Machine Learning,* (pp. 115-123).

Cohen, J. (1968). Weighed kappa: Nominal scale agreement with provision for scaled disagreement or partial credit. *Psychological Bulletin, 70*(4), 213–220. doi:10.1037/h0026256

Cohn, D. A. (1996). Neural network exploration using optimal experiment design. *Neural Networks, 9*(6), 1071–1083. doi:10.1016/0893-6080(95)00137-9

Colorni, A., Dorigo, M., & Maniezzo, V. (1991). Distributed optimization by ant colonies. In *Proceedings of First European Conference on Artificial Life,* (pp. 132-142). Cambridge, MA: MIT Press.

Comon, P. (1994). Independent component analysis, a new concept? *Signal Processing, 36*(3), 287-314. doi: http://dx.doi.org/10.1016/0165-1684(94)90029-9

Coombes, L. R., & Culverhouse, P. F. (2003). Pattern recognition in cervical cytological slide images. In D. P. Mukherjee & S. Pal (Eds.), *The 5th International Conference on Advances In Pattern Recognition (ICAPR) 2003* (pp. 227-230). New Delhi, India: Allied Publishers Pvt. Ltd.

Cotrans, R. S., Kumar, V., & Robbins, S. L. (1999). *Robbins pathologic basis of disease* (6th ed.). London, UK: W. B. Saunders Co.

Cozzarini, C., Fiorino, C., Ceresoli, G., Cattaneo, G., Bolognesi, A, Calandrino, R., & Villa, E. (2003). Significant correlation between rectal DVH and late bleeding in patients treated after radical prostatectomy with conformal or conventional radiotherapy (66.6-70.2Gy). *International Journal of Radiation Oncology • Biology • Physics, 55,* 688-694.

Craft, D., & Bortfeld, T. (2008). How many plans are needed in an IMRT multi-objective plan database? *Physics in Medicine and Biology, 53,* 2785–2796. doi:10.1088/0031-9155/53/11/002

Craven, M., DiPasquo, D., Freitag, D., McCallum, A., Mitchell, T., & Nigam, K. (2000). Learning to construct knowledge bases from the World Wide Web. *Artificial Intelligence, 118*(1-2), 69–113. doi:10.1016/S0004-3702(00)00004-7

Crini, G. (2006). Non-conventional low-cost adsorbents for dye removal: A review. *Bioresource Technology, 97,* 1061–1085. doi:10.1016/j.biortech.2005.05.001

Cruz, R., Cavalcanti, G., & Ren, T. (2009). An ensemble classifier for offline cursive character recognition using multiple feature extraction techniques. *IEEE International Joint Conference on Neural Networks* (pp. 744-751).

Cui, Y., Dy, J., Alexander, B., & Jiang, S. (2008). Fluoroscopic gating without implanted fiducial markers for lung cancer radiotherapy based on support vector machines (SVM). *Physics in Medicine and Biology, 53*(315-N), 327.

Cui, Y., Dy, J., Sharp, G., Alexander, B., & Jiang, S. (2007). Robust fluoroscopic respiratory gating for lung cancer radiotherapy without implanted fiducial markers. *Physics in Medicine and Biology, 52,* 741–755. doi:10.1088/0031-9155/52/3/015

Cunningham, S. J., Littin, J., & Witten, I. H. (2001). *Applications of machine learning in information retrieval.* Hamilton, New Zealand: University of Waikato.

Cybenko, G. (1989). Continuous value neural networks with two hidden layers are sufficient. *Mathematics of Control, Signals, and Systems, 2,* 303–314. doi:10.1007/BF02551274

D'Souza, W., Malinowski, K., & Zhang, H. (2009). Machine learning for intra-fraction tumor motion modeling with respiratory surrogates. *Proceedings of 8th International Conference on Machine Learning and Applications,* (pp. 463-467).

Dagher, I., & Nachar, R. (2006). Face recognition using IPCA-ICA algorithm. *IEEE Transactions on Pattern Analysis and Machine Intelligence, 28*(6), 996–1000. doi:10.1109/TPAMI.2006.118

Damasio, A. R. (2000). *The feeling of what happens: Body and emotion in the making of consciousness.* Fort Washington, PA: Harvest Books.

Das, S., Chen, S., Deasy, J., Zhou, S., Yin, F., & Marks, L. (2008). Decision fusion of machine learning models to predict radiotherapy-induced lung pneumonitis. *Proceedings of 7th International Conference on Machine Learning and Applications,* (pp. 545-550).

Dasarathy, B. V., & Sheela, B. V. (1979). Composite classifier system design: Concepts and methodology. *Proceedings of the IEEE, 67*(5), 708–713. doi:10.1109/PROC.1979.11321

Dawoud, A., & Kamel, M. S. (2004). Iterative multimodel subimage binarization for handwritten character segmentation. *IEEE Transactions on Image Processing, 13*(9), 1223–1230. doi:10.1109/TIP.2004.833101

De Mántaras, R. L. (1991). A distance-based attribute selection measure for decision tree induction. *Machine Learning, 6*(1), 81–92. doi:10.1023/A:1022694001379

De Marchi Triglia, R., Metze, K., Zeferino, L. C., & De Angelo Andrade, L. A. C. (2009). HPV in situ hybridization signal patterns as a marker for cervical intraepithelial neoplasia progression. *Gynecologic Oncology, 112,* 114–118. doi:10.1016/j.ygyno.2008.09.047

Deb, S. (2010). *Using relevance feedback in bridging semantic gaps in content-based image retrieval.* The Second International Conference on Advances in Future Internet (AFIN2010), Venice/Mestre, Italy, July 18 - 25, 2010

Deb, S., & Kulkarni, S. (2007). Human perception based image retrieval using emergence index and fuzzy similarity measure. *The Third International Conference on Intelligent Sensors, Sensor Networks and Information Processing (ISSNIP07),* Melbourne, Australia, December 3-6, 2007, (pp. 359-363).

Deb, K. (2001). *Multi-objective optimization using evolutionary algorithms.* New York, NY: John Wiley & Sons, Inc.

Deb, K., Pratap, A., Agarwal, S., & Meyarivan, T. (2002). A fast and elitist multiobjective genetic algorithm: NSGA-II. *IEEE Transactions on Evolutionary Computation, 6*(2), 182–197. doi:10.1109/4235.996017

Deerwester, S., Dumais, S. T., Furnas, G. W., Landauer, T. K., & Harshman, R. (1990). Indexing by latent semantic analysis. *Journal of the American Society for Information Science American Society for Information Science, 41*(6), 391–407. doi:10.1002/(SICI)1097-4571(199009)41:6<391::AID-ASI1>3.0.CO;2-9

Dehing-Oberije, C., Yu, S., De Ruysscher, D., Meersschout, S., Van Beek, K., Lievens, Y., ... Lambin, P. (2009). Development and external validation of prognostic model for 2-year survival of non-small-cell lung cancer patients treated with chemoradiotherapy. *International Journal of Radiation Oncology • Biology • Physics, 74,* 355-362.

Dekker, A., Dehing-Oberije, C., De Ruysscher, D., Lambin, P., Komati, K., & Fung, G. ... Lievens, Y. (2009). Survival prediction in lung cancer treated with radiotherapy - Bayesian networks vs. support vector machines in handling missing data. *Proceedings of 8th International Conference on Machine Learning and Applications,* (pp. 494-497).

Demirci, M. F., Shokoufandeh, A., Keselman, Y., Bretzner, L., & Dickinson, S. (2006). Object recognition as many-to-many feature matching. *International Journal of Computer Vision, 69*(2), 203–222. doi:10.1007/s11263-006-6993-y

Demiroz, G., & Guvenir, A. (1997). Classification by voting feature intervals. In *9th European Conference on Machine Learning*, (pp. 85-92).

Denkowski, M., Chlebiej, M., & Mikołajczak, P. (2004). Segmentation of human brain MR images using rule-based fuzzy logic inference. *Studies in Health Technology and Informatics, 105*, 264–272.

Desai, A. (2010). Gujarati handwritten numeral optical character reorganization through neural network. *Pattern Recognition, 43*(7), 2582–2589. doi:10.1016/j.patcog.2010.01.008

Detry, R., Pugeault, N., & Piater, J. H. (2009). A probabilistic framework for 3D visual object representation. *IEEE Transactions on Pattern Analysis and Machine Intelligence, 31*(10), 1790–1803. doi:10.1109/TPAMI.2009.64

Dietterich, T. G. (2000a). Ensemble methods in machine learning. In J. Kitler & F. Roli (Eds.), *1st International Workshop on Multiple Classifier Systems, Lecture Notes in Computer Science, 1857*, (pp. 1–15).

Dietterich, T. G. (2000b). Experimental comparison of three methods for constructing ensembles of decision trees: Bagging, boosting, and randomization. *Machine Learning, 40*(2), 139–157. doi:10.1023/A:1007607513941

Ding, C. H. Q. (2005). A probabilistic model for latent semantic indexing. *Journal of the American Society for Information Science and Technology, 56*(6), 597–608. doi:10.1002/asi.20148

Domeniconi, C., Gullo, F., & Tagarelli, A. (2009). Projective clustering ensembles. In *Proceedings of 2009 Ninth IEEE International Conference on Data Mining, ICDM09* (pp. 794-799). Miami, Florida, USA.

Dorko, G., & Schmid, C. (2005). *Object class recognition using discriminative local features*. INRIA - Rhone-Alpes.

Dozier, C., Jackson, P., Guo, X., Chaudhary, M., & Arumainayagam, Y. (2003). Creation of an expert witness database through text mining. *Proceedings 9th International Conference on Artificial Intelligence and Law*, (pp. 177-184). Edinburgh, Scotland: ACM Press.

Drucker, F. P. (1954). *The practice of management: An introductory view of management*. New York, NY: Harper & Row.

Dubois, D., & Prade, H. (1980). *Fuzzy sets and systems: Theory and applications*. New York, NY: Academic Press.

Dubuisson, M. P., & Jain, A. K. (1994). *A modified Hausdorff distance for object matching*. Paper presented at the International Conference on Pattern Recognition Jerusalem, Israel.

Duda, R. O., Hart, P. E., & Stork, D. G. (2001). *Pattern classification* (2nd ed.). Wiley-Interscience.

Durai, R., Duraisamy, V., & Sahasranaman, K. (2011). Content based image retrieval using fuzzy relaxation and rotational invariance for medical databases. *Proceedings of International Conference on Process Automation, Control and Computing*, (pp. 1-3).

Dworkin, R. (1977). *Taking rights seriously*. Cambridge, MA: Harvard University Press.

Eberhart, R. C. (1992). The role of genetic algorithms in neural network QBL and explanation facilities. In *Proceedings of the international Workshop Combinations of GA and NN*, (pp. 169-183).

Eberhart, R., & Kennedy, J. (1995). A new optimizer using particle swarm theory. In *Proceedings of the Sixth International Symposium on Micro Machine and Human Science*, (pp. 39-43).

Eberhart, R., & Shi, Y. (2001). Particle swarm optimization: Developments, applications and resources. In *Proceedings of Congress on Evolutionary Computation*, (pp. 81-86). Seoul, Korea.

Eberhart, R., Simpson, P., & Dobbins, R. (1996). *Computational intelligence PC tools*. Boston, MA: Academic Press Professional.

Edelman, S., & Intrator, N. (1997). Learning as extraction of low-dimensional representations. In Medlin, D. L., Goldstone, R. L., & Philippe, G. S. (Eds.), *Psychology of learning and motivation* (*Vol. 36*, pp. 353–380). Academic Press.

Eglin, V., Bres, S., & Rivero, C. (2007). Hermite and Gabor transforms for noise reduction and handwriting classification in ancient manuscripts. *International Journal on Document Analysis and Recognition, 9*(2-4), 101–122. doi:10.1007/s10032-007-0039-z

Egmont-Petersena, M., Ridderb, D., & Handelsca, H. (2002). Image processing with neural networks-A review. *Pattern Recognition, 35*.

Eisbruch, A., Ten Haken, R., Kim, H., Marsh, L., & Ship, J. (1999). Dose, volume, and function relationships in parotid salivary glands following conformal and intensity-modulated irradiation of head and neck cancer. *International Journal of Radiation Oncology • Biology • Physics, 45*, 577-587.

Eisbruch, A., Ship, J., Kim, H., & Ten Haken, R. (2001). Partial irradiation of the parotid gland. *Seminars in Radiation Oncology, 11*, 234–239. doi:10.1053/srao.2001.23484

El Naqa, I., Bradley, J., & Deasy, J. (2005). Machine learning methods for radiobiological outcome modeling. *AAPM Symposium Proceedings, 14*, 150-159.

El Naqa, I., Bradley, J., & Deasy, J. (2008). Nonlinear kernel-based approaches for predicting normal tissue toxicities. *Proceedings of 7th International Conference on Machine Learning and Applications*, (pp. 539-544).

El Naqa, I., Bradley, J., Blanco, A., Lindsay, P., Vicic, M., Hope, A., & Deasy, J. (2006). Multivariable modeling of radiotherapy outcomes, including dose-volume and clinical factors. *International Journal of Radiation Oncology • Biology • Physics, 64*, 1275-1286.

El Naqa, I. (2010). Machine learning as new tool for predicting radiotherapy response. *Medical Physics, 37*, 3396. doi:10.1118/1.3469271

El Naqa, I., Bradley, J., Lindsay, P., Hope, A., & Deasy, J. (2009). Predicting radiotherapy outcomes using statistical learning techniques. *Physics in Medicine and Biology, 54*, S9–S30. doi:10.1088/0031-9155/54/18/S02

El Naqa, I., Yang, Y., Galatsanos, N., Nishikawa, R., & Wernick, M. (2004). A similarity learning approach to content based image retrieval: Application to digital mammography. *IEEE Transactions on Medical Imaging, 23*, 1233–1244. doi:10.1109/TMI.2004.834601

El Naqa, I., Yang, Y., Wernick, M., Galatsanos, N., & Nishikawa, R. (2002). A support vector machine approach for detection of microcalcifications. *IEEE Transactions on Medical Imaging, 21*, 1552–1563. doi:10.1109/TMI.2002.806569

Elías, A., Ibarra-Berastegi, G., Arias, R., & Barona, A. (2006). Neural networks as a tool for control and management of a biological reactor for treating hydrogen sulphide. *Bioprocess and Biosystems Engineering, 29*, 129–136. doi:10.1007/s00449-006-0062-3

Elit, L. (2008). Cervical cancer. In Elit, L. (Ed.), *Resource compendium available for cervical and breast cancer control and prevention in the majority world*. New York, NY: Nova Science Publisher, Inc.

Elnagar, A., & Alhajj, R. (2003). Segmentation of connected handwritten numeral strings. *Pattern Recognition, 36*(3), 625–634. doi:10.1016/S0031-3203(02)00097-3

Espana-Boquera, S. (2010). Improving offline handwritten text recognition with hybrid HMM/ANN models. *IEEE Transactions on Pattern Analysis and Machine Intelligence, 99*.

Espejo, P. G., Ventura, S., & Herrera, F. (2010). A survey on the application of genetic programming to classification. *Transactions on Systems, Man, and Cybernetics. Part C, 40*(2), 121–144.

Estrada-Gil, J. K., Fernandez-Lopez, J. C., Hernandez-Lemus, E., & Silva-Zolezzi, I., Hidalgo- Miranda, A., Jimenez-Sanchez, G., & Vallejo-Clemente, E. E. (2007). GPDTI: A genetic programming decision tree induction method to find epistatic effects in common complex diseases. *Bioinformatics (Oxford, England), 23*(13), i167–i174. doi:10.1093/bioinformatics/btm205

Euthman's Images Collection. (2010). *Pathology cases*. Retrieved from http://www.flickr.com/photos/euthman/collections/72157603641714831

Fagin, R. (1996). Combining fuzzy information from multiple systems. *Proceedings of Fifteenth ACM Symposium on Principles of Database Systems*, (pp. 216-226).

Fan, R.-E., Chang, K.-W., Hsieh, C.-J., Wang, X.-R., & Lin, C.-J. (2008). LIBLINEAR - A library for large linear classification. Retrieved May 10, 2010, from http://www.csie.ntu.edu.tw/~cjlin/liblinear/

Fan, R.-E., Chen, P.-H., & Lin, C.-J. (2005). Working set selection using second order information for training SVM. *Journal of Machine Learning Research, 6*, 1889–1918.

Fausett, L. (2002). *Fundamentals of neural networks: Architectures, algorithms and applications*. Englewood Cliffs, NJ: Prentice Hall.

Feng, C., Shuzhen, C., & Libo, Z. (2007). New abnormal cervical cell detection method of multi-spectral Pap smear. *Wuhan University Journal of Natural Sciences, 12*(3), 476–480. doi:10.1007/s11859-006-0108-z

Fern, X. Z., & Brodley, C. E. (2004A). Solving cluster ensemble problems by bipartite graph partitioning. In *Proceedings 21st International Conference on Machine Learning ICML'04*, Vol. 69. New York, NY: ACM.

Fern, X. Z., & Brodley, C. E. (2004). Cluster ensembles for high dimensional clustering: An empirical study. *Journal of Machine Learning Research*, 2004.

Ferragina, P., & Gulli, A. (2004). *The anatomy of a hierarchical clustering engine for web-page, news and book snippets*. Paper presented at the Fourth IEEE International Conference on Data Mining.

Ferragina, P., & Guli, A. (2008). A personalized search engine based on Web-snippet hierarchical clustering. *Software, Practice & Experience, 38*(1), 189–225. doi:10.1002/spe.829

Feuer, A., Savev, S., & Aslam, J. A. (2009). Implementing and evaluating phrasal query suggestion for proximity search. *Information Systems, 34*(1), 711–723. doi:10.1016/j.is.2009.03.012

FeuRosa. P. V. (2000). The electronic judge. *Proceedings of AISB'00 – Symposium on Artificial Intelligence & Legal Reasoning*, Birmingham, UK, April, (pp. 33-36).

Filkov, V., & Skiena, S. (2004). Heterogeneous data integration with the consensus clustering formalism. In *Proceedings of Data Integration in the Life Sciences*, (pp. 110-123).

Fiorino, C., Sanguineti, G., Cozzarini, C., Fellin, G., Foppiano, F., Menegotti, L., … Valdagni, R. (2003). Rectal dose-volume constraints in high-dose radiotherapy of localized prostate cancer. *International Journal of Radiation Oncology • Biology • Physics, 57*, 953-962.

Fisher, D. (1987). Knowledge acquisition via incremental conceptual clustering. *Machine Learning, 2*(2), 139–172. doi:10.1007/BF00114265

Flickner, M., Sawhney, H., Niblack, W., Ashley, J., Huang, Q., & Dom, B. (1995). Query by image and video content: The QBIC system. *IEEE Computer, 28*(9), 23–32. doi:10.1109/2.410146

Forrest, S. (Ed.). (1991). *Emergent computation*. New York, NY: Elsevier.

Forsythe, G. E. (1977). *Computer methods for mathematical computations*. Prentice Hall Press.

Fournier, J., Cord, M., & Philipp-Foliguet, S. (2001). Back-propagation algorithm for relevance feedback in image retrieval. *Proceedings of International Conference on Image Processing*, (Vol. 1, pp. 686-689).

Frank, E., & Witten, I. H. (1998). Generating accurate rule sets without global optimization. In *15th International Conference on Machine Learning*, (pp. 144-151).

Franstrom, F., & Lewis, J. (2000). *Fast, single-pass K-means algorithms*. Retrieved December 27, 2009, from http://citeseerx.ist.psu.edu/viewdoc/summary?doi=10.1.1.36.7008

Freeman, J. A., & Skapura, D. M. (2002). *Neural networks, algorithms, applications and programming techniques*. Addison –Wesley Publication Company.

Freeman, J. S., Jackson, H. D., Steane, D. A., McKinnon, G. E., Dutkowski, G. W., Potts, B. M., & Vaillancourt, R. E. (2001). Chloroplast DNA phylogeography of Eucalyptus globulus. *Australian Journal of Botany, 49*, 585–596. doi:10.1071/BT00094

Freund, Y., & Mason, L. (1999). The alternating decision tree learning algorithm. In *Proceedings 16th International Conference on Machine Learning* (pp. 124-133). Bled, Slovenia.

Freund, Y., & Schapire, R. E. (1996). Experiments with a new boosting algorithm. In *Proceedings 13th International Conference Machine Learning* (pp. 148-156). San Francisco, USA.

Freund, Y., & Schapire, R. E. (1997). A decision-theoretic generalization of on-line learning and an application to boosting. *Journal of Computer and System Sciences, 55*(1), 119–139. doi:10.1006/jcss.1997.1504

Friedman, J., Hastie, T., & Tibshirani, R. (2000). Additive logistic regression: A statistical view of boosting. *Annals of Statistics, 28*(2), 337–374. doi:10.1214/aos/1016218223

Fukunaga, K. (1990). *Introduction to statistical pattern recognition.* San Diego, CA: Academic Press.

Fukuyama, Y., & Yoshida, H. (2001). A particle swarm optimization for reactive power and voltage control in electric power systems. In *Proceedings of Congress on Evolutionary Computation (CEC2001)*, Seoul, Korea.

Fumera, G., Roli, F., & Serrau, A. (2008). A theoretical analysis of bagging as a linear combination of classifiers. *IEEE Transactions on Pattern Analysis and Machine Intelligence, 30*(7), 1293–1299. doi:10.1109/TPAMI.2008.30

Garcia-Pedrajas, N. (2009). Constructing ensembles of classifiers by means of weighted instance selection. *IEEE Transactions on Neural Networks, 20*(2), 258–277. doi:10.1109/TNN.2008.2005496

Gatts, C. E. N., Ovalle, A. R. C., & Silva, C. F. (2005). Neural pattern recognition and multivariate data: Water typology of the Paraíba do Sul River, Brazil. *Environmental Modelling & Software, 20*(7), 883–889. doi:10.1016/j.envsoft.2004.03.018

Gelman, A., Carlin, J. B., Stern, H. S., & Rubin, D. B. (2003). *Bayesian data analysis* (2nd ed.). Boca Raton, FL: Chapman and Hall/CRC.

Gennari, J. H., Langley, P., & Fisher, D. (1990). Models of incremental concept formation. *Artificial Intelligence, 40*, 11–61. doi:10.1016/0004-3702(89)90046-5

Gero, J. S., & Maher, M. L. (1994). *Computational support for emergence in design.* Information Technology in Design Conference, Moscow, September 1994.

Gero, J. S. (1993). Visual emergence in design collaboration. *International Journal of CADCAM and Computer Graphics, 8*(3), 349–357.

Gersho, A., & Gray, R. M. (1991). *Vector quantization and signal compression.* Kluwer Academic Publishers.

Ghosh, R., & Ghosh, M. (2005). An intelligent offline handwriting recognition system using evolutionary neural learning algorithm and rule. *Journal of Research and Practice in Information Technology, 37*(1), 73–87.

Gluck, M., & Myers, C. (2001). *Gateway to memory: An introduction to neural network models of the hippocampus in learning.* Cambridge, MA: MIT Press.

Goder, A., & Filkov, V. (2008). Consensus clustering algorithms: comparison and refinement. In *Proceedings Tenth SIAM Workshop on Algorithm Engineering and Experiments, ALENEX 2008,* (pp. 109-117). Retrieved from http://www.siam.org/proceedings/alenex/2008/alx08_011godera.pdf

Goldberger, J., Roweis, S., Hinton, G., & Salakhutdinov, R. (2004). *Neighborhood component analysis.* Paper presented at the Neural Information Processing Systems (NIPS'04).

Gonzalez, R. C., & Woods, R. E. (2006). *Digital image processing* (3rd ed.). Prentice-Hall, Inc.

Google. (2006). *Google AdWords: Keyword tool.* Retrieved April 2, 2010, from https://adwords.google.com/select/KeywordToolExternal

Google. (2009). *2008 year-end Google zeitgeist.* Retrieved April 2, 2010, from http://www.google.com/intl/en/press/zeitgeist2008/index.html

Gopal, R., & Starkschall, G. (2002). Plan space: representation of treatment plans in multidimensional space. *International Journal of Radiation Oncology • Biology • Physics, 53*, 1328-1336.

Gorrell, G., & Webb, B. (2005). *Generalized Hebbian algorithm for incremental latent semantic analysis.* Paper presented at Interspeech 2005.

Gottumukkal, R., & Asari, V. K. (2004). An improved face recognition technique based on modular PCA approach. *Pattern Recognition Letters, 25*(4), 429–436. doi:10.1016/j.patrec.2003.11.005

Granger, S., Dagneaus, E., Meunier, F., & Paquot, M. (2009). *International corpus of learner English: The ICLE Project, Version 2.* Belgium: UCL Presses Universitaires de Lovain.

Grauman, K., & Darrell, T. (2005). *Efficient image matching with distributions of local invariant features.*

Graves, A., Liwicki, M., Fernandez, S., Bertolami, R., Bunke, H., & Schmidhuber, J. (2009). A novel connectionist system for unconstrained handwriting recognition. *IEEE Transactions on Pattern Analysis and Machine Intelligence, 31*(5), 855-868. Retrieved from 10.1109/TPAMI.2008.137

Gudivada, V. N., & Raghavan, V. V. (1995). *Content-based image retrieval systems.* IEEE, September 1995.

Gujarati, D. N. (1995). *Basic econometrics* (3rd ed.). New York, NY: McGraw-Hill.

Günter, S., & Bunke, H. (2004). HMM-based handwritten word recognition: On the optimization of the number of states, training iterations and Gaussian components. *Pattern Recognition, 37*(10), 2069–2079. doi:10.1016/j.patcog.2004.04.006

Günter, S., & Bunke, H. (2005). Off-line cursive handwriting recognition using multiple classifier systems--On the influence of vocabulary, ensemble, and training set size. *Optics and Lasers in Engineering, 43*(3-5), 437–454. doi:10.1016/j.optlaseng.2004.01.004

Gupta, A. (1996). *Visual information retrieval: A Virage perspective.* Technical Report, Revision 4. San Diego, CA: Virage Inc. Retrieved from http://www.virage.com/wpaper

Gusfield, D. (1997). *Algorithms on strings, trees, and sequences. Computer Science and Computational Biology.* Cambridge, MA: Cambridge University Press. doi:10.1017/CBO9780511574931

Haidar, I., Kulkarni, S., & Pan, H. (2008). Forecasting model for crude oil prices based on artificial neural networks. In *Proceedings of ISSNIP2008, Fourth International Conference Intelligent Sensors, Sensor Networks & Information Processing*, December 15-18, 2008, Sydney, (pp. 103-108).

Hall, M., Frank, E., Holmes, G., Pfahringer, B., Reutemann, P., & Witten, I. H. (2009). The WEKA data mining software: An update. *SIGKDD Explorations, 11*(1), 10–18. doi:10.1145/1656274.1656278

Hamad, H., & Zitar, R. (2010). Development of an efficient neural-based segmentation technique for Arabic handwriting recognition. *Pattern Recognition, 43*(8), 2773–2798. doi:10.1016/j.patcog.2010.03.005

Hämäläinen, M., Hari, R., Ilmoniemi, R., & Knuutila, J., & Lounasma. (1993). Magnetoencephalography, theory, instrumentation, and applications to noninvasive studies of the working human brain. *Reviews of Modern Physics, 65*(2), 413–497. doi:10.1103/RevModPhys.65.413

Hamm, J., & Lee, D. D. (2008). *Grassmann discriminant analysis: a unifying view on subspace-based learning.* Paper presented at the 25th International Conference on Machine Learning, Helsinki, Finland.

Hand, D. J., Mannila, H., & Smyth, P. (2001). *Principles of data mining.* MIT Press.

Han, J. (2001). *Data mining: Concepts and techniques.* San Francisco, CA: Morgan Kaufmann Publishers Inc.

Han, J., & Ma, K. (2002). Fuzzy colour histogram and its use in colour image retrieval. *IEEE Transactions on Image Processing, 11*(8), 944–952. doi:10.1109/TIP.2002.801585

Hansen, L. K. (2000). Blind separation of noicy image mixtures. In Girolami, M. (Ed.), *Advances in independent components analysis* (pp. 159–179). Springer-Verlag. doi:10.1007/978-1-4471-0443-8_9

Hansen, L. K., & Salamon, P. (1990). Neural network ensembles. *IEEE Transactions on Pattern Analysis and Machine Intelligence, 12*(10), 993–1001. doi:10.1109/34.58871

Haralick, R. M. (1979). Statistical and structural approaches to texture. *IEEE Transactions on Systems, Man, and Cybernetics, 67*, 786–804.

Harandi, M. T., Bigdeli, A., & Lovell, B. C. (2010). *Image-set face recognition based on transductive learning.* Paper presented at the International Conference on Image Processing (ICIP2010), Hong Kong.

Harandi, M. T., Nili Ahmadabadi, M., & Araabi, B. N. (2009). Optimal local basis: A reinforcement learning approach for face recognition. *International Journal of Computer Vision, 81*(2), 191–204. doi:10.1007/s11263-008-0161-5

Hart, H. L. A. (1958). Positivism and the separation of law and morals. *Harvard Law Review*, *71*, 593–629. doi:10.2307/1338225

Hastie, T., & Tibshirani, R. (1998). Classification by pairwise coupling. In *Advances in Neural Information Processing Systems*.

Haykin, S. (2009). *Neural networks and learning machines* (3rd ed.). New Jersey, USA: Pearson Education Inc.

Haykin, S. S. (1999). *Neural networks: A comprehensive foundation*. Upper Saddle River, NJ: Prentice Hall.

He, Z., Wei, C., Yang, L., Gao, X., Yao, S., Eberhart, R., & Shi, Y. (1998). Extracting rules from fuzzy neural network by particle swarm optimization. In *Proceedings of IEEE International Conference on Evolutionary Computation (ICEC '98)*, Anchorage, Alaska, USA.

Heikkilä, M., & Pietikäinen, M. (2006). A texture-based method for modeling the background and detecting moving objects. *IEEE Transactions on Pattern Analysis and Machine Intelligence*, *28*(4), 657–662. doi:10.1109/TPAMI.2006.68

Heikkilä, M., Pietikäinen, M., & Schmid, C. (2009). Description of interest regions with local binary patterns. *Pattern Recognition*, *42*(3), 425–436. doi:10.1016/j.patcog.2008.08.014

Hemanth, D. J., Vijila, C. K. S., & Anitha, J. (2010). Performance improved PSO based modified counter propagation neural network for abnormal MR brain image classification. *International Journal of Advances in Soft Computing and its Applications, 2*(1).

Hemanth, D. J., Selvathi, D., & Anitha, J. (2010). Application of adaptive resonance theory neural network for MR brain tumor image classification. *International Journal of Healthcare Information Systems and Informatics, 5*(1), 61–75. doi:10.4018/jhisi.2010110304

Hendler, J. (1997). Intelligent agents: Where AI meets information technology. *IEEE Expert*, *11*(6), 20–23. doi:10.1109/MEX.1996.546578

Heppner, F., & Grenander, U. (1990). A stochastic non-linear model for coordinated bird flocks. In *The ubiquity of chaos*. Washington, DC: AAAS Publications.

Hernandez-Lobáto, D., Martinez-Muñoz, G., & Suárez, A. (2009). Statistical instance-based pruning in ensembles of independent classifiers. *IEEE Transactions on Pattern Analysis and Machine Intelligence*, *31*(2), 364–369. doi:10.1109/TPAMI.2008.204

He, T., Clifford, G., & Tarassenko, L. (2006). Application of independent component analysis in removing artefacts from the electrocardiogram. *Neural Computing & Applications*, *15*(2), 105–116. doi:10.1007/s00521-005-0013-y

Heusch, G., Rodriguez, Y., & Marcel, S. (2006). *Local binary patterns as an image preprocessing for face authentication*. Paper presented at the 7th International Conference on Automatic Face and Gesture Recognition.

He, X., Yan, S., Hu, Y., Niyogi, P., & Zhang, H. J. (2005). Face recognition using Laplacianfaces. *IEEE Transactions on Pattern Analysis and Machine Intelligence*, *27*(3), 328–340. doi:10.1109/TPAMI.2005.55

Hobson, J. B., & Slee, D. (1994). Indexing the Theft Act 1968 for case based reasoning and artificial neural networks. *Proceedings of the Fourth National Conference on Law, Computers and Artificial Intelligence*. Exeter.

Hochbaum, S. (1985). A best possible heuristic for the k-center problem. *Mathematics of Operations Research*, *10*(2), 180–184. doi:10.1287/moor.10.2.180

Hofmann, T. (1999). *Probabilistic latent semantic indexing*. Paper presented at the 22th Annual International SIGIR Conference on Research and Development in Information Retrieval.

Hofmann, T. (2001). Unsupervised learning by probabilistic latent semantic analysis. *Machine Learning*, *42*(1), 177–196. doi:10.1023/A:1007617005950

Hofmann, T. (2004). Latent semantic models for collaborative filtering. *ACM Transactions on Information Systems*, *22*(1), 89–115. doi:10.1145/963770.963774

Holland, J. (1975). *Adaptation in natural and artificial systems*. PhD thesis, University of Michigan, Ann Arbor.

Horiguchi, S., & Inoue, K. (1977). Effects of toluene on the wheel-turning activity and peripheral blood findings in mice: An approach to the maximum allowable concentration of toluene. *The Journal of Toxicological Sciences*, *2*(4), 363–372. doi:10.2131/jts.2.363

Hornik, K., Stinchcombe, M., & White, H. (1989). Multilayer feedforward networks are universal approximators. *Neural Networks, 2*, 359–366. doi:10.1016/0893-6080(89)90020-8

Hosseini, A. E., Amini, J., & Saradjian, M. R. (2003). Back propagation neural network for classification of IRS-1D satellite images. *Proceedings of the Conference of High Resolution Mapping from Space*, Hanover, Germany.

Hotho, A., Maedche, A., & Staab, S. (2001). *Ontology-based text clustering. Text Learning: Beyond Supervision*. Seattle, Washington: IJCAI.

Hsu, C.-W., Chang, C.-C., & Lin, C.-J. (2003). *A practical guide to support vector classification*. Dept. Computer Science, National Taiwan University. Retrieved April 15, 2010, from http://www.csie.ntu.edu.tw/~cjlin

Huang, R., Liu, Q., Lu, H., & Ma, S. (2002). *Solving the small sample size problem of LDA*.

Hunter, D. (1994). Looking for law in all the wrong places: Legal theory and neural networks. In Prakken, H., Muntjewerff, A. J., Soeteman, A., & Winkels, R. (Eds.), *Legal knowledge based systems: the relation with legal theory*. Lelystad, The Netherlands: Koninklijke Vermende.

Hwang, J. N., Choi, J. J., Oh, S., & Marks, R. (1991). Query-based learning applied to partially trained multilayer perceptrons. *IEEE Transactions on Neural Networks, 2*(1), 131–136. doi:10.1109/72.80299

Hyvarinen, A., Cristescu, R., & Oja, E. (1999). *A fast algorithm for estimating overcomplete ICA bases for image windows*. Paper presented at the International Joint Conference on Neural Networks, IJCNN '99.

Hyvärinen, A. (1999). Fast and robust fixed-point algorithms for independent component analysis. *IEEE Transactions on Neural Networks, 10*(3), 626–634. doi:10.1109/72.761722

Hyvärinen, A., Karhunen, J., & Oja, E. (2001). *Independent component analysis*. Wiley-Interscience. doi:10.1002/0471221317

Hyvärinen, A., & Oja, E. (1997). A fast fixed-point algorithm for independent component analysis. *Neural Computation, 9*(7), 1483–1492. doi:10.1162/neco.1997.9.7.1483

Hyvärinen, A., & Oja, E. (2000). Independent component analysis: algorithms and applications. *Neural Networks, 13*(4-5), 411–430. doi:10.1016/S0893-6080(00)00026-5

Ikeda, K., Yanagihara, T., Matsumoto, K., & Takishima, Y. (2009). Unsupervised text normalization approach for morphological analysis of blog documents. In A. Nicholson & X. Li (Eds.), *Advances in Artificial Intelligence, AI 2009, Lecture Notes in Artificial Intelligence, 5866*, 401-411.

Ikeda, S., & Murata, N. (1999). A method of ICA in time-frequency domain. *Proceedings of the International Workshop on Independent Component Analysis*.

International Commission on Illumination (CIE). (2011). *Selected colorimetric tables*. Vienna, Austria: CIE Central Bureau. Retrieved March 14, 2011, from http://www.cie.co.at/index.php/LEFTMENUE/ index.php?i_ca_id=298

Ionescu, M., & Ralescu, A. (2005). Image clustering for a fuzzy hamming distance based CBIR systems. *Proceedings of the Sixteen Midwest Artificial Intelligence and Cognitive Science Conference, MAICS-2005*, (pp. 102-108).

Ionescu, M., & Ralescu, R. (2004). Fuzzy hamming distance in a content based image retrieval systems. *Proceedings of FUZZ-IEEE 2004*, Budapest.

Isaakson, M., Jalden, J., & Murphy, M. (2005). On using an adaptive neural network to predict lung tumor motion during respiration for radiotherapy applications. *Medical Physics, 32*, 3801–3809. doi:10.1118/1.2134958

Ishibuchi, H., Nakashima, T., & Nii, M. (2004). *Classification and modeling with linguistic information granules: Advanced approaches to linguistic data mining*. Berlin, Germany: Springer.

Islam, M. (2006). *Reducing semantic gap in content based image retrieval using region based relevance feedback techniques*. Retrieved from http://www.gscit.monash.edu.au/gscitweb/seminar.php?id=41

Islam, M. M., Yao, X., Shahriar, S. M., Islam, M. A., & Murase, K. (2008). Bagging and boosting negatively correlated neural networks. *IEEE Transactions on Systems, Man, and Cybernetics. Part B, 38*(3), 771–784.

Jackson, A., Skwarchuk, M., Zelefsky, M., Cowen, D., Venkatraman, E., Levegrun, … Ling, C. (2001). Late rectal bleeding after conformal radiotherapy of prostate cancer (II): Volume effects and dose-volume histograms. *International Journal of Radiation Oncology • Biology • Physics, 49,* 695-698.

Jackson, A. (2001). Partial irradiation of the rectum. *Seminars in Radiation Oncology, 11,* 215–223. doi:10.1053/srao.2001.23481

Jacobs, R. A., Jordan, M. I., Nowlan, S. J., & Hinton, G. E. (1991). Adaptive mixtures of local experts. *Neural Computation, 3,* 79–87. doi:10.1162/neco.1991.3.1.79

Jain, A. K., & Dubes, R. C. (1988). *Algorithms for clustering data.* London, UK: Prentice Hall.

Jain, A. K., & Li, S. Z. (2005). *Handbook of face recognition.* New York, NY: Springer-Verlag, Inc.

Jain, A. K., Murty, M. N., & Flynn, P. J. (1999). Data clustering: A review. *ACM Computing Surveys, 31*(3), 264–323. doi:10.1145/331499.331504

Jain, A., & Zongker, D. (2002). Feature selection: Evaluation, application, and small sample performance. *IEEE Transactions on Pattern Analysis and Machine Intelligence, 19*(2), 153–158. doi:10.1109/34.574797

Jang, J.-S. R., Sun, S.-T., & Mizutani, E. (1997). *Neurofuzzy and Soft-computing: A computational approach to learning and machine intelligence.* New Jersey, USA: Prentice-Hall Inc.

Janruang, J., & Kreesuradej, W. (2006). *A new Web search result clustering based on true common phrase label discovery.* Paper presented at the International Conference on Computational Inteligence for Modelling Control and Automation and International Conference on Intelligent Agents Web Technologies and International Commerce.

Jayarathna, U., & Bandara, G. (2006). New segmentation algorithm for offline handwritten connected character segmentation. *First International Conference on Industrial and Information Systems,* (pp. 540-546).

Jeong, B. R., Chung, J. B., Kim, S. H., Lee, Y. D., Cho, H. J., & Baek, N. J. (2003). Rhizosphere enhances removal of organic matter and nitrogen from river water in floodplain filtration. *Korean Journal of Soil Science and Fertilizer, 36,* 8–15.

Jeong, J., Sekiguchi, K., & Sakamoto, K. (2004). Photochemical and photocatalytic degradation of gaseous toluene using short-wavelength UV irradiation with TiO_2 catalyst: Comparison of three UV sources. *Chemosphere, 57,* 663–671. doi:10.1016/j.chemosphere.2004.05.037

Jepson, A. D., & Fleet, D. J. (2007). *Image segmentation.* Retrieved from www.cs.toronto.edu/~jepson/csc2503/segmentation.pdf

Jing, L., Zhou, L., Ng, M., & Huang, J. Z. (2006). *Ontology-based distance measure for text mining.* Sixth SIAM International Conference on Data Mining (SDM), Bethesda, Maryland.

Jing, F., Li, M., Zhang, H. J., & Zhang, B. (2004). An efficient and effective region-based image retrieval framework. *IEEE Transactions on Image Processing, 13*(5), 699–709. doi:10.1109/TIP.2004.826125

Joachims, T. (1997). A probabilistic analysis of the Rocchio algorithm with TF-IDF for text categorization. In *Proceedings 14th International Conference on Machine Learning,* (pp. 143-151).

Joachims, T. (1999). *Transductive inference for text classification using support vector machines.* Paper presented at the Sixteenth International Conference on Machine Learning.

Joachims, T. (2003). *Transductive learning via spectral graph partitioning.* Paper presented at the International Conference on Machine Learning (ICML).

Jodogne, S. (2006). *Closed-loop learning of visual control policies.* PhD thesis, University of Liege. Retrieved from http://www.montefiore.ulg.ac.be/\~{}jodogne/jodogne-phd.pdf

Jodogne, S., & Piater, J. H. (2005). *Interactive learning of mappings from visual percepts to actions.* Paper presented at the 22nd International Conference on Machine Learning, Bonn, Germany.

Jodogne, S., & Piater, J. H. (2007). Closed-loop learning of visual control policies. *Journal of Artificial Intelligence Research, 28,* 349–391.

Joho, M., & Rahbar, K. (2003). *Joint diagonalization of correlation matrices by using Newton methods with application to blind signal separation.*

Joho, M., Mathis, H., & Lambert, R. (2000). Overdetermined blind source separation: Using more sensors than source signals in a noisy mixture.

Joshi, A., & Motwani, R. (2006). *Keyword generation for search engine advertising.* Paper presented at the Sixth IEEE International Conference on Data Mining.

Justino, E., Bortolozzi, F., & Sabourin, R. (2005). A comparison of SVM and HMM classifiers in the off-line signature verification. *Pattern Recognition Letters, 26*(9), 1377–1385. doi:10.1016/j.patrec.2004.11.015

Kab´an. (2000). *Clustering of text documents by skewness maximization.*

Kanarek, A., & Micheal, M. (1996). Groundwater recharge with municipal effluent: Dan region reclamation project, Israel. *Water Science and Technology, 34,* 227–233. doi:10.1016/S0273-1223(96)00842-6

Karnik, N. N., & Mendel, J. M. (2001a). Centroid of a type-2 fuzzy set. *Information Sciences, 132*(6), 195–220. doi:10.1016/S0020-0255(01)00069-X

Karnik, N. N., & Mendel, J. M. (2001b). Operations on type-2 fuzzy sets. *International Journal on Fuzzy Sets & Systems, 122,* 327–348. doi:10.1016/S0165-0114(00)00079-8

Karnik, N. N., Mendel, J. M., & Qilian, L. (1999). Type-2 fuzzy logic systems. *IEEE Transactions on Fuzzy Systems, 7*(6), 643–658. doi:10.1109/91.811231

Karp, G. C. (2005). *Cell and molecular biology: Concepts and experiments* (4th ed.). Jefferson City, MO: Von Hoffman Press.

Karthikesh, R. (2000). *Sparse priors on the mixing matrix in independent component analysis.* Paper presented at the Workshop on Independent Component Analysis and Blind Signal Separation (ICA2000).

Karypis, G., & Kumar, V. (1998). *METIS: A software package for partitioning unstructured graphs, partitioning meshes, and computing fill-reducing orderings of sparse matrices.* Technical Report, University of Minnesota, Department of Computer Science and Engineering, Army HPC Research Centre, Minneapolis.

Karypis, G., & Kumar, V. (1999). A fast and high quality multilevel scheme for partitioning irregular graphs. *SIAM Journal on Scientific Computing, 20*(1), 359–392. doi:10.1137/S1064827595287997

Kato, M., Chen, Y.-W., & Xu, G. (2006). *Articulated hand tracking by PCA-ICA approach.* Paper presented at the FGR '06: The 7th International Conference on Automatic Face and Gesture Recognition.

Kaufman, L., & Rousseeuw, P. J. (1990). *Finding groups in data: An introduction to cluster analysis.* New York, NY: John Wiley & Sons.

Kavallieratou, E., Stamatatos, E., Fakotakis, N., & Kokkinakis, G. (2000). Handwritten character segmentation using transformation-based learning. *15th International Conference on Pattern Recognition,* (Vol. 2, pp. 634-637).

Keerthi, S. S., Shevade, S. K., Bhattacharyya, C., & Murthy, K. R. K. (2001). Improvements to Platt's SMO algorithm for SVM classifier design. *Neural Computation, 13*(3), 637–649. doi:10.1162/089976601300014493

Keerthi, S. S., Shevade, S. K., Bhattacharyya, C., & Murthy, K. R. K. (2001). Improvements to Platt's SMO algorithm for SVM classifier design. *Neural Computation, 13*(3), 637–649. doi:10.1162/089976601300014493

Kelarev, A., Kang, B., & Steane, D. (2006). Clustering algorithms for ITS sequence data with alignment metrics. *Advances in Artificial Intelligence, 19th Australian Joint Conference on Artificial Intelligence, AI06, Lecture Notes Artificial Intelligence, 4304,* (pp. 1027-1031).

Kennedy, J. (1999). Small worlds and mega-minds: Effects of neighborhood topology on particle swarm performance. In *Proceedings of the 1999 Conference on Evolutionary Computation,* (pp. 1931-1938).

Kennedy, J., & Eberhart, R. (1995). Particle swarm optimization. In *Proceedings of International Conference on Neural Networks (ICNN'95),* (Vol. 4, pp. 1942-1948). Perth, Australia.

Kennedy, J., & Eberhart, R. C. (1997). A discrete binary version of the particle swarm algorithm. In *IEEE International Conference on Systems, Man and Cybernetics,* (Vol. 5, pp. 4104-4108). Orlando, Florida, USA.

Kennedy, J., & Mendes, R. (2002). Topological structure and particle swarm performance. In *Proceedings of the Fourth Congress on Evolutionary Computation (CEC-2002)*.

Kennedy, J., & Eberhart, R. (2001). *Swarm intelligence*. Morgan Kaufmann Publishers.

Khemchandani, R., & Chandra, S. (2007). Twin support vector machines for pattern classification. *IEEE Transactions on Pattern Analysis and Machine Intelligence, 29*(5), 905–910. doi:10.1109/TPAMI.2007.1068

Khosla, A., Kumar, S., & Aggarwal, K. K. (2005). A framework for identification of fuzzy models through particle swarm optimization algorithm. In *Proceedings of IEEE Indicon 2005 Conference*, Chennai, India.

Kim, T.-K., Arandjelovic, O., & Cipolla, R. (2007). Boosted manifold principal angles for image set-based recognition. *Pattern Recogn., 40*(9), 2475-2484. doi: http://dx.doi.org/10.1016/j.patcog.2006.12.030

Kim, J., Choi, J., Yi, J., & Turk, M. (2005). Effective representation using ICA for face recognition robust to local distortion and partial occlusion. *IEEE Transactions on Pattern Analysis and Machine Intelligence, 27*(12), 1977–1981. doi:10.1109/TPAMI.2005.242

Kim, K. I., Jung, K., & Kim, H. J. (2002). Face recognition using kernel principal component analysis. *IEEE Signal Processing Letters, 9*(2), 40–42. doi:10.1109/97.991133

Kim, S.-H., Chung, J.-B., Lee, Y.-D., & Prasher, S. O. (2003). Electron affinity coefficients of nitrogen oxides and biodegradation kinetics in denitrification of contaminated stream water. *Journal of Environmental Quality, 32*, 1474–1480. doi:10.2134/jeq2003.1474

Kittler, J., Hatef, M., Duin, R. P. W., & Matas, J. (1998). On combining classifiers. *IEEE Transactions on Pattern Analysis and Machine Intelligence, 20*(3), 226–239. doi:10.1109/34.667881

Knowledge System Laboratory at Stanford University. (2003). *The BB1 Blackboard control architecture*. Retrieved from http://www.ksl.stanford.edu/projects/BB1/bb1.html

Ko, A., Cavalin, P., Sabourin, R., & Britto, A. (2009). Leave-one-out-training and leave-one-out-testing hidden Markov models for a handwritten numeral recognizer: The implications of a single classifier and multiple classifications. *IEEE Transactions on Pattern Analysis and Machine Intelligence, 31*(12), 2168–2178. doi:10.1109/TPAMI.2008.254

Koerich, A. L., Sabourin, R., & Suen, C. Y. (2005). Recognition and verification of unconstrained handwritten words. *IEEE Transactions on Pattern Analysis and Machine Intelligence, 27*(10), 1509–1522. doi:10.1109/TPAMI.2005.207

Kogilavani, A., & Balasubramanie, P (2009). Ontology enhanced clustering based summarization of medical documents. *International Journal of Recent Trends in Engineering, 1*.

Kohavi, R. (1995). The power of decision tables. In *Proceedings 8th European Conference on Machine Learning* (pp. 174-189).

Kohavi, R., & John, G. (1996). Wrappers for feature subset selection. *Artificial Intelligence, 97*(1-2), 273–324. doi:10.1016/S0004-3702(97)00043-X

Kohonen, T. (1989). *Self organization and associative memory*. New York, NY: Springer – Verlaag Publication.

Koknar-Tezel, S., & Latecki, L. J. (2009). Improving SVM classification on imbalanced data sets in distance spaces. In *Proceedings 2009 Ninth IEEE International Conference on Data Mining, ICDM09* (pp. 259-267). Miami, Florida, USA.

Kolda, T. G., & O'Leary, D. P. (1998). A semidiscrete matrix decomposition for latent semantic indexing in information retrieval. *ACM Transactions on Information Systems, 16*(4), 322–346. doi:10.1145/291128.291131

Kolenda, T. (2000). Independent components in text. In Girolami, M. (Ed.), *Advances in independent components analysis* (pp. 229–250). Springer-Verlag. doi:10.1007/978-1-4471-0443-8_13

Konar, A. (2005). *Computational intellingence: Principles, techniques and applications*. Heidelberg, Germany: Springer-Verlag.

Kontostathis, A., & Pottenger, W. M. (2002). *Detecting patterns in the LSI term-term matrix.* Paper presented at the ICDM'02 Workshop on Foundations of Data Mining and Discovery.

Koppel, M., Schler, J., & Zigdon, K. (2005). Determining an author's native language by mining a text for errors. In *Proceedings 11th International Conference Knowledge Discovery and Data Mining, ACM SIGKDD* (pp. 624-628). Chicago, Illinois, USA.

Koza, J. R. (1991). Concept formation and decision tree induction using the genetic programming paradigm. In *PPSN I: Proceedings of the 1st Workshop on Parallel Problem Solving from Nature,* (pp. 124–128). London, UK: Springer-Verlag.

Kretowski, M. (2004). An evolutionary algorithm for oblique decision tree induction. In *International Conference on Advances in Soft Computing,* (pp. 432–437).

Kruschke, J. K. (1992). ALCOVE: An exemplar-based connectionist model of category learning. *Psychological Review, 99,* 22–44. doi:10.1037/0033-295X.99.1.22

Kulkarni, S., Verma, B., Sharma, P., & Selvaraj, H. (1999). Content based image retrieval using a neuro-fuzzy technique. *Proceedings of IEEE International Joint Conference on Neural Networks,* (pp. 846-850). Washington, USA.

Kulkarni, S., & Haidar, I. (2009). Forecasting model for crude oil price using artificial neural networks and commodity future prices. *International Journal of Computer Science and Information Security, 2*(1), 1–8.

Kulkarni, S., & Verma, B. (2002). An intelligent hybrid approach for content based image retrieval. *International Journal of Computational Intelligence and Applications, 2*(2), 173–184. doi:10.1142/S1469026802000567

Kumar, C. P. (2003). *Fresh water resources: A perspective, international year of fresh water - 2003.* Roorkee, India: National Institute of Hydrology. Retrieved August 10, 2010, from http://www.angelfire.com/bc/nihhrrc/documents/fresh.html

Kumar, R., & Singh, A. (2010). Detection and segmentation of lines and words in Gurmukhi handwritten text. *Advance Computing, IEEE International Conference on* (pp. 353-356).

Kumar, V., Abbas, A., Fausto, N., & Mitchell, R. (2007). *Robbins basic pathology.* Philadelphia, PA: Saunders Publishing Co.

Kuncheva, L. I., Rodríguez, J. J., Plumpton, C. O., Linden, D. E. J., & Johnston, S. J. (2010). Random subspace ensembles for fMRI classification. *IEEE Transactions on Medical Imaging, 29*(2), 531–542. doi:10.1109/TMI.2009.2037756

Kuncheva, L. I., & Whitaker, C. J. (2003). Measures of diversity in classifier ensembles and their relationship with the ensemble accuracy. *Machine Learning, 51*(3), 181–207. doi:10.1023/A:1022859003006

Kunjikutty, S. P., Prasher, S. O., Patel, R. M., Barrington, S. F., & Kim, S. H. (2007). Simulation of nitrogen transport in soil under municipal wastewater application using LEACHN. *Journal of the American Water Resources Association, 43,* 1097–1107. doi:10.1111/j.1752-1688.2007.00086.x

Ku, Y., Tseng, K. Y., & Wang, W. Y. (2005). Decomposition of gaseous acetone in an annular photoreactor coated with TiO_2 thin film. *Water, Air, and Soil Pollution, 168,* 313–323. doi:10.1007/s11270-005-1778-4

Kwak, K. C., & Pedrycz, W. (2007). Face recognition using an enhanced independent component analysis approach. *IEEE Transactions on Neural Networks, 18*(2), 530–541. doi:10.1109/TNN.2006.885436

LaGrega, M. D., Buckingham, P. L., & Evans, J. C. (2001). *Hazardous waste management* (2nd ed.). Singapore: McGraw Hill.

Lai, L. B., Chang, R. I., & Kouh, J. S. (2007). *A time-series predicative model using query-based backpropagation neural networks.* Asia Pacific Industrial Engineering & Management System and 2007 Chinese Institute of Industrial Engineers Conference.

Lai, L. B., Chang, R. I., & Kouh, J. S. (2006). Mining data by query-based error-propagation. *Lecture Notes in Computer Science, 3610,* 1224–1233. doi:10.1007/11539087_162

Lai, L. B., Chang, R. I., & Kouh, J. S. (2009). Detecting network intrusions using signal processing with query-based sampling filter. *EURASIP Journal on Advances in Signal Processing, 2009.*

Lam, L., Lee, S., & Suen, C. Y. (1992). Thinning methodologies-a comprehensive survey. *IEEE Transactions on Pattern Analysis and Machine Intelligence, 14*(9), 869–885. doi:10.1109/34.161346

Langley, P., & Simon, H. (1995). Applications of machine learning and rule induction. *Communications of the ACM, 38*(11), 55–64. doi:10.1145/219717.219768

Langton, G. L. (1989). *Artificial life*. Addision-Wesley.

Lassouaoui, N., Hamami, L., & Nouali, N. (2005). Morphological description of cervical cell images for the pathological recognition. *World Academy of Science. Engineering and Technology, 5*, 49–52.

Lawler, R. (1964). *Stare decisis* and electronic computers. In Schubert, G. (Ed.), *Judicial behaviour: A reader in theory and research* (pp. 492–505). Chicago, IL: Rand McNally & Company.

Lee, H., & Verma, B. (2009). Binary segmentation with neural validation for cursive handwriting recognition. *IEEE International Joint Conference on Neural Networks, IJCNN 2009* (pp. 1730-1735).

Lee, K.-C., Ho, J., & Kriegman, D. J. (2005). Acquiring linear subspaces for face recognition under variable lighting. *IEEE Transactions in Pattern Analysis and Machine Intelligence, 27*(5), 684-698. doi: http://dx.doi.org/10.1109/TPAMI.2005.92

Lee, T.-W., Lewicki, M., & Sejnowski, T. (1999). *Unsupervised classification with non-Gaussian mixture models using ICA*. Paper presented at the 1998 Conference on Advances in Neural Information Processing Systems II.

Lee, H. M., Huang, C. C., & Hung, W. T. (2007). Mining navigation behaviors for term suggestion of search engines. *Journal of Information Science and Engineering, 23*, 387–401.

Lee, H., & Yoo, S. (2001). A neural network based image retrieval using nonlinear combination of heterogeneous features. *International Journal of Computational Intelligence and Applications, 1*(2), 137–149. doi:10.1142/S1469026801000123

Lee, H., & Yoo, S. (2001). Applying neural network to combining the heterogeneous features in content-based image retrieval. *Proceedings of SPIE Applications of Artificial Neural Networks in Image Processing, 4305*(13), 81–89.

Lee, T.-W. (1998). *Independent component analysis: Theory and applications*. Kluwer Academic Publishers.

Lee, T.-W., Lewicki, M. S., Girolami, M., & Sejnowski, T. J. (1999). Blind source separation of more sources than mixtures using overcomplete representations. *IEEE Signal Processing Letters, 6*(4), 87–90. doi:10.1109/97.752062

LegalXML. (2004). Retrieved March 15, 2004, from http://www.legalxml.org/

Leibe, B., & Schiele, B. (2003). *Analyzing appearance and contour based methods for object categorization*.

Lennernas, B., Sandberg, D., Albertsson, P., Silen, A., & Isacsson, U. (2004). The effectiveness of artificial neural networks in evaluating treatment plans for patients requiring external beam radiotherapy. *Oncology Reports, 12*, 1065–1070.

Leuski, A., & Allan, J. (2000). Improving interactive retrieval by combining ranked list and clustering. *Proceedings of RIAO,* College de France, (pp. 665-681). Paris.

Levenberg, K. (1944). A method for the solution of certain non-linear problems in least squares. *Quarterly of Applied Mathematics, 2*, 164–168.

Lewicki, M. S., & Sejnowski, T. J. (2000). Learning overcomplete representations. *Neural Computation, 12*(2), 337–365. doi:10.1162/089976600300015826

Lewis, D. (1991). Learning in intelligent information retrieval. *Proceedings of the International Workshop on Machine Learning,* (pp. 235–239). Evanston, Illinois.

Li, R., Lewis, J., & Jiang, S. (2009). Markerless fluoroscopic gating for lung cancer radiotherapy using generalized linear discriminant analysis. *Proceedings of 8th International Conference on Machine Learning and Applications,* (pp. 468-472).

Liang, Q., & Mendel, J. M. (2000b). Interval type-2 fuzzy logic systems. In *Proceeding of FUZZ IEEE '00,* San Antonio, TX.

Liang, Q., Karnik, N. N., & Mendel, J. M. (2000). Connection admission control in ATM networks using survey-based type-2 fuzzy logic systems. *IEEE Transactions on Man, Cybernetics Part C. Applications and Reviews, 30*, 329–339.

Liang, Q., & Mendel, J. M. (2000a). Equalization of non-linear time-varying channels using type-2 fuzzy adaptive filters. *IEEE Transactions on Fuzzy Systems, 8*, 551–563. doi:10.1109/91.873578

Liang, Q., & Mendel, J. M. (2000c). Interval type-2 fuzzy logic systems: Theory and design. *IEEE Transactions on Fuzzy Systems, 8*(5), 535–550. doi:10.1109/91.873577

Liang, Q., & Mendel, J. M. (2000d). Overcoming time-varying co-channel interference using type-2 fuzzy adaptive filter. *IEEE Transactions on Circuits and Systems-II: Analog and Digital Signal Processing, 47*(12), 1419–1428. doi:10.1109/82.899635

Liang, Q., & Mendel, J. M. (2001). MPEG VBR video traffic modeling and classification using fuzzy techniques. *IEEE Transactions on Fuzzy Systems, 9*(1), 183–193. doi:10.1109/91.917124

Lian, H. C., & Lu, B. L. (2007). Multi-view gender classification using multi-resolution local binary patterns and support vector machines. *International Journal of Neural Systems, 17*(6), 479–487. doi:10.1142/S0129065707001317

Li, F., & Wechsler, H. (2005). Open set face recognition using transduction. *IEEE Transactions on Pattern Analysis and Machine Intelligence, 27*(11), 1686–1697. doi:10.1109/TPAMI.2005.224

Linden, A., & Kindermann, J. (1989). Inversion of multilayer nets. In *Proceedings of the International Joint Conference on Neural Networks,* (pp. 425-430).

Lin, T., Cerviño, L., Tang, X., Vasconcelos, N., & Jiang, S. (2009a). Fluoroscopic tumor tracking for image-guided lung cancer radiotherapy. *Physics in Medicine and Biology, 54*, 981–992. doi:10.1088/0031-9155/54/4/011

Lin, T., Li, R., Tang, X., Dy, J., & Jiang, S. (2009b). Markerless gating for lung cancer radiotherapy based on machine learning techniques. *Physics in Medicine and Biology, 54*, 1555–1563. doi:10.1088/0031-9155/54/6/010

Li, S. Z., Lu, X. G., Hou, X., Peng, X., & Cheng, Q. (2005). Learning multiview face subspaces and facial pose estimation using independent component analysis. *IEEE Transactions on Image Processing, 14*(6), 705–712. doi:10.1109/TIP.2005.847295

Liu, B., Cao, L., Yu, P. S., & Zhang, C. (2008). Multi-space-mapped SVMs for multi-class classification. In *Proceedings Eighth IEEE International Conference on Data Mining, ICDM08* (pp. 911-916). Pisa, Italy.

Liu, X., & Randall, R. B. (2005). *Redundant data elimination in independent component analysis.* Paper presented at the Eighth International Symposium on Signal Processing and Its Applications, 2005.

Liu, Y., Zhao, T., & Zhang, J. (2002, November). *Learning multispectral texture features for cervical cancer detection.* Paper presented at the IEEE Symposium on Biomedical Imaging: SBI 02. Macro to Nano. Retrieved from IEEE Xplore: http://ieeexplore.ieee.org/ xpl/free-abs_all.jsp? arnumber=1029220

Liu, C. (2004). Gabor-based kernel PCA with fractional power polynomial models for face recognition. *IEEE Transactions on Pattern Analysis and Machine Intelligence, 26*(5), 572–581. doi:10.1109/TPAMI.2004.1273927

Liu, C., Nakashima, K., Sako, H., & Fujisawa, H. (2003). Handwritten digit recognition: Benchmarking of state-of-the-art techniques. *Pattern Recognition, 36*(10), 2271–2285. doi:10.1016/S0031-3203(03)00085-2

Liu, C., & Wechsler, H. (2000). Evolutionary pursuit and its application to face recognition. *IEEE Transactions on Pattern Analysis and Machine Intelligence, 22*(6), 570–582. doi:10.1109/34.862196

Liu, C., & Wechsler, H. (2003). Independent component analysis of Gabor features for face recognition. *IEEE Transactions on Neural Networks, 14*(4), 919–928. doi:10.1109/TNN.2003.813829

Liu, H., & Motoda, H. (1988). *Feature extraction, construction and selection: A data mining perspective.* Dordrecht, The Netherlands: Kluwer.

Liu, Y., Wang, X. L., Wang, H. Y., Zha, H., & Qin, H. (2010). Learning robust similarity measures for 3D partial shape retrieval. *International Journal of Computer Vision, 89*(2-3), 408–431. doi:10.1007/s11263-009-0298-x

Liu, Y., & Yao, X. (1999). Simultaneous training of negatively correlated neural networks in an ensemble. *IEEE Transactions on Systems, Man, and Cybernetics. Part B, 29*(6), 716–725.

Li, Y., & Guo, L. (2007). An active learning based TCM-KNN algorithm for supervised network intrusion detection. *Computers & Security, 26*, 459–467. doi:10.1016/j.cose.2007.10.002

Llewellyn, K. (1962). *Jurisprudence*. Chicago, IL: University of Chicago Press.

Llora, X., & Garrell, J. M. (2001) Evolution of decision trees. In *Proceedings of the 4th Catalan Conference on Artificial Intelligence,* (pp. 115–122). ACIA Press.

Long, C., Huang, M. L., Zhu, X. Y., & Li, M. (2009). Multi-document summarization by information distance. In *Proceedings Ninth IEEE International Conference on Data Mining, ICDM09* (pp. 866-871). Miami, Florida, USA.

Lorigo, L. M., & Govindaraju, V. (2006). Offline Arabic handwriting recognition: A survey. *IEEE Transactions on Pattern Analysis and Machine Intelligence, 28*(5), 712–724. doi:10.1109/TPAMI.2006.102

Loveard, T., & Ciesielski, V. (2002) Employing nominal attributes in classification using genetic pro- gramming. In L. Wang, K.C. Tan, T. Furuhashi, J.H. Kim, & X. Yao (Eds.), *Proceedings of the 4th Asia-Pacific Conference on Simulated Evolution And Learning (SEAL'02),* (pp. 487–491). IEEE, Orchid Country Club, Singapore.

Loveard, T., & Ciesielski, V. (2001). Representing classification problems in genetic programming. *Evolutionary Computation, 2*.

Lowe, D. G. (2004). Distinctive image features from scale-invariant keypoints. *International Journal of Computer Vision, 60*(2), 91–110. doi:10.1023/B:VISI.0000029664.99615.94

Lu, Z., Wu, X., & Bongard, J. (2009). Active learning with adaptive heterogeneous ensembles. In *Proceedings 2009 Ninth IEEE International Conference on Data Mining, ICDM09* (pp. 327-336). Miami, Florida, USA.

Lua, A. C., & Jia, Q. (2009). Adsorption of phenol by oil-palm-shell activated carbons in a fixed bed. *Chemical Engineering Journal, 150*, 455–461. doi:10.1016/j.cej.2009.01.034

Lui, Y. M., Beveridge, J. R., Draper, B. A., & Kirby, M. (2008). *Image-set matching using a geodesic distance and cohort normalization.*

Lu, J., Plataniotis, K. N., & Venetsanopoulos, A. N. (2003). Face recognition using kernel direct discriminant analysis algorithms. *IEEE Transactions on Neural Networks, 14*(1), 117–126. doi:10.1109/TNN.2002.806629

Lu, J., Plataniotis, K. N., Venetsanopoulos, A. N., & Li, S. Z. (2006). Ensemble-based discriminant learning with boosting for face recognition. *IEEE Transactions on Neural Networks, 17*(1), 166–178. doi:10.1109/TNN.2005.860853

Lukas, L., Devos, A., & Suykens, A. K. (2004). Brain tumor classification based on long echo proton MRS signals. *Artificial Intelligence in Medicine, 31*, 73–89. doi:10.1016/j.artmed.2004.01.001

Lula, P., & Paliwoda-Pekosz, G. (2008). An ontology-based cluster analysis framework. *Proceedings of the First International Workshop on Ontology-Supported Business Intelligence*, (pp.1-6), Karlsruhe, Germany.

Lycos. (2008). *Top search terms for 2008.* Retrieved April 2, 2010, from http://www.lycos.com

Ma, B., Li, H., & Tong, R. (2007). Spoken language recognition using ensemble classifiers. *IEEE Transactions on Audio, Speech, and Language Processing, 15*(7), 2053–2062. doi:10.1109/TASL.2007.902861

Mackay, D. J. C. (1996). *Maximum likelihood and co-variant algorithms for independent component analysis.*

MacKay, D. (1992). Information-based objective functions for active data selection. *Neural Computation, 4*, 590–604. doi:10.1162/neco.1992.4.4.590

Mackey, M. C., & Glass, L. (1987). Oscillation and chaos in physiological control systems. *Science, 197*, 287–289. doi:10.1126/science.267326

Maclin, R., & Shavlik, J. W. (1995). Combining the predictions of multiple classifiers: Using competitive learning to initialize neural networks. *International Joint Conference on Artificial Intelligence*, (pp. 524–531).

Mäenpää, T., & Pietikäinen, M. (2004). Classification with color and texture: Jointly or separately? *Pattern Recognition, 37*(8), 1629–1640. doi:10.1016/j.patcog.2003.11.011

Maier, H. R., & Dandy, G. C. (1998). The effect of internal parameters and geometry on the performance of back-propagation neural networks: An empirical study. *Environmental Modelling & Software, 13*(2), 193–209. doi:10.1016/S1364-8152(98)00020-6

Maier, H. R., & Dandy, G. C. (2001). Neural network based modelling of environmental variables: A systematic approach. *Mathematical and Computer Modelling, 33*(6-7), 669–682. doi:10.1016/S0895-7177(00)00271-5

Malik, H. H., & Kender, J. R. (2008). Classifying high-dimensional text and web data using very short patterns. In *Proceedings 2008 Eighth IEEE International Conference on Data Mining, ICDM08* (pp. 923-928). Pisa, Italy.

Marinai, S., Gori, M., & Soda, G. (2005). Artificial neural networks for document analysis and recognition. *IEEE Transactions on Pattern Analysis and Machine Intelligence, 27*(1), 23–35. doi:10.1109/TPAMI.2005.4

Marquardt, D. (1963). An algorithm for least-squares estimation of nonlinear parameters. *SIAM Journal on Applied Mathematics, 11*, 431–441. doi:10.1137/0111030

Martin, J. (1995). Clustering full text documents. *Proceedings of the IJCAI Workshop on Data Engineering for Inductive Learning at IJCAI-95*. Montreal, Canada.

Martin, M. A., Keuning, S., & Janssen, D. B. (1998). *Handbook on biodegradation and biological treatment of hazardous organic compounds* (2nd ed.). Dordrecht, The Netherlands: Academic Press.

Mat-Isa, N. A., Mashor, M. Y., & Othman, N. H. (2003). Classification of cervical cancer cells using HMLP network with confidence percentage and confidence level analysis. *International Journal of The Computer. The Internet and Management, 11*(1), 17–29.

Matsuoka, K., Ohya, M., & Kawamoto, M. (1995). A neural net for blind separation of nonstationary signals. *Neural Networks, 8*(3), 411–419. doi:10.1016/0893-6080(94)00083-X

Matthew, J. (2004). *Perceptrons*. Generation5.org website. Retrieved March 16, 2011, from http://www.generation5.org/ content/1999/ perceptron.asp

Ma, W., & Manjunath, B. (1999). NETRA: A toolbox for navigating large image databases. *Journal of ACM Multimedia Systems, 7*(3), 184–198. doi:10.1007/s005300050121

McCormick, D. N. (1978). *Legal reasoning and legal theory*. Oxford, UK: Clarendon Press.

McCue, C. (2007). *Data mining and predictive analysis intelligence gathering and crime analysis*. Elsevier, Inc.

McCulloch, W., & Pitts, W. (1943). A logical calculus of the ideas immanent in nervous activity. *The Bulletin of Mathematical Biophysics, 7*, 115–133. doi:10.1007/BF02478259

Medin, D. L., & Schaffer, M. M. (1978). Context theory of classification learning. *Psychological Review, 85*, 207–238. doi:10.1037/0033-295X.85.3.207

Mehta, D., Diwakar, E. S. V. N. L. S., & Jawahar, C. V. (2003). *A rule-based approach to image retrieval*. Retrieved from www.iiit.net/techreports/2003_8.pdf

Mei, Q., Zhou, D., & Church, K. (2008). *Query suggestion using hitting time*. Paper presented at the 17th ACM Conference on Information and Knowledge Mining.

Melin, P., & Castillo, O. (2005). *Hybrid intelligent systems for pattern recognition using soft computing: An evolutionary approach for neural networks and fuzzy systems*. Heidelberg, Germany: Springer-Verlag.

Mendel, J. M. (1999). Computing with words, when words can mean different things to different people. In *Proceedings of Third International ICSC Symposium on Fuzzy Logic and Applications*, Rochester University, Rochester, NY.

Mendel, J. M. (2000). Uncertainty, fuzzy logic, and signal processing. *Signal Processing, 80*(6), 913–933. doi:10.1016/S0165-1684(00)00011-6

Mendel, J. M. (2001). *Uncertain rule-based fuzzy logic systems: Introduction and new directions*. Upper Saddle River, NJ: Prentice-Hall.

Mendel, J. M. (2007). Computing with words and its relationships with fuzzistics. *Information Science, 177*(4), 988–1006. doi:10.1016/j.ins.2006.06.008

Mendel, J. M., John, R. I., & Liu, F. (2006). Interval type-2 fuzzy logic systems made simple. *IEEE Transactions on Fuzzy Systems*, *14*(6), 808–821. doi:10.1109/TFUZZ.2006.879986

Mendes, R. (2004). *Population topologies and their influence in particle swarm performance*. PhD thesis, University of Minho.

Mendez, G., & Castillo, O. (2005). Interval type-2 TSK fuzzy logic systems using hybrid learning algorithm. In *Proceeding of IEEE FUZZ Conference*, (pp. 230-235). Reno, NV.

Merkl, D., Schweighofer, E., & Winiwarter, W. (1999). Exploratory analysis of concept and document spaces with connectionist networks. *Artificial Intelligence and Law*, *7*(2-3), 185–209. doi:10.1023/A:1008365524782

Metzler, D., & Croft, W. B. (2007). *Latent concept expansion using Markov random fields*. Paper presented at the 30th Annual International ACM SIGIR Conference on Research and Development in Information Retrieval.

Meyer, R., Zhang, H., Goadrich, L., Nazareth, D., Shi, L., & D'Souza, W. (2007). A multi-plan treatment planning framework: A paradigm shift for IMRT. *International Journal of Radiation Oncology • Biology • Physics, 68*, 1178-1189.

Meyer, C. D. (2000). *Matrix analysis and applied linear algebra*. Cambridge, UK: Cambridge Press. doi:10.1137/1.9780898719512

Microsoft. (2006). *Microsoft adCenter*. Retrieved April 2, 2010, from http://adcenter.microsoft.com/

Mikolajczyk, K., Leibe, B., & Schiele, B. (2005). *Local features for object class recognition*.

Mikolajczyk, K., & Schmid, C. (2005). A performance evaluation of local descriptors. *IEEE Transactions on Pattern Analysis and Machine Intelligence*, *27*(10), 1615–1630. doi:10.1109/TPAMI.2005.188

Min, R., Stanley, D., Yuan, Z., Bonner, A., & Zhang, Z. L. (2009). A deep non-linear feature mapping for large-margin kNN classification. In *Proceedings Ninth IEEE International Conference on Data Mining, ICDM09* (pp. 357-366). Miami, Florida, USA.

Mitra, P., Mitra, S., & Pal, S. K. (2000). Staging of cervical cancer with soft computing. *IEEE Transactions on Bio-Medical Engineering*, *47*(7), 934–940. doi:10.1109/10.846688

Mizumoto, M., & Tanaka, K. (1976). Some properties of fuzzy sets of type-2. *Information and Control*, *31*, 312–340. doi:10.1016/S0019-9958(76)80011-3

Moghaddam, B. (2002). Principal manifolds and probabilistic subspaces for visual recognition. *IEEE Transactions on Pattern Analysis and Machine Intelligence*, *24*(6), 780–788. doi:10.1109/TPAMI.2002.1008384

Mo, J. H., Zhang, Y. P., Xu, Q., Lamson, J. J., & Zhao, R. (2009). Photocatalytic purification of volatile organic compounds in indoor air: A literature review. *Atmospheric Environment*, *43*, 2229–2246. doi:10.1016/j.atmosenv.2009.01.034

Momani, F. A. (2007). Treatment of air containing volatile organic carbon: Elimination and post treatment. *Environmental Engineering Science*, *24*, 1038–1047. doi:10.1089/ees.2006.0162

Momma, M., Morinaga, S., & Komura, D. (2009). Promoting total efficiency in text clustering via iterative and interactive metric learning. In *Proceedings 2009 Ninth IEEE International Conference on Data Mining, ICDM09* (pp. 878-883). Miami, Florida, USA.

Monari, E., Maerker, J., & Kroschel, K. (2009). *A robust and efficient approach for human tracking in multi-camera systems*.

Montazer, G. A., Saremi, H. Q., & Khatibi, V. (2010). A neuro-fuzzy inference engine for Farsi numeral characters recognition. *Expert Systems with Applications*, *37*(9), 6327–6337. doi:10.1016/j.eswa.2010.02.088

Montgomery, D. C. (2005). *Design and analysis of experiments* (5th ed.). New York, NY: Wiley.

Morris, C. G., & Maisto, A. A. (2001). *Psychology: An introduction*. Prentice Hall Press.

Mosher, J. C., Lewis, P. S., & Leahy, R. M. (1992). Multiple dipole modeling and localization from spatio-temporal MEG data. *IEEE Transactions on Bio-Medical Engineering*, *39*(6), 541–557. doi:10.1109/10.141192

Mozaffari, S., Faez, K., Margner, V., & El-Abed, H. (2008). Lexicon reduction using dots for off-line Farsi/Arabic handwritten word recognition. *Pattern Recognition Letters, 29*(6), 724–734. doi:10.1016/j.patrec.2007.11.009

Muhlbaier, M. D., Topalis, A., & Polikar, R. (2009). Learn++. NC: Combining ensemble of classifiers with dynamically weighted consult-and-vote for efficient incremental learning of new classes. *IEEE Transactions on Neural Networks, 20*(1), 152–168. doi:10.1109/TNN.2008.2008326

Muneesawang, P., & Guan, L. (2002). Automatic machine interactions for CBIR using self organized tree map architecture. *IEEE Transactions on Neural Networks, 13*(4), 821–834. doi:10.1109/TNN.2002.1021883

Munley, M., Lo, J., Sibley, G., Bentel, G., Anscher, M., & Marks, L. (1999). A neural network to predict symptomatic lung injury. *Physics in Medicine and Biology, 44*, 2241–2249. doi:10.1088/0031-9155/44/9/311

Murphy, M. (2008). Using neural networks to predict breathing motion. *Proceedings of 7th International Conference on Machine Learning and Applications,* (pp. 528-532).

Murphy, M., Jalden, J., & Isaksson, M. (2002). Adaptive filtering to predict lung tumor breathing motion during image-guided radiation therapy. *Proceedings of 16th International Congress on Computer Assisted Radiology and Surgery,* (pp. 539-544).

Murphy, M., & Dieterich, S. (2006). Comparative performance of linear and nonlinear neural networks to predict irregular breathing. *Physics in Medicine and Biology, 51*, 5903–5914. doi:10.1088/0031-9155/51/22/012

Mustafa, N., Mat-Isa, N. A., Mashor, M. Y., & Othman, N. H. (2008). Capability of new features of cervical cells for cervical cancer diagnostic system using hierarchical neural network. *International Journal of Simulation, Systems. Science & Technology, 9*(2), 56–64.

Nadeau, C., & Bengio, Y. (2003). Inference for the generalization error. *Machine Learning, 52*(3), 239–281. doi:10.1023/A:1024068626366

Nadler, D. A. (1977). *Feedback and organization development: Using data based methods.* Reading, MA: Addison-Wesley.

Naik, G., Kumar, D., & Palaniswami, M. (2008). *Multi run ICA and surface EMG based signal processing system for recognising hand gestures.* Paper presented at the 8th IEEE International Conference on Computer and Information Technology, CIT 2008.

Naik, G., Kumar, D., & Weghorn, H. (2007). *Performance comparison of ICA algorithms for isometric hand gesture identification using surface EMG.* Paper presented at the 2007 3rd International Conference on Intelligent Sensors, Sensor Networks and Information, Melbourne, Australia.

Naik, G., Kumar, D., Singh, V., & Palaniswami, M. (2006). *Hand gestures for HCI using ICA of EMG.* Paper presented at the VisHCI '06: The HCSNet Workshop on Use of Vision in human-Computer Interaction.

Naik, G., Kumar, D., Weghorn, H., & Palaniswami, M. (2007). *Subtle hand gesture identification for HCI using temporal decorrelation source separation BSS of surface EMG.* Paper presented at the 9th Biennial Conference of the Australian Pattern Recognition Society on Digital Image Computing Techniques and Applications (DICTA 2007), Glenelg, Australia.

Naka, S., Genji, T., Yura, T., & Fukuyama, Y. (2001). Practical distribution state estimation using hybrid particle swarm optimization. In *Proc. of IEEE Power Engineering Society Winter Meeting, Columbus, Ohio, USA.*

Nakajima, S., Tatemura, J., Hino, Y., Hara, Y., & Tanaka, K. (2005). Discovering important bloggers based on analyzing blog threads. In *Proceedings 2nd Annual Workshop on the Weblogging Ecosystem: Aggregation, Analysis and Dynamics.*

Nanni, L., & Lumini, A. (2008). Local binary patterns for a hybrid fingerprint matcher. *Pattern Recognition, 41*(11), 3461–3466. doi:10.1016/j.patcog.2008.05.013

Nara, K., & Mishima, Y. (2001). Particle swarm optimisation for fault state power supply reliability enhancement. In *Proceedings of IEEE International Conference on Intelligent Systems Applications to Power Systems (ISAP2001),* Budapest.

Natarajan, P. (2009). Stochastic segment modeling for offline handwriting recognition. *International Conference on Document Analysis and Recognition,* (pp. 971-975).

Nath, A. K., Rehman, S. M., & Salah, A. (2005). An enhancement of k-nearest neighbour classification using genetic algorithm. *Proceedings of the MICS*, (pp. 1-12).

Nattkemper, T. W. (2004). Multivariate image analysis in biomedicine. *Journal of Biomedical Informatics, 37*(5), 380–391. doi:10.1016/j.jbi.2004.07.010

Negi, S., Joshi, S., Chalamalla, A. K., & Subramaniam, L. V. (2009). Automatically extracting dialog models from conversation transcripts. In *Proceedings Ninth IEEE International Conference on Data Mining, ICDM09* (pp. 890-895). Miami, Florida, USA.

Nemr, A. E. (2009). Potential of pomegranate husk carbon for Cr(VI) removal from wastewater: Kinetic and isotherm studies. *Journal of Hazardous Materials, 161*, 132–141. doi:10.1016/j.jhazmat.2008.03.093

Newell, A. (1990). *Unified theories of cognition.* Cambridge, MA: Harvard University Press.

Newell, A., & Simon, H. A. (1961). Computer simulation of human thinking. *Science, 134*, 2011–2017. doi:10.1126/science.134.3495.2011

Newman, D., Hettich, S., Blake, C., & Merz, C. (1998). *UCI repository of machine learning databases.* Retrieved from http://www.ics.uci.edu/~mlearn/mlrepository.html

Ni, X., Xue, G. R., Ling, X., Yu, Y., & Yang, Q. (2007). Exploring in the weblog space by detecting informative and affective articles. In *Proceedings of the 16th International World Wide Web Conference, WWW2007* (pp. 281-290).

Niblack, W., Barber, R., Equitz, W., Flickner, M. D., Glasman, E. H., Petkovic, D., et al. (1993). *QBIC project: Querying images by content, using color, texture, and shape.*

Nilsson, N. J. (1998). *Introduction to machine learning.* Stanford, CA: Stanford University, Department of Computer Science.

Nishikawa, T., Abe, H., Saruwatari, H., & Shikano, K. (2004). *Overdetermined blind separation for convolutive mixtures of speech based on multistage ICA using subarray processing.* Paper presented at the IEEE International Conference on Acoustics, Speech, and Signal Processing, 2004 (ICASSP '04).

Nopsuwanchai, R., Biem, A., & Clocksin, W. F. (2006). Maximization of mutual information for offline Thai handwriting recognition. *IEEE Transactions on Pattern Analysis and Machine Intelligence, 28*(8), 1347–1351. doi:10.1109/TPAMI.2006.167

Norouzi, E., Nili Ahmadabadi, M., & Nadjar Araabi, B. (2010). Attention control with reinforcement learning for face recognition under partial occlusion. *Machine Vision and Applications, 22*(2), 1–12.

Nosofsky, R. M. (1986). Attention, similarity, and the identiδcation-categorization relationship. *Journal of Experimental Psychology. General, 115*(1), 39–57. doi:10.1037/0096-3445.115.1.39

Nunez, C. (1998). VOCs: Sources, definitions and considerations for recovery. In *EPA, Volatile Organic Compounds (VOC) Recovery Seminar*, September 16-17, Cincinnati, OH, (pp. 3-4).

Ogle, V., & Stonebraker, M. (1195). Chabot: Retrieval from a relational database of images. *IEEE Computer, 28*(9), 40-48.

Oh, J., & El Naqa, I. (2009). Bayesian network learning for detecting reliable interactions of dose-volume related parameters in radiation pneumonitis. *Proceedings of 8th International Conference on Machine Learning and Applications,* (pp. 484-488).

Oh, J., Al-Lozi, R., & El Naqa, I. (2009). Application of machine learning techniques for prediction of radiation pneumonitis in lung cancer patients. *Proceedings of 8th International Conference on Machine Learning and Applications,* (pp. 478-483).

Oh, I., & Suen, C. (2002). A class-modular feedforward neural network for handwriting recognition. *Pattern Recognition, 35*(1), 229–244. doi:10.1016/S0031-3203(00)00181-3

Oja, E., Laaksonen, J., Koskela, M., & Brandt, S. (1997). Self organising maps for content based image database retrieval. In Oja, E., & Kaski, S. (Eds.), *Kohonen Maps* (pp. 349–362). Amsterdam.

Ojala, T., Pietikainen, M., & Maenpaa, T. (2002). Multi-resolution gray-scale and rotation invariant texture classification with local binary patterns. *IEEE Transactions on Pattern Analysis and Machine Intelligence, 24*(7), 971–987. doi:10.1109/TPAMI.2002.1017623

Osinski, S., & Weiss, D. (2005). A concept-driven algorithm for clustering search results. *IEEE Intelligent Systems, 20*(3), 48–54. doi:10.1109/MIS.2005.38

Pajunen, P. (1998). Source separation using algorithmic information theory. *Neurocomputing, 22*, 35–48. doi:10.1016/S0925-2312(98)00048-4

Palaniappan, R., & Eswaran, C. (2009). Using genetic algorithm to select the presentation order of training patterns that improves simplified fuzzy ARTMAP classification performance. *Applied Soft Computing, 9*, 100–106. doi:10.1016/j.asoc.2008.03.003

Paletta, L., Fritz, G., & Seifert, C. (2005). *Q-learning of sequential attention for visual object recognition from informative local descriptors.* Paper presented at the 22nd International Conference on Machine Learning, Bonn, Germany.

Palmer, J. D. (1985). Comparative organization of chloroplast genomes. *Annual Review of Genetics, 19*, 325–354. doi:10.1146/annurev.ge.19.120185.001545

Pan, H., Haidar, I., & Kulkarni, S. (2009). Daily prediction of short-term trends of crude oil prices using neural networks exploiting multimarket dynamics. *Frontiers of Computer Science in China, 3*(2), 177–191. doi:10.1007/s11704-009-0025-3

Parikh, D., & Polikar, R. (2007). An ensemble-based incremental learning approach to data fusion. *IEEE Transactions on Systems, Man, and Cybernetics. Part B, 37*(2), 437–450.

Park, L. A. F., Leckie, C. A., Ramamohanarao, K., & Bezdek, J. C. (2009). Adapting spectral co-clustering to documents and terms using latent semantic analysis. In A. Nicholson & X. Li (Eds.), *Advances in Artificial Intelligence, AI 2009, Lecture Notes in Artificial Intelligence, 5866*, 301-311.

Parra, J., & Kalitzin, S., & Lopes. (2004). Magnetoencephalography: An investigational tool or a routine clinical technique? *Epilepsy & Behavior, 5*(3), 277–285. doi:10.1016/j.yebeh.2004.02.003

Parsopoulos, K. E., & Vrahatis, M. N. (2002). In Recent approaches to global optimization problems through particle swarm optimization. *Natural Computing, 1*(2-3), 235–306. doi:10.1023/A:1016568309421

Paterno, M., Lim, F., & Leow, W. (2004). Fuzzy semantic labelling for image retrieval. *International Conference on Multimedia and Expo*, (Vol. 2, pp. 767-770).

Pedrero, F., Kalavrouziotis, I., José Alarcón, J., Koukoulakis, P., & Asano, T. (2010). Use of treated municipal wastewater in irrigated agriculture-Review of some practices in Spain and Greece. *Agricultural Water Management, 97*, 1233–1241. doi:10.1016/j.agwat.2010.03.003

Pennebaker, J. W., Chung, C. K., Ireland, M., Gonzales, A., & Booth, R. J. (2007). *The development and psychometric properties of LIWC2007.* Retrieved October 20, 2010, from http://www.liwc.net

Pentland, A., Picard, R., & Sclaroff, S. (1996). Content-based manipulation of image databases. *International Journal of Computer Vision, 3*, 233–254. doi:10.1007/BF00123143

Peterson, M. R., Doom, T. E., & Raymer, M. L. (2005). GA-facilitated classifier optimization with varying similarity measures. *Proceedings of the IEEE Conference on Genetic and Evolutionary Computation*, (pp. 2514-2525).

Philipps, L. (1989). Are legal decisions based on the application of rules or prototype recognition? Legal science on the way to neural networks. In *the Pre-Proceedings of the Third International Conference on Logica, Informatica, Diritto*, (p. 673). Florence, Italy: IDG.

Phillips, L., & Sartor, G. (1999). From legal theories to neural networks and fuzzy reasoning. *Artificial Intelligence and Law, 7*(2-3), 115–128. doi:10.1023/A:1008371600675

Plamondon, R., & Srihari, S. N. (2000). Online and offline handwriting recognition: A comprehensive survey. *IEEE Transactions on Pattern Analysis and Machine Intelligence, 22*(1), 63–84. doi:10.1109/34.824821

Platt, J. (1999). Fast training of support vector machines using sequential minimal optimization. *Advances in kernel methods: Support vector learning,* (pp. 185-208).

Plötz, T., & Fink, G. A. (2009). Markov models for offline handwriting recognition: A survey. *International Journal Document Analysis and Recognition, 12*(4), 269–298. doi:10.1007/s10032-009-0098-4

Polettini, N. (2004). *The vector space model in information retrieval - Term weighting problem.* Department of Information and Communication Technology, University of Trento.

Polikar, R. (2006). Ensemble based systems in decision making. *IEEE Circuits and Systems Magazine, 6*(3), 22–44. doi:10.1109/MCAS.2006.1688199

Ponce, J., Hebert, M., Schmid, C., & Zisserman, A. (2007). *Toward category-level object recognition.* Lecture Notes in Computer Science New York, NY: Springer-Verlag, Inc.

Pound, R. (1908). Mechanical jurisprudence. *Columbia Law Review, 8,* 605. doi:10.2307/1108954

Powers, W. T. (1973). *Behavior: The control of perception.* New York, NY: Wiley.

Prastawa, M., Bullit, E., & Moon, N. (2003). Automatic brain tumor segmentation by subject specific modification of atlas priors. *Medical Image Computing, 10,* 1341–1348.

Pratt, W. K. (1991). *Digital image processing.* New York, NY: John Wiley & Sons.

Prayitno, A. (2006). Cervical cancer with Human Papilloma Virus and Epstein Barr virus positive. *Journal of Carcinogenesis, 5*(13), 1–4.

Proedrou, K., Nouretdinov, I., Vovk, V., & Gammerman, A. (2002). *Transductive confidence machines for pattern recognition.* Paper presented at the 13th European Conference on Machine Learning.

Qasim, S. R. (1999). *Wastewater treatment plants: Planning, design, and operation* (2nd ed.). CRC Press.

Quinlan, J. R. (1996). Bagging, boosting, and c4.5. In *Proceedings of the Thirteenth National Conference on Artificial Intelligence,* (pp. 725–730). AAAI Press.

Quinlan, J. R. (1986). Induction of decision trees. *Machine Learning, 1,* 81–106. doi:10.1007/BF00116251

Quinlan, R. (1993). *C4.5: Programs for machine learning.* San Mateo, CA: Morgan Kaufmann.

Quinney, D. (1985). *An introduction to the numerical solution of differential equation.* Hertforshire, UK: Research Studies.

Rachev, S. T. (1985). The Monge--Kantorovich mass transference problem and its stochastic applications. *Theory of Probability and Its Applications, 29*(4), 647–676. doi:10.1137/1129093

Radovanović, M., & Ivanović, M. (2006). CatS: A classification-powered meta-search engine. *Advances in Web Intelligence and Data Mining, 23*(1), 191–200. doi:10.1007/3-540-33880-2_20

Rajapakse, J. C., Cichocki, A., & Sanchez. (2002). *Independent component analysis and beyond in brain imaging: EEG, MEG, fMRI, and PET.* Paper presented at the 9th International Conference on Neural Information Processing, ICONIP '02.

Ramírez, M. C. V., Velho, H. F. de C., & Ferreira, N. J. (2005). Artificial neural network technique for rainfall forecasting applied to the São Paulo region. *Journal of Hydrology (Amsterdam), 301*(1-4), 146–162. doi:10.1016/j.jhydrol.2004.06.028

Ramos-Pollán, R., Guevara-López, M., Suárez-Ortega, C., Díaz-Herrero, G., & Franco-Valiente, J., Rubio-Del-Solar, … Ramos, I. (2011). Discovering mammography-based machine learning classifiers for breast cancer diagnosis. *Journal of Medical Systems*; epub ahead of print. doi:10.1007/s10916-011-9693-2

RapidKeyword. (2006). *Rapid keyword -Keyword research software and keyword generator tools.* Retrieved April 2, 2010, from http://www.rapidkeyword.com/

Rasmussen, C. E., & Williams, C. K. I. (2006). *Gaussian processes for machine learning.* Cambridge, MA: MIT Press.

Raubeson, L. A., & Jansen, R. K. (2005). Chloroplast genomes of plants. In Wallingford, H. R. J. (Ed.), *Plant diversity and evolution: Genotypic and phenotypic variation in higher plants* (pp. 45–68). doi:10.1079/9780851999043.0045

Ravi, R., Philip, L., & Swaminathan, T. (2010). An intelligent neural model for evaluating performance of compost biofilter treating dichloromethane vapors. In *Proceedings of the 2010 Duke-UAM Conference on Biofiltration for Air Pollution Control*, (pp. 49-58).

Read, J., Pfahringer, B., & Holmes, G. (2008). Multi-label classification using ensembles of pruned sets. In *Proceedings 2008 Eighth IEEE International Conference on Data Mining, ICDM08* (pp. 995-1000). Pisa, Italy.

Reed, R., Marks, R. J., & Oh, S. (1995). Similarities of error regularization, sigmoid gain scaling, target smoothing, and training with jitter. *IEEE Transactions on Neural Networks, 6*, 529–538. doi:10.1109/72.377960

Rekimoto, J. (2001). GestureWrist and GesturePad: Unobtrusive wearable interaction devices. *Proceedings Fifth International Symposium on Wearable Computers*, (pp. 21-27).

Ren, J., Lee, S. D., Chen, X., Kao, B., Cheng, R., & Cheung, D. (2009). Naive Bayes classification of uncertain data. In *Proceedings Ninth IEEE International Conference on Data Mining, ICDM09* (pp. 944-949). Miami, Florida, USA.

Rene, E. R., Maliyekkal, S. M., Swaminathan, T., & Philip, L. (2006). Back propagation neural network for performance prediction in trickling bed air biofilter. *International Journal of Environment and Pollution, 28*, 382–401. doi:10.1504/IJEP.2006.011218

Rene, E. R., Murthy, D. V. S., & Swaminathan, T. (2005). Performance evaluation of a compost biofilter treating toluene vapors. *Process Biochemistry, 40*, 2771–2779. doi:10.1016/j.procbio.2004.12.010

Rene, E. R., Veiga, M. C., & Kennes, C. (2009). Experimental and neural model analysis of styrene removal from polluted air in a biofilter. *Journal of Chemical Technology and Biotechnology (Oxford, Oxfordshire), 84*, 941–948. doi:10.1002/jctb.2130

Reproductive Health Technologies Project. (2008). *HPV vaccine update*. Retrieved from http://www.rhtp.org/fertility/cervix/documents/HPVVaccineUpdateFinal.pdf

Reynolds, C. W. (1987). Flocks, herds and schools: A distributed behavioral model. *Computer Graphics, 21*(4), 25–34. doi:10.1145/37402.37406

Riedmiller, M., & Braun, H. (1993). A direct adaptive method for faster backpropagation learning: The RPROP algorithm. In *Proceedings of the IEEE International Conference on Neural Networks 1993* (ICNN – 93).

Rissland, E. L., & Friedman, M. T. (1995). Detecting change in legal concepts. *Proceedings of the 5th International Conference on Artificial Intelligence and Law*, Melbourne, Australia, June 30 – July 4, (pp. 127-136). New York, NY: ACM Press.

Rodriguez, J. J. (2006). Rotation forest: A new classifier ensemble method. *IEEE Transactions on Pattern Analysis and Machine Intelligence, 28*(10), 1619–1630. doi:10.1109/TPAMI.2006.211

Romeijn, H., Dempsey, J., & Li, J. (2004). A unifying framework for multi-criteria fluence map optimization models. *Physics in Medicine and Biology, 49*, 1991–2013. doi:10.1088/0031-9155/49/10/011

Rosario, B. (2000). *Latent semantic indexing: An overview*. Retrieved April 2, 2010, from http://people.ischool.berkeley.edu/~rosario/projects/LSI.pdf

Rosen, I., Liu, H., Childress, N., & Liao, Z. (2005). Interactively exploring optimized treatment plans. *International Journal of Radiation Oncology • Biology • Physics, 61*, 570-582.

Rosenblatt, F. (1958). The perceptron: A probabilistic model for information storage in the brain. *Psychological Review, 65*, 365–408. doi:10.1037/h0042519

Rosenfeld, A., & Kak, A. C. (1982). *Digital picture processing* (*Vol. 2*). New York, NY: Academic Press.

Roth, D., & Tu, Y. C. (2009). Aspect guided text categorization with unobserved labels. In *Proceedings Ninth IEEE International Conference on Data Mining, ICDM09* (pp. 962-967). Miami, Florida, USA.

Ruan, D., & Keall, P. (2010). Online prediction of respiratory motion: multidimensional processing with low-dimensional feature learning. *Physics in Medicine and Biology, 55*, 3011–3025. doi:10.1088/0031-9155/55/11/002

Rubner, Y., Tomasi, C., & Guibas, L. J. (2000). Earth mover's distance as a metric for image retrieval. *International Journal of Computer Vision, 40*(2), 99–121. doi:10.1023/A:1026543900054

Rumelhart, D. E., Hinton, G. E., & Williams, R. J. (1986). Learning internal representations by error propagation. In Rumelhart, D. E., & McClelland, J. L. (Eds.), *Parallel distributed processing* (pp. 318–362). Cambridge, MA: MIT Press.

Rumelhart, D. E., & McClelland, J. L.PDP Research Group. (1986). *Parallel and distributed processing (Vol. I-II)*. Cambridge, USA: MIT Press.

Rumelhart, D. E., & Norman, D. A. (1978). Accretion, tuning, and restructuring: Three modes of learning. In Cotton, J. W., & Klatzky, R. L. (Eds.), *Semantic factors in cognition*. Hillsdale, NJ: Lawrence Erlbaum Associates.

Russell, S. J., & Norvig, P. (2003). *Artificial intelligence: A modern approach* (2nd ed.). Prentice Hall.

Saeed, K., & Albakoor, M. (2009). Region growing based segmentation algorithm for typewritten and handwritten text recognition. *Applied Soft Computing, 9*(2), 608–617. doi:10.1016/j.asoc.2008.08.006

Sahoo, G. B., Ray, C., Wang, J. Z., Hubbs, S. A., Song, R., Jasperse, J., & Seymour, D. (2005). Use of artificial neural networks to evaluate the effectiveness of riverbank filtration. *Water Research, 39*, 2505–2516. doi:10.1016/j.watres.2005.04.020

Saini, J. S., Gopal, M., & Mittal, A. P. (2004). Evolving optimal fuzzy logic controllers by genetic algorithms. *Journal of the Institution of Electronics and Telecommunication Engineers, 50*(3), 179–190.

Saleem, S., Cao, H., Subramanian, K., Kamali, M., Prasad, R., & Natarajan, P. (2009). Improvements in BBN☐s HMM-based offline Arabic handwriting recognition system. *International Conference on Document Analysis and Recognition,* (pp. 773-777).

Salerno, J. (1997). Using the particle swarm optimization technique to train a recurrent neural model. In *Proceedings of 9th International Conference on Tools with Artificial Intelligence (ICTAI'97)*.

Salton, G. (1989). *Automatic text processing: the transformation, analysis and retrieval of information by computer*. Addison-Wesley Longman Publishing.

Schapire, R. E. (1990). The strength of weak learnability. *Machine Learning, 5*(2), 197–227. doi:10.1007/BF00116037

Scherg, M., & Von Cramon, D. (1985). Two bilateral sources of the late AEP as identified by a spatio-temporal dipole model. *Electroencephalography and Clinical Neurophysiology, 62*(1), 32–44. doi:10.1016/0168-5597(85)90033-4

Seaborn, M., & Hepplewhite, L. (1999). Fuzzy colour category map for content based image retrieval. *Tenth British Machine Vision Conference*, (pp. 103-112).

Segev, A., Leshno, M., & Zviran, M. (2007). Context recognition using Internet as a knowledge base. *Journal of Intelligent Information Systems, 29*(3), 305–327. doi:10.1007/s10844-006-0015-y

Seliya, N., & Khoshgoftaar, T. M. (2010). Active learning with neural networks for intrusion detection. In *Proceedings of the 11th IEEE International Conference on Information Reuse and Integration,* Las Vegas.

Selman, B. (1989). Connectionist systems for natural language understanding. *Artificial Intelligence Review, 3*, 23–31. doi:10.1007/BF00139194

Serre, T., Wolf, L., Bileschi, S., Riesenhuber, M., & Poggio, T. (2007). Robust object recognition with cortex-like mechanisms. *IEEE Transactions on Pattern Analysis and Machine Intelligence, 29*(3), 411–426. doi:10.1109/TPAMI.2007.56

Shahabi, C., & Chen, Y. (2000). Soft query in image retrieval systems. *Proceedings of the SPIE Internet Imaging (EI14), Electronic Imaging, Science and Technology*, San Jose, California, (pp. 57-68).

Shan, C., Gong, S., & McOwan, P. W. (2005). *Robust facial expression recognition using local binary patterns*. Paper presented at the IEEE International Conference on Image Processing, 2005. ICIP 2005.

Sharma, R., Singh, K., Singhal, D., & Ghosh, R. (2004). Neural network applications for detecting process faults in packed towers. *Chemical Engineering and Processing, 43*(7), 841–847. doi:10.1016/S0255-2701(03)00103-X

Sharp, G., Jiang, S., Shimizu, S., & Shirato, H. (2004). Prediction of respiratory tumour motion for real-time image-guided radiotherapy. *Physics in Medicine and Biology, 49*, 425–440. doi:10.1088/0031-9155/49/3/006

Shechtman, E., & Irani, M. (2007). *Matching local self-similarities across images and videos*.

Shevade, S., Keerthi, S., Bhattacharyya, C., & Murthy, K. (2000). Improvements to SMO algorithm for SVM regression. *IEEE Transactions on Neural Networks, 11*, 1188–1193. doi:10.1109/72.870050

Shi, Y., & Eberhart, R. (1999). Empirical study of particle swarm optimization. In *Proceedings of Congress on Evolutionary Computation*, (pp. 1945-1950).

Shi, Y., & Eberhart, R. C. (1998). A modified particle swarm optimizer. In *Proceedings of the IEEE International Conference on Evolutionary Computation*, (pp. 69-73).

Shi, X. H., Liang, Y. C., Lee, H. P., Lu, C., & Wang, Q. X. (2007). Particle swarm optimization based algorithms for TSP and generalized TSP. *Information Processing Letters, 103*, 169–176. doi:10.1016/j.ipl.2007.03.010

Shi, Y., Eberhart, R., & Chen, Y. (1999). Implementation of evolutionary fuzzy systems. *IEEE Transactions on Fuzzy Systems, 7*(5), 109–119. doi:10.1109/91.755393

Shrivastava, S., & Singh, M. P. (2010). Performance evaluation of feed-forward neural network with soft computing techniques for hand written English alphabets. *Applied Soft Computing, 11*(1), 1156–1182. doi:10.1016/j.asoc.2010.02.015

Siebert, U., Sroczynski, G., Hillemanns, P., Engel, J., Stabenow, R., & Stegmaier, C. (2006). The German cervical cancer screening model: Development and validation of a decision-analytic model for cervical cancer screening in Germany. *European Journal of Public Health, 16*(2), 185–192. doi:10.1093/eurpub/cki163

Silva, C., Lotrič, U., Ribeiro, B., & Dobnikar, A. (2010). Distributed text classification with an ensemble kernel-based learning approach. *IEEE Transactions on Systems, Man and Cybernetics. Part C, Applications and Reviews, 40*(3), 287–297. doi:10.1109/TSMCC.2009.2038280

Silverstein, C., Henzinger, M., Marais, H., & Moricz, M. (1998). Analysis of a very large AltaVista query log. Retrieved July 1, 2010, from http://www.hpl.hp.com/techreports/Compaq-DEC/SRC-TN-1998-014.pdf

Sim, T., Baker, S., & Bsat, M. (2003). The CMU pose, illumination, and expression database. *IEEE Transactions in Pattern Analysis and Machine Intelligence, 25*(12), 1615-1618. doi: http://dx.doi.org/10.1109/TPAMI.2003.1251154

Simon, D. (2008). Biogeography-based optimization. *IEEE Transactions on Evolutionary Computation, 12*(6), 702–713. doi:10.1109/TEVC.2008.919004

Simpson, P. (1990). *Artificial neural systems: Foundations, paradigms, applications, and implementations.* New York, NY: MPergamon Press.

Sindhwani, V., & Melville, P. (2008). Document-word co-regularization for semi-supervised sentiment analysis. In *Proceedings Eighth IEEE International Conference on Data Mining, ICDM08* (pp. 1025-1030). Pisa, Italy.

Singh, S., Srivastava, V. C., & Mall, I. D. (2009). Fixed-bed study for adsorptive removal of furfural by activated carbon. *Colloids and Surfaces A: Physicochemical and Engineering Aspects, 332*, 50–56. doi:10.1016/j.colsurfa.2008.08.025

Sirovich, L., & Kirby, M. (1987). Low-dimensional procedure for the characterization of human faces. *Journal of the Optical Society of America. A, Optics and Image Science, 4*(3), 519–524. doi:10.1364/JOSAA.4.000519

Smith, J., & Chang, S. (1996). Querying by colour regions using the VisualSEEK content-based visual query system. In Maybury, M. T. (Ed.), *Intelligent multimedia information retrieval* (pp. 23–41). AAAI Press.

Song, Y. S. (2006). Lecture Notes in Computer Science: *Vol. 4223. Fuzzy c-means algorithm with divergence-based kernel* (pp. 99–108). Berlin, Germany: Springer-Verlag.

Sorenson, P. A., Winther, O., & Hansen, L. K. (2002). Mean field approaches to independent component analysis. *Neural Computation, 14*, 889–918. doi:10.1162/089976602317319009

Sözen, A., Arcaklioglu, E., Özalp, M., & Çaglar, N. (2005). Forecasting based on neural network approach of solar potential in Turkey. *Renewable Energy, 30*(7), 1075–1090. doi:10.1016/j.renene.2004.09.020

Spicer, C. W., Gordon, S. M., Holdren, M. W., Kelly, T. J., & Mukund, R. (2002). *Hazardous air pollutant handbook. Measurements, properties and fate in ambient air.* Boca Raton, FL: CRC Press. doi:10.1201/9781420032352

Spink, A., Wolfram, D., Jansen, M. B. J., & Saracevic, T. (2001). Searching the Web: The public and their queries. *Journal of the American Society for Information Science and Technology, 52*(3), 226–234. doi:10.1002/1097-4571(2000)9999:9999<::AID-ASI1591>3.0.CO;2-R

Sticker, M., & Dimai, A. (1997). Spectral covariance and fuzzy regions for image indexing. *Machine Vision and Applications, 10*, 66–73. doi:10.1007/s001380050060

Stone, J. (2004). *Independent component analysis: A tutorial introduction*. The MIT Press.

Stone, J. V. (2002). Independent component analysis: an introduction. *Trends in Cognitive Sciences, 6*(2), 59–64. doi:10.1016/S1364-6613(00)01813-1

Stranieri, A., & Zeleznikow, J. (2005). *Knowledge discovery from legal databases*. Berlin, Germany: Springer, Kluwer Law and Philosophy Series.

Stranieri, A., Zeleznikow, J., Gawler, M., & Lewis, B. (1999). A hybrid rule- neural approach for the automation of legal reasoning in the discretionary domain of family law in Australia. *Artificial Intelligence and Law, 7*(2-3), 153–183. doi:10.1023/A:1008325826599

Stranieri, A., Zeleznikow, J., & Yearwood, J. (2001). Argumentation structures that integrate dialectical and monoletical reasoning. *The Knowledge Engineering Review, 16*(4), 331–348. doi:10.1017/S0269888901000248

Strehl, A., & Ghosh, J. (2002). Cluster ensembles — A knowledge reuse framework for combining multiple partitions. *Journal of Machine Learning Research, 3*, 583–617.

Sugiura, M. (1989). The chloroplast chromosomes in land plants. *Annual Review of Cell Biology, 5*, 51–70. doi:10.1146/annurev.cb.05.110189.000411

Su, M., Miften, M., Whiddon, C., Sun, X., Light, K., & Marks, L. (2005). An artificial neural network for predicting the incidence of radiation pneumonitis. *Medical Physics, 32*, 318–325. doi:10.1118/1.1835611

Suryatenggara, J., & Ane, B. K. Pandjaitan, & M., Steinberg, W. (2009, December). *Pattern recognition on 2D cervical cytological digital images for early detection of cervix cancer*. Paper presented at the World Congress on Nature & Biologically Inspired Computing (NaBIC 2009). Retrieved from http://ieeexplore.ieee.org/xpl/freeabs_all.jsp?arnumber=5393710

Sutton, R. S., & Barto, A. G. (1998). *Introduction to reinforcement learning*. MIT Press.

Su, Y., Shan, S., Chen, X., & Gao, W. (2009). Hierarchical ensemble of global and local classifiers for face recognition. *IEEE Transactions on Image Processing, 18*(8), 1885–1896. doi:10.1109/TIP.2009.2021737

Suzuki, K., Armato, S., Li, F., Sone, S., & Doi, K. (2003). Massive training artificial neural network (MTANN) for reduction of false positives in computerized detection of lung nodules in low-dose CT. *Medical Physics, 30*, 1602–1617. doi:10.1118/1.1580485

Suzuki, K., Li, F., Sone, S., & Doi, K. (2005a). Computer-aided diagnostic scheme for distinction between benign and malignant nodules in thoracic low-dose CT by use of massive training artificial neural network. *IEEE Transactions on Medical Imaging, 24*, 1138–1150. doi:10.1109/TMI.2005.852048

Suzuki, K., Shiraishi, J., Abe, H., MacMahon, H., & Doi, K. (2005b). False-positive reduction in computer-aided diagnostic scheme for detecting nodules in chest radiographs by means of massive training artificial neural network. *Academic Radiology, 12*, 191–201. doi:10.1016/j.acra.2004.11.017

Suzuki, K., Yoshida, H., Nappi, J., Armato, S., & Dachman, A. (2008). Mixture of expert 3D massive-training ANNs for reduction of multiple types of false positives in CAD for detection of polyps in CT colonography. *Medical Physics, 35*, 694–703. doi:10.1118/1.2829870

Suzuki, K., Yoshida, H., Nappi, J., & Dachman, A. (2006). Massive-training artificial neural network (MTANN) for reduction of false positives in computer-aided detection of polyps: Suppression of rectal tubes. *Medical Physics, 33*, 3814–3824. doi:10.1118/1.2349839

Swain, M. J., & Ballard, D. H. (1991). Color indexing. *International Journal of Computer Vision, 7*(1), 11-32. doi: http://dx.doi.org/10.1007/BF00130487

Takemura, A., Shimizu, A., & Hamamoto, K. (2010). Discrimination of breast tumors in ultrasonic images using and ensemble classifier based on the adaboost algorithm with feature selection. *IEEE Transactions on Medical Imaging, 29*(3), 598–609. doi:10.1109/TMI.2009.2022630

Takeuchi, Y., & Hisanaga, N. (1977). The neurotoxicity of toluene. EEG changes in rats exposed to various concentrations. *British Journal of Industrial Medicine, 34*(4), 314–324.

Tandon, V. (2000). *Closing the gap between CAD/CAM and optimized CNC end milling*. Master's thesis, Purdue School of Engineering and Technology, Indiana University Purdue University Indianapolis.

Tang, A., & Pearlmutter, B. (2003). *Independent components of magnetoencephalography: Localization* (pp. 129-162).

Tan, P. N., Steinbach, M., & Kumar, V. (2005). *Introduction to data mining* (1st ed.). Boston, MA: Addison-Wesley Longman Publishing Co., Inc.

Tan, X., & Triggs, B. (2007). Enhanced local texture feature sets for face recognition under difficult lighting conditions. *LNCS, 4778*, 168–182.

Tata, C. (1998). The application of judicial intelligence and "rules" to systems supporting discretionary judicial decision-making. *Artificial Intelligence and Law: International Journal, 6*(2-4), 203–230. doi:10.1023/A:1008274209036

Tenenbaum, J., Silva, V., & Langford, J. (2000). A global geometric framework for nonlinear dimensionality reduction. *Science, 290*(5500), 2319-2323. doi: citeulike-article-id:266187

Thagard, P. (1989). Explanatory coherence. *The Behavioral and Brain Sciences, 12*, 435–502. doi:10.1017/S0140525X00057046

Thangavel, K., Jaganathan, J. P., & Easmi, P. O. (2006). Data mining approach to cervical cancer patients analysis using clustering technique. *Asian Journal of Information Technology, 5*(4), 413–417.

Thompson, P. (2001). Automatic categorization of case law. *Proceedings of the Eighth International Conference on Artificial Intelligence and Law, ICAIL 2001*, May 21-25, 2001, St. Louis, Missouri, (pp. 70-77). ACM Press. ISBN 1-58113-368-5

Topchy, A., Jain, A. K., & Punch, W. (2003). Combining multiple weak clusterings. In *Proceedings IEEE Internat. Conf. on Data Mining* (pp. 331-338).

Topchy, A., Jain, A. K., & Punch, W. (2005). Clustering ensembles: models of consensus and weak partitions. *IEEE Transactions on Pattern Analysis and Machine Intelligence, 27*(12), 1866–1881. doi:10.1109/TPAMI.2005.237

Touretzky, D. S., & Pomerleau, D. A. (1989). What's hidden in the hidden layer? *Byte, 14*(8), 227–233.

Trelea, I. C. (2003). The particle swarm optimization algorithm: Convergence analysis and parameter selection. *Information Processing Letters, 85*, 317–325. doi:10.1016/S0020-0190(02)00447-7

Trier, I. D., & Taxt, T. (1995). Evaluation of binarization methods for document images. *IEEE Transactions on Pattern Analysis and Machine Intelligence, 17*(3), 312–315. doi:10.1109/34.368197

Tsai, C., McGarry, K., & Tait, J. (2003). Using neuro-fuzzy technique based on a two stage mapping model for concept-based image database indexing. *Proceedings of the Fifth International Symposium on Multimedia Software Engineering*, Taiwan, (pp. 10-12).

Tsur, O., & Rappoport, A. (2007). Using classifier features for studying the effect of native language on the choice of written second language words. In *Proceedings Workshop on Cognitive Aspects of Computational Language Acquisition* (pp. 9-16). Prague, Czech Republic.

Tu, C. J., et al. (2008). Feature selection using PSO-SVM. *IAENG International Journal of Computer Science, 33*(1).

Tumer, K., Ramanujam, N., Ghosh, J., & Richards-Kortum, R. (1998). Ensembles of radial basis function networks for spectroscopic detection of cervical precancer. *IEEE Transactions on Bio-Medical Engineering, 45*(8), 953–961. doi:10.1109/10.704864

Tür, G., & Güvenir, H. A. (1996). Decision tree induction using genetic. In *Proceedings of the Fifth Turkish Symposium on Artificial Intelligence and Neural Networks*, (pp. 187–196).

Turaga, D. S., Vlachos, M., & Verscheure, O. (2009). On k-means cluster preservation using quantization schemes. In *Proceedings 2009 Ninth IEEE International Conference on Data Mining, ICDM09* (pp. 533-542). Miami, Florida, USA.

Turaga, P., Veeraraghavan, A., & Chellappa, R. (2008). *Statistical analysis on stiefel and grassmann manifolds with applications in computer vision.*

Turk, M., & Pentland, A. (1991). Eigenfaces for recognition. *Journal of Cognitive Neuroscience, 3*(1), 71-86. doi: http://dx.doi.org/10.1162/jocn.1991.3.1.71

Uestuen, B., Melssen, W. J., & Buydens, L. M. C. (2006). Facilitating the application of support vector regression by using a universal Pearson VII function based kernel. *Chemometrics and Intelligent Laboratory Systems, 81*, 29–40. doi:10.1016/j.chemolab.2005.09.003

Vacca, J. R. (2009). *Computer and information security handbook.* Morgan Kaufmann.

Vamvakas, G., Gatos, B., & Perantonis, S. J. (2010). Handwritten character recognition through two-stage foreground sub-sampling. *Pattern Recognition, 43*(8), 2807–2816. doi:10.1016/j.patcog.2010.02.018

van Dijk, J., Choenni, S., & Leeuw, F. (2009). Analyzing a complaint database by means of a genetic-based data mining algorithm. *Proceedings of the 12th International Conference on Artificial Intelligence and Law*, Barcelona, Spain, (pp. 226-227). ACM Press.

Vapnik, V. (2000). *The nature of statistical learning theory* (2nd ed.). New York, NY: Springer-Verlag, Inc.

Vasilescu, M. A. O., & Terzopoulos, D. (2005). *Multilinear independent components analysis.*

Venterink, H. O., Wiegman, F., Van der Lee, G. E. M., & Vermaat, J. E. (2003). Role of active floodplains for nutrient retention in the river Rhine. *Journal of Environmental Quality, 32*, 1430–1435. doi:10.2134/jeq2003.1430

Verma, B., Gader, P., & Chen, W. (2001). Fusion of multiple handwritten word recognition techniques. *Pattern Recognition Letters, 22*(9), 991–998. doi:10.1016/S0167-8655(01)00046-0

Verma, B., & Kulkarni, S. (2007). Neural networks for content-based image retrieval. In Zhang, Y. (Ed.), *Semantic based visual information retrieval* (pp. 252–272).

Verma, B., & Rahman, A. (2011). Cluster oriented ensemble classifier: Impact of multi-cluster characterisation on ensemble classifier learning. *IEEE Transactions on Knowledge and Data Engineering, 24*(4).

Vertan, C., & Boujemaa, N. (2000). Embedding fuzzy logic for image retrieval. *19th International Conference of the North American Fuzzy Information Processing Society*, (pp. 85-89).

Vidal, R., Ma, Y., & Sastry, S. (2005). Generalized principal component analysis (GPCA). *IEEE Transactions on Pattern Analysis and Machine Intelligence, 27*(12), 1945–1959. doi:10.1109/TPAMI.2005.244

Vigário, R., Jousmäki, V., Hämäläinen, M., Hari, R., & Oja, E. (1998). *Independent component analysis for identification of artifacts in magnetoencephalographic recordings.* Paper presented at the NIPS '97: The 1997 Conference on Advances in Neural Information Processing Systems, Denver, Colorado, United States.

Vigário, R., Särelä, J., Jousmäki, V., Hämäläinen, M., & Oja, E. (2000). Independent component approach to the analysis of EEG and MEG recordings. *IEEE Transactions on Bio-Medical Engineering, 47*(5), 589–593. doi:10.1109/10.841330

Vinciarelli, A. (2002). A survey on off-line cursive word recognition. *Pattern Recognition, 35*(7), 1433–1446. doi:10.1016/S0031-3203(01)00129-7

Vinciarelli, A. (2005). Application of information retrieval techniques to single writer documents. *Pattern Recognition Letters, 26*(14), 2262–2271. doi:10.1016/j.patrec.2005.03.036

Waismann, F. (1951). Verifiability. In Flew, A. (Ed.), *Logic and language*. Cambridge, UK: Blackwell.

Walker, E. (2002). Image retrieval on the Internet - How can fuzzy help? *Proceedings of the Annual Conference of the North American Fuzzy Information Processing Society, NAFIPS '00*, (pp. 526-528).

Wang, R., Shan, S., Chen, X., & Gao, W. (2008). *Manifold-manifold distance with application to face recognition based on image set.*

Wang, X., Gong, H., Zhang, H., Li, B., & Zhuang, Z. (2006). *Palmprint identification using boosting local binary pattern.*

Wang, J. H., & Ray, M. B. (2000). Application of ultraviolet photooxidation to remove organic pollutants in the gas phase. *Separation and Purification Technology, 19*, 11–20. doi:10.1016/S1383-5866(99)00078-7

Wang, J., Mo, Y., Huang, B., Wen, J., & He, L. (2008). Web search results clustering based on a novel suffix tree structure. *Lecture Notes in Computer Science, 5060*(1), 540–554. doi:10.1007/978-3-540-69295-9_43

Wang, L., Wang, X., & Feng, J. (2006). Subspace distance analysis with application to adaptive Bayesian algorithm for face recognition. *Pattern Recognition, 39*(3), 456–464. doi:10.1016/j.patcog.2005.08.015

Wang, X., & Tang, X. (2006). Random sampling for subspace face recognition. *International Journal of Computer Vision, 70*(1), 91–104. doi:10.1007/s11263-006-8098-z

Wan, X. (2009). Combining content and context similarities for image retrieval. *Lecture Notes in Computer Science, 5478*(1), 749–754. doi:10.1007/978-3-642-00958-7_79

Wassestrom, R. (1961). *The judicial decision. Toward a theory of legal justification.* Stanford, CA: Stanford University Press.

Wei, J., Wang, S., & Yuan, X. (2010). Ensemble rough hypercuboid approach for classifying cancers. *IEEE Transactions on Knowledge and Data Engineering, 22*(3), 381–391. doi:10.1109/TKDE.2009.114

Weinberger, K. Q., & Saul, L. K. (2009). Distance metric learning for large margin nearest neighbor classification. *Journal of Machine Learning Research, 10*, 207–244.

WEKA. (n.d.). *Waikato environment for knowledge analysis.* Retrieved October 30, 2010, from http://www.cs.waikato.ac.nz/ml/weka

Werbos, P. J. (1974). *Beyond regression: New tools for prediction and analysis in the behavioral sciences.* (Unpublished PhD thesis). Harvard University, Cambridge, USA.

Wesche, T., Goertler, G., & Hubert, W. (1987). Modified habitat suitability index model for brown trout in southeastern Wyoming. *North American Journal of Fisheries Management, 7*, 232–237. doi:10.1577/1548-8659(1987)7<232:MHSIMF>2.0.CO;2

WHO. (1981). Recommended health-based limits in occupational exposure to selected organic solvents, Geneva, World Health Organization. In *Technical Report Series 664.*

Widrow, B., & Hoff, M. E., Jr. (1960). Adaptive switching circuits. In *1960 IRE WESCON Convention Record*, Part 4, (pp. 96–104). New York, NY: IRE.

Wiering, M. A., & Hasselt, H. (2008). Ensemble algorithms in reinforcement learning, *IEEE Transactions on Systems, Man, and Cybernetics. Part B, 38*(4), 930–936.

Wikipedia. (n.d.). *Segmentation (image processing).* Retrieved from http://en.wikipedia.org/wiki/Segmentation

Wilson, A. (1977). Architecture for a self organizing neural pattern recognition machine. *Computer Vision. Image Processing, 37*, 104–115.

Wilson, L. G., Amy, G. L., Gerba, C. P., Gordon, H., & Johnson, M. (1995). Water quality changes during soil aquifer treatment of tertiary effluent. *Water Environment Research, 67*, 371–376. doi:10.2175/106143095X131600

Windeatt, T. (2006). Accuracy/diversity and ensemble MLP classifier design. *IEEE Transactions on Neural Networks, 17*(5), 1194–1211. doi:10.1109/TNN.2006.875979

Witten, I., & Frand, E. (2005). *Data mining: Practical machine learning tools and techniques* (2nd ed.). San Francisco, CA: Morgan Kaufmann.

Wolberg, W., Street, W., & Mangasarian, O. (1994). Machine learning techniques to diagnose breast cancer from image-processed nuclear features of fine needle aspirates. *Cancer Letters, 77*, 163–171. doi:10.1016/0304-3835(94)90099-X

Wolberg, W., Street, W., & Mangasarian, O. (1995). Image analysis and machine learning applied to breast cancer diagnosis and prognosis. *Analytical and Quantitative Cytology and Histology, 17*, 77–87.

Wolf, L., & Shashua, A. (2003a). Learning over sets using kernel principal angles. *Journal of Machine Learning Research, 4*, 913–931.

World Health Organization. (2007). IARC monographs on the evaluation of carcinogenic risks to humans: *Vol. 90. Human Papillomaviruses.* Lyon, France: International Agency for Research on Cancer.

World Health Organization. (2010). *Human Papillomavirus and related cancers.* Geneva, Switzerland: WHO/ICO HPV Information Centre.

World Health Organization. (2010). *World Health Report 2010: The path to universal coverage.* Geneva, Switzerland: WHO Media Center.

Wróblewski, M. (2003). *A hierarchical WWW pages clustering algorithm based on the vector space model.* Master thesis, Department of Computing Science, Poznań University of Technology.

Wshah, S. (2009). Segmentation of Arabic handwriting based on both contour and skeleton segmentation. *International Conference on Document Analysis and Recognition,* (pp. 793-797).

Wu, Y.-F., & Chen, X. (2003). *Extracting features from Web search returned hits for hierarchical classification.* Paper presented at the International Conference on Information and Knowledge Engineering.

Wuthrich, M. (2009). Language model integration for the recognition of handwritten medieval documents. *International Conference on Document Analysis and Recognition,* (pp. 211-215).

Wu, X., Kumar, V., Quinlan, J. R., Ghosh, J., Yang, Q., & Motoda, H. (2007). Top 10 algorithms in data mining. *Knowledge and Information Systems, 14*(1), 1–37. doi:10.1007/s10115-007-0114-2

Xing, E., Ng, A., Jordan, M., & Russell, S. (2002). *Distance metric learning, with application to clustering with side-information.* Paper presented at the Advances in Neural Information Processing Systems 15.

Xing, L., Li, J., Donaldson, S., Le, Q., & Boyer, A. (1999). Optimization of importance factors in inverse planning. *Physics in Medicine and Biology, 44,* 2525–2536. doi:10.1088/0031-9155/44/10/311

Xu, Q., Lam, L., & Suen, C. (2003). Automatic segmentation and recognition system for handwritten dates on Canadian bank cheques. *Seventh International Conference on Document Analysis and Recognition* (Vol. 2, pp. 704-708).

Yahoo. (2006). *Start advertising with Yahoo! Search marketing.* Retrieved 2 April, 2010, from https://sign-up13.marketingsolutions.yahoo.com/signupui/signup/loadSignup.do

Yahoo. (2009). *Top 10 - Yahoo! 2008 year in review - Top 10 searches for 2008.* Retrieved April 2, 2010, from http://buzz.yahoo.com/yearinreview2008/top10/

Yamaguchi, O., Fukui, K., & Maeda, K. (1998a). *Face recognition using temporal image sequence.* Paper presented the 3rd International Conference on Face and Gesture Recognition.

Yamaguchi, T., Mackin, K. J., Nunohiro, E., Park, J. G., Hara, K., & Matsushita, K. (2009). Artificial neural network ensemble-based land-cover classifiers using MODIS data. *Artificial Life and Robotics, 13*(2), 570–574. doi:10.1007/s10015-008-0615-4

Yang, M. H., Ahuja, N., & Kriegman, D. (2000). *Face recognition using Kernel eigenfaces.*

Yang, J. (2001). An image retrieval model based on fuzzy triples. *Journal on Fuzzy Sets and Systems, 121*(3), 459–470. doi:10.1016/S0165-0114(00)00056-7

Yang, J., Frangi, A. F., Yang, J. Y., Zhang, D., & Jin, Z. (2005). KPCA plus LDA: A complete kernel fisher discriminant framework for feature extraction and recognition. *IEEE Transactions on Pattern Analysis and Machine Intelligence, 27*(2), 230–244. doi:10.1109/TPAMI.2005.33

Yang, J., Zhang, D., Frangi, A. F., & Yang, J. Y. (2004). Two-dimensional PCA: A new approach to appearance-based face representation and recognition. *IEEE Transactions on Pattern Analysis and Machine Intelligence, 26*(1), 131–137. doi:10.1109/TPAMI.2004.1261097

Yang, Y., & Zheng, C. (2005). Fuzzy C-means clustering algorithm with a novel penalty term for image segmentation. *Opto-Electronics Review, 13*(4), 309–315.

Yan, S., Xu, D., Zhang, B., Zhang, H. J., Yang, Q., & Lin, S. (2007). Graph embedding and extensions: A general framework for dimensionality reduction. *IEEE Transactions on Pattern Analysis and Machine Intelligence, 29*(1), 40–51. doi:10.1109/TPAMI.2007.250598

Yearwood, J., Webb, D., Ma, L., Vamplew, P., Ofoghi, B., & Kelarev, A. (2009). Applying clustering and ensemble clustering approaches to phishing profiling. *Proceedings of the 8th Australasian Data Mining Conference: AusDM 2009 Data Mining and Analytics 2009,* 1-4 December 2009, Melbourne, Australia, (pp. 25-34).

Yearwood, J. L., Bagirov, A. M., & Kelarev, A. V. (2009). Optimization methods and the k-committees algorithm for clustering of sequence data. *Journal of Applied & Computational Mathematics, 1*, 92–101.

Yearwood, J. L., & Mammadov, M. (2010). *Classification technologies: Optimization approaches to short text categorization*. Hershey, PA: Idea Group Inc.

Yeh, J. Y., & Fu, J. C. (2008). A hierarchical genetic algorithm for segmentation of multi-spectral human brain MRI. *Expert Systems with Applications, 34*, 1285–1295. doi:10.1016/j.eswa.2006.12.012

Ye, N. (2003). *The handbook of data mining*. Lawrence Erlbaum Human Factors and Ergonomics Series.

Yorke, E. (2003). Biological indices for evaluation and optimization of IMRT. *Intensity-Modulated Radiation Therapy: The State of the Art: AAPM Medical Physics Monograph Number, 29*, 77-114.

Yoshida, H., Kawata, K., Fukuyama, Y., & Nakanishi, Y. (1999). A particle swarm optimization for reactive power and voltage control considering voltage stability. In *Proceedings of International Conference on Intelligent System Application to Power Systems (ISAP '99)*, (pp. 117-121). Rio de Janeiro, Brazil.

Yoshitaka, A., Kishida, S., & Hirakawa, M. (1994). Knowledge-assisted content-based retrieval for multimedia databases. *IEEE MultiMedia*, (Winter): 12–21. doi:10.1109/93.338682

Yu, H. (2001). A direct LDA algorithm for high-dimensional data — With application to face recognition. *Pattern Recognition, 34*(10), 2067-2070. doi: citeulike-article-id:5907405

Yu, S., & Dunham, M. (2011). A graph-based fuzzy linguistic metadata schema for describing spatial relationships. *Proceedings of International Symposium on Visual Information Communication*, Article no. 14.

Yuen, P. C., & Lai, J. H. (2002). Face representation using independent component analysis. *Pattern Recognition, 35*(6), 1247–1257. doi:10.1016/S0031-3203(01)00101-7

Yu, Y. (1997). Multiobjective decision theory for computational optimization in radiation therapy. *Medical Physics, 24*, 1445–1454. doi:10.1118/1.598033

Zadeh, L. A. (1975). The concept of a linguistic variable and its application to approximate reasoning. *Information Sciences, 8*, 199–249. doi:10.1016/0020-0255(75)90036-5

Zeleznikow, J., & Bellucci, E. (2003). Family_Winner: Integrating game theory and heuristics to provide negotiation support. In D. Bourcier, (Ed.), *Legal Knowledge and Information Systems. JURIX 2003: The Sixteenth Annual Conference*. (pp. 21-30). Amsterdam, The Netherlands: IOS Press.

Zeleznikow, J. (2000). building judicial decision support systems in discretionary legal domains. *International Review of Law Computers & Technology, 14*(3), 341–356. doi:10.1080/713673368

Zeleznikow, J., & Hunter, D. (1994). *Building intelligent legal information systems: Knowledge representation and reasoning in law, 13*. Kluwer Computer/Law Series.

Zhang, H., D'Souza, W., Shi, L., & Meyer, R. (2009a). Modeling plan-related clinical complications using machine learning tools in a multiplan IMRT framework. *International Journal of Radiation Oncology • Biology • Physics, 74*, 1617-1626.

Zhang, H., Shi, L., Meyer, R., & D'Souza, W. (2009b). Machine learning for modeling dose-related organ-at-risk complications after radiation therapy. *Proceedings of 8th International Conference on Machine Learning and Applications*, (pp. 457-462).

Zhang, R., & Zhang, Z. (2002). A clustering based approach to efficient image retrieval. *14th IEEE Conference on Tools with Artificial Intelligence*, (pp. 339-346).

Zhang, H., Gao, W., Chen, X., & Zhao, D. (2006). Object detection using spatial histogram features. *Image and Vision Computing, 24*(4), 327–341. doi:10.1016/j.imavis.2005.11.010

Zhang, H., Meyer, R., Shi, L., & D'Souza, W. (2010). The minimum knowledge base for predicting organ-at-risk dose-volume levels and plan-related complications in IMRT planning. *Physics in Medicine and Biology, 55*, 1935–1947. doi:10.1088/0031-9155/55/7/010

Zhang, J., He, L., & Zhou, Z. H. (2006). Ensemble-based discriminant manifold learning for face recognition. *LNCS, 4221*, 29–38.

Zhang, J., & Liu, Y. (2004). Cervical cancer detection using SVM based feature screening. In Barillot, C., Haynor, D. R., & Hellier, P. (Eds.), *Medical Image Computing and Computer-assisted Intervention - MICCAI 2004* (pp. 873–880). Heidelberg, Germany: Springer-Verlag. doi:10.1007/978-3-540-30136-3_106

Zhang, J., Marszałek, M., Lazebnik, S., & Schmid, C. (2007). Local features and kernels for classification of texture and object categories: A comprehensive study. *International Journal of Computer Vision, 73*(2), 213–238. doi:10.1007/s11263-006-9794-4

Zhang, P., Bui, T. D., & Suen, C. (2007). A novel cascade ensemble classifier system with a high recognition performance on handwritten digits. *Pattern Recognition, 40*(12), 3415–3429. doi:10.1016/j.patcog.2007.03.022

Zhang, T. Y., & Suen, C. Y. (1984). A fast parallel algorithm for thinning digital patterns. *Communications of the ACM, 27*(3), 236–239. doi:10.1145/357994.358023

Zhang, X., Wang, X., Dong, L., Liu, H., & Mohan, R. (2006). A sensitivity-guided algorithm for automated determination of IMRT objective function parameters. *Medical Physics, 33*, 2935–2944. doi:10.1118/1.2214171

Zhao, C., Shi, W., & Deng, Y. (2005). A new Hausdorff distance for image matching. *Pattern Recognition Letters, 26*(5), 581-586. doi: http://dx.doi.org/10.1016/j.patrec.2004.09.022

Zhao, Q., & Shirasaka, M. (1999) A study on evolutionary design of binary decision trees. In P. J. Angeline, Z. Michalewicz, M. Schoenauer, X. Yao, & A. Zalzala (Eds.), *Proceedings of the Congress on Evolutionary Computation*, Vol. 3, (pp. 1988–1993). Washington, DC: IEEE Press.

Zhao, T., Zhang, J., & Liu, Y. (2002, August). *Does multispectral texture features really improve cervical cancer detection?* Paper presented at the International Conference on Diagnostic Imaging and Analysis (ICDIA 2002). Retrieved from http://www.ri.cmu.edu/ publication_view.html?pub_id=4034

Zhao, G., & Pietikäinen, M. (2007). Dynamic texture recognition using local binary patterns with an application to facial expressions. *IEEE Transactions on Pattern Analysis and Machine Intelligence, 29*(6), 915–928. doi:10.1109/TPAMI.2007.1110

Zhao, H. (2007). A multi-objective genetic programming approach to developing pareto optimal de- cision trees. *Decision Support Systems, 43*(3), 809–826. doi:10.1016/j.dss.2006.12.011

Zhao, Q., Yang, Z., & Tao, H. (2010). Differential earth mover's distance with its applications to visual tracking. *IEEE Transactions on Pattern Analysis and Machine Intelligence, 32*(2), 274–287. doi:10.1109/TPAMI.2008.299

Zhao, W., Chellappa, R., Phillips, P. J., & Rosenfeld, A. (2003). Face recognition: A literature survey. *ACM Computing Surveys, 35*(4), 399–458. doi:10.1145/954339.954342

Zhau, R., & Grosky, W. I. (2002). *Bridging the semantic gap in image retrieval.* Retrieved from http://citeseer.ist.psu.edu/497446.html

Zhong, L., Haghighat, F., Blondeau, P., & Kozinski, J. (2010). Modeling and physical interpretation of photocatalytic oxidation efficiency in indoor air applications. *Building and Environment, 45*(12), 2689–2697. doi:10.1016/j.buildenv.2010.05.029

Zhou, B., & Pei, J. (2009). *Answering aggregate keyword queries on relational databases using minimal group-bys.* Paper presented at the 12th International Conference on Extending Database Technology: Advances in Database Technology.

Zhou, S., Krueger, V., & Chellappa, R. (2003). Probabilistic recognition of human faces from video. *Computer Vision and Image Understanding, 91*(1-2), 214-245. doi: http://dx.doi.org/10.1016/S1077-3142(03)00080-8

Zhuang, X. S., & Dai, D. Q. (2005). Inverse Fisher discriminate criteria for small sample size problem and its application to face recognition. *Pattern Recognition, 38*(11), 2192–2194. doi:10.1016/j.patcog.2005.02.011

Zhuang, X. S., & Dai, D. Q. (2007). Improved discriminate analysis for high-dimensional data and its application to face recognition. *Pattern Recognition, 40*(5), 1570–1578. doi:10.1016/j.patcog.2006.11.015

Zhu, X., Goldberg, A. B., Brachman, R., & Dietterich, T. (2009). *Introduction to semi-supervised learning.* Morgan and Claypool Publishers.

Zibulevsky, M., & Pearlmutter, B. (2001). Blind source separation by sparse decomposition in a signal dictionary. *Neural Computation*, *13*(4), 863–882. doi:10.1162/089976601300014385

Zimmermann, M., Chappelier, J., & Bunke, H. (2006). Offline grammar-based recognition of handwritten sentences. *IEEE Transactions on Pattern Analysis and Machine Intelligence*, *28*(5), 818–821. doi:10.1109/TPAMI.2006.103

Zuo, G. M., Cheng, Z. X., Chen, H., Li, G. W., & Miao, T. (2006). Study on photocatalytic degradation of several volatile organic compounds. *Journal of Hazardous Materials*, *B128*, 158–163. doi:10.1016/j.jhazmat.2005.07.056

Zurada, J. M., Malinowski, A., & Cloete, I. (1994). Sensitivity analysis for minimization of input data dimensions for feed forward neural network. In *IEEE International Symposium on Circuits and Systems*, London, May 30-June 1, (Vol. 6, pp. 447-450).

About the Contributors

Siddhivinayak Kulkarni (Sid) is currently working as a Senior Lecturer at the University of Ballarat. Prior to that, he was working as an Assistant Professor at Nipissing University, Canada. He has organized workshops on Machine Learning and Algorithms in 2007 and 2008 in Australia and attracted many research papers from various countries. Dr. Kulkarni has served on organizing and program committees for more than twenty-five conferences organized in various countries at an international level. He has served an editorial board member and reviewer for many reputed journals. He has published significant papers in reputable peer reviewed journals and presented papers at the international conferences. His research interest includes machine learning/computational intelligence, pattern recognition, and their applications in image/video retrieval, biometrics, and in health informatics.

* * *

Bernadetta Kwintiana Ane is a Research Fellow at the Institute of Computer-aided Product Development Systems, Universitaet Stuttgart in Stuttgart, Germany. She received MSc. (cum laude) degree from Bandung Institute of Technology, Indonesia in 1996 and PhD. (excellent) degree from Tokyo Institute of Technology, Japan in 2003, both majoring in Industrial Engineering and Management. She has been 15 years working in industry and academy. She published more than 40 scientific papers in the referred international journals and conferences, as well as book chapters, white papers, international research reports, scientific oratio, and owned international registered patent. Since 2008, she has chaired the International Symposium on Manufacturing and Application (ISOMA) track of the bi-annual World of Automation Congress. At the same time, she serves also several international conferences organized by Machine Intelligence Research Laboratory (MIR Labs.). Presently, as a Humboldtian she serves internationally as a research fellow at CeSDeS, Toyo University in Japan, Hagiwara Laboratory at Tokyo Institute of Technology in Japan, and the International Institute for Applied Systems Analysis (IIASA) in Laxenburg, Austria. Meantime, she also contributes as an Associate Editor for the *Journal of Intelligent Automation and Soft Computing,* University of Texas, USA, as well as research grant assesor for Czech Science Foundation and reviewers for the international journals of *Neural Network World* (Czech Republic), *Technovation, Technological Forecasting and Social Change, Computer Aided Design*, and *Information Sciences* (Elsevier Sciences), and *IEEE Transaction on Information Technology in Biomedicine* (IEEE Society).

J. Anitha received her B.E degree from Bharathiar University and M.E degree from Anna University. She is pursuing the Doctoral degree in the area of Medical Image Processing. Currently, she is working as Assistant Professor (SG) in the Department of ECE, Karunya University, India. Her research interests include evolutionary algorithms, image processing, modelling, et cetera. She has published 14 research papers in reputed international journals/IEEE conferences. She is a member of IACSIT, ISTE, & IAENG.

Adil M. Bagirov received a Master's degree in Applied Mathematics from the Baku State University, Azerbaijan in 1983, and the Ph.D degrees in Mathematical Cybernetics from the Institute of Cybernetics Azerbaijan National Academy of Sciences in 1989 and in optimization from the University of Ballarat, Australia in 2001. He was a Research Fellow at the University of Ballarat from 2001 till 2005, and a Senior Research Fellow from 2006 till 2009. Since 2010 Adil has been working as an Associate Professor at the University of Ballarat. His main research interests are in the area of nonsmooth and global optimization and their applications in data mining and regression analysis. Adil has been the Chief Investigator of several discovery and linkage grants from Australian Research Council in these areas.

Márcio Porto Basgalupp is an Associate Professor at UNIFESP, São Paulo, Brazil. He obtained his BSc in Computer Science from UFPel-RS, Brazil, in 2005; his MSc in Computer Science from PUC-RS, Brazil, in 2007; his PhD in Computer Science from University of São Paulo, Brazil, in 2010. In 2010, he held a post-doc position at NTNU, Trondheim, Norway, where he worked with bio-medical data mining. He has published papers in peer-reviewed journals and conferences. His current research interests are machine learning, data mining, and bio-inspired computation.

Rodrigo Coelho Barros received the B.Sc. degree from Universidade Federal de Pelotas, Brazil, and the M.Sc. degree from Pontifícia Universidade Católica do Rio Grande do Sul, Brazil, both in computer science, in 2007 and 2009, respectively. He is currently working toward the Ph.D. degree in Computer Science with Universidade de São Paulo, where he works with machine learning and data mining topics. He has published papers in peer-reviewed journals and conferences. His current research interests include machine learning, data mining, knowledge discovery, and biologically-inspired computational intelligence algorithms.

Shishir Kumar Behera obtained his Master's in Chemical Engineering from Indian Institute of Technology Madras, India in 2002, and PhD in Environmental Engineering from University of Ulsan, South Korea in 2010. He has published over twenty research articles in various international and national journals as well as conferences. He has taught various subjects in Chemical Engineering during 2002-2006. His research interests include; biological and physico-chemical techniques for the removal of high ammonium concentration and recalcitrant organics, including pharmaceuticals and personal care products in wastewater, reclamation and reuse of wastewater, waste management, industrial symbiosis, and eco-industrial park.

Constanţa-Nicoleta Bodea is Professor at the Academy of Economic Studies (AES), Bucharest, Romania. She taught Project Management and Artificial Intelligence. She is the President of the Project Management Romania Association, and chair of the Education & Training Board of the International Project Management Association - IPMA since 2007. She managed more than 20 R&D and IT projects in the last ten years. She is author of 11 books and more than 50 papers on project management, information systems, and artificial intelligence, being honored by IPMA with the Outstanding Research Contributions in 2007.

André C. P. L. F. de Carvalho received his B.Sc. and M.Sc. degrees in Computer Science from the Universidade Federal de Pernambuco, Brazil. He received his Ph.D. degree in Electronic Engineering from the University of Kent, UK. Prof. André de Carvalho is Full Professor at the Department of Computer Science, Universidade de São Paulo, Brazil. He has published around 80 journal and 200 conference refereed papers. He has been involved in the organization of several conferences and journal special issues. His main interests are machine learning, data mining, bioinformatics, evolutionary computation, bioinspired computing, and hybrid intelligent systems.

Ray-I Chang received the Ph.D. degree in Electrical Engineering and Computer Science from National Chiao Tung University, Hsinchu, Taiwan, R.O.C., in 1996. He then joined the Computer Systems and Communications (CSCL) Laboratory, Institute of Information Science, Academia Sinica. In 2003, he joined the Department of Engineering Science, National Taiwan University, Taipei, Taiwan.

Lin-Chih Chen is an Assistant Professor in the Department of Information Management at National Dong Hwa University, Taiwan. His research interests include Web Intelligent and Web Technology. He develops many Web Intelligent systems include *Cayley Search Engine, VLDP_KRG term suggestion system, Cayley Digital Content system, iClubs Community, Language Agent, and Web Snippet Clustering system*. He is also a leader of Cayley Group.

Maria-Iuliana Dascălu has a Master's Degree in Project Management from the Academy of Economic Studies, Bucharest, Romania (2008) and a Bachelor's Degree in Computer Science from the Alexandru-Ioan Cuza University, Iasi, Romania (2006). She is a PhD student in Economic Informatics at the Academy of Economic Studies, combining her work experience as a programmer with numerous research activities. Her research relates to computer-assisted testing with applications in e-learning environments for project management, competences development systems and their benefits to adult education. Maria Dascălu is a Certified Project Management Associate (2008). She also conducted a research stage at the University of Gothenburg, Sweden, from October 2009 to May 2010.

Warren D'Souza is an Associate Professor and Chief of Medical Physics of the Department of Radiation Oncology of University of Maryland School of Medicine. He obtained his Ph.D. in Department of Medical Physics in 2000 and his Therapeutic Radiologic Physics certificate from American Board of Radiology in 2003. He is member and leader of various institutional and national committees, including AAPM and ASTRO. His research is supported by NSF, NIH, and leading industry vendors. He has authored or co-authored 2 editorials and invited articles, 3 book chapters, more than 40 top-ranked journal papers, and more than 100 abstracts and conference proceedings. His research addresses both clinical practice and basic science problems and covers fields of medical physics, radiation oncology, computer science, operations research, and bioengineering.

Sagarmay Deb is an international consultant and researcher in Information Technology. He has been to many places of the world for consulting and research. He did a Master of Science in Statistics from Gauhati University, India, a Master of Business Administration from Long Island University, USA and a Ph.D. from The University of Southern Queensland, Australia. His research interests are multimedia databases, content-based image retrieval, various indexing techniques, and electronic commerce. He contributes to books on multimedia databases. He attends international conferences and also writes research papers for international journals. Also, he is a reviewer of contributions to international conferences and journals. He edited two research publications and wrote one book on multimedia which are in the market. Currently, he is with The University of Central Queensland, Australia and is involved in the teaching and research works. Marquis Who's Who, a well-known publisher of biographies of people of notable achievements, has included his biography in their 7th Edition of Who's Who in Science and Engineering. Also his biography has been included in the 2000 Outstanding Scientists of the 21st Century issue of International Biographical Centre, Cambridge, England in 2004 as recognition of his achievements in the field of scientific research.

Alex A. Freitas received the BSc degree in Computer Science from FATEC-SP, Brazil, in 1989; the MSc degree in Computer Science from UFSCar, Brazil, in 1993; the PhD degree in Computer Science (in the area of data mining) from the University of Essex, UK, in 1997; and the MPhil (a research-oriented master's degree) in Biological Sciences (in the area of ageing) from the University of Liverpool, UK, in 2011. He is currently a Reader in Computational Intelligence (position equivalent to Associate Professor) in the School of Computing, University of Kent, UK. He has authored or co-authored three research-oriented books on data mining, and has published over 45 peer-reviewed journal papers and over 100 peer-reviewed full papers in conference proceedings. His current research interests are data mining, the biology of ageing, bioinformatics, and biologically-inspired computational intelligence.

Mehrtash Harandi is a research scientist at NICTA and an Adjunct Lecturer at the University of Queensland. He received the PhD degree in 2009 from University of Tehran (Tehran, Iran) for his work on face recognition. His current research interests are in the areas of machine learning and computer vision with applications such as automated surveillance.

D. Jude Hemanth received his B.E degree from Bharathiar University and M.E degree from Anna University. He is pursuing the Doctoral degree in the area of Artificial Intelligence. Currently, he is working as Assistant Professor in the Department of ECE, Karunya University, India. His research interest includes soft computing, machine vision, pattern recognition, et cetera. He has published 22 research papers in reputed international journals/IEEE conferences and 1 book with VDM-Verlag Publishers, Germany. He is serving as the Editorial Board Member of several international journals and has organized several special issues in reputed journals. He is a member of Index Copernicus (IC) Scientists, ISTE & IAENG.

Andrei Kelarev received his PhD degree in 1989 and has 15 years of full-time teaching experience in several universities in Australia and USA. Andrei was the Chief Investigator of one Discovery grant of Australian Research Council. He has published two books, a volume of refereed conference proceedings, and over 170 refereed articles, mainly in international journals. Andrei has been working on several research grants at the Graduate School of Information Technology and Mathematical Sciences in the University of Ballarat. His research is devoted to the machine learning methods for analysis of data and to the optimization of various mathematical constructions for internet security applications.

Arun Khosla is presently working as Associate Professor in the Department of Electronics and Communication Engineering, Dr. B. R. Ambedkar National Institute of Technology, Jalandhar. India. His areas of interest are fuzzy modeling, biologically inspired computing and high performance computing.

He is a reviewer for various IEEE and other national and international conferences and journals. He also serves on the editorial board of *International Journal of Swarm Intelligence Research*. He has conducted a number of tutorials in the domain of soft computing at various national & international conferences.

Jen-Shiang Kouh received the Ph.D in Department of Shipbuilding Engineering, Fachhochschule Hannover, Germany. He is now a Professor in the Department of Engineering Science and ocean Engineering, National Taiwan University, Taiwan. His current research interests include Computer graphics and computational fluid dynamics, design and performances evaluation wind turbine blades, Web-based modeling and motion simulation of underwater vehicles, and moving particle semi-implicit method.

Jagannathan Krishnan received his Bachelor's degree in Chemical Engineering in the year 1997, from Bharathiar University, India. After serving in a petrochemical industry for a short period, he started his teaching career at Priyadarshini Engineering College, India. Later on, he pursued his higher studies and obtained his Master's and PhD degrees in Chemical Engineering in the years 2002 and 2007, respectively from Indian Institute of Technology Madras (IITM), India. He worked at the School of Biotechnology and Chemical Engineering, Vellore Institute of Technology (VIT) University, for a couple of years, before taking up his present teaching and research career at the Faculty of Chemical Engineering, MARA University of Technology (UiTM), Malaysia. His research interests are biological and physico-chemical treatment of pollutants, advanced oxidation processes, process modeling and modeling of environmental processes using artificial neural networks.

Dinesh Kant Kumar received the BE degree in Electrical engineering from the Indian Institute of Technology (IIT) Madras, India, in 1982, and the PhD degree from IIT, Delhi, India, in 1990. He has worked in the engineering industry for over ten years in various capacities. Since 1996, he has been an academic with RMIT University, Melbourne, Australia. His research interests include iterative signal processing, computer vision, and intelligent systems for application such as biometrics, human computer interface, and helping the disabled. He is an Associate Editor for *IEEE Transactions on Neural Systems and Rehabilitation Engineering*.

Liang-Bin Lai received the B.S. degree in information management from the National Yunlin University of Science and Technology, Yunlin, Taiwan in 1999. Since 2004, he has been studying toward the Ph.D. degree. His research interests include neural networks, fuzzy logic, data mining, and database applications.

Hong Lee is currently a PhD student in CQUniversity Australia. His research is contributing towards improvements in character segmentation methodology for offline cursive handwriting recognition. His major research interests are handwriting recognition and segmentation, pattern recognition and neural networks. He is an active member of IEEE and IEEE Computational Intelligence Society. He is actively engaged in annual IEEE post-graduate symposium to present his research methodology for peer discussion. He is also involved in teachings of various information technology related subjects within CQUniversity. He also received research excellence awards from Bundaberg City Council and Bundaberg Drink Brewers, and travel grants to IJCNN from IEEE CIS.

Shu-Yu Lin received the B.S. in Information Management from National Central University, Taipei, Taiwan, ROC, in 2004; the M.S. in Engineering Science from National Taiwan University, Taiwan, in 2006; and now is a Ph.D. student. He is also now working in Institute of Information Science at Academia Sinica. His current research interests include query-based learning, swarm intelligence, green computing, and image retrieval.

Adina-Lipai is working as a software developer. She has a Bachelor's Degree in Informatics from the Academy of Economic Studies, Bucharest, Romania. Adina Lipai earned a PhD in Economic Cybernetics and Statistics at the Academy of Economic Studies. Her research relates to the Web search engines, the innovative approaches for increasing the search performance.

Artem A. Lenskiy received the BS degree in Computer and Information Science and his MS degree in Digital Signal Processing and Data Mining from Novosibirsk State Technical University (NSTU), Russia. He received his PhD degree in Electrical Engineering from University of Ulsan, Korea in the year 2010. Prior to his assignment in Korea, in the year 2005, he was working as a Lecturer and Head of IT Laboratory at NSTU. His current research interests include computer vision, machine learning algorithms and applications of self-similar random processes.

Brian C. Lovell was born in Brisbane, Australia in 1960. He received the BE in Electrical Engineering (Honours I) in 1982, the BSc in Computer Science in 1983, and the PhD in Signal Processing in 1991: all from the University of Queensland (UQ). Professor Lovell is Project Leader of the Advanced Surveillance Group in NICTA and Research Leader of the Security and Surveillance Group in the School of ITEE, UQ. He served as President of the International Association of Pattern Recognition 2008-2010, and is a Senior Member of the IEEE, Fellow of the IEAust, and voting member for Australia on the Governing Board of the International Association for Pattern Recognition since 1998. Professor Lovell was Program Co-Chair of ICPR2008 in Tampa, Florida, and is General Co-Chair of ACPR2011 in Beijing, and ICIP2013 in Melbourne. The Advanced Surveillance Group works with port, rail, and airport organizations as well as several national and international agencies to identify and develop technology-based solutions to address real operational and security concerns.

Robert Meyer is a Professor Emeritus of the Computer Sciences Department of the University of Wisconsin-Madison. He served as Chair of the Computer Sciences Department from 1981 to 1984. Over the course of his career, he has authored or co-authored more than 100 published journal papers and book chapters, and edited several volumes of conference proceedings and special journal issues. His research since his Ph.D. in Computer Sciences in 1968 has spanned a wide variety of areas including nonlinear regression, nonlinear programming, discrete optimization, network optimization, and logistics, and his current research, supported by an NIH grant, is focused on radiation treatment planning for IMRT and IMAT with emphasis on the use of advanced optimization tools, machine learning, and parallel computing. He served as an associate editor of *Mathematical Programming*, the leading journal in optimization, from 1992 to 1999.

Tomoharu Nakashima received his Bachelor, Master, and Ph.D. degrees in Engineering from Osaka Prefecture University in 1995, 1997, and 2000, respectively. He joined at Department of Engineering, Osaka Prefecture University in 2000 as a Research Associate. He was promoted as an Assistant Professor in 2001, as an Associate Professor in 2005. In 2012, he was promoted to a Professor of Department of Sustainable Systems Science at Osaka Prefecture University. His research interest includes fuzzy rule-based system, RoboCup soccer simulation, pattern classification, agent-based simulation of financial engineering, evolutionary computation, neural networks, reinforcement learning, and game theory.

Ganesh R. Naik received B.E. degree in Electronics and Communication Engineering from the University of Mysore, Mysore, India, in 1997, M.E. degree in Communication and Information Engineering from Griffith University, Brisbane, Australia, in 2002, and Ph.D. degree in the area of Digital Signal Processing from RMIT University, Melbourne, Australia, in 2009. He is currently an academician and researcher at RMIT University. As an early career researcher, he has authored more than 60 papers in peer reviewed journals, conferences, and book chapters over the last five years. His research interests include pattern recognition, blind source separation techniques, audio signal processing, biosignal processing, and human–computer interface. Dr. Naik is a member of the organising committee for IEEE BRC2011 Conference, Vitoria, Brazil. He is a recipient of the Baden–Württemberg Scholarship from the University of Berufsakademie, Stuttgart, Germany (2006–2007).

Hung-Suck Park obtained his Master's in Environmental Engineering from the Korea Advanced Institute of Science and Technology, in 1986, and subsequently his PhD in Environmental Engineering from the same institute in 1990. He joined University of Ulsan as an Assistant Professor in 1993. At present, he is a Full Professor in the same Department. He has published over 70 papers in international and national journals of repute and presented many papers at seminars/workshops. His major areas of specialization are environmental biotechnology, environmental management with special emphasis on hazardous waste management, eco-industrial parks, life cycle analysis, and environmental impact assessment. He has carried out many industrial consultancies and sponsored research projects and guided several students for their PhD and Master theses.

Ashfaqur Rahman received his Ph.D. degree in Information Technology from Monash University, Australia in 2008. Currently, he is a Research Fellow at the Centre for Intelligent and Networked Systems (CINS) at Central Queensland University (CQU), Australia. His major research interests are in the fields of computational intelligence, data mining, multimedia signal processing and communication, and artificial intelligence. He has published more than 20 peer-reviewed journal articles and conference papers. Dr. Rahman is the recipient of numerous academic awards including CQU Seed Grant, the International Postgraduate Research Scholarship (IPRS), Monash Graduate Scholarship (MGS), and FIT Dean Scholarship by Monash University, Australia.

Eldon Raj Rene obtained his PhD in Chemical Engineering from Indian Institute of Technology Madras, India in 2005. He worked as a Research Professor at the Department of Civil and Environmental Engineering, University of Ulsan, South Korea during the academic year 2005-2006, where he was engaged both in teaching and research. Subsequently, he joined the Chemical Engineering Laboratory, at the University of La Coruña, Spain for his post-doctoral fellowship, where his research focus was on developing novel bioreactors for air pollution control. Presently, he works as a researcher with a contract under the Juan de La Cierva fellowship programme from the Ministerio de Ciencia e Innovación, Spain. His research interests include; biofiltration, odor management, VOC abatement, treatment of high strength wastewaters through various bioreactor configurations, and the application of artificial neural networks and fuzzy systems for modeling complex biological systems.

Dieter Roller holds the position of Director of the Institute of Computer-aided Product Development at the University of Stuttgart. He is full Professor and Chair of Computer Science Fundamentals. Additionally he has been awarded the distinction as a honorary Professor of the University of Kaiserslautern and also serves as liaison Professor of the German computer science society "Gesellschaft für Informatik e.V." for the University of Stuttgart. He is Chairman of several national and international working groups and former President of the ISATA forum, on of the world-wide largest technological associations. Furthermore he is organiser and chairman of symposia, congresses, and workshops in the field of product development and automation. Professor Roller serves as reviewer for the Commission of the European Communities in Brussels as well as for the Baden-Württemberg Ministry of Science and Research for project grants. He is also reviewer for well-known scientific journals and member of several national and international programme committees. As former research and development manager with world-wide responsibility for CAD-technology within an international computer company, he gathered a comprehensive industrial experience. He is the inventor of several patents and is well-known through numerous technical talks in countries all over the world, 70 published books and over 160 contributions to journals and proceedings books. With his wealth of experience, he also serves as a technology consultant to various high-tech companies.

J. S. Saini received his B.Sc.(Engg.) degree (Hons.) in Electrical Engg. from Punjab University, Chandigarh, India in 1983. He did his M.Tech. in Control Engg. & Instrumentation from I.I.T, New Delhi (India) in 1989, standing first in his discipline despite crediting excess number of subjects. He was awarded Ph.D. degree in Electrical Engg. by M.D. University, Rohtak, Haryana (India) in 2003. He served for different periods in faculty of Electrical Engg. Department, G. N. Engineering College, Ludhiana, Punjab; Punjab Engineering College, Chandigarh; TTTI, Chandigarh and REC Hamirpur (HP). He had a brief stint with the industry, serving as Appr. Engineer in D.C.M. Engg. Products, Ropar, Punjab. He is currently working as Professor, Department of EE and & Dean College at Deenbandhu Chhotu Ram University of Science & Technology, Murthal, Sonipat (India). He has published about 50 research papers in journals such as *IEEE Transactions, Journal of IE(I), Journal of Instrument Society of India, Journal of Systems Society of India, IETE Journal of Research,* & Proc. of National & International Conferences. He has been a referee for IEEE, International and National Conferences. He was awarded Systems Society of India's High Quality Presentation Award for one of his research papers and Certificate of Merit for another paper by Institution of Engineers (India). His current interests include Genetic Algorithms, Chaotic Systems, Fuzzy Logic & ANN applications in Control, Instrumentation & Optimization.

Gerald Schaefer gained his BSc. in Computing from the University of Derby and his PhD in Computer Vision from the University of East Anglia. He worked at the Colour & Imaging Institute, University of Derby (1997-1999), in the School of Information Systems, University of East Anglia (2000-2001), in the School of Computing and Informatics at Nottingham Trent University (2001-2006), and in the School of Engineering and Applied Science at Aston University (2006-2009) before joining the Department of Computer Science at Loughborough University. His research interests are mainly in the areas of colour image analysis, image retrieval, physics-based vision, medical imaging, and computational intelligence. He has published extensively in these areas with a total publication count of about 250. He is a member of the editorial board of several international journals, reviews for over 50 journals and served on the programme committee of more than 150 conferences. He has been invited as plenary speaker to several conferences, is the organiser of some international workshops and special sessions at conferences, and the editor of several books and special journal issues.

Leyuan Shi is a Professor in the Department of Industrial and Systems Engineering at University of Wisconsin-Madison. She received her Ph.D. in Applied Mathematics from Harvard University in 1992. Her research interests include simulation modeling and large-scale optimization with applications to operation planning and scheduling, supply chain management, transportation, and health care systems. Her research work has been published on journals such as *Operations Research, Management Science, JDEDS, IIE Trans.,* and *IEEE Trans.* She is serving on editorial board for *IEEE Trans on Automation Science and Engineering, Journal of Discrete Event Dynamic Systems,* and *Journal of Methodology, and Computing in Applied Probability.* She served on editorial board for *Manufacturing & Service Operations Management* and *INFORMS Journal on Computing.* She also served as General Chair, co-Chair, and program committee for many national and international conferences. She is the recipient of the Vilas Associate Award in 2006. She is an IEEE Fellow.

Satvir Singh was born on Dec 7, 1975. He received his bachelor's degree (B.Tech.) from Dr. B.R. Ambedkar National Institute of Technology, Jalandhar with specialization in Electronics & Communication Engineering in 1998, master's degree (M.E.) from Delhi College of Engineering with distinction in Electronics & Communication Engineering in 2000 and doctoral degree (Ph.D.) from Maharshi Dayanand University, Rohtak in 2011. During his 12 years of teaching experience he served as Assistant Professor and Head, Department of Electronics & Communication Engineering at BRCM College of Engineering & Technology, Bahal, (Bhiwani) Haryana, India and as Associate Professor & Head, Department of Electronics & Communication Engineering at SBS College of Engineering & Technology, Ferozepur Punjab, India. His fields of special interest include Artificial Neural Networks, Type-1 & Type-2 Fuzzy Logic Systems and other nature inspired evolutionary algorithms such as GA, PSO and BBO etc. for solving engineering problems. He is active member of an editorial board of *International Journal of Electronics Engineering* and published nearly 10 research papers in Journals and Conferences. He has delivered more than 10 expert talks in National and International Conferences, seminar, symposiums and workshops.

Andrew Stranieri is an Associate Professor and the Director of the Centre for Informatics and Applied Optimisation in the School of Science, Information Technology & Engineering at the University of Ballarat. He adapted his training in psychology and counselling experience to inform his research into cognitive models of argumentation and artificial intelligence. This research was instrumental in modelling decision making in refugee law, copyright law, eligibility for legal aid, sentencing, and research ethics with Professor Zeleznikow. His research in health informatics spans data mining in health, complementary and alternative medicine informatics, telemedicine, and intelligent decision support systems. He is the author of over 80 peer reviewed journal and conference articles and has published two books.

T. Swaminathan is Professor at the Department of Chemical Engineering, IIT Madras, India. His major areas of specialization are environmental engineering with special emphasis on hazardous waste management, biotechnology, membrane technology, and environmental risk assessment. He contributes regularly to the media through his comments and opinions on scientific issues which relate to his areas of knowledge. Prof T. S often extends his research collaboration with a larger community (both national and international) of researchers and professors who are actively exploring all aspects of pollution abatement processes (air, water, and solid waste). He has guided 16 PhD and several Master theses and has published over 100 research manuscripts in international and national journals. He has also carried out many industrial consultancy and sponsored research projects.

Javid Taheri received his Bachelor's and Master's of Electrical Engineering from Sharif University of Technology, Tehran, Iran in 1998 and 2000, respectively. His Master's was in the field of Intelligent Control and Robotics. His Ph.D. is in the field of Mobile Computing from the School of Information Technologies in the University of Sydney, Sydney, Australia. He is currently working as a Postdoctoral research fellow at same school. His main areas of research are optimization techniques, artificial intelligence, vehicular ad-hoc networks, scheduling, parallel and cloud computing.

Rosemary Torney is a Research Assistant in the School of Science, Information Technology and Engineering at the University of Ballarat in Australia. She is also currently a PhD student within the University of Ballarat's Internet Commerce Security Laboratory, where her research focuses on the application of machine learning techniques to profile the demographic characteristics of the authors of anonymously published online texts.

Peter Vamplew is a Senior Lecturer in the School of Science, Information Technology, and Engineering at the University of Ballarat. He is Deputy Director of the Centre for Informatics and Applied Optimisation (CIAO), and is involved in the leadership of CIAO's Data Mining and Informatics Research Group and also its Internet Commerce Security Laboratory. Prior to joining the University of Ballarat he was a Lecturer at the University of Tasmania, where he completed his PhD on the application of neural networks to automated recognition of sign language. His primary research interests are in the fields of machine learning (particularly reinforcement learning) and data mining, including mining of information from text documents.

Brijesh Verma is a Professor in the School of Information and Communication Technology at Central Queensland University (CQUni), Australia. His main research interests include pattern recognition and computational intelligence: neural and evolutionary learning algorithms, ensemble and fusion of classifiers, feature extraction and selection, image segmentation and analysis, handwriting recognition, face recognition and digital mammography. He has published thirteen authored/co-authored/co-edited books, seven book chapters, and over hundred papers in journals and conference proceedings. Dr. Verma has served on the organizing and program committees of over thirty national and international conferences such as IJCNN, CEC, ICONIP, ARC ISSNIP, IEEE CIDM, and ICCIMA. He is currently serving as IJCNN Special Sessions Chair for IEEE World Congress on Computational Intelligence (WCCI 2012). He has served as editorial board member or associate editor for six international journals, such as *IEEE Transactions on Information Technology in Biomedicine, International Journal of Computational Intelligence and Applications,* and *International Journal of Hybrid Intelligent Systems.* He is currently serving as Editor-in-Chief of *International Journal of Computational Intelligence and Applications* published by World Scientific/Imperial College Press. Dr. Verma is a member of International Neural Network Society (INNS) and a senior member of IEEE. He has served on IEEE CIS outstanding chapter award subcommittee (2010) and senior members sub-committee (2010). He has also served as a Chair of IEEE Computational Intelligence Society's Queensland Chapter (2007-2008) and received 2009 IEEE CIS outstanding chapter award.

John Yearwood is Professor of Informatics and the Head of the School of Science, Information Technology, and Engineering in the University of Ballarat. His research spans areas of pattern recognition, argumentation, reasoning, and decision support and its applications in health and law. John has been the Chief Investigator on a number of ARC grants in these areas. His work has involved the development of new approaches to classification based on modern non-smooth optimization techniques, new frameworks for structured reasoning and their application in decision support and knowledge modelling. John is an Associate Editor for the *Journal of Research and Practice in Information Technology* and has over 200 refereed journal and conference articles.

John Zeleznikow is a Professor of Information Systems and Director of the Laboratory of Decision Support and Dispute Management in School of Management and Information Systems at Victoria University. His expertise is in the use of machine learning to enhance decision-making – in law, negotiation, business, and support. He has obtained over $US 7 million in competitive national and international research grants, successfully supervised thirteen PhD students, and published over 250 refereed journal and conference articles as well as three research monographs.

Hao Zhang is an Instructor of the Department of Radiation Oncology of University of Maryland School of Medicine. He obtained his Ph.D. in Industrial and Systems Engineering with a concentration in applying Operations Research/Numerical Methods to Radiation Oncology. Among his contributions during his thesis work was the development of a machine learning predictive model for radiotherapy outcomes including xerostomia and rectal bleeding. Even at the early stage of his research career as a junior research faculty, Zhang has published 7 total peer-reviewed journal papers and 30 abstracts and conference proceedings. In 2008, one of his abstract contributions was selected as a finalist for the Young Investigator Symposium at the AAPM annual meeting. One of his papers was selected as a Pierskalla Prize Finalist at the Informs Annual Meeting in 2009. In 2011 Zhang was one the two junior researchers who received AAPM Research Seed Funding Initiative Awards.

Index